MARK ROSEMAN

The Past in Hiding

PENGUIN BOOKS

PENGUIN BOOKS

Published by the Penguin Group
Penguin Books Ltd, 27 Wrights Lane, London w8 5TZ, England
Penguin Putnam Inc., 375 Hudson Street, New York, New York 10014, USA
Penguin Books Australia Ltd, Ringwood, Victoria, Australia
Penguin Books Canada Ltd, 10 Alcorn Avenue, Toronto, Ontario, Canada M4V 3B2
Penguin Books India (P) Ltd, 11, Community Centre, Panchsheel Park, New Delhi – 110 017, India
Penguin Books (NZ) Ltd, Private Bag 102902, NSMC, Auckland, New Zealand
Penguin Books (South Africa) (Pty) Ltd, 5 Watkins Street, Denver Ext 4, Johannesburg 2094, South Africa

Penguin Books Ltd, Registered Offices: Harmondsworth, Middlesex, England

First published by Allen Lane The Penguin Press 2000
Published in Penguin Books 2001

1

Printed in England by Clays Ltd, St Ives plc

Contents

Illustrations

Acknowledgements

My biggest debt is to Marianne Ellenbogen, the subject of this book, for embarking on our painful journey – and to her son Vivian (for whom the journey was no less painful), for staying the course to the end. I hope this book will serve to commemorate those whom Marianne lost in the Holocaust, above all her parents, Siegfried and Regina Strauss, her brother, Richard and her fiancé, Ernst Krombach.

I am grateful to the Nuffield Foundation and Keele University for financing travel to the Americas and to Israel, and the Alexander von Humboldt Stiftung for a fellowship to work in Germany. My thanks also to Jürgen Reulecke and Siegen University, my official hosts for the Fellowship; Professor Düwell and the University of Düsseldorf kindly provided additional facilities.

Alongside Marianne, a large number of individuals generously agreed to be interviewed or to provide information: Eric and Nancy Alexander, Stamford; Uri Aloni, Beit Lochamei Hagetaot; Paul Alsberg, Jerusalem; Hanna Aron, West Hartford, Connecticut; Lily Arras, Walbeck; Christian Arras, Essen; Waltraud Barkhof-Kreter, Essen; Saul and Clara Bender, Chester; Thomas Toivi Blatt, Issaquah, Washington; the late Fritz Briel, Remscheid; Wolfgang Briel, Barsinghausen; Chaja Chovers, Haifa; Jane Dalton, Romsey; Ruth Davidsohn, Haifa; Inge Deutschkron, Berlin; Edith Dietz, Karlsruhe; Ruth Elias, Israel; Gershon Ellenbogen, London; Michael Ellenbogen, Liverpool; Vivian Ellenbogen, Liverpool; Ruth Gawse, Jerusalem; Karin Gerhard, Essen; the late Tove Gerson,

ACKNOWLEDGEMENTS

Essen; David, Sandra and Rob Gray, London; Werner, Thomas and the late Hannah Hoffmann, Buenos Aires; Waltraud Horn, Bad Dürrheim; Elisabeth Jacobs, Paderborn; Hanna Jordan, Wuppertal; Ellen Jungbluth, Wuppertal; the late Meta Kamp, Niefern-Öschelbronn; Enrique Krombach, Buenos Aires; Jakov and Tsofia Langer, Kiryat Tivon; Rosemarie Lange, Bobingen; Hilde Machinek, Wuppertal; Monte and Phyllis Miller, Liverpool; Eva Morting, Sundbyberg, Sweden; Imo Moszkowicz, Ottobrunn; Elfrieda Nenadovic, Göttingen; Johannes Oppenheimer, Berlin; the late Lew Schloss and Trudy Schloss, Teaneck, New Jersey; Hermann Schmalstieg, Göttingen; Aenne Schmitz, Wuppertal; Armgard Schubert, Seeheim-Jugenheim; the late Eva Selig, London; Robert Selig, Denmark; Tillie Stein, Atlanta, Georgia; Ernst Steinmann, Achim; the late Liesel Sternberg, Birmingham; Reinhold Ströter, Mettmann; Uri Weinberg, Jerusalem; Hélène Yaiche-Wolf, Paris; and Kurt Zeunert, Berlin. I thank them as well as those respondents who wished to remain anonymous. I am very grateful too to a number of specialists who shared valuable knowledge and resources: Jochen Bilstein, Hanns W. Gummersbach, Jürgen Fehrs, Ulrich Föhse, Helena Fox, Monika Grüter, Gudrun Maierhof, Winfried Meyer, Gabriel Milland, Steve Paulsson, Michael Treganza and E. Thomas Wood.

I am also indebted to the archives and archivists who provided material and information: Zdenek Schindler, Academy of Sciences of the Czech Republic; Franciszek Piper, Panstwowe Muzeum, Oswiecim (Auschwitz); Edna Brocke, Judith Hess and Monika Joosten, Alte Synagoge, Essen; Beith Terezin (with thanks to Ruth Elias); Berlin Document Centre; BBC Written Archives Centre; Frau Maerten, Bundesarchiv, Berlin; Andreas Matschenz, Landesarchiv Berlin; Hermann Simon, Centrum Judaicum; Deutsche Bank, Essen; Reinhard Frost, Deutsche Bank Historisches Institut, Frankfurt; Stadtarchiv Dinslaken; Anselm Faust, Hauptstaatsarchiv Düsseldorf; Klaus Wisotzky, Stadtarchiv Essen; German Historical Institute, London; Institut für Zeitgeschichte, Munich; Vera Bendt, Frau Freidank and Leonore Maier, Jüdisches Museum, Berlin; Diane R. Spielman, Leo Baeck Institute, New York; Ulrich Borsdorf, Mathilde Jamin and Ernst Schmidt, Ruhrland Museum, Essen; David Cesarani and Jo Reilly, Wiener Library, London; Stadtarchiv Wuppertal; and Judith Kleimann, Jacob Borut and Mordechai Paldiel,

Yad Vashem, Jerusalem; Zentrum für Antisemitusmusforschung, Berlin. Benno Reicher of the Jüdische Gemeinde, Essen and Ingrid Kuschmiers of the Luisenschule–Altschülerinnenverband allowed me to benefit from their knowledge and connections.

I wrote this book while at Keele University, and had the good fortune to be in a history department that was high-powered but good-natured. Thanks to my colleagues and the office staff for making it so. Historians at Keele and elsewhere who have been particular sources of advice and encouragement on this project are: Jakob Borut, Patricia Clavin, Richard Evans, Angela Genger, Chris Harrison, Liz Harvey, Marion Kaplan, Philip Morgan, Alexander and Alice von Plato, Norbert Reichling, Colin Richmond, Nick Stargardt, Charles Townshend, Falk Wiesemann, Peter Witte and Michael Zimmermann. Colin Richmond, Nick Stargardt, Falk Wiesemann and Michael Zimmermann gave extremely generously of their time in reading and making valuable suggestions on the manuscript.

For assistance in turning the idea into a book I am very grateful to Peter Robinson of Curtis Brown, who in his good humoured way forced me to define what kind of book I was writing and then explained to others what I was about. My editor at Penguin, Simon Winder, has been a real pleasure to work with. Thanks to Volker and Marion Berghahn for making connections in the USA and for their enduring support and friendship. Thanks also to my US agent, Jill Grinberg of Anderson, Grinberg Literary Management. The manuscript benefited immeasurably from the editorial input of Joan Roscman and of Sara Bershtel of Metropolitan; I am indebted to them both for the skill, energy and time they devoted to the task.

As any writer knows, completing a project on this scale depends on the emotional support of others. In Germany, I looked to Alexander and Alice von Plato and Falk and Lisa Wiesemann. In Britain, my friend Frankie Zimmerman, my cousins Joe Hyames Mernane and Janet Davies and above all my children, Jacob, Abigail and Kate, were my significant others. Thanks too to Sarah Montagu, particularly for support with childcare during my extended residence in Germany.

Those who know me well will recognize how much the spirit of enquiry in this book draws on the intellectual environment in which I grew up. This book is respectfully dedicated to my parents, Nat and Joan Roseman.

If any one faculty of our nature may be called *more* wonderful than the rest, I do think it is memory. There seems something more speakingly incomprehensible in the powers, the failures, the inequalities, of memory, than in any other of our intelligences. The memory is sometimes so retentive, so serviceable, so obedient – at others, so bewildered and so weak – and at others again so tyrannic, so beyond controul! – We are to be sure a miracle every way – but our powers of recollecting and forgetting, do seem peculiarly past finding out.

Fanny in Jane Austen, *Mansfield Park*

Introduction

In a very literal sense, Marianne Ellenbogen née Strauss spent her past in hiding. A German Jewess born in the 1920s, Marianne survived the Nazi killing machine by going underground. But her extraordinary journey into and out of the Holocaust had little of the passivity and isolation we associate with being hidden. Between 1941 and 1943, she and her parents were protected by contacts with the Nazi Wehrmacht's own counter-intelligence organization, the Abwehr. When Marianne's fiancé was deported to a Polish ghetto, she managed for six months to maintain a unique chain of communication to him there. And when the rest of her own family were eventually deported, she went on the run. For two years, a hitherto virtually unknown resistance group helped her to survive in the heart of Nazi Germany. She surfaced in Düsseldorf at the end of the war, joined the Communist Party and threw herself into rebuilding a better Germany.

In the months and years that followed, it was Marianne's past itself that went into hiding. In 1946 she came to Britain, married and tried to bury her memories. She led an ordinary life as housewife and mother until her death in 1996. Even her closest relatives knew next to nothing about her wartime experiences. And yet the clues to that past had not quite disappeared. For more than fifty years, an astonishing profusion of letters, diaries, official records and memories lay dormant, ready to bear witness to her survival. The tale of how they eventually came to life again is no less extraordinary than that of her survival itself.

This book is the search for a past in hiding.

Marianne's report

In 1984, at the behest of her wartime helpers, Marianne Ellenbogen wrote one brief article about her underground life for an obscure journal, *Das Münster am Hellweg*, published in Essen, the town of her birth. Entitled 'Escape and life underground during the Nazi years of persecution, 1943–5', it began:[1]

On a Monday morning at ten o'clock in August 1943, the two most feared Gestapo officials in Essen appeared at our house. They gave us just two hours to get ready for 'transport to the East'. At this point we were almost the last full-Jewish family left in Essen. In 1941 we had already been condemned to deportation and assigned to a transport. But at the last minute, in full view of all the other hundreds of people waiting for an unknown and frightening future, we were sent back by the Gestapo to our sealed-up house. Now, in 1943, the deportation order came like a bolt out of the blue.

The Gestapo officials did not let us out of their sight. The allotted two hours were filled with feverish packing of the few things that we were allowed to take with us – clothing which, in the unknown destination of a 'work camp', should be practical, warm and with luck keep us alive. Then came my moment. The two officials disappeared into the basement, probably to find some loot – all the household goods that we still possessed and did not need for day-to-day use were stored in the cellar in crates and cases. These helped to support the cellar roof and give us a bit more security from the bomb attacks since, as Jews, we were not allowed to use the public air-raid shelters. Unable to say goodbye to my parents, my brother and my relatives, I followed the impulse of the moment, ran out of the house just as I was, with some hundred-mark notes which my father had stuffed into my pocket just a few moments before. I ran for my life, expecting a pistol shot behind me any minute. To go in that way seemed to me a much better fate than the unimaginable one that might await me in Auschwitz or Łodz, in Treblinka or Izbica. But there was no shot, no one running after me, no order, no shouting!

That evening the twenty-year-old Marianne Strauss made her way to a building in southern Essen which belonged to the 'Bund', a locally based group founded by a man named Artur Jacobs. Meanwhile, with the Gestapo still hoping they would recapture the missing girl, Marianne's family were held in an Essen prison. After a few days, they were deported to Theresienstadt.

For several weeks, Marianne Strauss hid out in Essen. But because bomb attacks and surveillance made remaining there too risky, she began to travel, staying in towns across north and central Germany with members of the Bund:

It was decided that I should never stay for more than three weeks with any one person. We had to prevent the relatives or neighbours of my hosts from getting suspicious. In any case, I had no food coupons, so my friends carried the great burden of having to feed me from their rations. But I had some money and access to suitcases containing clothes and linen that my parents had hidden some weeks before their deportation, so I was able to barter their contents with farmers in the country in exchange for food or clothing coupons. This was an essential but very dangerous operation. I also hand-crafted countless felt flowers, which were in hot demand at various fashion shops with little to sell. In the course of time, I found a small fashion shop in Braunschweig whose owner paid for my goods largely in the so-crucial coupons. She became my main customer and I had a suspicion that she had half-guessed my situation and wanted to help.

For almost two years Marianne Strauss travelled without papers or ration cards, never staying for longer than three weeks with any of her hosts.

On 7 June 1944 – on my twenty-first birthday, I was . . . in Beverstedt and heard on the BBC that the occupants of the transport that had gone from Theresienstadt to Auschwitz on 18 December 1943 had been gassed there in the last few days. I knew that my parents and my brother had been on this transport to Auschwitz.

As Germany's military situation worsened, so did the hazards of travel. Marianne was twice nearly killed by bombing raids and often only narrowly escaped detection from the Gestapo. But she survived, enduring the last weeks of the war in embattled Düsseldorf.

A picture for the exhibition

I first saw the article some five years after it was published, in September 1989. Its arrival in the post was preceded by a call from Dr Mathilde Jamin of the Ruhrland Museum in Essen. Dr Jamin was in search of witnesses for a forthcoming exhibition on wartime life in the Ruhr. Did I know of a member of Essen's pre-war Jewish community, Marianne Ellenbogen, now living in Liverpool? It was reasonable to assume that I might at least have encountered her name: in the early 1980s I had conducted historical research in Essen, and my wife and I had been active in the town's tiny Jewish community. But most of the congregation had been post-war refugees from Eastern Europe and, with a few exceptions, Essen's pre-war Jews were present only as ghosts, their names on gravestones or memorial plaques in the Jewish cemetery. Their synagogue – the 'Old Synagogue' – once one of the finest in Germany, was now just a shell, housing another museum. So, no, I had never heard of Marianne Ellenbogen.

Dr Jamin asked whether, if Mrs Ellenbogen were amenable, I would be willing to talk to her about her experiences during the war. I readily assented. It sounded interesting. In any case, I'd enjoyed the support of the Ruhrland Museum's energetic director Professor Uli Borsdorf in the past and was happy to return the favour. And I'd just taken up a post in modern history at Keele University, so Liverpool wasn't too far away.

And then the article arrived in the post. I found it astonishing. Although I had heard of the so-called 'U-boats' in Berlin, Jews who hid in the cellars or attics of non-Jewish friends, this was the first time I had ever heard of a German Jew moving about the country in this way. I wondered what kind of young woman would have had the nerve to survive like this, to travel without papers, deal with shopkeepers and barter with farmers when any denunciation would have meant her death. And what kind of group was it that had kept her alive? I knew the research on the Ruhr in the Nazi period well but I had never heard of the

'Bund' – or at least not this particular organization, which had nothing to do with the better-known Jewish Bund in Poland. Not only was the name new to me, so was the idea of a network managing to provide a Jew with shelter in one town after another across the middle of Nazi Germany. Could this really have happened? I had grave doubts about some of the details in Marianne Ellenbogen's account, in particular the story about the BBC. Given the current state of the historical debate about what the Germans had or had not known about the Holocaust, I did not believe that the BBC could have been transmitting information with anything like that kind of precision. Even so, the interview which I had taken on partly as a favour now looked like a privilege.

But first, Mrs Ellenbogen had to agree.

Whether because of the natural circumspection of Dr Jamin's genera-tion in relation to former Jewish residents of Germany, or because of Mrs Ellenbogen's particular sensitivity, I didn't yet know which, the museum were approaching the issue extraordinarily carefully. As a first step, Dr Jamin had asked colleagues from the Old Synagogue (the principal contact point for Essen's former Jewish residents) to ask Mrs Ellenbogen if she would be willing for the Ruhrland Museum to contact her at all in relation to the exhibition. Only then did Dr Jamin write to Mrs Ellenbogen herself. After thanking her for being 'so friendly as to hear my request' she went on:

Your article . . . in Das Münster am Hellweg (1984) impressed me very much – and not just because you are one of only two people I have heard of who are still today in a position to report on Jews' experiences of war in the Ruhr. It seems to me that you and people in your situation were exposed just as much to the dangers and hardships of war as the German majority population, indeed even more so (for example, you could not enter the air-raid shelters). Yet these dangers and hardships must have seemed almost irrelevant compared with the terrible experience of Nazi persecution. Anyone who has understood this must be proof against the potential danger of the 'German self-pity' which an exhibition about the war might arouse – against our intentions – amongst its visitors. Partly for this reason, we would like to give the strongest emphasis to the victims of German policies and their experiences.

After explaining how oral testimony would be used in the exhibition, and with the assurance that 'Your voice would of course remain anonymous – unless you should wish it not to be so', Dr Jamin introduced me, 'a young English historian [. . .] who from 1981–4 was a member of the Jewish community in Essen'. A few days later she called me to say all was well.

When I rang Marianne Ellenbogen to fix a date there was something very civilized and confident about her manner, but she did say one slightly odd thing. The Jewish festival of Tabernacles was approaching and she said that she would be unavailable on a certain date because 'the Jewish festivals are observed in this house'. I wondered about this strangely passive formulation. Did she live with children who were more Orthodox, or was there perhaps still a problem with her grasp of English?

In the autumn of 1989 I drove up to Liverpool. The address I had been given turned out to be in a leafy, prosperous-looking suburban road of solid, semi-detached 1920s houses. I arrived at the same time as a good-looking man whom I judged to be in his early fifties. Marianne appeared at the door – full of energy and charm, but looking distinctly older than he. Presumably, this was the son who observed the festivals in this house. Before I had a chance to say the wrong thing, he was revealed as Basil, Marianne's husband, six years her senior. There was some small talk and Basil hovered. He did not really want to leave us to it and wondered aloud if he could contribute something to the interview. But since he had met Marianne only after the war, and as I was then under the mistaken impression that he didn't speak German – the language in which we had to record the interview – I didn't see how he could. In any case, Marianne was clearly not keen for Basil to take part.[2] Only in retrospect did I come to see the symbolic significance of this transaction – of his desire to be involved and her desire to exclude him. At the time, I had no sense of the family burdens such memories could bring.

I had, however, been right to detect something odd in the way Marianne had alluded to the festivals on the phone. Married to an Orthodox Jewish husband, she had gone along with a level of Jewish observance that went well beyond what she was used to from her acculturated

German-Jewish background and what she would have chosen for herself. Later, I came to see a sadly ironic continuity here. Both in Nazi Germany and in post-war Britain, the outside world imposed her Jewish identity on her to a degree that went well beyond her own sense of its significance. From 1933 until her death, Marianne's Jewishness was both her fate and her burden.

Our conversation on that autumn day in 1989 was enormously warm and stimulating. After I had admired the antiques, beautifully made furniture and family paintings which Marianne seemed to have somehow salvaged from her parental home, we sat down to strong black coffee and swirly biscuits of a kind I usually had only ever received in Germany. Marianne had intense, jet-black eyebrows and striking dark eyes, a full smiling mouth and hair pulled back tautly behind her head in continental style. The voice was cultured and slightly husky. Like many Germans who speak English almost perfectly (my doubts on this score had been completely unfounded), her accent was delightful, particularly the 'oh' sound, as in the charming 'hello' that had greeted me on the doorstep, which took on a fragrant, sophisticated quality. I, of course, was constantly studying the housewife in her sixties to detect the qualities that had enabled the twenty-year-old girl to survive. I was struck by the strength and character of her face, her energy. She was charming with a hint of steel.

In response to Marianne's request for the questions in advance, Mathilde Jamin had sent both of us a check-list, and we obediently worked through it. Marianne talked about life in Essen during the war and the double threat of Gestapo persecution and Allied bombing. But though she would never learn to make the grammatical mistakes that I would never learn to avoid, German had become a somewhat awkward tool for her. And memory – that was a *very* awkward tool. The whole interview took on a rather dutiful character. Somehow, Marianne conveyed to me that beyond this brief encounter she would not be induced to talk about the past. She took pleasure in my company, I could see, and at one point there was just a hint that I might be her amanuensis. But really, what bonded us at the end of the afternoon was that we had survived together a painful immersion in her memory. And now it was over.

Conceiving this book

In the following months and years I often thought of Marianne, and we spoke occasionally on the phone, but nothing more. That the story did not end there was almost an accident. In 1996, I was involved in the preparatory work for a TV documentary on the Allied Occupation of Germany, and I knew that Marianne had remained in Germany for a year and a half after the end of the war. Like the Ruhrland Museum before me, I thought Marianne's testimony would 'disrupt' mainstream German perceptions of what had been going on. Marianne did not want to be on camera, but was very pleased I had rung. She was a widow now (Basil had died in February), and very ill. She had thought of me a lot lately because she wanted me to look at some papers in her possession and see if they should go into a public archive. Would I come and visit her?

When she opened the front door to me in July 1996, my initial impression was that the intervening seven years had not changed her very much. There was sadly no Basil, of course; I registered that she stooped a little more and I noted the stair lift. But as far as I was concerned, it was the same face full of energy, power and charm. Later, I saw some family snaps taken in the late 1980s and realized she had lost weight since then – her recent ill health had done her the ironic favour of slimming her down. It was rather fitting, as it turned out, that the (photographic) record proved that my memory had in a small way deceived me.

The good strong coffee and the biscuits were, however, definitely the same. We went upstairs to a study piled high with books and papers. Not with ceremony, quite, but with a mixture of hesitancy and portent Marianne handed me some folded, yellowing sheets of paper on which neat lines of German text had been written in pencil. This, she said, was a letter from her fiancé, Ernst Krombach. I hadn't realized that she had had a fiancé before Basil. The letter was sent in August 1942 from Izbica which, Marianne said, was a Polish concentration camp. Considering the conditions under which it was written and the events it described, it was an enormously composed, careful and sober document. Indeed, the mixture of normality and horror, the juxtaposition of extraordinarily adverse circumstances and the writer's modest optimism, made the letter at once approachable and elusive. It was vivid, it was there in my hands, but it was also beyond imagining.

I was very conscious of Marianne's watchful eyes on me. I did not realize at the time how little is known about Izbica, a ghetto rather than a camp, which in 1942 was a point of interim resettlement for thousands of German, Austrian and Czech Jews. Neither did I realize that this was only part of a truly unique extended correspondence that Marianne and Ernst had managed to maintain between Essen and Izbica. But I said that I thought something *should* be done with the letter.

I asked Marianne how she managed to avoid the deportations that had taken away her fiancé. I had always wondered about the striking reference in her article to the family having been once nearly deported in 1941 and then reprieved. She was not sure, but she thought that the family had been protected by the Abwehr. The Abwehr – the Wehrmacht's counter-intelligence organization? Marianne was clearly somewhat nervous about the whole thing, worried that there might be something slightly shameful involved. It did seem hard to understand that the German Wehrmacht should have been trying to protect any Jews – and why her family?

I also asked how Ernst had managed to get the letter from Izbica to her (and how, as shown by the letter, she had managed to get life-saving goods to him). Marianne said that her uncle and then she herself had got to know a young SS man whose family owned a garage in Essen. Under cover of his contract work for the SS, he had taken out parcels from her to Ernst and brought back the letter. An SS man entering the ghetto, delivering parcels and returning with uncensored letters to the Jewess who commissioned him? I could only shake my head.

We went out for lunch. Despite her illness, Marianne was still driving and, after she had gingerly eased herself into the driving seat of her solid-looking Rover, drove us confidently the short distance to a nearby Chinese restaurant where we were joined by her son, Vivian, a grave, bearded man in his forties. It was Vivian who put the idea of recording his mother's life story openly on the table. After the meal, he took me aside briefly. He told me that Marianne might have only weeks to live and I should act fast. Later, I learned that he had heard this from the doctor only that morning and had spent the last couple of hours driving aimlessly around, wondering what to do with the news and his feelings.

We agreed that I would return soon with a tape recorder. In the course of 1996, Marianne and I had three long conversations, and fragments of her life gradually began to fall into place. I learned much more about the central dramas in Marianne's life – the moment of near deportation, the love affair and correspondence with Ernst, the escape from the Gestapo, the dramatic twists and turns of her two years underground, and the eighteen months spent in the ruins of post-war Germany.

These conversations were moving and enthralling, but they were anything but easy. Marianne was deeply ambivalent about talking to me. She wanted to commemorate Ernst and the help that had been given her by her friends in the Bund. But she found the act of remembering very painful. Our exchanges sometimes became rather combative. She did not want anything written about her life after 1946 when she came to England – she was worried that what she said might appear disloyal to Basil and hurt surviving relatives. She also could not bring herself to talk about what was probably the greatest tragedy in her life: the death in 1969 of her eighteen-year-old daughter Elaine, following a protracted struggle with anorexia. I insisted that we had to talk about the burden of the past on the present – about restitution, guilt and her surviving links to Germany. All right then, but we were not to probe into her family life in Britain. And so, with this uneasy agreement, we carried on. Marianne produced more documents – an extended correspondence between her and Ernst before September 1942 and a wealth of family photos. She had been a most striking-looking girl with huge, burning eyes.

As Marianne's health declined, each time she talked to me involved a major effort to psych (and drug) herself up. On a pharmacologically induced high, she would talk for hours and then by the evening would be utterly drained and take days to recover. I felt increasingly guilty that in what might be her last weeks I was adding to her burden. Did a Holocaust survivor not have a right to die in peace? Towards the end of October we had our longest, most intensive session. She kept putting off the next meeting until she felt stronger. In the meantime, I arranged that

I would go to Germany in January to try to meet some of the surviving members of the Bund and to find out what records were still available. In November, Marianne went for a spell of convalescence to a nearby hospice. The stay seemed to do her good and she returned home in December. But, unexpectedly, her condition deteriorated and she died in the early hours of 22 December 1996.

Remembering, recording and forgetting

Marianne's death caught me unawares. I felt a deep sense of loss – and sadness that I would never be able to show her the finished product. I wondered, in fact, if there could now *be* a 'finished product'. A novelist would find in what I had already learned the plot for a marvellous survival story. But I did not want to blur fact and fiction – I wanted to write history. Quite apart from my general training and temperament, I believe that dealing with the Holocaust demands special care. One has to be very clear about what happened and what did not happen. I could not bring myself to invent details for the sake of the narrative. And that left me wondering whether I had enough material to do justice to Marianne's life. I also wondered, though I had been very hesitant to challenge her directly, whether some of the things Marianne told me could really be true.

Thus, when I took my long-planned trip to Germany just a fortnight after Marianne's death, I did so with a feeling of considerable uncertainty. My first port of call was the Hauptstaatsarchiv in Düsseldorf, which held the records from the Düsseldorf district of the Gestapo (of which Essen was part). I was lucky that this was one of only two regions in the Federal Republic where the Gestapo files had not been destroyed. When the bulging folders for Marianne's father and uncle appeared, it was clear that I had found something special. The Strauss family proved to be one of the best documented cases showing how resistance groups within high-ranking official organizations had intervened to try to protect Jews. The records even contained information about Marianne's escape.

On that and subsequent visits to Germany further remarkable sources revealed themselves. But, as in a detective story, many of the most vital clues turned out to be close to home. In early 1997, Marianne's son Vivian began what was for him the psychologically arduous process of clearing out her belongings. It was only now that he and I discovered how many important documents the Strausses had managed to deposit with friends for safe-keeping. Several times, I made journeys to Liverpool to look through the latest piles of paper that Vivian had found. Even after we had cleared the house there turned out to be another huge trunkful in the shed. The papers included some extraordinary postcards, letters and diaries from wartime Nazi Germany. I did not know whether to be more struck by their existence or by the fact that Marianne had never mentioned them while she was alive.

As in a detective story, I also felt my way, initially rather blindly, along an extending chain of witnesses. I found business contacts of her parents, distant relatives, ex-schoolmates, members of the Bund and post-war friends. It was a poignant reminder of what happened to German Jewry that my search led me across Germany, Israel, the USA and Argentina and brought me correspondents and contacts in Canada, Australia, France, Sweden, Poland and the Czech Republic. But not all my respondents were so far from home. In one instance, a conversation with the helpful archivists in Essen's Old Synagogue led to the discovery that a ninety-year-old friend of Marianne's fiancé's family was now living in Birmingham, just a couple of miles from my home.[3]

So often, the testimony of the Holocaust survivor is just one lonely voice relating a story in which almost everything and everyone described has been destroyed. But in Marianne's case, though she undoubtedly had been robbed of so much, her 'lost' world was still able to speak alongside her. It was thus possible both to be true to my craft *and* to piece together a vivid story. The gaps that remained were almost welcome, as reminders that this picture of the past had been reassembled, like a puzzle. The documentation allowed me not only to supplement but also to corroborate Marianne's testimony. All of her more implausible claims – about the Abwehr, about the underground, about the BBC – proved to be true.

At the same time, these new sources raised questions about authenticity and truth that became a central part of the story. Discrepancies began to emerge. The Gestapo's account of Marianne's flight largely mirrored her own, but there were some subtle and interesting differences which, at the time, I could not interpret. It became clear that Marianne had subtly changed some incidents, forgotten others or 'appropriated' memories that in fact belonged to other people. These changes caught my imagination, not least because they affected episodes remembered so forcefully by Marianne that they had seemed etched in stone. Even traumatic memories, it seemed, and perhaps particularly and peculiarly them, were subject to change.

Sometimes, the 'discrepancies' were not factual errors at all. Except in a few minor particulars, Marianne's memory of events on the run, for example, did not contradict the facts described in the underground diary that I found after her death. Nevertheless, the picture that emerged from the diary of what illegal life was like, and above all of what the young woman was like who had been living that life, was very different from the one she had painted for me. It became clear Marianne had lost sight of the person she had once been. The documents and witnesses thus put me on the trail not just of Marianne's past, but of the painful story of remembering and forgetting.

Surviving Nazi Germany

As a professional historian concentrating on recent German history, one of my main preoccupations over the years has been to try to understand what went wrong in Germany between 1933 and 1945. Indeed, it was the threatening mystery of the Holocaust that provoked me into becoming a historian in the first place. But when I initially decided to write this book, it was to preserve an extraordinary survival story rather than because I expected to gain major insights into the Third Reich and the Holocaust. Marianne's life seemed too much a one-off to offer more than peripheral insights into the nightmare from which she had so unusually managed to escape. Survival was so much against the normal run of things for a Jew caught in Germany or German-occupied Europe after 1939 that in telling Marianne's story I felt guilty almost of fostering a kind of distortion. Jews did not normally thrive in the period

1938–41, have protection from the Abwehr, slip away from the Gestapo or live underground for two years. Out of the quarter of a million Jews still in Germany in 1939, fewer than 3,000 survived in hiding, and half of those were in Berlin.

At the time Marianne and I were having our first conversations, Britain and the USA were enjoying a round of German-bashing. In Britain, Germany's response to Britain's BSE crisis, the prospect of a single currency and football's European Championship were the main reasons for this latest wave. In the USA, there was a continuing, more diffuse unease at the implications of German reunification. The academic analogue to all this was the Goldhagen controversy, which gathered momentum in the summer and autumn of 1996. In his powerful study *Hitler's Willing Executioners*, published the year before, Daniel J. Goldhagen had demonstrated how widespread and wilful was German participation in the killing of Jews. Far from the 'Final Solution' being a clinical mechanical procedure carried out by a tiny few, Goldhagen argued, ordinary Germans from all walks of life showed that they shared the moral calculus which made the killing of Jews seem not only acceptable but even desirable. Powerful descriptions of death marches and forced labour buttressed the argument. Goldhagen attributed this widespread involvement to a distinctive 'exterminatory' anti-Semitism that had evolved in German culture over the centuries, creating a general German propensity to kill Jews. Goldhagen's book has been enormously influential at a popular level, and even for academics doubtful whether German anti-Semitism was so simple and direct a cause of the Holocaust the force of the book's explanation is not easily answered.

The more material and testimony accumulated, however, the more I began to feel that Marianne's story revealed, in microcosm, the complex nature of Germany's relations with its Jews. As with Viktor Klemperer, whose diaries appeared just before I began this research,[4] Marianne's story, indeed her survival, rested on the interrelationships between the Jewish and non-Jewish world. Between herself and her family on the one hand, and the non-Jewish world on the other, a whole variety of ties – ties of sentiment, of business or merely of short-term mutual advantage – were carried across the threshold of 1933 or, indeed, arose thereafter.

Even while the Strauss family was under persecution, I found nuances and differentiation I had not expected. Gestapo attempts to turn various denunciations into prosecutions collapsed because the state prosecutor or the judiciary refused to play ball. As the tax authorities squeezed the family for the special levy on Jews in 1938/9, it proved possible within the narrow limits set by the law to negotiate improvements or concessions. Even in 1941, there was still some small scope for negotiations with the city about the terms of the sale of the Strauss apartments.

As I came to know Marianne's helpers and saviours through the letters and diaries of the time, and through meetings and conversations with those still living, I learned also that the exceptional and the ordinary were closely bound up with each other. Artur and Dore Jacobs, the leaders of the Bund, were clearly exceptional personalities. But many of the individuals whom they inspired to take extraordinary risks, though upright, deeply committed and showing immense moral courage, were quite 'ordinary Germans'. Although the Bund had important distinguishing features, the values it drew on were in many ways typical of a broad grouping within the Weimar left. In short, although the drama of Marianne's survival was unique, the backdrop was so well illuminated and the cast of players so large that her story shed light on the whole theatre in which it took place.

The burdens of the past

There were many moments – for example, when I revived some contact that had lapsed for fifty years or more, or when I discovered some discrepancy between Marianne's recollections and the documents – when I so wished that Marianne were still alive to discuss my findings. The painful truth, however, was that if Marianne had not died, many of the papers, and the names and addresses to which they helped me gain access, would have remained hidden from me. During my conversations with her she had known, as I then did not, that the house was heaving with records and mementoes. She evidently could not bring herself to confront them. Vivian told me that his mother was normally orderly, filing everything in its proper place. Yet these papers were all stuffed into envelopes and folders, nothing thrown away but nothing catalogued, in nooks and crannies all over the house. From some of the things Marianne had said to me, I do not think even she remembered exactly what was there. In other words, her story could be told only because I had been able to talk to her while she lived and gain access to her papers after she died.

For almost fifty years this knowledge, this documentation, lay dormant. No questions were asked, no discussion was allowed. In 1945, it seemed, Marianne had come out into the open – but her past had gone into hiding. A few days after Marianne's death, I had my first long talk with Vivian. I was stunned to learn that his mother had told him virtually nothing of her past. He was waiting to hear about it from a stranger, from me. At the same time, it was clear that he was fiercely protective of her memory and did not want me to intrude too deeply into her privacy. The same intimate, respectful, wary, guilty clinch that had characterized my relationship with Marianne would now continue with him. And thus I learned something of the silent, awful burdens which, in indefinable ways, the past had placed not just on Marianne but on her whole family. Those burdens of a past in hiding are also the subject of this book.

I

Childhood in a German-Jewish Family

Marianne told me the story of a much-prized family document. It was an elaborate family tree commissioned by her mother, Regina Strauss, and produced by a professional artist. Regina, or Ine as everyone called her, was, like her husband Siegfried, immensely proud of their ancestors' long years of respectable settlement in Germany and had carried out a great deal of research. On both sides of the family, forebears could be traced back to 1740. The assiduously collected dates and names of Strausses, Rosenbergs, Weyls, Sterns, Reisses, Behrendts and Nördlingers were incorporated into the beautiful chart of almost 200 years of births, deaths and marriages in Germany.

Marianne told me that Ine was so proud of the result that she sent it off to the Jewish Museum in Berlin for safe-keeping and display. At the time, Marianne said, she gave the document very little attention. 'All that' meant little to her as a girl. Now she wished she had been more involved. But above all she was sorry to have lost so much evidence of her family roots. She told me that on Kristallnacht[1] the Jewish Museum in Berlin went up in flames and with it the family tree. The burning of the family tree seemed to me poignantly symbolic. It represented the destruction of a German-Jewish identity. It was also full of sinister portent. Modifying Heine's famous dictum about books and people, we sense that where you begin by burning family trees you end up by burning families.

Some time after Marianne died I was researching in Berlin. I took a tour through the recently built extension to the Jewish Museum, with its striking modern design based on a fractured Star of David. Because the artefacts had not yet been installed, our guide, a final-year architecture student, talked mainly about the building's design. But he did say one or two significant things about the museum's history. I had not realized that the original Jewish Museum was created in January 1933, only six days before the Nazis came to power. I later found out that in 1936 the museum put on an exhibition titled 'Our Forebears', and it was for this exhibition that Ine submitted the family tree.[2] For me, her gesture now took on a different quality. I had made the mistake at first of seeing in it ostentatious pride. Now I saw a more conscious act of self-assertion at a time when the Nazis were trying to deny German Jews their right to call themselves German.

On 10 November 1938, the day after Kristallnacht, the museum was closed but, I now learned, had not been set alight. Indeed, a number of the museum's paintings turned up after the war and some of the former owners recovered their works. No one knows what happened to the rest. When Marianne told me the museum had gone up in flames she had, probably unconsciously, created a literary metaphor dressed up as memory. The uncertainty about what had actually happened to the family tree must have been too painfully reminiscent of her lack of final knowledge about her family's fate.

Marianne's grandparents

Marianne must have met one of her great-grandparents, since her great-grandmother Sophie Stern died aged 100 in 1928 when Marianne was five. But Marianne's recollections go back only as far as her paternal grandparents, Leopold and Saly (Rosalie, née Stern) Strauss, as well as her mother's parents, Isaak and Anna Rosenberg. Both couples were settled in little towns on the fringe of the Ruhr valley, the Strausses in the lower-Rhinish community of Dinslaken, the Rosenbergs in Ahlen, a Westphalian market town. Both families combined positions of great respectability in their respective communities with a reasonably observant Jewish way of life.

Marianne's Family

Great-grandparents

Seligman Strauss	Bina née Reis	Alexander Stern	Sophie néeNördlinger	Philipp Rosenberg	Therese née Windmüller	Kappel Weyl	Marianne, née Behrendt

Grandparents

Leopold Strauss	Rosalie Stern	Isaak Rosenberg	Anna Weyl
b. 30.11.1861, Hessen	b. 5.4.1867 Pflaumloch,	b. 25.5.1863 Ahlen	b. 4.1.1867 Haltern
d. 15.6.39 Essen	Wuerttemberg	d. 8.5.1932 Ahlen	d. 9.1.1944 Theresienstadt
	d. 28.5.1934 Essen		

Parents

Siegfried Strauss	Regina Rosenberg
b. 24.4.1891 Battenberg	b. 13.1.1898 Ahlen
d. July 1944[?] Auschwitz-Birkenau	d. July, 1944[?] Auschwitz-Birkenau

Marianne's paternal uncles and aunts	*Marianne's maternal uncles and aunts*
Alfred b. 24.4.1891 Battenfeld; m. Lore *née* Dahl; d. Sept. 1944[?] Auschwitz-Birkenau, Lore died Jan. 1945 Kurzbach, nr. Breslau	Hannah b. 5.11.1894 Ahlen; m. Ernst Weinberg; d. ? (deported Lodz Oct 1941); children: Alexander (Eric); Alfred(Uri); Otto (Gerald)
Richard b. 10.1.1893 Battenfeld; d. 14.12.1916 Gumbinnen	Adolf b. 30.4.1896; m. Erna Hertz; d. Florida 1970s; son: Rolf (Ralph)
Bertel b. 13.6.1900 Dinslaken; m. Ferdinand Wolf; d. August 1942[?] Auschwitz-Birkenau; son: Richard (René) Wolf	Karl b. 1909; m. Diane Doutreport; d. Spain 1980s; daughter: Marie Anne

Siegfried m. Regina 27.8.22 Ahlen

Children: Marianne b. 7.6.1923 Essen; m. Basil Ellenbogen; d. 22.12.1996 Liverpool
Richard b. 26.10.1926 Essen; d. July 1944[?] Auschwitz-Birkenau

The Ellenbogens

Max Ellenbogen m. Gertie *née* Hamburg
children: Gershon, b. 7.1.1917 Liverpool
Basil b. 22.12.1917 Liverpool; d. 21.2.1996 Liverpool

Raymond b. 1.7.1924 Liverpool
Basil m. Marianne 29.12.1946 London
children. Vivian b. 23.11.1947, m. 2.3.1975
Elaine b. 18.1.1951; d. 29.9.1969

Leopold Strauss was the only one of eleven siblings to receive second-ary education. He trained as a rabbi and teacher, and in 1896 was appointed headmaster of Dinslaken's Jewish school. He was also cantor[3] for Dinslaken's Jewish community. At the same time, he was invited by the mayor to be a teacher and later honorary director of the town's vocational school (the letter in elegant copperplate Gothic script still survived in Liverpool). He became a town councillor and served on the town's Youth Welfare Committee. When Leopold retired from teaching in 1927, the Dinslaken mayor made a formal announcement to the council and gave Leopold the town's best wishes.[4]

One of Marianne's vivid recollections was of her grandparents' wonderful garden, which, to a child at least, seemed enormous. Grand-mother Saly grew apples and pears and other fruit, from which she would make vast quantities of bottled fruit and jellies. They also kept poultry, and Marianne remembered feeding the chickens and the plea-sure of a fresh egg every morning for breakfast. These happy memories lay alongside the less happy experience of having to receive extracurricu-lar Hebrew lessons and tuition in mathematics from grandfather Leo-pold. Coming as they did in the holidays, Marianne found the extra lessons 'very unfair', but she was compensated by the time she spent with Saly, a 'lovely person'. Saly and Marianne would go out shopping, meeting and greeting other members of the Jewish community. After Saly, a chronic asthmatic, died in 1934, Marianne used to stay in a room of her own on the second floor of the Strausses' house. 'It was very nice and very, very snug and very comfortable . . . I always loved having this room to myself, away from everything.'

Marianne had equally warm recollections of her mother's parents, the Rosenbergs, whom they visited regularly. If the family went to Dinslaken for Passover one year, they would go to the Rosenbergs in Ahlen the next. 'It was all done with great style' in Ahlen, Marianne told me. Isaak Rosenberg's father had established a successful grain and fodder business and Isaak, the fifth of seven children, had taken it on to become one of Ahlen's most prosperous citizens. He played a leading role in local civic associations such as the Bürgerschutzverein and the voluntary fire service. He was also a member of the nationalist-patriotic Kyffhäuser-Bund.[5]

Like Leopold Strauss, Isaak remained a religious man and was presi-

Leopold and Saly Strauss at a spa

dent of Ahlen's small Jewish community. Marianne remembered that, at Passover, Isaak would sit at the head of the table in his kittel[6] and talet.[7] Once, when very young, Marianne asked why her grandfather was wearing the kittel. He said that was what you wear when you get buried. Wearing it reminds you that life is fleeting and that everybody has to die. This was Marianne's first remembered encounter with the idea of death. When Isaak died of heart disease in 1932, the eight-year-old Marianne had her first encounter with the reality of death. The firemen's band turned out to play at his funeral.

The Rosenbergs' house, on one of Ahlen's main streets, fascinated Marianne. It was step-gabled like a Dutch house and inside there was a large winding staircase. Even as a small child Marianne had an eye for art, and remembered the top gallery being chock-a-block with old copper engravings. Halfway up the stairs was a dark room stuffed full with sacks of sultanas, currants and sugar. In the attic, there was storage for grain and a large hook outside for lifting sacks up on chains. Behind the house were offices and a yard. The family did its own slaughtering. Twice a year the butcher would come and they would make sausages and smoke the meat. Isaak used to go pheasant shooting, and Marianne remembered braces of pheasant being sent to her parents in Essen. Marianne's overall impression of Isaak was of a larger-than-life character, picking people up off the street to invite them to dinner, and with a house full of family, guests and servants.

Marianne's parents

Though remaining observant Jews, the Strausses and Rosenbergs were part of a trend of acculturation[8] that had begun in Germany in the eighteenth century, as a result of which Germany's Jews came to resemble their Eastern European counterparts less and less.[9] Whilst Marianne's grandparents had all come from large families, for example, both couples chose to have only four children. They gave their offspring, and particularly their sons, fine-sounding Teutonic names rather than biblical ones. There was Siegfried (Marianne's father) and his twin brother Alfred, born in 1891, followed two years later by a younger brother, Richard. Only their sister Bertel, born in 1900, had a Yiddish-sounding name. The Rosenbergs for their part produced a Johannah (Hannah) (1894), Adolf (1896), Marianne's mother Regina (Ine) (1898) and Karl (1907).

Equally characteristic of the trend was that the Strausses and Rosenbergs placed greater emphasis on a good secular education than on religious instruction. Leopold sent Siegfried and Alfred to a state elemen-

Marianne's father and uncles as children

tary school in nearby Duisburg rather than to his own Jewish school in Dinslaken. A photo of the two boys at primary school survives, with their round, thin-lipped, intense faces and their identical sailor-suits. In 1902, the twins transferred to secondary school, a *Realgymnasium* in Duisburg-Meiderich. The Rosenbergs made similar choices. At this time, German-Jewish families probably took the education of their daughters more seriously than their non-Jewish counterparts. The typical pattern was that the girls were educated for a career which they then did not pursue after marriage. Isaak and Anna sent Ine to a convent lyceum run by Ursuline nuns, because of the good classical education on offer there. According to Marianne, her mother also absorbed much of the moral atmosphere of the place.

The Strauss boys' choice of career – the grain trade – was also characteristic of Jews in the region. For all their efforts to acculturate, German

Jews both in the Ruhr area and elsewhere retained a highly distinctive occupational profile. By the time of the First World War, the Ruhr was dominated by heavy industry, but very few of the region's Jews went into coal, steel or engineering. Instead, the majority remained in trade and, of those, by far the largest group were in clothing and food.[10]

Siegfried, Alfred and their younger brother Richard trained as apprentices to a Duisburg merchant. After completing their apprenticeships, they gained practical experience in the processing and storage of grain and fodder with the company Siegfried Heineberg, Jewish corn brokers in Düsseldorf. Some of Siegfried's references and curricula vitae survive. They tell us that he and his brother mastered, amongst other things, business correspondence, book-keeping, stock management – and telephone conversation. Evidently, telephone conversation was still considered sufficiently arcane to rank as an acquirable skill. In those days, of course, the receiver and mouthpiece were two separate parts. One of Siegfried's nephews told me that Siegfried and Alfred were such a double-act that, later, when they had their own business, one of them would do the speaking and the other the listening.[11] After a year's military service in 1910–11, Siegfried spent three years working for Heineberg as a grain, seed and animal fodder salesman. The First World War interrupted his career.[12]

For her part, Ine attended a commercial college, graduating with good results in March 1916.[13] She then trained as a teacher and was briefly employed in a commercial college in Münster, where a surviving reference suggests that she was a great success.[14] A cultured and intelligent person, in a later generation she would surely have gone to university. She had some training as a painter, and until her marriage painted for pleasure with considerable success. She was also a great linguist, one of her life-long interests being the local dialect, the Westphalian Platt.

The call to arms

For both Siegfried and Alfred, as Marianne remembered, the First World War was a defining experience. Keen members of the Reserve before the war, both rushed to the colours and spent the whole of the war in the field. Marianne's documents include Alfred's army pay book, which shows that he joined the Reserve Infantry Regiment 220 on 1 October 1911, at the age of twenty, was called up on the second day of mobilization and rejoined the regiment for war on 30 August 1914. He served with the regiment, primarily on the eastern front, until July 1918 and then with the mine-laying Batallion 20. Siegfried, for his part, fought on the western front with Füsilier-Regiment 39 Düsseldorf. In total, about 100,000 Jews, 18 percent of the entire German-Jewish population, served in the course of the war.[15]

For the brothers, the war instilled a powerful identification with the fatherland and a strong sense of having merited official recognition and honour. Amongst Marianne's papers are hundreds of photo-cards from the front which her father and uncle collected to mark the experience. Marianne told me that her father was an officer in the German army, and this presumably was the way the family liked to think of him. In fact, the two Strauss brothers did not make it to full officer class, both remaining at non-commissioned officer level – Siegfried as corporal, his brother as sergeant. Of course, for Jews even this level of promotion was not easy to achieve and only 2,000 made it further to become officers.[16] Marianne also told me that her father had been awarded the Iron Cross. Again, this may well have become family lore, but does not seem to have been quite the truth. It is certain that both Siegfried and Alfred were among the 35,000 Jewish soldiers who were decorated for valorous service, and both received the Honour Cross of Front Fighters, but it seems that only Alfred was awarded the more prestigious Iron Cross (Second Class), on 4 April 1915.[17] Warm letters sent from his lieutenant convalescing at home to Alfred at the front testify to the esteem in which the latter was held by his superior officer.[18]

Although Siegfried and Alfred had a good war, the conflict also brought tragedy to the family. Among the family papers, I found the last correspondence between their brother Richard and their father, dating from early December 1916. On 14 December 1916, aged twenty-three years and eleven months, Richard died of malaria on a transport in East Prussia.[19] So the Strauss family felt it had made ample sacrifice for the fatherland.

We now know that the First World War and Germany's subsequent defeat were key moments in the resurgence of politically aggressive

On the eve of war: Siegfried as soldier

anti-Semitism.[20] In 1916, in reaction to accusations that Jews were shirking their duty at the front, the Prussian War Ministry ordered a count of all Jews in active service. The figures showed that Jews were at least as well represented as the rest of the population but, shamefully, the Ministry refused to publish them.[21] Defeat further poisoned the atmosphere, and a Reich Association of Jewish Combat Veterans (Reichsbund jüdischer Frontsoldaten; RjF) was formed with the intention of combating the defamation of Jewish participants in the war effort.[22] Yet, for the Strauss brothers and so many others like them, it was unthinkable that their services to the country should be forgotten.[23]

Business and marriage

For a brief period after the war, Siegfried worked in Dinslaken's municipal food administration.[24] But on 26 August 1919, he and Alfred founded the grain and cattle-feed firm Gebrüder Strauss OHG, operating from Essen, then a major industrial centre of around 500,000 inhabitants in the heart of the Ruhr valley.[25] At corn exchanges in Essen, Duisburg, Cologne and elsewhere the brothers bought grain from overseas suppliers. Then they travelled around the region and sold grain mixes as cattle-feed to local farmers, retailers and other large customers.[26] It was a far from easy time to start up in business. The unsettled post-revolutionary political atmosphere and galloping inflation bankrupted many enterprises. But the brothers prospered. There is circumstantial evidence to suggest that they knew how to turn the inflation to advantage, since they invested Reichsmarks of little value in property and other fixed capital that was to make a good return in later years. In 1922 they bought land and in 1923 they made their first property deal on the Brunnenstrasse in Essen. On the other hand, they were too solid to indulge in speculation. The company's listing of its debtors and creditors shows that throughout the inflation years the company was consistently owed more by its debtors than it owed to its creditors.[27]

From the start, the brothers took a scientific approach to the right fodder mix for farm animals. With leaflets such as 'The hen is an egg machine', picturing a proud hen strutting against the background of an industrial factory, they appealed to the 1920s commitment to rationaliz-ation.[28] The other key factor in their success, according to one of the company's salesmen, was the brothers' methodical approach to selling. In 1923, the business acquired its first car, enabling the firm's salesmen to drive round and visit the thousands of farms in the area.[29]

Werner Hoffmann joined the company in April 1924, when it was already a flourishing concern. Still upright and square-shouldered despite being almost ninety when I met him in Buenos Aires in 1998, he remembered the Strauss brothers as born officer types. He and another youngster with the company, Hans Goldschmidt, used to laugh behind their backs at Siegfried's stiff military style. Alfred at least had a jovial touch in dealing with the customers; Siegfried had never been known to smile. There was no doubt that the brothers ran a tight ship. Employees were not allowed to be unoccupied for a moment. Werner remembered one example of the brothers' no-nonsense approach to the business: he was out selling in 1934 when he heard that Saly Strauss had died and rang in, offering to come back. 'There is no cause to take a holiday,' was the stern reply. He laughed at the memory. Now, with a successful business career in Argentina behind him, he said he had learned a lot about business methods from the brothers. In later years he would often catch himself applying some maxim or other that he had gained from them.[30]

By 1921, the now thirty-year-old Siegfried felt sufficiently established to consider marriage. There were various ways for Jews to meet a suitable partner at the time but a common one was to go to one of the seaside or cure resorts favoured by Jews. Norderney, a North Sea island off the Fresian coast, was a popular destination for Jews from the Ruhr, and it was here that Siegfried and Regina met, possibly introduced by a cousin. The courtship proceeded rapidly. An elegant card survives, announcing the couple's engagement in December 1921. They were married on Sunday 27 August 1922, 3 Ellul 5682 in the Hebrew calen-dar, at 1.30, in the Hotel Piper in Ahlen. Siegfried's father officiated at the wedding.

What did the pair see in each other? She was not particularly beautiful, nor he especially handsome. Both tended even then towards a certain rotundity. But by the same token, both had stature and gravitas. Their backgrounds were similar. Both were very serious people, though Nord-

Marianne's parents at the time of their engagement

erney would have brought out their gayer sides. In Marianne's photo collection, the snaps where her parents are smiling tend to be those taken at the seaside – at Norderney, or at the Dutch resort of Noordwijk. Marianne believed that her parents had a very good relationship. It was not an outwardly passionate marriage, and initially possibly not even a love match. 'Perhaps all the better because of it,' said a seventy-six-year-old Marianne with her own long years of marriage behind her. She felt her parents had had a great deal of respect for each other. Siegfried was not artistically inclined but admired Ine's talent, whilst she probably saw in him the honest, forceful, hard worker that he was. For Siegfried, Ine's dowry of RM60,000 was no bad thing, either, and he invested it immediately into the purchase of a marital home.

In later years, Marianne's mother would tell her that respectable people waited a little after marriage before having their first child. However, if Marianne was conceived the statistically average thirty-nine weeks before she was born, a rough calculation back from Marianne's birthday, 7 June 1923, suggests that Ine conceded less than two weeks to propriety.

About the birth itself, we know very little. The only family paper to shed some light on the occasion was a little note, dated 7 June 1923, from Marianne's father to her mother. Written on the back of one of his business cards, he thanked her 'for the new happiness which has been bestowed upon me by you'.[31] Seemingly nondescript as a historical source, in fact the card hints at three Strauss characteristics. First, Siegfried Strauss was undoubtedly very proud to have children. Second, if sentiment was articulated at all in the Strauss family then it was stiffly and formally. And, third, Siegfried was not a man to spend money on such fripperies as a greetings card, when the back of a business card would serve. Family pride, stiffness and great care with money were dominant themes in Marianne's childhood.

The house Siegfried and Ine bought in February 1922, Ladenspelder-strasse 47, was a substantial building with three stories and a cellar. The attic rooms were let out to a tenant, Fräulein Remkes, to help pay for the mortgage. A couple of months after Marianne was born, with the French occupation of the Ruhr still ongoing, the Strausses were obliged to put up a French officer for a while.[32] When Marianne's brother Richard was born in 1926, conditions became rather cramped and the maid had to sleep on a chaise longue in the living room. Eventually, the Strausses were able to help Fraülein Remkes to find a room elsewhere. In 1928, the family had a struggle to prevent the city authorities from imposing another tenant on them.[33]

The house itself was nicely furnished. There was Chippendale furniture

Siegfried and Ine on honeymoon, 1922

and heavy Persian carpets in many of the rooms, and a number of valuable paintings.[34] When I talked to Marianne, some of the pieces were still on display in Liverpool. A relative, Eva Selig, claimed that the house of Marianne's parents was one of the most beautiful she had visited.[35]

The neighbourhood was not particularly Jewish – indeed, there was no real Jewish quarter in Essen – which is hardly surprising since the

5,000 odd Jews in the town made up only 1 per cent of its population.[36] Poorer Jews tended to live north of the centre around the Viehofer Platz, whilst the most affluent gravitated south of the city, into Bredeney or in Rüttenscheid. The Strausses lived in between, just to the west of the centre, in Essen-Holsterhausen. Ladenspelderstrasse was a reasonably well-to-do street of new houses, in which a few other Jewish families had also found residence. Bernd Simon, who as a young German Jew had lived across the road from the Strausses, remembered them as respectable if rather distant neighbours.[37] Later, Siegfried's brother Alfred moved into a new house at number 74.

In 1997 I made a pilgrimage to Ladenspelderstrasse. I knew that the Strausses' house had been destroyed by a bomb in the war. What I hadn't bargained for was that there would be no number 47 at all. I walked up and down the street, and enlisted the assistance of a young man in one of the Ruhr's typical little street kiosks, but he couldn't help. Then an elderly resident told me that when the houses were rebuilt in a different style – squat ugly 1950s blocks – there were fewer buildings than addresses, so some numbers had been dropped. It seemed eerily appropriate for victims of the Holocaust that there should not even be a sign of the space the Strausses' house had once occupied.

Marianne's childhood

'I wasn't a very happy child,' Marianne said, 'and didn't have a very happy temperament.' And on another occasion she said: 'My mother didn't have an easy time with me – but I didn't have an easy time with my mother.' She remembered her parents with great love and respect and tended to blame herself for her unhappy memories; indeed, she felt an enormous amount of guilt in relation to her parents, but she could not look back on the 1920s with much pleasure:[38]

'I was very dependent on my mother. We always had a nanny, later on a governess. When I was young, I missed my mother very much. My parents would go on skiing holidays and we would have a nanny. I was utterly miserable when they were away. I don't know why I was so relieved when they returned.'

Life before Richard: Marianne at the seaside, 1925

One of Marianne's early memories was of being 'very, very naughty indeed' when her mother was away. The nanny wanted her to put on some clothes, but Marianne 'absolutely refused'. Her grandmother was 'quite scandalized'. The memory was particularly significant because the event took place soon after her brother was born – 'I was sitting there on my brother's changing table and didn't want to put some shoes on.' Marianne told me that when she was very small she adored her father and he seemed to adore her. 'He was a wonderful dad to have around.' But as soon as her brother was born, his whole interest focused completely on the boy. In telling me this, Marianne leaped to protect her father; she was sure that the problem 'never occurred' to him, but she 'really resented' his shifting attentions which coloured her relationship with him. Again, she was self-critical, 'I wasn't an easy child by any means.' Her brother was a charming child, she wasn't so charming, and so he got a lot of attention. Richard was quieter, more serious and easier and therefore also a more cosseted child.

'We were brought up in a very autocratic way. Looking back on it, my parents were very Victorian in their attitudes. We had a very, very

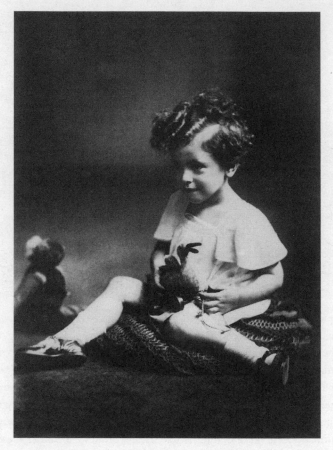

Marianne, 1925–6

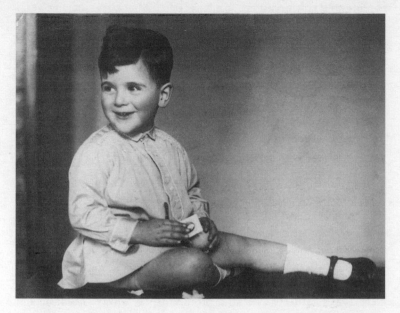

Marianne's younger brother Richard

austere upbringing in many ways.' When the children were young, a lot of time was spent with 'well-trained nannies' who would take them out to Essen's new Gruga park and in later years supervise their homework. When she was older, Marianne suffered from the very strong emphasis on prowess at school. She could remember having bad marks and being absolutely terrified of coming home from school. Her mother took 'all that very seriously':[39]

'My mother had a very volcanic temper, so if things didn't go the way she wanted them to go she'd let you know soon enough. And she was also a very moral sort of person, having been brought up by nuns. She'd been to a convent school and of course she had all the prejudices that went with being brought up in a convent school. Which then was transmitted on to me, who was a natural rebel. So that really was not a very easy milieu to be brought up in. The pressure formed a cloud over my childhood – I hated school I really did.'

A few letters survive which the schoolgirl Marianne wrote to her parents on family occasions. In a letter dated May 1932, the nine-year-old wrote in a painfully correct German hand:[40]

> *Dear Daddy,*
> *Today is father's day. I thank you for all the love you have shown me. You have always worked for us. I wish you a long life, much happiness and health. I will pay good attention at school so that I can get into higher school next year and I will give you much happiness. Now I give you, dear Daddy, best wishes for today.*
> *Your,*
> *Marianne*

A mother's day note from the same month recorded rather stiffly: 'you are very dear to me, my Mama', and promised again 'I want always to bring you happiness. When I am bigger I will always help you.'[41] (Across the top of the note, Marianne's mother has written 'on the day my dear father died' – Isaak Rosenberg died on 8 May 1932.) Earnest promises of more work and more devotion continually recur. An undated Jewish New Year's card began with a promise to be 'always obedient and diligent'.[42] In a card for the Jewish New Year in 1935, the twelve-year-old Marianne wrote 'I promise you that I will always be good and diligent'.[43] And another note, written to offer her parents greetings for the 1936 secular new year, struck a similar chord: 'I have the firm intention that this year I will bring you only happiness. I want to make a special effort at school.'[44]

The children were given little freedom or responsibility. 'We never had pocket money because my father had the feeling that we had everything we needed, and I found that very difficult.' Looking back as a trained kindergarten teacher who had raised her own children, Marianne allowed herself to be critical of her parents on this point. As it was, she had had no sense of the value of money. Money was never short in the family – unlike so many of her contemporaries, Marianne had no special recollection of the Depression. Yet, 'here we were . . . leading a luxurious life, worry-free, on the one hand; on the other hand, every penny had to be accounted for.'[45] If friends gave her money, it had to go into a savings box. Once, she opened the box surreptitiously and took some money

Letter, Marianne to parents, New Year 5695 (September 1934):
I have the firm intention of bringing you only happiness this
year. I will make particular efforts at school.'

for sweets. Her mother noticed, and 'all hell broke loose – because of the dishonesty'.[46] Even in 1941, when Marianne was already eighteen and living away from home in Berlin, and when the entire world was falling apart around them, her father did not allow her to use her whole stipend[47] – she had to send some home, 'which I did religiously. One day, when I overspent, I had sleepless nights to have to explain to my father how I'd overspent. My father took that very seriously; they were very moral, everything was a moral issue.' There was a whole correspondence about the missing money. 'So that's how money was regarded, with great seriousness in a most extraordinary way.'[48] 'An awful lot was expected from us as children – probably more than most other children. It wasn't very carefree or easy going.'[49] Werner Hoffmann remembered Marianne as an intelligent child but rather withdrawn and quiet and without a large circle of friends.[50]

Marianne's social life was focused very much on the extended family. Her fondest memories, apart from those of her grandparents, were of her aunt, Lore 'Oe' Dahl, Alfred's wife. Lore Dahl, the daughter of David and Else Dahl, came from a well-established family in Wuppertal-Elberfeld. She married Alfred in 1927 when he was thirty-five and she not quite twenty. They made a much more relaxed couple than Marianne's parents. Lore had come to Alfred on the rebound. She had fallen deeply in love with a cousin of hers but, although such a match would not have been forbidden by Jewish tradition, her family were against it, above all worrying about the health of any offspring. It was a bitter irony when it transpired after her marriage that she was unable to have children. For Alfred and Lore, Richard became a surrogate son, 'as much their child as my parents'', said Marianne. 'He adored Lore and she adored him. When she came into the family, he couldn't pronounce Lore and made it Oe, as that was all he could say. So she became Oe in the family.'[51]

When Marianne and Richard went on holiday trips to Norderney with their parents, Alfred and Lore would often travel up afterwards and Richard would stay on with them. This special favouritism was not easy for the young Marianne to take, but over time, her relationship with Oe grew extremely close.[52] Marianne admired Oe's energy and enthusiasm and her talent for getting on with young people.[53]

Marianne with grandmother Saly Strauss in Dinslaken

After Alfred and Lore had moved into a building further down the Ladenspelderstrasse, one of the treats for the Strauss children was to go down on their own to their uncle and aunt's flat on Sunday mornings and have breakfast with them:[54]

'When we went there, sometimes they hadn't got up yet, and the greatest fun was to crawl into bed with them. They called it the Cave of Machpele, from the Bible story; my uncle made a sort of cave in the bedclothes and my brother would disappear into these bedclothes and that was a game they played quite frequently on a Sunday morning.'

Apart from visiting family, other happy childhood memories included Marianne's dance classes. She had a teacher trained by Rudolf von Laban and Marie Wigman, and learned modern and group dance, coupled with a little philosophy. Marianne said she was absolutely determined to become a professional dancer, an idea that horrified her mother. Marianne also took piano lessons. Then there were regular weekend visits to the Folkwang museum, Essen's art gallery. Although the museum's behaviour to its many Jewish benefactors in the 1930s was far from laudable, Marianne maintained her affection for it up to her death and bequeathed the gallery a Chagall lithograph in her will. At weekends too, the family would often go out for coffee and cakes to one of the many pleasant cafés in southern Essen, Schwarzer Lene or the Heimliche Liebe with its spectacular views of the city forest, the Baldeney lake, the Ruhr and the Villa Hügel, the Krupp family home.

For holidays, the family would often go to Norderney for six weeks, with 'full trunks and the nanny and everybody'. Or to the Dutch resort of Noordwijk, on the North Sea near Leiden, where they stayed in an elegant hotel, the Haus der Dönen.[55] These holidays were a pleasure, though, here, too, there were memories of being at odds with her parents. Marianne told me that her father was riding on the beach in Noordwijk one day when it started to rain. 'I said, "Oh, the poor horse!", and my mother was scandalized that I worried about the horse and not my father!'

Alexander and Alfred, Eric and Uri

My contact with one of Marianne's two surviving close relatives, her cousin Eric Alexander (formerly Alex Weinberg), began with a rather engaging letter to Vivian Ellenbogen.

Stamford, Lincs,
19 January 1997

Dear Vivian,

As you know, I had a phone call from a Mr Roseman. I have written down such meagre details as I can remember and I am posting a copy of these to you. I am also enclosing the copy intended for Mr Roseman. I am sending this to you rather than directly to him to give you an opportunity to consign it to the wastepaper basket if you so wish. As you will see, my views about your grandfather are not very positive. However, in my view it would not be fair to the memory of your mother and to the memory of your grandmother – my favourite aunt – to concoct a distorted picture from the one I remember . . .

The people swallowed up by the Holocaust were human beings, not plaster-cast saints, and human beings, alas, have faults as well as virtues.

Best wishes and regards to your family,
Alex

Eric Alexander was the oldest son of Ine's sister Hannah. Alongside the refreshing honesty, what emerged from his letter was a prickly persona with somewhat contested identity. For one thing, I did not know how to address him – was he Eric or Alex? The note to Vivian was signed Alex, the attached letter to me was signed Eric Alexander. For another, in the letter to me he managed to be extremely critical not only, as the cover-note promised, of Marianne's father but also of Germany ('every self-respecting (?) town' had a concentration camp), the hypocrisy of his parents' German-Jewish identity ('In Erkelenz[56] Hebrew was gabbled parrot fashion') and the attitudes of Eastern European Jewry ('still very much influenced by . . . the Shtetl').

In a subsequent letter, Eric Alexander invited me up to Stamford to talk about 'Germany and the whole ghostly/ghastly cavalcade'. So, on a sunny summer morning, I drove across from Birmingham to Stamford. He and his second wife Nancy lived in an attractive modern complex of flats near the city centre. In keeping with the gardens outside, which were bright with flowers, the Alexanders' flat was full of floral designs. Sofa and curtains were in chintz. There was some nice china and generally a slightly old-fashioned, genteel English feel. Nancy, a tall, graceful presence in a floral dress, had put her stamp on the apartment. Alex, kindly looking and somewhat rounder, reminded me of German-Jewish émigrés I had known from the Reform-Jewish community in which I grew up, in Leeds.

Eric Alexander had grown up as Alexander Weinberg, the oldest of three brothers, in Erkelenz, a small town to the south of Mönchen-

Marianne with her cousins, the Weinberg boys,
in Erkelenz, 1928

Gladbach, north-west of Cologne. His father, Ernst Weinberg, had been born and bred in the town, knew everybody, was well-connected and served on the town council. He ran the family store, A. Weyl Nachfolger, selling clothes and later toys. His war service had been even more illustrious than the Strausses'. While still a sergeant, he was with his men in a dugout when a nearby explosion destabilized some poison-gas canisters. Until he himself collapsed, Ernst repeatedly went into the dugout and dragged his men out, saving many of them from death. His commanding officer put him up for a commission and he became a lieutenant. His sabre remained on permanent display in Alex's grandmother's room. 'It was ironic,' said Alex, 'he was saving his men from gas only to be gassed himself.' 'Surely he wasn't gassed,' I said, since

Alex's parents had been killed in Łodz as far as I knew. But it is true, the fate of many of the deportees is not certain.[57] 'Łodz, Majdanek, Treblinka – who knows?' said Alex. Later I learned that many of the economically 'inactive' Jews of Łodz were gassed at Chelmno as early as January 1942.[58]

After the First World War, Ernst married Hannah Rosenberg and the boys were born: Alexander in 1921, Alfred in 1923 (just a couple of weeks before Marianne) and Otto in 1924. In 1937, as persecution worsened and it became apparent that the family store could not be maintained, the family moved to Cologne. In 1939, the boys came to Britain, Alex first and then the other two with a special transport organized by their Jewish school. Later Alex and Otto both volunteered for the British army, and it was in the army that they changed their names. Gerald (Otto) ended up fighting in Germany with the Glasgow Highlanders, Eric (Alex) was in the Middle East, interrogating German POWs. Alfred was interned as an enemy alien in Liverpool and later in Australia, whence he went to Israel. He is the only one of the brothers to have retained the name Weinberg, but in Israel the Alfred metamorphosed to Uri.

In the early part of the war it was possible for the boys and their parents to write to each other, thanks to the Red Cross, but the letters were few and far between. I had seen a letter sent out by Marianne's grandmother, Anna Rosenberg, in 1940–1, in which she said of Hannah and Ernst, 'Sadly, they very seldom hear from the boys.' I'd noted this down on my pad and Alex, when he saw it, said rather gruffly, 'Well, not at all, I should think, yeh, well, there you are.' His parents were deported to Łodz in October 1941. After the war, one of his uncles told Alex that someone had 'seen my father gathering nettles to eat, you see, but there again, whether true or not, who knows . . . It's impossible to tell. You have to excuse me for a minute . . .' And he went into the other room for a moment or two.

In the 1920s, the Weinbergs did not have a great deal of contact with the Strauss family and tended to see rather more of relatives on Ernst's side of the family, the Alsbergs. This was partly a question of distance, as Erkelenz was a good couple of hours' journey from Essen, but also because, according to Alex, Siegfried Strauss was not particularly liked in the Weinberg family. Alex's parents used to refer to a little raised area in the centre of the Strausses' sitting room as 'the heights of Siegfried'. Alex's mother later told him that in 1923–24, after the hyperinflation, the business in Erkelenz was foundering:

'My mother went to see her father in Ahlen to obtain further funds. He gave her a second dowry of – I believe – another 60,000 marks. When Siegfried got wind of this – so the story goes – he threatened to divorce Ine unless he got the same. I am not sure that Marianne even knew this story. I rather hope she did not.'

Alex confirmed Marianne's impression that the Strausses were very careful with money – though in this he felt they were very much of a piece with his grandfather Rosenberg's household. Marianne had remembered Isaak as a very generous and outgoing individual, always with guests at the table, but Alex's perception was different. He felt the Rosenbergs' wealth didn't show at all. For example, Alex's mother had told him the story of her courtship by his father, Ernst. Before Ernst's visit to inspect and be inspected by the two available Rosenberg daughters, Hannah had thought it expedient to trim the frayed linoleum floor-covering with a carving knife. Still, Alex, like Marianne, had very much enjoyed visiting the Rosenbergs. Going to Ahlen with its spacious courtyard and its horses was the highlight of the year.

Alex's own perceptions of Siegfried were particularly negative. Before the meeting he had written to me:

When the Strauss family were together, one could not fail to see how Siegfried Strauss doted on Marianne's young brother Richard. I cannot recollect similar displays of paternal affection towards Marianne. I never discussed with Marianne her relationship with her parents, but I would not be surprised if at least for some part of her growing up period the relationship with her father was rather fraught.

Much of this confirmed Marianne's memories, but in Alex's eyes, Siegfried appeared far more wilful and bitter and less august. And in his letter, Alex's view of Marianne's mother both reinforced and differed from hers:

I loved my mother very much, but I always thought that aunt Ine was both better educated and more intelligent than my mother, who liked the lighter side of life. In Ahlen, they had oil paintings done very competently by Ine. My impression is in retrospect that Ine's marriage was not a happy one. I might be mistaken, but my impression is that Ine was afraid of her husband. I thought Siegfried was a petty domestic tyrant.

About Marianne herself, Alex had little to say. As a child he had liked her very much, and in the 1930s, when Marianne had come to stay with the family, there had been a brief, very innocent relationship between them. This had come to an abrupt end when they were found holding hands. But in Alex's memory, it was the negative relationship with Siegfried which had stuck.

Since the war, Alex had had intermittent contact with Marianne. Nancy said she'd only met Marianne a couple of times, but remembered her as very charming and sophisticated. 'She was a big girl,' she said, but when she walked 'it was as if she floated. You didn't see her move.' When Nancy said Marianne had been a big girl, Alex – who clearly still had a soft spot for his cousin – gallantly said it was the cortisone.

Several times on and off the tape, Alex came back to the moment of parting with his own parents when he left for England at the age of eighteen. I wondered at what point he had learned of his parents' deaths. He said he'd always known what was coming. When he and his father parted at the station in early 1939 his father said maybe they'd see each other again, and Alex had said, coldly, 'I don't think so.' And this brusqueness, plus the fact that he'd complained his mother wasn't there – she was involved in a sweet-making course in Munich, but probably also just couldn't bear to come – still haunted Alex.

Alex had arrived in Britain with a fierce hatred of Germans. His father wrote to him that he shouldn't volunteer for the British army because the Germans would shoot him as a traitor if he were caught, but Alex was 'raring to go'. But despite feeling so anti-German, he felt at odds with his Jewishness. He felt that there were only two choices: to live in Israel, or to cease being a Jew. And since his first wife did not wish to live in Israel, he converted to the Anglican faith. He did not wish his children to go through what he had suffered.

Yet Alex still felt deeply tied to his former fatherland:

'I'm a German man, I suppose. I am really, what with the accent and what have you. I would have *liked* to be in Germany, yes. I might have got my chips in Russia, I suppose. Germany was my country, my father brought me up that way, you see. That's why I hated the Germans so much.'

Thus, when Alex talked to me about Siegfried, I knew that, whilst some of his dislike clearly resulted from his own observations – for example the relative neglect of Marianne – mapped on to those observations now was a complex love–hate relationship with all the values that German-Jewish fathers had stood for.

Less than a fortnight after this conversation, I was in Israel. My aim, among other things, was to talk to Uri, Alex's brother. On the phone, Uri had a much stronger accent than Alex, still clearly German but now mixed with something else – it sounded more Yiddish than German. He lived in Batei Ungari, part of Me'a Sharim, Jerusalem's ultra-Orthodox quarter and home to some of the most observant Jews in the world. Evidently, Uri's address wasn't going to be easy to find, since the house numbers did not follow any conventional order. The directions were complex: go past a print shop and round a corner to a gap in the wall; pass through into a courtyard; up some steps into another courtyard and then turn right; more steps, a left turn and the second door along the balcony was his.

The street with the print shop was full of hurrying men in black suits, some in black stockings and streimels.[59] There were signs periodically enjoining visitors to dress modestly. Then, there really was a gap in the wall, and suddenly I found myself in a different world. In the courtyard, young mothers draped in simple, heavy dresses looked up suspiciously from playing with their children. I bounded up the stone steps and counted down the doors. Uri's was open. From the balcony, I entered straight into a room that could have been in a Polish ghetto town. A penetrating smell of a meat stew floated in from the back somewhere. The wallpaper was peeling and filthy. There was very little furniture – just a wooden table, a couple of chairs, and cupboards full of books in Hebrew. Uri, who had been sweeping out the room, put down his broom. I saw only one characteristic that constituted any kind of link with Alex's or Uri's German past: Uri's luminous blue eyes, which looked out from a face adorned with a magnificent white beard.

I'd worried whether he might have reservations about my using a tape-recorder, but Uri was very uncomplicated about such things. He began – and it takes up a good forty minutes on the tape – by telling me the story of his trip on the notorious ship the *Dunera*, which took a mixture of German prisoners of war and Jewish internees from Liverpool to Australia for internment. Uri was something I have never encountered before – a truly gifted raconteur of the old school. The story began in the middle, on the gangplank out to the ship, then swept back in widening circles of explanation before plunging to its ironic conclusion.[60]

I mentioned Alex's view that Siegfried Strauss had not been well liked in the family:

'Alex has some funny memories; well, not funny . . . He was and he was not – he was liked and he wasn't liked, you can't say. He was more exact like, you know. He was more of a soicher [a businessman] than my father. My father was a bad merchant, like me. We are too easy-going. We can't go after every penny.'

Uri's memories circled more around the amusing quirks of each individual.

'The Strauss family? Well, let's see, there were two brothers and two wives. It was known, the two brothers . . . nothing came between them . . . One said something, the other helped him a bit. The wives, it's just the same. They were not fighting. Never.'

It was Uri who told me about the Strauss brothers telephoning, one holding the receiver, the other speaking into the mouthpiece. And he had a similar account of family life in Essen:

'Yes, always my mother said, "In Essen it goes like this: Siegfried shouts 'The kids should go to bed'. The kids shout back and the women say, 'Oh, let them stay', first Oe then Ine and then Alfred says 'No, no, the kids into bed.'" That's how it was always.'

Uri's laugh was infectious. He, like Alex, had a dowry story in his pocket, but it was a different one, concerning the original dowry. Siegfried and Alfred had gone to Ahlen to collect it:

'It was the middle of the inflation. My father was there . . . The whole dowry was on the table and in Germany they had these big baskets you could lock up, like trunks. They filled up the whole basket with the dowry . . . but it didn't all fit in, so Siegfried and Alfred took a flour bag or whatever, a corn bag, and with the rest of the dowry, the corn bag was also full . . . It was a rainy day. My father never laughed so much as when the two of them, just as they got the dowry – they didn't barely say goodbye yeh – they grabbed the basket to make the train to Essen, one of them holding the bag, I don't know who held it, Alfred or Siegfried, both holding the trunk, one on each side, and running all the way to the station. When they arrived in Essen an hour later the money was only worth half. My father laughed his head off at the time.'[61]

Uri's story too captured the Strauss brothers' hard-headedness, but in a less angry way – perhaps reflecting the fact that Uri's account stemmed from his father, whilst Alex had heard his story from his mother.

Uri's take on Ine differed, also – both from Alex's and from Marianne's own memory. Whereas Alex had seen in Ine the intellectual, and Marianne remembered her mother as something of a firebrand, Uri felt that she was more relaxed. In fact, Uri's judgement on almost every aspect of family life was different from that of his brother. He did, however, share Alex and Marianne's pleasure at visiting Ahlen. But whereas both Marianne and Alex had remembered the Rosenbergs as very religious, for Uri, measured against the Me'a Sharim scale of religious observance, Isaak hadn't been so Orthodox. The really religious member of the family, he told me, had been his paternal grandfather, whom he'd never met.

Before I left, Uri asked after his brother. Though their post-war diaspora had taken them in such different directions, the two retained a great deal of affection for each other and telephoned occasionally. Uri had maintained intermittent contact with Marianne, too, though he had actually seen her only once since the war. She and Basil had come to visit him in Jerusalem, but stayed only ten minutes. Why was that? The meeting had been fraught. Uri had asked after the children, but unbeknown to him it was just a few months after Elaine's death:

'I said to Marianne, "You have a son and a daughter, how are they?" And then she told me right out. She could keep herself. I can also. But Basil broke down.'

The Weinberg boys now (Eric Alexander and Uri Weinberg)

On the Ellenbogens' later trips to Israel, Basil returned to visit, but Marianne did not come with him. The thought of one of her own family choosing a life so wholly alien was, I think, unbearable for her.

The Strausses, the Jewish community and anti-Semitism

What little social contact Marianne's parents cultivated outside the family tended to be with Essen's Jewish community, which by the 1920s had grown from just a couple of hundred a century earlier to over 5,000. It had also become more affluent, largely through the success of self-employed businessmen such as the Strauss brothers, who made up a majority of the community. A growing number of Jewish professionals – particularly lawyers and doctors – added to the congregation's wealth and prestige. In 1913, a new synagogue had been consecrated, one of the grandest and most imposing works of Jewish architecture in Germany, whose striking green cupola became (and remains) a dominant feature of the Essen skyline.[62]

The community increasingly moved away from traditional Orthodox practice. The Strausses themselves were intermittent rather than regular synagogue-goers, though Marianne's mother was active in the Jewish Women's League. In this, they resembled most of the community – only the recently arrived immigrants from Eastern Europe, the so-called *Ostjuden*, were more observant.[63]

Apart from periodic synagogue visits, Marianne's other main contact with the community began in 1929, when she began attending the Jewish school. Located in a modern building within easy walking distance of her home, the school was quite large, with 450 boys and girls – indicating that many members of the community sent their children there, at least for the elementary years. Marianne had no particularly strong memories of the school, though her general recollection was positive. She believed she gained a very good grounding in Jewish history and Hebrew. When I later found records of her performance at the Yavne Jewish school in Cologne and the Jewish kindergarten college in Berlin, however, Hebrew turned out to be by far her worst subject.[64]

Marianne had no sense that her German-Jewish identity was in any way

Marianne at the Jewish school, 1932 (back row, centre)

problematic before 1933. Her memories do, however, reveal considerable social segregation. Her parents' social life was restricted to family and Jewish community. Marianne went to a Jewish school. She did not recall ever playing with non-Jewish neighbours on the street. Her cousins, too, remembered social intercourse being largely restricted to other Jews. But this does not necessarily indicate that there was a 'problem'. It could, for example, have been a sign of an active choice among German Jews to maintain their identity, to have both 'Goethe *and* Gemeinde' – both German culture and Jewish community.[65] It is often forgotten that Catholics and Protestants, too, did not mix socially at the time.

The lack of social intercourse with non-Jews does, however, limit what we can learn from Marianne's testimony. Because she had not yet reached secondary-school age and was still very much within the family orbit before the Nazis came to power, social segregation prevented her from being aware of her differentness. So, all her own memories can tell us is that anti-Semitism had not at the time reached a level which impinged on a well-protected child in an affluent family.

From the latter part of the nineteenth century, anti-Semitism had undoubtedly gained ground as a social force among broad sections of the middle class. Even in the Ruhr, one of the most tolerant regions in Germany, Jews were left bewildered and dismayed by their encounters with renewed manifestations of anti-Semitic sentiment.[66] Particularly, after the First World War, politically aggressive anti-Semitism never really went away. In Essen and elsewhere, new Jewish organizations emerged, reflecting the community's sense that it needed to assert itself.[67] On the other hand, the Weimar Republic was not a one-way street leading to Nazism.[68] It was only after 1929, in the disastrous economic and social conditions of the Depression, that extreme right-wing radicalism in the form of the Nazi Party came to dominate the political stage.

In fact, for Marianne's family, as for Marianne herself, the family history before 1933 held remarkably few clues as to what was to follow. The Strausses' and Rosenbergs' success stories before 1933 did not presage disaster. On the contrary, even the Depression was weathered by the brothers with relative ease. And as far as Marianne herself is concerned, the often subdued and occasionally contrary daughter of strict middle-class Jewish parents gave barely a hint of the independent and courageous fighter she was to become.

2

Schoolgirl in the
Third Reich

Marianne was always going to find the tenth year of her life a challenge. Some children stayed on at the Jewish school until school-leaving age, but Marianne's parents had long planned for her to change after the four primary years to the Luisenschule, a highly respected *Lyzeum*, or girls' grammar school, not far from their home. The Luisenschule represented not only a new academic atmosphere, but also Marianne's first venture into non-Jewish circles. So, she was inevitably going to experience 1933 as something of a shock. However, there was an additional factor: Marianne's arrival at the Luisenschule in April 1933 took place just over two months after Adolf Hitler became Reich Chancellor.

Many Jews had feared what would happen if the Nazis came to power. Their vague forebodings were more than confirmed by the rapid succession of measures that followed Hitler's appointment on 30 January 1933. First came attacks on left-wing Jews and local boycotts of Jewish businesses.[1] On Saturday 1 April there was an official national boycott, with SA (Sturmabteiling, the Nazi paramilitary wing) guards positioned outside Jewish shops to deter potential customers. Local newspapers, among them the Essen *Nationalzeitung*, published lists of Jewish doctors, businessmen and lawyers so that right-thinking citizens would know whom to avoid. Because our sense of proportion is distorted by the horrors that came later, it is hard for us to appreciate how shocked the Jewish community was in 1933 by official state involvement in such activities. The boycott was followed by laws of restriction and exclusion. Later in April, Jews were purged from the Civil Service and denied the right to practise law (though exceptions made for First World War veterans meant that many Jewish lawyers continued to practise for the time being).

Schools everywhere proved very responsive to the new regime. In neighbouring Dortmund, for example, Jewish children were excluded from school on the day of the anti-Jewish boycott, though possibly to protect them.[2] 'Wrong-thinking' and Jewish teachers were purged from all German schools a few days later. Non-Nazi youth groups were rapidly banned and youngsters encouraged, cajoled and later forced into the Hitler Youth. Marianne was thus changing schools at a most ominous time.

Business as usual

But before we follow her into the classroom, we should look first at how her parents fared in the new conditions. For one of the defining elements of Marianne's own experience (and indeed, the reason that she continued to attend the Luisenschule) was the extraordinary insouciance with which her parents, particularly her father, met the Third Reich.

Vivian told me about the huge brown trunk in Marianne's outhouse a long time before he managed to clear a path to it. The trunk, engraved with Siegfried's initials and the number 5, was presumably the fifth in a series of cases belonging to Marianne's father. It seems that during the war it was deposited with the family banker for safe-keeping. When we finally manhandled it into Vivian's living room, we discovered a very comprehensive collection of Strauss business records which showed that the brothers had survived the 1930s in much better economic shape than I would have believed. True, in 1933 they abandoned plans for major expansion,[3] but in 1934, company turnover at RM643,432 was almost 50 per cent higher than it had been a year earlier.[4] Company profits did even better. In 1933, Alfred (for whom we have better information than for Siegfried) enjoyed pre-tax earnings of only RM11,500; his earnings in 1934 jumped to RM21,152. To give a sense of comparison, in the

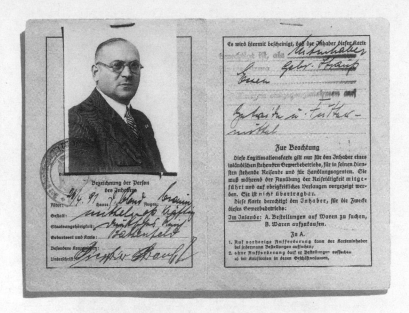

Weathering the storm; Siegfried Strauss, 1936

mid-1930s the pay of a top worker in the best-paid armaments sector was between RM2,500 and 3,000 a year before tax. Many workers would be earning only a tenth of what Alfred and Siegfried were taking home.[5] In August 1934, they felt able to enlist the help of the German consulate in Sofia to deal with a dispute arising out of a Bulgarian export ban.[6] Most striking of all was Werner Hoffmann's recollection that in February 1936, when he left for Argentina, the business was still operating without hindrance. As he drove round his customers for the last time in early 1936, making his farewells, he found that few could understand why he was going.[7]

The brothers' success is all the more surprising in that even after the national boycott was abandoned, 'unofficial' economic discrimination against Jewish businesses and workers increased apace. Within three years, many small business sectors would be effectively cleared of Jews. By 1936, a good fifth of the Jewish population was dependent on

Siegfried's employee, Werner Hoffmann, and his fiancée Hanna
Heumann at the time of their departure to Argentina 1936

Jewish welfare.[8] The Strauss brothers, however, possessed a number of advantages. First, though Essen's town administration supported anti-Jewish measures, the region was relatively tolerant. Most Jews who lived there felt somewhat protected from the excesses they heard of elsewhere. Indeed, up to 1938, Jewish emigration from the Rhineland area, to which Essen belonged, was proportionately lower than for the country as a whole.[9] Secondly, the regime was initially very hesitant to do anything that might disrupt the food trade. But probably the most important factor favouring the Strauss brothers was that they went to their customers, not the other way round, and their customers were in farms away from the public gaze.[10]

Even if they had thought of selling up, there were also serious economic disincentives to leaving the country. It was increasingly hard to get a proper price for Jewish assets. Potential customers assumed the seller would be desperate enough to accept any price. Then, the so-called Reich Flight Tax (*Reichsfluchtsteuer*) had to be paid. This tax had been introduced in 1931 to hinder the emigration of wealthy asset holders. After 1934, its main thrust changed to fleecing Jewish emigrants, and a wealthy individual like Siegfried could reckon on losing 25 per cent of his assets to the tax. But there was more. With foreign currency at a premium in the German economy, there were very tight restrictions on conversion. Again, to economic necessity was added anti-Semitic logic. The result was that a Jew in Siegfried's position leaving Germany before 1937 would be lucky to take 50 percent of his assets abroad. The only exception to these restrictions was emigration to Palestine. But Palestine, with its primitive conditions and limited business opportunities, had no appeal for a man like Siegfried Strauss, who had always been hostile towards the separatism of the Zionists.[11] After 1937, the screw was tightened further, with ever more punitive currency conversion rates being applied. For the Strauss brothers, Werner Hoffmann told me, the idea of getting out of Germany with a small remnant of their wealth 'was simply brushed aside.'[12]

But economics was only part of the explanation for the brothers' refusal to leave. Werner remembered much talk of the imminent collapse of the regime. And then there was their utter conviction that the debt to a former front-line soldier would not be forgotten. Marianne noted with a trace of irony how her father used to quote General Ludendorff's statement: 'The gratitude of the fatherland is surely yours.' Werner quoted almost word for word the same phrase about the '*Dank des Vaterlandes*'.[13] Among Marianne's surviving papers was a certificate belonging to Feldwebel Alfred Strauss, awarded on 16 April 1934, bestowing on Alfred the Remembrance Cross in 'faithful memory' of his service to the Königliches Preussiches Füsilier Regiment 39. How could anything bad happen to such loyal servants of the Reich?

In their faith, the Strausses were far from unique.[14] Often it was Jewish men rather than their wives who felt more tied to German soil, though there is no evidence that Ine thought differently from her husband.[15] Perhaps she too believed that the brothers' military background and prosperity would protect them. For a long time, there was always some hope they could cling to. After the promulgation of the Nuremberg Laws, many Jews felt they now knew the legal position and would be able to cope. During 1936, the year of the Olympics, the regime largely refrained from intensifying anti-Jewish measures. Jewish emigration remained low.[16] But even at the time, Werner Hoffmann found the brothers' confidence almost incomprehensible. For example, he remembered that when there was an amnesty for repatriating foreign accounts in 1934 or so, the brothers dutifully brought their foreign exchange holdings back into Germany. Even harder for Werner and his colleague Hans Goldschmidt to comprehend was the brothers' decision to invest in property in the mid-1930s. 'We could not understand it.'[17]

The brothers' property dealings are, indeed, the best evidence that they believed they could outlive the regime. By 1935 they had clearly decided that the prospects for their grain business were poor, at least in the short term. So, in October 1935 they bought land on the Hufeland-strasse, a street at the bottom of the Ladenspelderstrasse. Marianne remembered the excitement surrounding the building project, to which the brothers committed well over 200,000 Reichsmarks.[18] A Swiss archi-tect, Rudolf Zbinden, was employed to build two luxury apartment blocks. Because all the business records are preserved, we can see that the brothers had no particular barriers put in their way. On one or two occasions, irate tradesmen adopted an anti-Semitic tone, but because the brothers were unflappable and never allowed themselves to be intimi-dated, normal courtesies were soon resumed.[19] In one of those touching examples of childhood response untouched by adult realism, Marianne assured me that the houses were the 'talk of the town' at the time.[20] In October 1936 the first tenants moved in and in 1937, with the block fully occupied, Alfred's pre-tax income was as good as in any year since the 1920s:[21]

> 2,999 from grain business
> 9,934 dividends
> 8,462 rents
> 21,395 total
> 20,150 after deductions.

In one sense, the brothers were far-sighted. They had chosen the one economic activity, property letting, in which Jews would be able to operate longer than any other. In another sense, of course, they had not been far-sighted at all.

Siegfried and Ine cannot have been unaware of the worsening conditions around them. In October 1933, the Nazi Veterans' Organization tried to bring a prosecution against them relating to their house-purchase ten years earlier. It came to nothing, but it must have given them pause. After the Nuremberg Laws in 1935, they were no longer allowed to employ non-Jewish maids. Non-Jewish acquaintances and neighbours began to look the other way from Marianne's family:[22]

'The neighbours never talked to us. They used to be quite friendly, ordinary people. Who'd been living there all our lives, as long as we'd been there. I can never remember ever talking to any of them after 1933. So we were completely isolated.'

On one side of the house lived a family with children of Marianne's age. Ine had been on friendly terms with the mother, a Frau Salk. 'And suddenly not a word, over the garden fence or whatever. And on the other side I don't even know – I can't remember the people or who lived there.' The only sign of life Marianne could remember from that side was wonderful music:[23]

'Somebody played the piano beautifully. I could have listened all day to whoever it was. I don't even know if it was somebody playing or if it was one of those mechanical things, it was so good. But that was the only contact with those neighbours on that side. I never saw anybody. Extraordinary, extraordinary.'

Social life was focused more and more on the family. Every Sunday relatives would visit, cousins, aunts, for tea or supper, or they would go out in the afternoon. Grandfather Leopold in Dinslaken became the object of particular attention after his wife Saly died in May 1934. But even family life began to suffer. Years earlier, Ine's cousin, Greta Rosenberg, had married a non-Jewish doctor, Dr Untiedt. Marianne remembered visits to Ahlen in the 1920s when she used to play with the Untiedts' daughters. Dr Untiedt himself was an enormous man; in the 1920s, whenever Marianne was ill in Ahlen, he would lumber in looking more like a vet than a doctor, and she would be terrified. But now the

The family together, 1934

contact was broken. Grete's daughters had joined the female equivalent of the Hitler Youth, the League of German Girls (Bund deutscher Mädel or BDM). Greta would cross the road so that she would not have to say hello to her aunt, Marianne's grandmother, terrified of being implicated by the Jewish connection. Grandmother Rosenberg, of course, found this very upsetting. But such developments still did not persuade Marianne's parents that they should go. Werner Hoffmann sadly shook his head at the Strauss brothers' obstinacy. It was harder to elicit a direct view from Marianne of her parents' reluctance to leave. Once, though, Marianne described to me an argument she had after the war about whether the Holocaust could have happened in Britain, and in doing so indirectly offered a judgement of her parents:

'People just won't see it, they just will not . . . because it demands some sort of reaction or action or anything. Nobody wants to leave their home and pack up and go into the unknown. Particularly not if you're pretty well off and you've worked for it very hard and are very much self-made. And you think you've done your duty by your country. Now it's the turn of your country to do its duty by you. You're a German like everybody else. But not only that, it's sort of . . . you don't want to be inconvenienced, I don't know what you can say . . . it's something you don't want to face up to.'

The same theme recurred in my interviews with Marianne's later wartime helpers. Whenever they talked about her parents' fate, they always emphasized the fact that her father had waited too long to leave. The uniformity and emphatic way in which this view was put forward suggested that it stemmed from Marianne. Throughout her interaction with me, though, she tended to defend their behaviour and only occasionally allowed herself some veiled criticism.

At the Luisenschule

For Marianne's parents the 1930s were unpleasant but bearable. For Marianne, the period was very different. She recalled her time at the Luisenschule as unredeemed misery. In the tape we made in 1989, she said:[24]

'Anti-semitism in Essen was always palpable . . . My childhood was very coloured by such things, particularly my experiences at school. My fellow pupils were all in the BDM and there was strong anti-Semitism in the school and in the class . . . I can remember only one or two teachers who one felt were at all distanced from the situation and were completely neutral. Never did anyone express any form of sympathy or fellow feeling.'

When we came back to the issue in 1996, she told me that 'we weren't allowed to forget that we were Jewish.' There was a lot of jeering. 'Children can be very cruel.' In fact, she was adamant that she had no positive memories of school whatsoever: 'There was nothing at all enriching about it.' In a later conversation she was even more damning: 'It was absolute hell, really.'[25] To reinforce the point, I discovered that, shortly after the war, Marianne had written a report recalling how at the age of eleven, 'I heard for the first time the word *Jew* being hissed behind my back,'[26] and how it had taken her a long while to recover the sense that there was no disgrace to being a Jew.

Marianne remained bitter about her fellow students until the end. During the 1980s, the Alte Synagoge in Essen informed her that a former fellow pupil, a Frau Barbara Sparrer,[27] had visited the exhibition in the synagogue and asked after Marianne, seeking to make contact. Would Marianne like to respond? She most certainly would not. The woman, she told me, had been 'one of her biggest tormentors'. I didn't think much more about the story until after Marianne died and I found the letter from the Alte Synagoge. I wrote to Frau Sparrer, explaining that I had found the letter and asking if she would be willing to talk to me.

Frau Sparrer lived in a very pleasant block of flats in the south of Essen. Her building was on a steep hill and with the colourful canopies over the balconies the neighbourhood might have been some Swiss holiday resort. I rang the door and she came down to meet me. Her face when I introduced myself was expressionless. We went upstairs and had coffee on the balcony, a rather cramped affair off the pleasant living room. She started off by trying to work out who I was.

'Are you, how shall I say, Israeli?' she asked.

'Do you mean Jewish or Israeli?' I responded.

She persisted: 'There are the three religions – Christianity, Jewish, Muslim – or have I got the sequence wrong?'

I clarified the difference between being a Muslim, an Israeli and a Jew, but Frau Sparrer had some difficulty understanding that I could be both English and Jewish at the same time. After I briefly mentioned the death of Marianne's daughter, Frau Sparrer looked nervously out over the balcony (we were several floors up) and said we'd better go inside. At this point I realized why she had been so expressionless downstairs. For some reason, she was paralysed with fear.

Frau Sparrer told me that she had tried to contact three Jewish fellow pupils and none had responded. The last time she saw Marianne was during the war. Nervously, she began to ask about Marianne's wartime experiences. Her questions, hesitant and broken off, were hard to follow. 'Could I then ask . . .' she began, and there was a very long pause. Then she pointed to her chest: 'Here, you know? The yellow star with the word *Jew* on it. I once saw Marianne on the street, but quite a way distant on the other side; I think it was Krupp Street, she must have been there then.'

Hmm.

Then she asked me a series of questions about Marianne's life after the war and about her children. She repeatedly sought to clarify my relationship with Vivian and the motive behind my project, almost as if she feared that some dossier was being put together against her. The ensuing exchanges revealed both great discomfort and much confusion:

'Now tell me; Marianne, you've just spoken about her parents . . . how is it possible, didn't they . . . Marianne must surely have in some way . . . oh, I see she lived in the – what did you say – underground?'

I confirmed that Marianne had remained in Germany illegally. 'Illegally', repeated Frau Sparrer, curiously relieved she had found the right word. 'Ah, *that's* how she saved her life.' She went on, 'There are many who left Germany early.' I agreed that there were. 'Yes? And . . .' there was another of her very long pauses, '. . . how is it possible that the parents, for example, with all the concentration camps and so on, how is it possible that her parents didn't leave in time?' Was she asking, I wanted to know, seeking to provoke her into an admission of knowledge, because it was so clear what was about to happen to them?

'Well, I know, people, I've heard that . . . but you must remember that, when I say that, I was just a child then, yes? How is it that . . . ah, now I know what I wanted to say, they said that those who had read Hitler's *Kampf* knew what was coming . . . Have you heard this said?'

'Hmm, hmm. Yes, sort of, hmm.'

We then talked about the concentration camps. Frau Sparrer had problems telling one from another and there were repeated confusions between Theresienstadt and Auschwitz, which she had visited. She had been shocked by Auschwitz, but she had an explanation: 'They did that while the German men were at the front.' And she cast doubt on the whole thing by wondering where all the bodies had gone, if there had been so many. I was able to help her out on the last point.

'They were burned,' I said.

'Ach, so.'

We moved on to Kristallnacht. Frau Sparrer remembered the devastation clearly:

'They destroyed everything. Terrible. The synagogue, it's now the museum, that was destroyed too . . . it was one of the most beautiful museums. [She meant synagogues.] Dortmund also had a beautiful synagogue . . . Yes and . . . yes what did they do? They . . . I think, they poured petrol into the synagogue and set it on fire.'

Sensing that I was dutifully being offered all this, I said that we were all agreed in condemning what had happened in retrospect, but that my interest was not in passing judgement. What I wanted to know was what her feelings, expectations and perceptions had been *at that time*. Frau Sparrer responded by asking how long Marianne was at the Luisenschule. As far as I knew, Marianne had been there until Kristallnacht. 'Yes?' said Frau Sparrer, surprised. 'But she must have . . . the parents were no longer in Essen, isn't that right?' No, the parents had still been there. Again Frau Sparrer looked surprised. When I added that Marianne had had to leave the school in 1938, she asked anxiously 'Had to? . . . What form did that take, this *having* to leave? I don't know.'

Suddenly, in a very lively voice, she launched into something else: 'Now then, you know, this probably is not appropriate here because it's not really very factual but Marianne . . . black hair, I think she had a centre parting and plait and curls . . . that's right, isn't it? Then she had a kind of old-fashioned dress and something . . . a kind of smock which, ach at that age you didn't wear any more . . . And in addition, please don't take offence, that I'm telling you this ... she wore a little girl's petticoat, I still remember that about Marianne.'

Her good cheer remained as she remembered the day the three Jewish girls had shown their classmates a book, 'the Talmud', Frau Sparrer called it:

'That's their bible that you read from right to left, that's right isn't it? ... They showed us that once. All three. Otherwise, you wanted to know, how we co-pupils behaved towards the Jewish girls. 1-A, 1-A. I think also –'

'What does that mean, "1-A"?'

'The best.'

Frau Sparrer told me that her father was against Hitler, that her parents protected her, that she was a sheltered girl and that her parents didn't want her to go to BDM. She said she didn't go to the younger version of the BDM, the Jungmädel, with much enthusiasm, either. Then I asked her again about the '1-A'.

'That's how I experienced it.'

'Yes. I mean, normally when one reads, er, reports about Jewish pupils at normal school in the 1930s, one could not say that the relationship was 1-A; quite the contrary.'

'No? I think it was. You mean that the Christian pupils behaved very badly towards the Jewish ones?'

'Yes.'

'That's what you want to say.'

'That pupils were discriminated against, that after a certain point they had to sit separately –'

'No. I have no memory of that. No, no ... I normally have a good memory of where we sat. I can't remember that.'

'And that the lesson material itself made clear distinctions, for example –'

'History? Or –'

'For example,' I persisted, 'racial teaching in biology. And –'

Frau Sparrer interrupted by asking if biology was a principal subject in the curriculum at the time, something to which I did not know the answer. I then asked her how she experienced school and she said it was a good time. They had good teachers, amongst other things a priest's son, Dr Rollenberg, who taught German and history. 'Yes, well,' she said, 'so that would probably be about it. Did you have any other questions which I haven't addressed?'

I took a deep breath:

'Well, now I . . . I would like to say something that will perhaps be a little difficult for you to hear or . . . well, let me ask a question. Have you wondered, when I tell you that Marianne received your letter, why she did not reply?'

'All three did not respond. I didn't give it any thought. That was how it was, I accepted it. One didn't know what kind of fate they had faced.'

'Well, Marianne said to me, before she died –'

'That she knew me?'

'She didn't give me your name; I found out your name only when I found the letter. But she said that someone from her school had tried to get in touch –'

'That must have been me . . . and now you want to know why I did that?'

'No. It's that Marianne referred to you as one of her tormentors.'

'Me?'

'That's what she said.'

'I'm absolutely shocked . . . I don't know what she means by that. We were never together. We were in the same class and that was it.'

There was a long pause. 'Now, I want to say something to you', said Frau Sparrer, and she hit the table several times while talking. 'It was out of purely positive, human reasons. I didn't do that out of nosiness. I am really shocked about this . . . I don't know what you mean by tormentor. I was not in her parents' house, nor did I sit next to her; I can't remember that at all. How should one . . . how should one understand "tormentor"?'

The exchanges which followed contained an odd contradiction. Frau Sparrer expressed more than once amazement that the Strauss family managed to survive in the Ruhr until 1943. Yet when I tried to get at why this should be surprising, she claimed to know nothing about the deportations that would have made her see 1943 as very late for them still to be in the Ruhr. She was 'too much a child'. (In 1943 Frau Sparrer celebrated her twenty-first birthday.) Again and again, she came back

to the word 'tormentor' and to the fact that her father had been against
Hitler, with the implication that this provided a blanket dispensation
for the rest of the family. For example, there was the time when a Jewish
acquaintance of her mother wanted to make her farewells and her father
insisted she be able to do so in the Sparrers' house:

'Everyone was frightened and said, "For God's sake, do anything but
let a Jewess into the house." "No," said my father, "there's no question.
This is where she will make her farewells."'

Who was everyone, I wanted to ask. After lots more of the same, I
asked:

'Am I the first who has asked you about the past?'

'Yes, and you see that I know so little . . . I did say that on the phone,
that I know very little. And I really don't know if it helped you.'

'I found it very interesting.'

Shortly afterwards I took my leave. I found myself angrily pleased at
having delivered this late bit of emotional restitution. I was proud that
I'd had the nerve to be so brutally open. So much of what she had told
me fitted into the pattern of post-war apologia. The not having known
anything. The explanation that the Jews were murdered while the German
soldiers were at the front – those honest German men who would have
put a stop to it. At the very time we were talking, the travelling exhibition
'Crimes of the Wehrmacht' was on in Essen. It showed just how deeply
the Wehrmacht was implicated in the crimes. As in the war so now, it
seemed, Frau Sparrer was ignoring the information available to her.
BDM-generation girls typically took refuge behind the judgements and
political positions that their parents, particularly their fathers, had held
before Hitler came to power. A single moment of helping a Jew – here the
graciousness with which a friend had been able to make her farewells –
became the exculpatory proof of innocence. On the other hand, was I so
certain that Marianne had got it right? And who was I to be the avenging
angel? Had I been a German Aryan in the 1930s, would I have been
braver? Guilt followed pride. I felt bad at having left Frau Sparrer in such
obvious distress. Her worst fears had been realized. She was never going
to look back on her school days in the same way again.

I did learn one more interesting thing from Frau Sparrer – that the
Luisenschule had an Old Girls' association that held annual meetings.

In August 1997, I wrote to the organizer, Frau Ingrid Kuschmiers. A couple of months later, Dr Rosemarie Lange, living in southern Germany and a year younger than Frau Sparrer, wrote to me that Marianne Strauss had joined her class for a short period in 1938:

I think that she came after the summer holidays after a lengthy cure by the sea. After the cure she had been kept back a year, since she started the school in 1933 whereas my class began in 1934.

I can remember that she lived in the Ladenspelderstrasse. Otherwise I know nothing of her family, siblings, or her father's career. That surprises me now because we sometimes cycled home together, but my journey was a lot shorter than hers. What did we talk about: school and music lessons?

Marianne was a pretty girl, with dark eyes, fresh skin colour, brown curly hair done up in a braid.

Dr Lange followed with details of Marianne's last day at school after Kristallnacht and continued

. . . we never heard anything more of her. I have often thought of her. Evidently, she succeeded in getting to Britain. I would be interested to hear about her subsequent life. She was the only Jewish person I ever met.

I wrote back, intimating that Marianne had not, as Dr Lange clearly assumed in the wake of the previous correspondence, been able to escape before the war, but had survived the Nazi period inside Germany. In January 1998, Dr Lange responded:

For your friendly letter many thanks . . . You cannot know how much your letter has occupied my thoughts. I must say to you that, try as I can, I cannot recall any more memories.

Like most of the pupils, I was in the BDM, in a performance group, which primarily did music. Since I also had violin lessons, my leisure time after school was pretty well filled, particularly as I had to catch up on all the work I'd missed through illness.

Marianne thus became known to me only in September after the summer holidays. I can remember one thing clearly, that on a beautiful warm day we came out of the school gates with our bikes and Ferrucio, the Italian,[28] was there and we all said hello. I had told him that we had a Jewess in the class. I'm sure he was very pleasant to her.

I really do not know whether Marianne and I regularly went home together. Her way home was somewhat further than mine. In order to avoid making a big detour, she really had to go in a different direction and the tram also went her way. How strongly she was integrated into the class, I don't know. But she was actually only in our class for about eight weeks.

The only other thing I remember is a school excursion, in rather poor weather, with our class teacher. He was a fine man and belonged to the parish circle of Pfarrer Gräber and Gustav Heinemann.[29] (There's more that could be said on that score.) Our headmaster Dr Lindenberg was probably in the party, but he behaved correctly and was not servile, as far as I could judge that as a pupil.

[. . .]

I remember that she came with us on the first excursion. Whether she was attacked or isolated I don't know . . . Perhaps one didn't seek out her company. It is always hard for new people in a class to be integrated, and in her case surely particularly difficult.

[. . .]

What astonishes me and what I had thought was impossible is that there were Jews who survived in Germany. After everything that I've heard since then, I find it miraculous.

I found Dr Lange's correspondence rather moving. The picture was more complicated than I had originally thought. When Marianne had referred to fellow pupils in the BDM, I had had an instant vision of ideologically committed, anti-Semitic young German girls making her life miserable. But here an implicit distinction was being drawn between those who belonged to the BDM or the party but remained correct in their behaviour, and those who were not so correct.

Other members of Dr Lange's class told me that Marianne had joined it in 1936. One, Frau Horn, was clearly one of those observant children who retain their early memories all their lives:

Marianne Strauss belongs to the classmates whom I remember as vividly as ever after six decades. [. . .] At the beginning of gymnastic lessons we

*Two views of the Luisenschule: (above) Marianne's later school
class, probably taken in 1935 (before she joined); (below)
Marianne at school in 1937*

would line up in order of size. She stood on my right and looked attentively forward at the teacher. Now and then I would look sideways and admire her beautiful dark hair, plaited into a thick braid around her head.

Marianne made me think. Despite the initially only slight difference, I felt she was much bigger than I and, despite being the same age, well beyond me in age and in sense. (As the youngest child I was over-protected but at the same time subject to an unusually strict upbringing. I was unworldly, lost in books and dreams.)

Sometimes, before the first lesson in class I would already be sitting in my place and I would see her come in. I would register with pleasure her natural but well groomed appearance. Her clothes were stylish and a little sporty, in an unostentatious, classy way. I would register too the calm look in her big dark eyes. In language lessons (French or English) I noticed that she responded more than the others and also that the teacher (of both languages) was particularly friendly towards her, both in her manner and in what she said, which of course I saw as very appropriate.

One lunchtime I was one of the last to leave and met a group of fellow pupils who were taking turns trying out a new bicycle. It belonged to Marianne. Although I had been standing there for only a little while, she quickly noticed me, and instead of calling me over loudly came up to me and asked quietly, 'Would you like to have a go?' Her sensitivity moved me very much, but I said shyly 'No, thanks', stood for another few minutes and then went home.

Once at the start of a summer trip we met accidentally in the train. My father went into a compartment where there were unoccupied seats. Opposite us sat Marianne's parents, Marianne and her brother (perhaps ten years old), who was deeply immersed in a Karl May book.

Marianne waited for a few minutes, then called me cheerfully, 'Come on, let's go outside to the open window!' We did that and looked out for a long time and enjoyed the trip and the wind, until Father and I had to change trains. It was only years later that I asked myself – why this often overpowering shyness towards such a delightful young human being? After all, whenever I met our neighbours, an old Jewish couple, on the street I spoke to them freely and without inhibition. And this *remained so until perhaps two years after the beginning of the war. Then it was said that they, like other pensioners, fled the increasing air raids on Krupp-dominated Essen and went to the Netherlands. Not long after that, their house, like ours, was completely destroyed.*

It was in the beginning of 1943 when, very early one morning after a long night in the air-raid shelter – the all-clear had only just been sounded – I saw Marianne again on an almost deserted street, after more than four years. We hurried from different directions and to different destinations, looked at each other without saying anything and went on, without stopping.

How big and how grown-up she looked now, and yet still wore her hair as she had as a child.

Elsewhere, Frau Horn noted that when she met Marianne's father in the train he had not stood up. 'Although I assumed that he had sustained a war injury, I'm no longer sure, after such a long time, whether this really was the case.' There followed more information about Frau Horn's visiting Yad Vashem with the Society for Christian–Jewish Co-operation. In a later letter, Frau Horn added further details, remembering that there had been one occasion, but only one, when a male teacher had shouted something anti-Semitic at Marianne.

Both Frau Horn and Dr Lange were in deepest southern Germany, and not so easy to reach, but another correspondent, Waltraud Barkhoff-Kreter, was in Essen. On the phone, her gravelly voice was direct and to the point. Was she willing to meet? Certainly, come tomorrow morning at eleven.[30] And so I did. She lived in a neat block of flats on a long and rather lively street of shops and restaurants. A smiling, round-faced rather solid figure opened the door. It was clear she was still professionally active as a homoeopath – she was in the middle of a telephone consultation when I came in and there were to be several more calls in the course of our interview. I went into the sitting room and looked around. There were Chagall prints on the walls and a Menorah, the nine-armed candelabra for the Chanukah festival, on the sideboard. I remembered that Frau Barkhoff-Kreter had written that she had paid some visits to Israel. In the kitchen, making coffee, she told me about her father's pre-war contacts with the wealthy Jewish Hirschland family.

Herr Hirschland had become her godfather. After the war, Jewish friends from the USA had sent them 'care packages'.

Like her contemporaries, Frau Barkhoff-Kreter's first point of reference was Marianne's beauty:

'Yes, and then Marianne Strauss, I always admired her, a beautiful girl. I was, you know, the blonde type, with round cheeks, long arms and long legs, and Marianne Strauss was already really womanly! And to me she was beautiful. I would very much like to have been like that.'

She laughed loudly with an agreeable, slightly hoarse, smoker's laugh. Beyond that, she could remember little direct contact. What was interesting, though, is that she was a latecomer to the class, having previously been at an anthroposophical school until it was forcibly closed in 1936 and only then relocated to the Luisenschule, and her memories were closer to Marianne's. Arriving at the Luisenschule after the Waldorf school had been a shock, and she had never learned to feel at home there.

'I don't remember much of the class. When I joined as a twelve-year-old it was as if I came from another planet. And there were these girls preening themselves in their BDM uniforms.'

She pulled out a photograph of the class, taken before she or Marianne had arrived, and sure enough, a good proportion of the class was sitting there in BDM uniform.

'I wasn't old enough to realize that, for all that, they might be all right . . . I was a stranger in the class, a real stranger. When school was over I would just pack my things and go.'

She also identified rather more teachers as being real Nazis than had other pupils. Though she too, made distinctions, in her vocabulary those teachers whom others had described as '*korrect*', she designated as fellow-travellers.

How was one to make sense of it all? On the specific point of dropping back a year, the evidence was in favour of Marianne having moved in 1936. With some remorse, I realized therefore that Frau Sparrer had been partially correct in remembering that Marianne had 'disappeared' from the class before 1938. She would have had no direct memories of Marianne after 1936. Nevertheless, Frau Sparrer's recollections still stuck out from the rest. The contrast between her mirthful memory of

Marianne's odd appearance and Frau Horn's paean to her sporty look seemed crass (though it was possible that Marianne's style changed between joining the school in 1933 and dropping back in 1936).

In any case, could one assume that the more positive memories were necessarily authentic? A lot of the letters contained a kind of philo-Semitism all too familiar in post-war Germany, in which the old anti-Semitic stereotypes are replaced by philo-Semitic ones.[31] Out of the hook-nosed, exploitative, rootless Jews arose brilliant minds, helpful shopkeepers and beautiful children. In such a context, the memory of Marianne's father failing to stand up had now to be interpreted as the result of a war injury. On the other hand, the stereotypical philo-Semitism was rarely accompanied by such detail about individual personalities, encounters and incidents as here. And Marianne, after all, *had* been beautiful. That was no imposition of a stereotype.

Frau Kuschmiers, the Luisenschule archivist, sent me a copy of the volume *125 Years Luisenschule 1866–1991*. The last page was devoted to 'A letter', from Jerusalem, dated August 1991, the only letter included.[32] The writer, Ruth Gawze, née Ferse, a Jewish woman one year older than Marianne, had attended the Luisenschule from 1932 to April 1938 and had managed to reach Israel early in 1939. She wrote now of her re-encounters with Essen and with the Luisenschule in the 1980s:

I myself have positive memories of the years spent at the Luisenschule. Neither from the teachers nor my fellow pupils did I hear anti-Semitic remarks.

Ineluctably, I found my perception of Marianne's school days changing into something more ambiguous. Perhaps, at least until Kristallnacht, the climate was not as anti-Semitic and hostile as she had said. Perhaps, in retrospect she had exaggerated.

Jewish pupils remember school

A few months after these exchanges, I made my trip to Israel. I was there, amongst other things, to talk to two of Marianne's former Jewish fellow pupils. Ruth Gawse, born in 1922, had written the friendly letter to the Luisenschule, and Ruth Davidsohn, née Mendel, was one of the three Jewish girls in Marianne's class whom Frau Sparrer had tried to contact. I also wanted to meet Jakov, formerly Klaus, Langer, another of Marianne's contemporaries.

Ruth Davidsohn and Jakov Langer both lived in the north, Mrs Davidsohn above Haifa, in the leafy heights of Mount Carmel. I hired a car and drove up the winding, tree-lined roads, getting lost more than once, until I found her pleasant flat. In her youth, Ruth Mendel had been plain and plump. Now, a widow in her seventies, she was slim, spry and good looking. We waited on her balcony for Chaja Chovers (formerly Klara Kleimann), another of Marianne's contemporaries from Essen, to join us.[33] Ruth told me that, decades after the war, she and Chaja had met up again by chance, when Ruth was teaching traffic regulations to Israeli children. There was a pause while this sank in. We agreed with a chuckle that her teaching hadn't had much effect on Israeli driving standards.

Mrs Chovers arrived and Mrs Davidsohn served a delicious cold lunch of bread and salads, with watermelon to finish. We drank raspberry tea, something I've only had elsewhere in German youth hostels. Our conversation began with a sad acknowledgement. I showed them the photograph of Marianne as a teenager, then I showed them the photograph of Marianne a few weeks before she died. They were both shocked by how she had aged. 'Um Gottes willen! She must have suffered,' said Ruth, who kept switching between English, German and occasionally Hebrew. 'She must have suffered terribly . . . If someone had told me that that was Marianne I wouldn't have believed it.' After that, our conversation turned to school days. As it turned out, Mrs Davidsohn had been at the Luisenschule for only a year. Her memories of the place were at least as unfavourable as Marianne's. On the phone, she had already told me that all she remembered was feeling miserable and being thrown out of the religious education lessons.[34] Now, she added:

'I was *such* a bad student! . . . I had managed to get into the school. But I was bored to death there. I can remember the French lessons. To learn French, we first had to learn how to roll our r's. So we sat for hours and went "rrrr". That's how we learned French – when you think about that today . . . !'

Chaja Chovers and Ruth Davidsohn in Israel

Of course, there was nothing particularly National Socialist about bad French teaching, but Ruth went on:

'You noticed the anti-Semitism. And then there was the fact that I was so terribly fat, so there was *the fat Jew*, and this kind of stuff. I was happy to get out of the school. And there was something else. I was very often ill. Whether that was psychological or not, I don't know, but I was at home more often than I was at school. I think it was my parents who said, "There's no point, the child is simply miserable." But around this time, they were all thrown out.'

A little later, she reaffirmed that anti-Semitism had been evident from both staff and students. The Jewish school, which she rejoined after this one year, was much more comfortable.

I showed her the letter from Ruth Gawse, which suggested that the Luisenschule had been a positive experience. At this, Mrs Davidsohn became unsettled. She said she could remember so little, she had a 'blackout' of the period at the Luisenschule. All she could remember was being miserable, the French lessons, and the religious instruction. She could remember nothing else.

Before I left, we looked through her family photo album. There was a snap of her mother's family in 1921, a couple of years before Ruth was born. Her parents had survived, and so had an aunt, but as for the rest ... We went down the row of comfortable faces: 'She was in Theresienstadt, deported, deported, deported, deported, deported, everyone deported . . .' And on that sad note, we parted.

Ruth Davidsohn's school memories may have been limited, but they were more than I gleaned from Mrs Gawse later in the week.[35] In an earlier letter, Mrs Gawse had written to me that she found it 'very surprising that Marianne Strauss suffered, which I did not know anything about and have no memory of'.[36] When I interviewed her, her recollection was so limited I felt unable to use her as a witness. Perhaps she had had a clearer memory in 1991 when she had sent the letter to the Luisenschule. If not, then it should be seen only as a gesture of conciliation – none the less meaningful for that – rather than any kind of description of the past.

On the other hand, it was clear Jewish pupils *did* have conflicting memories of school days in Essen.[37] My most reflective witness on this point was Jakov Langer. I had come across his name in Marianne's correspondence – yet another of the people from the past who had sought contact with her in the 1980s and to whom she had not responded. He lived in Kiryat Tivon, also in the northern part of Israel, and so after taking my leave from Ruth Davidsohn and Chaja Chovers I drove down to visit him.[38] The wooded, hilly country on the way to Tivon was lovely. The Langers lived in a beautiful, simple bungalow, set back from the road up some steps and surrounded by trees and a pond. It was a little paradise. I didn't yet know that Jakov Langer was a nature lover and bird-watcher and had been one of the pioneers of conservation in Israel. His wife Tsofia, a cultivated but somewhat ailing woman of Dutch origin, answered the door. A little later, Jakov himself came bounding in, shirtless, healthy and active. We sat down to a simple meal of bread and cheese. Before, while washing my hands, I'd noticed a calendar on which various dates and names had been inscribed. Here was Westerbork and a date, there was Sobibor and a date, there was Auschwitz and a date. These were the anniversaries of the dates on which family members had been deported or murdered. Jakov's father had been deported to Izbica in April 1942. His wife's family were the victims in Westerbork and Sobibor. His wife had survived in hiding in Holland. Her mother, Clara Asscher-Pinkhoff, had survived Belsen and been released to Palestine before the war ended, as part of an extraordinary deal with the Nazis. Her book *Sternkinder* had been a post-war best-seller.[39] Everywhere I turned in Israel, there were such miracles and tragedies.

Jakov Langer was born in 1924 and, like Marianne, had started secondary school soon after the Nazis came to power. For the first few years he had been in Gelsenkirchen, a period he remembered as relatively relaxed, playing with classmates and making mischief. But by 1936, when he came to Essen and transferred to the Humboldt Oberrealschule in Steelerstrasse, things were already different. His parents told him to be cautious. In 1937–8 he was the only Jewish boy out of 700 pupils. His fellow-pupils didn't talk to him much in the playground. And, one

Jakov and Tsofia Langer in Israel

day, he found himself sitting alone on his bench in the classroom – his neighbour must have been told to move. But, according to Jakov Langer, there was no abuse. He drew my attention to the book *A Boy in Your Situation*, written by Charles Hannam, which describes a miserable experience of persecution at the Goethe school in Essen.[40]

Langer said that he himself had 'never heard "dirty Jew" or that kind of thing. I didn't have strong contacts with fellow-pupils, that was only natural. They had been indoctrinated along those lines in the Jungvolk [the Hitler Youth's junior wing], but there was no taunting or remarks from pupils or from teachers.'

A friend of his, who had been at the Goethe school, did not share Hannam's memory, either. Langer felt that the differences were a function of individual perception or the bad luck to land in a class where there was real anti-Semitism. The fact that Langer had been sporty, though smaller than the average, may have helped. In class he was allowed to contribute normally. Only twice – during a lesson on Nazi ideology and during a biology lesson – was he asked to leave the classroom. Ironically, he was asked to guard the school gate to make sure no 'foreign elements' came into the school.

My perception of Marianne's school days had swung back again. Her recollection of misery had regained its emotional force, a force for a while diluted by the different tide of memory flowing from her non-Jewish contemporaries. It was almost shocking how differently individuals could experience the same events. Marianne's non-Jewish contemporaries had simply not understood how, for Marianne, the absence of easy interaction coupled with the odd exclusion from lessons, or outbursts from a teacher, or the occasional anti-Semitic remark in the playground, could add up to a hostile environment. For her non-Jewish contemporaries, the fact that most teachers and students behaved in a *korrekt* manner most of the time, that little overtly anti-Semitic was said or done, was evidence that the school was OK. And for some Jewish pupils, such an environment was bearable. If, like Langer, they were armed with a clear-cut interpretative framework which acknowledged the conditions shaping the behaviour of their fellow-pupils, then they were able to understand the silence around them as not particularly hostile. But for others, like Marianne, the experience overall was negative and depressing. We know that Marianne was more the rule than the exception.[41]

What made school even harder to bear for Marianne was that her parents were as keen as ever that she should perform well academically. In 1935, the Jewish newspaper *Jüdische Rundschau* felt obliged to warn parents of the situation faced by their children. It cited the example of a girl attempting to reassure her younger sister that the horse near-by would not hurt her. 'Go on,' the older girl says, 'the horse doesn't know we're Jewish.'[42] For Siegfried and Ine, however, nothing was to disrupt their daughter's education.[43]

In addition, Marianne also had ill health to contend with. Asthma and bronchitis often kept her away from school. When she was thirteen, she suffered particularly from bronchitis and was sent away for a cure.[44] This enforced absence resulted in poor marks, as she told me with regret:[45]

'Both my parents [were] very bright, particularly my mother, who'd been a high flyer and very ambitious . . . To do well at school was probably the most important thing . . . So I knew I was a great disappointment to my parents, and that didn't help me any.'

Jewish youth together

There was one thing on which all the Jewish witnesses agreed: by 1935, at the latest, the only time they felt relaxed or confident or could really enjoy themselves was when they were with other Jews, above all with other Jewish youngsters. They met at Jewish youth groups, at organized events in the Jewish Youth Centre, or in each other's houses. Jakov Langer, for example, remembered bumping into Marianne occasionally at the Makkabi Hazair youth group, to which they both belonged. His most vivid memory, though, was of meeting her at a concert evening in a private house. The Langers always attended such events, being very much part of the Essen musical scene, and both Jakov (then Klaus) and Marianne were taking lessons from the same piano teacher. They chatted during the concert. 'I remember that she was pretty. That her appearance made a real impression on me – I remember that, too.'

At Ruth Ferse's party, 1937 (Marianne and Ruth in front)

I noticed with surprise that the Langers had a very impressive NAD stereo system, which didn't fit at all with their simple rustic life-style. Much later, in the States, when I told Hanna Aron, another contemporary, that I'd visited the Langers and Ruth Gawse she exclaimed, 'Oh, you visited the elite!' That took me aback. She was remembering them the way they had been. Herr Ferse, Ruth's father, had been a judge who had trained the later Federal President, Gustav Heinemann. Jakov's father had been a judge, too. Both his parents had been talented and enthusiastic musicians. I was going to respond that there was nothing upper-class about them now. But then I suddenly saw Jakov's stereo-system and record collection as a last echo of that German-Jewish cultural and musical life of which he and Marianne too had been a part in the 1930s.

Although in her reminiscences Marianne did not make a particular feature of the youth groups of the 1930s, we know that she took part in them and there is good reason to think that the values of the youth movement had a lasting influence on her. After 1933, Jewish youth groups continued to be allowed to operate fairly freely and took on a new significance. Whereas before 1933, only a quarter of Jewish youngsters in Germany had been organized in Jewish youth groups, now the proportion rose to over half, and by 1937 had reached around 60 per cent.[46] The youth groups were strongly influenced by the so-called free German youth, a movement that could trace its roots back to the so-called *Wandervogel* groups that emerged in the nineteenth century.[47] The *Wandervogel* had emphasized young people's right to lead themselves, removed from adult society, and had criticized modern, urban life. During the 1920s, a new German youth movement had emerged, the so-called *bündische* youth, less anarchic than the *Wandervogel* and seeking to create a separate ordered community with strong inner leadership. Surviving publications from Marianne's youth group, Makkabi Hazair – since 1934 combined with the Jewish Scouts into the JPF–MH (Jüdischer Pfadfinder–Makkabi Hazair, the largest Jewish youth organization in Germany)[48] – show that it was very much shaped by the Bündisch atmosphere. Alongside support for Zionism, it called for 'discipline, order, cleanliness, a simple life-style and clothing, calm behaviour in public, comradeship, work for the community, preparedness'.[49] Some of its dicta could just as easily have stemmed from the Hitler Youth – its emphasis on performance and effort as the principle of leadership selection, for example.[50] But whereas the Hitler Youth was increasingly regimented and controlled from above, the Jewish youth movements retained their independence. Paradoxically, the Jewish groups were probably the last in Germany to still honour the spirit of the free German youth movements of the pre-1933 period.[51] Jakov Langer remembered the group's uniform of blue shirts, with white shirts for special occasions. They would hold a roll call and march within the Youth Centre. In the 1936–8 period, Marianne's age group was very active, with regular evening and weekend meetings, talks, plays and trips.[52]

From Ruth and Chaja, I learned of another Essener of their generation, Hans Eulau, now working in the Museum of the Ghetto Fighters, Beit Lochamei Hagetaot. So, after staying over at the Langers', I drove back past Haifa to visit the museum, where Hans Eulau, now Uri Aloni, worked as a volunteer. Having learned only the day before that he was there, I turned up unannounced.[53] He received me very pleasantly, excited by the Essen connection, but also frustrated at the lack of advance notice. He had a tour group of Americans to look after, so I sat in his office and asked him questions in ten- to fifteen-minute bursts (to which he responded in faultless English) between his assignments. While we were talking, Chaja arrived. The two hadn't met before, so I felt oddly part of a kind of Essen reunion.

More strongly than any of the others, Uri Aloni emphasized the emotional and psychological reinforcement provided by the youth groups. His memory of the classroom was one of defiance; when the class had to say 'Heil Hitler', the Jewish boys shouted 'Drei Liter'. He missed not being able to go to the cinema or the public swimming baths. The youth movement was his compensation; it 'straightened our backs'. Though in his seventies, Uri Aloni had kept his 'straight back'. He had been a keen boxer in Hakoach, a Jewish sports movement, as evidenced by his flattened nose and cauliflower ears. I wouldn't have wanted to go in the ring with him in the 1930s. I wouldn't want to go in the ring with him now. He said something that I think was to be true of Marianne later, too, namely, that during the 1930s Jewish parents' and children's roles began to shift. Home had once been the place of security, but now it was a place of uncertainty. Suddenly, the parents were more unsure what to do than the children were. 'Suddenly, we knew better,' Uri said. The youth movement 'gave us just what we were lacking at home'.

Uri Aloni was at pains to point out that the youth movement had also given him a strong commitment to Zionism and a belief in the future. Clearly used to making professional presentations for visitors, he offered a smooth and well-paced account. Particularly on the subject of the youth movement, his line was so clear that I couldn't help feeling I was being given some kind of propaganda. After he left me to look after his Americans, I visited the Museum of Jewish Resistance. Its re-creation of the ghettoes was subtle and complex. But, when we came to the youth movement and its role in the resistance, the exhibition drew the same clear and direct line from the solidarity learned in Habonim or Makkabi Hazair, through anti-Nazi resistance, to the contribution of the young immigrants of the 1930s and 1940s to the foundation of the state of Israel. Here, even more than in the interviews, I had a strong sense of public ideology.

At once, my perception of the conflicting testimony changed again. I had initially been conscious of the changes and omissions in particular individuals' testimony. Then, I had realized that many discrepancies did, in fact, faithfully reflect different contemporary perceptions of events. Now, I saw how important the public context was in which individuals recalled their past. My non-Jewish German correspondents had remembered the Luisenschule within a specific German public context of post-war philo-Semitism and forgetfulness. Not only that, but when I thought about it there had been a much more specific ex-Luisenschule community which had helped to shape memory. Many of the pupils told me they had learned after the war that their teacher, Herr Schammel, had been more anti-Nazi than they had realized.[54] Their former teachers had helped disseminate the idea that the bulk of the school had resisted the tide.[55] For their part, my Israeli interlocutors were, consciously or unconsciously, speaking from the background of a battle-hardened, tenaciously self-assertive Israeli state.[56] For Marianne, however, on whom Zionism had never rubbed off very strongly, there was no such obvious public context to shape her memories.[57]

Respite in Wyk

In Marianne's recollection, the experience from the 1930s that had given her the most emotional reinforcement had been not the youth groups but her cure in Wyk, on the North Sea island of Föhr.[58] Föhr was a health resort for respiratory diseases. The flat shores provided an ideal recreation ground for young people and there were several children's convalescent homes. The Jewish Women's League (Jüdischer Frauenbund, JFB) had set up its own children's home there in 1927. After 1933, it began to advertise the home not only as a place of convalescence but also as a refuge for children suffering under the current political conditions.[59] During 1936, more youngsters than ever stayed at the home, nearly 300 – perhaps a sign of growing parental awareness of the strains of being in

Germany.[60] In that year, Marianne had severe problems with asthma and bronchitis, possibly exacerbated by stress. Marianne's memory was that she spent almost six months in Wyk. The usual length of a cure was seven weeks, and it is possible that Marianne had extended the time in her memory, but the comments of one of her teachers suggest that she may well have been there for longer than the customary stay.

An article written in 1937, celebrating ten years of the children's home, gives the impression of a delightful environment but a highly structured regime. Run by Clara Simons from Cologne with a team of some twenty kindergarten, school and gymnastics teachers, each day was tightly planned. For Marianne, a rather protected thirteen-year-old, such an environment was probably ideal. Even in 1936, the home was still able to offer the children such treats as trips to the small, bare but inhabited islands round about.[61] Within this child-centred regime, Marianne found being away from home and school and encountering some of the more open-minded staff especially liberating.

In particular there was Edith Caspari, whom Marianne was to meet again in Berlin during the war. Caspari, trained by the educationalist Helene Lange, was among other things a disciple of Jung and a graphologist. Marianne recalled that Caspari could gain the most astonishing insights from a small sample of someone's writing. She introduced Marianne to a new world of ideas.[62] In a letter written to Marianne in January 1943, Edith Caspari found emotional space amid the utter horror of that time (many of her closest colleagues had recently been murdered), to recall in rather literary style their first encounters:[63]

I often still see little Marianne and her pigtails before me, just as she was when she arrived aged fifteen[64] with her father. She grew very fast and tried to enjoy life. She was frivolous in lessons and in spending money on pretty things and on the care of her own pretty body. But it is good to go through such phases too. They are not wasted. Humans are not angels. And in this period, Marianne still gave joy to other people, and not only because of her appearance (I see her still in the pretty, dark blue dress and in the colourful dressing gown).

But while, to outsiders, Marianne was experimenting with charm and frivolity and the unusual freedom of having a little spending money, her own memory is of an independent identity that was taking shape for the first time. She arrived, as Edith Caspari observed, still a young girl, but she left on the way to maturity.

The end of the illusion

After a lull during 1936, the pace of repression speeded up again. Between autumn 1936 and spring 1937, conditions deteriorated rapidly for many Jews. The Aryanization of Jewish firms accelerated. In February 1937, the head of the German Labour Front Robert Ley announced that a key goal of the four-year plan was to eliminate Jews from German economic life. Even so, by January 1938 only 135,000 of Germany's 525,000 Jews had emigrated. The next twelve months were to see a decisive difference, both locally and nationally.

From January 1938, Jewish citizens crossing the border into Switzerland and France had their passports confiscated, as the government attempted to restrict travel to those who were emigrating. By April 1938, only 40,000 businesses remained in Jewish hands out of 100,000 in 1933. Approximately half of all Jewish workers were now unemployed. In June 1938, Hitler ordered the Munich synagogue to be razed to the ground. Closer to home for the Strauss family, the synagogue in Dortmund was destroyed and the community cheated out of the funds they were supposed to be paid for the building.[65] From July onwards, all Jews, including infants, had to carry Jewish identity cards. In August, a new law expelled all Jewish doctors from the profession, effective from the end of September.[66] Jews were no longer allowed to own cars and the Strausses were forced to sell their smart *Wanderer*.[67] In October, Jews of Polish origin, including several hundred from Essen, were expelled from the country under appalling conditions.[68] But still Siegfried and Ine made no move to leave.

3

Shattered G
Shattered Li

On 7 November 1938, a German official at the Paris embassy was shot by Herschel Grünspan, a young Jew of Polish origin, protesting against his parents' inclusion in the October expulsions. On 9 November, at around 9 p.m., the Nazi leadership, most of whom were in Munich celebrating the fifteenth anniversary of Hitler's beer hall putsch of 1923, learned that the official, Counsellor Ernst vom Rath, had died from his injuries. Soon after the news came in, Hitler withdrew, leaving Goebbels to take the initiative and incite those present to take 'retribution'. At 10.30, the assembled Nazi, SA and SS prominence rushed off to make their telephone calls to the provinces. In this almost casual way, the stage was set for a pogrom.

In Essen, as elsewhere, local activists were deep in their cups celebrating the anniversary of the putsch. As midnight approached, SA and SS, drunk and surprised, were ordered into action and, on foot and by car, they piled off to the Essen synagogue. Thanks to the fact that one of their ranks was in charge of the carpool for the Nazi leadership in the region, the SS men managed to obtain petrol canisters and bring them into the synagogue. The fire service was so supportive that the news went round Essen in the following weeks that the firemen had 'put the fire out with petrol'. A wave of attacks on Jewish shops and homes followed, which lasted until 11 November.[1]

Delayed reaction

...denspelderstrasse, for some reason, the houses remained ...touched both on 9 November and on the following days of destruction. According to one surviving Jewish witness who had lived in that part of Essen, the local district SA chief was relatively decent, and this helped spare the area.[2] Curiously, the myth of the decent local SA was relatively common in Jewish accounts of Kristallnacht. For example, the story was often told that SA units were brought in from other towns and regions to avoid local ties of friendship getting in the way of the violence. Yet subsequent research has often demonstrated such claims to be false.[3] Whatever the reason, on the night of 9 November, the Strauss family slept undisturbed.

The following morning, having no inkling of what was taking place all across Germany, Marianne went to school as usual. Rosemarie Lange wrote to me:

Her last day at school was terrible . . . We had music lessons on the stage in the big hall. The teacher was late, and while we waited some of the girls were discussing what had happened in the town, what they'd seen and all the places that had been destroyed and smashed up. Maybe that was the first moment that Marianne heard about these things. It certainly was for me – we didn't have a radio, my parents were away at the time and the way to school led through a residential area . . . That class must have been absolute hell for Marianne. During the break, she left school unobtrusively, and we never heard from her again. I have often thought of her.

Another correspondent, Vera Vahlhaus,[4] also described that day:

On the morning after Kristallnacht (which neither Marianne nor I knew anything about because we lived in areas where 'nothing' had happened) I was standing on the steps by the school entrance. As Marianne Strauss came slowly towards me, another girl, Gudrun P.,[5] greeted her with the words, 'You old Jew, get lost, you've no business here,' and hit her on the head with an atlas. Without thinking, I walked over to Gudrun and shoved her head against the wall. The bell prevented me, thank God, from causing any further injury. It was the first and only time that I've ever been violent against another creature. Marianne Strauss ran from the school and I never saw her again.

I tried to clarify the contradiction between the claim that Marianne ran away from the school before classes even started and Rosemarie Lange's account. I also asked if I could have the full name of Gudrun P. Mrs Vahlhaus wrote back:

About the music lesson: I had had the incident with Gudrun and had to go to the headmaster. After a telephone call to my father I was sent home. I was completely out of control, and the headmaster knew I was in danger of saying or doing things that might have got my parents into trouble.

On balance, it seems that Marianne probably did not leave school immediately and went to the music lesson as Dr Lange had said. Frau Vahlhaus would not give me Gudrun P.'s full name. She said the time for revenge was past and, although revenge was not really the point, I left it at that.

Only one of my correspondents made a point of recollecting that Marianne was *not* in school at all the day after Kristallnacht, a Mrs Gudrun Hochwald.[6] She wrote:

In contrast to the reminiscences of Rosemarie Hahn [Lange], I do not think that Marianne appeared on the day after Kristallnacht. After the war, when the whole tragedy of the Jews became known, I often wondered about Marianne's fate, because I can't remember a conversation about it in our class. I think I sensed at the time that injustice was being done, but I was too reserved to act. Our class teacher at that time was Herr Schammel, who emerged after the war as a convinced opponent of the Nazis. He might well have talked his way into a death sentence if he had spoken openly about all the terrible things that happened that night.

Later, I had the opportunity to interview Frau Vahlhaus. I brought along all the correspondence I had received from different Luisenschule pupils – given the uncertainties about exactly when Marianne had repeated a year, I wanted to check which of my correspondents had actually been together. I also brought a copy of the class photo that Waltraud Barkhoff-Kreter had given me in Essen. Frau Vahlhaus looked at the correspondence from Gudrun Hochwald and managed, which I had failed to do, to decipher the handwritten note of her unmarried name. She gave a start. Frau Gudrun Hochwald had been Fräulein Gudrun Plumpe, and Fräulein Gudrun Plumpe had been the girl who had attacked Marianne on the steps. Looking at the photo, she picked out a girl with glasses and identified her. I tried to find some resonance of a violent attack in the friendly letter I had received from Mrs Hochwald, in which, in addition to the section about Kristallnacht already quoted, she had written:

Marianne sat diagonally left from me and I was always admiring her thick long plaits. I remember her as a quiet, reserved girl. Whether that was her nature or stemmed from the situation in those days, I can't say. I can't remember that she had any special status in the class. In my memory, my relationship to her was not awkward, particularly as our contact was restricted to lessons. Beyond that, there were no school activities. I don't know anything about her personal details (parents, siblings, where she lived).

During my last lengthy stay in Germany, I asked Frau Hochwald for an interview without mentioning any details. She wasn't sure if she could remember enough to make it worth my while, she said, but I was very welcome to come. A few days later, I took the train to the sizeable industrial centre in which she lived, followed by a long taxi ride into the pleasant hills overlooking the town. As I walked towards the smart two-storey house, I felt even more peculiar than when interviewing Frau Sparrer, Marianne's 'tormentor'. I knew that if I told her of my specific interest this disclosure would distort the interview and provoke a purely apologetic response. On the other hand, I am no poker player. Frau Hochwald answered the door with a smile in which I discerned friendly politeness but also wariness. She was dressed smartly and conservatively and the house was full of expensive, very good quality heavy furniture. Her husband was there too, a friendly but firm man with a successful business career behind him, who would clearly stand no nonsense. The fact that we were to have the conversation *à trois* made me even more nervous.

The interview took the usual course. Even before I had started the tape, Frau Hochwald began by talking about Marianne's exotic beauty. And when I asked her to repeat the comment, once the tape was running, she was off on her father's positive attitude to the Jews. Apparently, Jewish employers had helped him weather the Depression. She didn't think the girls had normally worn BDM uniform in class and got into a muddle trying to explain away the photo, in which many of the girls were dressed in uniform. The photograph must have been taken on a Saturday, she claimed, although BDM girls did not attend school on Saturday. Her husband got into a similar contradiction, repeatedly asserting for most of the interview how little he was aware of politics, but when we got to his military career, he stressed his knowledge of contemporary affairs, which had got him through an important interview. And there was more sincere but apologetic detail that did not quite ring true. Frau Hochwald had, as she openly admitted, been an enthusiastic leader in the Jungmädel, the junior section of the BDM, and had risen through the ranks. But it had been an ideology-free zone, according to her. As time went on, though, I became less and less sure of my ground. Frau Vahlhaus had remembered Marianne's assailant's father as an apothecary and Nazi Party member. Frau Hochwald's father had been neither. Frau Vahlhaus had identified Gudrun Plumpe on the photo as a dark-haired girl with glasses. It was perfectly clear that the naturally blonde Gudrun Hochwald could not have been she. And when I finally put the specific accusation to Frau Hochwald, various aspects of her reaction made me pretty confident that, if she was concealing something, it was not at a conscious level.

Could I now be sure that the accusation was authentic, particularly as Marianne herself had never mentioned her last day at school? It was reasonable that Marianne's own memories should be dominated by the horrors that emerged later that day, but would she not have remembered an assault? Those who have conducted interviews in contemporary Germany know that post-war memories about Jews in the 1930s typically cluster around Kristallnacht. The historian Frank Stern has discerned in this pattern a kind of defensive forgetfulness – the long development of anti-Semitic measures and attitudes to which so many were party has been compressed in retrospect and loaded on to these few violent days.[7] Should the attack on the steps be seen as one such compressed symbolic memory, standing-in for tens of little incidents over a longer period of time that Marianne's contemporaries did not want to remember? Or had Kristallnacht really been a turning point in the schoolyard: tipping over into brutal action girls who previously had not been violently anti-Semitic, while shocking others into recognition of what was really happening? I was never going to find out.

The assault on the Strauss family

What is clear is that soon after Marianne came home from school, the family learned that the previous night's orgy of destruction was giving way to something even more sinister. Reinhard Heydrich, the head of the Gestapo and the Sicherheitsdienst (SD), the SS security service, had given the order that as soon as the pogrom had died down a little, each district was to arrest as many Jews – in particular affluent Jews – as could feasibly be incarcerated. Initially, only healthy, male Jews were to be taken, and contact was established immediately with the concentration camps to achieve rapid transfer of the prisoners.[8] In Essen, the first Jewish men were rounded up on 10 November 1938. We know that at least 319 were taken into 'protective custody' in the police cells on the Haumannshof. As news of the round-up reached the Strauss family, Siegfried and Alfred decided to go into hiding. Marianne's great uncle Abraham Weyl (the brother of her maternal grandmother) had recently moved to Essen and was not yet well-known in the town. So Alfred and Siegfried travelled to his home at Hermann-Göringstrasse 316, Essen Bredeney, and spent two anxious days cooped up there. 'So there was hope,' Marianne said, 'that they might have been saved there. Which they might well have been had not the Gestapo put the screws on and come every few hours and said that if they didn't turn up they would take my mother and me. That brought my father and my uncle out pretty quickly, unfortunately. I don't think they would have taken us, but even so . . .'[9]

As persecution intensified, the records of the persecutors become more detailed; from this point on the Gestapo records, for example, begin to contain surprising detail on the Strausses' lives. We know from the records that the Strauss brothers eventually turned themselves in to the police on the afternoon of 12 November and were taken into protective custody as part of Heydrich's round-up. The files also include a statement Siegfried made after he gave himself up. Timed at 3 p.m. on the afternoon of the 12th, the statement runs as follows:[10]

I have been resident in Essen since 1919. I fulfilled my military duty before the war and spent the whole war in the battlefield at the front . . .

By birth, I am of the Israelite religion. My ancestors have always been in Germany and I can prove this back to 1740. I possess German citizenship and feel myself a German in other respects too.

It does not seem too much to say that we have here, preserved in the records, the last point in Siegfried's life, almost to the hour, when that proud sense of national identity could be uttered with any confidence.

Marianne's memories gain a new sharpness and depth from Kristallnacht onwards which they did not have for earlier phases of her life. Shortly after the end of the war, she recalled in a BBC broadcast 'the burning synagogues, the fear-filled days and nights in which, more clearly than ever before, we felt we were in the clutches of a power from which there was little chance of escape'.[11]

While her father was hiding, Marianne and her family began to learn what had happened to her grandparents, Leopold Strauss and Anna Rosenberg. Marianne's maternal grandmother, Anna Rosenberg, had been living alone on Adolf-Hitlerstrasse in Ahlen. Both Marianne and her cousin Uri Weinberg told me that the marauding SA came from other towns, but this was probably another myth.[12] Uri told me that Anna had a non-Jewish tenant in her house. When the SA was heard downstairs, Anna Rosenberg rushed into her tenant's rooms and hid in her bathroom. The tenant told the SA Anna had left. The men became suspicious when they found Anna's door open, but the tenant had the presence of mind to say that Frau Rosenberg was so absent-minded she regularly did such things. As Anna cowered in her tenant's bathroom, she heard her flat being destroyed.[13]

Meanwhile, Marianne and her aunt Oe telephoned Leopold Strauss in Dinslaken to see if he was all right. There was no answer. So they asked someone to drive them to Dinslaken. The house at Duisburgerstrasse 100 was empty and completely smashed to pieces. The curtains had been torn down. The mess was 'absolutely indescribable'. The bottled fruit that her grandmother had made before she died and stored in the attic, 'all beautifully, neatly labelled' was 'smashed to smithereens'. The destruction was so terrible that the conserves were dripping through the ceiling from the attic. Eventually, they found grandfather Leopold in a nearby hospital.

Of all the family members, Leopold's fate is the best documented, though some of the sources are ones to which Marianne never had access. Her own memory was dominated by her recollections of uncertainty about his welfare, and the terrible discovery of the empty house. After the war, though, Marianne's cousin obtained this description from Leopold's non-Jewish tenant, Herr Johann Mund:[14]

The first to arrive at the house were some four to five SA men who turned up on the morning of 10 November 1938 at 9 o'clock. I opened the door and they asked me if I was Herr Strauss. I answered that they could see that I wasn't Herr Strauss. So then they went up to the first floor to look for Herr Strauss. The SA men immediately began smashing things to bits, but left after twenty to thirty minutes. Then came some twenty-five or thirty boys who immediately took up the destruction. They pulled doors off their hinges and threw them down, smashed the jars of jam and preserves and threw clothes into the jam. Much of Herr Strauss's clothing, china and cigars were thrown out the window.

After they'd done this, the boys wanted to destroy the stairwell as well. I said enough was enough and they left. The things remained in the street and the house was surrounded by police. Not a single pane of glass in the house was intact when the boys left. The following morning, when the police had gone, everything on the street that was still usable was stolen. I myself swept up the glass.

Herr Strauss sustained severe injuries to the head. He ran to Dr Kurz, who has since died, to be bandaged and was then taken to the hospital, where he stayed for a while. After being discharged, Herr Strauss went to his son Alfred in Essen, at Hufelandstrasse 23. Shortly afterwards I and my family visited Herr Leopold Strauss. When I entered Herr Alfred Strauss's apartment I had the impression I was entering a palace.

On the afternoon of 10 November 1938 they had wanted to set fire to Duisburgerstrasse 100. Uniformed men pulled up in a truck loaded with straw. But since I was living in the house they decided not to set it alight.

Johann Mund's report was inaccurate in one respect: Leopold did not manage to go straight to either doctor or hospital. At the Leo Baeck Institute in New York, I came across an account of the events in Dinslaken on 10 November by Yitzhak Sophoni Herz, teacher at the Dinslaken orphanage.[15] Herz and the children in his charge were forced into a side alley, from where they witnessed the demolition of the orphanage. A baying crowd of more than a hundred looked on, among them people who only a week before had been happy to do business with the institution. Like a medieval rite, the children were forced in procession through the streets, then herded into a schoolyard and finally into the school hall along with several Jewish women, some of them barely dressed, and some older men. Leopold Strauss was among them, as Yitzhak Herz recalled:[16]

The retired old Jewish teacher of Dinslaken, a particularly venerable looking old gentleman (he was at one time a town councillor and head of the commercial college) sat groaning in a corner. His head was bleeding from the injuries the Nazis had inflicted upon him. With the help of a used envelope, I managed to bring some water to the suffering man. I did this in a brief moment when no one was looking, because we were in fact forbidden to leave the hall.

Only at this point did a Nazi official in civilian clothing come to assure the detainees that they need not fear, 'they were not in Soviet Russia', and to say that the elderly Jews could be taken to the hospital. He also assured them that the cow which belonged to the orphanage was being properly looked after. A doctor arrived, who treated the elderly with 'visible compassion'. From here, Leopold must have made his way to the hospital where Marianne found him.

There was one last set of documents on the incident: among Marianne's papers I found a letter sent to Leopold Strauss twelve days after his attack. The head office of the Health Insurance Association for teachers wrote:[17]

> *Re: termination of membership*
>
> *The damnable crime against the German legate, Ernst vom Rath in Paris, has raised feelings of the greatest anger towards the Jewish population in the entire German people. Among German educators too there has been the sharpest condemnation of the fact that Jews are still members of a health insurance association belonging to an organization attached to the National Socialist German Workers' Party. Many Aryan members of the association threaten to leave if the remaining Jews are not expelled as quickly as possible.*
>
> *The Board of the Association has therefore decided to move forward the expiration date of your membership ... which will now terminate on 30 November.*
>
> *Our cancellation department in Berlin has been instructed to remove you from the list of members on that date.*

This letter was filed with three letters to Leopold Strauss from the teachers' fire insurance association. The first was a hand-written note from the Teachers' Fire Association of Rhineland and Westphalia sent in 1913, cordially welcoming Leopold in his new role as the association's district head for Dinslaken.[18] The next was an equally cordial typed note dated 1 August 1933. Evidently, Leopold had stood down and a new district administrator was elected for Dinslaken:[19]

> *We would not wish to miss the opportunity of extending to you our heartfelt thanks, both on behalf of the Association you have so strongly supported in your district and on our own behalf. All matters in your district have always been dealt with promptly and in an orderly manner. Correspondence between you and the Board has always been businesslike, calm and pleasant. Please therefore*

accept our thanks for the efforts you have devoted to the Fire Insurance Association. We wish you all good fortune and beg you to retain your interest in the Association.

With collegiate greetings,
[Signature illegible]

The last note was an anonymous looking circular from the by now renamed Fire Association:[20]

Your membership of the Fire Association of West German Teachers and your insurance against fire damage and theft expires – as does that of all Jewish members – on 31 December 1938.
The Board.

Dachau and its impact

Meanwhile, Siegfried and Alfred sat in an Essen jail. Some older Jews were released, but on 16 November, 175 'younger' Jews – including Siegfried and Alfred – were deported to Dachau. Walter Rohr, then a fit, young twenty-two-year-old, vividly remembered the transport. The train became increasingly overcrowded until at some point they were ordered to switch to a cattle car with no lights or sanitary facilities. They arrived at Dachau at four in the morning and were sent stumbling through the drizzle. There was no food on the first day. For Rohr, the ensuing routine of rising at five to stand at attention for hours on end, arduous labour, hunger and other 'horrors of life in a concentration camp' made these 'the most gruesome days' of his life.[21]

Marianne's mother was in despair. Uri Weinberg remembered a weeping aunt Ine coming to see his parents in Cologne. The only option was to seek clemency from the Gestapo. Ine sent her first letter on 23 November, a week after Siegfried's deportation:[22]

My husband is forty-seven. As a non-commissioned officer he served in the First World War from 1 August 1914 to the end of the war, and was the recipient of several honours. Recently, he suffered from a serious inflammation of the veins which kept him in bed for weeks. His heart has suffered heavily as a result of this illness and from rheumatism. In addition, my husband is needed to administer the houses he owns. I am not informed about the business and am not in a position to pay taxes, welfare payments and other ongoing commitments.

The sale of land for the purpose of Aryanization has to be initiated immediately. It is our desire to emigrate to North America as soon as possible. I received the affidavit a few days ago.

Four days later, Ine sent a second letter, the most notable feature of which was that Frau Strauss knew Siegfried Strauss's exact address down to his cell number: KL Dachau 3K, Block 21, Stube 2b. Here was the first intimation of a persistent element in Marianne's story – the startling amount of information flowing in and out of the camps. This second letter reinforced the arguments of the first; Siegfried was urgently needed to raise the money for the first instalment of the *Judenvermögen-sabgabe* or Jewish property tax,[23] a reference to the compensation payments demanded of the Jewish community to cover the costs of repairing their own damaged property.[24] On 2 December, the regional Gestapo headquarters (Staatspolizeileitstelle) in Düsseldorf telegraphed Dachau that Strauss's wife had appeared with proof of his military service and had declared the family's intention to leave for the USA (the evidence she presented will have also established Alfred's intention to leave). Frau Strauss had been instructed to transfer to Dachau the money for her husband's train journey. The Dachau commandant was requested to release prisoner 29826[25] and order him to report to the Gestapo in Essen.[26]

The brothers were released together on 9 December, just over three weeks after their arrival in Dachau. In Marianne's memory, the period of internment had grown to six weeks. Elsewhere she wrote of eight weeks.[27] As so often, Marianne, Eric Alexander and Uri Weinberg all retained different memories of the event. Marianne believed that the Dachau internment was an absolutely decisive experience for her father. He came back a changed man, she said, shrunken and embittered. He never talked about what had happened to him and became very 'silent, very quiet indeed, very intractable'. I wondered whether he even talked to his wife about Dachau. Marianne did not know, and quite possibly he could share it with no one. The wife of the rabbi in nearby Dortmund remembered that 'it was an almost unbearable pain to see our friends return, their spirit so broken that they did not speak of their experiences even to their wives'.[28] For the young Marianne, the blow to her father's self-esteem was heart-rending. The most difficult thing for him, Marianne felt (perhaps only later on in life) must have been the stripping away of civilized behaviour and the confrontation with one's own naked instinct to survive. 'Because that really is the moment of truth – how you cope, how you behave, not how the others behave, though that was terrifying enough.'[29]

Typically, Uri Weinberg's memory was gentler. He did not remember that Siegfried had come back so changed, though he had certainly said little about his experiences. He remembered Siegfried volunteering that the train journey to Dachau was bearable, but that after that ' "a different wind was blowing" '. Eric Alexander, by contrast, remembered Siegfried indulging in rather unappetizing and unconvincing bravado. It wasn't so bad, Siegfried had said, the exercise had been good for them.

Other evidence, too, supports the idea that, in public at least, the fight had by no means gone out of the Strauss brothers. But in private it was another matter.

Paying for the damage

The after-shocks of Kristallnacht continued to buffet the Strauss family. As Ine's letter to the authorities has shown, there was now the task of paying for the damage. In one of the regime's most cynical exercises, Hitler called for the Jews to pay one billion Marks to 'atone' for the destruction. The tax authorities struggled to determine the percentage of Jewish assets required to meet the figure. In the end, it was decided that 20 per cent would be required in instalments and an elaborate schedule of payments was drawn up. (Later, the rate would be raised to 25 per cent and an additional instalment required). So, the Strauss brothers were barely able to catch their breath after Dachau before they were struggling to meet the official timetable set for the new tax.

Among Marianne's papers is a letter written by Alfred Strauss on 13

December 1938, informing the south Essen tax office of the depreciation of family property since the assessment in the summer. Reading this solid businesslike document, one can hardly believe that it was written just three days after Alfred's return from Dachau. The taxes subsequently imposed show that the revisions were accepted. But the bill was still massive. In all, Siegfried, Ine and the children paid just over RM75,000, a sum in excess of Siegfried's entire earnings over the preceding three years. Alfred and Lore paid still more.[30] Together, Siegfried, Alfred and Leopold paid around 2.5 per cent of the entire Essen levy.[31]

The documents kept by the brothers on the process are revealing in a number of ways. Deadlines were tight, and the procedure full of pitfalls and humiliations. On 13 December, for example, Anna Rosenberg (whose affairs were being handled by Siegfried) ordered the Deutsche Bank in Essen and the Sparkasse Münster to make securities available for the first payment, due on 15 December. Both banks subsequently confirmed that on 14 December they had notified the relevant tax office, Beckum, that the shares were available. However, a week later Frau Rosenberg received a letter from the tax office, dated the 14th but franked 21 December, announcing that payment was late; a fine of RM117 was payable, and in addition a 'security deposit' was required equal to the full amount of the remaining payments. (Curiously this letter was dated before the due date for the first payment, and thus before it could even have been established that payment *was* overdue. Perhaps the date was an error, or the letter may have been drawn up in advance in the hope that Frau Rosenberg's payment would be late). On 4 January, Frau Rosenberg wrote, advising that she had made shares available before the due date and that her order was confirmed by the bank. Five days later the tax office responded that it did not agree and pointed out that the Deutsche Bank's letter had arrived only on 24 December, nine days after the deadline. The fine still stood, but, without any explicit acknowledgement of a modification, the penalty was reduced, based on the fact that one part of the transfer had arrived in time. On 12 January, possibly before the letter of the 9th had arrived, Frau Rosenberg wrote again, saying that there were no grounds for paying the requested security deposit, indeed that she was not in a position to pay it, since she had already made one such deposit against future payment of the Flight Tax. On the 16th she responded to the letter of the 9th, enclosing proof from the Deutsche Bank that it had indeed notified the tax office before the deadline, and appealing against the penalty. She also asked that the interest paid on the shares after their arrival in the tax office be taken into account. On the 18th, the tax office agreed that the security deposit was not necessary. On the 19th, the tax office wrote again, arguing that the note which the Deutsche Bank had sent on the 14th was insufficient; the proper form, in triplicate, had been sent only on 22 December, arriving on the 24th. However 'as a courtesy' the fine would be waived.

The subsequent instalments raised similar problems. Though the whole operation was punitive, degrading and nerve-rackingly arbitrary, there were still dim messages of hope for the Strauss family. In almost every case, letters requesting the reversal of harsh penalties, or alerting the tax office to property depreciation and so forth, were accepted. While the tone of communications from the tax office offered little comfort, letters from the Deutsche Bank continued to convey the traditional deference commanded by possession of a sizeable bank account. Where money counted, the correctness of German institutions had not yet disappeared.

But more remarkable than the remaining vestiges of correctness was the faith that the Strauss family continued to put in those institutions. The Rosenberg case again serves as an example. In October, Germany's Jews were dismayed to find that the tax had been raised to 25 per cent of their property value and thus another 5 per cent was due in a fifth instalment. Around this time, Anna Rosenberg moved to Essen and her brother, Abraham Weyl, became her trustee, though there is good reason to believe that Siegfried was keeping her accounts. On 31 October 1939, Herr Weyl wrote to the Finance Office in Düsseldorf (Oberfinanzpräsident, OFD) asking for Anna Rosenberg's fifth instalment to be waived, on the grounds that her property was over-rated, and that she herself was elderly, in ill-health and had very limited income.

The Essen tax office now responsible for Anna Rosenberg agreed to suspend collection while the matter was looked into by Düsseldorf, but warned that if Düsseldorf did not agree, Frau Rosenberg would be fined. On 10 November, Abraham Israel Weyl received a one sentence reply

Anna Rosenberg in Essen, 1940

from the OFD, 'I reject the application of Frau Anna Sara Rosenberg, Essen, Cäsarstr. 22, for release from the payment of 5,750.' No explanation, no nothing. But the family did not leave it there. On 14 November 1939, Abraham Weyl wrote to the Reich Finance Minister in Berlin again asking for the final payment to be waived. Simultaneously, however, the fifth instalment *was* paid as a precaution. On 9 January 1940, the OFD wrote to say that the Herr Reichsminister had rejected the application.

In this case, the family achieved nothing through their intervention. But the fact remains that even after Kristallnacht, after Dachau, they still thought they might obtain justice from the authorities. Or even more remarkably, since the law was fairly clear that Anna Rosenberg *would* have to pay, they still expected reasonableness from the civil service. And they were not yet so cowed into submission as to be frightened of asking for it. Their persistence was testimony to the enormous faith which the Strauss family had once placed in German institutions. Or perhaps the possibility that justice was no longer to be had was just too frightening to contemplate.

Kristallnacht as a turning point

Kristallnacht is well known as a day on which Jewish houses of worship, public institutions and businesses were destroyed. It is also common knowledge that the pogrom marked a dramatic though somewhat unplanned radicalization of Nazi policy. But until I talked to Marianne, I had not fully realized how devastatingly the events of those days reached into the private sphere of every German-Jewish family.[32]

Yet, astonishingly, given Marianne's own memories and descriptions, when I made this observation to her, she refuted the idea. She said she didn't feel that Kristallnacht had been a turning point. The family had been aware for years of the way things were deteriorating. Then she said something odd:

'My father, we could have gone out, I used to, we had always. You asked whether there was a lot of social intercourse, there was, but with relations . . .'

Did this sentence really begin as a statement about social life in the

1930s? Or had Marianne started to tell me the family could have left the country earlier – and then changed the topic? My sense was that she could not allow Kristallnacht to be a transformative experience (though elsewhere her comments clearly indicated that it was) because she felt that her parents should have read the writing on the wall earlier. But when it came to openly articulating the criticism, she could not allow herself to do that either, and ended up telling me about social intercourse with relations.

One family member for whom Kristallnacht was indisputably a turning point was Marianne's grandfather, Leopold. Among the surviving family papers are two of Leopold's identity cards. The photo on Leopold's card from 1926 is of a vigorous, ebullient man in his prime. The Jewish Identity Pass from January 1939 depicts a man looking not thirteen but thirty years older, distinguished still, but aged and exhausted. Still lively of mind before the attack, Leopold rapidly developed Alzheimer's disease. After a miserable few months in Essen, he died on 15 June 1939 in Alfred's apartment.[33] A careful letter from Ine Strauss to a relative in New York, Fritz Stern, noted:[34]

His state of health since the end of last year left much to be desired. He had remained healthy, calm and adaptable to change for such a long time, but the recent dislocations left their mark. And so we must allow him his eternal rest and allow ourselves to accept the loss of this good man.

Leopold's grave can still be found in the Essen cemetery. He was the last member of the family to be given a proper burial on German soil.

Kristallnacht and emigration

Marianne said that it was only after Kristallnacht and the imprisonment of the Strauss brothers that the family took steps to leave Germany. Initially, I did wonder if she was exaggerating their obstinacy. Was it not possible that her parents had in fact begun their efforts to leave rather earlier? But among Marianne's papers I discovered extensive correspondence with the family's American relatives, including several

Leopold Strauss, 1926 and 1939

affidavits of support filled out by Siegfried's cousin, Fritz Stern (his mother Bertha had been one of Leopold's sisters), who had been in the United States since 1907. The purpose of these affidavits was to guarantee that the Strauss family would have financial backing in America. Stern, the President of Great American Knitting Mills in Pennsylvania, with a substantial annual income of $25,000, was a credible sponsor.[35] But what was most noteworthy was the date of the very first one: 2 December 1938. This was the same day the Gestapo recorded Ine Strauss as having arrived at their headquarters with proof of Siegfried's intention to leave. Ine must have been anxiously waiting for the affidavit to arrive and gone straight to the Gestapo offices when it did so.[36] The fact that this was the earliest affidavit I found among the Strauss papers suggested strongly that it really was only the crisis provoked by Siegfried's imprisonment that had propelled the family to seek to emigrate. Incidentally, on 24 November 1938, Regina went to the local register office to get a copy of Marianne's brother Richard's birth certificate, having presumably mislaid the original. By now, every scrap of official paper had taken on a new significance. They could make the difference between acceptance and rejection of an emigration application and thus (though this was not yet fully clear) between life and death.[37]

A series of new persecutory measures gave the family further encouragement to leave. At the end of 1938, Jewish passports were declared invalid and could be reissued only with a special 'J' stamp. From 1 January 1939, Siegfried and Richard, along with all Jewish men, had to adopt the middle name Israel, whilst Ine and Marianne were assigned the middle name Sara. Siegfried had to surrender his driving licence for which, with bureaucratic thoroughness, the authorities issued him a 'confirmation of receipt'. (With the same thoroughness, Siegfried and his daughter ensured the receipt's survival until now.)[38] The car was already gone, anyway. In February 1939, the Strausses had to surrender all articles in their possession made of gold, silver, platinum, pearls or gems, with the exception of wedding rings. There is good reason to believe that they did not in fact submit all their valuables, but instead made a judicious selection, making it seem as if they had.[39]

As Siegfried's business activities were effectively limited to his responsibilities as landlord, an increasing proportion of Marianne's

Marianne's identity pass, January 1939

parents' time, energy and emotion could be invested in preparing for emigration; their money, however, was harder to deploy, since it was now subject to official controls. Marianne was away at college for most of this time and so did not experience much of this effort, but the considerable number of surviving family papers give a good idea of what her parents were doing. The papers include carefully cut-out sections of the Jewish newspaper, the *Jüdisches Nachrichtenblatt*, on emigration and English lessons. In May, Siegfried applied to enter New Zealand and Australia, stressing his particular skills in the grain trade. But access to these countries was extremely restricted. The Australian application was rejected in June, the refusal from New Zealand followed in July.

The Strausses also considered Britain. The Jewish Veterans' Association (RjF), informed the Jewish Ex-Servicemen's Legion in London that Siegfried was an RjF member and urged the Legion to provide 'the comrade with advice and help and all necessary information in a comradely way', adding that the assistance sought was not of a material nature. Siegfried will not have been unaware of the irony of the RjF appealing to the 'comradely' instincts of the former enemy.

In May, the family received medical certificates in English, confirming that none of them was 'mentally or physically defective in any way' and none afflicted with tuberculosis or any other 'infectious, loathsome or contagious disease', including 'favus, leprosy, framboesia or yaws, trachom, syphilis or scabies'.[40] In July 1939, the synagogue wrote letters of recommendation for the family. Marianne Strauss was:[41]

a well-educated girl. She is intelligent, amiable and has especially good manners. She went to the Girls' High School, which she left with the finishing certificate. Since Easter 1939 she has attended the Nursery Training College in Berlin. She easily gets adapted to her surroundings and will very well fit into an English family and into English Nursery Training-College. We can recommend her from every point of view, as she seems particularly fit for the work she wants to train for.

The German Jewish Aid Committee, based in Britain, wrote to the Strauss family on 19 July to advise that a visa application had been made on their behalf, and again on 15 August advising them to apply for a visa in Berlin.[42] On 17 August, a letter from the British Consulate-General in Cologne arrived to verify their address and finally, on 21 August, a short letter from the same source confirmed that their visas were now ready for collection.[43] The family had finally been granted permission to enter Great Britain. The sense of relief in Essen can be imagined.

Twelve days later, Britain and Germany were at war, and emigration to Britain became impossible.

4

Blossoming in a
Harsh Climate

'I really must say,' Marianne summed up for me, 'in spite of everything, the war and whatever happened . . . it was really like beginning another life. It was most enriching. It was wonderful training, a great deal of experience in every way, human, social, apart from the training itself. So, it was a very, very wonderful time for me.'[1] If I had not known better, I would have assumed Marianne was talking about her life after the war. It was scarcely credible that she was referring to the years 1939–41, when she attended the Jewish Training College for Kindergarten Teachers in Berlin.[2] Her verdict on the Yavne school in Cologne, where she studied from the end of 1938 until March 1939, was almost as positive.

Up to 1938, it had been Marianne's parents' ability to carry their prosperity and confidence through the storm that had been remarkable. While Marianne suffered at school, they had managed, like cartoon victims already over the cliff edge, to tread on air for five years of Nazi rule. Now, following Kristallnacht, the roles were reversed. At a time in which the Jewish community suffered 'social death'[3] in advance of its physical death, for Marianne 'that's when life began!'

Changing schools

Though the formal legislation was issued only on 15 November 1938, the Luisenschule, like many other schools, seems to have dismissed its remaining Jewish pupils on the 10th. Certainly, Marianne's final school report dates from then. Naturally, along with so much else, the report is still preserved. By 1938, almost all German schools were too cowardly to grade Jewish pupils any higher than 'adequate' or 'satisfactory'. The overall judgement that 'Marianne made an effort to meet the demands of the school' and the series of 'adequate' or 'satisfactory' marks has the authentic ring of cowardly begrudging. On the other hand, the marks gain some plausibility in that Marianne did receive a 'good' for English, which Frau Horn remembered her as performing so well in, and for music, where her piano lessons had presumably stood her in good stead.[4]

For Siegfried and Ine, as soon as they could give thought to anything other than the family's survival, the question was what to do about the children's education. The Reich Education Ministry decree of 15 November 1938, forbidding Jews from attending state schools, made a return to the Luisenschule out of the question.[5] Instead, Siegfried and Ine – perhaps advised by the Weinbergs – decided to send their children to the Yavne school in Cologne. Yavne, founded in 1919, was the only Jewish secondary school in the Rhineland.

Until 1933, Yavne pupils had been recruited largely from Orthodox families. The bulk of the liberal-minded Jewish middle class sent their children to secular state schools. This changed dramatically after 1933. By 1934, pupils from non-Orthodox backgrounds accounted for 85 per cent of the new intake, and the overall number grew steadily, peaking in 1937. That youngsters from liberal backgrounds could be absorbed into a school run on Orthodox Jewish lines had much to do with the role and personality of Dr Erich Klibansky (1900–42) Yavne's headmaster from 1929. As his reputation grew, so did the proportion of youngsters coming from outside Cologne – by 1938 they made up a quarter of the school body.[6]

Marianne and her brother Richard were thus part of the growing trend of non-Orthodox outsiders seeking a safe and stimulating environment for study. They stayed with their cousins, the Weinbergs, recently installed in Cologne. Boycotts and local pressure had induced Ernst Weinberg to sell his Erkelenz shop and, like many Jews at the time, the Weinbergs had decided that the anonymity of the big city offered a better chance of protection than their close acquaintance in the small town. The three boys, Alex, Alfred and Otto, were all sent to the Yavne.

It did not surprise me by now that Marianne, Alfred and Alexander should each have different memories of the school. For Marianne, it was the first step on a personal journey of intellectual growth and liberation. She remembered above all the cultured atmosphere, the qualifications and high quality of the teachers. Partly because there were no employment prospects elsewhere, the school was staffed by a marvellous array of talent. The well-known artist Ludwig Maidner, abstract painter of the Düsseldorf school, had been at Yavne since 1935 and was Marianne's art teacher. The distinguished translator, Else Nussbaum, at the school since 1935, taught Marianne English. The staff's approach to ideas and education also appealed to her. As early as 1933, given that Jewish students' access to German universities was now severely restricted,[7] Klibansky recognized that the function of the school had changed. It was no longer to accredit youngsters for their university place, but to provide true learning.[8] In retrospect, Marianne said, 'it was the first time in my life that I enjoyed school and really got something' out of it.

Alfred, now Uri, recalled the school with similar pleasure. For him, too, it was a place of freedom. He remembered having to be very careful at his old grammar school in Erkelenz. In Erkelenz he had had to learn to judge people's character very carefully, he said. But at Yavne you felt free. He remembered that when he first joined the school, he arrived to find Klibansky teaching the class history. Klibansky asked the class a question to which Alfred, with his good grammar school education, was bound to know the answer – Frederick II. Alfred duly put his hand up, but used the description obligatory in German schools, 'Frederick the Great'. Klibansky said, 'We don't say Frederick the Great here, or if we do, we say Frederick the Great Windbag.' Alfred felt the question was designed to test which 'side' he was on: was he still (like his brother) hankering to be a German, or did he primarily see himself as a Jew?

Alfred's answer was clear, and in that one exchange he felt a stone fall from his shoulders and knew he was among friends. The school was to be an important step on his journey towards a religious Jewish life. Tears came to his eyes as he remembered Rabbi Stein, who had befriended him at Yavne; it was his first encounter with a vibrant Orthodoxy.

I had expected that Marianne, too, would recall the school as having given her a sense of a vital Jewish identity. The historian Joseph Walk noted that, partly because Klibansky managed to be Orthodox on the one hand and tolerant on the other, the school strengthened its pupils' Jewish identity, leading many to embrace religious observance and even to pass it on to their parents.[9] But Marianne said nothing of this. After she told me about the 'celebrities' on the staff, and mentioned Nussbaum and Maidner, I discovered that another distinguished teacher had been Kurth Levy, an important academic dismissed from the Oriental Seminar in Bonn, who now taught Hebrew and Latin at the school. Marianne had no memory of him or of the Hebrew lessons.[10] I wondered whether this meant she had had no positive religious experiences at the time or whether her subsequent development – be it the identity she assumed in wartime or her years of living with a more Orthodox husband after the war – had meant she forgot such experiences in later life.

For Eric Alexander, the Yavne school represented a personal defeat – the final nail in the coffin of his dream of becoming a successful German boy. He found it hard going, not least because, having attended classical grammar schools, he had not studied English and now found himself in an all-English class. He worked hard, though, and in 1939 his teacher secured him passage to Britain, so in the end Yavne served him well. But he had not made the school his own. Laughing, he told me that Alfred was 'well in with the rabbi there and I think he must have told him about me, because I remember the rabbi once passed me in the street, and if looks could kill . . .'[11]

At first, Marianne and Richard stayed in the Weinbergs' flat. After a while, though, they moved back home and commuted daily to the school from Essen. Marianne said they ended the arrangement because the flat was too small, but Eric Alexander recalled it differently. He was then about seventeen and Marianne was fifteen and they had a 'little love affair, well, you could hardly call it that really, holding hands . . . Then

Siegfried came and "ohhhh!" ' Siegfried wasn't happy about it? 'No, not at all, so she had to move out again.'[12]

Marianne might have forgotten this, but she was probably being discreet. I was later to discover that a relationship with a French prisoner of war in 1944 and a brief romance after the war were similarly passed over. What Marianne did mention was that she and Richard now had to get up at crack of dawn, and make a nearly two-hour journey every day during a very cold winter. The Kriminalpolizei would come through the trains and inspect the special authorization she said they needed to travel by rail.

Leaving the Yavne

At Easter 1939, Klibansky managed to organize the departure of a group of children to England. The group included Marianne's class and, Marianne thought, was also open to Richard. In all, 130 children got to England in this way.[13] Alexander Weinberg had already gone with an earlier group. Now Alfred and Otto followed. Marianne and Richard did not, because Siegfried did not want them to go abroad on their own.

What on earth was Siegfried thinking of? The rabbi's wife in nearby Dortmund, for example, remembered parents literally begging the rabbi 'to send their children away as soon as possible', since the parents 'could no longer stand to see them suffer from hatred and abuse'.[14] Thanks to the various *Kindertransports* – above all to Britain – the bulk of German youngsters were getting out. By the outbreak of war, teenagers were few and far between. Of the Jews left in Germany, 75 per cent were over forty.[15] So it is hard to understand Siegfried's position. It is just possible that in March 1939, with the affidavit from Fritz Stern in his pocket, he was so confident that the US application would soon come to fruition that the risk of separating the family at this stage seemed too great. That confidence might also explain why he waited as late as May to begin applying to Britain, Australia and New Zealand. But what seems evident is that, despite Dachau, Siegfried still had not fully realized what the regime was capable of. How else to explain the fact that he thought it safer for the children to make a lengthy train journey from Essen to

Cologne every day rather than risk the danger of Alexander and Marianne holding hands?

Marianne said she didn't question her father's stance at the time. Siegfried made the decisions. However, she would have enjoyed the adventure. She felt already 'very grown up and rather restricted in my home set-up.' Her brother, who was more timid, might not have enjoyed it, she said. As to what she thought of the decision now, she made no comment.

By March 1939, Marianne had completed her fifth year of secondary school. That entitled her to the intermediate school qualification, the Mittlere Reife. The Yavne school's final report recorded her general behaviour as good but, interestingly, the marks were not so different from those of the Luisenschule. The overall grade was only adequate. Marianne did well in German and again music, but poorly in art and mathematics. In the remarks section, the report stated only that 'The school bids Marianne farewell with the best wishes for her future.'[16]

Marianne's parents were once again faced with a decision about their children's future. The local Jewish school in Essen had no higher-level education to offer. There was nowhere in Germany she could study for the Abitur, the qualifying university entrance examination, and, in any case, German centres of higher learning were closed to her. However, because of official Nazi 'support' for Jewish emigration, Jewish vocational colleges had been allowed to proliferate at a time when all other opportunities were falling away. In Berlin, in particular, there was a range of colleges offering skills useful for emigrants.[17] True, the options available specifically to girls were fairly circumscribed. There were some places at agricultural schools to prepare girls for emigration to Palestine, but the Strausses were not thinking of Palestine. There was domestic science training. There were nurses' training courses in several Jewish hospitals such as the Neonatal and Children's Hospital in Berlin. The Jewish College for Kindergarten Teachers in Berlin was unique in that it provided a state-recognized qualification.[18] Typically, the chance at an official accreditation was the crucial advantage in Marianne's parents' eyes. It was so important that Siegfried was even prepared to allow his fifteen-year-old daughter to go to Berlin, alone.

The move to Berlin was in many ways to be Marianne's liberation, but in retrospect she associated it also with the sadness of leaving Richard behind. Older children, particularly at the point where they outgrow the parental home, often lose contact with their younger siblings. In normal conditions, this can be remedied later. But one of the most painful experiences for Marianne was that there was never a later point of remedy. Even the things Marianne could tell me were not always accurate. For example, in telling me that after the Yavne school Richard was educated privately at home it is clear that she lost sight of three years of his schooling – the years, in fact, when she was largely away from home.

In December 1939, Richard celebrated his barmitzvah, a very reduced affair compared with family celebrations past. The Oberpräsident, Düsseldorf, Devisenstelle had to give his permission for Siegfried to draw RM100 from his account for 'confirmation fees,' presumably to pay the rabbi.[19] By then in Berlin, Marianne did not come back for the occasion. She said to me at one point that she could not get permission. But in a later conversation she said that she could not face the disruption and her parents had not been particularly encouraging, more interested that she should continue the course. Now, with hindsight, she was very sorry she hadn't gone. 'At the time nothing like that seemed to matter.'[20] Marianne felt guilty about losing track of her brother, and at the same time guilty towards her parents that she, and not the academically more able brother, had survived.[21]

Kindergarten college

Now largely unknown even to experts on Jewish history, the Berlin College for Kindergarten Teachers was created in 1934 and, despite some wavering on the part of the Prussian Cultural Ministry, received state recognition. 'While Jews are still living with us,' went the official argument (and this in May 1934!), 'it would be both impractical and undesirable to deny them training for work in Jewish nurseries in proportion to the size of the population.'[22] To restrict the number of Jews obtaining a state qualification, though, the Ministry limited the intake to thirty, refused to accredit any other college within the entire Reich and insisted on extending the course to two years instead of the proposed eighteen months. At Easter 1938, the school was allowed to introduce a second class, and in summer 1938 Margarete Fraenkel,[23] previously a teacher at the school, took over as head.

Marianne's memory was that the school normally required pupils to have their Abitur and that her mother had to obtain special dispensation for Marianne to enter so young. Probably this memory reflects the sense of awe and trepidation with which Marianne went to Berlin. In fact, with her Mittlere Reife, Marianne met the minimum requirement for admission. Even so, the school normally required its pupils to be aged at least seventeen. Marianne may have been right in thinking that when she set off for Berlin in April 1939, two months short of her sixteenth birthday, she was the college's youngest entrant.[24]

When she arrived in Berlin, she found the college located at Wangenheimstrasse 36, in the affluent western Berlin district of Grünewald. It was 'a very good address, like The Bishop's Avenue', Marianne assured me, unconsciously slipping into a British register for her comparison.[25] The luxurious villa, donated by a Jewish banker, housed not only the school but also the hall of residence for girls from outside Berlin.[26] Marianne remembered the place as 'enormous, with I don't know how many really splendid 1920s bathrooms' and a large garden. The most desirable bedroom, which everybody wanted, was the 'plum room' on the top floor, a corner room with two little turrets, one of them looking down the Wangenheimstrasse, the other down the Lynarstrasse. In 1940, Marianne managed to move in there.

Here, as at Yavne, the elimination of opportunities elsewhere was a boon for the school as a glittering array of intellectuals and inspired teachers had joined the teaching staff. Aware that in different circumstances many of the students would have sought a more academic education, the college offered a far more intellectual and wide-ranging course than was usual for kindergarten teachers. An advertisement in the newsletter of the Jewish Women's League (JFB) in 1935 gives a hint of this breadth and depth:[27]

The academic instruction covers the history of education and an introduction to educational literature, psychology and educational theory, kindergarten studies, health studies, contemporary affairs, children's literature, nature study, cultural studies, German, Hebrew, Jewish history and Jewish knowledge. Candidates will be expected to have a basic knowledge of Hebrew. The course will place considerable emphasis on arts and crafts such as music, handicrafts, drawing, modelling, needlework, gymnastics and movement.

Marianne told me that the core teaching team at the college had all been trained at the Pestalozzi-Fröbel-Haus – the famous social-work institution founded by Helene Lange. The College director, Margarete Fraenkel, had been a pupil not only of Helene Lange but also of Jung and Adler. The Institute's board included several very prominent Jews, among them Leo Baeck. The teaching staff numbered among its ranks inspiring figures such as Hannah Karminski, a leading member of the JFB until its dissolution in 1938, who herself had trained as a kindergarten teacher and social worker. Karminski's correspondence reveals that she found teaching in the college a source of satisfaction and compensation amid her otherwise miserable and largely hopeless duties in the welfare department of the Reich Association of Jews (Reichsvereinigung der Juden, RV). There were also musicians, sociologists, specialists of all kinds. Marianne recalled 'a pupil of Gundolff – *the* translator of Shakespeare into German – who was our teacher on Shakespeare. We had a teacher just on Shakespeare . . . It was quite unheard of.'[28]

For Marianne, the college was liberation. 'Suddenly I was away from this very strict parental control. I *really* blossomed, I really sort of grew up in no time at all.'[29] Marianne was not the only student to see her studies as a liberating experience. Edith Dietz started at the College a year earlier and graduated in 1940. In her memoirs,[30] she too recalled the quality and depth of the teaching and the feeling of freedom in Berlin.[31]

The staff were well aware of Marianne's enthusiasm and responsive to her talents.[32] Her practical training outside the college, in kindergartens or with families, was equally appreciated.[33] But while Marianne was full of energy and enthusiasm, she soon found that she was 'really very innocent':[34]

'The head of the school said, "We'll throw you to the wolves, you're the youngest." So that was learning very fast, very fast indeed. Working with families and coming across their problems. People who were impoverished and demoralized. Mothers who had mental breakdowns. Children who were the result of incest. I worked in the only Jewish baby home which still existed, and the misery of the abandoned children there . . . It's just not imaginable.'

It was one of the many incongruities of this period that the conditions Marianne encountered were reminiscent of those portrayed in anti-Semitic propaganda films. Marianne had to do 'practical work in the most appalling slum conditions. I'd never known such destitution would exist among Jews . . . inadequacies, incest, anything you could think of.' Marianne remembered one particular family, 'called Fleischhammel, which was the most extraordinary name but it suited them beautifully. It was like something out of Dickens, or even worse.' She would turn up with new clothing for the children, but the next day:[35]

'. . . it was all gone, had been sold for whatever. The wallpaper was off the walls, and even during the day the cockroaches were crawling around there. I not only had to look after the children, but clean the place up, and the children didn't go to school because they had no clothes to go in. And they all slept more or less in two beds, the parents and children, and the sheets they were given away or sold or whatever. The filth was indescribable. Every day I went there I found the same thing. I took one clean lot packed one day and the next day it started all over again.'

As a sixteen-year-old who thought 'you could alter the world overnight and make decent human beings out of people' this imperviousness to assistance was hard for Marianne to bear. 'There were times when I felt quite suicidal.' At the same time, coming back each night to the very civilized existence in the Grünewald was so rewarding 'you forgot really what was going on outside. There was always something interesting going on. There were lots of interesting people still living ordinary lives in Berlin – very public well-known figures, friends of the organization. Musicians would come and give concerts and they would come and play records, we'd have get-togethers . . . folk singing, lectures . . . wonderful social things going on all the time.'[36]

Marianne's new-found independence and sociability brought her into contact with a wide circle, including a literary and cultural set. Despite the restrictions, life for her was full of undreamed-of freedom. 'When I went to Berlin I had never been out late at night, so really, I was very lucky I was of a very careful disposition. If I hadn't been, I could probably have landed in a great deal of trouble, suddenly being let off the leash as it were.'[37]

Meeting Inge Deutschkron

In Germany, Inge Deutschkron's book *Outcast: a Jewish Girl in Wartime Berlin*[38] is the most famous autobiographical account of a so-called 'U-Boat', as the Jews protected by friends in Berlin were known. A younger generation recently learned her story anew because of the success of *From Today Your Name Is Sara*,[39] a play based on Inge Deutschkron's life. I read the book to see if there were parallels between Deutschkron's and Marianne's experiences. What I had not expected to find was that Inge Deutschkron, a year Marianne's senior, had studied at the kindergarten college at exactly the same time. I wrote to Frau Deutschkron on the off-chance that she might remember Marianne and, when a glowing tribute came back, arranged to see her next time I was in Berlin.

Inge Deutschkron lived in a large block of flats with a marvellous view over the city. She herself was clearly a toughie who didn't suffer fools gladly, but at the same time was lively and engaging. She produced a delicious late breakfast of watermelon and regaled me with the details of her Al Italia flight from Israel the previous day, including a short, miserable stopover in Milan. The final straw had been the stewardess wanting to refuse her an aisle seat, because, with her cane, she might impede the egress of the others. I'd like to have been there to see the explosion.

And then we turned to the past. It soon became clear that the college had not had the same significance for Inge Deutschkron that it had for Marianne. As a local girl, she had lived at home and missed the intensity of the boarding experience. In any case, thanks to her parents she had already been part of a lively, left-wing circle and the college's intellectual and cultural effect on her was thus far more limited. Moreover, she hadn't particularly enjoyed working in kindergarten. 'I learned that all the frustrations a kindergarten teacher has she passes on to the children. So I decided if ever I had children I would never send them to kindergarten!'[40] Nevertheless, she too remembered the villa on the Wangenheimstrasse with great pleasure. It was huge, with a lovely garden, 'just a wonderful place to live. I even remember wood panelling which shows you a rich house!'

In her book, Inge Deutschkron wrote that Frau Fraenkel 'conducted the college as though there was nothing more important in the world than to prepare young girls for their vocation.'[41] The girls lived in a separate little world, and 'acted as if nothing happened outside'. But like Marianne, she too encountered in her work with families a degree of poverty and misery she had not believed possible. 'I mean it was good,' she said, 'I saw life. From a different angle, you know.'

The main thing she remembered about Marianne was her appearance and deportment. There was something – Inge Deutschkron searched for a word – there was something *royal* about her:

'It was very intentional, of course. I mean it was not that this came natural to her. But . . . she had this wonderful hair, I don't know if that was still the case when you met her, very strong. And in a long pigtail. She wore it mostly in one, very thick. And sometimes she took that pigtail and turned it around her, what do call that?'

'Like a braid?'

'Like a braid, yes, of course that made her look even more, you know. And she was tall and slim and had a very good figure . . . I was impressed by her, I must say. And her demeanour, that's probably the word for it, it was something, so quiet, I don't know. This is also what I wrote to you, something peaceful came from her, emanated from her. She was definitely a personality, no question.'

Not only Marianne's manner and general level of education but also the quality of her clothes conveyed the impression that she came from a wealthy family. 'But I must say the girls I remember from that time, most of them were from very educated families and they were really good – it was a good place to be.'

Frau Deutschkron lived near the college's old address, though she herself never went there. So after taking the bus for a couple of stops, and then walking through still-affluent Grünewald, I found myself in front of number 36 Wangenheimstrasse. I looked up at the windows and wondered whether Marianne, in her 'plum room', had gazed out over the city from one of them.[42] The street was quiet. At lunchtime on a warm summer weekday only children and tradesmen were about. What kind of people had lived in this street then? Marianne once told me that next door to the school lived a close friend of Hermann Goering. On one occasion this friend had a party to which Goering was invited and the College members were quietly asked beforehand not to be in evidence.[43]

I walked to the other end of the street, savouring the fact that this had been Marianne's territory almost sixty years ago. A little footbridge at the end took me without warning over the Stadtring, the urban motorway that circles the city. Out of the quiet and shade of the Wangenheimstrasse I was suddenly plunged back into the noise and heat and ceaseless stream of traffic of 1990s Berlin.

Wartime Berlin

In September 1939, the girls were in quarantine because of a case of diphtheria. On a very hot summer's day, they were sitting in the wonderful conservatory attached to the house:[44]

'I remember it was about midday,' said Marianne, 'and we were having a sewing lesson and sitting there doing some embroidery when news came over the radio that war had been declared and it was a most, really, a most devastating thing. Even though we had all thought probably that that would happen – the Germans I think wanted it – it was a devastating, quite unforgettable day.'

Initially, Marianne's life was not too affected by the outbreak of war. A curfew was introduced for Jews in Berlin from 9 p.m. to 5 a.m. in the summer months and from 8 p.m. to 6 a.m. in the winter,[45] but I don't think she took it very seriously.

Life was full of incongruities. The College members were invited to take part in air-raid precautions. Representatives of the Fliegerabwehr came and gave the students lessons in first aid and protective measures during an air raid. The girls were even issued with gas masks. 'Imagine!' said Marianne. In 1939, the regime was still protecting Jews from gas. It was also training them as air-raid wardens – Marianne's papers include a certificate confirming that Marianne Sara Strauss had taken part in a Luftschutzlehrgang (air raid course) run by the LS-Hauptschule der Ortsgruppe X/Charlottenburg (the air-raid training school of the Charlottenburg district) from 11–21 October 1940.[46] There were few actual raids, but frequent warnings that sometimes lasted all night. Marianne would have liked to stay up in her plum room, looking at the sky. But 'it was de rigueur, as soon as the bloody sirens went' that they should go down to the cellar. At first, they would sit in the cellar nearly all night, but gradually they stopped taking the warnings quite so seriously.

More incongruity: during the summer of 1940, Marianne worked at a Jewish institute for deaf and dumb children, earning her first salary.[47] The head of the institute was away at the time, leaving his three children behind. His son fell in love with Marianne, and one of the daughters had an SS officer lover. On weekends, this SS 'fellow used to come and on a Saturday night we would sit there and the lights would go out eventually, and we were all in the same room. They were quite openly going about their business and he knew who these people were and yet he was carrying on a love affair with this beautiful girl. What became of them, I don't know.'[48]

Marianne had taken the job as a means of obtaining a rather more tangible forbidden fruit – her first gramophone. She was short of money, not because of the regime's restrictions but because of her father's. With many of the family's funds frozen by the regime, each family member was granted an official personal allowance. Siegfried felt that Marianne's allowance was far too generous for a girl of her age and she was under strict instructions to send most of it home. She vividly remembered her anxiety on the one occasion when for some reason the money she sent home was a little short. The result of her father's strictures was that she didn't even have the means to buy a swimsuit in the sales, although in the heat of the summer she longed for one. 'I always was a great shopper but a very frustrated one ... but I made up for it later on,' laughed Marianne.[49] But, still, she did want the gramophone. For the six weeks' summer job she earned RM35 and bought the cheapest, tiniest, portable wind-up gramophone she could find. Marianne was very proud to have earned it herself. Her sympathetic aunt, Oe, supplied the first records.

At some point at the end of 1940 or the beginning of 1941, the villa was requisitioned by the Gestapo. The college was allocated another building belonging to the Jewish community, this time a large house on the Meineckerstrasse.[50] The new accommodations were more spartan and Marianne found herself sharing rooms with other girls, 'quite a different thing', but still 'all right and civilized'.[51] The new location had at least one thing to recommend it; the immediate proximity of one of the world's most exciting streets, the Kurfürstendamm, full of seductive possibilities:

'On a Saturday night, we would go out on the razzle, walking along the Kurfürstendamm in twos and threes. I remember one particular occasion going with a friend window-shopping on a Saturday evening and two SS chaps were following us. We suddenly realized that we were being followed. Of course, that's how far their racial instincts went! We didn't know how to shake them off. They were obviously making overtures and making quite clear they would have liked us to join them ... so the only way out was to get a taxi. That happened several times and in the end it became like a game of Russian roulette, a dare.'

Marianne would think 'the *Herrenrasse*, the *Herrenvolk*, and they can't even tell a Jew when they see one!' But after a while the girls felt it would be better not to tempt fate too much and grew more circumspect. In June 1941, Marianne celebrated her eighteenth birthday in Berlin.

We should not be seduced by such memories into imagining that life for Berlin's Jews was still happy. By the first winter of the war, one in four depended on Jewish welfare. The city authorities were vicious. Minor traffic offences, an infringement of the blackout or curfew, crossing the street at the wrong place or shopping at the wrong time could lead to very high fines of 40 marks or more, imprisonment, concentration camp or even death. Berlin was often the first to promulgate anti-Jewish legislation later adopted for the whole Reich.[52]

On the other hand, the size of the Jewish community, and the cosmopolitanism of much of the non-Jewish population, prevented Nazi measures from having the same impact in Berlin as in the provinces. Marianne said:[53]

Marianne, 1939/40

'In Berlin there was quite a different sort of attitude to Jews still from the rest of the country. Very much more cosmopolitan, not so narrow, somehow people behaved in a much more civilized way to us than we were expecting or knew of in the provinces; particularly after Kristallnacht, when it hit everybody what exactly might be in store.'

The sheer size of the city also meant that it was easier to be anonymous and ignore the regulations without being spotted. Thus, in the summer of 1941, it was still possible for Marianne to wander down the Kurfürstendamm without being racially attacked.

But even these special factors could not shield the community from the decisive changes of 1941.[54] Suddenly, without formal announcement, trips to the woods around Berlin were declared illegal for Jews.[55] The children remaining in the Jewish schools were forced to seek their exercise in the Jewish cemetery, the one place still open to them.[56] By the autumn of 1941, almost every store on the Kurfürstendamm carried the sign 'No entrance to Jews'. Most Berlin Jews of working age were conscripted into forced labour and suffered the humiliation and exhaustion induced by unfamiliar work, lengthy journeys to and from the factories, and a wage that after all deductions (Jews paid the highest tax rate) often barely covered the most basic needs. In July and August, Berlin Jews were denied the extra rations granted for heavy work or long hours.[57] Marianne remembered that many of the spouses of teachers at the College were conscripted into war work. 'They looked dreadful, they would hardly get any money, it was slave labour.'[58]

Shock after shock hit the community. It was suddenly announced during March 1941 that more than a thousand Jewish apartments must be vacated within five days. A further major mass eviction took place in August.[59] It rapidly became common knowledge that the Jewish official in charge of housing had pleaded for a bit more time, and had promptly been incarcerated in a concentration camp. He died there a few months later.[60] During the summer, it also became known that the RV's former chairman, Dr Otto Hirsch, had died in Mauthausen camp in June 1941.[61]

Thus, Marianne's happy memories cannot be explained by Berlin's special situation. But young people like herself were in a privileged position. The adult world ensured they were shielded as far as possible from the worst effects of persecution. Even in the terrible year 1941, the teachers at the college clearly managed to maintain their pupils' spirits. This was not just Marianne's recollection. Former pupils often retained close contact with the college. Edith Dietz, for example, qualified in 1940 and was caring full time for the often seriously disturbed children of the Berlin community. But she continued to come to classes in education and psychology.[62] Frau Fraenkel had the talent to keep her students motivated and outward-looking; she even included theology and philosophy in their curriculum. In her moving contemporary record of forced labour at Siemens in 1940–1, Elisabeth Freund writes of meeting kindergarten-college trained young women and wondering at the enthusiasm with which these women sought to continue their studies.[63]

Berlin via Riga, Essen and New Jersey

Within this protected niche, Marianne benefited from the simple solidarity of living, studying and working together with a small group of young people. From May to August 1941 Marianne worked at the Neonatal and Children's Hospital on the Moltkestrasse in Berlin Niederschönhausen.[64] While I was researching this book, a lawyer approached the Jewish community in Essen, asking if they knew the whereabouts of a Marianne Strauss. His client, Mrs Trudy Schloss, needed to authenticate her claim to a pension for having worked in the Niederschönhausen Hospital. The name Schloss meant nothing to me at the time, but I later came across some post-war letters from Marianne's relatives, referring to her 'best friend Trude Schloss'.[65] I contacted the lawyer, sending some letters that helped to confirm the connection between the two women and asked him to pass on a letter to Mrs Schloss. She turned out to live in New Jersey, and since I was shortly to be in New York, to work in the Leo Baeck Institute, I arranged to interview her at the same time.

In August 1998, Lew and Trudy Schloss picked me up from my hotel in Manhattan in a very smart new Mazda. She was petite, with a lively, smiling and still very attractive face. He was tall, broad-shouldered and engaging, but also conveyed the air of taking no nonsense from anybody. Nothing about this couple even hinted at the horrific journeys that lay

Lew and Trudy Schloss in New Jersey

behind them. They had first met, in fact, in labour camps in Riga, bumped into each other again on a forced transport in and out of Stutthof – one of the most nightmarish of all the camps – and managed to meet after the war. 'Hitler was our *schadchen* [Jewish matchmaker]', said Lew in the car as we drove over the Washington Bridge on our way to New Jersey. I assumed he'd made his joke many times, but Trudy laughed and I laughed and he said he'd just thought of it.

Their house, on a typical American suburban street, was pleasant and roomy. The children's houses were much bigger, they told me. The son was personnel director for a large company and the daughter was also something high-powered. They both lived near by. By this stage I'd learned to my amazement that *both* Trudy and Lew Schloss had known Marianne, though by completely different routes, and before they knew each other. Lew, then Ludwig, Schloss had grown up near Essen in Gelsenkirchen, had moved in Essen circles and had even had a girlfriend,

Klara Stamm, who was the Strauss family maid 1940–1. And Trudy, then Trude Ullmann, had worked in Berlin as a nurse in the children's hospital and met Marianne there. I began by interviewing Lew, but although his stories were fascinating, he couldn't tell me much about Marianne's life in Essen. Had his girlfriend talked about what it was like working for the Strausses? 'No. We weren't interested in, you know, working conditions.' We all laughed. 'She was a nice looking girl.'

In the late 1930s, Lew had sometimes met Marianne socially. What did he remember of her? 'She was a little bit uppity. That I remember. She was a nice-looking girl. That's basically, you know, what you were interested in, in those days. I didn't analyse,' and he laughed again. Trudy interjected that Marianne had been fairly tall, but Lew said that compared to her, anybody was tall, and we all laughed again. Lew said Marianne had got on well with his girlfriend and hadn't treated her patronizingly. Could he remember her brother? 'No, I wasn't interested in her brother at the time.' I got the message and turned to Trudy. What were her memories of meeting Marianne in the hospital?

'Well I remember she was, like Lew said, a little bit *hochnäsig* [snooty] at times. But in Berlin it was a different story, she was with all the girls, you know, she used to talk quite a bit about home, like I guess we all did. Because let's face it, we were fifteen years old and we missed our families, all of us, you know? She was basically very, how would you say . . . ?'

'Lively,' said Lew.

'Lively,' Trudy agreed.

'Outgoing,' I volunteered.

'Vivacious,' said Lew.

'Outgoing, very outgoing,' said Trudy. 'We used to sit sometimes in the evening telling all kinds of stories. And then, once in a while, if we met a fellow or something, you know, like young girls are . . . what can I tell you?'

Trudy remembered she once had a visitor from her home town – a young man who 'never made it either'. Trudy received the message that there was someone there to see her.

'They called me, they said someone's here to visit you, a young man, so I don't have to tell you they were all very anxious to see who the young man was. But that's . . . I have *nice* memories of that.'

'Of that time, yes, Marianne did, too,' I told her.

'It was an encapsulated community,' said Lew.

The girls worked very hard, caring not just for sick children but also for youngsters whose parents were working. Sometimes if there was an air raid they had to take the kids into the shelter. But 'it wasn't really that bad. I mean we couldn't go into a lot of things, but we had each other and we used to have a lot of fun, you know, just socializing with each other'. They were limited in where they could go, and in any case felt very self-conscious in public, even before they had to wear a yellow star. Lew agreed. Jews were so conditioned, he said, that people could practically identify a Jew on sight. Jews 'were afraid, afraid to do something wrong, because you always lived with the sword over your head. Any second something could happen.'

Trudy returned to her theme. 'I couldn't say that we *suffered* in Berlin, because we had food, we didn't have to worry, we had a place to stay, it was very clean. I don't even have to tell you how particular they were, you know what I mean.'

'They were German,' said Lew.

'I remember how they used to watch us when we sterilized the instruments and everything. Ach Gott, they used to stand behind you, you know. These kinds of things you don't forget.'[66]

Marianne worked at the hospital from the beginning of May to the end of August 1941. Her report from the head of the hospital, Dr Rosenberg, was very satisfactory, attesting to her hard work, skill and conscientiousness.[67] The hospital itself survived until March 1942, and most of its staff were deported only in autumn of that year.[68] But by then Trudy was long gone. In 1940, her parents had been deported to the Gurs camp in France. Later they would be murdered in Auschwitz. In November 1941, Trudy's aunt was due to be deported to Riga and Trudy joined her rather than be left on her own in Germany. Only when they arrived did she realize the murderous conditions she had opted for.

An exam

Memory can be a great harmonizer. Compared with Riga and Stutthof, for example, or with Marianne's years underground, it is easy to imagine that in retrospect the time in Berlin looked like paradise. That does not necessarily mean it was experienced as such at the time. But at an early stage in our conversations Marianne offered me letters from her time in Berlin, and they are the most striking evidence yet of Marianne's ability to draw sustenance from the most barren environment.

In August 1941, the Berlin community was reeling from the news that Jewish men and women aged between eighteen and forty-five were banned from emigrating. The law affecting women was particularly alarming because it clearly had no military basis. On 1 September 1941 came the proclamation that all Jews over six years of age had to wear the yellow star, and this had a much greater impact in Berlin than elsewhere. The many small evasions of regulations by Jews which Berlin's size had made possible now became much more difficult and dangerous.[69]

The Jewish Kulturbund was proscribed on 11 September 1941.[70] Then in early October came a round of eviction notices with the even more chilling instruction that those affected should not seek new apartments. The first deportation followed on 18 October 1941 to Łodz (Litzmannstadt) ghetto.[71] Hundreds were crowded into the great synagogue on the Levetzowstrasse and held there for several days before the deportation; the lack of space meant that many were left outside in the rain for hours at a time.[72] Morale among Berlin's Jews reached an all-time low.[73] Many of the children in the care of the college-trained kindergarten teachers were caught up in the deportations.[74]

Marianne returned to Essen in October, when she and her family only narrowly missed being sent to Łodz. Marianne then remained in Essen for several months, during which time she met a young man, Ernst Krombach, the son of lawyer David Krombach, the leading figure in what still remained of Essen's Jewish community. Marianne and Ernst, who had himself studied for a while in Berlin, were soon deeply in love. In February 1942, she received a letter from the RV confirming her admission to the final state exam beginning on 9 February and ending on the 20th.[75] (The letter survives among Marianne's papers, as does Ernst and Marianne's correspondence. As if circumstances had conspired to preserve every document pertaining to Marianne, Ernst at a later date returned all Marianne's letters to her, for safe-keeping.)

Marianne left for Berlin on Thursday 5 February. When I told Trudy Schloss about this trip, she was astonished and also somehow delighted. She and Lew batted the idea back and forth between them:

'Oh, she went back to Berlin and . . .'

'She did get the exam?' asked Lew.

'Oh she got her Staatsexamen? Because by that time a lot of the young nurses weren't there any more . . . But that is *interesting* that she went back to make her exam. Because I wasn't there any more at that time. You see I never knew this! . . . I have to call Ruth Arndt[76] after we finish!'

There *was* something deeply affecting about the thought of Marianne's journey. The infamous Wannsee conference, which clarified responsibility and procedures for the murder of Europe's Jewry, had taken place in Berlin a couple of weeks earlier. The deportation programme was in full swing. And yet here was Marianne returning to the Nazi capital for the sake of a qualification.

The night before her departure, Ernst put pen to paper. The unfamiliar business of communicating with Marianne by letter was rendered even more odd by the fact that at that moment Marianne was still in Essen. Ernst's pet name for Marianne was Jeanne, or Jeanny, after Joan of Arc:[77]

Wednesday evening

Dearest Jeanny,

Welcome to our old Heimat.[78]

I hope the trip was pleasant and at least interesting. I'm not enjoying having to write to you, even though I know you're not yet physically far apart from me. I might possibly be able to get to the station tomorrow morning, but since I don't know if you'll be on your own – maybe it's better if I communicate to you this way . . .

Now, you must promise me something: as soon as you arrive, forget about Berlin, sit yourself down in your room, and study as hard as you can. I hope you can make up for the time you lost here. Do you feel that you've lost ground? You know by now that I'm quite capable of telling you off!

I was just interrupted, but now my mother is playing patience and this time, thank God, she's managed to collar my father. My parents, incidentally, are full of sympathy. They know what a sacrifice we're making!

So, I must stop now, my eyes are closing. There was a moderate turn-out at the gymnastics class, but it was still tiring.

If possible I'll write every day, sometimes more, sometimes less as time allows and events dictate.

Give my best wishes to our mutual friends. Here's a loving good night kiss from your

Ernest[79]

I'll write in the evenings and then get the letter to the morning train. Let me know when you've received this one.

Will the time pass quickly?

Marianne wrote as soon as she reached Berlin:

Berlin, 5 February 1942.

Iranischestrasse 4[80]

My love,

This is my first chance to write to you. It's already late. One person after another dropped in to break into happy screams at seeing me. (Am I being conceited to write that?!) Now I'm writing letters in my old bed; everything is as it was; at least at first sight; the same untidiness as before – Bohemian is nothing compared to this – though I'm more conscious of it now that I'm less used to it. In fact, the untidiness is like everything else – I know it all, and all so well, and yet I have to get used to it again. But let me tell you everything in order:

My travelling companions were awful. Did you pray to the Lord

not to lead me into temptation? Three nuns especially for my
entertainment. One had rattling dentures, the second drank con-
tinuously from a bottomless thermos, while the third preferred not
to drink because she thought she would have to go too often.[. . .]

But the journey through the white world was beautiful. Do you
know what I wished . . . ? We passed by fields; sometimes there
were horses pulling an old cart through the snow, once even a
sleigh. The snow swallows up the colours, you see only nuances
from white to black. And yet you don't get tired of looking. I think
you can guess how much work I did (are you pulling a cross face?).

And now I'm here. Everything is as it was and yet completely differ-
ent. Do you know what I mean? It's a feeling I can't explain, but
maybe it's not important – tomorrow it will all look different anyway.

At the moment, I have the feeling that everything is too much
for me. But I'm writing that only because we want to tell each other
everything. It doesn't sound good, but since I'm so honest . . . !

Inge is tired, so I won't write any more. I hope I get a letter from
you soon. I was so, so pleased to get the wallet and your photo,
Ernest. Thank you. Your photo is next to me, so at least I have
something of you.

[. . .]

Don't be angry if this letter isn't up to much; put it down to
tiredness and interruptions. Sleep well, my love, and write soon to
your Jeanny.

By the time she wrote the next day, she had received her first letter
from Ernst.

Friday 6.II.1942

Iranischestrasse 4

Tel 460441

My dear Ernest,
I found your letter early this evening when I got home, tired and
freezing cold. You can imagine how happy I was. Particularly as it

was written under such *difficult conditions! I'm facing similar difficulties: it's just past midnight, your Jeanny has been very good, studying until now (though not from fear of you being cross!).*

Today was a memorable, uplifting day: the big welcome assembly with Frau Dr Fraenkel in front of all the assembled students. As I sat there among them, I had to pinch my arms to see if I was dreaming. But I quickly came back to earth, thanks to the discussion of our exam subjects. For my optional subject I'm taking kindergarten theory; the compulsory subject is health studies. I haven't been able to revise either until now. Then there's educational theory and subjects which they may question me about for a 'quick check': Pestalozzi, Fröbel, school reform, and so on. You see, my love, that I didn't need your strictures at all!

Tomorrow Inge and I are going to 'sneak' into the residence of a former fellow sufferer, who took the exam last year. Have I told you about Marianne Levy? You know, I lived with her in the Wangenheimstrasse. Since then she has strapped the yoke of marriage to her fragile frame; tomorrow we shall visit her to study with her and her husband. You probably agree with all the people here who say that I won't fail the exams!

On Thursday I give a teaching demonstration. I've been assigned to a kindergarten. I'm going to do fun gymnastics with the children. I have a group of 6–8 children, as usual. Hannah Karminski, one of our teachers and the people who work at the kindergarten are the 'audience'. I hope it'll be OK. It's more a matter of luck than anything else. But I'm sure to fail in Hebrew; Frau Fraenkel tried to console me: 'The worst that can happen is that you get an unsatisfactory mark for your writing.' Poor consolation!

I wanted to visit Uta today during a free period. But I couldn't find them. They left their flat because of the cold and moved in with their parents. This morning we had our lessons in Marburgerstrasse and this afternoon in the Joachimsthalerstrasse because the Wilsnackerstrasse has been 'burned down'.

Coal is a real problem. It's freezing in the hall of residence. And travelling around in unheated trams is freezing too. The first thing we do when we get home is take a hot bath and then get into bed.

Tomorrow, however, I'm going to be a hero and work through the night. In the education theory exam on Monday we're afraid they'll ask about Pestalozzi and Fröbel – lots of work to do for that. But I see I've written about nothing but me. I hope you had a few happy hours with Hilde. Give her best wishes from me if you like. Above all, though, best wishes to your parents.

You ask if the time will pass quickly. Don't let it get you down, my love. It's tougher for you than for me. Every day, I have some new experience to help the time pass quickly, while for you life follows its familiar course. But I've found that it's possible to think of several things at the same time . . . !

Now I must finish. Tomorrow, another hour with you, if at all possible.

A kiss from your
Jeanny

At first glance, these letters are a more trustworthy source than memories related fifty years later. They are indubitably still just as they were in 1942. Yet they raise problems of interpretation that are no less intractable. What should we make, for example, of the fact that there is no mention of wearing the yellow star, of official harassment or of so many other aspects of life for Jews in Germany in 1942? How much self-censorship is being imposed here on mail which, after all, had to pass the surveillance of a police state? Life under the conditions of Nazi Germany, it seems, is almost by definition unobservable. Every faint ray of light that manages to escape from that dark era is bent out of shape in one way or another – either filtered and refracted through long years of memory, or else a reflection, bounced off the surface of contemporary documents whose reliability and faithfulness we cannot know. That is why the interplay *between* letters and reminiscences in this case is so helpful. The letters confirm that Marianne's positive memories of her little Berlin world were not a retrospective invention. The memories suggest that, if she was leaving negative experiences out of the letters, it was not because her real views were being constrained by censorship – since they don't appear in her memories either.

On Monday 9th, Marianne reported an eventful day:

My love,

The first round of terror has passed; now Lilly and I are sitting with Marianne, gorging on coffee and jam and memories of old times when everything was better! (what kind of face are you making?) ... both of them are thoughtfully being very quiet because they know that I am writing to you, my love. You should be very impressed that I'm managing to write at all, after this morning. We had three topics:

1. *'He who seeks to lead others must be capable of great sacrifice.'*[81]
2. *The importance and scope of co-operation between the Hort [the after-school club for school-age children] the family and the school.*
3. *The depiction of child development in literature.*

I chose the third topic to start with, and do you know which book I wanted to review? ... Fall Maurizius. But after I'd already written lots, one of the girls advised me to ask Dr Fraenkel, who said I shouldn't use the book. So then, I decided to do topic two. Of course, none of this was good and I think I've thoroughly messed up the exam. Lilly has read the essay and doesn't think so, but I've got a definite feeling.

Tomorrow morning there's the handicrafts or drawing exam; I'll do a drawing or a collage. In the afternoon it's written Hebrew!!!! ...

At five we've got lessons again and now that I've written to you I feel so much better that I'm sure they'll go very well. Only, I've got to make the big trip from Alexanderplatz to Joachimsthalerstrasse. So, I'm going to stop now. If possible I'll write again in an hour.

It's evening now. This is the first chance I've had to write more to you. No post from you today so now I've got to wait until tomorrow evening – an awfully long time away! I think of you all the time, Ernst, and I wish you were with me. Then we wouldn't need to write. It's strange – I thought that the things I'd like to say but can't would be easier to write, but now, with you, I'm finding I can't write them either. My letters to you always end up differently from how I wanted – maybe that will change. My love, there's so much I should say to you, but easier said than done. Anyway, you can always read between the lines!!!!

In the meantime, all I want is for everything that I've got to do this evening to be done so that I can sleep, sleep and sleep. I'm so tired. Two nights without sleep are making themselves felt. Incidentally, there was a promising start to the day. At around 1 a.m. Inge and I were sitting with a pile of books and sweets when we heard a sudden hullabaloo in the corridor. A guard had noticed that the hall wasn't fully blacked-out. When we heard the noise in the corridor we quickly switched off the light and fell into a 'deep sleep' in our beds. The warden's wife ran through all the rooms in a panic and couldn't find a light on anywhere. We all lay like sleeping beauties. Here and there, someone groaned sleepily as the warden's wife flung open a door (we did too, of course). That was the first blow. The second came soon after. We were supposed to be in the Wilsnackerstrasse by 9 a.m. At 8 some charitable soul found me dreaming peacefully in my bed. I swore, prayed, ran, tripped and . . . arrived on time! But I sat there the whole morning starving and desperate for a certain small room. First I hadn't had anything to eat – (later a couple of girls took pity on me) and second . . . ! And third, you're not allowed to leave the room during the exam.

My love, now you know everything there is to know about my bad luck. I hope that tomorrow brings me better luck and at least two letters from you!
Thinking of you always
Your
Jeanny

When Ernst saw the reference to the 'round of terror' he might have thought Marianne had suffered some terrible act of persecution, perhaps a near escape from the Gestapo. But it soon becomes clear that she is referring only to her exams. Even in the Germany of the Wannsee conference, of restrictions and deportations, Marianne was able to focus all her energies and emotions on the conventional challenges of exams. There is a poignant irony in the fact that for this German Jewish girl there was only one threat worth five exclamation marks: her written Hebrew exam. Frau Fraenkel, with her knowledge of the grim events outside, tries to reassure her that the worst that can happen is a bad mark. But this, for Marianne, is only a weak consolation. By contrast, the guard checking on the light and the house warden's wife scurrying through the block in a panic, is registered merely as a comic interlude.

Marianne was not the only person to have an eventful Monday. That day, Ernst returned home to find that the elderly Frau Austerlitz, with whom the Krombachs were sharing an apartment, had died:[82]

> *Sad piece of news awaited me when I got home: Frau Austerlitz had died. It's been a real challenge to write this letter because there's been so much to organize: visits to pay our condolences, the doctor, the nurse, informing the night watch, dealing with telegrams and so on. I'm continually interrupted. Only one thing really shocked me – that her death left me completely unmoved. No feelings, nothing. A sign of the times? Probably, yes. Partly also I've been expecting it for some time and so got used to the idea. It seems just the natural outcome. Whatever – it didn't frighten me.*

People in their situation 'who only live for the present moment', Ernst continued, had to create a certain distance from the misery around them, though that did not mean they lost the ability or the desire to feel sympathy.[83] Marianne's reply by return of post was equally revealing:[84]

> *Love,*
>
> *I think the death of Frau Austerlitz affected you more than you think, because as I read the opening lines of your letter I had a very odd feeling that something must be wrong. Until now I had never believed that you could sense a person's mood just from reading their letter ...*
>
> *Do you remember our conversation about death and life?[85] You just have to find the right attitude to death and then it no longer seems so horrifying. It is both salvation and a biological necessity. That's why you weren't so disturbed, at least on the surface: it was the natural outcome. You don't need to worry about*

your feelings, love. Your attitude is the more natural one, in earlier times it was the natural attitude. Today, human beings with their 'culture' have modified these attitudes and customs. Of course we are sad when a loved one passes on; but death should be no more than a fact of nature. (I'm coming closer to your scientific approach to life.)[. . .]In the end these issues always confront us with a problem, no matter how old we are; every opinion and every belief is simply an attempt to avoid uncertainty. Because unfortunately we try to understand everything in terms of reason and we want to know everything. How much wiser the Indians are, for example. We should learn from them. They embody so much that our modern psychology is seeking. It would be really good if, after Freud, we read something about Indian life?! I will ask around, all right? It is fantastic to be here again and I have really settled in marvellously.

Over the next four years, Marianne's letters and diaries turned again and again to the issue of death and how to cope with it. At the college, Jungian ideas were in vogue and Marianne shows some of their influence here.[86] Another frequent theme in her writing was the lessons to be learned from pre-modern peoples whose 'natural' way of life should serve as a model. In this, she echoed a common preoccupation among youth-movement and 'life-reform' circles in Weimar.

Wednesday brought new experiences and a telling observation on the sad decline around her:[87]

This afternoon we outsiders – there are five of us – had an educational theory lesson with Frau Dr. I really enjoy that. It's a bit of continuity that consoles me for all the other changes, makes them trivial and insignificant. Then I'm less upset by the fact that the quality of life in the hall has fallen so much. It's now an iceberg and has lost all its physical appeal. There's no intellectual life here any more, no musical evenings, no discussions about God and the world, no meetings in beautiful, cosy rooms until late at night. Whenever we 'veterans' meet, we hark back nostalgically to the time when there was still an 'elite' here. But it's only to be expected that as the external framework collapses so too does the life within.

Nevertheless, Berlin was so rich in interesting people that, provided one was able to ignore the daily horrors, one could still have a wealth of stimulating encounters even in February 1942. There was the artist Bielefeld, whom Marianne charmed into giving her a drawing. And there was Alfred Selbiger, a former youth worker now employed by the RV, with whom she had a 'fantastic conversation' about the problems faced by young people in the current conditions. She wrote to Ernst:[88]

> *He is a perfect youth movement type, and I liked him enormously. It seems the feeling was mutual because he proposed introducing me to a group with similar attitudes to his. I'm excited by the idea, of course, and I'll see what I can manage with the little time I have [. . .]I realized how good it would be for us to live a* bündisch *life. And if only for that reason it would be interesting to get to know the group and see if we would fit in or if all our ideas are illusions.*

On Saturday 14th Marianne wrote again. She had spent the day in Grünewald, with friends of her parents who had managed to keep their house in that elegant suburb. They had as a guest a young Chinese man who had spent five years in Germany training to be an engineer. Here was another fascinating encounter.[89]

Neither Marianne nor Ernst, however, was under any illusion that conditions would improve. Prophetically, Marianne wrote:[90]

> *I often have the feeling that life is offering me as much as it can before a door is slammed shut. So much is happening and I wonder why it's different from the last 2½ years. But perhaps it just seems different because I'm living in the moment and see the fact that I'm here as a gift. If only you could always be with me! There, we don't really live – there are more choices here, even now. Perhaps it is self-centred to think like this; we have each other – unthinkable if we didn't; but nothing comes to us from the outside world. It's sad! But at least this evening we laughed as we haven't done for ages: we managed to make fun of every teacher in college.*

According to Marianne's schedule, her last oral exam took place on the morning of 20 February. Among her papers I found a telegram sent from Berlin at 15.10 on Friday 20 February to Ernst Krombach,

Marianne's Staatsexamen certificate

Semperstrasse 5, Essen. The text ran: 'ALL TERRORS SUCCESSFULLY OVERCOME – MARIANNE'.

One of Marianne's claims about which I was most sceptical was that the kindergarten college exams still enjoyed any official status. On 25 June 1940, the Reich Education Ministry had published a general decree stating that examinations at Jewish higher schools would no longer be regarded as state exams.[91] True, Marianne's post-war CVs and applications always referred to a 'Staatsexamen', and she assured me that she had sat the official examination. My scepticism was heightened, however, by the restitution correspondence in which Marianne was unable to authenticate the official status of her qualification.[92] But then, when her son Vivian finally worked his way through the bric-à-brac in the outhouse to the huge trunk at the back, we found her final transcript. Marianne had gained an overall mark of 'good' (though just as she had predicted, her Hebrew *had* been 'unsatisfactory', as indeed had her exam essay). But most remarkable was that the transcript came complete with the eagle and swastika stamp of the Reich and the signature of the Stadtpräsident der Reichshauptstadt Berlin. In February 1942, a month after the Wannsee conference, Jewish kindergarten teachers in Berlin *were* still graduating with the Staatsexamen, even as their potential charges were being transported to Łodz, to Minsk and to Riga.[93]

5

The Family, the Gestapo, the Abwehr and the Banker

After the outbreak of war with Britain, the Strausses again looked to the USA for salvation. They had two advantages over many other would-be emigrants. They had an affidavit – from cousin Fritz Stern – and they could afford to pay their passage (assuming they received permission to withdraw money from their blocked accounts). Yet, when the Nazis finally stopped all Jewish emigration from Germany in August–September 1941, the Strausses were still in Essen. Marianne firmly believed that the family's American relatives had let them down. Her father pleaded with them, she said, but 'they didn't do a thing'.

The correspondence between Marianne's parents and their US relatives from 1939 to 1941 does not really bear out her view, however. The Strausses' main problem was simply timing: because their application was made so late, they were far down in the queue for US visas: number 28,972.[1] The US consulate in Stuttgart did not even call for their application papers until January 1941.[2] And submitting the papers was merely the start of a protracted second stage which would culminate in an interview at the consulate and, with luck, the visa.

Nevertheless, in January 1941 the family grew hopeful. Siegfried and Ine attended intensive lessons in English and US accountancy. A poem presented to Siegfried on his fiftieth birthday by fellow students mentions his hard work and his difficulties with English pronunciation. From May to July, the couple attended 'preparatory lessons for the profession of an Accountant'.[3] Siegfried gave the English class weekly lectures on the customs and character of the different American states.[4] A cousin, Hugo Strauss, sent them useful information on living in the USA: furniture was light and simple; people used gas stoves and refrigerators, toasters and vacuum cleaners; men's ties were narrow and brightly coloured.[5] Marianne's parents found the details so important, or so reassuring, that they typed them out again. But in July 1941, just before the family's interview in Stuttgart, all the US consulates in Germany were closed and applications would now be dealt with in Washington. There was a whole new procedure and the number of visas would probably fall sharply. The US relatives genuinely could do nothing.

It is easy to understand, though, why the Strausses felt uncertain about how much support they could expect from their American cousins. Their principal correspondents were their cousins Hugo and Grete Strauss, to whom they were very close. But Hugo and Grete themselves had reached the USA only in 1938, and as new arrivals in difficult circumstances were in no position to provide a plausible affidavit of financial support. By contrast, Fritz Stern, the relative who since 1938 had acted as Siegfried's guarantor, was, though financially very well-placed to provide support, someone whom the Strausses hardly knew.

In January 1940, the family had asked Fritz Stern to renew his affidavit. He replied fairly rapidly, on 23 February, but the uncertain post meant his letter did not arrive until mid-April. The delay was worrying enough. In May, Marianne's parents received a letter from Hugo Strauss written in January (after their own request for a new affidavit had reached the States, but before Fritz Stern had responded). Hugo wrote, trying out his English:

> *Dear Folks,*
>
> *I want to inform you that I spoke to Fritz Stern today with regard to the renewal of your affidavits. We agreed in the fact, that you should let him know as soon as this renewal is, actually necessary. If it is urgent, you may wire to him and he will send out the papers immediately. To have always best results for the common benefit, in avoiding any work, not necessary for the very moment. But don't hesitate and let me know it immediately, when*

it is the right time. Fritz is a very nice man, clearcut and short in his decisions. Let me know as soon as you make your request to him, that I may follow it up.

Fritz may have been very nice, but wasn't there something worrying about Hugo having to reassure them? Why had Hugo written and not Fritz? Next to 'clearcut', either Siegfried or Ine has written a German translation in pencil, suggesting that they didn't know what it meant and had looked it up in a dictionary. Since their lives might depend on this man, it was important to understand every adjective.

The family's uncertainty about the help they might expect must have been heightened by Siegfried's sister's experience. Whereas Siegfried and Ine were not seeking financial assistance to enter the States, as they emphasized more than once, Siegfried's sister Bertel was in a different position. On 22 October 1940 Bertel, her husband Ferdinand Wolf and son Richard were caught up in the Bürckel-Action, in which 6,504 Jews from Baden and some 1,000 from Alsace and Lorraine were deported to various concentration camps in Vichy France.[6] Siegfried wrote to Hugo begging him to do something for them:[7]

We are convinced that cousin Fritz and the other relations will be willing to help our dear ones with passage to the USA. You know Bertel and Ferdinand and know that they are hard-working, ambitious and undemanding and will not be a burden to you. I thank you heartily, dear Hugo and the other relatives who are working for our transfer to the USA.

Hugo's reply, posted in January 1941 but not received by the Strausses until March, was not encouraging. He had tried all sorts of things for relatives in similar difficulties with little success. Fritz Stern was hard to contact in New York:[8]

Luckily I reached him yesterday. He doesn't think we will be successful with the Wolfs. This is understandable given our experiences. He didn't make any promises re the fare but left the possibility open. I will . . . ask him to send an affidavit to the consulate in Marseilles. I will also try to get him to send a confirmation to the consulate about paying the fare. He is a very fine man. That is the lucky thing. Given the misfortunes that have afflicted everyone, most people won't even listen to you. I approach the thing cautiously to avoid a rejection. It is difficult to push him towards a decision. I will do my best. Fritz is my only hope . . .

Later in the year, the Strausses were very distressed to learn via Grete Strauss that their hopes of Bertel's emigration had come to nothing. She was now interned in the Rivesault camp, separated from her husband and her son. Marianne's aunt Lore could not hide her disappointment:[9]

We thought she would be with you in July and were so disappointed when you, dear Grete, wrote she had been unsuccessful because of the cost of the passage. Bertel and Ferdinand are so reliable that as soon as they were able to work they would certainly pay back every penny that was advanced to them.

If Grete's information was correct, the Wolfs failed to escape ultimately because the American relatives had been unwilling to pay.[10] Bertel and Ferdinand were eventually murdered in Auschwitz. Their son Richard, however, escaped and survived.

Among Marianne's papers, I found a small address book. It appears to have been prepared in advance of deportation, in case she might manage to reach the USA on her own and need help. It lists at least six different sets of cousins in the USA. With so many connections, could the money not have been found? Marianne's resentment might thus have been justified in the case of the Wolfs, but is inappropriate with regard to her immediate family. Certainly, Fritz Stern did all that was asked of him for relatives he hardly knew. Not for the last time, I wondered if some of Marianne's criticism of others was in fact a deflection of the anger she felt towards her parents for having left it too late.

Expropriation and persecution

For Marianne's parents, the period 1939–40 was characterized by the drip, drip of persecution rather than by radical change. Life was miserable but bearable. After the outbreak of war, the family was restricted to RM700 a month, which, though hardly generous, was enough to live on, particularly as Siegfried was allowed to make additional monthly transfers to pay for Marianne's schooling.[11] The introduction of rationing after the outbreak of war gave German officialdom scope to deprive Jews of food and other goods. There were no more clothing coupons for Jews,[12] and from 18 December 1939 onwards, Jews were permitted only the basic food rations and denied the supplementary card available to others. Non-rationed foods were forbidden them altogether.[13] Still, up to 1941, the Strausses had no pressing material worries, even if their standard of living had become far more modest.

In early 1941, however, the regime's threats to their well-being and survival took on a new quality. Their core assets – particularly the two blocks of flats in the Hufelandstrasse – were now in jeopardy. Not surprisingly, these smart apartment buildings were attractive to would-be 'Aryanizers', including Essen's city council. The records of the city's transactions, preserved in detail in the city archives, give an illuminating picture of the process that was set in train.[14]

The council's interest in the Hufelandstrasse seems to have arisen in autumn 1940, when a nearby hospital needed accommodation for doctors and nurses. The council first approached the brothers' architect, R. Zbinden, in November 1940, and on 5 December 1940 one councillor Schlicht sent the Oberbürgermeister a detailed description of the hospital's accommodation problems. 'For this reason, a survey of the area has been carried out to identify houses which could either be purchased or else acquired by Aryanization.'[15] At the end of December 1940, a Nazi Party official, Schwarzlose, asked the city's Land Department to find out if the brothers were willing to sell. If not, he would seek approval from the Reich Economics Minister for 'compulsory dejudification'.[16]

On 28 January 1941, Siegfried Strauss had a meeting with city officials. The minutes record the following:[17]

Herr Strauss came to discuss the matter on the 28th of the month. He stated that there are currently 28 tenants in the two houses, only two of whom are Aryans. He requested us not to take over the properties and to acquire others in the area, in deference to the fact that he is a combat veteran and has at no time had any kind of criminal records. He believed that such a request was the more justified in that he intended to leave for America as soon as possible. In this connection, he suggested that we propose to the Currency Office an exchange whereby he would acquire the property of a German returning from the USA against the property he gave up here.[18]

I advised Herr Strauss that the city must pursue the purchase of the Hufelandstrasse properties as a matter of urgency and that it will if necessary seek approval for compulsory dejudification. I also rejected the idea of an application to the Currency Office. I agreed only that if Strauss identified a possible exchange, the city might support such a proposal to the Currency Office by emphasizing the public interest of the Hufelandstrasse properties.

A day later, there was another meeting. Siegfried, with customary obduracy, reiterated his position, stressing his intent to emigrate. The official showed his ignorance of the Jewish situation by doubting that emigration was possible in wartime. Siegfried responded that several boats had recently sailed from Lisbon to the USA and again asked for an exchange with US property. The city official, on this occasion, simply said this was not feasible. Siegfried emphasized that, as First World War combatants, he and his brother enjoyed a certain level of protection against compulsory 'dejudification' and urged the city not to take over the houses at present. The officials then asked if he would be willing to part with one block and Siegfried rejected the proposal.[19] So now the city, with the backing of the regional economic chamber, began to set the wheels in motion to force the brothers to sell.

The city was not the only would-be tenant. In June 1941, the mayor received a letter from a businessman, Diplom Kaufmann Ricco Arendt:[20]

I write to you on the advice of my father-in-law, Herr Dr Paul Redlich of the Essen Chamber of Industry and Commerce. I would be most grateful if you would allow me to visit you during business hours to discuss the following.

I have been trying to find an apartment in Essen since January of this year. Because I have so far failed to do so, my wife and I have been obliged to rent furnished rooms since our marriage and are at present subtenants at Billrothstrasse 32. While looking for a flat, I discovered that the most attractive houses in my area, Hufelandstrasse 23 and 25, are occupied almost exclusively by Jews. I cannot understand why here in Essen the best flats should be occupied by Jews when married couples like ourselves are obliged to live in furnished rooms. Moreover, my wife is pregnant and I therefore apply to you in the hope of possibly finding a flat by this means.

I await your reply as to when I may come and discuss the matter with you and remain yours,
   Heil Hitler

Such everyday participation in the expropriation of Jewish property had long fuelled the Nazi Aryanization campaign.[21] Herr Arendt was no doubt disappointed to learn from the city administration that the houses were already designated for hospital use.

Aryanization was not the only weapon deployed against the Strausses. On 10 May, the local block official, an engineer called Kemmerer, together with the Gestapo, knocked on the door of Hufelandstrasse 23 late in the evening, to complain about the lack of proper blackout at a second-floor window. The window was in Alfred's flat. The consequence for an Aryan, assuming that the complaints were at all justified, would probably have been a gruff warning. Not for a Jew. Alfred Strauss was taken into custody. On 22 May, the Gestapo urged the state prosecutor to initiate proceedings. The indictment, statements and state prosecutor's response are all preserved in the Gestapo records in Düsseldorf.

According to the Gestapo, the block official, Kemmerer, claimed that:[22]

The (NSDAP) Essen-Holsterhausen local group had entrusted him with the task of monitoring the blackout in his block. The buildings at Hufelandstrasse 23 and 25 belonged to his block. In the two houses, which were occupied only by Jews, there had often been gross infringements of the blackout regulations which had been reported to the local group.

Within the Nazi political system, the rank and file party member often had disappointingly little power, particularly after 1934. Making a nuisance of himself about blackout regulations was one of the local block official's remaining perks. Here was a chance to flex his muscles against the wealthy owner of a big house and, what was more, a Jew. This was grist for the Gestapo's mill, which concluded that 'The suspicion that from time to time the Jews here *deliberately* fail to abide by the police blackout regulations in full is therefore probably justified.'[23]

The vague language of the memo – 'from time to time', 'fail to adhere in full', 'probably justified' – speaks for itself. And in an internal memorandum to their Düsseldorf superiors, the Essen Gestapo admitted they were seeking a prosecution 'mainly so that, if St. [Strauss] is prosecuted, he can be declared an enemy of people and the state. He owns property worth RM150,000'.[24]

In the official submission to the state prosecutor, Kriminal-Assistent Kosthorst of the Essen Gestapo did his best to establish the seriousness of the case. First, the culprit was a Jew and thus a notorious enemy of the state. It was well known that the Jews aimed to undermine the rule of law. Second, repeated breaches of the blackout law showed the infringement to be deliberate. Third, given the proximity of the hospital, patients would be endangered if a bomber saw the light.[25]

In his own submission, Alfred Strauss provided a detailed account of his military service in the First World War. He also emphasized his lack of political activity before 1933 and his understanding that it was particularly incumbent on Jews to keep the law, and that there was, therefore, no question of deliberate infringement. As for the particular accusations, Alfred noted that the window had both a blackout curtain and a blackout screen. On the evening in question, the curtain had undoubtedly been closed, but he might have forgotten the screen, so that some light could have been visible. Finally, Alfred noted that he hoped to leave for the United States in the near future and asked that no impediment be placed in the way of his emigration.

The state prosecutor dismissed the case on two grounds. In the first place, it was still only twilight when the offence had been committed. Second, there was no proof that the other breaches had been observed in Alfred Strauss's apartment. It was irrelevant that other occupants of the building might have committed the same offence.[26] The Gestapo was of course very disappointed and decided to order twenty-one days' protective custody for Alfred. The Essen police president was invited to think of further measures that might be undertaken.[27] Interestingly, while the Gestapo thought the police had agreed on twenty-one days' detention, Alfred actually spent only six days in custody, although this detail does not appear in the files. He also paid a fine of RM30.50.[28]

Just as after Kristallnacht, when the Strausses had managed to obtain some concessions from the tax authorities, the legal process conveyed mixed messages for the family. Clearly, there was still justice of a sort to be had from some servants of the state. The judicial system still enjoyed a degree of independence from Himmler's police empire. On the other hand, the grounds cited seem a woefully inadequate response to the arbitrariness of the case. For what must have been clear to the prosecutor is that the Gestapo imprisoned Alfred Strauss on the flimsiest ground – a partial failure to black-out a window, observed when it was not yet even dark.

On 26 June, the authorities' assault on the Hufelandstrasse flats entered a new phase. The Regierungspräsident in Düsseldorf informed the brothers that as of July 1941, 'on the basis of paragraph §2 of the Decree on the Utilization of Jewish Property from 3.12.1938',[29] a Dr Gilka would be appointed commissioner for their property. The state was willing to offer a purchase figure equal to the construction cost of the building. This was not the market price, but at least bore some relation to the apartments' value. The brothers bowed to the inevitable.[30]

The city file on the matter contains a small but telling indication of the atmosphere in the council offices. The housing department drafted a letter to the Hufelandstrasse tenants, to notify them that their tenancy would end at the end of October. It was addressed to 'Herrn Israel NN.' 'NN', for Nomen Nescio was a standard abbreviation, for which the real name would be substituted. Since the tenants were Jewish they would, if male, have the middle name Israel. So 'Mr Israel NN' was a playful short-hand, meaning 'to the Jew it may concern'. It is the playfulness which most disturbs.

The pace of persecution continued to accelerate. In July 1941, the US consulates were closed. August 1941 saw the ban on emigration and September the introduction of the yellow star. In early October, the Strausses left the Hufelandstrasse and moved back to their old house on

Ladenspelderstrasse.[31] In a rare moment of complaint, Ine wrote to relatives in the USA about how much they regretted having to give up their beautiful, comfortable apartment.[32] But worse was to come. Hardly had they unpacked when they were informed by a local party boss and the city official Schwarzlose that Ladenspelderstrasse too was about to be expropriated.[33] And they had hardly digested *that* when they were notified of their imminent deportation to the East.

Snatched from the gravedigger's spade

In October 1941, Marianne was in Berlin. The first she heard of the deportation was a telegram from her parents telling her to come home immediately. The college hurriedly gave her a provisional graduation certificate[34] and Marianne arrived in Essen on 25 October.[35] The transport to which Siegfried and his family had been assigned was scheduled for 26 October 1941 and bound for Łodz, 'Litzmannstadt' in German.[36] This was the first major deportation from Essen since the expulsion of Polish Jews in 1938, and involved some 250 people.[37] It was part of a wave of transports from all over Germany, which deported 8,000 German Jews to Łodz up to the beginning of November. Ine's sister Hannah and her husband Ernst Weinberg were scheduled for a transport from Cologne as part of this wave.

Siegfried Strauss and his family may have been placed on this first list by chance, but one rather significant detail suggests otherwise. Although the Hufelandstrasse sale had been agreed upon in July, the Oberbürgermeister approved the transfer of payment only on 24 October 1941, just a few days before the deportation. Actual payment could not be made until the exchange control office in Düsseldorf had given its approval, so it seems at least reasonable to assume that Essen Council hoped to avoid paying Siegfried altogether.[38] At the same time, the city had its eye on the fine property on the Ladenspelderstrasse. Deporting the family would make expropriation easier and obviate the need to rehouse them.

The Strausses may not have known their exact destination – Marianne remembered something about a 'work camp in the East'.[39] Nor could they know the kind of conditions awaiting them. For one thing, this was the first major deportation from Essen. Marianne's parents had, of course, gained some idea of the misery which the victims of the 1940 deportations to France, in this case Siegfried's sister, had suffered. But clearly they were unaware of the true horror ahead, because when I checked in the Gestapo records I discovered, to my amazement, that Marianne was not on the deportation list.[40] I think Marianne may never have known – she certainly never said – that her parents were taking her with them voluntarily. Just as they had prevented Marianne and Richard from leaving for Britain in March 1939, so now too they placed absolute priority on keeping the family together. It is unlikely that Siegfried and Ine would have insisted had they known what they were going to.

Marianne told me they spent three tense days packing. As on other occasions, a traumatic episode had expanded in her memory – in reality she was at home for only one day.[41] The official instructions specified that each transport member could take up to RM100, one suitcase containing household goods, a complete set of clothing, bedclothes and food for eight days. Valuables, other money, jewellery (apart from wedding rings), pets and ration cards could not be taken.[42] Among Marianne's papers, tucked into the address book containing the family's foreign contacts, I found a hand-written list:

Rucksack filled with essentials
Woollen blanket and pillow with pillow case
Thermos flask
Plastic cup and plate with suitable bag (for hygiene reasons)
Cutlery and bag
Butter dish
Needle and thread in a bag
Soap, soap powder, candles, torch, toilet paper, writing
instruments, comb and washing stuff in an oilcloth bag
Pharmaceuticals Borax ointment, sticking plaster, burn plaster,
cotton wool, cotton bandage, absorbent cotton wool, acetate of
alumina, 'Novaletten' (Valerian in solid form), quinine for
temperatures, charcoal for constipation, diuretics, insect powder,
thermometer, scissors, tweezers
One light suitcase Underwear, clothing, warm slippers, shoes, two
smocks as substitute for lightweight clothing, two sleeping bags, if

possible made of easily washable coloured materials, towels and clothes

To wear Thick stockings, underwear, clothing, coat, raincoat with a hood in the pocket

Address book with addresses of relatives and friends abroad

4 passport photos

Photocopies of important papers, incl. school certificates, birth and marriage certificate

1 bag with several days' food.

On the morning of the 26th an official appeared, took the house keys and sealed up the house. Siegfried, Ine, Marianne and Richard set off on foot for the collection point in Haumannshof, site of the police headquarters and the district court. Carrying their luggage, they walked down the Ladenspelderstrasse, round the corner into the Hufeland-strasse and down to the Haumannshof. Here, a crowd of deportees awaited them.

Marianne's memory was that they queued up to board a tram taking them to the station, whence the transport would go on to Łodz:[43]

'I shall never forget the moment when we were standing there and the people were all being loaded into the tram. In front of everyone, the two Gestapo officials, notorious officials from the Gestapo headquarters in the Kortumstrasse, told my family that we were not to get on but should go back home.'

The hatred on the faces of fellow Jews as the Strausses were let go was an unforgettable experience:[44]

'We were sent back home, and that was the most dreadful experience anybody had, to hear this animal howl go up, that was really quite something which I never forgot. It took me quite a long time to get that out of my ears . . .'

So the family walked back up Ladenspelderstrasse and took the seals off their front door. Siegfried said that they had been 'snatched from the gravedigger's spade'.

Up to this point, the family's experience and behaviour was more or less the same as that of many other patriotic, well-to-do, provincial, middle-class German Jews. On 26 October 1941, however, the Strausses' story took on a new quality. What had happened – something for which Siegfried had been working but to Marianne was unexpected and inexplicable – launched the family on a different trajectory, one that in the end would enable Marianne to survive.

In retrospect, Marianne herself regarded the moment on the Haumannshof as a turning point. On one occasion, she was talking to me about the influence cast on her by left-wing friends whom she met later in the war. They were the most formative influence on her life, she said:[45]

'I felt that I had to move away from all of this Jewish ballast as I felt it then, and the hypocrisy . . . I realized how these people behaved and we were sent back you know, from this meeting point where everybody was gathered and we were in full view of everybody, quite with the intent of causing this frisson. . . . And all these things were building up and I thought I don't want anything more.'

The bitter cry of her fellow deportees took on a special significance in her memory. Marianne was torn between a feeling of injury as the object of unjust envy and wrath and a sense of unease at being unfairly privileged. This double burden of anger and guilt made the scene on the Haumannshof one of the pivotal moments of her life. She came to interpret it as a crucial stage in her alienation from the Jewish community.

Why had the Strausses been saved?

Why was the family sent home? The Jewish community in Essen had its suspicions. When I contacted the daughter of the Essen Jewish Community's former secretary, who had settled in the States, I was shocked to hear her say with some certainty that the Strausses had bribed the Gestapo and paid a poor mother to send one of her sons in their place. She even knew the woman's name, Moszkowicz.[46] I was even more shocked as the Gestapo list of deportees to Łodz confirmed that there was indeed a young man of that name on the transport, albeit spelled slightly differently: Jakob Moschkowitz. What I found disturbing was not so much the shadow cast over Marianne's family – though, if true, the incident was distressing enough – but more the idea that places on the transports could be bought and sold. It did not fit into the conventional picture of the Third Reich at all.

By an extraordinary coincidence, I was already in touch with Imo
Moszkowicz, the sole surviving member of this family. I wrote to him
with some trepidation, asking about the story:[47]

*I heard that the Strauss brothers were hated for the fact that they had
paid a poor woman to send one of her sons in the place of the family
Strauss. Then I learned that the woman was your mother and the son
your brother. I looked in Schröter,* Geschichte und Schicksal der Essener
Juden, *and saw that Jakob Moschkowitz (this is how it is spelled but I
assume it is your brother) really did go on this transport. On the other
hand, both he and the Strauss family appear at the same time on the
list [. . .]*

*If it is not too painful for you to tackle this subject, my question to
you is, do you have any memory of this? I don't understand in any case
how one person – in this case your brother – can 'replace' a whole
family. Were other people involved?*

The more I thought about it, the less plausible the story seemed and,
when I talked to him, Imo Moszkowicz did not confirm it. Jakob wasn't
his brother but his cousin, he said, and there had been some question of
volunteering, but not to replace the Strauss family. His cousin, who had
simply been idling his time away in Essen, had agreed to accompany two
elderly ladies on the transport. Money might have changed hands, he
wasn't sure. Certainly, the fact that both Jakob *and* the Strausses were
on the same Gestapo list at the same time makes the substitution story
particularly suspect. Imo told me that he and his friends had assumed
the Strausses were protected because Marianne's father had invented the
famous Krupp stainless steel, Nirrosta Stahl.[48] This was a string to Siegfried's bow I knew nothing about. In fact, as it later transpired, Imo Moszkowicz and other contemporaries had confused Siegfried with another
Essen Jew, Bruno Strauss, who had indeed invented the steel.

These variant narratives suggested that it may indeed have been
possible to influence the lists (and there was certainly a great deal of
corruption); but above all I was being offered some insight into the way
rumour worked in those fevered times. When ineffable decisions from
on high could mean the difference between life and death, there was
bound to be speculation about what lay behind them. Once the com-

munity had construed the Strausses' protection in a particular way, the rumour machine rapidly spread speculation as hard fact.

For Marianne, much of the background to her family's reprieve from deportation was shrouded in mystery. Siegfried Strauss remained true to his habit of not discussing his affairs with the family, or at least with the children, even though these affairs now held the key to their survival. We know that he worried about their ability to keep a secret, and the people he was dealing with had undoubtedly impressed upon him the need for discretion. The more people knew, the less plausible the enterprise. What Marianne did find out was astonishing enough. Her family, it seems, was being protected by no less an organization than the Abwehr, the counter-intelligence arm of the German Wehrmacht.

In parallel with the SD, the security organization belonging to Himmler's police empire, the Abwehr sought on behalf of the Wehrmacht to monitor foreign intelligence activity and to gain its own intelligence abroad. Most of its employees were loyal supporters of the regime. At the very top, however, the Abwehr contained a number of individuals increasingly hostile to the Nazis. Initially, the most active was General Major Hans Oster, head of the Abwehr's Central Section. In 1938, supported by his direct superior and overall chief of the Abwehr, Admiral Wilhelm Canaris, Oster developed contacts with other generals illdisposed to Hitler, above all General Beck. Hans von Dohnanyi, the brother-in-law of the oppositional Christian, Dietrich Bonhoeffer, and himself a long-term opponent to the Nazis, joined the Abwehr in August 1939. Alongside Canaris, Oster and Dohnanyi, the other key anti-Nazi conspirator in the Abwehr was Helmuth James von Moltke, who joined its Ausland Abteilung at the outbreak of war.[49]

Nowadays, it is widely known that the Abwehr was implicated in wartime conspiracies against Hitler, and many of its leaders were executed shortly before the end of the war. Far less well known is its involvement in helping German Jews to get abroad. Almost as surprising to me was that the organization should be in contact with the Strauss brothers. The family was not particularly prominent, and their business hardly functioned on a scale that gains access to government circles. But Marianne believed that the link to the Abwehr was the family banker, Friedrich H. Hammacher.

Looking back, I realized that Marianne felt there was something unworthy about all this. There is a section in the tape of our conversation in September 1996, when Marianne was responding to my first draft. Her reaction makes it clear that she would be quite happy not to have the episode mentioned. After Marianne's death, I discovered that the Gestapo files on her father and uncle revealed an extraordinary cat-and-mouse game the Abwehr and Gestapo had played with agonizing slowness for almost two years. The material was so detailed and offered so much clarification that I cursed the fact I'd discovered it two weeks after Marianne's death. I wished I could have shown it to her to reassure her.

Later on, though, as Vivian and I worked through Marianne's papers, we found that she had copies of the Gestapo documents, sent her by researchers in the Alte Synagoge in the 1970s or 1980s. This was one of many areas where it turned out that Marianne knew or had once known more than I realized. Later still, I came across her testimony in restitution hearings in 1952 which showed she had known things that were not even in the Gestapo records. Perhaps no amount of detail could have eased her worries about being singled out for special protection.

The Gestapo and the Abwehr

The first hint in the Gestapo files that the Strausses might escape the deportation is a telegram sent on 22 October at 8.10 p.m. from the Gestapo in Bremen to the Gestapo in Essen. Headed 'Secret' and 'Urgent. For immediate consideration', the telegram ran:[50]

Strauss has declared himself willing to go to the USA for the Bremen office of the Abwehr division of the Oberkommando of the Wehrmacht. Since Strauss is due to be transported to Poland in an action against the Jews on 26.10.1941, the Bremen office requests that Strauss be withdrawn from the transport since he is needed for Wehrmacht purposes in the USA.

Unsure what to do, Gestapo officials in Essen telephoned their superiors in Düsseldorf that night. Düsseldorf's Kriminalsekretär

Ommer advised them not to remove the Strausses from the deportation until he had made enquiries.[51]

The following day, Düsseldorf evidently did nothing. On the 25th, while Marianne was travelling back from her Berlin haven, Siegfried, presumably now extremely anxious about the impending deportation, went to the Gestapo headquarters in Essen. There he reported a visit by an Abwehr representative from Bremen the previous day. The visitor had been unable to come to the Gestapo in person, but had advised him to obtain confirmation that he was exempted from the transport.[52] The head of the Essen Gestapo, Kriminalrat Vaupel, cabled Düsseldorf again asking whether the Strauss family was to be 'evacuated', as the Gestapo euphemistically described deportation.[53]

The Düsseldorf officials were sceptical. But they now sought guidance from their superiors in the Reich Security Main Office (Reichssicherheitshauptamt, RSHA) in Berlin, the body that co-ordinated the activities of police and Gestapo:[54]

It is suggested that the request from Bremen be rejected. Strauss was here and said that the man from Bremen visited him yesterday in his apartment and told him to come here today and confirm that he is released from the evacuation. The man from Bremen in question could not come himself because he had to travel further at 7.45. Strauss did not want to give the man's name. Strauss's story seems suspect. He probably just wants to evade evacuation. Strauss is very wealthy.

I request a clear decision. As of this moment the evacuation is still planned because Strauss's story seems too suspect.

Whether Berlin responded during the day we do not know, but towards the evening, a senior official in Düsseldorf, Regierungsrat Ventner, felt called upon to make a decision.[55] At 7.40, Ommer cabled Essen that the Strauss family was to be given a temporary reprieve until the next available transport.[56]

The Gestapo officials in Essen did not transmit this information to the Strauss family immediately, but chose to play out the charade at the collection point. Perhaps they wanted to prolong the psychological torture. Perhaps, as Marianne suspected, they wanted to create a rift between the Strausses and the rest of the community. Perhaps they felt

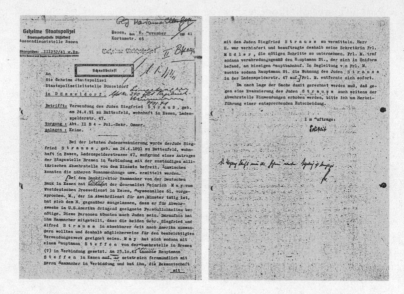

*Gestapo document of 6 November 1941 showing the fruits of its
investigations into Abwehr, Hammacher and Strauss*

outwitted and sought to emphasize their power. Whatever the interpretation, they were not simply following orders. They were making up their
own game.

Meanwhile, the Düsseldorf Gestapo officials tried to work out what
kind of opposition they were up against and the extent of Abwehr
support for Siegfried Strauss. On 28 October, they cabled their colleagues in Bremen to establish whether Siegfried Strauss's account of his
dealings with the Abwehr had been correct.[57] The Bremen Gestapo
cabled back on 4 November, confirming Strauss's account and asking
for his family to be exempted from future transports.[58]

Unable to fathom why the Strausses should have been singled out,
Essen officials now investigated the local background. They discovered
that Heinrich May, a journalist for the Westdeutscher News Agency who
was also working for the Abwehr office in Münster, had told Friedrich
Hammacher, a Deutsche Bank director in Essen and the Strauss family's

banker, that the Abwehr were looking for suitable people for intelligence work in America. These people 'could also be Jews'. Hammacher had suggested the Strauss brothers, since they were planning to emigrate to the USA in the near future. May then got in touch with a Captain Steffen, who met the Strausses in Essen on 23 or 24 October. Hammacher's secretary acted as go-between, collecting the uniformed Steffen from Essen station and taking him to Ladenspelderstrasse 47.[59]

Historians and the Abwehr

For a long time little was known about the Abwehr's operations involving Jews. The key figures were killed before the end of the war. The few references to saving Jews in the memoirs of other Abwehr figures are often inaccurate. Recently, however, an outstanding study by Winfried Meyer has explored one particular Abwehr action, Operation Seven, in great detail.[60] Initiated by a small number of anti-Nazi conspirators at the very top of the Abwehr (including its chief, Admiral Canaris), Operation Seven saved the lives of fifteen Jews and half-Jews. Hans von Dohnanyi played the leading role.[61] The operation began in 1942, when Dohnanyi attempted to protect some Jewish colleagues from deportation. At the behest of Bonhoeffer and Canaris, further names were added to the list of protégés. The conspirators invented a cover story that the Jews would be used as agents in South America. In August and September 1942, after months of difficult negotiations and preparation, the Abwehr was able to get them into Switzerland. There the fifteen Jews survived the war, thanks as well to the Abwehr's financial assistance.

Meyer's account rightly and understandably draws attention to the heroism and principle of the men behind the rescue effort. Dohnanyi and his senior colleague Hans Oster were already under close surveillance by the SD, and it took great courage to persist with their plans. In the end, Operation Seven led to Dohnanyi's imprisonment and contributed to his execution in April 1945, though the main charge against him, as against Bonhoeffer, Oster, Canaris and Moltke, who were also all murdered in January or April 1945, was their involvement in plans to topple the regime.[62]

Elsewhere, though, the Abwehr's relationship with Germany's Jews appears to have been far less benign. Sections of the Abwehr worked closely with the SS and SD in promoting Nazi racial policy, for example, and in carrying out murders of Jews in Poland and Russia.[63] On the other occasions when the Abwehr protected Jews from deportation, the motives were far less obviously altruistic than in Operation Seven. In some cases, Jews were genuinely used to spy for the Reich, usually forced to do so by the fact that family members remained behind in Germany under threat of persecution and deportation. In other cases, the line between aiding Jews and exploiting them was very blurred, and nowhere more so than in Operation Aquilar, which was probably the source of the Strauss brothers' protection.

Operation Aquilar came into being because of a very ambiguous character, Harry W. Hamacher (no relation to the family banker, Friedrich W. Hammacher, as far as is known), the well-connected proprietor of an Aryanized travel and transport company. Well-connected in Abwehr circles, Hamacher sought official assistance to enable some Dutch Jews to emigrate. Hamacher may have been partially animated by humanitarian motives, but he was certainly making very good money out of providing assistance to desperate Dutch Jews.[64] The Abwehr representative in The Hague with whom Hamacher had contact may have had humanitarian motives, too. His primary interest, however, seems to have been in increasing the flow of intelligence from the Americas. 'Disguised' as refugees, Dutch and German Jews could plausibly travel to North and South America in a way which non-Jewish Germans could not. Canaris gave Aquilar his backing and, in April, the relevant SS official in the Netherlands gave provisional approval for the emigration of 250 people to North, Central and South America. Clearly, the story of Operation Aquilar is far from being the same sort of edifying tale as Operation Seven. Financial motives, the need for information and the desire to rescue Jews were mixed up in a not very appetizing brew. On the other hand, Aquilar was more effective. Under its auspices, 174 people managed to emigrate during 1941 and even as late as 1942, the majority to Central and South America.[65] And the inclusion of the Strauss family with all their relatives in the operation (thus leaving no hostages behind who could be used to extort information) adds credence to the idea that many of those recruited were not really expected to spy.

Although the operation was based in Holland, the Bremen office features in the telegrams in the Strauss file because it had overall responsibility for espionage in the Americas. While many would-be emigrants came from Holland, several regional Abwehr offices outside the Netherlands, including offices in the Ruhr, were notified that Jews interested in emigration were also potential recruits. Of the Abwehr representatives in the region, we know, again from Meyer, that the Heinrich May mentioned by the Gestapo had been in the Abwehr's employ since 1939. US security services had evidence that May had been gathering information about the British, French and American aircraft industries.[66]

Bank director Hammacher

How did the Strauss brothers come to be included? One point in their favour was that the Abwehr liked to use Jews with a good war record. But there were many Jewish veterans who did not enjoy Abwehr protection. According to Gestapo records and Marianne's memory, the key link between the Abwehr and the Strauss family was the Deutsche Bank director Hammacher. Did he act out of simple loyalty to two long-standing customers with whom he had a relationship of trust and co-operation? There is no doubt that the Deutsche Bank correspondence with the brothers remained cordial and respectful to the end.

Direct information about the man is hard to come by. We know that Friedrich Wilhelm Hammacher was a manager with the Essener Credit-Anstalt from before the First World War. By the early 1930s, he had the rank of deputy director with the Deutsche Bank in Essen, becoming a departmental director sometime between then and 1937.

The clues to his role in the affair came from testimony in post-war restitution disputes between Marianne and Hammacher and from the deposition of one of Hammacher's former tenants, Hanna Aron, living in the USA. Hammacher's intervention was tied up with the purchase of the Strauss house on Ladenspelderstrasse. In a letter to the Gestapo in 1943, he stated that with permission of the Wehrmacht High Command (Oberkommando der Wehrmacht, OKW) he had capitalized his war pension to acquire Ladenspelderstrasse 47 from the 'Jew Siegfried Israel Strauss' on 30 October 1941, just four days after the aborted deportation.[67] When the Strauss family finally left Essen in 1943, Hammacher did indeed move into their house. After the war, in the context of Marianne's restitution claims against him, Hammacher emphasized his role in protecting the Strauss family, but admitted that it was linked to the house purchase:[68]

The help which I promised before we agreed on the purchase consisted amongst other things of my providing, with the support of my friends in the Abwehr as it then was (Canaris' group), eight passports with travel visa to Sweden. The men involved are still alive, two of them in Essen.

Hammacher claimed that the Strauss family's right to remain in Ladenspelderstrasse until their departure was enshrined in a secret codicil attached to the house sale. There is certainly no evidence that he pressured the family to leave.

Marianne's own testimony in the restitution process adds another dimension to our understanding of the conditions at the time. According to her statement to the Essen Regional Court in 1952, Schwarzlose, the party figure who informed her father in October of the imminent expropriation of Landespelderstrasse 47, was a good acquaintance of Herr Hammacher. Despite the fact that the council was about to acquire the property, she said, Herr Hammacher was subsequently allowed to purchase it.[69] Hanna Aron, who had lived with the Strausses and remained after Herr Hammacher took over the building, remembered also that he had very good connections with the Gestapo. On the Strausses' departure in 1943, he had arrived with Gestapo officials to claim some of the family's furniture.[70] This connection explained something that had been puzzling me, namely that the Gestapo reports contained nothing against Hammacher despite having identified him as the original link between the Abwehr and the Strauss family. In the restitution hearings after the war, another witness also intimated that payments had been involved.[71] Marianne herself swore under oath that there had been considerable payments under the table to keep the Gestapo sweet. Her father once told her that he had had to pay out forty-odd thousand marks to get a visa.[72]

There is a lot we will never know. Many of these statements were made in the context of restitution hearings and may not quite be what they seem: Marianne was at pains to achieve compensation, Hammacher to prove his innocence. Yet, I felt I had at least glimpsed a murky world hidden from the official records. The connections between Hammacher and the Abwehr, Hammacher and the Party, Hammacher and the city administration, Hammacher and the Gestapo were, I believe, not unusual in the Third Reich. Siegfried's protection involved a hidden local network, within which a degree of sympathy felt by a banker for an upright client merged with legal opportunities for enrichment, which in turn merged with outright corruption on the part of Gestapo and city officials. In the course of my investigation, enough such examples emerged to suggest that corruption in the Third Reich was far more widespread than has been assumed. Hanna Aron, who was not only a tenant of Hammacher's but also the daughter of the Jewish Community secretary, remembered other examples. When the last leader of the Jewish Community, Herr Ostermann, was put on a list for a future transport:[73]

'Herr Kosthorst said to Herr Ostermann, "Herr Ostermann, when you go away, I can have your briefcase." And my mother came home and she said she cried her heart out over this, that they already planned to plunder him while he was still there.'

Arthur Prinz, a leading member of the RV, wrote in his memoirs that:[74]

... corruption had by that time become so general, even down to the lowest level, that some officials – in our own case, e.g. one of our district policemen – would tell emigrants about to break up their household just what they wished and expected to get 'for free'.

Because there were several instances where individual Gestapo and police members were prosecuted by the Nazis for personally enriching themselves at the cost of the deportees, many historians still assume that most participants in Jewish persecution stuck to the rules. But the Strausses' case is one where private testimony undermines the official record. The full history of corruption in the Third Reich has yet to be written.

The privilege of their own four walls

Whatever the precise reasons for their protection, the fact remains that Siegfried and his family were safe for the time being. In this, they were luckier than Ine's sister Hannah and Ernst Weinberg. True, Hannah and Ernst too were sent home from the first Cologne transport to Łodz on 21 October, but only because it was full. They were told to come back in six days and went off on 27 October.[75] When I worked through Uri (Alfred) Weinberg's collection of letters from his parents, sent by the Red Cross to his internment camp in Australia, their very last letter before deportation proved to be missing, something that upset Uri very much. But I did find a letter to him from Marianne's grandmother Anna Rosenberg, reassuring him that his parents had gone off in courage and good faith and equipped with the skills to survive. Cards came back from Łodz for a time, the last one in May 1942.[76] Subsequent enquiries through the Red Cross proved fruitless.[77]

In Essen, having failed to deport Siegfried, the Gestapo turned its attention to Siegfried's brother, Alfred.[78] Alfred now had the same nerve-racking wait as Siegfried, but at least he had a measure of confidence that the protection would extend to him.[79] In the end, the outside pressure worked again and within a few weeks Alfred and Oe quit the Hufelandstrasse and joined Siegfried and his family in Ladenspelderstrasse 47. Oe's mother Else Dahl was also officially listed as living in the house, but in fact continued to live as a tenant elsewhere, at Brahmstrasse 10.

Permission to stay in the family home was an increasingly rare privilege for Essen Jews. The city authorities had been concentrating Jews in a few designated 'Jew-houses' since 1 May 1941. In April 1942, many were forced to move to Holbeckshof, a barracks complex in the eastern suburb of Essen-Steele, favoured because it was next to the railway line. Even those not sent to the barracks were crowded into ever more dismal apartments.[80] In June 1942, Leopold Sternberg wrote from Holbeckshof to his son Walter in Chile that Walter's former employers, Siegfried and Alfred Strauss, were 'almost the only ones who still lived in their own home'.[81] Small wonder that envious rumours grew in the dwindling community about what the Strauss brothers could have done to deserve such privilege.

Cuba

For the Strausses, the priority was to get out of Germany. In mid-October, before they knew they were to be reprieved, Siegfried had contacted his US relatives again, this time to obtain a visa to Cuba. On 17 November 1941, Siegfried wrote to Fritz Stern:[82]

Dear Fritz,

The upheavals of the last few weeks have left me no time to write the letter I have been wanting to send for some time. I want to thank you and the others involved for your help and the promptness with which you acted. As you indicated in your cable of the 24th of the last month, on 14 November we received a cable from Hugo telling us that notification of our visas awaits us in the Cuban legation in Berlin. In the meantime the transfer has been partially made. The rest follows. We expect the visa's arrival any day now and hope to begin our journey as soon as possible. Alfred and Lore have their visas for Cuba and are waiting for the next opportunity to travel. My brother-in-law, Adolf Rosenberg, will have received our letters in the meantime and will know that we and our mother, who will travel with us, are well. Sadly, since the end of October we have heard very little from my brother and sister-in-law, Ernst and Hannah Weinberg. They are in the same situation as our sister Bertel. We hope very much to see you and all our relatives soon.

With thanks again for all your efforts and many greetings for you, dear Fritz and your family, I remain your cousin Siegfried

Dear Fritz, Accept my heartfelt thanks too for your help and family-mindedness and best wishes to you and yours from your cousin Ine.

In relation to their earlier efforts to leave the country, the Strausses now faced two even more formidable obstacles. Above all, Nazi Jewish policy had now officially changed from emigration to murder. Up to 1939 or so, Nazi policy had been primarily to force Jews to leave the country. Over the next two and a half years, Nazi leaders experimented with various forms of territorial concentration of Jews. The last versions of this territorial solution were still being discussed in spring and summer 1941, when it looked as if the SS leadership was considering creating a kind of reservation on Russian soil. By then many Jews had been killed in Poland, but not yet as part of a systematic policy of extermination. During the Russian campaign from June 1941, however, the sporadically murderous operations against indigenous elites, partisans and Jews which had already characterized the occupation of Poland metamorphosed into systematic killing. A variety of SD, army, police and other units liquidated local Jewish populations with unimaginable brutality and thoroughness, wiping out half a million Russian Jews in a relatively short period (and many more over the longer term). By the end of 1941 the murder of all European Jews was firmly established as the principal goal of Nazi Jewish policy.[83]

A second hurdle which the family had to surmount was that, even assuming that with the Abwehr's help they could successfully leave the country, the Japanese attack on Pearl Harbor and Hitler's declaration of war against the USA on 11 December ended any possibility of going straight to North America. It also vastly reduced the scope for help from relatives in the States, since direct communication was now prohibited. The letter to Fritz Stern of November 1941 is, as far as we know, the last between the Strausses and their transatlantic cousins.

The only improvement in the brothers' situation was that, through the Abwehr's intervention, they regained partial control of their bank accounts. Without access to those accounts, they would never be able to find the resources necessary to obtain visas, travel documents, and foreign currency. Now, at last, in a manner not possible since October 1938, they could make their assets work for them. In 1940, the Essen tax office had put Siegfried's assets at:[84]

½ property Essen Mackensenstr. 69	RM12,550
Hufelandstr. 25	RM82,900
Ladenspelderstr. 47	RM15,800
Claim on estate of Leopold Strauss	RM5,500
Current account Deutsche Bank	RM768
Securities held by Deutsche Bank	RM74,742
Life assurance Gerlingcompany	RM10,374
	RM202,634
after liabilities	RM201,501

Alfred, for his part, was worth some RM274,000, including RM173,000 in securities and similar.[85]

From having largely lain dormant over the past few years, Siegfried's bank account suddenly registered a series of huge transactions in November 1941, with something like RM150,000 flowing into the account and around RM100,000 flowing out again.[86] On 8 November, for example, the brothers sold Mackensenstrasse 69 to a Josef Vertschewall for RM26,000 (if the 1940 valuation is anything to go by, this seems to have been a fair price).[87]

The records of these transactions show not simply how busy the brothers were, but also how the Reich engaged in legal robbery at every turn. On 13 October, just before Siegfried's aborted deportation, Alfred had made a huge transfer of RM150,337.50 to Cuba.[88] But since foreign currency was offered at only 4 per cent of the original value, the transfer generated only 2,000 to 4,000 dollars.[89] And the punitive exchange rate was not the only problem. There were also other special taxes, levies to pay for the Jewish community's welfare bill, and so on. Alfred finally received the purchase price for Hufelandstrasse 23 in December, but out of the RM115,000 agreed, almost RM20,000 was immediately confiscated by the Reich.[90] Of the remainder, RM68,624 was placed in a blocked account for future payment of Reich Flight Tax, RM17,454.30 earmarked for the Jewish Community in Essen and RM2,000 for sundry other payments. Only RM9,544.52 was actually transferred to Alfred's account – to which, in any case, he had only partial right of access.[91] In other words, when all the deductions are made, it is clear that the Strauss brothers were able to transfer abroad only a tiny proportion of their wealth, certainly well under 1 per cent.

Still, they had no choice but to go on liquidating their assets.[92] By the beginning of 1942 virtually all the properties were gone, and the brothers' assets were largely held in the form of securities and shares in the blocked accounts.[93] Finally, in March 1942 – and only then – did the brothers accede to the official removal of their grain business from the business register.[94]

The Gestapo hovered between reluctant authorization and doing what it could to frustrate the process of emigration. On 20 November, Essen Gestapo officials informed their superiors in Düsseldorf that the Deutsche Bank had been commissioned to transfer RM4,000 to Cuba for the Strauss family and that permission had been granted by the Currency Office in Düsseldorf. All seemed in order, but the official, Horn, could not refrain from adding that, 'should the Strausses in fact *not* be permitted to leave the country, please let me know if they can now be evacuated'.[95] On the 24th, the Essen Gestapo wrote to the head of the Essen police saying that, as an exception and in the interests of the Reich, Siegfried and Regina Strauss could be issued with passports. However, a supplementary memo noted that there was as yet no passport authorization for Regina's mother. Whether it was this that prevented their departure to Cuba we do not know.[96]

Meanwhile, the Düsseldorf officials sought to establish with Berlin whether the Abwehr really intended to use the Strauss family once they were abroad. 'Berlin' in this case meant the section within Division IV (Gestapo) of the RSHA under Adolf Eichmann responsible for Jewish emigration and deportation. Pending clarification from Berlin, the Düsseldorf office provisionally assigned the Strauss brothers to a transport to Riga scheduled for 11 December.[97] The Strauss file now contains something remarkable, a direct intervention from Adolf Eichmann showing that the RSHA intended to use the family as a test case to challenge the Abwehr. In a telegram dated 2 December and addressed to the head of the Düsseldorf Gestapo, SS Obersturmbannführer Oberregierungsrat Dr Albath, Eichmann outlined the fundamental issues involved:[98]

In response to your message of 20.11.1941, this is to inform you that the recent evacuation transports have been accompanied by a noticeable number of interventions on behalf of Jews from individual Wehrmacht offices or officers.

Recently, accompanied by the most diverse types of explanation, applications have been made for Jews' exemption from evacuations and for the issuance of emigration permits on the grounds that the Jews are ostensibly to be used for Abwehr purposes after their emigration.

In the light of experience the suspicion cannot be dismissed that, in the majority of such cases, personal interests lie behind the applications.

Exemption of the Jews in question from the evacuation and the issuance of an emigration permit cannot be approved prior to receipt of a letter from the OKW, specifically confirming the use of these Jews for Abwehr purposes.

The Abwehrstelle in Bremen should be informed that an appropriate letter from the OKW must be sent to the RSHA.

In other words, the RSHA, which was suspicious of the whole enterprise, wanted the Abwehr to compromise itself by formally declaring its support for Jews. On 6 December, the Düsseldorf SS duly told their colleagues in Bremen that the Wehrmacht should make a formal request in relation to the Strauss brothers. In the absence of such a request, the brothers would remain on the list for a future transport. Since no formal request was received over the ensuing weeks, it would seem that telephone communication, or simply a sense that there were important institutions involved, stopped the Gestapo from pursuing its threatened course of action.[99]

Once again, then, an agonizing waiting game was underway. At every stage, the authorities took an unconscionably long time to issue the necessary permits. It was not until the end of March 1942, more than five months after the Abwehr had first offered protection, that Gestapo approval from the top in Berlin was granted (probably by now including Anna Rosenberg and Else Dahl as well).[100] Now it was the tax authorities' turn to procrastinate. On 11 May 1942, Siegfried Strauss obtained their stamp of approval allowing him to emigrate to Cuba. He sought permission from the Currency Office (ODD) in Düsseldorf to transfer funds to Cuba and to take his luggage, packed with linen, clothing and items for individual use, out of the country. The ODD did not give permission there and then and on 2 June turned to the Gestapo in Düsseldorf for confirmation.[101] Almost another three weeks passed before the Düsseldorf officials conveyed that there were no grounds for refusal.[102] That was 19 June. When Anna Rosenberg applied to Düsseldorf for permission to transfer funds to pay for *her* ticket, the ODD *again* felt obliged to seek permission from the Düsseldorf Gestapo. By the time the Gestapo gave its approval it was 8 August.[103]

In response to a request for a progress report on the case, Kriminalrat Nohles of the Essen Gestapo informed his superiors that all that was required now was the transit visas from the countries through which the Strauss family would have to pass.[104] Whether this was one hurdle too many, or there was some other complication, we do not know, but by mid-August the Strauss family knew they were not going to succeed in emigrating to Cuba.[105] Probably the formalities within Germany had taken so long that the Cuba visa had lapsed. From correspondence after the war between Marianne and one Marcus Cohn, a Basel-based lawyer who did some work for the family, we know that the family also tried to obtain exit visas to Mexico.[106] This too came to nothing.

The Gestapo's attitude began to harden, partly because of a bureaucratic mistake. On 2 July 1942, Aunt Oe's mother, Else Dahl, sought written confirmation from the police president in Essen that she was excluded from deportations. She had been told she needed such a document in order to obtain from the RV in Berlin a further document authorizing her continued presence.[107] After the usual consultation with the Gestapo the confirmation was duly given and, in September 1942, Else Dahl presented a copy to the RV. This fetched up with a different sub-section of the RSHA which had, or claimed to have, no knowledge of the approval granted the Strauss family the previous March. As a result, in October 1942 a letter arrived in Düsseldorf from this particular RSHA sub-section, asking the regional Gestapo chiefs what was going on.[108] The officials in Düsseldorf realized immediately that Berlin had got its wires crossed but sensed an opportunity once again to question the whole exemption procedure. They telegraphed Essen asking why the police president had provided Else Dahl with written confirmation, suggesting that it endangered the secrecy essential to any Abwehr operation.[109] This in turn was grist to the mill of the Essen officials, unhappy at repeatedly having to exempt the Strauss family. Essen cabled back with the background details and heartily endorsed Düsseldorf's criticisms. Indeed, they went further:[110]

Your view that the issuance of such certificates undermines the secrecy of the grounds for emigration is most strongly to be endorsed. Moreover, the fact that the evacuation of the Jew Strauss and his family to the East has been repeatedly deferred must also have undermined the secrecy.

So, back went a letter from Düsseldorf to the RSIIA, wondering whether, in light of these facts and the changed political and military situation, the Strauss family emigration was still seen as appropriate.[111] This galvanized Adolf Eichmann's office into a new attempt on the Abwehr on 14 December 1942:[112]

The application for exceptional approval of the emigration of the above-named Jews to the USA was passed on 23.12.1941[113] in the interests of the Reich's counter-intelligence. The emigration has not yet taken place. In view of the lengthy interval, I assume that the case is no longer of any interest. In this context, it should also be noted that as a result of the efforts of the Jews Strauss to achieve their own and their families' emigration at all cost, significant groups, particularly Jewish organizations, have learned about the exceptional treatment, so that in our view the procedure is no longer secret. Communication of your views on the matter is requested.

Despite the provocative new tone with which Eichmann 'assumed' that there was no further need for the Strauss family, he still asked the Düsseldorf HQ to await further instructions. Over the next few months, it seems, the Abwehr bought time for the Strauss family by simply not replying.[114]

The sad fact was that at the end of 1942, four *years* after their first attempts to leave the country, the Strauss family were back to where they had started. The only sense in which they had achieved anything at all was that they had avoided the fate of their fellow Jews in Essen.

6

Love Letters in the Holocaust

In October 1941, Marianne found herself back in Essen, away from her friends and studies in Berlin. There was the near-deportation, the reprieve, and suddenly Marianne found herself with nothing to do. And just as suddenly, she found living at home unbearable. Although she had done and experienced so much in Berlin, her parents still expected her to be the dutiful daughter.[1] She found very little to appeal to her in the Essen Jewish community. There was no cultural life any more. The waves of deportations were causing everyone to panic. And there were so few young people left. It was against this background that Marianne fell in love with Ernst.

Marianne and Ernst Krombach had had some contact in Jewish youth groups during the 1930s. A friend of Marianne's, Ute Unger, had met Ernst in Berlin in 1937 or so, while he was studying at a technical college. In 1939, long after Ernst had left Berlin, Ute became close to Marianne and informed her that Ernst 'would be perfect for her'. By May 1940 the Krombachs had moved into Hufelandstrasse, becoming tenants and neighbours of the Strausses,[2] and Marianne's aunt Oe worked alongside Ernst, organizing activities for the Jewish children still in Essen. Oe too thought Ernst and Marianne would get on well. Matchmaking friends and relatives do not always get it right, but in this case they did.[3]

Marianne did not tell me a great deal about Ernst, though she made no bones about his having been the first great love of her life. She said

Ernst Krombach

he was very handsome and the photos tell a similar story. The two shared a love of children. Ernst wanted to be a paediatrician and Marianne told me he would have made a very good one.[4] In Marianne's 1942 diary I later found fantasies about how she would work to support Ernst in their future life together so that he could recover the medical training denied him under the Nazis.[5] To me, she recalled his touching care for her when she had to see a doctor because of a badly swollen toe. In the summer of 1941 she had gone boating (illegally) on a Berlin lake and had afterwards dropped the boat on her toe, causing such pain that she 'nearly died'. On more than one occasion back in Essen, Josef Löwenstein, one of the remaining Jewish doctors, had to remove the nail under local anaesthetic and Ernst went with her each time and 'held my hand'.[6] Later, in one of Ernst's little notes, dated 30 March 1942, I found a tender admonishment to Marianne: 'Don't overdo it with your foot!'[7] Marianne said to me, 'I could never imagine Basil [her later husband] going with me.' But she said it laughingly, and I never had the feeling she was saying that Ernst had been *the* love of her life (though I do think it was easier for her to talk about him after Basil's death).

The view from Buenos Aires

Marianne did not need to speak at length about Ernst, because she gave me so much to read. Letters from Ernst, copies of letters to Ernst, Marianne's diary from the time spent with Ernst – these were the only documents I had from the very beginning, all handed over at our first and second meetings. In addition, Marianne gave me letters she received at the end of the 1980s from Ernst's brother Heinz (now Enrique) Krombach from Argentina. Though he wrote several times, she could never bring herself to reply.

I wrote to Enrique, and established a warm rapport by fax and letter. His first letter, from 31 December 1996, in reply to mine of November, was in reality partly addressed to Marianne:[8]

Thank you for your letter of 18 November. Memories are usually tied up with pain, but I have come to the conclusion that we who were able to survive the terror years of the 1930s have a historical duty to report on the events. Thus we are connected, since you as historian have made research into the past your life's work.

Yes, you are of course right that Marianne's relationship with my brother Ernst will have been the most painful episode in her life and I tried several times to make contact. I would be very grateful if you would tell Marianne about our correspondence because she should and must know that she does not carry those years alone and that our loved ones live on as long as we remember them.

Your work in particular should help us preserve the memory of our lost ones and show that the sacrifices were not in vain. One should forgive but not forget.

[...]

I could not pass this message on to Marianne. Unbeknown to Enrique, she had died a week before he put pen to paper.

Over the following months, it became clear that memories of the family were so painful for Enrique that he found it almost as difficult as Marianne did to write about the past. It is true too that he did not have much time. Although in his mid-seventies, he was still very active professionally. In fact, I came to feel that his friendliness and generosity towards me, though undoubtedly sincere, were almost defensive – designed to guard himself against the pain my researches might bring. More than six months went by before he sent me a still not very detailed description of his brother. Enrique travelled to Germany regularly for business reasons and I hoped to meet him there; as it turned out we only met in June 1998, when I visited him in Buenos Aires.[9] We had arranged that Enrique would pick me up at my hotel and I waited downstairs in the lobby, looking through the window at the people passing by to see if I could spot him. It seemed impossible that the man who approached me was Enrique – the haircut and moustache made him look so Spanish. But then I recognized the sensitive heavy-lidded eyes I had seen in a photo of his mother. We embraced. At seventy-eight, Enrique was still vigorous and active, though he grew increasingly melancholy as the day went on. He propelled his new silver Escort confidently round the broad streets of Buenos Aires, straddling lanes as is de rigueur in Argentina, and giving me an interesting condensed tour: the old synagogue, the law courts, the government quarter. Enrique conveyed the sense of someone fully at home in his adopted country.

We were now out of Buenos Aires and driving alongside a tributary of the river Plate to the town of Tigre. There were rowing clubs along the river, little cafés and pleasant bungalows. The warm weather (despite its being mid-winter in June) gave the scene a real holiday feel. We sat down at a café filled with families and groups of youngsters enjoying Saturday out. I asked Enrique if he would like to see the photos I had brought. He stiffened. 'Are there some of Ernst?' Yes. It turned out he had none. The handsome, clear-eyed boy slipped out of my wallet and tears came to Enrique's eyes. I let him keep the photos to copy them. So the tone had been set: I was there with explosive material and he was there to be hurt. I realized that, with the exception of Vivian, of all my interviewees Enrique was the most vulnerable. He was the one most likely to experience pain at the things I had to ask and the things that I could tell. Drying his eyes, Enrique plunged into the past.

Ernst's background had been strikingly similar to Marianne's. Like Marianne's parents, the Krombachs had distinguished forebears. Ernst's father, David, could trace his German ancestry back to the eighteenth century and his mother, Minna, née van der Walde, came from a wealthy, well-connected Hamburg family. Like the Strauss brothers, Krombach had volunteered at the outbreak of the First World War, and like them he had reached the rank of non-commissioned officer and earned the Iron Cross Second Class. David Krombach had come to Essen just after the war as they had, but, having a university career behind him, he followed a different career path and Abel, Herzfeld and Krombach became one of the region's better known legal practices. The Krombachs belonged to the same assimilated, patriotic wing of the Essen Jewish community as the Strausses. Unusually, even among the more accultur- ated Jews, David Krombach was an enthusiastic rider and was regularly to be seen exercising one of the horses belonging to an Essen-based riding club. The boys Heinz and Ernst were born in 1920 and 1921 respectively, and, like Marianne and Richard, were sent to the Jewish Volksschule. Though as with Siegfried and Ine, David and Minna pre-

Enrique (Heinz) Krombach

ferred a secular humanistic education at the secondary level and so sent the boys to the Goethe Gymnasium.

In Enrique's recollection, the family 'felt themselves to be completely German but lived as conscious Jews'. David Krombach was extremely active in the Jewish community, a leading member of the local and regional associations of the principal group for representing Jewish interests before 1933, the Central Association of German Citizens of the Jewish Persuasion (Central-Verein deutscher Staatsbürger jüdischen Glaubens, CV), as well as part of its national committee. He was also active in the Jewish youth associations. In 1933, he worked with his law partner and friend Ernst Herzfeld in an important Essen initiative that led to the creation of the Reich Association of German Jews (Reichsver-tretung der Deutschen Juden, RV).[10]

In 1933, the Krombachs, like the Strausses, thought that the law-loving German people would surely not tolerate Nazism for long; they were certain their own credentials as citizens could not be called into question. David and Minna did not think of emigrating, though Enrique told me that as a result of some frightening and degrading incidents he himself decided as early as 1933, at the age of thirteen, that he wanted to leave. As a former front-line soldier, David Krombach was allowed to continue practising law for much of the 1930s. During this period, he became even more important in local Jewish life than before, Chairman of the Essen and Rhineland-Westphalian regional branches of the CV and, with Ernst Herzfeld, in charge of a legal-financial advice centre for the Jewish community.[11] For the Krombachs, as for the Strausses, Kristallnacht was the turning point in their attitude to emigration. Heinz left for Argentina in early 1939, but Ernst wanted to stay on with his parents until they all had US visas. In another grim parallel to the Strausses' experience, the visas never materialized.

Enrique had a great deal to tell me about his father – information augmented by a number of published tributes.[12] There was David Krombach's courage, visiting a client in an Essen jail on the day after Kristallnacht.[13] And there was David Krombach's insistence on doing everything by the book, which prevented him from reacting quickly enough to take advantage of some Chilean visas Heinz procured in Paris on the way to Argentina.[14] But as with Marianne's recollections of Richard, Enrique's memories of the younger sibling were far more patchy. In the late 1920s and early 1930s, he was the more outgoing of the two boys and spent much time outside the family in the non-Zionist Jewish Youth movement, the CV Youth.[15] Ernst was also involved, but he was far more home-based. Denied the right to take the Abitur exam, Heinz left the Goethe school before his younger brother did and, since sons of active combatants were still allowed to attend technical schools, studied away from home in a technical college in Mettweiler. Soon after Kristallnacht, he left with a youth group seeking to create a kibbutz-like community in South America.[16] So Enrique could not tell me much beyond a brief résumé of Ernst's education. In 1936 or 1937, Ernst too had been forced to leave the Goethe school before taking the Abitur and began studying as a chemist in Berlin. Kristallnacht ended his studies as well. After returning to Essen for a while, Ernst enrolled in a horticulture course at the Israelite Agricultural School in Ahlem, one of the educational institutions for Jews allowed to continue until 1942.[17] In 1941 or so Ernst returned to Essen and was drafted into forced labour in nearby Velbert.

Like Marianne, Enrique thus bore the pain of being an older sibling who had never known his younger brother properly. He felt guilt: if the brothers had been closer, Ernst might have decided to go with him to Argentina. For Enrique, the pain had become acute recently, because in accordance with Marianne's wishes and at his own request, I had forwarded to him copies of the letters Ernst had sent Marianne in 1942. Enrique was deeply impressed by the young man who emerged from the letters – this was a far more mature brother than he had known. Enrique told me how much he now missed having a brother and how well he thought they would get on. He was moved and impressed too by the degree to which Ernst had devoted himself to their parents.

The last letters Enrique received from Ernst were sent in 1941. His voice hoarse and emotional, Enrique told me that Ernst had written 'that I didn't understand him. And when I look back today I can understand why he wrote that. *Evidamente*, we had no idea what life was like for the people who could not get out.'

I asked him if still had those letters. 'Not all of them but I have one or two letters, also my father's last letter before he was transported in April 1942. He wrote, "a new task stands before us". Even as he was about to be deported, looking after others – which in the end cost my father his life – was of such significance for him that he saw a new task in it.'

Enrique went back to Germany for the first time in 1984. From then on, however, he'd returned regularly, above all to Düsseldorf, promoting co-operation between the regional governments of Buenos Aires Province and North-Rhine Westphalia (NRW). He had got on well with the then SPD parliamentary leader, Mathesen, who had been deeply moved by Enrique's life story. Enrique was even asked to inaugurate a new beer – the Krombacher Pils. These meetings were clearly extremely important to him, as was the relationship which developed with an Essen lawyer, Bernd Schmalhausen, who had devoted himself to ensuring that Essen's Jewish lawyers be properly remembered.[18]

I asked Enrique how he had found life in Argentina since the war. It would have been different in Germany, he said, much easier. Unconsciously echoing his father's sentiments, he went on that it had been an advantage not having things so easy, because it is the challenges we face that help us develop. Looking back now, he could feel content. The recognition he had received showed him that he had played his part. What recognition? Well, said Enrique, the German embassy in Buenos Aires had said that the relationship between Buenos Aires and North-Rhine Westphalia would not function smoothly without Herr Krombach. We were driving back into town in the Saturday evening twilight. I looked out of the window at the pleasant suburbs in an area once the preserve of the wealthy in Buenos Aires, touched by the irony that even now German approbation was Enrique's yardstick of success.

The Krombachs seen from Birmingham

Even before meeting Enrique, I had heard another account of the Krombachs' family life. Through Essen's Alte Synagoge I had asked for information about the family, and the search threw up, among other things, a letter of 1945 from a lady in Birmingham to a former CV colleague, seeking information about David and Minna Krombach and the children.[19] I discovered that the author of the letter, Liesel Sternberg, was, in 1997, still in friendly contact with a member of the Alte Synagoge and, above all, that she still lived in Birmingham, within three miles of my own home. Miss Sternberg was very small and a little unsteady on her feet following two recent accidents, but she was in spirit unbowed, an alert and lively ninety-one-year-old with the strong deep voice of a singer. She had an almost comic German accent despite, as she laughingly acknowledged, almost sixty years in Britain. Born in 1905, she had grown up in Essen, attending the Luisenschule a generation before Marianne.[20] Walter, her brother, had worked for Siegfried and Alfred in the 1920s, and had then put the experience in import–export to good use in Chile, becoming director of a very substantial cork factory there. So the Strauss brothers figured in Liesel Sternberg's memory as the people who had equipped her brother for success.

Liesel had been active in the non-Zionist youth movement, which was how she had come to know David Krombach. She went to work for Krombach's partner, Herzfeld, in the late 1920s and managed Krombach's front office in the 1930s. When asked about the family her reply was full of energy and enthusiasm. David Krombach she both liked and admired exceedingly. Minna was a delightful and cultured person. Among other things, Minna and Liesel had shared a love of music. Liesel had trained as a singer and Minna was a delightful soprano:

'I liked them both very, very much. She was charming, and the house had a lovely atmosphere. It was a very affectionate household. I remember the boys when they were very small. And of course David was very eminent in Jewish life in Essen . . . the house was full of books, full of music.'

Liesel Sternberg remembered the brothers as normal, lively boys, though very different from each other. Heinz, the elder, was much more down to earth and practical; Ernst, the younger, was the more intellectual. Liesel Sternberg recalled her last encounter with the family: at a Chanukah party in the Krombachs' in December 1938. She had little sense of what the two boys were up to on that occasion, preoccupied as she was by a number of the guests, including her brother Walter, who had returned shaven-headed from Dachau just a few days before. Soon after that, she herself was in Britain, working as a maid for a family in Birmingham. She never saw the Krombachs again.[21]

Letters between Essen and Berlin

Marianne and Ernst had so much in common by way of background, shared interests, good looks and isolation in an otherwise ageing community, that it is hardly surprising they were drawn to each other. Within two months of meeting, the two were already deeply in love. From the vantage point of 1 January 1943, after a devastating year, Marianne looked back to 'our New Year's walk last year and the church with the organ that was privy to our countless wishes. My love! I can't comprehend the awful thing that has happened!'[22]

In February 1942, Marianne's final exam at the Kindergartenseminar meant leaving behind her beloved and returning to Berlin. The correspondence between Ernst and his 'Jeanne' gives vivid insights into the nature of their burgeoning relationship. They were clearly in love. On the back of the scrap of paper carrying Marianne's exam timetable, she wrote out some lines from M. Hausmann:[23]

For each other
You are for me and I am for you selected
As word for word in writing down a verse
Each is nothing when to the other unconnected

Their attitudes and values had much in common. Like many influenced by the German youth movement, both Ernst and Marianne were extremely critical of conventional marriage. Their criticism did not concern the joys of free sex – indeed, the letters are chaste and never go beyond offering 'a thousand kisses' or allusions to the pleasures of the other's physical proximity.[24] Instead, they were scornful of the hypocrisy and show of the bourgeois marriage and the stereotypical roles it enforced. Ernst, for example, reported on a wedding he had recently attended in Essen:[25]

> *Incidentally, the ceremony was grotesquely typical. Quite apart from [the officiant's] stumbling reading, the inappropriateness of his clichés and phrases stood out clearer than ever. 'Remember that after the first torrent of young love . . .'(six years engaged) or: 'You, my dear groom, have taken on the duty of leading your bride carefully and surely through life . . .'(You know who wears the trousers?) Can you imagine my ironic smile? I found it terribly difficult to keep a straight face.*[26]

Marianne's attitude to marriage was if anything even more critical. Her friend Marianne Levy had 'strapped the yoke of marriage to her fragile frame'.[27] With Freudian consistency, Marianne failed to remember the married names of her formerly single friends.[28]

Both were critical of their parents. But Ernst was happy to acknowledge his parents' touching and unoppressive interest in his new love affair and to keep them informed; Marianne, by contrast, starved Siegfried and Regina of news from Berlin. Ernst, who was making the fairly typical discovery that the terrible oppressors described by his beloved were, at least in their interaction with him, 'very friendly and nice',[29] dropped in on the Strausses on Sunday 15 February:[30]

> *to congratulate your dear parents on the successes to date of their daughter, young Miss Strauss. You almost got into hot water*

because I suddenly realized that your parents had not the faintest idea what I was talking about and had not heard from you since Tuesday!. . . Incidentally, their reception of me was very nice and kind (particularly worthy of note).

In normal circumstances, their different relationships with their parents would have been of little import. But part of what burdened Marianne throughout her life was the feeling that she and Ernst had suffered different fates because he had loved his parents more than she had loved hers.

The correspondence did not always run smoothly. Not for the last time, the couple had to learn to cope with the vagaries of the mail. Marianne left for Berlin on Thursday 5 February. By the Sunday, after *three whole days*, Ernst had not received a letter:[31]

Yesterday I was cross with you. Today too I had good reason. I have still had absolutely no mail from you! Terrible. The days seems like weeks. Actually, I didn't want to write to you today. I'm already half undressed and ready for bed. But I can't help writing. Probably the post's to blame.

His waiting finally ended the next day. Two letters at once! To enhance Ernst's pleasure, his parents held back the second letter and gave it to him five minutes after he had read the first.[32]

In the second week, however, Ernst's principal problem was coping with Marianne's descriptions of one stimulating experience after another, many of them involving interesting men. More than once Ernst abandoned a paragraph he was writing, too churned up to continue. One young man in particular provoked his anxiety. Alfred Selbiger, with whom Marianne had had a 'fantastic conversation' about the youth movement, was someone whom Ernst himself had met and had initially been very drawn to, indeed who had provided him with something of a role model:[33]

On the surface he makes a fantastic impression and everyone must find him sympathetic. But sadly he knows this all too well and has to struggle not to abuse those attached to him. Räqui's mother, incidentally, was also one of his 'girlfriends' . . .

Now, Jeanny, I'm counting on you! You will find the right path!

The following day, when Marianne contrasted the lack of stimulus in Essen with all that Berlin had to offer, Ernst gave way to anxiety again. Recognizing, indeed having predicted, how different Berlin would be for her from Essen, he sought to reassure himself under cover of reassuring her:[34]

> What a difference there is between living in the backwoods with limited people and a limited horizon and living in a world where there are still real people, real experiences and real stimulus![. . .]It is only natural that you should feel you are leading a fuller life there.[. . .]So I will share your pleasure in your stay, but, just one thing: in all this enjoyment, don't lose your healthy common sense! (See my letter of yesterday).

Marianne received the first of these two letters on Wednesday, and she had to take a bath to recover from the letter's contents. She resolved to send Ernst a photo of herself straight away:[35]

> This picture is proof that I think of you all the time. Doesn't that tell you everything? Doesn't it show in everything I write? But we can discuss the problem when we are together again (which thank God is very soon).

She continued, alternating rather amusingly between contrition and irritation:[36]

> I wish I could be with you to remove all your worries. Actually, it's sad you have so little trust in me. But the fault is no doubt mine – 'seek the faults of your children in yourself' (Salzmann). Everything I've done to wrong you, my love, I'll make good.
>
> Actually, a bit of jealousy never did any harm. But this seems to be too much for you. Don't worry.
>
> Think of me as much as I think of you.

On Thursday, the second of Ernst's anxious letters arrived and Marianne responded with more reassurance:[37]

> Although tomorrow threatens to be the most horrible day since ancient times, I want to write to you this evening. Today was

awful. My marks in Hebrew: 5! And in Jewish knowledge 4! Not exactly uplifting! I'm quaking about the results.

Now to you! Another letter like yesterday's. The only good thing is that we'll be together again soon. I'm looking forward to it so much. It's the shining light that keeps me going. These last few days I've realized how much we belong together. Everyone I've met or who has impressed me or whom I've enthused about pales into insignificance when I think of you. I'm so happy to feel this way, my love. Because that is the only real proof of the strength of one's feelings and ties to another person.

If I were with you, I could tell you everything that I want to say.

I am so fond of you.

Your J

That is the last of Marianne's letters from Berlin. Ernst wrote one on the Wednesday, noticeably more cheerful, and particularly pleased at Marianne's response to his rather depressed musings of the weekend. Marianne sent her telegram announcing she had passed. A card in Ernst's handwriting, dated Monday 23 February 1942 and delivered by hand, bears the text 'After successfully surmounting all challenges, welcome home!'

A secret engagement

When Marianne returned to Essen, she found the Jewish community waiting for the next disaster and her family hoping to leave for Cuba. The nervous, restless atmosphere at home was intolerable. So Marianne did what came naturally – flung herself day and night into service for the community. Inspired by her training, she set out to organize a kindergarten for the children in the city; her first step was to buy the equipment. In conversation with me she looked back wryly at her enthusiasm. 'I remember going and really doing this in the very classical manner as I had been taught.'[38] The kindergarten was established on Hindenburgstrasse in what was then the community centre, an old ramshackle house with one large room which might once have been a shop. Downstairs in the basement were smaller rooms, and these Marianne converted into the kindergarten.

She had her work and she had her relationship with Ernst. First love at eighteen is often all-consuming; to be in love at a time when one is trying to 'squeeze out every last drop of experience' is something different again. The sense that theirs was a relationship for life developed fast, even though Ernst's work and Marianne's responsibilities meant that the couple could only spend the day together on Sundays. The stresses of separation in Berlin were soon forgotten; indeed, wrote Marianne in her diary, 'the separation showed us for the first time how much we belong to each other'.[39]

Marianne told me that at some point during the next six weeks they were secretly engaged. I wasn't sure how formal this understanding was, since Enrique had never heard of it. There is no explicit mention of it in the letters, but Ernst did later write of the rings they had exchanged, and in her conversations with me, Marianne certainly referred to Ernst as her former fiancé. There is a hint that they had become engaged before 26 March, since a note from Ernst hints at some secret 'theatre' in which they were both involved.[40]

A few days later, in another note, written just before going to bed after a long Sunday spent together, Ernst sighed:[41]

Jeanne, how lovely it would be if you could be with me now or I with you! I can hardly imagine what it will be like when this is possible every day! We cannot avoid yearning for such a time – it's the logical conclusion to all our plans and feelings. But until then, we must set ourselves more modest goals. That's the only way we can get through this period until we can live just for each other.

10 o'clock, Jeanne. I'm quickly getting my bed ready, organizing my stuff for tomorrow, and then I'm all yours again!

. This note and others like it suggested that the relationship had not been consummated. Towards the end of 1942, Marianne confided to her diary: 'We should have spared ourselves all the barriers and all our bourgeois decency. But who could have predicted all that!'[42] However, before I came across that entry, I had already asked Marianne the delicate question. Had they . . . ? 'Alas, alas.' Marianne 'would have liked to', but Ernst was 'too much a gentleman'.[43]

The major bombing raids on Essen began on 10 March 1942.[44] The Strausses' house was not affected but the Krombachs were less lucky. We know a little about their experience because of the diary of Artur Jacobs, a non-Jew, who with his (Jewish) wife and a group of politically minded friends was making it his business to maintain links with the Jewish community and provide help where possible.[45] In spring 1942, Artur Jacobs had regular contact with the Krombachs ('Dr K'). On 13 March, Artur wrote:[46]

At Dr K's, the house devastated – roof gone, ceilings down, windows blown in, doors torn off their hinges. 'We are experiencing Polish conditions in advance,' he said, 'One gets used to them.' No water, no heating, dirt and rubble. The last pieces of furniture also destroyed. But when one has no expectations, such disasters don't hit so hard.

On the morning of the disaster, they rescued the woman next door who had been trapped.

Their reward came quickly the following day.

A policeman with an officer: 'You have to quit the apartment and make room for Aryan citizens who have lost their homes.'

Having to move out of demolished rooms is not so bad. But that this should be their thanks, that makes one bitter.

This was the Krombachs' relationship to their fatherland in a nutshell. David Krombach with his generous sense of duty and responsibility; the regime with its determination to drive them out.

It is striking that neither the later letters, nor Marianne's reminiscences, contain any reference to the destruction of the Krombachs' house. For ordinary non-Jewish residents, the experience of bombing raids, particularly the destruction of their homes, was the major, unforgettable experience of war. The date that one's home was hit was one of those key fixed points around which all narrative revolved. How striking an illustration of the threat facing Essen's Jews, then, that the destruction should not figure in their communications or their memories! The Krombachs and the widower Austerlitz moved from their comfortable home on Semperstrasse to cramped quarters at Lindenallee 61, joining a number of Jewish families already there.[47]

David Krombach's comment to Artur Jacobs about experiencing

'Polish conditions' in advance strongly indicates that by mid-March he was expecting to be deported. With his RV connections he will have known that the 1941 expulsions were not the end of the matter.

Preparing for deportation

In fact, unbeknown to Marianne and Ernst, an administrative process had started which would soon tear them apart. Even as Marianne was making her way from Essen to Berlin in February 1942, a letter was travelling from Berlin to Düsseldorf demanding up-to-date statistics on the Jews in the district and the total number that could be deported. On 6 February the regional Gestapo headquarters in Düsseldorf passed the letter on to the local police and Gestapo officials, demanding an answer within twenty-four hours. On 7 February, the Essen Gestapo cabled back that 455 Jews fell into the relevant categories.[48]

A note from Ernst to Marianne dated 26 March refers for the first time to the threat of deportation, though Ernst was at pains to reassure Marianne that the danger – 'on this occasion' – seemed to have passed. Ernst and Marianne were probably unaware of the grotesque bureaucratic infighting in the background. The labour exchange, seeking to retain its conscript workers, wanted to restrict the number of deportees to 100 – a figure which would certainly have removed Ernst from the transport. But eventually the Gestapo and labour exchange compromised on 353. By 8 April at the latest, Ernst knew that he and his family, along with several hundred other Essen Jews, had been assigned to a transport due to leave for the East on 22 April.[49] All but a few of Marianne's kindergarten children were also on the list. The letter informing the victims did not, of course, tell them where they were going.

The Krombachs now had to facilitate the expropriation of their own property. A prepared form had to be filled in with details of everything they owned, including clothing, valuables and all other assets. 'No allowances would be made' if they failed to fill the forms in correctly. In addition, they had to provide RM 50 per person for conversion to zloty.[50] Many of the deportees, including the Krombachs' friend Austerlitz, had to move to the Holbeckshof barracks a few days before deportation, leaving virtually all their possessions behind them.[51]

Unseen by the human 'cargo', another set of decisions was taking place in the background. The first major wave of deportations from the Reich in October 1941 had been to Łodz, the second in November to Minsk and Riga. After the Wannsee conference, early in March 1942 Eichmann's office ordered that the bulk of deportation from the Third Reich be re-routed to ghettoes and camps in the Lublin district within the General Government, the rump area of Poland originally designated as a dumping ground for 'non-Aryan' Poles and Jews (as opposed to those areas like the Warthegau, claimed for 'Aryan' resettlement).[52] By 1942, the General Government's function for Jews had changed into an extermination centre, and the onset of transports to the region coincided with the opening of the death camp at Belzec in mid-March and the building of Sobibor and Treblinka. A series of locations – Trawniki, Piaski, Izbica Lubielska among them – were designated as temporary holding bays.[53] Initially, the Krombachs' transport was supposed to go to Trawniki, but technical difficulties meant that Ernst's destination was to be Izbica Lubielska in the Lublin administrative district.[54]

Although it became a transit point for many German, Austrian and Czech Jews in 1942, Izbica's role in the Holocaust remains almost unknown, and there is no entry for it in most Jewish encyclopedias or encyclopedias of the Holocaust. In Martin Gilbert's *Atlas of the Holocaust*, one of the few references to Izbica Lubielska appears in the context of the initial deportations to Belzec, 17 March 1942. The map shows that Izbica was roughly equidistant between Lublin and Belzec, some forty miles from the death camp.[55] As well as having drawn little attention from historians, there are very few contemporary documents about Izbica in 1942–3. According to the voluminous memorial volume for the Jewish victims of persecution (*Gedenkbuch Opfer der Verfolgung der Juden*), produced by the Federal Archive in Koblenz:[56] 'No records survive providing information about the methods adopted in the camp, about the arrivals and departures or about the fate of the prisoners who passed through.'

As we shall see, the designation 'camp' is somewhat inappropriate. And as we shall also see, some records *do* survive.

An honourable departure

During the Krombachs' last fortnight in Essen, Ernst was freed from labour. Only now were he and Marianne able to spend almost every waking hour together. They would go for long walks through the Essen forest above Lake Baldeney. Meanwhile, Ernst's parents prepared themselves for departure. Artur Jacobs, who had long concluded that the Nazis could not be tackled by lawful means, recorded his despair at Frau Krombach's desire to stick to the rules. It would seem that Jacobs had suggested making some extralegal provision for protecting family property:

15 April
Frau K wants to travel with 'her conscience clean' and therefore not do anything which is 'forbidden'! Should one curse, should one laugh?

How much immorality resides in such 'morality'! How much bourgeois pseudo-morality! Worn-out, old legalistic thinking, how weak!

Perhaps Artur Jacobs did not understand the psychological boon to the deportee of knowing that at least one was in the clear, had done no wrong. But it is hard not to agree with Jacobs when we recall that the family failed to leave the country because of David Krombach's insistence on doing everything by the book. In an immoral society, the time for law abiding had passed.

Nevertheless, there is no disguising Jacobs' admiration for David Krombach's final words, spoken the night before the deportation:

20 April
A final word from Dr Krombach (as, drained and overtired, he bade me farewell. Tomorrow they start on their journey[57]):
'We have had to shoulder many burdens. Often we thought we would go under. But we have also experienced much that gave us hope. Selfish feelings fade away – one is ashamed of them. We pull together and learn something of the power of the whole.
'It may be,' he added after a pause, 'that later, when we've got through this, we'll look back on this as the most important time of our lives and won't regret having gone through it, brutal as it was.'

There are strong echoes here of David Krombach's last words to Enrique – 'A new task awaits us'.[58]

Borrowed memory

On the night before Ernst's departure, Marianne remembered meeting Artur Jacobs in the Krombachs' apartment – a fateful encounter, as later events were to prove. At this stage, however, they did not know each other very well. Artur and David Krombach withdrew into the back room for private discussion – it may have been then that David Krombach uttered the noble sentiments noted above. Marianne helped the family to pack.

Marianne told me that she accompanied the family to the barracks in Holbeckshof and spent the night pleading with Ernst to make a run for it.[59] It seemed an astonishing act of courage to accompany them since she would have run the considerable risk of being deported too. It also crossed my mind, afterwards, to wonder what kind of escape she had in mind. She had only just met Artur Jacobs and could not yet know the possibilities he represented. But when I asked her, Marianne told me she had heard that he had offered help to the family.[60]

Among the letters from Ernst that Marianne gave me I found the following:

20/21 April
Jeanne!

The last night in the apartment and therefore a moment of 'peace'. Ours is an unusually hard fate to shoulder, there is no doubt about that. It will certainly be hard for us, faced with all these other challenges, suddenly to find ourselves without each other – especially since we've been together every day recently, living almost like a married couple. How could we be satisfied with anything less? How rich and good it was to be together at a time of the most appalling conditions, and how great it will be when we can live together as free human beings! There are no words for the happiness that comes from our being together, a togetherness that is not bound to time or place or anything . . .

*My dear 'love', you must know and feel that I will always be
with you.[. . .]I hope that you will be able to leave Germany as
soon as possible. That would be a source of great comfort for me,
even if we are geographically further apart. We will find each other
again, we must. A hard test has been put before us, but in the end
a happy golden time awaits us! Let's look to work and people to
occupy and divert us, always with an eye to gathering valuable
experience for our future life together.*

    Jeanne, good luck! You live always and eternally in
        Your Ernest

I was so moved by Ernst's sentiments that it was only after Marianne's
death that I recognized a problem raised by the letter. It is clear from
the split date (20/21 April) that it was written across midnight, into the
small hours. We know that the Krombach's transport left on the 21st.[61]
The letter makes it clear that Ernst was writing in the Krombachs'
apartment and that he was alone. In other words, on the last night
before deportation, Ernst was not in the barracks and he was not with
Marianne. Jacob's entry of the 20th, incidentally, also indicates that the
Krombachs were in their apartment. Marianne's memory of accompanying the family to the barracks cannot be accurate.

Sometime after Marianne's death I was in Essen, reading a collection
of essays about Essen's Jewish life put together under the auspices of the
Alte Synagoge. In it, Hanna Aron wrote that her boyfriend was sent to
Holbeckshof with his mother. He was included on the second deportation list to Izbica on 15 June 1942. Aron wrote that the night before
deportation she went to Holbeckshof and spent the night with her friend,
pleading with him not to go. But he would not abandon his mother.[62]
This seemed strikingly close to Marianne's account. I made a point of
going through Marianne's book collection; she did not own the book in
which the account appeared. I then learned that Hanna Aron and
Marianne had known each other well at one stage, and in 1998 I visited
Hanna Aron in Connecticut. She told me that in March 1943 she, her
mother and brother had moved in with the Strausses. Not only that, but
it transpired that Hanna's friend had been Richard Fuchs, a former tutor
to Marianne's brother and someone well known to the Strauss family.

So it came to seem highly credible that Hanna had told Marianne about her last night in the barracks while living with the Strausses and that Marianne later came to believe the story was her own.[63] Marianne was very probably with Ernst earlier on the eve of his deportation, but then went home. There is a hint in letters written a few weeks later that Marianne had contemplated accompanying Ernst to Izbica and blamed her parents for preventing her from doing so. Whatever her deliberations, the trip to Holbeckshof never happened.[64]

When Vivian read my conjectures here, he was angry with me. I was challenging one of the few things which his mother had told him, and on more than one occasion. It seemed unfair to his mother when she could not answer back. And why should she invent things? This was something she remembered so vividly. It was one of the great traumatic departures in a life which had had more than its fair share. I could understand his unease and felt not entirely happy about it myself. It *was* one of those moments that Marianne had talked about as if it were yesterday. And yet, the evidence was overwhelming that she had appropriated a story that was not her own. It was only when I encountered other discrepancies in Marianne's memory that I began to discern a pattern to the changes she wrought upon the past.

The Krombachs' journey to Izbica

On the morning of 21 April 1942 the Krombachs were deported from Essen. Marianne was waiting at the main station to give Ernst a last wave, but evidently he did not realize she was there and by the time he went to the window the train was almost out of the station. After the train had left, Marianne went back to the Krombachs' apartment with the family's loyal former housekeeper, Änne. Here she collapsed in despair.[65] She was in such a state, she said, that the alarmed housekeeper contacted her parents. In the 1980s, Enrique wrote to Marianne that Änne still remembered 'What a pretty girl you were, how much you felt for Ernst and how often you placed yourself in danger in order to do something for them.'[66]

For Marianne, the memory was of the deepest despair she had ever felt. 'That was the last time in my life,' she told me, 'that I really cried.'[67]

Our natural assumption is that the moment of separation was the last time the two lovers heard from each other. We think of deportees as cut off from the rest of the world. Possibly we *want* to think of them like this, so that we do not have to stay with the thinking, feeling, suffering participants to the end.

One of the first things Marianne gave me, however, was a padded envelope, on the front and back of which she had written 'Marianne – not to open! 29.VII.46'. The inscription suggests that while Marianne was still in Germany in 1946, she sent the envelope on ahead to Britain (possibly with other personal effects) and wanted to make sure that no one looked at the contents. Had they done so, they would have found some twenty-odd communications from Ernst dating from April to August 1942 and some lengthy, typed half-diary entries, half-letters from Marianne to him. Other Essen deportees had managed to mail an initial card from Izbica,[68] but there is no other known example of such a sustained correspondence having been preserved.

Marianne's fifty-nine single-spaced, typed A4 pages begin with an entry for 22 April 1942, the day after the Krombachs left Essen. She did not have a great deal of spare time to write. With the deportation of most of the children to Izbica, the kindergarten was closed and the community rooms were now an old-age home. The very elderly had been largely excluded from the Izbica transport, and thus found themselves left behind in Essen without family support or carers. So they were installed in the community rooms on Hindenburgstrasse, each bringing a bed, a wardrobe and a cupboard into the makeshift home. The Jewish community still had a number of nurses and Marianne joined them, initially as an unpaid auxiliary.

In her entry for 22 April 1942, Marianne wrote:

My love, I wonder how you slept. I spent last night in your mother's bed. Änne and I had so much to do. So I had another night in your presence and that was good. I will find much to do and I am happy about that. Everyone is very kind to me and, knowing how you would be, I shall be kind to them. Oh, that I didn't manage to see you again yesterday! We three waited for the train. When you came to the window,

-1-

den 22.4.42.

Lieber,wie Du wohl geschlafen hast?Ich habe heute nacht im Bett Deiner Mutter geschlafen.Anne und ich hatten noch so viel zu tun.So war ich noch einer Nacht in Deiner Atmosphäre und das war gut.Ich werde viel zu tun finden und darüber bin ich froh.Die Menschen sind liebe voll mit mir und ich will ihnen ein Gleiches tun im Gedanken an Dic

Dass ich Dich gestern nicht noch mal gesehen habe!wir 3 haben noch den Zug erwartet.Als Du ans Fenster kamst,war der Zug schon in weiter Ferne.Es war vielleicht besser so.Im Büro gab Herta mir Deinen Brief.Dank Dir,Lieber.Wir beide,Du und ich,wir wollen danach leben; egal,was kommen mag.Ich habe den Eindruck,dass die Sache,die geplant ist,wirklich ernst wird.Nicht zu meiner Freude.Aber es ist ha alles Schicksal und wir müssen sehen,für uns beide das Beste daraus zu machen.Einmal werden wir wieder zusamme sein.

Ich werde Dir über jeden Tag einen Bericht geben.Wie ein Tagebuch. Diese Blätter werde ich dann nach einer bestimmten Zeit gesammelt schicken.So weisst Du,was hier vorgeht.Sobald ich Deine Adresse habe,bekommst Du die ersten Blätter.

Um eins mein Lieber,kann ich Dich nicht oft genug bitten: sieh und sorge,dass Du gesund bleibst.

23.4.42.

Mein Lieber,inzwischen sind Deine ersten beiden Nachrichten von Duisburg und Düsseldorf angekommen.Härchen,und ich sind so glücklich mit der Post,die wir beide bekommen.wir sind gute Freunde,und werden immer bessere werden.Über Deine zweite Karte war ich etwas beruhigter,nachdem ich nämlich vorher nur Gegenteiliges gehört hatte.Die Hauptsache ist,Lieber,dass man selbst versucht,alles leichte anzusehen und mit allem sich abzufinden und fertig zu werden.Dazu müssen wir uns erziehen,wollen wir selbst uns nicht verrückt machen. Ausserdem ist Arbeit das beste Mittel.Heute hatte ich meinen ersten Dienst-Tag im Betsaal.Jetzt kommt mir viel mehr das Unerfreuliche dort zum Bewusstsein.Aber man wird sich daran gewöhnen.Ausserdem tröste ich mich in dem Gedanken,dass jeder Tag,den man hinter sich bringt,uns beide näher zusammen führt.

Was soll ich Dir sonst schreiben?Du weisst ja alles,denn jeder Gedanke gehört Dir.

Gestern kam ein Brief an Dich von Manfred K.en,den ich gleich beantwortete.An Theodor will ich auch baldmöglichst schreiben.Schreiben hilft mir sehr über das Denken hinweg.Es ist unbedingt die Beschäftigung,die am zwingendsten die Gedanken in andere Bahnen lenkt.

Manfred schreibt,dass er jetzt in der Friedhofsgärtnerei arbeitet. Die Arbeit macht ihm Freude;vor allem das Pflanzen.Nur kann er das leider nicht immer tun,denn es müssen sehr oft Gruften geschaufelt werden.Er klagt,dass er s o sehr allein ist und Post seine einzige Abwechslung bedeutet.Ein Grund mehr für mich,ihm gleich zu antworten.

Page 1 of Marianne's letter-diary

the train was already in the far distance. It was probably better so. In the office, Herta gave me your letter. Thank you, my love. We must try and live up to its sentiments no matter what may come. I have the impression that the plans here are really serious.[69] *Not to my satisfaction. But it is all fate and we must see how we can best turn things to our advantage. One day we will be together again.*

I shall write a report for you every day. Like a diary. After a time I shall send the pages together. So you'll know what is happening here. As soon as I have your address, you'll get the first pages.

There's one thing, my love, which I can't ask you enough: be sure to look after yourself.

For his part, Ernst wrote his first postcard as the train left Essen: the address given is 'just after Mülheim' – the next station on the line – and from the postmark we see it was mailed in Duisburg, the station after that. It is from this letter that we learn that Ernst had caught a last glimpse of Marianne at Essen station:[70]

Another quick hello from me! At the last moment, I saw you on the platform as we travelled through. I was 'visiting' with Else Bär and the Löwensteins. In Mülheim, we were joined by loads of acquaintances. The next stop seems to be Duisburg, where I will post this card.

Best wishes to your parents, Oe and Kurt K. To a rapid reunion! Your Ernst

Ernst's next card was sent from Düsseldorf, where the Essen deportees were kept overnight. Only now was Ernst able to ascertain where the train was actually going, though still without absolute certainty.[71]

From the historian Michael Zimmermann we know that this first leg of the transport ended in Düsseldorf Derendorf, where Jews from various parts of the region and destined for Izbica were gathered. Derendorf is now a regular, though rather desolate, train stop, currently under renovation. Whenever I flew to Germany I would land at Düsseldorf airport and take the S-Bahn into town. The train passed through Derendorf, and when we pulled into the station I would recall that this was where Ernst's group had been deposited and marched over to the abattoir near by. The station had been used by the Gestapo because of its long platform. As my S-Bahn glided off, rolling past metre after metre of desolate platform under scaffolding, one had a faint frisson of the misery of families standing in line, over-burdened with luggage and anxiety.

Ernst's train arrived there around 14.30 and the group was led by policemen (one for every twenty deportees) into the large hall of the neighbouring municipal abattoir. Now began the sifting and confiscation of much of the luggage. At the same time, court officials handed out official papers confirming that, under the Reichsbürgergesetz (Reich citizenship law) of 25 November 1941, the property of Jews leaving the country was deemed automatically to accrue to the Reich.[72]

The deportees were now restricted to taking one suitcase or rucksack with essential items, including food for fourteen days (which was supposed to comprise largely bread, flour and nuts), a woollen blanket (in which the food for the first three days was to be wrapped) and a spoon and plate. Everything else was confiscated. The German Red Cross was the beneficiary. From the thank-you letter it sent to the Gestapo, we know that the spoils in Derendorf included bandages, medicines, candles, towels, torches, washing powder, soap, razor blades, shaving cream, shampoo, toilet water, matches, eau-de-Cologne, creams, shoe polish, sewing materials, tooth brushes, tobacco and chewing tobacco, cigarettes, cigars, tea, coffee, cocoa, sweets, sausages, oranges and lemons and other fruit.[73] That was just the bounty enjoyed by the Red Cross. Confiscated clothing, by contrast, went to the National Socialist Welfare Organization. We do not have a full list of the clothing, under-wear, bed linen, table cloths, umbrellas, rucksacks and pillows that were their portion, but we know that the confiscated outer clothing alone comprised 192 coats, 82 jackets, 69 ladies' jackets, 345 dresses, 181 blouses, 5 swimsuits, 330 pairs of stockings, 21 pairs of slippers, 37 hats and caps, 93 scarves, 165 ties, 171 pairs of men's trousers, 19 dressing gowns, 485 woollen items, 133 pairs and 30 single shoes, 22 pairs of over-shoes, 145 pairs of gloves and 41 scarves.

The official documents convey the impression of nameless, passive victims, having no choice but to see their belongings extracted by the Gestapo. Enrique, too, felt the Jews left in Germany could do nothing but submit to what happened to them. Yet Ernst's correspondence does not portray such passive victimhood. Undoubtedly, his cards sought to protect Marianne from some of the worst. He was also mindful of censorship. But his letter from Düsseldorf on Wednesday 22 April suggests that he had not only managed to survive and evade the demoralizing business of the plundering remarkably well, but had even been able to provide strength and good cheer to those around him:[74]

After a second sleepless night, thousands of loving greetings. Despite minor irritations I am content. Unfortunately, not everyone was so lucky, but it was a source of satisfaction to be able to help improve the situation of others. Including the luggage business!

An uncensored letter in August added further details and revealed that it was Ernst's position as a Jewish orderly that had helped him circumvent the worst:[75]

Up to Düsseldorf the trip was pleasant. Taken by gendarmes and Gestapo to the abattoir; the bundles and suitcases were then checked through and much depleted. Through special care and with my armband[76] I managed to get our bundles and ourselves through the control without loss.

Early in the morning of that same day, the Essen deportees were herded out of the Derendorf abattoir on to train Da 52. The deportees were 'lucky' in that they were transported in normal passenger cars rather than in the goods and cattle cars usually deployed outside Germany. Having boarded the train, they sat and waited for hours. Finally, they left at 11.06, stopping at Erkrath, Hagen, Soest, Paderborn, Ottbergen, Northeim, Nordhausen, Wolferode, Halle, Falkenberg, Cottbus, Sagan and Glogau, reaching Izbica two days later.[77]

Ernst's next card and a letter were written on Thursday 23 April as the train was leaving the Reich proper for German-occupied Poland:[78]

Dearest, We travel on. Time travels too and brings us closer to the point when we can meet again! That is our consolation, that every day brings us closer. This will probably be the last time I write from

*the transport. It is getting harder and harder to do so. However, I
learned that we will be able to write from the camp. It will be in
the Lublin area, not, however, in the two places mentioned but
near by.*[79] *As soon as we find out, you will too, of course.*

*Our separation, Jeanne? Hard! Inescapable![. . .]What's clear is
that it's harder for you than for us. For you, our absence must make
itself felt from the start. For us, the challenges we face provide a
distraction. I'm being open about this so that you don't worry about
us. My love, we can get through many difficulties. We'll probably
have it harder once we're settled and have time to reflect again.*

*I feel myself strong enough now, even if I was sometimes a bit
doubtful in Essen whether I was up to this. I would be happy if
you could say and think the same for yourself. To a very small
extent we can draw a parallel to our separation in Berlin. But the
roles are now reversed. I'm always happy to be among people I
can talk to about you. I was just talking for a while with
Rudi.*[80]*[. . .]I am not getting on particularly well with my parents
at the moment. The reason: my father is too self-centred when I
want to take care of others. Well, thank God I don't need them.
Now, dearest Jeanne, the page is full. I've written the whole afternoon, with interruptions. Some things may be a bit confused.*

I take you in my arms and kiss you fervently! Your Ernst

A card sent that same day, postmarked Ostrowo, was even more
upbeat:[81]

My dear Marianne!
*Today you are fated to hear from me again. We are in good form
but would be very happy to reach our destination soon. I'll write
to you all the time, of course, as soon as it's possible. The landscape
has been very interesting. We are now in the General Government.
One can see from the cleanliness that this was once a German area.
We brought so much food with us that we haven't even got through
the sandwiches. One shopping bag is still full. So do not worry. In
the meantime, the train has started moving again.[. . .]*

Even more than Marianne's letters from Berlin, these sources present us – and presented Marianne – with a problem of interpretation. Do they convey in any way the reality of conditions on the train? Clearly, Ernst was trying to reassure Marianne and, in protecting her, probably giving himself courage too. And he will also have again been mindful of the censor. Later, in a letter that went by private channels, Ernst was able to provide different details of the train journey. For example, that they had travelled twelve to a compartment[82] (which presumably meant two people per seat, not to speak of all the luggage), and that in Lublin, the wagon taking the bags of those who couldn't carry their own luggage was uncoupled and left behind.

But assuming that Ernst's early letters withheld some details, there is much we can believe. There is the strange mixture of information and ignorance. The deportees are able to communicate with Essen, send cards from the train, yet their destination is shrouded in mystery. It is clear from the letters that rumours were flying back and forth in the train – where they were going, what conditions would be like. Someone evidently claimed to know that letters would be permitted, and Ernst has chosen to believe it, but in reality no one could be certain of such things. Clearly, the deportees have no knowledge of the larger context; that their first destination is merely a holding bay before they are murdered.

Ernst's courage and generosity of spirit are evident. Obviously his parents, seeking to conserve their strength and their resources, felt he was doing too much for others, perhaps taking too many risks on other people's behalf. And then there is Ernst's ineradicable Germanness. His pleasure at the cleanliness and signs of German roots could hardly have been greater were he a young 'Aryan' travelling out to the Warthegau area of Poland reserved for German settlement, rather than a Jew condemned to the General Government ghettoes.

While she waited for news, Marianne threw herself into her new work, caring for the elderly in the Jewish community. Her task was made much lighter by the speed with which Ernst's cards arrived. The two dispatches from Duisburg and Düsseldorf reached her on 23 April. Both their upbeat content and their speedy arrival were enormously reassuring. 'Mein Lieber' Marianne tapped out on the keys of her borrowed Jewish community typewriter:

your first two messages from Duisburg and Düsseldorf have arrived. Bärchen and I are so happy with the post we have both received. We are good friends and are becoming ever better ones. I was somewhat reassured by your second card, because what I'd been hearing was rather the opposite.[83] *The main thing, my love, is to try to see the brighter side, to come to terms with everything and to deal with it. We must school ourselves if we are to avoid going mad. Also, work is the best answer. Today I had my first working day in the prayer hall [where the elderly were being accommodated]. I'm much more conscious now of the many grim aspects to the work there. But I'll get used to it. And also I console myself with the thought that every day we manage to get through brings us closer together.*

What else should I write? You know everything already because all my thoughts are with you.

Bärchen ('little bear'), incidentally, was Herta Byttiner, née Behr, then thirty-three, who worked as a typist for the Jewish Community.[84]

On 24 April 1942, Ernst's train trundled into Izbica. For an agonizing week, Marianne had no news; a card on the 30th confirmed Ernst's arrival, but gave no address. By 3 May, however, she had received two more communications from Ernst, sent on 25 and 28 April, while Ernst was taking stock of the Krombachs' new home, Izbica Lubielska, Kreis Krasnystaw, in the Lublin administrative district of the General Government.[85]

The first exchanges with Izbica

While Marianne waited for mail she wrote about her work, her problems with the family and, of course, how much she missed Ernst:[86]

My love, I want to spend a while longer with you before I go to bed. How will you sleep?[. . .]I am with you in every thought. If only I could be with you fully. Does God mean well with us? We must believe in him and hope that he will help us. Only in that thought can we find solace.

If I could only know that you are managing to overcome everything and deal with it, I would rest easy. You must try. I will too, my love.

I'm so pleased that there's so much here for me to do. Every minute is taken up. At night I drop, dead tired. It's good. (Don't worry, I've remembered my promise and won't overtax myself.) Life has become harder. Two weeks ago we were happier. It is unbelievable how quickly fate can turn and strike. The main thing is not to lose sight of the light – the light of hope. We must carry our light before us. Then others will see it and live accordingly. I think I mean a lot to the old people, they're happy when they see me and that makes me happy. The place is depressing, but one must have courage and ignore the bad things with a smile. It's often awfully difficult. But if we're given time and space and everything isn't torn down as soon as it is put up, then we'll certainly be able to make many improvements. Today we finished building a medi-cine cupboard and one for the instruments. If we carry on working as we are we'll surely achieve something. Willy H is much better and his mother too. He's my favourite patient – you know, my son. Now that I don't have any little sons any more, I have to replace them with big ones.

The one thing, my love, is to take care of yourself. I can do it only in my thoughts. More tomorrow. In my letters to you I am trying every typewriter in the Community: Hindenburgstrasse, Steele, home. At the moment I'm sitting at home. In front of me on the desk I've still got your picture from Lake Baldeney in the little frame I found at your house. There are always fresh twigs next to your picture because we both want to have something from spring!

[. . .]

Now, really, a very good night, Ernest.

Though Marianne's workload grew steadily, she relished the challenge:[87]

The number of patients is growing[. . .]The ward is packed to the rafters, but still not full enough for the 'management'. From time to time his lordship rushes in and gives us the benefit of his opinion. It looks as if we might be moving. But that has its advantages: you don't get out of practice, and they say that change is as good as a rest.[. . .]I may earn some pocket money; then I can send my loved ones countless parcels.

I can't tell you any more today. It's late and I've got to clear the decks because I'm keeping Oe and Alfred awake. I'm typing up here because I can't stand it downstairs. I get on with my parents like you do with yours. Now my wish is that you sleep well and peacefully. Every night I pray for you and I pray that we will see each other soon and that nothing but death will ever part us again.

One of Marianne's consolations in those early days was to visit friends still living in the Holbeckshof barracks in Steele:[88]

This morning I spent a little while in Steele. It helped me bounce back a bit. The atmosphere there is excellent. I'm just sad I can't always be there with them. I feel cut off from everyone and everything. An awful feeling. They are planning communal evenings. Someone different is in charge of organizing the evening each time. It's marvellous how quickly people can fill the gaps in their ranks, even though they're always aware of them. Don't think that people here have forgotten you.

It was symptomatic of the divide that had grown between Marianne and her parents that, while Siegfried and Ine wanted at all costs to avoid being transferred to Holbeckshof with its lack of amenities and communal living, Marianne felt so much freer there. She revelled in the barracks' enforced communality and group spirit, and welcomed the change from the heavy material objects of the family home. Her response was a further sign of the enormous generational differences in the reaction to Nazi measures. Young people in their teens or early twenties who had not yet established a fixed way of life and had not yet acquired social status and material goods were capable of adapting to conditions simply unacceptable for older people. Within a week of Marianne writing these thoughts, for example, Artur Jacobs noted in his diary:[89]

In the barracks [. . .]
How many challenges do they have to face! Overnight, 300 people from every class, every age group, every occupation are thrown together, in a mad rush, without even the most basic things. (They can bring with them only what they are later allowed to take to the East, in effect nothing, compared with a normal existence.) No furniture, no cupboard,

no table, no mattresses (instead, straw sacks, sometimes filled with paper), one big stove (on which almost 100 women are supposed to do their cooking!). Under such conditions – who could expect everything to go smoothly? Particularly among people who are not used to each other and who have to learn almost everything about living together. Who could be surprised that there's constant collision, friction, discontent, reasonable and unreasonable demands?

They have to fix up their living area (in order to live at all), but who has any desire to make everything nice and comfortable when tomorrow it could all be over?

A devastating scene – the old headmaster, who is supposed to look after the children (there are still some here), sits in despair among his piled-up books, unable to come to terms with his fate.

'We live like dead men,' he said, 'spiritually adrift, in dirt and misery. When I think how we used to live . . .'

Tears welled up in his eyes.

What consolation can one offer? Every false word of comfort only aggravates the injury.

The difference between Marianne's perception and that of the weeping headmaster could hardly be more stark.

There was probably some measure of illusion in Marianne's perception. She had not been forced to go to the barracks or to abandon all her possessions. Those who had, like Imo Moszkowicz, were far less romantic in their description of the place. In retrospect, Moszkowicz felt that they were being drilled for life later in Auschwitz. Undoubtedly, part of Steele's appeal for Marianne was that it was Not Home. Every experience seemed defined by the growing antagonism between her and her parents, an antagonism that sometimes led her to take some uncharacteristic stances. For example, though a great lover of children, Marianne argued to a friend in the barracks that, confronted with the choice of abandoning her husband or her children, a woman should always go with her husband. 'Parents must be able to free themselves from their children.'[90]

Finally, on 3 May, almost two weeks after the Krombachs left Essen, a letter from Ernst arrived offering a first glimpse into conditions in Izbica:

Dearest,

Sadly I have not yet had any post from you. So I am waiting for something nice. What shall I write about? In terms of food and cleanliness, the conditions here are more extreme than anything we imagined; it's simply impossible to put them into words. Words could never convey the reality of life here. The Wild West is nothing to this. The attitudes and approaches to life here are so incomprehensible. Anyone not firmly grounded will find himself spiritually derailed for ever. There is neither culture nor morality, two things we once thought we could manage without. Once you experience the extremity of this place, you're cured of that particular view. It is terrible not to be able to help people. One is simply powerless in the face of it all!

I'm trying to give you some insight into what it's really like here. But it's impossible. I could fill twenty pages and you still wouldn't know. I'll save it until I can tell you face to face. Don't worry about me. I'm strong enough, and as long as I don't have the misfortune to go the way of all flesh, we'll see each other again. I know what to do and the thought of you keeps me going, too. I'm writing all this so openly so that you on no account pursue the plan with Bärchen. I am really happy that you do not have to be here and I pray to God every day to carry you to safety! Jeanne, I know that this is doubly hard for you. But if you trust me, you must be strong. I know that what's asked of us is almost inhuman; but we always wanted to achieve great things; so here it is, our first and probably hardest test. The word MUST stands above us and reunion is the goal that keeps us going.

I don't work – working is not the custom here. Where possible, I try to help, but the problems are so great and so many and my resources so limited that I can offer little in relation to what is needed. Every day I meet nice young people my own age so that I have something for myself. My love, I keep realizing that, although comparisons are possible, there is no one who is right for me as you are. The difference is so great!

Postal transfers are not always accepted. But we are allowed to receive money via letters and letter-parcels do get here. It's prob-

ably better not to send proper parcels. It is possible to put old clothes in letter-parcels. It is possible to receive food.

You must be terribly curious about the appearance of this place. There are 7,000 Jews, ruled by a Council of Elders, and the Council is ruled by the Gestapo. That might sound fine, but the reality is different. You might be able to sketch a rough picture of the place, but I doubt it would bear much resemblance to the reality.

Now the page is used up, Jeanne!

[. . .]

Shocked, Marianne wrote:[91]

Your letter from 28.4 arrived today, and all I can say is we cannot, we should not, we must not lose courage and hope. We have a goal to live for and it must give us the strength to cope with every challenge. The clock keeps ticking and every move of its hands brings us a step closer to the light. God puts only the good to the test. He is always with us — let us draw solace from that. Only if we are strong can we complete the task that we have set ourselves: to help others. We should be proud, my love, that things have not been made easy for us. I feel you completely as part of me: how could I live otherwise! Don't think that it's easy for me. But let's set ourselves tasks and work and then everything will be easier. For you there must be endless things to do. Don't try and achieve everything at once. Have patience, have patience. I believe in you, always, and know that you will manage. Are all your ideals in pieces? Don't give up, even so. Later, the two of us will pick up the fragments and piece them back together. Much will be destroyed, it's war, but out of the rubble new and better things will arise. We have strong hands.

Reason and feeling

These and subsequent letters show how far Marianne and Ernst had advanced since Marianne's stay in Berlin. Then, the emotional tone of their correspondence had been fairly conventional, with all the repetition of sentiment, uncertainty and occasionally jealousy that separation can bring. Now, they were living on a different plane. Often the strongest evidence of their love lay in what they chose *not* to say, in their restraint, their selflessness, the determinedly optimistic tone for each other's sake. 'What struck me,' commented Ernst, when the first of Marianne's diary-letters finally reached him, 'was that independently of each other we found the same words and sentences to express our feelings of separation.'[92] Above all, the two had concluded that the language of love and feelings could only burden the other, arouse desires that could not be fulfilled, and render separation unbearable. Later, Ernst articulated this thought explicitly:[93]

> *Our relationship, I feel, is the same as it ever was; no, it has become far deeper. Our yearning for each other increases in direct proportion to the length of our separation. All the more wonderful our reunion and a future life that can build on such admirable foundations. I think it's natural that we can't always suppress our feelings and now and then ignore what's rational, even if sadly the rational must predominate. Or perhaps it's that the rational is really an expression of the emotional, because each of us feels that it's better for the other this way. Always the two key factors: reason – feelings!*

From some of the letters, it is clear that theirs was not the only correspondence passing between Essen and Izbica at the time. For example, 'Bärchen', Marianne's co-worker in the Essen Community office, was corresponding with her friend Rudi Löwenstein. But like most of the Jews still in Essen, Bärchen was deported to Theresienstadt in July. Probably, no correspondence like Marianne's survived not because none existed but because by the summer of 1942 the recipients had all been deported and their property destroyed.

More unusual than the fact of getting letters through was the scale of material assistance Marianne managed to provide. After a slow start, we know that by the end of May 1942 Ernst had received a number of parcels from her. A recurrent theme in the mail from Izbica was the sheer pleasure these parcels gave their recipients – by supplementing their diet, providing capital in an environment where everything could be had for barter or money, as a sign of love and sacrifice, as a link to the outside world – in short, as the source of everything vital for Ernst's and the family's continued existence. Or rather, Ernst's letters convey that the value of these parcels went beyond what could be expressed in words. An outsider simply could not imagine their significance.[94]

Much of the communication out of Izbica from May onwards was limited to postcards with officially prescribed text by which the deportees were allowed to acknowledge receipt of parcels: 'We are healthy. We are being treated well. Deepest thanks for your post.' Marianne's papers include cards of this type sent by Ernst on 28 June, 4, 10, 17, 24 and 31 July and 8 and 14 August, but even these responses do not give an indication of the sheer volume of parcels Marianne was managing to send. From late July until the autumn Marianne developed a veritable cottage industry, begging and bartering dry goods (or being given them by sympathetic friends, family members or a friendly pastor, W. Keinath, from Wuppertal) to send to deportees in general and the Krombachs in particular. Marianne lived, she wrote, for the help she could provide Ernst and his family:[95]

You know my life has a deeper meaning: I exist for you and the awareness that this is so has allowed me to grow and keep on growing. My greatest worry is for you and the people we both hold dear. I want to help you, help you, help you as well and as much as I can. But you must overcome your inhibitions and tell me with absolute clarity what I can do. I beg you to do this with all my heart.

A few days later, on 11 August, Ernst noted:[96]

Last week you really spoiled me again. A large number of parcels arrived. 131, 135, 114, 115 – those were the numbers from last week. I think the numbers themselves speak volumes for your unceasing love.

By mid-August, then, it seems that more than a hundred small parcels had reached their addressees. By now, Marianne was dispatching them at a rate of several a day. Again and again, Ernst struggled to explain their significance.[97]

It is incredible what you have achieved with your daily packets of love. Not just the help you give us but also the signs that you're there make me so happy. There are no words of thanks for something like this . . . It's incredible. A thousand deepest thanks for all this proof of your love, and what love it is! It's as limitless as the love we feel too! Special wishes to your parents, Oe and Alfred, and other friends. Loving greetings and countless wishes! Your Ernst

The ragged thread

A dramatic and inspiring lifeline was thus sustained between Ladenspelderstrasse 47, Essen and Block III/443c, Izbica. However, soon after I began to piece together which letter had arrived when, it became clear that the lifeline was a ragged thread. This was not a correspondence in the conventional sense. On the contrary, although most of Marianne's parcels managed to reach their destination (though not in order), the post was completely erratic, sometimes taking four days, sometimes four weeks. Some letters or packages arrived completely overtaken by events, others still so fresh from the pen that the two lovers felt that they had almost touched each other.[98] For long periods they were writing to one another without knowing whether the post was arriving and without getting anything in return.

Marianne did not at first understand what caused the long intervals between Ernst's letters.[99] It gradually became clear to her, however, that there were severe çonstraints on what could be said and how much could be written. 'If you hear little from us, don't worry. We will, of course, write when we can,' wrote Rudi Löwenstein in June.[100]

From early May to the beginning of June, Marianne had to suffer four weeks without word from Ernst.[101] Towards the end of May she became particularly anxious because of news filtering back from other deportees:[102]

In the last few days, vague reports have reached us about conditions there. We hear that most people have gone. Where they have gone to, nobody knows: God alone knows where you and your family are. I won't say what I think, but I don't need to. Teddy [Bärchen] and I have continued to write letters to the old address and send them out as before. Is there any point . . .

Today I wrote the Council of Elders and asked for information about where you are. Is there any point . . . Love, love, I pray and believe and hope. Our imagination cannot keep up with reality, try hard as it might.

Marianne's fears were not ill-founded. It is impossible to say with certainty who was deported when, but in his study of the extermination camps, Yitzhak Arad notes a deportation of some 400 Jews from Izbica to Sobibor death camp on 15 May, and from Ernst's letters we will see that there were other deportations not listed by Arad.[103] Even so, it seems that the majority of the Essen deportees were still in Izbica in May.

Then, miraculously, a few days before Marianne's birthday on 7 June, a birthday card arrived from Ernst, sent on 31 May. With a whoop of relief and renewed confidence – 'you can hardly imagine my joy', she wrote to a friend[104] – she rounded off the first section of diary entries and put them into the post:[105]

Today, love, love, after five weeks the first card from you arrived. I probably don't need to say how happy this made me, Ernest. I am endlessly happy that you received my parcels. Now I'm full of belief and courage and without more ado I am going to put these diary pages into the parcel. The daily reports continue.

For Marianne, Ernst's card was a sign that God had not abandoned them[106] though from then to the end of July she again received very little mail. On 6 August, a detailed letter arrived, dated 5 July, conveying an idea of what Ernst's work was like. Another letter soon followed but, once again, the thread slipped and became caught up in the ineffable machinery of German censorship and the postal system. Only later did Marianne learn that sending letters from Izbica was officially punishable by the death penalty.[107]

At Ernst's end, although Marianne was sending post on an almost daily basis,[108] almost ten weeks went by with no letters from Essen, broken only at the end of June by the arrival of the parcel containing the first part of Marianne's journal: 'That was really a piece of you, how you live and love,' he responded.[109] By then, however, Ernst had realized that personal letters were often not getting through to Izbica at all, although Marianne could not yet know this. Money orders and parcels *were* being passed, and letters hidden in parcels, such as Marianne's letter-diaries, had a chance of reaching their destinee.[110]

The misery and anxiety generated by the inconsistent post can hardly be imagined, but when letters did get through, confirming that the writer was still alive and still thinking of the other, what joy they brought. In early August, after a lengthy wait, Marianne finally received a long letter from Ernst. She had to put pen to paper straightaway:[111]

My love, this evening Oe came back from Melitta with the letter.[112] Each such message awakens so much within me. Above all, I am so infinitely grateful for such a tangible sign that you are alive. I reach into it to find you, as you are now and in my memories. [. . .]

Again and again, I read your letters, late in the evening when it's quiet all around and we too are rendered quiet by the night. Then it's our inner voice that speaks – the voice that we listen to in our dreams as well, my love. And I had the same moment with the stars as you did. God makes them speak to me at the same time as to you and in the same language. We had the same feelings here, do you remember?

The letters have their biggest impact on me when I read them for the first time. Then they are at their most immediate. Then I am with you and everything around me ceases to exist.

By then, Marianne had an inkling that their communication was about to take a dramatic new turn.

7

Report from Izbica

Early in 1942, or possibly even late in 1941, certainly before Ernst was deported, the Strauss family had come to know a Christian Arras, the twenty-eight-year-old son, partner and heir of the owner of a truck dealership and repair garage in Essen. Marianne's recollection was that the garage was doing contract work for the SS and that Christian himself had joined that organization opportunistically in order to enjoy the business opportunities that its contacts offered. Marianne told me that she and Ernst had met Christian and his fiancée, Lilli, at Oe and Alfred's apartment:[1]

'So he knew him and me of course, and knew where Ernst had gone. I had told him, he knew the whole story. And one day he told me that he was going there, and if I wanted to take some stuff.'

Marianne's comment sounded so innocuous, I almost missed it. Then it hit me. Christian, doing business in the General Government, had offered to take anything Marianne liked to a Jewish deportee, Ernst. Marianne wondered if Christian was supplying vehicles to Izbica – if so, it was an incredible coincidence that this little town, a tiny part of the SS killing empire, should have been serviced by someone she knew in Essen. And then there was the equally extraordinary fact that Christian was willing to perform what might prove to be a dangerous mission.

On 2 August, Marianne packed a suitcase of things for Christian to take to her lover. At last, she had something real to live for.[2] Stowed in with the clothes, foodstuffs and other items was a letter:[3]

Actually, I don't need to write much, Ernst. What do you think of this? I've lived this moment a hundred times in my thoughts and wished, wished that I myself could bring you my love and best wishes. But we must thank God and be grateful. It is another sign that He means well with us.

Stapled to the back of the copy of this letter, I found a copy of a 'questionnaire' which Marianne had also sent:[4]

Here is a questionnaire so that you can answer systematically the burning questions which so concern us and which you have not or not fully answered. Above all, I beg you to be completely honest and not to think that we will find the truth a burden. Only if I really know how things are for you all can I rest easy.

1) *What do you do during the day; work; working hours?*
2) *How are you treated?*
3) *Income?*
4) *Do you get a ration or do you have to pay for food out of your own pocket?*
5) *Can you move about freely or only with permission, and who gives the permission?*
6) *Which organization has authority there and how do you interact with it?*
7) *Exact description of the living conditions and the hygiene.*
8) *Leisure activities (books, music), friendships, attitude of the comrades to moral and ethical questions.*
9) *Can you get the food you need? In particular, what is the situation as regards fats (butter etc.)?*
10) *Do you have to pay duty on parcels and letters and what determines the level of duty?*
11) *Can you really make use of our parcels and what is most useful?*
12) *What do you need particularly for your own use?*
13) *Do all the parcels sent you reach their destination and do you feel they arrive complete???*
14) *Do you think it would be a good idea to put a contents lists in each parcel?*

15) Do you have any idea or definite reports of the whereabouts of people sent on from there?

16) How many have gone? Where are Arthur and Else? So far, no news from them.

17) Activities and food for the children.

18) As far as you can tell, will you stay there or be sent on further?

Initially, there were problems with Christian's rendezvouz with Ernst. By 17 August, however, Marianne had certain knowledge that Christian would be in Izbica two days later, and she was confident he would be able to see Ernst:[5]

. . . the day after tomorrow he will be there. Countless wishes and thoughts accompany him. Again and again I have lived through the meeting in my mind, just as though it were happening to me. For us it is a glimpse behind the door with seven seals – and that is an understatement.

On 26 August, a telegram arrived in Essen and the following day a postcard, both indicating that Christian would soon be back and implying that he and Ernst had indeed managed to meet.[6]

Marianne's next diary entry is dated 3 September:[7]

My only love, Christian has now been back for a whole week. Only now can I fully comprehend what's happened. So much post! The bell rang late Saturday evening and I knew immediately who it was. And on Sunday, after I had your letters, I went to our little hill from last April. There was no one to interrupt me and YOU were with me as you were then. Love, my love.

On 'their hill' in the Stadtwald, Marianne sat and read for hours.

In a two-page covering note, Ernst listed everything he had sent:[8]

1 Letter to your parents

1 Letter to your parents, O. and you from my father, with notes from Katzenstein

1 Letter to you from Rudi

1 Letter to you, that was lying here, that I couldn't get out, partially out of date

1 Eighteen-page report for you

1 task list for you – four pages – with two letters from my father.

The letters to Marianne's parents have not survived, nor the letters from Ernst's father which accompanied the task list. The partly out-of-date letter to Marianne may well be one of the many letters from Izbica which she saved, but it is no longer possible to identify it with certainty. The other letters have all survived and are clearly identifiable.

Rudi wrote just to thank Marianne for the things she had sent and for the unbelievable moment of contact she had arranged. Rudi's wife Grete also took the opportunity to write: 'You can hardly imagine what this means to us and how happy we were to receive your wishes through Chr.'[9] Both used the brief opportunity to ask her to maintain links with those of their relatives who had eluded deportation.

One real difference between Ernst's task list[10] and all previous communication was that he could, at last, openly name relatives and friends to contact, to provide with news, to beg for help and to engage in support; he lists name after name in Germany, Portugal, Holland, Spain and South America. If the prospect of material help from such quarters seemed somewhat illusory, since the letter also revealed to Marianne that currently no parcels or letters at all were being delivered to Izbica, there was yet hope that the conditions might change in the future. Also, it seems that the Krombachs still had a good collection of fine porcelain and other belongings in store in Essen, which could be used to reward assistance rendered. Again, taking advantage of this moment of open communication, Ernst also proposed a way of encoding information in the official postcards he was allowed to send acknowledging receipt of parcels:[11]

> *If the date is at the top left, you can't send anything. Top right: possibly (i.e., cautiously try to send something). Bottom left: you can write again. If the 'the' is abbreviated to 't.'[12] you can send only small packets with a value of less than 25 zloty duty. If it is written out in full then you can send larger parcels. If the month is written as a number, then be careful, because an evacuation is imminent. If I write 1942 everything is OK, if only '42', we will certainly be evacuated. Wait till news possibly gets through. This applies from now on. (Not to my card from 22.)*

Of course, such code could be of use only if the normal post started up again. Only the existence of the alternative channel opened by Christian made the suspension of communication seem less serious than it was.

But the main item in Ernst's package was the eighteen-page account of conditions in Izbica written in pencil in regular, even lines in Ernst's neat handwriting. The letter, which Marianne had handed me in June 1996, was the starting point for this book; it is one of very few extant contemporary accounts of Izbica as the Final Solution was underway, perhaps even the only one.[13] There are some post-war survivor reports which I was able to consult in Yad Vashem. There are also the recently published reminiscences of a survivor, Thomas (Toivi) Blatt, who had grown up in Izbica.[14] By email and later in a personal interview, Mr Blatt gave me further information and photographs. But Ernst's lengthy, measured, detailed contemporary report with its mixture of facts and perceptions is extraordinarily rare, not simply for Izbica, but for the experience of all German Jews deported to Poland generally.

22/VIII.42.

My love, my dearest!

You can imagine my feelings and my joy! Everything you sent us, which for a while has removed our worries about our daily bread! The conversations and encounters, everything all at once, raised our spirits and naturally filled me with excitement. It's all so extraordinary, thoughts come thick and fast. First of all, I can't stop thinking about what this means for us. Let me say something important about this right away. Like me, you're surely wondering how we can best use this bridge for us. How can we come together? Is it something we can take upon ourselves and how could we do it? But even if we assume that it would be possible for me to return: it would be very difficult and dangerous. There would be little chance of my staying there [in Essen], given all the checks and controls and the uncertainty of how long it would be for. The most important and impossible aspect, though, is that I would be exposing my parents to grave danger, indeed putting their lives at risk. So we must put the idea out of our heads.

Christian told me that your journey [out of the country] is no

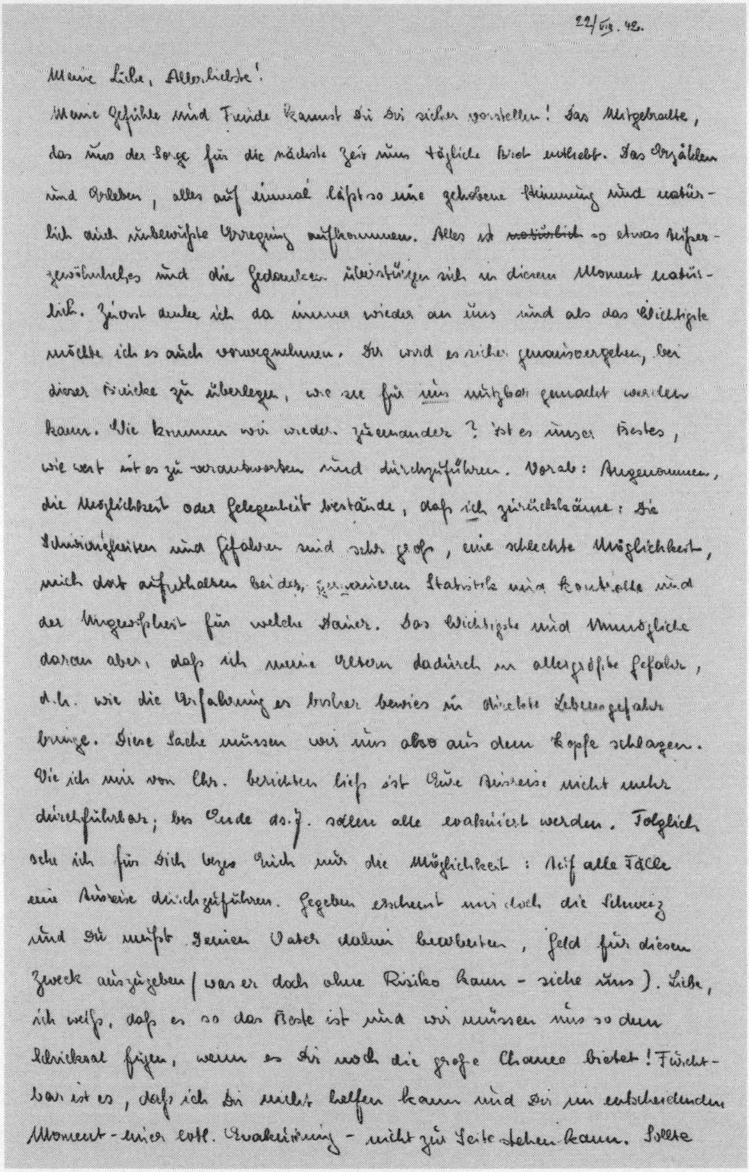

22/VIII. 42.

Meine Liebe, Allerliebste!

Meine Gefühle und Freude kannst Du Dir sicher vorstellen! Das Mitgebrachte, das uns der Sorge für die nächste Zeit ums tägliche Brot enthebt. Das Erzählen und Erleben, alles auf einmal läßt so eine gehobene Stimmung und natürlich auch unbewußte Erregung aufkommen. Alles ist ~~natürlich~~ so etwas Außergewöhnliches und die Gedanken überstürzen sich in diesem Moment natürlich. Zuerst denke ich da immer wieder an uns und als das Wichtigste möchte ich es auch vorwegnehmen. Dir wird es sicher genauso ergehen, bei dieser Brücke zu überlegen, wie sie für uns nutzbar gemacht werden kann. Wie kommen wir wieder zueinander? Ist es unser Bestes, wie weit ist es zu verantworten und durchzuführen. Vorab: Angenommen, die Möglichkeit oder Gelegenheit bestände, daß ich zurückkäme: Die Schwierigkeiten und Gefahren sind sehr groß, eine schlechte Möglichkeit, mich dort aufzuhalten bei der genaueren Statistik und Kontrolle und der Ungewißheit für welche Dauer. Das Wichtigste und Unmögliche daran aber, daß ich meine Retter dadurch in allergrößte Gefahr, d.h. wie die Erfahrung es bisher bewies in direkte Lebensgefahr bringe. Diese Sache müssen wir uns also aus dem Kopfe schlagen. Wie ich mir von Chr. berichten ließ ist Eure Ausreise nicht mehr durchführbar; bis Ende d.J. sollen alle evakuiert werden. Folglich sehe ich für Dich bezw. Euch nur die Möglichkeit: Auf alle Fälle eine Ausreise durchzuführen. Gegeben erscheint mir doch die Schweiz und Du mußt Deinen Vater dahin bearbeiten, Geld für diesen Zweck auszugeben (was er doch ohne Risiko kann – siehe uns). Liebe, ich weiß, daß es so das Beste ist und wir müssen uns so dem Schicksal fügen, wenn es Dir noch die große Chance bietet! Furchtbar ist es, daß ich Dir nicht helfen kann und Dir im entscheidenden Moment – einer evtl. Evakuierung – nicht zur Seite stehen kann. Sollte

Page 1 of Ernst's letter

*longer possible and that by the end of the year everyone will have
been evacuated [deported]. I see only one possibility for you and
your family: at all costs get out. Switzerland seems a possibility
and you must work on your father to spend money to this end
(which he can do without risk, as we learned). My love, I know
this is best. If fate should still offer you a chance, we must take it!
It is terrible that I cannot help you and that at the crucial moment
of a possible evacuation I cannot stand by your side. Should
the evacuation take place around the time of Christian's second
journey you will probably try to come with him.*[15] *As far as I can
judge this seems to involve the least risk. But – as I said – from this
end I can do nothing to help and I must advise you not to come
here voluntarily. We must try and stay alive for each other's sake,
and if you come here without being forced to do so any sensible
person would think you mad. But why should I go on about it? I'll
give you a report so you can see for yourself. I realize that I could
just as easily write a whole novel about it – a factual novel. But I
hope that I can capture the conditions on a couple of pages. It will
definitely not be easy given the abnormality of life here, which lacks
all formal or logical basis. Only someone who has experienced it
can really understand it. Perhaps Christian will be able to make
some of the incomprehensible things comprehensible. Perhaps I
should begin at the beginning, directing my thoughts back four
months.*

Here, Ernst gives the account of Derendorf and the crowded train
compartment cited earlier and goes on:

*In the evening, we arrived in Izbica in the rain. We were received
by the Jewish Police and SS and shoved into cave-like dwellings.
An optimist might think of Carmen if the reality hadn't been so
hard, particularly for the elderly.*

*Thus we arrived in Izbica and gradually we 'adjusted'. At this
point I must describe the environment. Izbica is a village hidden in
a valley. It used to be home to about 3,000 Polish Jews. Its
geographical situation is superb. The 'houses' are mainly built of
wood and clay and consist of one or two 'rooms'. Everything filthy*

and infested. A few of the houses have the luxury of beds, tables, chairs or cupboards. We ourselves live less comfortably than most but, on the other hand, we are closer to the outskirts. We look out on to greenery and freedom, in a peaceful, sunny and stink-free (no sewers) environment. 12 of us: 4 Rudis,[16] 3 Katzensteins,[17] 2 Meyers (relatives of Rudi's) and we 3 in a hole, 2×4 metres. At the front: 2 tables, 2 wooden benches we made ourselves, 4 chairs which we 'organized', 1 stove; at the back, on the luxury of a wooden floor (elsewhere clay) and sacks of straw the 'beds', side-by-side on the floor. As so often happens, the wives find it hard to co-operate – not least because of the limited space and the fact that three families have to share their cooking on one small wood-burning stove. This town of cave-like huts with its many hiding places would be absolute paradise for a scout group.

Now to the 'Jewish state'. Before the first transport arrived here, Izbica was cleansed of its Jewish residents.[18] I.e. the SS drove them out with weapons and clubs. The first transport arrived here in March from Czechoslovakia (from Theresienstadt where the people had been held for two months). The second transport also came from Czechoslovakia and thus the important positions were taken by the Czechs. After that the transports came thick and fast: Aachen, Nuremberg, Aachen-Düren, Breslau, Essen, Stuttgart, Frankfurt, two from Slovakia, two from Theresienstadt etc. So now there were three different categories [of Jews] here: Germans, Poles, Czechs. The German character you know: military discipline, reliable, hard-working. The Pole is the opposite: ill-disciplined, lazy, dirty, uncomradely, very good at business. One should not judge them too harshly. External conditions and pressures have made the Pole what he is. I was obliged to study the Polish character at length when I arrived. They are extremely intelligent, talented and quick on the uptake. An eight-year-old boy who has never had the opportunity to go to school writes his name with a speed and fluidity that are beyond some of our adults. Although he had certainly never seen a guitar before, he held mine correctly immediately. Even though he produced discords, he did so with rhythm. The Czechs, too, are hard to deal with. Why?

They see themselves solely as Czechs who were driven out of their
country by the German invaders (understandably, since they were
not affected until war started) and regard us as Germans. Unlike
us, they had not been forced to regard themselves as Jews and led
back to Judaism.[19] *The slogan of this motley crew is: 'Sauve, qui*
peut' or ME, ME, and after me my relatives (nepotism without
end), and forget about the rest.

The region contains several villages like Izbica, occupied by
Polish and other evacuated Jews, Polish Aryans and a few ethnic
Germans; there's no barbed wire (thank God). The district is ruled
by two SS men and a sub-machine gun. The village itself is run,
under SS supervision, by the so-called Judenrat, with responsibili-
ties such as law and order, sanitation, disinfection, burial, supplies,
firewood, housing, soup kitchen, etc., etc. The Judenrat is made
up of leaders of the individual transports. But in the course of time
so many arrived that the newcomers (the Germans, of course,
including my father) were stuck in a Working Committee. The
committee has no say in anything, and if anybody dares to open
his mouth, he is rendered harmless by the simple expedient of being
shoved on to one of the evacuation transports that leave here from
time to time. The Judenrat thus consists of Czechs whose level of
correctness and humanity is certainly open to criticism. Alongside
it there is a Polish Judenrat, whose leader has managed to grab
most of the power (i.e. over both councils). All in all, it's very
difficult for us Germans who came with so many illusions about
comradeship and co-operation.

The legal code is simple to describe: the death penalty. The
hangman's assistants who haul out unfortunates and sometimes
go looking for them are also Jews. Everything is forbidden; the
penalty as above. Leaving the ordained district before 7 a.m. or
after 7 p.m. Bartering, buying or selling or speaking to Polish
Aryans. Baking bread. Buying rationed groceries such as butter,
eggs, bread, potatoes, etc., etc. Sending letters or other messages.
Leaving the city limits. Owning gold, German money or indeed
any money, jewellery, silver, etc., etc. Unfortunately, such offences
(if that is what they are) have cost many lives. On arrival, the last

meagre possessions such as spare underclothes, suits, coats, shoes, leather goods, jewellery, wedding rings, etc. were confiscated. Some people were taken away and shot as a warning. This brings me to something that affects us both: the gold rings, our investment capital. An insufficient number was collected from our transport. So a few people were selected to collect rings. They were going to be shot.[20] The transport leader too looked as if he would lose his neck. A last attempt was made to buy up rings or slip in rolled gold. People went from house to house and took down names. At this point I sacrificed the most precious thing I have from you; our ring. You know what I am going to ask: send me another one, new! I feel the loss terribly. I miss it very much. My only consolation is the feeling that I helped and probably saved others. If it's no longer possible to send things, Christian can certainly bring it with him. If the post starts up again, put the ring in semolina (or similar), in blancmange powder (and reseal). I will always look carefully. For the moment, I hold on to your letter (which I carry around with me as a substitute) and your many larger and smaller presents (pendants,[21] pictures, etc.).

In the meantime, many transports have left here. Of the approximately 14,000 Jews who arrived only 2–3,000 are still here. They go off in cattle trucks, subject to the most brutal treatment, with even fewer possessions, i.e. only the clothes they are wearing. That is one rung further down the ladder. We have heard nothing more of these people (Austerlitz, Bärs, etc.) After the last transport, the men who were working outside the village returned to find neither wives, nor children, nor their possessions. (We've been somewhat lucky in any case because later transports have come in without any men. They'd already been taken out at Lublin.) If you know how, however, you can usually avoid such evacuations by going into hiding and simply reappearing after the transport has left. We learned this from the Poles . . . As far as punishments or shootings are concerned the Poles are usually 'favoured' – poor consolation to us. A German is seen as more of a human being – not surprising given the ragged appearance of the Poles (who have more money than one realizes). Whenever I've had the opportunity to join the

police I've always refused. Mainly because of the unpleasant work:
Jews against Jews. But I was unable to avoid getting involved in
the evacuation of Polish Jews. You have to suppress every human
feeling and, under supervision of the SS, drive the people out with
a whip, just as they are – barefoot, with infants in their arms. There
are scenes which I cannot and will not describe but which will take
me long to forget. But that only as an aside, because I just thought
of it. Basically I have, thank God, a healthy constitution and retain
a balanced, clear view. I only think of these inhuman experiences
in my dreams.

Food is a principal concern for everyone here. Many go under
through malnutrition. There's no one here to care for them. There
is some 'welfare', which provides hardly any help (water soup).
With exemplary inhumanity, the Czechs in the Judenrat put poor
people on the next available transport. Various private individuals
give lunch to people. We and the Rudis look after needy people
from Essen. Those who have no money, no relatives, no acquaint-
ances in Germany to send them things and nothing left to sell must
either starve or steal. At the moment the vegetable harvest is good.
We three can be very content. (We're eating off your plates.)
Vegetable or barley soup, potatoes (pancakes or salad) sometimes
with meat, blancmange, cucumbers, vegetables, beans, peas. Nutri-
tious fare, which lacks only fats. Sometimes we buy or barter butter
or oil. Because we are short of fats we eat a huge amount. But
there's another reason too: fear of starvation and the drive for
self-preservation. It has become such a mania that 90 per cent of
conversations are about food. And when everyone talks about it
so much you naturally feel hungry even if you are not really in
need of food. For example, today I had two large slices of bread in
the morning with cucumber and tomato (also stolen apples and
carrots). For lunch, I had potatoes and cabbage. In the evening
potato salad, beetroot soup and semolina pudding (with milk and
eggs). Coffee with half a large slice of bread. It's like this every
day, sometimes a bit more, sometimes a bit less. I haven't wasted
away yet. So, a satisfactory, adequate diet.

That brings me to monetary values. A Reichsmark is normally

2 zloty, on the black-market as much as 2.80. Otherwise the black-market prices are pure extortion.[. . .]You can get everything here from whipped cream, ice-cream and chocolate to Schnapps etc. at horrendous prices but excellent quality.[. . .]My love, I have written the whole afternoon. Tomorrow the report continues: work, hygiene etc. For today, good night! How well will I sleep?

Yours!

23/VIII.42

Dearest Jeanne!

The report continues. I am so happy, finally to be able to write to you freely in such detail and with no pressure, just as you have doubtless long wished me to. I wish I had much more time to write. Let me not forget to touch on a subject, if only very briefly. This morning, Sunday, I dressed just as I used to with you, only more summery in trousers and shirt. I lost some time looking for a new place to live. I found a room for us three and hope also to be able to organize some furniture and even some beds (bedframes). But send things to the old address until you hear for sure, because it's not 100 per cent certain that we'll move. Even if we do move into III/440 the post will definitely be forwarded. I'm particularly happy about this move for my parents: peace and more comfort. Rudi's parents are moving into the same house. The families will each have their own room and yet be next to each other. (In the meantime unclear if it will be approved for Rudi.) Yesterday I finished by talking about the post. Only money-orders are getting through at the moment. Should parcels be resumed, please do not send silk underwear (duty too high), peppermint or fruit teas – we've got loads and can't get rid of it; everything else is desirable. Thank God neither we nor you on our behalf need have any worries about our food for a while even if the post remains blocked (and we stay here). As the owner of a sweet tooth I must say that I often enjoyed your 'sweet' parcels even more than the others. We don't spend money on sweets or biscuits, and as a non-smoker and a 'solid individual', I often yearn for something sweet. The *home-baked biscuits were wonderful. You seem to have known my weakness and gave me particular pleasure with these regular dispatches. We received no letter post, only the three cards right at the beginning. Your letters in the packages all seem to have arrived. But you must be very careful about confirming receipt of my post, because I'm taking an enormous risk in sending it. You mention having written three letters, none of which reached me. Let's hope they don't get into the wrong hands[. . .]What a pity you didn't include a longer letter with the other things. Well, I can't complain – despite the external conditions I can call myself a happy man at the moment, the happiest man in Izbica! What you have done for us through Christian* is absolutely unbelievable. *But more on that later.*

Now, you'll be certainly be interested to hear about my daily routine and my work. My father has various responsibilities on the Working Committee, has lost weight and doesn't look particularly good; he spends all day in the office and has to listen to the woes of people looking to him for help which he is ill-placed to give. At best he can reduce their misery. My mother is on the go from morning till night. She too has got thin but does an enormous amount. The cooking alone takes a great deal of time, then shopping, selling (the Poles come to the house), washing and so on. My mother has a heavy work-load. Things which are no problem on a gas stove take hours in these primitive conditions. I myself probably look the best. Some say better than I did at home. I take good care of my body because I want to survive. I eat everything which comes my way and so far, without having done anything particularly to earn them, I have had some lucky breaks. Most people suffer because they are doing unaccustomed heavy work on inadequate rations. But from the first day, I've been doing a job of my choosing (I'm still doing the same job).[22] *Unlike many others I wasn't sent to a work camp or put to heavy labour with bad treatment. The earnings in these camps are meagre, usually an inadequate daily ration of a mere quarter-loaf of bread, coffee and water soup, perhaps a few zlotys a week – but usually less. I do not earn anything, or rather I earn a ration card for bread which entitles me to a 2kg loaf for 3 zlotys (4kg a month!!). Otherwise I have the advantage that I pay no rent or water rate (there are only six pumps in the whole of Izbica) and that I can use the bath (a wonderful invention, the nicest in the whole of Izbica, a shower bath) once a week for free. Sometimes I get an extra half a loaf where I work. It's a brickworks which is standing idle, a large complex of buildings and estates under the control of a German director from the SS. I work for this director as gardener in his private garden. The treatment is generous. I am cock of the roost because I have a whole harem of girls around me to whom I assign work. Thanks to my pedagogic talents I have managed to bring the Polish girls, who think any kind of work is crazy, to the point where the director is satisfied with the state of his fields. The tomatoes and cucumbers etc. we have managed to grow are real masterpieces. I get on well with the head gardener. My daily programme runs: get up 6.30 and wash; 7.00 report for work, allocation of tasks; at 8 I disappear off to the Order Police to give gymnastics lessons to the youth of Izbica. Something which provides me with stimulus and variety and contact with the police. At 10 back to the garden. 12–13 is lunch, 13–16 more work. The work is fabulous, on the hill in the open, with fresh, healthy air, surrounded by nature, almost naked, tanned – a contrast to all the misery down in the village. After work, I try to help my mother with the bartering. I am now the perfect cook, and licking the pot reminds me of times gone by. I am also a fireman and have to take part in drills twice a week.*

Unfortunately, the day is not as rosy or calm as this suggests. We have become used to shootings. No week goes by without something happening: evacuation, round-ups of people on the street for work in the vicinity, visits from outside SS, house searches, confiscation of particular items, etc., etc. Recently on one morning alone more than twenty Polish Jews were shot for baking bread ... Our lives consist of uncertainty and insecurity. There could be another evacuation tomorrow, even though the officials concerned say that there won't be any more. It becomes more and more difficult to hide, given how few people are here now –

particularly as there is always a given target that has to be met. The Wild West was nothing to this!

'Hygiene' is a joke. Everything filthy, lice (particularly clothes lice, which spread typhus), fleas, bugs. There are few latrines. Sewage flows through unpaved streets (stench, illness). One illness is very common here: a high temperature with no other symptoms. It goes as quickly as it comes, but it leaves you weaker. Diarrhoea is equally common. Your Tamalbein has been used up already. Perhaps you could provide some more, or tar compresses. Neusamag[23] is useful too to deal with the flu symptoms brought on by sudden changes in the weather. Sometimes a cloudburst in the morning sends such floods of water through the streets that no one can venture out and the houses suddenly have 'running water'. By the afternoon, the bright sunshine makes everything dry. At the moment, the days are hot and the nights cold. Otherwise, we are adequately provided for with medicines thanks to your so thoughtfully assembled parcels.

There is no 'social life' here to speak of. Understandable, given the conditions, worries and the sauve qui peut *complex. Concerts, lectures and music belong to another world; 25-zloty novels pass from hand to hand. Personal relations are limited to trade or remain purely superficial. You have to search for real friendships with a microscope. I myself don't feel the lack of these people. They have nothing to give me. There are people here from every country and of every kind. My knowledge of humanity will soon be complete! But no one even comes close to you! I'd need only to stick out my hand in this superficial place to conquer a heart or two. Conceited? No. First of all, there are more women than men. Second, my friendly manner, which stops short at a certain point, seems to exert an attraction on the girls. Perhaps it's a flaw in my character and I do it consciously, out of arrogance and confidence in our relationship. In general, I don't 'lust' after any of the girls, just after one person whom I can't find here.[. . .]Otherwise I yearn for books, which are a rare item. The Poles have only Polish or Yiddish books. The only better-quality book I managed to lay my hands on was* Niels Lyhne *by Jacobsen. I liked it and found it*

*dealt with real issues in an interesting way. The style didn't suit
100 per cent. Otherwise, I've read one of the better sort of trashy
novel, The Career of Doris Hart; vulgar, entertaining and many
pages! I also pore over old newspapers, rescued from parcels.*

*That is the end of my report, or rather sketch. Christian can
probably give you more detail about things I have only touched
on or not mentioned at all. I have written to you as it is, authenti-
cally. But there is so much misery that it can't be put into words.
A picture of Herr Simon, the father of Eugen from the Mas-
chinenstrasse, could speak more than three volumes. Half mad
with despair, undernourished, beaten black and blue, he returns at
the weekend from his work outside and finds nothing: his wife,
child and sister have been transported, his belongings have disappeared . . . a case of particularly bad fortune, but the daily misery
here.*

*Jeanne, this is not for you! Many more will perish, of that I am
sure. I have the will to survive, sustained by the thought of you.
We can draw only one conclusion, as I did at the beginning of the
letter. We need not flinch from saying that we miss and need each
other almost all the time. I can't make any pretence about that.
But only in my quieter moments. Otherwise, I am glad to know
that you are safe. Hard as life is for us at the moment, something
grand will emerge from it. This proof of our love for each other is
such a foundation for our future life! If only we were at that point
now! When I am with you in my thoughts and dreams, it seems
like a fairy tale. What a miracle it would be to feel you in my arms
again. How one learns here to see the value of life – and of bread,
food, chair and bed! It would be a good lesson for some, if only it
did not demand such a high price!*

*I have just reread your questionnaire. I think that these eighteen
pages have answered it satisfactorily. It is a time of insecurity and
unrest, but we will survive it with hope, confidence and . . . luck.
Now you know the harsh reality of my life, but at least you have
the certainty of definite knowledge. God will protect and help us
as He has done so far. He will bless us and steer us in the right
direction! So far I cannot complain! Stay strong and courageous*

*and do not worry! Easier said than done, but trusting one another
we can do it!*

    Fondest kisses! E

Understanding Ernst's letter

What can have been the impact of this extraordinary letter on Marianne?
Each line, each paragraph, must have sent her spinning from horror, to
hope, to amazement at the tenacity and strength of character of the
human spirit in general and of Ernst in particular, then to fear and back
again.

What must have made the letter especially hard for her to comprehend
was its mixture of normality and horror, 'liveability' and squalor. In
part, Marianne herself was responsible for this uneven picture: amidst
general squalor, she had provided the Krombachs with riches. Thanks
to her, they were eating remarkably well. It is also clear that Ernst
himself could make no overall sense of the conditions around him; even
within the confines of this one letter, Ernst's mood and judgement seem
to fluctuate. The letter's shifting perspective shows how a contemporary
account differs from post-war testimony. In 1942, when Ernst wrote
this letter, Europe's Jews were not operating with a collective concept
of the 'Holocaust' that gave shape and 'logic' to their experiences. They
probably did not yet know what the endpoint was. Until the moment
they were selected for murder, life went on, in the nooks and crannies
between the Nazi ordinances.

To some extent, the striking juxtaposition of the bearable and the
barbaric was also a product of the Lublin region's distinctive character.
In other parts of Poland or in Lithuania, Jews were cleaned out of the
countryside and concentrated in large ghettoes. But because Lublin had
originally been designated as a Jewish reservation, the Jews were not
concentrated but dispersed into the smaller communities. This explains
the background to Ernst's experience, close to nature on the edge of a
small town with no barbed wire.

Something Marianne will not even have noticed was how German

Ernst was. A wry insight into the 'Germanness' of the deportees was provided by the native of Izbica, Thomas Blatt. When we met in Frankfurt, I showed him some of Ernst's correspondence. He pointed out the address: Block III/443c, Izbica a./Wiepiz, Kreis Krasnystaw, Distrikt Lublin, General Government. He told me that a similarly formal address figured on other German postcards he had seen, something that had bemused him for a long time because Izbica wasn't divided into blocks. But as he had recently learned from a Polish survivor, the German and Czech *Jewish* Councils had introduced blocks to improve administration.

For his part, Ernst's impressions since leaving German territory were those of a young man used to order, cleanliness, efficiency and plain-dealing, expectations which even the years of Nazi rule had not completely dispelled. In April, on the train to Izbica, Ernst's enthusiastic assertion that the order and cleanliness of the landscape showed the German influence placed him squarely within his native culture.[24] Ernst shared many of the prejudices of his countrymen, as is particularly apparent in his attitude to the Polish Jews. His reaction to the dirt and disorder is understandable, but because they fit his pre-existing prejudices, he clearly assumed that the Polish environment he encountered had always been thus, rather than being the product of war. In fact, Thomas Blatt's autobiography shows Izbica had enjoyed a thriving social and cultural life before the war, which had been wiped out by the Germans. The Izbica community had undoubtedly been poor, but conditions were transformed by the German invasion. Up to the time when many of its Polish occupants were deported in March 1942, the town was overwhelmed by the influx of Jews from all parts of the country. Ernst saw nothing of the social and religious distinctions within the Polish community, about which Blatt informs us. He never suspected that the inflated prices for goods were the result of the wealth brought there by newcomers such as himself – prices which the locals could barely afford.[25]

But alongside such prejudices, in many ways Ernst embodied all that was best about German youth. It was typical that, as a former youth leader, Ernst could not help but notice that the opportunities for hiding in Izbica made it ideal territory for a scout group. He continued to provide gymnastics instruction for the young, sought to help his parents where possible. As a humane, generous and idealistic boy, he found the commitment to ruthless self-preservation of many of those on the Jewish Council unpalatable. But the truth was, as he acknowledged, that it was often difficult to do much different. No doubt the hopeless Polish victims, shoved on to the extermination train by Ernst on the occasion when he was drafted in to help, experienced him no differently from the other orderlies involved. Still, there *was* a difference. Ernst was not about looking after number one. He was aware that there was a chance to escape – but to do so would have abandoned his parents to the next deportation train, and that he was not willing to do. In the final note that came with the report, Ernst even found time to worry whether Marianne had found a niche at home that she could call her own, where she could read and write in peace. From someone living with eight people in one room, that took more than a small degree of empathy.

Despite Ernst's protestations, Marianne must have worried whether Ernst really was painting a faithful picture of conditions. His letter was clearly designed both to deter and to reassure: Marianne should not be tempted to follow him; she should be given enough realistic detail to feel she understood; but she should not be unduly alarmed. In survivor testimonies from Izbica, I read about events in the summer of 1942 with which Ernst must have been familiar but which he does not mention here. In the testimonies deposited at Yad Vashem, the regular beatings and shootings emerge more clearly. Thomas Blatt told me that the two Gestapo officials, Engels and Klemm, beat and executed Jews on the street on a regular basis.[26] Another survivor, Hejnoch Nobel, recorded that an ethnic German called Schultz, who became Izbica's mayor, trained his Alsatian to attack people wearing white armbands (i.e., Jews) for sport. Nobel saw a woman being murdered in this way as she returned from drawing water.[27] There is much more in this vein and worse. This kind of terror is largely absent from Ernst's account, though he must have been aware of it.

I wondered whether Ernst was telling Marianne all he knew about the so-called evacuations to the East. Given that the letter is so well informed on other points, is it possible that Ernst did not know the deportation trains' destination?[28] According to Yitzhak Arad, up to August 1942 news of the activities of Belzec and Sobibor extermination camps (the destination of most of the trains removing Jews from the Lublin region) had not yet permeated much of the General Government. In August and September, Warsaw Jews arrived in Belzec and Treblinka with no idea of their imminent fate.[29] Sobibor remained so secret that in January 1943 Jews were still arriving unaware of the implications. On the other hand, Thomas Blatt says that his family heard about the Chelmno gas vans as early as December 1941, and that soon after the first major deportation from Izbica in March 1942 they learned that the unfortunates had been murdered in Belzec.[30] Blatt's account is, of course, written with hindsight, and he himself acknowledges that his family was not sure whether to believe this information. Blatt also acknowledges that the German Jews were less aware and less inclined to believe such rumours than their Polish counterparts. From August/September 1942 on, though, rumours and information about the camps and the fate of the deportees spread fairly fast through the Jews remaining in the ghettoes and labour camps of the General Government. On 20 September, an underground newspaper in Warsaw gave details of Treblinka.[31] It is thus just possible that when Ernst wrote to Marianne, he still did not know the truth – but his ignorance would not last much longer. What he did know was that those who had been taken had left only with what they had on their backs. Nothing good could come of such a departure. What could their destination be?

Ernst's last words to Marianne were written in a cover note accompanying the letters. He expressed once again his sheer amazement at what Marianne and Christian had achieved and repeated that she could not imagine the value of her supplies. Christian had told him what efforts Marianne made to assemble the parcels. Only now do we learn the full scale of the gifts she sent with Christian – a suitcase full of sweaters, jackets, food and much more. Ernst said they would sell some of the things because they needed to ensure liquid assets in case of another evacuation. Ernst asked Marianne to reward Christian generously from the Krombach property in storage in Essen.

At last, Ernst had to put down his pen:

Although I often physically yearn for you, physical desire has taken second place to the strength and purity of our love. This despite or, rather, because of our hard separation. I had to struggle with physical desire but it is no longer a problem. Possibly it is still there, unconsciously adding to my yearning for you. I know that above all I want you as a person, and that is everything to me.

My love, you have no fewer worries than we do. I wish I had the strength to be with you and protect you. Daily air raids? God will and must help. Nothing else is conceivable! Every evening I pray for us. Despite the general harshness of conditions, there have always been some gestures of leniency. We all hope to return soon.

My dear Jeanne! Thank you for everything, everything! You are always with me, as I with you. I feel now as I did when the train was leaving. This letter must go or it will never get out and you won't get even a line from me. Anything that is missing, Christian will tell you!

If only I could take you in my arms and kiss you . . .

Eternally yours, Ernst

Marianne and Christian Arras

We can imagine the Krombachs' reaction when this tall German man in uniform turned up in the camp, laden with goodies. Ernst could not believe it – and neither can we. Marianne told me Christian Arras was in the SS. What kind of SS man was that?

Marianne felt very ambivalent about Christian Arras. She remembered that he and his girlfriend Lilli had come to know the Strauss family through a sale of household goods organized by Oe. Lilli and Christian were setting up house at the time and little was to be had in the shops. Lilli, a youthful and elegant young woman, whom Marianne remembered as 'a lovely girl, very nice', hit it off with Oe straight away and they became very friendly. Over the next few months Christian, too, became friendly with Alfred and Oe. Marianne remembered that Lilli and Oe shared a taste in clothes, and for her lively aunt, cut off from so much, any contact with the outside world was welcome. Moreover, there was the importance of getting cash and coupons in return for clothes and other items that the family could not use. Christian and Lilli used to bring Oe and Alfred foodstuffs 'because of course you couldn't get anything, really very nice'. But, she went on:[32]

'. . . he was an opportunist, entirely an opportunist. He became very wealthy, they were very well off, working for the SS, repairing all these things. So in a way that was how he became useful. And they were useful, but of course they were very well paid for it, and in the end they got a lot of my aunt's things, just to keep and give back after the war if they had returned. And after the war I only saw him once.'

I think, however, that Marianne herself realized that money was not a plausible explanation for Christian's action. There is no doubt that at a time when quality goods were very hard to come by, the Strauss family did provide some items on a permanent basis and others for safe-keeping which were very useful to a couple setting up home. The latter included some oil paintings, a brass chandelier, a wardrobe, a mirror and other items of exceptional quality. But there is clear post-war evidence that, unlike other recipients of Strauss family property, the Arrases regarded many of these goods as only temporarily in their possession.[33] In any case, whatever largesse the Strauss family were willing to bestow, it is unlikely that Marianne's parents would have wanted to spend heavily to benefit the Krombachs, whom they did not know particularly well. And although Ernst suggested rewarding Christian out of Krombach property, this arrangement had clearly not been worked out in advance. So it is just not credible that Christian took the parcels to Izbica for the material rewards.

Marianne had yet another interpretation of Christian's motives:[34]

'I think he just enjoyed taking risks. He was a . . . dare-devil type and would probably have been a bit of a juvenile delinquent in his time, like so many of the SS. I never trusted Christian Arras because he was too much of a wind bag. And I could never really fathom . . . why should a man like that do it? What was in it for him? I don't know . . . What was in it for him, I *assume*, was just the daredevilry of it . . .'

Christian had liked Ernst, he probably had liked Marianne, and he certainly had liked her uncle Alfred. But that, Marianne felt, wasn't enough reason to have stuck his neck out. And yet stick his neck out he certainly did.

The significance of the deed was indisputable, but it seemed that I would never be able to resolve the mystery of a man sufficiently integrated into the German killing system to be able to enter and leave an SS ghetto at will, yet sufficiently motivated to risk seeking out and helping a young Jew whom he barely knew.

Marianne and Lilli Arras

On my first research trip to Essen in January 1997, just after Marianne's death, I was drinking tea in the office of Mathilde Jamin – the historian at the Essen Ruhrland Museum who had originally introduced me to Marianne. I asked her if I could borrow her telephone directory to see if there were still a garage or truck company run by Christian Arras, not a particularly common name in Germany. There was a stunned silence when I discovered that there was. It was too late in the day to call, but that evening I turned over and over in my mind verbal strategies to prevent an ageing SS member from putting the phone down at the mention of the past.

The following morning I rang the company and asked for Christian Arras. A suspicious voice at the other end asked who wanted him, but cheered up enormously when I said who I was. It transpired that I was talking to Christian's son, also called Christian, and that the company had been named after Christian's father, yet another Christian. (For the sake of clarity I shall refer to Christian Arras Senior, Christian Arras and Christian Arras Junior.) Clearly, Christian Arras Junior had been expecting a call from someone he was reluctant to talk to, but he certainly had no reservations about historians. His father had died some years before. His mother, Lilli, however, was still alive and would be happy to speak to me.

A day or two later, I took a train out to the little town of Geldern, near the Dutch border. I arrived early, and hung around in front of the deserted station until a new-looking dark blue BMW pulled up. Lilli Arras was tall and elegant, though of course now quite elderly, her hair neatly coiffured, her long dark coat turned up at the collar. We drove to a small village outside Geldern, to the smart bungalow that had been her and Christian's home in retirement.

On the way a strange and striking conversation unfolded. Though I

Lilli Arras

marvelled at what her husband had done, I was also somehow suspicious. Because of Marianne's many ambivalences – the question of
Christian's SS membership, the suggestion that he had rendered service
for family property and so on – there was something about the story that
made me uneasy. And, undoubtedly, because I was in this hyper-sensitive
state, I was particularly aware of more jarring notes during the drive to
the bungalow. As we entered her little village, we saw a most un-German
sight – houses with washing outside blowing in the wind on this chilly
snowbound day. She said the houses belonged to Aussiedler (the ethnic
Germans recently repatriated from Russia, most having few linguistic
or cultural links to their former land). There had been plans for more,
but a local resident had complained and stopped the building of further
homes. 'That was right,' she said. And then she went on to talk about
the past. The worst time, she said, was after the war – 1946, 1947, when
there had been no food. And I thought – there was a much worse time
in Germany than 1946, 1947!

But then there was one of those heart-stopping moments. Lilli began to tell me about her children, about Marianne, born in 1947. I looked at her. 'Yes,' she said, 'on purpose.' Marianne had never known that the Arras family had named their daughter after her. I saw the gesture as a sign of the friendship and respect Marianne had earned. But more, I suddenly felt that I was not just leafing through paper scraps of the past, deciphering faint imprints of past events, but was actually reconstructing a story which had never been fully told, never been fully known even by those involved. And for the first of many times I lamented that I had not been able to do the research in Germany just a few months earlier, while Marianne was still alive.

We arrived at Lilli Arras's elegantly furnished bungalow and I began taking notes. Christian had been born in 1914, Lilli four years later. Christian's father, Christian Senior, hailed from the Palatinate. Trained as a blacksmith, he had come to Essen in 1904 and set up a smithy. The company moved into transport in 1928 and took on a dealership for Magirus trucks. Christian began working for his father in the 1930s, and during the war the company had done contract work for the German army. Lilli herself hailed from a fairly modest background. Her father had been a foreman with Krupp, and there had been five children to feed. Because Lilli's father was unemployed for a significant part of her childhood, she well knew the meaning of hard times. She met Christian through one of her sisters. Apparently Christian Senior, ambitious and enterprising, rather looked down on the girl from a modest home.

Lilli Arras no longer remembered in much detail how the relationship between Christian, herself and the Strauss family had been established. For Lilli, the memory of war revolved around one thing – the bombings. On three separate occasions, the house in which she and Christian had lived was destroyed. In the worst of these, she was trapped in the cellar. The escape route to the cellar of the neighbouring house had been boarded up and she and Christian feared they would die in the flames. It was only after knocking down the barrier that they escaped. This attack, incidentally, destroyed all their furniture, including most of the things loaned to them by the Strauss family. On the next occasion, she remembers the houses toppling as bombs rained down on the street. Again and again, my questions on other subjects would lead her back to the bombings. Her wartime chronology was structured around them. At first, I was wary. Didn't she know there were worse fates? But then I understood: this, after all, had been the main threat to her own survival.

Whereas Marianne remembered the link between the families beginning with a sale of household goods, Lilli seemed to think the relationship had originated through contacts of her husband. He had come to know another member of the Jewish community, Jakob Ackermann, very well, and they had been jointly involved in black-market slaughtering in one of the large basement rooms on the Arras business premises. Yes, she acknowledged there had been property transactions. A very colourful Strauss family couch had survived the war in the Arrases' possession. Lilli told me that Alfred and Lore were at their wedding celebration, which took place on 20 February 1943 at the couple's apartment, and gave them a small telephone table as a present. On 5 March, though, all the wedding presents were destroyed in a bombing raid.[35]

I got the feeling that for Lilli the Strauss family had represented above all a touch of class. Their elegance and good manners marked them out as people of quality. Lilli remembered her first meeting with Marianne. With her plaited hair, she looked like a 'baroness from an estate', Lilli said. 'She certainly caught my eye.'[36] In one of the many letters she sent me after that first interview, Lilli remembered with particular pleasure a moment when Alfred was showing her his war decorations. She told Alfred about her own father's distinguished service in the First World War – he too had received the Iron Cross. Then, as Lilli wrote (recalling in the process of writing that Alfred's wife had been called Lore):[37] 'Herr Strauss called out "Lore come over and listen to this!" (Lore! I'd forgotten).'

It was a story full of poignant irony. The loyal German ex-soldier Alfred taking so much pleasure in the war service of another German. And the young Lilli, taking such pride in the social recognition offered her by an outcast Jew.

Lilli remembered something else from those days which confirmed the strong sense of social propriety. One day during the war, when she was living with her parents, her own house having been bombed out for the second or third time, she came across some Dutch forced labourers crowded round a large pot of 'soup', which was nothing more than white cabbage leaves in water. The young men were aged between twenty and thirty, Lilli Arras wrote,[38] 'and I said: "The educated class!" They had good clothing, expensive glasses, a sympathetic air (like you!), conversation in German.'

Here again was that sense of social order disturbed, of sympathetic, polite, established men subjected to a degrading situation. That, I think she felt, could not be *in Ordnung*.

How was it, I asked, that Christian was in a position to provide such a service for the Krombach family? Lilli had or offered only vague ideas. She said that Christian did not tell her beforehand where he was going. She remembered him going to a camp, she thought Theresienstadt, though it may well have been Izbica, with suitcases full of clothes. She thought he had bribed the guards and presented himself as an SS man. I said he didn't have to pretend, he *was* in the SS. At this point, Lilli became very agitated and the issue became a central one in our conversation (and, for a while, in our subsequent correspondence). Lilli insisted that he had been purely military, he was in the Pioniere, did his military service in Königsberg 1935–7, but was never in the SS.[39] Later, Christian Junior gave me more details. His father had done his military service in the 1930s with a Pionierbatallion and had then been called up to the army in 1939, where he had the non-commissioned rank of Schirrmeister and was responsible for the transport of a technical battalion. He was posted first to Poland, then France, then Poland again, but old man Arras had managed to have his son declared essential for the firm and got him home. It was only later in the war that Christian was called up again.

After that interview, Lilli wrote to me twice on the subject. She sent me a photo showing Christian in army uniform and his discharge certificate from prisoner-of-war camp, which clearly showed him as being army rather than, say, Waffen SS. The Berlin Document Centre (BDC), which holds the records of former SS and party members, had no file for Christian Arras. This lent credence to the idea that Marianne had got it wrong.[40] Marianne herself had said that she had never seen him in uniform.

But if he wasn't in the SS, how had he been involved in work in Izbica? Or perhaps he was working for the army near by and had managed to

Christian Arras in Wehrmacht uniform

bribe his way into the village? I resigned myself to the fact that we would probably never know. Lilli did, however, remember that considerable bribery had been involved for the guards to let him meet the Krombachs.[41]

The other issue was *why* Christian had taken such risks. Here, Lilli was sure that his motives were not particularly ideological; he was simply a good-hearted man. Friendships had been established and, on the basis of these friendships, Christian had wanted to perform a service. I discovered later that the Ackermann family, to whom Christian had become particularly close, had been deported on the same transport as Ernst, and it is evident from Marianne's references to 'Jakob's Friend' that Christian's visits to Izbica were also designed to assist Jakob Ackermann. When I later met Christian Junior on the premises of the family garage, he painted a similar picture of his father. He had had no interest in politics, but he had grown up in the heavily Jewish Nordviertel and Segerroth districts, and as a youngster had been friends with many Jews. Above all he was a good-hearted *Mensch*. His army record had said 'a good comrade and a poor soldier'.

When Christian returned from Izbica, Lilli remembered seeing him with a thick pile of letters – presumably the letters from Ernst – but she did not read them. Christian told her a little of what he had seen, and that had been enough. She remembered his account of a family he had visited (possibly the Krombachs) where the wife had been very ill. She remembered something about them vegetating in holes, absolutely primitive. Christian had been very shocked. And then again Lilli expressed that sense of a social order disturbed. The family had come from a 'decent house, terribly ill. Absolutely awful.'[42]

As a result of these conversations and correspondence, and in the absence of any BDC record for her husband as a party member, my attitude began to shift. But I was still far from giving Christian Arras unequivocal hero status.

Other voices

After the Krombachs were deported, Marianne retained contact with Artur Jacobs, whose diary entries about the bomb attack on the Krombachs' house we have already encountered. On 4 September, Jacobs wrote an entry about Izbica, which made clear that Marianne had shown him Ernst's report.[43] Over the next few days, he included several direct quotations from Ernst's letters. On 16 September, Artur again made a lengthy extract from Ernst's long letters whose contents had clearly both impressed and depressed this sensitive man. But before the extract he noted:

Conversation with a man returned from the General Government (and was also in I.) A simple man, straightforward, just facts. Struck me as trustworthy – strengthened the horror of the earlier reports.

A tragedy is taking place that is comparable only to the tragedy of the Armenians in the First World War. Almost more horrific.

One keeps on putting one's head in one's hands:

Is it possible? Is it humanly possible?!

I often feel I have been dreaming, as if it were all a horrific nightmare and I could just wake up with a feeling of relief: Oh, if it was all only a dream.

But what mind could conceive such a dream?!

Artur's entry vividly reveals how a sensitive and sympathetic observer of the Jewish fate gradually discovered the enormity of what was happening in the East. But it also gives us a further glimpse of Arras. For he, surely, must be the man mentioned, since he has just returned from Izbica and is associated with Ernst's letter. Knowing that Jacobs was a tremendous judge of character, I considered his good opinion yet more evidence in Arras's favour.

About ten days later, while following up information about Marianne's maternal ancestors, the Rosenbergs from Ahlen, I came across some interviews between a local historian, Hans Gummersbach, and Imo Moszkowicz, a Jewish-German Auschwitz survivor who stayed on in Germany after the war.[44] At this stage I didn't know about the rumours linking Moszkowicz's cousin and the Strausses' reprieve in 1941. What I did learn was that, though he was born in Ahlen, Moszkowicz had gone to live in Essen in 1939. As I read on, I came across a startling passage. Sometime between April 1942 (when Imo Moszkowicz's mother was deported to Izbica) and February 1943 (when Imo himself was rounded up for deportation to Auschwitz) something happened which he still remembered vividly, and yet which was so strange that it was hardly believable. For 'unfathomable reasons' a 'high-ranking military man, perhaps even an SS man' came to the family home and told them what was happening in the East:[45]

'He reported on the extermination camps. We thought, stupidly, that he was a Gestapo spy come to draw us out[. . .]He said he had come from the East and we should leave the country, flee! We thought this was a provocation to catch us out. We distrusted this man enormously . . . And I remember that he went away shaking his head. That's my memory. He asserted that he had met Essen families in the East, he even had with him a handwritten greeting from some Essen Jews with whom he claimed to be friendly. He had a big car-repair shop in Essen towards Altenessen. He repaired trucks for the army and went with them to the East. He accompanied the transport, he said, because he wanted to know what was going on. To outsiders he acted as though he was a 100 per cent Hitler supporter and in reality he was trying to undermine everything.'

Unless there were several people with big repair shops in northern Essen travelling with Wehrmacht trucks to Poland, this must be Christian Arras. When I contacted Imo Moszkowicz about this, he was stunned after fifty-five years to be faced with the incident again. Thanks to his memory of the incident, at last I now had a more plausible account of how Arras came to be in the East: it was on the pretext of accompanying repaired Wehrmacht trucks. But even though the Wehrmacht contracts gave Arras an excuse for travel to Poland, he still needed enormous amount of courage (and probably not a little cash) to enter a place like Izbica.

Why did Christian Arras do it? Imo Moszkowicz himself was in no doubt, as he informed me in a subsequent letter:[46]

I tried to find Christian Arras after liberation, hoping that he would know something of the whereabouts of my family. But at a time when neither trains nor post were working properly (and when life beckoned me!), my intention soon faded. Particularly, as it is only now, through your letter, that I have been able to dredge the name Arras from my memory. At the time it simply would not come to me.

Yes, he organized truck repairs for the Wehrmacht and managed personally to accompany the repaired trucks back to the East. He was concerned, I seem to remember, about a Jewish friend, whose name I no longer recall. The friend had been sent to Izbica and Arras looked for him and apparently found him.

Arras was a hero.

Did they sing his praises in Essen?

Ach, do you know that we who survived are guilty of committing great sins of omission since that time. Through their deeds, all those good souls kept us from absolute despair, gave us the hope that was so essential for survival. But after 1945, after the horror came to an end, they were as if paralysed, struck dumb.[. . .]

I would gladly have met Arras again. Probably, though, I had the suffocating fear that I would learn more terrible things about the fate of the Essen Jews in Izbica – about the death of my mother, my siblings, my friends. And I simply did not have the strength to learn about that. My instinct for self-preservation protected me, I think, from the intolerably horrible reality, which Arras surely knew.

(Even now I still don't want to know the reality and I won't allow my imagination to produce a clear picture of what went on).

When I interviewed Hanna Aron, the woman whose memory of accompanying her lover to Holbeckshof Marianne had unconsciously borrowed, I found that she too had things to tell me about Arras. This sub-community of hidden knowledge! Hanna's mother, Irene Drucker, had been the secretary to the Jewish Community. Hanna said her mother had told her about Arras, a German soldier who was giving them help and information. But she mustn't talk to anybody about it:[47]

'I think he was a good guy, he put his own life in jeopardy. Why he did it, I don't know, because there was *so* much danger in it. He must really have felt an obligation, a conscience to do this. Otherwise you wouldn't do this. They all knew that you could be taken to the camp.'

According to Hanna, the Community would organize food parcels which Christian Arras then took to Izbica.[48] She told me that his visit to the Community offices was a turning point in their awareness of conditions in the East. Once he had told them what he had seen, the Jews in Essen lost all illusion that life after deportation could be survived.

Imo and Hanna put an end to my scepticism. Clearly, no material incentive had been involved, since the poverty-stricken Moszkowicz boys had nothing to offer Christian Arras. I no longer had any doubt: Christian Arras was an unlikely hero.[49]

Yet I could sympathize with Marianne's ambivalence, echoes of which I heard in both Imo Moszkowicz's and Hanna Aron's accounts. In the atmosphere of terror, almost every gesture must have seemed suspect. I could understand that both Marianne and Moszkowicz should blur German uniforms – whether the Wehrmacht, as in this case, or railway officials, or the police – into the evil, threatening outfit of the SS. I was to find the same lack of differentiation in others interviewed. It was also easy to see why they had found Arras's actions so hard to fathom. Here, after all, was an apolitical individual, not above a bit of black marketeering, engaged in a most dangerous deed – for what? When I asked Hanna Aron if she would put into writing the positive recollections she had given me, so that I might forward them to Yad Vashem with a view to a possible recognition of Arras as 'righteous gentile', she was very reluctant:[50]

At the time we believed he delivered the packages. Today I am not so sure any more. He also gave an account of the people who were still there. Today I must ask myself: How did he know? Was he in one of the Commandos himself? I recently read Daniel Goldhagen's book about the Commandos. Nothing would surprise me any more.

She wrote this even though Marianne's receipt of Ernst's letters proved Arras undoubtedly *had* delivered the parcels he was given. But Arras's actions went so much against the grain of accepted knowledge about

Germans and Germany that it was hard to maintain belief in their reality. It was easier to begin doubting what one had once known as fact.

Uncovering Ernst's fate

Sadly, Arras could not provide the lifeline that Marianne hoped. Izbica was simply a stopover on the way to the extermination camps. Ernst's survival for so many months was the result of a series of logistical hiccups in the killing machinery.[51] By April 1942, the facilities in nearby Belzec had become overwhelmed. For a time, deportations there were halted, the existing killing machinery torn down, and a new larger facility constructed. Sobibor took over briefly and there were deportations there from Izbica in May and June, but the summer offensive in the Soviet Union led to the cessation of non-military transports. In August, when Ernst wrote Marianne his letter, personnel and vehicles from the Lublin district were heavily involved in the 'Great Action' in the Warsaw Ghetto, in which 300,000 people were deported in just a few weeks, most of them to Treblinka.[52] It was not until the end of August 1942 that deportations from the Lublin district could resume in larger numbers. Even then, technical problems – for example, with the rail connection to Sobibor – limited the pace of deportations. In early October 1942, as the killing machine came closer, Izbica was again spared because the main extermination effort was to the north of the district.[53]

For Marianne, the only sign initially that things were not going well was that the post embargo continued. In early September, she wrote to the Red Cross in the General Government asking if they could forward parcels for her. A brief note from a Herr Michel, dated 14 September 1942, informed her that only parcels registered with the Presidium of the German Red Cross in Berlin could be forwarded. She should enquire in Berlin about the regulations.

Proof of Marianne's growing uncertainty about the possibility of future contact with Ernst was that, towards the end of September, she began a private diary alongside the letter diary for Ernst. Here she allowed herself bleaker reflections than she was willing to express in the letter diary. On 6 October 1942, she acknowledged for the first time that many people were saying that no one would come back from Izbica.[54] On 22 October, an extremely cautious entry in the letter-diary implies that 'our tall friend' (Christian) had been in Izbica again and that there was evidence that the Krombachs were still there. Perhaps Christian could visit Ernst soon: 'Now we hope that our tall friend will visit him because we have learned, finally, that they are still there.'[55] There is no record of news coming back.

Marianne could not have known, but in fact 22 October was the day on which the real purge of Izbica began. Overall, at least 50,000 Jews from the Lublin district were caught up in the deportation operation which ran until early November.[56] By then, most knew of their impending fate and great force had to be used. Many Jews fled from the ghettoes into the forest[57] and massive shootings followed; over 10,000 Jews were shot between October and December 1942 in the Lublin district alone.

Thomas Blatt vividly remembered 22 October 1942. The town was surrounded by SS soldiers and the Jewish leaders summoned to meet Engels, the local Gestapo chief. Many residents suspected that this was the end of Izbica. There was no longer any point in hiding because there was no longer any hope of moving freely once the operation was over. The local non-Jewish citizens would hand over anyone who tried to hide. So the Jews made their way to the station for a two o'clock deadline. Blatt did manage to hide, while the rest of his family went on. He heard screams and machine-gun fire from the station. Later, hearing talk in Yiddish, he looked out and saw groups of unguarded Jews returning to the town, some carrying pitiful belongings, others crying and covered with blood. Later he found his mother, father and brother alive and back home. The train's capacity had been too small, so Engels had made a selection. Resting his machine-gun on the shoulder of the Judenrat chairman he had mowed down a group of people and forced the others into the boxcars. They were packed so tightly that some suffocated even before the train left. Those for whom there was no room had been sent home.[58]

The Krombachs seem to have survived even this terrible operation, but there were further deportations in November.[59] On 25 November, Marianne made a coded reference to a recent visit by Christian Arras:[60]

Today my heart is so heavy. Someone coming from there told me that there is no one left in Izbica. He kept looking round and asking, but in recent weeks everyone had gone, perhaps to nearby Lublin. Who knows! Winter draws ever closer and makes me more anxious than ever. I think always of you, of how the winter may hit you and how you will survive it. Only in such crises is one forced to acknowledge how small and insignificant one is and how powerless.

In December came more news. Christian Arras had again had business in Izbica and again had carried post for Ernst. But the conditions he had discovered this time were very different from the last. On 30 December 1942, Marianne wrote in the private diary:

I don't know what to write because life is pointless. You go round and round in a circle from which there is no escape.

News finally after four months. Our dear friend brought it again, after having had no sign of life since his last report. But this was so much more awful. There are things we know are terrible but whose horror we never fully grasp, and in that way we're protected from madness. Just sometimes there is a flash of brief, crippling insight. Then we learn the true significance of the individual person, or rather his insignificance.

Somewhere my trust has been punctured and I can only watch fearfully and hope the hole doesn't grow . . . I fear for you now, that you are so alone and dependent on yourself. Your mother gone, no one knows where she and all the others have ended up – no one knows their fate. God must be with you. Your father . . . died, from pleurisy, they say.

One says and hears and writes words whose meaning one simply does not understand! And you, you, experience the ghastly reality and you must be strong so that you don't . . . do you hear, you must! How do you look, I want to know, how do you live? It all weighs on me endlessly, the not knowing and the not being able to help! I want to be so, so close to you. And I cannot be that, even by post.

Despite everything, you must stay strong and preserve your spiritual foundation, because if you lose that you have given up.

What a poor spectacle human beings are! I can't go on!

More than fifty years later, Marianne recalled what Arras had told her:[61]

'Of the few hundred people who went there in April 1942 there were only a handful left, about sixty people from that particular group. The rest had either been killed or sent away or just shot – tried to escape and been shot, or they just died of starvation and disease.'

Ernst was on his own, Arras reported to Marianne, his father had died, allegedly of pleurisy and his mother had disappeared. And Ernst himself? 'Ernst, he said, had been used for some medical experiment and lost his sight. Whether that was permanent or not he didn't know . . .'[62]

A copy of a very cautious letter from 8 January 1943, sent by Marianne to a Herr Austerlitz,[63] informed him of David Krombach's death, without mentioning the name. The son had been blinded as a result of an 'accident', whether irreparably so was not clear. At the same time, Marianne wrote to Emil Fuchs in Berlin to see if the RV had any means of contacting the deportees (or 'evacuees' as they were officially to be called). But Fuchs could offer no help:[64]

> *Dear Miss Strauss,*
>
> *To my very great regret I have to inform you that all, I mean all, possibility of communicating with the evacuees has been severed. For several months, every route we have tried has been barred. We suffer deeply over it. But we are helpless.*
>
> *Accept my deepest sympathy.*
>
> *Yours,*
>
> *Emil Fuchs.*

Typically, Marianne did not leave it there. Writing from the address of the Jewish Community office, she courageously approached the Red Cross again, asking if post could be sent to Ernst Krombach. At the end of January, she received a letter from the German Red Cross representative attached to the Generalgouverneur in Poland. In dry officialese, giving little away, it informed her that 'delivery of your letter to the above-named is not possible'.[65] One can well imagine the agonies of uncertainty that would follow the receipt of such a letter. Was it saying that letters or parcels generally could not be delivered, or that Ernst was not available to receive them? Marianne wrote again, and, on 10 February, a further letter arrived from the same office, grudgingly giving a little more information:[66]

With reference to your letter of 1.2.1943 I hereby inform you that it is generally possible to send messages to Jews, but that in this case your message cannot be passed on.

What did 'in this case' mean – Izbica, or specifically Ernst Krombach? Some moral constraint or some concept of public relations prevented the Red Cross from simply ignoring Marianne's letters, but they were being as unhelpful as possible. Undaunted, the tenacious Marianne wrote again:[67]

Marianne Sara Strauss, Hindenburgstrasse 75 to German Red Cross, Kracau, 17.2.1943

Re: delivery of letter to Ernst Israel Krombach reference: S-O/GG J/II NR.6084/43/1

With reference to your letter of the 10th, I trouble you once more with the following question, to which your last letter did not provide a completely clear reply.

Is it generally impossible to send messages to Izbica or is Ernst Israel Krombach no longer reachable there?

Is there any point in seeking his current address and which office or organization would be the responsible authority?

Thank you in advance for your efforts.

When no reply was forthcoming, she re-sent her request. This elicited the worst of all possible answers from the Red Cross:[68]

With reference to your letter of 8.3.1943, I would hereby inform you that the above-named can no longer be reached at the camp and further enquiries are pointless.

A letter that managed to be unequivocal about the pointlessness of further efforts, yet *still* avoid revealing Ernst's final fate. Realizing that nothing more was to be gained from this quarter, in April 1943 Marianne wrote to the Red Cross Head Office in Berlin to ask if there was a branch of the Swedish Red Cross in the General Government.[69] Again there was no reply and again she followed up with a further letter.[70] She was rewarded with a laconic three-liner stating that there was no Swedish organization. In all the correspondence she had received, there had been never a 'Dear' nor a 'Yours sincerely' nor even the tiniest human gesture.[71]

What exactly *was* Ernst's fate? So little is known about Izbica that it is virtually impossible to gain unequivocal information. I began to wonder, though, whether Marianne's memory of Christian Arras's report about medical experiments could be correct. Such experiments presupposed some kind of medical or research facility, which fitted less and less well with what I was learning about the place. I also noted that there was no reference to medical experiments in any of her communications or diaries at the time. For example, after giving up on the Red Cross, Marianne now turned abroad for help. I'd had no idea that German Jews were still able to communicate with friends and relatives in the neutral countries, but on 15 April 1943, and again on 16 May, Marianne wrote through the Red Cross to a former Essen community nurse, Sister Julie Koppel, living in Stockholm. Hoping that Julie Koppel's Red Cross connections would allow her to obtain further information about her beloved, Marianne provided effectively the same account of an accident as in the letter sent to Herr Austerlitz in January. Ernst, Marianne wrote, 'is said to have been blinded as a result of an accident.' Again, however, it is possible this was a neutral account to get past the censor.[72]

In his collection of tributes to Essen's Jewish lawyers, Bernd Schmalhausen's account of David Krombach contains a rather different story. According to Schmalhausen (and Enrique Krombach, who later told me exactly the same thing), Sister Julie Koppel wrote to Enrique in South America that Ernst was deliberately blinded by SS thugs after a failed escape attempt.[73] For this to be true, Julie Koppel would have needed another source of information about Izbica apart from Marianne. Yet in June 1943, Julie wrote to Marianne to say that she had no information about the Krombachs and that, though she would do her best, as things stood it was impossible to find out more.[74] From what I could tell, the letter from Koppel to Enrique no longer exists. Instead, Schmalhausen's account was based on Enrique's memory of receiving the letter.

I wrote to Thomas Blatt asking if he could remember either medical experiments or an attempted break-out by the German Jews. He was certain there had not been the former and was pretty sure there had been no escape attempts, either, at least on the part of the German Jews in Izbica.[75]

Artur Jacobs' diary offered another piece of the puzzle. On 31 December 1942, he wrote one of the bleakest entries of the war:[76]

Marianne has just gone. I feel numb. I keep thinking: it isn't so. You're dreaming, it can't be true, and I try to erase it.

Dr Krombach dead, his wife gone, the boy blinded . . .

The other fates similar. Only a tenth of the Esseners still there, the others dead or sent further on. Frau Krombach two days after her husband's death. That is the norm. If the husband dies, the wife is sent on.

The boy worked in an explosives factory and lost his sight in an explosion. Where he is, what he is doing, where he lives, whether someone is helping him, in a place where it takes a supreme effort just to look after yourself, no one knows.

I still see his father before me, on the last day before his departure[. . .]

Man dead, wife transported (who knows where? Is she even alive?) And the boy – blind!

The fate of the Jews is there before you in all its naked horror and hopelessness.

Here was yet another account – blinded by an accident in an explosives factory. Or *was* this different? It was virtually what Marianne had written to Austerlitz in January 1943 and to Julie Koppel in May. Influenced by what she told me about medical experiments, I had assumed the letters offered a self-censored version of the events and not the truth. Now it seemed they might have stated the plain awful facts. If so, that meant that since the war, living on separate continents, *both* Marianne and Enrique had created private and different legends about Ernst's fate.

There was further corroboration that an accident was involved. In August 1945, Liesel Sternberg wrote to a colleague in Essen trying to trace her former employer and friend, David Krombach.[77] Liesel's letter refers to post she had just received from Enrique Krombach, who had written to her to tell her he had learned from Julie Koppel in September

1943 that Ernst had been blinded in a factory accident. In other words, at the time of writing to Liesel at the end of the war, Enrique clearly believed that his brother had been blinded in a work accident. It is unlikely that Julie Koppel wrote later with different information. It was thus clear to me that the story of the escape, as indeed the story of a medical experiment, was a later invention.

Of course, this chain of letters and diaries leads us back only as far as Arras's original report, and we will never know how accurate that was. We do not know where he obtained the information about David Krombach. 'Pleurisy' sounds like the fake causes of death supplied by Nazi concentration camps when inquiries arose. What we *can* say is that, quite independently of each other, with no communication between them to hold their memories in check, Marianne and Enrique developed different versions of Ernst's fate from a common starting point. I could not ask Marianne about this process, because she died before my discoveries. But Enrique was surprised to hear what I had learned. He agreed that he had had no new information since the war. So why should his memory have changed? As he said, it was not that his version was more bearable. On the contrary, it was more horrific than the original report. In fact, not only he but Marianne too had, in their different ways, added an extra shade of horror to the story as told them. Later, as I found out more about the fate of Marianne's own family, I was to learn that there was a discernible pattern in these revisions.

One thing was for sure: Izbica was not a place in which a blind person could survive, certainly not a blind person deprived of his family. Amid all the horror of the place, the thought of the blind Ernst dragging himself around, friendless, is unbearable. 'Oh, those beautiful eyes which looked so trustingly on the world,' wrote Julie Koppel to Marianne in June 1943. 'Oh, if only what you know were untrue. We too hope for miracles.'[78] But there were no miracles in Izbica at the end of 1942. For a brief period, Jews were allowed to work in the town again. In April 1943 the final clearance took place and the last Jews were deported to Sobibor.[79]

As far as we know, Sister Julie's letter of June 1943 was the last communication Marianne ever received about Ernst. But he did leave behind one more palpable reminder of his presence. In the very last plastic bag of documents in Marianne's house, Vivian and I found a gold ring, inscribed 'Ernest, March 1942'. It must have been the engagement ring Ernst had given Marianne before his deportation.

8

Deportations, Death and
the Bund

For Marianne's parents, life in 1942 must have been one long miserable wait under steadily worsening conditions. It is a macabre fact that, even as the number of Jews in Germany dwindled, so the regulations making life unliveable became ever more comprehensive. In the course of the year, Jews were progressively denied eggs, white bread, bread rolls, cigarettes and many other goods, and Jewish rations effectively fell to starvation level. With their money and contacts, the Strausses managed to get by, but they certainly did not live well. Steadily intensifying decrees made it virtually impossible for Jews to use public transport. Communication, too, was extremely difficult. Having had their private telephones confiscated, Jews were now forbidden to use public phones. In March, they were even forbidden to buy newspapers and magazines. Segregation was rigorously enforced and Jewish houses had to be marked with a black star. Expropriation continued – a hand-written note among the Strauss family papers records that on 22 June 1942 they handed in three typewriters, one remaining bicycle and their binoculars. The list of decrees is almost endless.[1]

Within the legal framework, there were countless opportunities for small-scale official harassment. When Else Dahl, Aunt Oe's mother, moved to Essen at the end of 1941 a Frau Schweizer sent some of her belongings on to her in a parcel. The parcel did not arrive. Frau Schweizer complained to the post office, which duly informed her that the parcel had been confiscated because the addressee was a Jew. On 8 February,

Frau Dahl wrote to the post office that she was astonished that the parcel had been confiscated because it contained her underwear. Giving chapter and verse on when and where she had bought it and confirming that if need be she still had the receipts, she asked for the underwear to be returned as she had urgent need of it.[2] A gruff four-liner came back from the post office informing Frau Dahl that the (Essen) Gestapo had confiscated the parcel. 'You will direct your application to that office.'[3]

Up until Spring 1941, as we have seen, German officialdom had occasionally displayed some vestige of its former correctness. But after the autumn there was only the unfailing politeness of the Deutsche Bank to remind the Strausses of the respect they once enjoyed. To take one example of officialdom, a senior tax inspector from the Düsseldorf Finance Office approached the Gestapo with a blunt enquiry about transferring some funds to the Strauss family. 'Before I order the Payments Office to transfer the funds, please inform me now forthwith if we can assume that these Jews will soon be evacuated.'[4] More and more, the Strausses found officials treating them as non-persons who had overstayed their welcome and who should have gone East long ago.

The family's social isolation grew. Until 1942, Richard had managed to enjoy something of a social life. From 1939 to 1941 he had attended the Jewish Volksschule in Essen. Then, denied the more academic opportunities he would normally have pursued, he had trained in metalwork, commuting daily to a Jewish workshop in Cologne.[5] But on 20 June 1942, all Jewish training schools were closed. Almost all the young Jews remaining in Cologne were deported to Minsk and murdered shortly after arrival.[6] It was at this stage, probably, that Siegfried organized private tuition for Richard. It seems that neither Richard nor Marianne had to engage in forced labour, the fate of almost all surviving Jewish youngsters at the time.

After the summer of 1942, the only relatives with whom the family were in touch were Alfred Weinberg, who received Red Cross post in his internment camp in Australia, and a distant relative in neutral Sweden. Anna Rosenberg wrote forlornly to Alfred, 'You are the only person I can write to and get a reply.' When the family sent Alfred birthday wishes in 1943, the letter was noteworthy in that the Strausses had absolutely no news about themselves to offer.

The Strausses' only social contacts were gentiles willing to run the risk of trading with them. Alongside Christian and Lilli Arras there were others, including a Catholic pair, the Jürgens. Marianne explained:[7]

'My mother got to know this Frau Jürgens. My mother fed her the most wonderful items of silver and Meissen and God knows what else in return for a piece of meat or whatever. Frau Jürgens ended up with an awful lot of things and all the furniture and the pictures which she didn't all return. But that's how these sort of relationships were ... purely out of mutual need.'

For her part, Marianne felt more and more isolated. More than one former classmate recalled seeing her walking along on the other side of a road, wearing the yellow star, but none dared offer a sign of recognition.[8] (It did occur to me to wonder why they never remembered seeing her on the same side of the road.) In June 1942, most of Marianne's remaining young friends were taken away in a second deportation to Izbica.[9] On 20 July, all her elderly patients, together with the nurses and community workers on whom she had come to depend – Irma Ransenberg, Bärchen and the others – were loaded on to cattle trucks and deported to Theresienstadt.[10] Marianne's great uncle and aunt, Abraham and Anna Weyl, were also among the brutally dispatched human cargo. We know that after spending more than a year in Theresienstadt, most of the deportees were sent on to Auschwitz.[11]

Marianne wrote to Ernst on 21 July:[12]

Herr O [Ostermann] is still here, otherwise it would be intolerable. Torn from everything. Did you sense from my letters how my work fulfilled and satisfied me? There is no one left within reach whom I can care for. So I will devote myself all the more to looking after you.

For a while, Marianne's principal activity was collecting goods for her parcels. She told me:[13]

'I had developed a whole ... I wouldn't call it an industry, there wasn't enough of that to go around, but a sort of occupation, trying to find people who would give me foodstuffs to send away. Non-Jewish people, friends of friends and that sort of thing. It was amazing, there were one or two people who really were very kind. There was an old lady who had a very nice grocery shop, well it was at that time a grotty little shop in a side street somewhere. She became very rich during the war with all the black-market dealing. She also was dealing in all directions, but she knew what she was doing and she used to give me stuff, dry goods, like peasum,[14] that sort of thing . . . Some dry goods were not very highly rated on the coupon side – we did quite well with that.[. . .]

'People said try so and so, that priest or whatever – because the church was still the most likely way of getting some sort of echo. One always hoped that there was something someone might be able to do, hoping against hope.'

But by the autumn, when it became clear that no post was getting through, even this activity lost its purpose.

Marianne still did some clerical work for the Community.[15] She played a vital role answering enquiries from Jews who had emigrated about family members they had left behind.[16] Like Ernst, Marianne could not escape becoming a minor cog in the Nazi machinery. With the bulk of the community now deported to Łodz, Minsk, Izbica or Theresienstadt, there were a series of smaller-scale deportations to mop up the Jews left behind, and Marianne was given the responsibility of informing those assigned to the next transport. She remembered in particular one middle-aged lady:[17] 'who lived on her own, to whom I had to bring this news. She just nodded, she didn't say anything, and the next day they found her dead. She had hanged herself.'

Imo Moszkowicz and the Hindenburgstrasse

After summer 1942, the only Jews left behind were a few privileged individuals and those conscripted into essential war work. True, some life returned to the rooms at Hindenburgstrasse 22 when the remaining Jews from Holbeckshof moved in there, but, unlike the children or the elderly, they did not require special help. There was little Marianne could do for them:[18]

The sad remnant is moving tomorrow from Steele to 22. The bachelors, fifteen of them, will be in the main room, the couples are in the other

room and in 88. So there'll be some life in the place, which was com-
pletely dead last week. Those coming here are not particularly happy
about it and you can't blame them. They lived so much more freely
there.

In the summer of 1997 I gained an unexpected insight into Marianne's
effect on this group. The sixteen-year-old Imo Moszkowicz was among
the new residents of the Hindenburgstrasse. Imo has already surfaced
several times in this book, wherever his memories shed light on Marianne's story. However, my discovery of quite how intricately his life had
been interwoven with Marianne's was much more dramatic than might
appear from his intermittent appearances in this narrative.

It began with my visit to the historian Hans Gummersbach. From Dr
Gummersbach I learned that Imo Moszkowicz had grown up in Ahlen
and had some memories of the Rosenbergs – Marianne's maternal
grandparents, aunts and uncles. In 1939, Imo came to Essen. Then I
discovered that Imo's mother and most of his siblings were deported to
Izbica on the same transport as Ernst. Imo and Marianne had in
fact both been at Essen station seeing off the train. More dramatic still
was Imo Moszkowicz's encounter with Christian Arras, an encounter
he still remembered, but could hardly believe, fifty years later. Because
I was so taken with these connnections, Dr Gummersbach lent me the
video of a television programme he had made about Imo Moszkowicz's
life.

I didn't have a video player in Germany, and so had to wait a week
before seeing the tape. In the meantime, without realizing I was about
to uncover yet another link between Imo and Marianne, I went to
Wuppertal to interview Hanna Jordan, a celebrated stage designer. I
wanted to talk to her because I knew that she had been a friend of people
who had assisted Marianne. She herself, as it turned out, had vivid
memories of meeting Marianne during Marianne's underground years.
A few days later, I flew back home and finally watched the video. The
film followed Moszkowicz from his Ahlen childhood, through the years
in Essen to his deportation to Auschwitz in February 1943. Surviving
both Auschwitz and the subsequent death marches, Moszkowicz elected
to stay in Germany after the war. The second half of the film pursued

the handsome and charismatic Moszkowicz in his blossoming post-war career as theatre director and master of the new medium of television, for which he made over a hundred productions. And there in the film was yet another connection to Marianne: Moszkowicz's close collaborator on countless projects was Hanna Jordan, whom I had just interviewed in an entirely different context.

The film made clear just how reluctantly – and only after decades of silence – Moszkowicz had begun to delve into the past. But I could not refrain from writing to him. Almost immediately, back came a fax:[19]

> *Dear Doctor Roseman,*
> *I just received your letter. In a flash it shoved me back into that past which I – so unsuccessfully! – seek to flee. Is Marianne Strauss still alive?*

So he *had* known her. Imo promised to send a detailed answer before he took up a visiting professorship at the Academy for the Performing Arts in Graz. He concluded:

> *The Hanna Jordan connection, your mention of Ernst Krombach, Christian Arras, Izbica, simply take my breath away. A photo of Arras would help my vague memories.*

A day or two later, I received a six-page fax. He began with Marianne herself:[20]

> *I am trying very hard to transpose myself back to those years when I was in Marianne Strauss's presence. But I'm dredging up shadows rather than concrete facts.*
> *Marianne was adored by all who knew her. She mastered the challenges of the time with such ease and unaffectedness. If I am not mistaken, she wore her hair round her head in a braid, adding an extra touch to her good looks.*

The letter then repeated the widely held misperception that Siegfried had invented a particular steel for Krupp and had therefore been protected. For Imo Moszkowicz, there was another unexpected link – that Marianne was the niece of Carlos (Karl) Rosenberg of Ahlen, someone with whom he had become a close friend in the post-war period.

Imo Moszkowicz

He talked at length about the Essen deportation and about Arras. He went on:

Almost unbelievable, it seems to me, is the fateful link to my Hanna Jordan. I am simply speechless and have no further comment! I simply note that in Hanna's presence I often had to think of Marianne Strauss – Hanna had almost exactly the same kind of aura. Perhaps she also made me unconsciously aware of my failure to look for Marianne Strauss after the war.

'Does the name Marianne Strauss mean anything to you?' you ask me, and in doing so have hit a central element in my reflections on my own memories. You must understand that in our world at

that time, Marianne was an extraordinary phenomenon – and not
just in terms of her appearance.

[...]

Marianne comes (came?) from a very good background, from
an assimilated, almost goyish family, very rich and well educated.
I, on the other hand[...]come from a very poor, more or less
religious. East European cobbler's family. From my earliest child-
hood I have suffered from the difference between Eastern and
Western Jews. I understood that the Yiddish of my parents was
not pleasant to Western ears because it sounded like debased
German. Also kaftans and Peikeles [Peyot – the long side-curls
worn by very Orthodox Jews], which hardly anyone wore in the
Western world, were seen as repellent – a pretext for the racist
propaganda of Der Stürmer *and the carnival associations.*

Imo argued that the Nazis' failure to discriminate between Eastern
and Western Jews did not end the divisions and recriminations within
the community:

Even as a child I already felt burdened by the way the others
distanced themselves from us, and this depressed me deeply. Even
during the most dangerous times, when the gas chambers were
working to full capacity, there was no real mixing of Eastern and
Western Jews. One must remember that at that time, in 1938, as
the Polish Jews were driven out of Germany across the Polish
border, not even the German Jews living in safety abroad protested.
Because many Western Jews were not unhappy to be relieved of
this Eastern Jewish burden – by Hitler! – while they as German or
stateless Jews could, for a while at least, enjoy the fruits of this
contemptible distinction.

But Marianne approached us in a way that broke down all these
awful barriers. Although she could have got out abroad years
before, she didn't. She took up with us outcasts and used her
privileged status only when the situation was life-threatening.

Or was it just love for Ernst Krombach which bound her to that
time and place?

In my memory, Marianne has become a symbol of my dream of

unconditional Jewish unity. The way she turned this dream into reality in the most awful hell helped to stabilize my shaky belief in the necessity of Judaism.

For that I admire her, honour her, and have held her in my feelings and my memory through all the years.

He concluded:

'*Anything which you can remember from that time in Essen, would interest me,' you write. I have ventured back into those years for Marianne's sake; but I find it very painful. I had made a firm decision never to do it again. The Essen of those times, it's true, is always in my consciousness. But writing or speaking about it demands such an effort. It forces me to sink back into the past (which is always with us), and that I find unspeakably difficult.*

Only in honour of Marianne Strauss have I overcome my inhibitions and accepted the heavy duty of the historical witness. Perhaps also because as a young man, hungry for life, I felt such a strong attraction to her, one that it would be fair to call love.

And this indescribable feeling has been brought back into life by your letter.

For that, I thank you very, very much.

As long as there is memory, however painful it may be, then all those who once were still exist: Non omnis moriar, *says Horace in his Odes.*

Imo Moszkowicz's letters and his painful wonder at the hidden links brought out of the shadows fifty-seven years later made me feel, for a moment, like part of the story, a small link in the chain. Of course, there are always coincidences waiting to happen, connections and associations lurking round the corner, some to be discovered, others to remain forever hidden. But this was something more. The unwillingness or inability to face the past, the silence after 1945, had created a barrier to the resumption or resolution of relationships and friendships. Though I deeply regretted not being able to bring all these connections to Marianne, I wondered if she, had she been alive, could have coped with all this past brought back to life.

In any case, did Imo Moszkowicz's idealized Marianne, his almost literary construction of her as a bridge between East and West, bear any relationship to her own reality? For her, the interactions in the Hindenburgstrasse were far less significant. She did note in her diary some of the meetings with the boys in the Hindenburgstrasse. On 17 November, in deepest despair at the lack of news from Ernst, she recorded a meeting with the youngsters for an oneg Shabbat (an oneg, literally 'delight', is a Sabbath study-meeting). Marianne evidently went with much reluctance, protesting that out of respect to those who had been transported to the camps they should not enjoy their unearned freedom. With a little self-irony, she recognized something 'puritanical, blue-stocking' about her opinions, and in the end was able to enjoy the get-together. The group read 'Angst' by Stefan Zweig and sang old songs. But it is clear her thoughts were elsewhere.

'Does God mean well with us?'

One can see why the sixteen-year-old Imo felt the way he did about Marianne. It was not just her beauty. Her serenity and confidence, her openness and strength were inspiring. She proved there were still Jews who did not look bowed or crushed, despite everything the Third Reich had thrown at them. At the same time, she was alive to the worries of others and totally committed to providing help. She represented the best kind of Jewish elite. It's not surprising Imo should have fantasized that, had she wished to, Marianne could easily have left the country.

On the other hand, there seemed to be a kind of irony here. For Imo, Marianne stabilized his belief in Judaism. But for Marianne, Jewishness often seemed so irrelevant. It was surely no accident that at the kindergarten college, Hebrew and Jewish studies should have been her worst subjects. It was Marianne who had told me about the division between her and the community triggered by the cry of envy on the Haumannshof. And yet here she was figuring in Imo Moszkowicz's memory as a symbol of Jewish unity.

But when I looked again at Marianne's diary and correspondence from 1942, I realized that religion meant more to Marianne then than at any time before or since. It was noticeable how often God was mentioned in Marianne's letters to Ernst. In April she asked, 'Does God mean well with us? We must believe in him and hope that he will help us. Only in that thought can we find solace.'[21] When Ernst's card arrived in time for her birthday, she saw it as a sign from heaven. 'The Lord will help us, my love, I build my hopes on that.'[22] This is very different from the letters she wrote in Berlin or her diary entries in later years. In the whole of her 1944 diary, for example, God is mentioned only once.

In 1942, Marianne referred to the Jewish festivals as they occurred. Sometimes she noted simply that they were not being celebrated. But she also drew hope from the texts traditionally read on the day. On 21 May, she referred to the festival of Shavuot (Pentecost) and the associated period of reflection and contemplation.[23] The next major festival in the calendar is Rosh Hashanah, the Jewish New Year, and to celebrate the day, Marianne selected a present to send to Ernst as soon as the opportunity allowed. On the most solemn day of all, Yom Kippur, the Day of Atonement, Marianne wrote how consoling the prayers were, how much hope they gave. And she copied out in her letter diary for Ernst the Haftorah[24] portion from the prophet Isaiah read on the morning of Yom Kippur.[25] In his long report, as we know, Ernst distinguished between German Jews and their Czech counterparts. 'Unlike us,' he wrote, the Czech Jews 'had not been forced to regard themselves as Jews and led back to Judaism.' The implication was that the Nazis, by forcing Jewish identity to the fore, had effected among German Jews a positive, subjective return to Judaism as well. Ernst clearly felt Marianne would understand and identify with this proposition.

It is easy to make the mistake of assuming that other people have one unchanging identity. By contrast, having himself grown up in Weimar Germany, the historian Arno Klönne wrote of the identity of Jewish youth in Weimar and Nazi Germany:[26]

From my own experience I know that there's something one might call shifting consciousness. In a single year it was possible to go through three phases of self-identification all within the same youth organization: secular Jewish nationalism with a socialist tinge, German-focused anti-fascism, and a religious Jewish phase.

In later life, Marianne lost sight of the nourishment she had once drawn from her Jewish identity. But for a while in 1942 her Judaism was a real source of comfort and strength.

The depths of despair

Through October and November 1942, as Ernst's silence continued and the rumours and news grew worse, Marianne became ever more miserable. She often felt she was living in a dream. The blurring of reality and nightmare became complete following an operation on her toe. The old injury from Berlin had been giving her trouble – potentially a huge handicap when all forms of transport were forbidden to Jews. But where was she to go for treatment? There were no Jewish doctors left. There was, however, a Catholic hospital in Essen Steele and Aunt Oe, bolder than Regina, finally suggested they make an appointment there without giving too many details. The surgeon asked no questions and a date was set for Marianne's third operation at the end of September 1942.[27] Apparently, a fragment of bone had broken off and was floating loose in the toe. Marianne was given chloroform and the surgeon removed the fragment, the size of a pea. She told me that the traumatic experience of waking up from the operation, linked to her terror of having said something to reveal her identity, gave her a fear of anaesthetics she never lost.

In her diaries, I discovered her contemporary account of the experience, which continued to haunt her for weeks. She had had a vision, 'like a dream', she wrote on 7 October, that made her aware of 'how brutal life is, how badly mankind deals with it and yet that God is merciful enough to allow mankind to live'.[28] She was standing before a kind of divine court, a young boy clad in only a shirt was wandering around and playing a tune; she could sense the presence of others but not see them. And then suddenly:[29]

It is as if in this one minute my life were to be judged, as if in this single minute of CONSCIOUSNESS it were to be subjected to God's unsparing judgement; but I am no longer just me but to be held to account for the whole of humanity. The judgement: 'You are not fit to count as enlightened beings . . . but I will be merciful and tolerate you as before.'

The deathly fear from that moment has still not gone.

This epiphany, part nightmare, part prophecy, occupied her thoughts for weeks. On 18 October, she wrote in her private diary the bleakest entry yet:

Sunday, 18th October
My love, and now I don't know how I can write out of myself everything that lies so deeply within me. All the terrible fear that crawls around me. How should I fight it when the weapons and strength I need to confront it dwindle and dwindle? At night when I lie awake or sit upright in bed it creeps over me, closer and closer, all the horror. And then I experience everything that makes your life intolerable and threatens to destroy all of you physically and spiritually. And I curse my powerlessness and retreat into prayer, which gives me only a little consolation and you not even that. How long will God stand by and watch it all! I wish this awful life would come to an end. And still we accept whatever comes and grab it indiscriminately, knowing full well that all we're being offered are temporary expedients.

Now the shocks followed fast upon each other. At the end of the year, Christian Arras brought back the terrible news that Ernst had been blinded and was on his own. Then, just when Marianne must have thought she could not take any more, a letter arrived from Edith Caspari, her former teacher in the kindergarten college, written on 31 December.[30] Edith described the horrors which had hit the Berlin community. Mothers had been deported, leaving their children behind. In one case, a fourteen-year-old child had been left on its own because it had diphtheria at the time of deportations. But what will have depressed Marianne beyond words was the news about her many friends and teachers. The inspirational Hannah Karminski, her former teacher and examiner, had been held as a hostage and subsequently deported with five hundred other RV employees. Karminski died on the transport, although Edith Caspari would not have known this at the time.[31] Other hostages had been shot, including Alfred Selbiger, Marianne's handsome conversation partner of February of whom Ernst had been so jealous. The book of Job was now 'our book', wrote Edith Caspari, concluding the letter with a heartfelt 'Farewell! Let us hope for a better New Year! Remain my Marianne!'

This was the end. The news was so devastating, so appalling, the sense of helplessness so overwhelming that there was nothing to be done, nothing to be said. After typing out a final entry, Marianne abandoned the letter-diary:[32]

New Year 1943
New Year. And one so different from what we had imagined and hoped. What one year can do to a person, one day, one hour even ... don't think, don't think! Our New Year's walk last year, the church with the organ privy to our countless wishes. My love! I can't comprehend the awful thing that has happened! To be with you, to help you, to protect you! My love, my love, what have I done! That I didn't stand by you or bring you out of danger! We should have spared ourselves all the barriers and all our bourgeois decency. But who could have predicted all that! What the year brought us – and what will this one bring? I pray, pray, pray that God will give you back to me, very, very soon. Your dear, good eyes ... I can't think about it or imagine it. And the way I found out! – but that is irrelevant.

How wonderfully the year began for us, and how it has ended! Shooting stars and other signs – are they good or bad omens? I don't know anything any more, don't want to know anything, don't want to think any more. Only you. To help you, to liberate you.
God must help us!

The Bund

In these months of despair a force entered Marianne's life that was to be her spiritual salvation even before it saved her physically. But to understand it, we need to cast our eyes back briefly to the early 1920s. The term 'Bund' (meaning 'league' or 'federation') is common to numerous organizations. Perhaps best known is the socialist Jewish Bund, with its many supporters in Poland and Russia. In post 1949 West Germany, the shorthand 'Bund' came to be used to denote the Federal Government as opposed to the individual states. Neither of these has anything to do with the Bund in Marianne's story, which is not well known and was never a large organization. Even at its peak, the *Bund. Gemeinschaft für sozialistisches Leben*, the League. Community for Socialist Life, never had more than a few hundred members.

The Bund emerged in Essen in the early 1920s out of a group attending the Volkshochschule lectures of Artur Jacobs. The Volkshochschulen, literally Higher Education Institutions for the People, were created after the First World War, seeking to advance the cultural and educational level of the working class. Jacobs, the son of a craftsman, and from a very pious Protestant background, had been active in the German youth movement before the First World War. Despite his modest origins, he had managed to attend university and trained as a school teacher. But he proved too radical for the conservative parents of Essen and, taking early retirement, Jacobs became an enthusiastic and inspirational lecturer in the Volkshochschulen. In 1924, the close and persisting contacts with his students were formalized with the creation of the Bund.[33]

The Bund was one of a small number of left-wing circles in Weimar Germany that sought to bring together Marxist thinking about society with Kant's view of the objective ethical laws governing the individual.[34] Jacobs combined a belief in the historical mission of the proletariat with an intense concern for the moral choices that face individuals in their daily lives. 'He who puts into practice the most modest idea,' Jacobs declared in 1929, 'is closer to the truth than he who merely researches or declaims the most sublime.'[35] The Bund's members were as likely to discuss marital relationships or a group member's work problems as the development of the world economy.[36]

The 'socialist life' of the Bund's title was thus meant to convey a dual programme of campaigning for a better society and experimenting with new ways of living, or 'life reform', in Weimar parlance. The Bund's core members developed a regular pattern of Sunday meetings in which the group would spend the whole day together, discussing, eating, walking, playing music and dancing. During the 1920s, Bund members bought, built or rented so-called 'Bund houses'. The 'Blockhaus' in Essen was completed in 1927; there was also a second Essen house, in the Dönhof and one in Wuppertal. Some of the Bund members lived in them as collectives (though without the free love practised by their 1960s successors).[37]

The group sought also to find a new relationship to physical movement and the body. Artur Jacobs' Jewish wife Dore, née Marcus, had been trained in eurhythmics and began to develop her own philosophy of dance and movement, aimed particularly at non-professional dancers. In 1925, Dore Jacobs' school for rhythm and movement was formally constituted. Many later members came to the Bund via instruction at Dore's school or after seeing some of her pupils perform. It was not uncommon during the Weimar period for dance and movement to be seen as part of the political struggle, and no left-wing festival was complete without its dance group and theatre presentations. There was also a broad shift at that time away from narrow intellectuality and towards a reaffirmation of man's natural energy and physicality. But it was rare that a consciously political organization and a dance group should be as closely tied as here. The Bund's aim was to create a socialist way of life which would incorporate the whole person – body, mind and soul.[38] In contrast to their 1960s counterparts' use of drugs, the Bund members were hostile to all forms of artificial intoxication, including alcohol.

The Bund was influenced by the notion of the *Orden* or order, a popular concept in Weimar Germany. An *Orden* consisted of a group bound together by a common oath under the natural authority of a charismatic leader. The Bund drew on this cultural attraction to charismatic leadership and Artur and Dore were held in awe by the other members. The Bund was thus a kind of hybrid. It was a circle of friends rather than a formal organization. At the same time, it was a very tight-knit group of people who spent much time together, in some cases living together, who discussed everything and who swore a solemn oath or 'commitment' to one another.[39] *Verpflichtung*, or commitment, was the key concept. Initially just the core members, the so-called Inner Circle, ceremonially committed themselves, swearing an oath to the Bund. At later annual festivals, newcomers joined the ranks of the *Verpflichteten*. The group's excursions – every summer, for example,

Artur and Dore Jacobs in 1964

they would go to the same retreat in the Sauerland – provided an opportunity for members from further afield to bond with the core members and absorb the group's atmosphere.

One feature of the Bund that most impressed newcomers was its ability to transcend the class barriers that were otherwise so insurmountable in Weimar Germany. A number of the Bund's leading figures were teachers who had risen from modest backgrounds. Others, particularly some of the women, came from educated, bourgeois households, while many others were workers. The middle class Tove Gerson, for example, remembered being awe-struck in her first dance class by the way Dore related to a worker in the group:[40]

'The idea that without any awkwardness you could say to a worker,

"Fritz, come on show us [how you'd drive in that prop]", I'd never seen that. I was a bourgeois and the fact that we were working together there, in a flash I suddenly saw the Bund's attitude to the social question.'

The group was also more conscious than most of gender issues and was committed to equality in marriage. One of the most incisive and progressive pamphlets published by the Bund was the tract *Mann und Frau als Kampfgenossen* (*Man and Woman as Comrades in the Struggle*), which appeared in 1932.[41] This awareness of gender gave it a strong appeal for women (though, ironically, so did Artur's patriarchal role as father of the movement). Moreover, Dore's work with dance and movement offered women the chance themselves to become dance and gymnastics teachers, a career increasingly recognized as a profession in the 1920s and 1930s. Equally important for the shaping of the Bund's identity was the fact that gender issues were the most direct and challenging area of daily life in which to apply and test its principles.[42]

Racism was another core area of concern to the Bund. Remarkably, as early as 1920, Artur Jacobs wrote an article about racism in education which rejected selection based on racial or ethnic principles.[43] The presence in the group of Jewish and half-Jewish members, including Dore, sharpened the group's sensibility to such issues.[44]

The Bund in the Third Reich

After 1933, the challenges to the members' commitment became tougher. Many similar left-wing circles collapsed under the pressures, whether because they had underestimated the regime and took part in foolhardy protest actions, or because Nazi infiltration resulted in the group's destruction, or because opportunism and fear led to quiescence and silence. By and large, the Bund did not engage in open resistance. But its commitment to maintaining group meetings and communication and its low-key efforts to undermine and expose racism and fascism in the outside world demanded courage enough. In the early years, Bund members also protected individuals on the run from political persecution, and helped them get out of the country.[45]

For someone so idealistic and humane, Jacobs always had an extraordinary degree of political insight. For example, he worried that the very honesty and civil courage of many Bund members might lead to dangerous acts of opposition or a failure to make proper risk assessments. Lisa Jacob, one of Dore Jacobs' first pupils and a founder member of the Bund, recalled:[46]

Artur Jacobs taught us (and not a few tears flowed in this 'extra tuition') to fight the enemy with his own weapons. Faith in human decency or in the propriety of the judiciary was completely inappropriate. We learned to keep secrets, lie, camouflage and mislead.

Lisa was Jewish by background, and these lessons were later to save her life. In intensive workshops, the group systematically analysed the various elements of National Socialist ideology. Jacobs developed 'seventeen points', a kind of intellectual catechism listing all the weaknesses of the National Socialist creed. Another of the Bund's founder members and influential figures was Ernst Jungbluth. His widow Ellen recalled in an interview that the great strength of both Artur Jacobs and Ernst was their thoroughness. They never treated a particular incident, a mistake or a problem as a one-off accident but always went back to its roots. Group members would take part in role plays, acting out how they would respond to a specific eventuality, an interrogation, for example, and getting the group to criticize. They repeated the appropriate answers over and over again until they could say them in their sleep.[47]

Even in the Nazi years, the Bund groups managed to maintain their regular meetings and these were crucial in helping individuals find the right balance between personal safety and activism.[48] Above all, the Bund broke through each individual's sense of isolation. In an early post-1945 publication, the Bund tried to make foreign friends aware of just what it had meant to live in a situation where you could trust no one. Where anyone, any neighbour was a potential enemy. Where there was no free press, just a constant stream of lies and deceptions.[49] In Germany, unlike other countries that had national resistance movements against German occupation, there was no consensus of oppositional feelings or ideals that found a broad echo, no national ethos that could unite resistance.[50]

In contrast to many other left-wing opponents of Nazism, the Bund recognized from the start that the Nazi movement's anti-Semitism was at the heart of the problem. Particularly after Kristallnacht, the Bund showed its true colours. As Tove Gerson recalled, Artur's slogan was: 'Step forward and break through the isolation of the Jews.' It was liberating to know what one should do. Tove Gerson remembered, for example, having to run the gauntlet of a baying mob to visit a wealthy Jewish family in their destroyed apartment on the day after Kristallnacht. But her solidarity was not enough to prevent the couple from later committing suicide. Artur Jacobs' private diary contains ample testimony of his refusal to look the other way.[51]

When the deportations started, the Bund gave the deportees what assistance it could, helping them carry their luggage, offering psychological support and sending parcels to the ghettoes. In 1983, the German Radio Station WDR broadcast a moving selection of letters between Trude Brandt, who had been deported from Posen to Poland in 1939, and Lisa Jacob who, with the assistance of other Bund members, regularly sent her parcels of food and clothing.[52] In 1941, Artur Jacobs recorded his last conversation with a woman on the transport to Minsk. She thanked him for his help:[53]

'What for? For the tiny assistance that was more of a help to us than to you? We must thank you for being able to discharge a tiny portion of our guilt. It's more a token of goodwill than anything more material, but one suffocates if one does nothing . . .'

She (after weeks of holding herself together and forcing herself to appear calm) burst into tears. 'You don't know what comfort you give me.'

Most of the group's Jewish members managed to leave the country before the war. Others, like Dore Jacobs, lived in a 'privileged mixed marriage' (a mixed marriage where the male partner was not Jewish and the children had not been raised as Jews) and were for the moment safe from deportation. April 1942 brought the group's biggest challenge yet, when Lisa Jacob was put on the deportation list to Izbica. But the Bund had long prepared for this eventuality. Lisa went underground, to be fed and supported by the other Bund members for three years.

Marianne and the Bund

Marianne's first contact with the Bund had come much earlier, in 1933. In that year, Marianne and other Jewish pupils had been prohibited from receiving further dance lessons at the Folkwangschule. Marianne's parents sent her to train with Lisa Jacob and Dore Jacobs. One of Marianne's most endearing traits, so far as I was concerned, was her confident, dismissive judgement, particularly on things cultural, about which she was so knowledgeable. Whenever former Bund members talked to me about Dore Jacobs' marvellous approach to movement and dance I would replay in my mind Marianne's verdict: 'Utterly boring!' She said it was not nearly as constructive, lively or imaginative as the classes she had taken at the Folkwangschule. But at least the instruction gave Marianne her first contact with Bund members, in the communal house in the Dönhoff.

After a while, Marianne had discontinued the dance lessons and lost contact with the Bund. In the Krombachs' flat the night before Ernst's deportation, she was reintroduced to Artur Jacobs. He invited Marianne to call on him if she needed advice or support. Soon after, when Marianne was working in the nursing home with one of the community nurses, Artur came in with food coupons and again offered help. From time to time, Bund members would bring coupons or food for the home. Artur asked Marianne to keep him informed of developments because he was compiling a dossier on Nazi policies.[54] In the spiritual and emotional vacuum left by Ernst's deportation, Marianne did seek out Artur and his wife, at first hesitantly, then quite frequently. 'They always made me very welcome, and for me it was an enormous moral help, you know, to be able to talk about this dreadful business and unburden myself.'

Some passages from Artur Jacobs' remarkable diary have been quoted earlier. I was first alerted to the diary's existence when I discovered that Dore Jacobs, now a widow, had in the 1960s or 1970s sent Marianne an extract from it as a keepsake of Artur. As I gradually made contact with the surviving members of Jacobs' group, I asked them about the diary. None of them knew where it was, but one thought there might be something in the Essen city archive. Sure enough, the loose-leaf volumes, some in their original state, some copied out later, were in a large cardboard box in the vaults. They were to turn out to be one of the most dramatic sources for this book. The diary jumps between thoughts about Goethe, lyrical reflections on nature, moving accounts of Artur's attempts to support Essen Jews and extracts from an equally moving correspondence with Artur's son Gottfried, trapped in Holland and suffering terribly from the German occupation. There are also powerful insights into the Nazi system, a record of his growing awareness of the unique monstrosity of the Final Solution and acute descriptions of people he had met, including the Krombachs – and Marianne.

We first learn what Jacobs thought of Marianne in a diary entry written in August 1942. The entry is itself an extract from a letter Jacobs had just written to his son Gottfried. In the 1930s, Gottfried had been sent by his parents to the safety of the Netherlands, but now found himself living under German occupation and drafted into forced labour. His sad letters to his parents must have been almost unbearable to them. In June 1942, Gottfried had written that he fainted at work from under-nourishment and was not sure he could continue to bear the demands placed on him. In July, he had sent an even more distressing letter, describing the deportation of his lover, Gina, from Holland. Artur sought various ways to persuade Gottfried to shake off his depression and throw himself into helping others. Finally, he tried a positive role model:[55]

Yesterday evening a young girl was with me, whose best friend had to go to the East. She has always had a rich and varied life with many friends, books, music etc. Now everything has been taken from her. And how does she live? I asked her. She told me: from early to late I sit in the office, then at home, to help my mother, then I make up parcels [inserted in pencil below 'for deported Jews'] and then I think how else I can help. By then, it's usually after midnight. This is not the life I was used to, but it satisfies me. The only unsatisfying thing about it is that it is much too little.

Hers is certainly not a happy life in the usual sense of the term. But isn't it nevertheless worth living? And don't you think that it can yield moments of deep satisfaction that a worry-free, 'happy' life can never offer? And what a different complexion life has when it triumphs over such difficult conditions!

Although Marianne was not named, the details and her explicit mention in other entries make her almost certainly the person described. As in Imo Moszkowicz's memory, here, too, Marianne Strauss emerges as a role model. To earn the respect of a man as rigorous with himself and others as Artur Jacobs was some achievement.

In early September, Artur's diary is full of comments about Izbica and excerpts from Ernst's letters. On the 18th it refers to the meeting with Christian Arras and a further quotation from Ernst. Then on the 22nd:[56]

Singing with Marianne Str.

Folk songs and serious ones from Brahms.

That's what she wished. But one does it with ambivalent feelings.

How could someone so caught up in the thick of things,* for whom life consists of nothing but waiting for something terrible to happen or hearing about something terrible that's already happened, how could she open herself up to this beautiful serious world. It seems so far away, so unreal, like a cruel joke?!

A front-line soldier, hearing these old songs for the first time, suddenly began to cry – so terrible, so unnerving, so unsettling was the contradiction . . .

Yes, crying seems almost more natural than such carefree immersion in the stream of feeling that flows from the songs.

* *She was awaiting her deportation [Pencil addition at bottom of page].*

Although Marianne's self-discipline was implicit in the restraint of her own letters, it was clearly evident to perceptive outside observers as well. As Uri Weinberg told me in Jerusalem, 'She could keep herself. I can also.' The soldier weeps, but Artur and Marianne, with iron self-control, kept their feelings and thoughts to themselves.[57] Just as in Berlin, but now in even more difficult circumstances, Marianne managed to concentrate on the present and set aside her burdensome knowledge of terror and loss. This capacity for self-control and ruthless focusing was a crucial weapon in her armoury for survival and was later transmuted into a strategy for dealing with the past.

In November, Marianne visited Artur Jacobs, seeking courage to face an impending Gestapo interrogation. Jacobs noted:[58]

Earlier with Marianne – in personal difficulties. She has to attend tomorrow. Perhaps something minor – perhaps not. One has to be ready for anything.

She was very calm.

Meeting Marianne on 31 December, just after the desperate news about Ernst had reached Essen, Artur Jacobs could only shake his head at Marianne's rigid composure:[59]

Strange the way the girl is, with her apparent calm.

Terrible things must be going on inside – how could it be otherwise?

But on the outside she keeps up the conventions, like a suit of armour that prevents the failing body from collapsing.

How much more natural one would find any kind of wild cry. But perhaps this is the best part of conventional behaviour. Otherwise, such a young person would fall apart.

And yet one senses that she is frozen, rather than finding release in sorrow and experiencing new life and depth.

On the one hand total pessimism, which brusquely rejects every consoling word, every tiny trace of hope, even the smallest shadow of a possible way forward. On the other, a web of illusions in which the soul staggers around like a drunkard, with no sense of reality.

Marianne herself was aware of how strange her calm demeanour must have seemed to others. She noted in her diary:[60]

Sometimes they must all think that the most important things barely affect me (that's the feeling I have), but I push everything deep down and let no one near.

If Jacobs was impressed with Marianne, she, for her part, was increasingly influenced by the Bund. To me she said, 'It really was the most formative influence on my life.'[61] In her diary and letters of the time she was naturally extremely cautious about mentioning her contacts with the group. True, we find a former nurse of the Jewish Community, Sister Tamara (not Jewish herself), with whom Marianne was in correspondence, expressing her pleasure in spring 1943 at learning that Marianne had found a regular sanctuary at the Blockhaus in Essen-Stadtwald.[62] But for the most part, contemporary evidence of the Bund's influence on Marianne is less direct. From November 1942, for example, Marianne's diary displays a new interest in the wider political and military picture. Of course, the changing military situation began to offer a glimmer of hope with the result that, in any case, world news was now more palatable and worthy of note. Nevertheless, it is noticeable that, from then on, Marianne's diary is interspersed with descriptions of national and international affairs. Elements of the Bund's ethical teaching also appear from this time. Here she is, writing in her diary in response to a new threat from the Gestapo:

Yesterday they gave me a moment of fear. I received some orders, well, I can tell you the details later, I hope it's all sorted out. But the thing about it is: one simply has to submit to whatever happens. The question of lawful or unlawful is an illusion. One has to build one's own ethical code to live by. It is so important that one can justify one's actions to oneself and say: it was right. Whatever the consequences. The world is unpredictable and unjust and therefore one must be at peace with oneself.

This approach to ethics and the law was exactly that of Artur Jacobs and the Bund – bow to force majeure when one had to, but live by one's own ethical code as far as one was able.

As Marianne sought to regain her footing after the shocking news from Izbica, she adopted Jacobs' strategy of trying to identify the root of the problem so as to make it more manageable. 'Explain, investigate, prove, understand, everything, everything. Not this permanent state of being thrown out of balance,' she wrote in January.[63] And during spring 1943, a little of her old vigour gradually returned.

Family tensions

For Marianne, drawing closer to the Bund meant pulling away from her parents. Rather than forging family unity, the stress and strains of everyday life served further to inflame the tensions. In November 1942, conflict worsened after Marianne received a summons to visit Gestapo HQ.[64] The Gestapo had, it seems, confiscated two letters addressed to her which contained some money. The interrogation, Marianne noted in her diary, was not very serious. But, as she also noted:[65]

It was the perfect opportunity to open my box of letters and diary entries and to go through everything and read it most carefully. Afterwards they could claim such pious reasons for having done so; for example, that there should be no incriminating material in case of a search, or worrying about me . . .

At first, I thought it was the Gestapo who had searched through Marianne's things. But then I realized that it was the family who had done so. Marianne was left feeling violated and bitter; it felt, she said, like a rape. As a result, she cut herself off from them, and removed all her things from the house. In her diary, she wrote:[66]

Unspoken and spoken accusations against the bad, cold daughter who shows her loved ones only ingratitude, egotism and lack of trust. I am used to them, and they affect me no more now than before.

Fifty years later we can feel more sympathy with desperate parents, anxious about their daughter's activities at a time of such danger, seeking to understand what was going through her mind. As Dore Jacobs reported, the Bund itself had a similar philosophy:[67]

Leave no one to their own devices. Don't rely blindly on even the most dependable; for example, in relation to their room, their letters and papers. Periodic checks essential (we called it 'house cleaning').

In their concern that nothing should jeopardize their plans to leave the country, Marianne's parents must have seen her as rather selfish. Every risk she took could affect the fate of her brother, her parents, her aunt and uncle, her grandmother and Lore's mother. But we can also sympathize with Marianne. Her every impulse moved her to help others. Moreover, she was only nineteen and faced with the common teenage challenge of emotional disengagement from rather overbearing parents. It was her tragedy that her fight for independence had to take place under such horrendous conditions. A few days later, the violation was still very much on her mind:[68]

I think with horror of the events of last Thursday and want to thrust them away from me as far as possible, but the memories are more resistant than I would like and make everything even more difficult than it would otherwise be. Also, they ensure that there is nothing left to tie me to my parents. I feel more burdened than I can say. I wish there were some way to make a physical separation so that I would not be continually reminded how unnatural our relationship is.

I wonder if Marianne ever looked back at this passage. In the light of later events, it must have been unbearable.

The Strausses observed

As 1942 became 1943, the family's protective bubble grew thinner and thinner. The remaining 'privileged' members of the community were picked off one by one for deportation. When Marianne's former boss in the Jewish Community, Fritz Ostermann, was deported to Theresienstadt in June 1943 with his wife Else and the last remaining Community officials, the Strauss family were left behind as probably the last full-Jewish family in the city, perhaps in the region.[69]

Another major source of anxiety was the increasingly intensive bombing. The industrial Ruhr area, with Essen at its heart, was a prime target for the Royal Air Force. On the night of 5 March 1943, Essen suffered something quite outside its previous range of experience. In little over an hour, 50,000 civilians were rendered homeless, 1,600 injured and 479 killed. A further 20,000 had to leave their homes temporarily. Hardly had the town begun to recover when it suffered another massive raid a week later, on 12 March. In that one night, Essen was hit by

500,000 explosive bombs and 200,000 incendiary devices, over five times the number of incendiaries dropped during the whole of 1942. For the next few weeks there was something of a lull as other cities in the region received the same treatment, but in May and July there was more heavy bombing – in July there were another 509 deaths in Essen.[70]

Denied access to the public air-raid shelters, the Strauss family took refuge in their own cellar, surrounded by packing cases full of their belongings. In our conversations, Marianne remembered the air raids as a time of terror. But she also remembered watching from the windows and fantasizing that an aeroplane might touch down and lift them away from it all.[71]

'My uncle Alfred being such a war buff, he had a map on the wall and would put little stickers in, hoping that the British would soon be licking the Germans. Every night he would sit with this map, like a general. That was his pastime, hoping for the best. Well, it kept him busy, he didn't have much else to do, unfortunately.'

Barely once in the whole of the war do the bomb attacks figure in Marianne's letters or diary. Even Artur Jacobs, so selfless and universal in his perspective, became obsessed by them for a while in 1943. It is a sign of how enormous were the other threats and pressures on Marianne that even the most damaging raids did not feature as significant events in her wartime experience.

With the growing housing shortage in Essen, the Strauss family had to share their home with even more people. Marianne told me that in March 1943 she rescued the secretary to the Jewish Community, Irene Drucker, who had become homeless, and brought her home with her son and daughter. When a mixed-marriage couple, the Rosenbergs, were assigned to a second room a month or so later, the Strausses effectively lost the use of their own ground floor.

When I was given Hanna Aron's phone number in Connecticut, and told that she had known Marianne, I did not immediately realize that Hanna was Irene Drucker's daughter, and thus someone who could give me a brief glimpse inside the Strauss household during the family's last months in Essen. In August 1998, I took a Greyhound bus down from New York to Hartford, Connecticut. That evening, Mrs Aron and I had dinner in my hotel in Farmington, and I began to learn about her life.

Hanna Aron in Connecticut

Though very lively, round-faced and cheerful at seventy-three, she had recently had a stroke, so I was a little worried when she drove off into the night whether she would get home. Happily, the following morning she returned to take me to her house, where we were due to tape an interview.[72]

Hanna gave the same kind of feisty account of herself as had Marianne's schoolfriends whom I interviewed in Israel. Born in 1925, she was two years younger than Marianne. In 1940–1 she had gone to the Yavne school in Cologne, and she too had found it a marvellous experience. The school was 'beautiful . . . so many lights went on, it was just gorgeous. Not the building but the people.' For a brief period after April 1942, Hanna, her parents Bernhard and Irene and her younger brother Wolfgang had been assigned to the Holbeckshof barracks. But because Hanna's mother was a convert to Judaism and thus 'racially' an Aryan, the family was allowed to return home.

In June 1942, Hanna's friend Richard Fuchs was on the deportation list to Izbica, and it was then that Hanna spent the much-discussed night with him in Holbeckshof, pleading with him to go underground. Hanna told me that on the morning of the deportation, the deportees were made to stand on the platform in the pouring rain for hours. When the train finally arrived from Cologne, where it had taken other deportees on board, the Essen Jews were soaking wet. As they boarded the train, somebody shouted that there were corpses on board. Some of the infirm pushed on to the train in Cologne must have died in the time it had taken to get to Essen.

A couple of weeks after losing Richard Fuchs, Hanna lost her father. Bernhard Drucker had been conscripted into clerical work in a warehouse in Essen-Katernberg. He died when a heavy load fell from a crane under mysterious circumstances. Another Jewish conscript was to die in similar fashion not long after. Hanna's sixteen-year-old brother Wolfgang was working on the same site and had to endure the experience of one hospital after another refusing to take his father. By the time a Catholic hospital finally deigned to admit him, it was too late.

And then came the massive air raids of March 1943. Living near the Krupp factory, the Druckers were very exposed to the risk of destruction. Hanna had a vivid memory of the night her house went up:

'We were in there and every time a bomb came down you'd hear this szhszhszhszhszh boom! This went on for twenty minutes, and it was just awful [. . .] My brother threw down a mattress from the third floor and he threw down some clothes, which we put into a big basket and that was all we saved. We couldn't save anything else. The house was burning, we had to get out. This was during the night [. . .] Krupp's had a shoe-repair shop and we sat there, all by ourselves, just crying. The next morning I don't know whether my mother went to work. I think she tried to go. And my brother and I, we were sitting alone [. . .] and Marianne came and said, you can come to us we will give you a room'.

Like an angel, Marianne had appeared, scooping the family off the pavement and inviting them back to live in Ladenspelderstrasse.

'So my mother somewhere found a *Schubkarre*, what's this in English?'
'A cart.'
'Yes, to take the little leftovers that we had because this was far away: Holsterhausen. So we pushed them on a cart, my brother and I, to

Holsterhausen . . . and so we got there and the Straussen gave us there a front room. I remember the front room was empty, I don't think it was empty before, they must have done this quickly. I give them so much credit for this, you know. We had nothing, of course.'

Her mother managed to organize a couple of beds after a few weeks and Hanna's brother slept on the floor on a mattress. By this time the other tenants, the Rosenbergs, had moved in:

'Now there were three women who had to share the kitchen, Frau Strauss, Frau Rosenberg and my mother. You can imagine . . . But Frau Strauss, the *kleine* Frau Strauss, she must have been very tolerant. I can tell you one thing, when we were in the barracks, it was always terrible to cook in the main kitchen, but here in the Strauss house it was OK. Everybody got along because everybody made an extra effort to get along, you knew you couldn't get on each other's nerves.'

Hanna said Ine had been wonderful and very generous. Generous in what sense? 'Well in sharing, the sense of, you know, women in the kitchen, it's not easy to do. She also shared food.' Did they have food, then? 'They had food. If you had money, you had food.' In retrospect, Hanna felt Ine was a rather subservient wife:

'Looking back at it some years afterwards, she was the typical traditional housewife who did what the husband says. I think she got up when he said get up and she lay down when he said lie down. Was this Marianne's impression?'

'Not absolutely.'

'Because I always thought of her as a very obedient wife, you know. I did not see this in my parents, but of course my parents' situation was different. Siegfried was a big heavy strapping guy, she was a little itsy bitsy of a woman. In public at least she always seemed to be doing what he wanted. She was definitely the traditional housewife, no question about it. Marianne always had fights with her father. Loud fights.'

How did Hanna know? Had the noise come down from upstairs, I wondered. Hanna said it had. She had a notion that Marianne's mother used to leave the room when there was a fight. What did they fight about? Hanna said it was more ideological than anything else:

'Marianne at that time was very much into Communism. Socialism, to put it in a more acceptable word today, you know. Communism at that time was not a bad thing. It is today. But at that time it was not a bad thing. And Marianne really fought for the idea of equality among the people.'

This fitted very well with the impression Marianne's writings gave of her developing identity. In 1943, she must have been testing out the Bund's ideas against her parents. Not surprisingly, the solid businessman Siegfried Strauss didn't like the sound of it at all. Hanna had some sympathy for Siegfried:

'It must have been terrible, you know, for the men too, can you imagine? To be at home day after day. First of all, with your wife; I mean, I married you for better or worse but not for lunch and here you have the men sitting there all day long. And with no outlet, nowhere to go really, nothing to do. It must have been terrible.'

But for company, Hanna preferred Alfred and Lore. They were not quite so stiff as Siegfried and Ine.

After we finished the interview, I took some photos of Hanna outside her house. She lived in the sort of classic leafy American suburb that I knew from a thousand films. It was an area where one would be absolutely lost without a car. When Hanna had her stroke, she told me that the brief spectre of carlessness had been a terrifying prospect. In this area, I felt, to take away your car ownership was almost to take away your citizenship. Not for the first or last time, I heard an odd echo. For a moment, I caught a glimpse of the ageing process as a malevolent regime, gradually, incrementally laying down new restrictive laws and ordinances – shutting down this right, that pleasure, blocking off opportunities and marking out the victims.

That evening, a friend of Hanna's collected me from the hotel and drove me to the temple. At the synagogue, I met up with Hanna, her son Michael and Michael's wife and children. Hearing Hanna's enthusiastic participation in the service was a particular pleasure. It established a different kind of connection to her former self, giving a different resonance to the answers she had given to my questions about Jewish identity. For Hanna, those 'lights that went on' in the Yavne had never gone out.

I had agreed to give a brief talk after the service about Marianne's story and about Hanna's relationship to her. Afterwards, I didn't feel particularly happy with my talk. I wasn't sure that you could turn a

Holocaust experience into Sabbath evening fare. It seemed somehow American to believe that you ever could. But Hanna looked radiant. Earlier, she had told me about the crying fits she had had in past years about 'how they destroyed us'. If the public narration of the past gave her some satisfaction, I felt she was well entitled to it.

There was one other remarkable moment in the question and answer session. Someone stood up and said he had been a good friend of Heinz Krombach. They had taken gymnastics classes together in the Krombachs' front room. It seemed I could arrive on any foreign shore in the world and find that a small piece of Marianne's past had washed up there.

9

The Escape

For almost four and a half years the Strauss family had sat and waited. Their attempts to leave the country had met with reversal after reversal. But sometime in spring 1943, they gained new reason to hope. Marianne's recollection was that the Abwehr had obtained visas for them to go to Sweden. The records show, though, that the Gestapo believed the family was poised to go to Switzerland.[1] Since I knew that Switzerland had become the prime destination for the Abwehr's protective efforts, I thought that Marianne had probably misremembered. Subsequently, however, I found ample evidence that the family had indeed set its sights on Sweden. The Abwehr may have deliberately kept the Gestapo in the dark. The Gestapo's information was that the Strauss family was due to depart on 30 August 1943. Possibly the Gestapo was as misinformed about the timing as about the destination.

The Deutsche Bank records in Frankfurt show that in May 1943 Siegfried emptied his account with the Deutsche Bank – showing that he really was expecting to leave the country very soon.[2] He sold his last assets – RM65,000 in securities held in his blocked account – with the proceeds going to a notary, Ivor Morting, in Sweden, the son-in-law of Ine's distant relative Grete Sander. The Deutsche Bank confirmed the instruction on 10 May, noting that the securities had been accepted by the Deutsche Golddiskontbank at the usual exchange rate of 4 per cent. With a loss of value of 96 per cent, the transfer produced only 4,368 Swedish kronor.[3] Another transfer of RM32,626.95 netted some 2,192 kronor.[4] On 2 June, Alfred wrote to the Deutsche Bank, asking for his remaining bank holdings to be converted too. Because he had to pay RM21,908 flight tax, his assets of over RM75,000 were reduced to a yield of just 3,700 kronor.[5]

There is further evidence that the family was poised to leave. On 23 June, Sister Tamara wrote to Marianne, rather incautiously naming her destination: 'I personally fear very much that I shall not find you there in late autumn. For *you* I wish *deeply* that you soon land in Sweden,'[6] and going on to enthuse about the qualities of the country and the possibilities for Marianne to use her child-caring talents and energies there. She also hoped that Marianne would convey a message to her former colleague, Julie Koppel.

On 2 July, bank director Wilhelm Hammacher wrote to the Gestapo asking permission to buy the Strausses' furniture. The letter explained that the family would soon be emigrating, and that Hammacher himself had been bombed out. Attached was a note signed by Siegfried Strauss, listing the furniture he wished to sell.[7] On 19 July the Gestapo agreed.[8] The family also deposited goods in various places for collection after the war. The Jürgens received for safe-keeping several trunks, containing clothes, linen, silver, pictures, chairs, other furniture and some Persian rugs. Business papers were left with Herr Hammacher.[9]

The Bund gave Marianne its good wishes and a more practical offer. Artur Jacobs told her that, if it came to the crunch, she should turn to the Bund for help. Something which Marianne never told me, and which I can no longer fully corroborate, was reported to me by Bund member Tove Gerson. Tove, by 1943 safe in the USA with her half-Jewish husband, herself heard it only after the war from another Bundist, Else Bramesfeld, a life-long friend of Marianne's who died long before I had a chance to meet her. So the story, at two removes, may be apocryphal, but it has the ring of Artur Jacobs' honest clarity. Apparently, Artur said to Marianne, 'You can't save your parents, but you can save yourself.'[10]

Everything seemed set for emigration, yet Marianne did take one precautionary step, though we know neither why nor how she did it. On 12 August 1943 she obtained – or perhaps renewed – an international postal ID card, made out to Marianne Strauss, leaving out the obligatory

Marianne's wartime pass

'Sara' and thus all visible sign that she was Jewish. The card identified her as a *Kindergärtnerin*, resident in Essen.

The SS, the Abwehr and the Strauss brothers

Until July 1943, the Gestapo's efforts to pierce the Strauss brothers' protective shield continued to fail. On 27 May, the Düsseldorf Gestapo sent a telegram to Berlin, stating that there seemed little prospect of the Strauss family leaving Germany and asking if they could be included in the next deportation to Theresienstadt.[11] From other Gestapo files we know that a transport was due to leave on 16 June 1943.[12] But when Eichmann replied on 9 June, stating that he had again approached the Oberkommando of the Wehrmacht, he once more asked the Düsseldorf office to hold fire.[13] Nevertheless, the local officials may have been encouraged by Eichmann's involvement to think the matter would be soon resolved. They fielded an enquiry from the Düsseldorf Finance Office as to whether the Strausses would soon be evacuated[14] with a telephone call to say they would hold off replying formally for about three weeks. They clearly hoped that three weeks was sufficient time for Eichmann to confirm the Strausses' deportation.[15] But by the end of July, they were still unable to respond.

As Eichmann's interventions in the Strausses' case have shown, the RSHA had been questioning the Abwehr's use of Jewish agents ever since 1941. In February 1942, Heinrich Himmler complained directly to Hitler about it. In summer 1942, however, the Abwehr's chief, Admiral Wilhelm Canaris, had been able to regain some of the initiative. An espionage disaster and the death of several German agents had led Hitler to make a wild comment proposing the use of 'criminals or Jews' for such work. But by early 1943, the SD began Operation 'Deposit Account', reviewing the Abwehr's use of Jews as agents. In June 1943, Dietrich Bonhoeffer, at that stage held in an army prison in Berlin-Tegel, was interrogated on the matter. It seems that sometime in July Hitler also explicitly rejected using Jews for espionage work.[16]

Then, Himmler made a rather surprising deal with the increasingly powerless Canaris. Himmler had his own reasons for not wanting to dissolve the Abwehr completely – not least the fact that he was putting out peace feelers, and needed the Abwehr to act as go-between with the Allies. The Abwehr was allowed to survive, but the quid pro quo was that it should stop using 'unreliable elements' as agents. A reorganization followed. Hans von Dohnanyi was imprisoned and placed under investigation. Hans Oster was suspended and placed under house arrest. The registry of the Abwehr's Bremen section indicates that it received key instructions concerning the use of Jewish agents in mid-July. On 24 July, Bremen responded by letter, appending a ten-page list of the Jewish informants run by the Bremen office which has not been preserved but which, presumably, identified the Strauss brothers by name.[17]

Death sentences come in different forms. On 6 August 1943, unbeknown to the Strauss family, theirs arrived in Düsseldorf in the form of a short telegram, signed by Eichmann's deputy SS-Sturmbannführer Günther. It announced that the Wehrmacht High Command was 'no

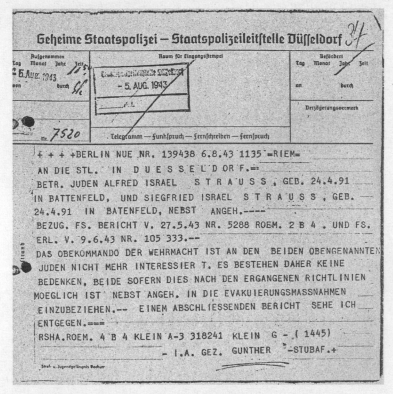

*Gestapo telegram – Wehrmacht has no further interest in the
Strauss family*

longer interested' in Siegfried and Alfred Strauss. There were no objec-
tions, 'insofar as existing guidelines allow', to including the Strauss
family as well as their dependants in the evacuations.[18] A couple of days
later, these instructions were passed on to Essen, but with a macabre
twist. The draft text of the letter to Essen said that there was now no
reason to *include* the Strauss family in the evacuation measures. Perhaps
the Gestapo officials were confused by their own euphemisms, mixing
up 'emigration' (survival) with 'evacuation' (murder). In any case, a
stroke of the pencil hastily changed the reprieve to a death sentence:[19]

*There are no longer any grounds for ~~including~~ excluding the Strauss
brothers and their families ~~in~~ from the evacuation measures.*

The Essen Gestapo was instructed to prevent the Strauss family's
emigration and to await further directions with regard to a transport to
Theresienstadt. An additional memo on 8 August, some two months
after the initial enquiry, advised the Düsseldorf Finance Office to abandon the transfer of funds.[20]

Whether Siegfried and Alfred received warnings of the change in their
status, we do not know. Marianne's memory was that, up to the end,
they were still expecting to leave in a few days' time. They may have
suspected something was wrong on 30 August, if that really was their
departure date, since they did not receive their passports. On that same
day, Kriminalsekretär Kosthorst of the Essen Gestapo telephoned his
superiors in Düsseldorf to warn them that the Strauss family might well
try to make a run for it; it was decided to imprison them on the 31st.[21]
The family was once again within reach of the 'gravedigger's spade'.

Could they, should they, have got away earlier? Were they still
finessing, waiting for the last transfers of money to be effected, however
pitiful the amount to be paid into the Swedish accounts? In May,
Siegfried had authorized the sale of his final assets. But Alfred's transfer
of assets, though initiated in June, was not finalized until 24 August.[22]
Had the brothers really been waiting for the funds to clear? According
to a letter from Wilhelm Hammacher after the war, 'The chance to
leave the country had existed since the beginning of 1943. Why the
unfortunate victims should have hesitated so long is something I wonder
about to this day.'[23] But Hammacher's testimony is not really to be
trusted. In the context of Marianne's restitution claims on Strauss family
property in his possession, he had a strong interest in emphasizing the
quality of his aid. The failure, he was trying to argue, lay not in the
degree of support provided but in the family's own unwillingness to
leave. I was not sure if I should simply discount his letter. What held me
back from doing so, though, was that Hammacher's assertion was so
reminiscent of the Strauss family's reluctance to leave in the earlier
period. It is just possible that their assets were still delaying their departure in 1943.

Amongst Marianne's papers I found a copy of a letter sent in 1961 from Ernst Dahl, Lore's brother in Canada, to Marianne's cousin René Wolf in France. These two, together with Marianne, were Alfred and Lore's surviving legal heirs. From Ernst Dahl's letter, I learned that in the summer of 1943 Alfred had not simply transferred money to Sweden – he had sent on some of his suits. I understood Alfred's logic: if the brothers were going to live in Sweden and seek employment there, they would need respectable clothing. After reading about so many family disappointments, I found this evidence of careful bourgeois planning right up to the end almost unbearable.

The clothes arrived in Stockholm and awaited their owner for the rest of the war.[24]

A *few minutes before* 12

Among Marianne's papers are several drafts of the article she published in *Das Münster am Hellweg*. With very minor differences they all say that on 31 August at 10 a.m. two of the most feared members of the local Gestapo, Kriminaloberassistent Kosthorst[25] and Kriminaloberassistent Hahn, appeared at Ladenspelderstrasse 47. They gave the family two hours to prepare for a forthcoming transport. The arrival of the Gestapo, Marianne wrote, was like a bolt from the blue. Up to that moment, the family had still been expecting to get away in the next few days. Now, in just two hours, they had to adjust to their new fate and scramble everything together for deportation.

Shortly before midday, Marianne's father passed her a few hundred marks, which she stuffed into the pocket of her tracksuit.[26] Meanwhile, the Gestapo went down into the cellar to inspect the substantial family belongings stored there in packing cases. Seizing her chance, and without being able to say goodbye to the family, Marianne slipped down the stairs to the front door and left:

'I ran for my life, expecting a pistol shot behind me any minute. But it had always seemed to me better to end my life like that than to await an unimaginable fate in Auschwitz or Łodz, Treblinka or Izbica. But there was no shot, nobody running after me, no order, no shout!'

In our conversations, Marianne added a few details to the picture. She told me that when the Gestapo arrived, a friendly churchman, Pastor Keinath, was visiting the family.[27] He hid on the balcony and tried to get away while the Gestapo were down in the cellar. Unfortunately, the stairs squeaked. Marianne said that when the Gestapo appeared, Keinath looked like a ghost. After answering questions he was allowed to go. Marianne's memory was that he got away with a heavy fine, which the church paid, perhaps because Keinath's wife was related to Bishop Galen. We know that Keinath survived because Marianne remained in friendly contact with him until his death, and afterwards continued to correspond with his family.[28] What struck me as odd about this story at the time was that if Keinath had tried and failed to escape while the Gestapo were in the cellar, it seemed almost unimaginable that, having apprehended him, *both* officials would later have returned to the cellar, or that Marianne herself would have attempted and succeeded with exactly the same ruse.

The family were not told the destination of the transport. They were given to understand, though, that it was Theresienstadt.[29] Marianne's mother put on her one pair of sensible footwear, a sturdy pair of walking shoes. But one of the Gestapo men said it wasn't worth her putting the boots on, they'd have them off her at the police station before she was sent away. Marianne erupted. Weren't they taking enough of the family's property without taking the clothes off their backs as well? She remembered the Gestapo official standing on the stairs and drawing a pistol. Marianne said, go on shoot me, it's better than going off on a transport. In our last interview, she said that it was this episode that made her realize she would be a liability for her family.[30]

In our conversations, Marianne added that when the Gestapo arrived, her father had slipped her a wad of 200-mark notes which he had in the house, 'which was naturally illegal'[31]. She couldn't remember the exact amount, but felt that it ran to several thousands. 'I swore that he would get it back in its entirety when he came back.'[32] She told her father she wanted to run and asked if she could take Richard. Her father agreed, but Richard wouldn't go. In Marianne's written account, when the Gestapo went into the cellar (again), she saw her moment, caught sight of her mother in the kitchen and gave a brief wave. Her mother nodded, the front door opened noiselessly, and she was gone.

Once she had made it down the street, Marianne criss-crossed through different parts of Essen so that, if she were being followed, her pursuers would not know where she was headed. She kept to side-streets, put on a scarf and even varied her usual gait. She telephoned from a call box to a contact number her father had given her. She remembered having heard that it belonged to the head of the Canaris group, who lived with his butler in some style. 'I don't know who answered the phone, a man answered, and I asked if I could speak to so and so.' Marianne used a code she'd been given. She was not sure if the person at the other end knew what she was talking about. If he did, he did not let on. Marianne told him her family was in jail in Essen. Then she hung up quickly and ran on.

I asked her if she could remember what went through her mind as she left the house. She said she only had one thought:[33]

'To get away. I was expecting any minute now, absolutely – I was quite clear about that – that there would be some shooting and I would have had it. But that's what I wanted . . . To go to one of the camps was to me one of the most horrifying, nightmarish things and I just could not, I just could not do that.'

For the rest of that day she stayed with a former assistant of David Krombach. Later, I learned that she may also have dropped in on Martin Schubert, a Krupp manager with links to the Bund.[34] As night fell, Marianne made her way to Essen-Stadtwald. Jacobs had suggested that in the event of having to make a run for it, Marianne should go to the Blockhaus to stay with Sonja Schreiber, which she now did.

Thinking about Marianne's escape, it struck me that this was not a period of technological surveillance. Nowadays – though ironically this is truer of a country like Britain, where the lack of a public commitment to civil liberties has allowed video and close-circuit cameras far greater intrusion than in Germany – it would not be possible to run away from the house and not be spotted. The Gestapo staffs were surprisingly limited and, indeed, the same two or three officials have surfaced regularly in this story. They relied for their effectiveness on denunciations from the public.[35] The fact that no police reinforcements were used also shows that the Gestapo was accustomed to depending on the passivity of its victims. Two officials were considered quite enough to keep an eye on the eight members of the Strauss entourage.

The Gestapo reports Marianne's disappearance

Only at 11 o'clock on the morning after the escape did the Essen Gestapo summon the courage to cable their superiors in Düsseldorf:[36]

> *Telegram. Gestapo Essen Office to Stapoleitstelle Düsseldorf, 1.9.1943 11.07*
>
> *Re: Evacuation of the Jews Strauss.*
>
> *Refers: Telephone instructions from 30.8.1943.*
>
> *The Jewess Marianne Sara Strauss, born 7.6.1923, resident here Ladenspelderstrasse, due to be taken into custody for the purpose of evacuation to Theresienstadt, has escaped. A letter to her parents found here, runs: 'I am not going with you, I am taking my life, God protect you, Marianne.'*
> *Signed, Nohles*

Because I found these documents only after Marianne's death, I couldn't ask her about the suicide note. The Gestapo officials may have invented it – no copy of the note appears in her file. A dead Jew was less of an admission of failure than one on the run. I discovered that after the war the Gestapo official Kosthorst himself disappeared, faking his own suicide with a note, so perhaps Marianne's too stemmed from his imagination.[37]

On the same day, the Düsseldorf Gestapo (now based in nearby Ratingen because of bomb damage to their headquarters) cabled Theresienstadt:[38]

Urgent, present immediately.

Re: change of address of Jews to Theresienstadt

Refers: Telegram 31.8.1943

For technical reasons the Transport of the Jews in the above-mentioned telegram cannot take place on 6.9.1943 but only on 9.9.1943. Consequently, the transport will arrive in Theresienstadt on 8.9.1943 with the normal timetabled D-Train at 2.57.
 Confirmation is requested.

Not noticing that Düsseldorf had designated an arrival time a day before departure, Theresienstadt cabled back acceptance. Only a day later was the error spotted in Düsseldorf and a correction made.

The mere three-day delay shows that the Gestapo assumed Marianne would not last long on her own. They did not believe anybody would shelter her for any length of time. As Marianne learned later from the Druckers, after sealing up the Strauss family apartments Gestapo officials kept returning to Ladenspelderstrasse 47 at different times of the day and night in the expectation of finding her there.[39]

On 3 September, Kosthorst evidently felt compelled to make a lengthier report about the escape:[40]

On 31 August 1943, accompanied by Kriminaloberassistent Hahn, I made my way to the apartment of the Jews Strauss. I informed them of the impending expulsion to Theresienstadt. I gave the Jews a fixed-time period by which to pack the things to take with them. During the packing, I supervised the family of Siegfried Israel Strauss living on the first floor (five people). Kriminalober-assistent Hahn supervised the family of Alfred Israel Strauss (three people) on the second floor. For the purpose of taking food for the journey I allowed the Jewess Marianne Sara Strauss to go to the kitchen in the ground floor. She then left the house in an unsupervised moment. After about five minutes, her absence was noticed. The aforementioned farewell note was discovered in the hall.
 Signed, Kosthorst.

This was slightly different from Marianne's account. Marianne had remembered the corrupt officials rooting around for loot among the family possessions in the cellar. Kosthorst seemed to be concealing the dereliction behind a picture of the humane Oberkriminalassistent allowing the daughter of the house to get food. His trust had been abused by the deceitful Jewess. Encountering this document in the reading room of the Düsseldorf State Archives, it struck me that I was probably the first person to read it who knew it contained a lie.

Not long after seeing the Gestapo records, I spoke with Lilli Arras. She had met Marianne once or twice after the war and Marianne had told her about her escape. Completely unprompted, Lilli told me how the Gestapo had been with the family and Marianne had asked to go and get bread and had then disappeared. Suddenly, it seemed the Gestapo story was true. And that on this point Marianne's account was inaccurate.

Later echoes of the escape

Lilli Arras was not the only person to whom Marianne had said something about what happened that day. When I talked to her friends from Liverpool and surviving relatives, I found that they generally knew about her escape even if they knew little else about her past. By and large, their recollections closely resembled Marianne's written account: the Gestapo in the cellar, her quick escape down the stairs and out of the front door. Some understood that she might have gone through a back door or climbed out of a window. Her second cousin, Robert Selig, emailed me from Denmark:[41]

Marianne never mentioned her past and any information I have about it comes from other sources, mainly my parents. As far as I know, she lived in Essen with her parents, her grandmother and her younger brother Richard. The Gestapo (or possibly other police) came to arrest them, but Marianne climbed out of a window at the rear of the house and escaped. She wanted to take her brother with her, but her mother would not allow it as he was thought to be too young. She spent the

Essen, den 3. September 1943. 59

Betrifft: Flucht der Jüdin Marianne Sara S t r a u s s ,
geboren am 7. 6. 1923 in Essen, wohnhaft hier, Laden=
spelderstr. 47.

────────

Am 31. 8. 1943 begab ich mich mit dem Krim.-Ober-Assistenten
H a h n in die Wohnung der Juden S t r a u s s , um sie von
der bevorstehenden Abschiebung nach Theresienstadt in Kenntnis
zu setzen. Ich gab den Juden eine befristete Auflage zum Packen
der mitzunehmenden Sachen. Während des Einpackens beaufsichtigte
ich die Angehörigen der in der 1. Etage wohnenden Familie Sieg=
fried Israel Strauss (5 Personen), während Krim.-Ober-Assistent
H a h n die in der 2. Etage wohnenden Angehörigen der Familie
Alfred Israel Strauss (3 Personen) beaufsichtigte. Zwecks Mit=
nahme der Reiseverpflegung hatte ich der Jüdin Marianne Sara
Strauss gestattet, die im Erdgeschoss gelegene Küche aufzusuchen.
Sie hat dann in einem unbewachten Augenblick das Haus verlassen.
Nach etwa 5 Minuten wurde ihr Fehlen festgestellt. Im Hausflur
wurde der bereits erwähnte Abschiedsbrief vorgefunden.

Krim.-Sekretär.

Geheime Staatspolizei
Staatspolizeileitstelle Düsseldorf
Außendienststelle Essen   - 6. SEP. 1943   Essen, den 3. September 1943.
II B 4/4472/43.

Urschriftlich

der Staatspolizeileitstelle Düsseldorf
in
R a t i n g e n
────────────────

gemäss fernmündlicher Anordnung vorgelegt.

Im Auftrage:

Gestapo report on Marianne's escape

*next years living underground until she walked into a British camp near
the front line.*

I assumed the details that differed from Marianne's original had
simply been misreported by the listeners. Indeed, the story of her walking
into a British camp near the front line was so at odds with what actually
happened that Marianne could never have asserted it. But among her
restitution papers I found a declaration made by Marianne herself in
1961 to the effect that she had jumped out of a window. This made me
wonder if Selig's comment that Regina had been unwilling for Richard
to go had also emanated from Marianne.[42]

Flight from memory

The escape was one of the two most vivid and traumatic episodes of
Marianne's life. The memory never really left her. Above all, it stood
under the twin stars of liberation and betrayal. It was both the moment
of decision, when her survival was balanced on a knife-edge, and the
moment when she abandoned her family, probably for ever. It was a
moment etched into Marianne's consciousness.

And yet her account of the escape began to change relatively early on.
In 1984, when her article was published in *Das Münster am Hellweg*, it
was no surprise that a woman in her sixties should have lost track of a
few details of an event that had happened over forty years before. But,
in fact, in the context of restitution proceedings we find Marianne
making a written declaration as early as 1957, and under oath referring
to the Gestapo as being in the cellar.[43] A few years later, she made
another declaration containing a slightly different version; this time she
left the house by the window.[44] Within a few years of the end of the war,
the details were slipping and changing.

Three key aspects of leaving the house were ambiguous. There was
the issue of how premeditated the escape was. In Marianne's published
account, her escape appeared as a last-minute decision, with her father
slipping her cash just before. In her verbal account to me she said she had
received the money early on, and her decision to leave was made after she

had the altercation with the Gestapo on the stairs. Then there was the question why Richard did not go with her. In the published account, the issue is not raised. In conversation, Marianne said that Richard did not want to come. The Seligs heard that Ine would not allow it. Finally, there was the question of how she got out of the house. The episode of Marianne asking whether she could get some bread seemed too powerful and memorable to have 'gone into hiding' from her memory.

At this stage, I had no real theory about why Marianne should have lost this particular memory. But I was already beginning to feel that the traumas of separation were at once the most painful and the most elusive events in Marianne's enormous collection of sad memories. I could see strong echoes of the way Marianne's account of Ernst's departure had evolved. Here was another painful moment of separation. Perhaps, too, here was another 'borrowed' journey in the sense that Pastor Keinath's attempted escape while the Gestapo was in the cellar had metamorphosed into her own path to flight, just as Hanna Aron's night in Holbeckshof had become her own last journey with Ernst. But why should Marianne have been borrowing other people's journeys? That I did not yet understand.

And that was it

I had read and heard Marianne's own accounts. I had consulted those close to her to whom she had spoken at various times from the 1940s to the 1980s. And I had worked through the Gestapo records with all their astounding (though sometimes mendacious and often misleading) detail. I felt I had found more evidence about an escape from an ordinary house in wartime Nazi Germany than even the most obsessive historian could require.

Then I spoke to Hanna Aron:[45]

'As a matter of fact, the day they were picked up I had played hooky.[46] And I had gone to a movie theatre in Essen West, which was of course forbidden. I had taken off my star, gone to see the movie, come back home and when I came in the door – there are the stairs, there, just like these stairs. When you came into the house you could see right into the

kitchen and up the flight of stairs – when I came in I immediately saw
Mr Hahn from the Gestapo standing there. I knew him quite well and
he knew me. And I went to the right, past the kitchen, into our room
because I'd seen him and, boy, was I in dire straits because I had taken
the star off! Well, I put it on and he came into the room right away, and
he saw that I had just put it on there with a pin. And he said to me,
"You know, I could send you to camp right away." I don't know, I
think I apologized, I must have, very low key, being so afraid. Somebody
must have called my mother at work. It certainly wasn't me, because
"You stay in the room!" So of course I did, being so afraid. I think it
was Rosenberg who called my mother and she came home. And when
she walked into our room, Herr Hahn came in again and told her what
had happened. That he had caught me without the star and so forth.

'But before my mother came home, before, Marianne opened the door
of the room. She looked in and I was sitting there, you know, very afraid,
just sitting there, frightened. Marianne opens the door, looks in, and
makes a movement with her head, doesn't say anything. Leaves the door
a little bit ajar. And I think, what the heck is she doing now?! I am in so
much trouble already! I didn't think any more about her. Then my
mother was home and when Hahn came into the room she said to him,
"Herr Hahn can we leave?" And he said, "Yes, you can leave." And she
took me and we went to these friends that we had in Essen West. Later
we came home, it was dark already and we had of course the curfew[. . .]

'We came back and Herr Rosenberg, Fritz, was all upset. "My God,
Frau Drucker, you don't know what happened!" "What happened,
what is so terrible?" "Marianne ran away! And if they catch her, they'll
kill her!" And my mother smiled and said, "Thank God, at least she got
away." So then he told us that by the time they were ready to leave,
everybody had their things together, Marianne was not there, she was
not to be found, and then they realized the front door was open. She
had left through the front door, carrying nothing with her, leaving the
front door ajar not to make any noise. And she must have gone out of
the house very silently, you know. And Rosenberg was so upset about
it and my mother said to him, "Fritz, you know, I can't get very excited
about it, it's good for her that she left."

[. . .]

'The next day the Gestapo came, they took everything that wasn't nailed down. They took the artwork, they took the huge steamer trunks that weren't in the basement. I saw it myself. And they worked hard at it because those trunks were heavy.'

Hanna wasn't sure where the Gestapo were at the point when Marianne left. She felt that Marianne had probably left just after poking her head round Hanna's door. Later, it occurred to me that this raised the problem that Hanna and her mother seemed to have gone out between the moment Marianne left the house and the moment when others found the door ajar. I wrote to her about this, and she said that she and her mother found the door open and left it so. But whether this was a genuine memory or something she felt she had to come up with to fit my question, I wasn't sure.

Her memory pushed the evidence forward a little on two points. One, Marianne had certainly used the door and not the window. Second, no one in the house mentioned that Marianne had left a note. 'No, nothing, nothing, absolutely nothing,' Hanna said. 'She just looked into my room and afterwards I realized she had been saying goodbye.' So it did look as if this element of the Gestapo communication might have been a lie.

Hanna said that when her mother came home she saw Ine in the kitchen. And what did Ine say?

'Well, I don't know but I think they embraced, cried a little bit.'

'Did your mother say this, or this is just a sense that you have?' I asked.

'No, this is what my mother said. First of all, you couldn't do very much in front of the Gestapo, and you didn't want to let yourself go. Because once you start crying, you can't stop. So I think Ine pretty much kept a stiff upper lip and my mother probably also, you know. They just hugged each other, and that was it.'

10

Memories Underground:
August 1943 – Spring 1944

For a long time, my perception of the dangers and stress of Marianne's escape was focused on what lay behind her, on the risks and pain of leaving. I thought of the trauma of abandoning her parents and Richard. I imagined her spine arched in anticipation of the pistol shot from behind. I thought of the chance that someone on Ladenspelderstrasse might see her running and do what the Gestapo relied upon Germany's citizens to do: inform on her. These were the threats, the uncertainties that I imagined going through her head.

But when after some months I listened again to the tape Marianne and I had made in September 1996, I heard something which had not initially caught my attention. Marianne said of the Bund's offer to help her:[1]

'Maybe somebody else would have felt squeamish about it and thought, well, people say these things and they don't mean them. But I took that risk, you see. And I thought, if they don't want me they can say so. But by that time I knew Artur well enough to think I could believe that they did mean it. And there you are, they saw me through.'

She sighed audibly on the tape and I realized the obvious. At the moment of escape, Marianne was not at all sure if the Bund would be willing or able to help her. She was fleeing into the unknown. What she faced was as uncertain and threatening as what lay behind her was traumatic and dangerous.

The day before Marianne's escape, Bund members had held one of their summer meetings. Artur Jacobs was full of concerns. A few days earlier, a card had arrived from his son's Amsterdam landlady to say that Gottfried had been missing for weeks. Artur had sent letters to the German consul and to the police in Amsterdam. Now at the end of August came the news of Gottfried's arrest.[2] But typically, his anxieties about Gottfried did not prevent Artur from taking the keenest interest in his neighbours, and in Marianne's fate in particular. The Bund would remain true to its word.

A day or two after her escape Artur noted in his diary:[3]

Marianne is in the Blockhaus. She eluded disaster at the last minute.

What an upright, mature, intelligent, active, courageous young person! And one discerns hardly a glimmer of what she's going through!

What people like her have learned to deal with! And with unbroken courage.

That young people of this calibre can still evolve, even in such an environment should make us think. It is proof, surely, that good seeds will germinate in the most unpropitious soil.

Marianne: again and again, she simply amazes me. The thought of all she carries on her shoulders! She stands there unbowed, with her heavy burden and an uncertain and difficult life before her . . .

What sources does she have to draw on? First, there is the boundless energy of the young; second, a certain caution in expressing her views which she has learned to practise since childhood; and, not least, the strength built up during a long period of suffering and growth.

The Blockhaus

On the evening of 31 August 1943, Marianne arrived at the Blockhaus. When I went there in the summer of 1997 to take photographs, I realized that it was only a quarter of a mile away from where I had once lived in Essen. The hill which Marianne must have climbed was one I had walked up and down many times. But the Blockhaus had never caught my attention – and I would not have understood its significance even if it

The Blockhaus

had. Now, of course, the little wooden building, clearly unchanged since Marianne's time, was bursting with significance. And yet, for passers-by, it was a nondescript structure, perhaps slightly out of place, on an ordinary suburban street with little Sunday traffic. The Dore Jacobs school, which – with the exception of the Nazi years – had used the Blockhaus as its premises since 1927, was closed for the summer holidays. So I was left to contemplate alone the irony that of all the buildings in which Marianne had lived, the only one to have survived was made entirely of wood.

In May 1999, I was back at the Blockhaus, this time to interview Karin Gerhard, the Dore Jacobs school director. Inside, I discovered that the building was almost exactly as it had been during the war. Seeing my excitement, Frau Gerhard gave me a tour. For once, I was able to move through rooms in which Marianne had lived during that time – the little kitchen, the bedroom where she stayed, the hall where the Catholic church had held services. For a moment, the past was so present it was hard to breathe.

Almost immediately after her arrival, Marianne cut and bleached her hair because she had heard from Frau Drucker that the Gestapo had put up a wanted poster for her.[4] Many who met her during the war years retained an abiding vision of Marianne's vital, animated face and her reddish hair. For the moment, though, Marianne had little human contact with anyone apart from her host, Sonja Schreiber. Marianne felt immediately that the forty-nine-year-old Sonja had taken on responsibility for her; indeed, Sonja became her substitute mother.[5]

Sonja Emmi Schreiber was one of many socially conscious middle-class women drawn to the Bund. Born in 1894, the daughter of an Essen town councillor, she attended Marianne's school, the Luisenschule, some thirty years before Marianne. She studied in Bonn and at the left-leaning Frauenakademie in Düsseldorf, and was a member of the free German youth movement. After the First World War she taught at an experimental, non-denominational school in Essen-Rellinghausen. Like many others, she was drawn to Artur Jacobs' circle by his lectures on Kant at the Volkshochschule; she became one of the Bund's founders and a member of its inner circle.[6]

From 1927 until the last years of her life, Sonja lived in the Blockhaus. Dore's school was closed down after 1933 and the practice rooms in the building were handed over to the Catholic church in Essen-Stadtwald. The church held services there and organized a kindergarten in the building. But Sonja lived on in the rooms upstairs, which became a place of refuge for those helped by the Bund. In 1940, Sonja had been denounced to the Gestapo for publicly declaring her outrage at the treatment of the Jews, and had only narrowly escaped with a warning.[7] But the experience did not make her hesitate to help Marianne.

During the day, Marianne was confined to those rooms:[8]

I could leave the house for short walks only after dark. I was known in Essen, and denunciation represented the biggest threat to my safety and to that of everyone involved in my escape. During the day I had to stay in my little room because the kindergarten brought many outsiders into the house. Cooking soon became my responsibility and I cooked for the

Sonja Schreiber

first time in my life, mainly vegetables and salads, and above all cabbage, and also whatever Sonja got on her rations and as gifts from our friends. She shared everything with me, the danger above all.

Only after seeing the house myself and discovering how small it was did I realize that a short, narrow staircase and a closed door were all that separated Marianne from those who might betray her.

Last contacts with her parents

While Marianne was in the Blockhaus, her parents, brother, aunt, uncle, grandmother Anna Rosenberg and great aunt Else Dahl were held in the cells at police headquarters. A Bund member, Grete Ströter, who was at this stage living with the Jacobs in the Bund house in the Dönhof, visited the family in prison and gave them a gift from Marianne. In this way, Siegfried and Ine received silent reassurance that their daughter was free and safe with friends. Marianne told me that the contact was rendered a little easier because of another unexpected twist in the story. One of the warders turned out to be a wartime comrade of Alfred Strauss and, possibly with a bit of bribery, was willing to close an eye now and then.[9]

Even so, a visit to imprisoned Jews in 1943 was an act of enormous courage. Unfortunately, by the time I came to interview Bund members, Grete Ströter had died. I did speak to her husband, Reinhold, but he had been away in Hamburg at the time and had heard about her prison visit only after the event. Grete, like many of the Bund members, had been so discreet about her heroism that others such as Ellen Jungbluth and her step-daughter Ursula heard about her action only from me. 'Typical Grete!' said Ursula Jungbluth.

Marianne told me that the family was held for three weeks while the Gestapo returned to Ladenspelderstrasse day and night in the hope of finding her.[10] In fact (just as in relation to her father's imprisonment in Dachau and the time she had spent in Essen before the aborted deportation) a traumatic time had again expanded in her memory: her parents were held for just over a week. Marianne was dreadfully afraid that she had exposed her family to all kinds of torture. 'I put my parents at risk, I put my whole family at most dreadful risk; the Gestapo could have done anything they wanted with them.

'I don't even know how big the[ir] cell was. Quite frankly I didn't ask too many questions. I really didn't want to know. Because there was nothing I could do about it. And I had nightmares, as you can well imagine.'[11]

Aware that her parents were detained at least in part to put pressure on her, Marianne asked herself over and over whether she should give herself up:

'And then my, I don't know what it was, whether I was just yellow or whether it was my better sense, or a combination of both got the better of me and I thought: there's nothing I can do. If I join them that only does the Gestapo a favour, not my parents or me, because the Gestapo can then send them off to wherever they send them to. Whereas this way, my family is still here, while the Gestapo's hoping that they come across me somewhere so they won't have to report to Düsseldorf to the headquarters that out of eight people one went missing. That really pleased me.'

Among Marianne's restitution papers is a statement from Julia Böcker, who was ostensibly already incarcerated at police headquarters and witnessed the Strauss family's imprisonment. She wrote that she was surprised at the jewellery and other goods the Strauss family still had in its possession:[12]

One day after they were brought in, the family was stripped completely by the Gestapo and taken into another cell. They were given only a blanket to cover themselves with. Then Gestapo officials Kosthaus [sic] and Hahn made a thorough search of the cell in which they had been previously held. They even cut through the straw mattresses to search for jewellery. Then they packed all the items they had found into the family's suitcases and took the cases with them. They left behind only underwear and clothes which the Strausses were allowed to put on again after the search.

However, there is considerable doubt over the veracity of Frau Böcker's testimony. Another statement that she made at the same time suggesting Lore Strauss was murdered in Auschwitz was certainly not true.[13] She also claimed she could 'still assert today with absolute certainty' that Lore had a diamond ring – something which Marianne knew not to have been the case. In a subsequent statement, she dealt with the problem of how she could have known what the Gestapo took by claiming there had been a small hole in the wall through which she observed them.[14] Just as conveniently for Marianne's restitution claims, Frau Böcker claimed to have overheard the Gestapo men saying that they wanted the Strauss suits because they were 'very good suits'. The suspicion is, therefore, that Frau Böcker was a rather too obliging witness, perhaps in return for a small consideration.

Herr Hammacher also claimed to have had contact with the family in captivity. According to him, with the help of his chauffeur he was able 'continually to smuggle groceries and other goods into the prison'.[15] Marianne was sceptical. It was tendered, after all, as part of an attempt by Hammacher to strengthen his case at a post-war restitution tribunal. On the other hand, if anybody had the connections to smuggle goods into the prison, it was bank director Hammacher.

Occasionally, Marianne ventured out in the evening to try to stir the family's influential contacts into action. She wrote:[16]

As long as my parents were in jail, I had some hope that I would be able by telephone to activate the influential figures who had protected us for so long. But in the end . . . this proved unsuccessful.

The last time she tried to call, she 'was given a very strong indication that it would be very dangerous to contact them again. So I didn't', she said, 'and that was that'.[17]

The protection offered by Marianne's parents' world – the quiet relationships between established Jews and high-placed resistance circles – had thus indubitably failed. Now Marianne had to put her faith in the ethical socialism of the 'proletarian' Bund. Yet in a way, she none the less owed her good fortune to her father, at least in part. It was precisely because he had been a well-connected bourgeois member of the Jewish community that Marianne had been able to benefit from the Bund's protection. For a start, Artur Jacobs' concern for the plight of Essen's Jews had led him inevitably to such community leaders as David Krombach. Consequently, Jacobs was far more likely to meet those who moved in the Krombachs' circle. And as we know, only someone with clout and money, such as Siegfried Strauss, could have evaded deportation until 1943. The other Jews, the mass fodder of the deportations, were too numerous, too unknown, caught up too early in the process to have had the chance of falling into the Bund's protective net. By late 1943, with so few Jews left and clear signs that Germany was losing the war, it was psychologically possible for a group to take on the danger of sheltering individuals. This is not in any way to belittle the enormous risks taken by the Bund; but Siegfried's power and that of the circles he moved in had bought Marianne time. So now, the beautiful middle-class Jewish girl passed into the hands of the pro-proletarian Bund.

The family dispatched

On 6 September, the Gestapo contacted the German railway authorities in Mönchen Gladbach:[18]

To facilitate a prisoner transport we request that on 9 September 1943 (Thursday), two 3rd-class compartments in the time-tabled train DmW 311, if possible at the front of the train, be kept free and marked 'reserved'. Brief written confirmation is requested.

The train was due to reach Dresden at around ten at night. The Strausses would travel on from Dresden just after midnight and arrive in Theresienstadt shortly before three in the morning. Pre-war Theresienstadt, or Terezin, to give it its Czech name, was a small garrison town some forty miles north of Prague. In 1930, it had had just over 7,000 inhabitants. The garrison consisted of a number of barracks, many of them still as primitive as when they were built 150 years earlier, and a number of equally primitive private homes. Into these buildings, tens of thousands of Jews were concentrated in the first deportations in 1942. By 1943, there were over 40,000 people pressed into a ghetto 700m by 500m. Theresienstadt was designated a 'show camp' for prominent and aged Jews and some First World War veterans, but it was a model camp only in comparison with the benchmarks set by Auschwitz or Treblinka.

On 9 September, the family's hour had come. Maria Jürgens, who had enjoyed such profitable exchanges of food for family Meissen and silver, was at Essen station, whether by chance or design we do not know, and saw the family escorted on to the train. When Marianne met Maria a few days later, her description made it clear that the family, though deprived of most of their possessions, were travelling with at least some of their cases.[19] (Yet more evidence that Frau Julia Böcker had exaggerated.) A Gestapo memo from 21 September records that

'The transport took place smoothly and without incident. The Jews were escorted by Polizeisekretär Waldbillig and Polizeisckretär Pütz.'[20] RM770.42 was confiscated from the Strauss family, of which RM450 was handed over to Theresienstadt. On file is the receipt provided by Theresienstadt for the RM450.[21] The balance was paid to the Finance Office in Düsseldorf. Everything correct and in order.

One interesting legal point. I was puzzled that the Strausses' property was confiscated under the Reich Interior Ministry circular of 4 July 1942 concerning 'control of property of Jews of German nationality who have assisted measures hostile to people and nation'. The Krombachs' property had been taken away under the Reich Citizenship Law of 25 November 1941, whereby the holdings of Jews leaving the country were deemed automatically to have accrued to the Reich. Why was that law not invoked here? The answer is logical: Theresienstadt was a part of Czechoslovakia which had been made a German protectorate, and thus was not formally foreign territory. The 1941 law did not, therefore, apply, so a different decree was required.[22]

An internal Gestapo memo gave instructions for information about the family to be transferred to file cards and the remaining paperwork to be archived. The Strauss files were closed.[23]

The hissing bomb

In the Blockhaus, Marianne was now isolated from all former friends and family. Her life in September 1943 – a life of confinement indoors, apart from a few breaths of air in the evening – briefly resembled what we imagine a life in hiding might be like, influenced by the account of Anne Frank; a life of inactivity, of frustration, perhaps also, as in the case of Anne Frank, of intense inner life. And of waiting for denunciation, discovery or liberation, whichever came first. Such extended waiting vigils undoubtedly did take place in Nazi Germany. In Berlin in particular, there were people hidden in friends' apartments, sharing a two- or three-room flat until the end of the war.[24] However, in Marianne's case, her period of immobility was quite short. Indeed, of the very small number of Jews who survived in hiding, even fewer were able to stay in one spot.[25] Ironically, what often endangered the fugitives and, certainly, what dislodged Marianne was the increasing intensity of Allied air raids. Whether Marianne could have coped with two years' enforced idleness is another question.

One evening, an incendiary bomb fell on the Blockhaus gymnasium. Before it went off, Marianne told me:

'I summoned the courage to grab the hissing bomb, cross the long hall to the window and throw it into the garden, where it exploded immediately. Possibly, I saved the Blockhaus, whose memory is so precious to me, from burning down.'

This incident brought the precariousness of Marianne's position home to everyone. Made of wood, the Blockhaus was particularly vulnerable in an air raid. And since Marianne was still so close to home, she ran a great risk of being identified any time she went outside. Behind the scenes, the Bund's inner circle debated what to do. Artur and the others felt that it was simply too dangerous for her to stay in the Blockhaus. Her time of relative security thus came to an end within a few weeks.

None the less, even after Marianne was forced to start moving, Sonja remained a pivotal figure and the Blockhaus Marianne's physical and psychological base and refuge.[26] Indeed, the weeks she spent with Sonja in September 1943 marked the beginning of a life-long friendship. After Sonja died on 27 June 1987, Marianne wrote the warmest of tributes to her Bund friends, acknowledging Sonja's love and concern for others and reminding them of what she herself owed her former protector. 'I would so have liked to embrace her once more.'[27]

Marianne on the run

From October 1943 until February 1945, Marianne's life was characterized by a series of short stays with Bund members, occasionally with family friends or distant relatives, punctuated by journeys across Germany by train and tram. During the two years she made more than thirty, very probably more than fifty such journeys.

A novelist would accompany Marianne on her journey from place to place, family to family. The narrative would start in Braunschweig and

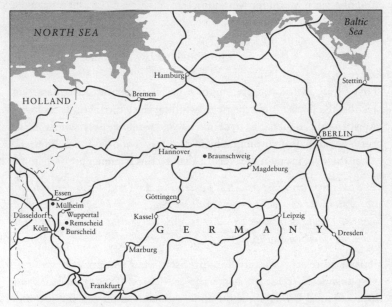

North-central Germany in the 1930s (including principal rail connections and towns where Marianne stayed)

then move on to Göttingen, taking Marianne from the Morgensterns to the Gehrkes, the two families the Bund leadership initially entrusted with Marianne's care. Then, in the shorter days of winter 1943–4, when it was easier to avoid being recognized, the story would follow her back closer to home, as she moves between Remscheid, Wuppertal, Mülheim, Essen and Burscheid. Here we would join her on the trams which she used to travel between her hosts, rather than the more intensively policed Reichsbahn.

But although we know Marianne's general destinations, we cannot recapture Marianne's time underground in anything like a continuous narrative, particularly in the period before April 1944. Marianne recalled some episodes very clearly, but many were no longer accessible to her memory. Some of her hosts had vivid memories to offer me, others had died or were too ill to meet. What we can do is attempt to construct a composite picture of her life underground in those first few months, and of what it meant for Marianne.

Trams and trains

First of all, it meant travelling in a police state without a pass. Lisa Jacobs, the Jewish Bund member in hiding since the Izbica transport of April 1942, had managed to obtain a forged identity pass, which carried her own photo but the biographical details of a non-Jewish Bund friend. After the war, Lisa wrote a small paean to this document:[28]

The pass was my most priceless possession. Life and death depended on its existence. I carried it in my shoulder bag, which I never let out of my sight. At night it always lay next to me. To grab it during an air-raid warning or when a visitor arrived became a reflex.

That 'priceless possession' was precisely what Marianne did not have. Her only usable ID was the international postal ID card she had somehow obtained before she went underground. On the left is a beautiful photo of Marianne with her hair up in a plait, big eyes looking coolly, but somehow also vulnerably, at the photographer. Superimposed on the lower part of the photo is a green 50-pfennig stamp with a solemn-faced Hitler gazing into the distance. Officially, the pass could only accredit the holder at post offices; it offered little protection elsewhere. Effectively, Marianne was travelling without papers.

Official controls to check papers were common on trains and trams at the time. When uniformed men boarded the train, Marianne sometimes stayed in the toilet and got off at the next station to avoid a check. Once or twice she moved slowly through the overcrowded train ahead of the guards and, luckily, reached a station before they reached her. In her deposition to the restitution authorities in the 1950s, Marianne mentioned two occasions when she was caught by the police on a train. Both times she managed to get away, once because of police inattention and the second time because she managed to escape in the press of the crowd as she left the station.[29] On trams, too, several times she edged slowly to the back as the control came in from the front.[30]

Listening to Marianne talk about her travels, it was almost impossible to imagine what it had been like. But what she said reminded me that earlier in the year I had been travelling from Dortmund to Essen – a stretch of track Marianne must have covered many times – with a British TV journalist and a German colleague. At the time, we had just been talking to an Auschwitz survivor and I had still been feeling overwrought from his unbearable testimony. At Dortmund station we ran for the S-Bahn, catching it with no time to buy a ticket. There are no conductors on the S-Bahn, but occasionally teams of men in plain clothes make surprise swoops through the train. Coupled with the gruelling interview behind us, I found the tension of travelling without a ticket almost unbearable. We weren't caught, but now hearing Marianne's account made me think of my reaction to this experience. What was the worst that could have happened to us? A 40 mark fine. For Marianne, the checks were about life and death.

Along with her own stories, I gradually collected a series of anecdotes which Marianne had told others – Bund members she had spent time with during the war, German friends she had spoken to immediately after the war, friends in Britain to whom she had let slip the odd snippet. In an affidavit to the German restitution authorities in support of Marianne's claim for compensation for loss of freedom, one of her former Bund friends, Hanni Ganzer, described a time when Marianne was stopped by the police on the train to Bremen and was only able to get away by chance.[31] The late Fritz Briel, a Bund member from Remscheid, vividly recalled Marianne's account of one narrow escape. She had hidden in the toilet on a train while a check was being carried out. Suddenly, there was a knock on the door, and when she opened it three young SS men were standing there. Evidently Marianne bawled them out: 'How dare you frighten a young girl like that?' The alarmed SS men never did check her papers.[32] (Incidentally, they were unlikely to have been SS. The blurring of uniforms in memory had probably taken place here, too.)

In 1997, while attending Marianne's stone-setting[33] in Liverpool, I discovered that Sol and Clara Bender, close friends of the Ellenbogens who lived in nearby Chester, also had something to tell me. Shortly before the end of her life (and during the period of our interviews),

Marianne had dropped in after one of her trips to Chester's antique shops, sat down and, for the first time in their many years of friendship, talked freely about the war years. The Benders wished they had noted down what she said, but some of what she related had stuck, especially her description of playing hide and seek at a station with guards and ticket inspectors.[34] A cinematic image came to mind of Marianne moving warily with the crowd, eyeing the guards and officials around her.

Then, when I went to the States, I heard another anecdote from Lew and Trudy Schloss. Before I even got to switch the tape recorder on they wanted to tell me the story which had stuck in their minds for the last fifty-odd years. It was when Marianne called on them in Essen unannounced in 1945 – the one time they'd seen her since the war. This is the version of the story I managed to get on tape:[35]

TRUDY: *I was startled when all of a sudden she rang the doorbell, do you remember?*

LEW: *Well, there were so few Jews there – you, and me and a few others.*

And here was Marianne, looking so like a German, they said, she could have been Scholtz Klink (the most senior woman in the Nazi movement, head of the National Socialist Women's League). They both laughed.

LEW: *When she came, she told us at the time that one of the reasons she survived was that she masqueraded as a Nazi; not as a Nazi, as an agent.*

TRUDY: *I don't know if this is true, I don't know.*

LEW: *She told us that she would go into compartments in trains where the hierarchy of the Nazis and the Gestapo officers would travel. That impressed us at the time and this is what I, we, both had foremost in our minds: that she told us that she survived because she was in the lion's den, and whenever somebody asked her what she was doing she said, 'I can't tell you that because I am under direct orders of the Führer.' Now I don't know if that's true . . .*

TRUDY: *But that's the story we remember . . .*

LEW: *But this is what I remember distinctly . . .*

[. . .]

TRUDY: *This is the story we didn't forget.*

LEW: *This was so unique at the time but, you know, since I survived under all kinds of circumstances, it made perfectly good sense to me that somebody could have done this. And certainly, when she walked in, I mean all she needed was to put on the uniform and she would have fitted perfectly.*

TRUDY: *She really looked like a German. When she walked in that time in our house I couldn't believe it.*

The memory of that incident was so strong that we came back to it a third time after lunch:

TRUDY: *In fact, we were sitting there and were absolutely . . .*

LEW: *Stunned . . .*

TRUDY: *Stunned when she told us that story. And how she used to sit in first class in the train, and they used to ask her . . .*

LEW: *It was always first class.*

TRUDY: *. . . and they used to ask her, you know what she was doing . . .*

LEW: *Direct order from Hitler,* direkter Befehl von Hitler. *Something like that.* Sie kann nicht darüber reden.

TRUDY: *And she told us, she used to dress very well, in order to look, you know.*

LEW: *How she managed to do that . . . ?*

TRUDY: *I don't know how she managed all that, I have no idea.*

Marianne's cousin Eric Alexander had another story. Some while after I had visited him and his wife in Stamford, I called him up to check on another matter, the call was almost over, and then he suddenly remembered Marianne telling him something. Shortly before the end of the war, a Gestapo officer in Düsseldorf had asked for her papers but then let her go, even though she didn't have satisfactory identification. Marianne had sensed that the official knew something was not in order, but the end of the war was so obviously imminent that he let her go.[36]

Thus, I gradually pieced together a mosaic of Marianne's daily life. Each of her interlocutors had held on to a fragment of her experiences, sufficiently arresting (or rather not) to lodge firmly in the listener's memory, sometimes for more than fifty years. But each fragment was different. Some of the differences were small enough to guess that they might be the same story, changed in the remembering, but often my impression was that Marianne had dropped into the laps of her friends one precious little pearl and no more. When I told Lew and Trudy what I knew of Marianne's survival, for example, they were struck that in the summer of 1945 she had said nothing to them about the Bund. She gave them her train story and that was their ration.

Marianne's hosts

On most occasions, Marianne's arrival at her destination meant putting herself in the hands of strangers – strangers whose background, experience and way of life often had little in common with her own. Not all Marianne's hosts were members of the Bund. Friends and family connections of the Strausses could also sometimes be used. There was a distant relative in Beverstedt, near Bremen. There was Grete Menningen, a sister of Marianne's former nursing colleague, Irma Ransenberg, who lived in Barmen in a mixed marriage and was comparatively safe until the regime's policy on mixed marriages hardened in summer 1944.[37] Emilie Busch, a resident of Wuppertal Elberfeld, was Oe's former housekeeper, and on several occasions Marianne was able to spend a few days in her little top-floor flat. But the Bund members were her principal protectors during the period. For Marianne it was a miracle

that in this fearful time there was always a safety net waiting to catch me; people who were complete strangers were willing to expose themselves to such dangers for my sake and for the sake of human rights.

What kind of people were her Bund helpers? Although each of her hosts – the Gehrkes in Göttingen, the Morgensterns in Braunschweig, the Briels in Remscheid, the Zenkers in Mülheim and the Schmitzes in Burscheid – were, of course, individuals in their own right, they also had much in common with one another. They were nearly all working class in origin, though the Morgensterns presented a colourful exception here, since Carlos, the husband, came from a very simple background, but his wife, Karin, was upper class. Theirs was an 'extraordinary marriage', Marianne said, 'so ill matched, yet it was very good and it worked.'[38] Almost all had had only limited formal education, having left school after the basic four years of secondary education to earn a living. For the most part they were fifteen to twenty years older than Marianne and married with small children. Generally of modest means, they typically lived in small apartments. Often they did not have a spare room and could offer Marianne only a couch.

Like Marianne, many had been influenced by the free German youth movement, but usually by groups on the left-wing of the youth spectrum such as the Naturfreunde (literally, Friends of Nature) or pacifist groups. Most had gravitated to left-wing parties in the 1920s. Some were members of the Social Democratic Party (SPD), whereas the Morgensterns, the Briels and the Zenkers were committed Communists. Some had encountered the Bund first through gymnastics lessons or seeing a troupe of Dore Jacobs' pupils perform. Others had attended Bund lectures at the Volkshochschulen in Essen or Wuppertal and had been won over.

It was all a million miles away from Marianne's own milieu, yet in many of her hosts she found inspiring, self-educated conversation partners and role models. Often, the men were away, either like Gustav Gehrke or Carlos Morgenstern because they were called up, or because the bombing had induced the wives to move out of town whilst the men stayed near their factories. Thus, it was the women of the Bund – above all Sonja Schreiber, Maria Briel, and later Meta Steinmann[39] – who meant most to Marianne.

Maria Briel, for example, was born in 1905 to a large family and soon learned the meaning of hardship and independence. Her father, a craftsman, died of tuberculosis in the early years of the First World War. Maria trained as a secretary and worked as office girl in a factory while she attended lectures at the Volkshochschule. Here she made her first contacts with the pacifist and anti-militarist movement, and ultimately with the Bund. It was, she recalled, a personal liberation. She went on long hikes with her new-found spiritual companions. 'That was the beginning of a wonderful time, I really felt, for the first time, that I had found my feet, that I was someone, that I had become "me"!'[40]

Maria Briel

Her husband Fritz Briel, born in 1907, also came from a working-class family. After the First World War, he apprenticed as a joiner and discovered the Bund in the 1920s. Both he and Maria attended monthly meetings at the Remscheid Volkshochschule and also maintained regular contact with the Essen group.[41] In 1933, they distributed anti-Nazi leaflets, but soon realized the risk of this kind of activity. Indeed, both were briefly imprisoned by the Nazis. Despite the danger and the hostility of many of their relatives, the Briels maintained their Bund links throughout the 1930s. Another Bund member, Grete Dreibholz, whose sister was married to the left-wing Jewish playwright Friedrich Wolf, made them aware of the Jewish community's problems.

Of all the relationships Marianne formed in the first months on the

Fritz Briel in recent times

run, she was probably closest to the Briels. In her short article on her experiences during the war, she made special mention of their fearlessness and generosity. And Maria Briel, like Sonja Schreiber, also became a kind of substitute parent for Marianne.

Because Maria died in the early 1990s and her husband Fritz was already very poorly when I was in Germany, I never came to meet her and had only a telephone conversation with him. I did have a pleasant meeting with their son Wolfgang, born in 1940, but he remembered little of the war years. Luckily, an extended video interview with Maria made in 1990 survives.[42] I was struck immediately by her sense of quiet strength. Her face was too severe to be charming, her spectacles were thick and chunky, but there was something very sympathetic about the

Ellen Jungbluth

whole. Extremely self-contained, modest and unheroic, volunteering nothing more than what was asked, Maria Briel was a real presence.

The only one of Marianne's hosts during her first year in hiding I managed to meet personally was Aenne Schmitz, with whom Marianne stayed in the spring of 1944. My first contact was with a rather shaky, nervous voice at the other end of the telephone. I wanted to arrange an interview, but Frau Schmitz was not sure she was up to it. Blind and living alone, she was understandably very reluctant to let a stranger into her apartment. Through the intercession of another Bund member, Ellen Jungbluth, it was arranged that we would both go to Frau Schmitz's home.

By the time the taxi had deposited me outside Frau Schmitz's flat it was already dark and very cold. I rang the bell, was ushered in, and immediately found myself in a scene of some confusion. Frau Jungbluth, physically rather frail-looking herself, whispered me into the spare room.

Aenne Schmitz

Frau Schmitz had had a turn for the worse and the doctor was with her. It was not clear whether we would be able to talk. With the cold gloom of a Wuppertal winter evening outside, I could not have had a starker reminder of how little time I had left to complete the project. How melancholy it was to see these once indomitable women reduced to such fragile and vulnerable selves. The doctor came out, consulted with Frau Jungbluth, and concluded Frau Schmitz might be well enough to have a brief chat. Round-faced and rather flustered, she greeted Frau Jungbluth warmly as she heard her voice. She was totally blind.

Aenne Schmitz had been born in 1906 into a working-class family.[43] Her mother was very religious, her father had been a Social Democrat and it was to him that young Aenne was most strongly drawn. Whilst her mother and siblings went to church, she would go for nature walks with her father, 'which upset my mother very much'. In the early 1920s, Aenne joined the Young Socialists and at nineteen became a member of the SPD, 'And I still am today,' she said. She was apprenticed as a

book-binder and also trained to become a member of the Workers'
Samaritans' League.

In 1928, she joined the Bund. Her first experience of the group had
been at a left-wing festival, an 'L-L-L' (Lenin, Liebknecht, Luxemburg)
celebration in Barmen. Dore Jacobs' dance group performed a piece
about the impact of machines on human beings and Frau Schmitz could
still remember vividly the great effect the simulated mechanical motions
on stage had had on her. Invited by Ernst Jungbluth, she joined a
Volkshochschule group in Wuppertal and later came to lectures given
by Artur Jacobs in Essen. At the mention of his name, Frau Schmitz
became animated. 'Artur already saw the dangers, already saw the
dangers,' she said in a quavery voice. Aenne's future husband, August,
also joined the Bund.

In the early Nazi years their flat was used as a stop-off point for
left-wingers who were being spirited out of the country. Frau Schmitz
never knew their names, but she had a spare room with a couch and was
thus able to help them hide for a day or two. They also had the advantage
that their neighbours were either Social Democrats, old Kaiser loyalists
or, at least, not ardent Nazis. At one stage, though, August was arrested
and imprisoned for six months. Frau Schmitz could still remember the
house-search, the jackbooted figures rifling through their books. Like
the Briels, the Schmitzes did not allow the experience to frighten them
into silence.

Meeting Aenne Schmitz was a memorable and moving occasion, but
in one sense it was rather a failure. Because I knew that the Bund
members who were blind communicated with each other by sending
tapes, I had assumed that Frau Schmitz had a cassette recorder in good
working order, and foolishly omitted to bring my own. In fact, her bulky
tape machine had only a short lead, which would not stretch to where
we were sitting, and had no external microphone. So although I recorded
a tape, on replaying it at home all I could hear was distant murmuring.
As Frau Schmitz's voice grew more tired, even the murmurs gradually
disappeared behind the hiss of the tape.

Cover stories

Sheltering Marianne, even for a couple of weeks, was not an act to be taken lightly. Above all, it meant finding a way to explain to neighbours, relatives – one's own children – who this stranger was. In the case of the Morgensterns in Braunschweig this was not so complicated. They lived in a rather isolated house on the edge of the town, and while Carlos was away Marianne and Karin lived a secluded life, eating the produce of the garden and, Marianne said, giving each other support and solace. With her kindergarten training, Marianne also enjoyed looking after the two daughters. At the Gehrkes, there was a problem in the form of Hedwig's mother-in-law, a 'terrible old tartar', to whom the truth could not be told. Hedwig found it difficult to explain away Marianne's presence, and during a later stay in 1944 the tensions were to reach breaking point.

When Artur Jacobs approached the Briels on Marianne's behalf, they did not hesitate. 'We were frightened, but we thought, it'll be fine.'[44] But it was no easy matter. They lived fairly centrally in a small apartment in Remscheid and in neighbouring apartment blocks there were a number of convinced Nazis as well as some right-wingers who had fought for the Phalangists in the Spanish Civil War. Not all the Briels' relatives were reliable either, and a cover story had to be invented for their benefit as well. Even their son, Wolfgang, then only three years old, had already picked up that the world was full of enemies and hidden dangers. Maria Briel remembered:[45]

'When he went out he asked "Mother, are the Ms [the name of some family acquaintance] on *our* side?" Although we never said anything, children soak up what is going on. He knew not everything was kosher.'

The principal problem was how to explain why such a physically fit young girl was not working. Artur Jacobs came up with the idea of borrowing a child from some other Bund members and presenting Marianne as a young mother. 'When we had the child here,' said Maria Briel, 'the neighbours said, "She's the spitting image of her mother"!' Some of Fritz Briel's acquaintances who bumped into Fritz on a walk with the attractive young Marianne decided that there was something

Marianne underground with Wolfgang Briel

illicit but enviable going on: Fritz remembered them ribbing him afterwards about his new 'Freundin'.

Proof that the cover stories worked for the Briels, at least, came when Marianne visited them some time after the war. Maria Briel remembered:

'When Marianne was here, my sister-in-law said, "Oh, I haven't seen you for a long time." "Yes," Marianne said, "Back then I was here illegally.". . . My sister-in-law didn't even know what "illegal" meant! Though we'd been swimming in illegals!'

With the Schmitz family, things were a little easier. Because they were bombed out in 1943, Aenne, her sister and two-year-old son Jürgen moved to live with their aunt in Berringhausen, a small village north of Burscheid. Burscheid itself is a modest town in the Bergisch region south of the Ruhr, not far from Cologne. The local squire helped the sisters obtain an apartment in an old farmer's house, just across the way from their aunt. The old lady who lived there then died, and it was here that Ernst Jungbluth made several visits. Ernst and Aenne went for a walk through the woods and Ernst said, 'I would like to introduce a friend to you'. 'Of course!' was the reply. But even in such a relatively secluded situation there were still authorities to deal with. The local mayor wanted to know who Marianne was. Aenne explained that she was an Essen resident who'd lost her papers in the bombing, and was not coming to stay permanently. Since she eventually planned on returning to Essen, she didn't want to register properly in Burscheid. 'I was very confident. We lived freely there,' was how Aenne Schmitz recalled a conversation which could have cost her her life.[46]

Sometimes, Marianne had to arrive without warning. Her grandmother had a distant cousin who had married a non-Jew and lived on the land in Beverstedt, near Bremen. All Marianne knew of them was their address, and she knew this only because some family packing cases had been sent there for safe-keeping. One day, Marianne simply turned up at the house. The husband was a ship's purser on the Bremen line, 'a real rough diamond', but they agreed to look after her and she stayed with them on several occasions.[47]

Between freedom and danger

I had assumed that when Marianne stayed with her hosts she would resume her Blockhaus routine, hiding in bedrooms and spare rooms and taking brief, nervous constitutionals in the early evening. But when Maria Briel's interviewer on the video asked her if it was true that she had hidden a Jewish girl in her apartment, she said, 'You couldn't say hidden, she lived openly with us, she could do that because she had changed her appearance and had no acquaintances here.'[48]

So, Marianne was not tucked away in an attic. At the Briels she slept on a fold-up bed in the living room. By day, Maria Briel said, 'We didn't stay in our apartment. No, we went out . . . we didn't act as though we were hiding someone. She lived completely openly.'

This was my first real inkling of the freedom that Marianne had wrung from her situation. Talking to me on the phone, Fritz Briel remembered Marianne as 'very courageous and cheeky' and, of course, very good looking.[49] Maria, too, was struck by Marianne's apparent lack of anxiety or concern. Of course, there were fearful moments – for instance when they had to go to the air-raid shelter.[50]

'The only time she showed fear was when we had to go into the air-raid shelter. She had no papers, and I know that the landlady, our landlady, once said, as we went down into the cellar, we had our bed clothes, you know, she said, "Ach, Marianne, she always crawls right under the bedclothes."'

If they had been asked there for their papers, it would have been disastrous. Maria remembered other moments too:[51]

'I know that we had to be careful to make sure we stayed on good terms with the landlady . . . She was angry once, Marianne had motioned to me, I was cleaning the steps and she motioned to me that I should come and listen to the English broadcaster, and then the landlady came and said, "Two women in the house and still they leave a bucket on the steps." She was really angry!'

As the story of the encounter with the landlady indicates, the Briels and Marianne listened to the BBC together, despite the consequences of being caught, particularly once the BBC began to broadcast more information about Nazi treatment of Jews.

One story Maria told (which Marianne, with her typical reticence, had never mentioned) was about Marianne's romance with a French prisoner of war. Near the apartment was an air-raid shelter that had been flooded. Conscript labourers assigned to clear the shelter included a young French soldier. Although it was strictly forbidden for Germans to make contact with the foreign conscripts, a friendship, actually signs of something more than friendship, began to develop between Marianne and the young man. This was the one event during Marianne's stay that had even the courageous Briels chewing their fingernails.[52]

Each of Marianne's hosts conjured a similar image. Aenne Schmitz remembered her gaiety and had a strong visual memory of her cheerfully washing the red dye into her hair of an evening. Indeed, so many of my interlocutors had a vivid memory of Marianne's hair colour that I began to feel there was some point that I was missing. To be sure, the result clearly looked attractive – Aenne recalled that the village boys had been *very* interested in the newcomer. Marianne's looks had been almost too good. A bit plainer, a bit more discreet, would have been better. But, still, there was something about the way Marianne's red hair shone like a beacon through different people's memories that I did not understand. But then, in the wonderfully written reminiscences of a Polish-Jewish survivor, Janina Fischler-Martinho, I came across a passage in which she describes running into her family's former manicurist, Lola, who – thanks to her liaison with an Aryan – has metamorphosed into something far more confident:[53]

She had had her hair hennaed. Today, a woman turns from a deep brunette into a golden blonde from one day to the next and nobody turns a hair ... But in those days, to change the colour of one's hair marked one as a female bold as brass, a pioneer, a revolutionary – almost. A mass of fiery, coppery, glinting waves and ripples. We were speechless with wonder and astonishment at the audacity and splendour of that transformation.

In Marianne's case, the point was not so much that people were struck by the sudden transformation. After all, many of them had never known

Marianne in her previous dark-haired incarnation. It was rather the boldness – under normal circumstances, the vulgarity – of changing one's hair colour that was the thing. There was, I realized, a kind of excited complicity among my respondents, in having been party to this brash subterfuge.

The same themes of beauty, transformation and freedom emerged powerfully from the testimony of Hanna Jordan. In her post-war career, Hanna Jordan had become a celebrated stage designer. On the day I visited her, I found her just back from her travels, ensconced in a sizeable apartment full of art, interesting clutter, fluffy toys and two noisy parrots. Hanna's mother had been Jewish, but she herself had become a Quaker after the war. Still, there was something Jewish in her style which I immediately felt at home with. She had a garrulousness, a sort of cosmopolitanism with attitude, which came as a welcome break from the steady, calm seriousness of many of my interviewees. I went to see her, expecting to learn something about her own fate during the war (I knew that she had had some contact with the Bund then). What I hadn't expected was that she herself had met Marianne.

Hanna Jordan was two years older than Marianne, having been born in Wuppertal in 1921, the daughter of two lively minded, left-wing parents.[54] None of her family were ever members of the Bund, but her parents moved in the same kind of circles, were regular participants in the Volkshochschule courses in Wuppertal and came to know a number of Bund members well. From an early stage they were deeply impressed by the Bund's seriousness and strictness. In the 1930s, Hanna was sent away to Holland to attend a school run by Quakers for the children of people subject to persecution in Nazi Germany. It was an experience that helped forge Hanna's own political and religious identity, and provided the basis for personal contacts, some of which continue until this day. She then rejoined the family, living in the progressively more circumscribed conditions attached to being a *Mischling 1. Grades* (first degree half-Jew).

In 1942, Hanna had direct experience of the Bund's willingness to help. In that year some Jewish relatives, a youngish couple with their son, were placed on the deportation list. The Bund offered to protect them. Hanna went to see the pair to give them the message, but they were too frightened to respond and, finally, the three were transported to the East and never heard of again. At the end of 1942, Hanna's mother was caught in one of the Berlin operations and interned, prior to deportation. Under the rules then in force, as a partner in a so-called 'privileged' mixed marriage, Frau Jordan should not have been imprisoned. Hanna's father travelled to Berlin and furnished the necessary papers to get her out shortly before she was due to be dispatched to the East.

The conversation took a new turn, and I was suddenly surprised and excited to learn that Hanna had met Marianne. Really? When was that? Had they met while Marianne was living underground? I thought it must have been then, because until that time Marianne had not had contact with Bund circles outside the Jacobs and Sonja Schreiber in Essen. But Hanna thought not:

'Well, I don't think that it can have been when she was hidden, because she would not have been able to go out, she couldn't have visited anybody. We experienced that ourselves, my parents and I, when we were hiding towards the end of the war. You stayed where you stayed, hidden, you couldn't move . . .'

Well, I went on, what impressions of Marianne had she retained?

'The main thing, which naturally made a particular impression on me as a woman, but also impressed all of us, was that she was so beautiful. I have never seen such a beautiful person, unbelievable. When you saw her, you thought, that's how I'd like to look. She had frizzy red hair tied at the back and a beautiful face, dark brown eyes . . . an absolute treat for an artist. She spoke very well, spoke beautifully, she moved, she had something that you don't usually find, but you held your breath and you looked and thought, My God! And I don't know, whether I've dreamed it or whether she really did, at some point, have black hair instead of red or . . .'

'Yes, she did.'

'Could that have been while she was hidden?'

'While she was hidden she had red hair.'

'She was red, then! I know her red and black, but I can't remember when red and when black.'

'So you *did* meet her in her the underground period!'

'Well, I mainly remember her red.' And then she went on: 'I can't remember any more, but that is not just a sporadic memory but a very personal impression of someone who was with us more than once and who stayed strongly in our memory – someone whom we spoke of later. I remember a very intelligent person, a very clever person, a very sensible person, she had a real personality, and impressed us very much. At that time, you know, that really stuck. I would very much have liked to meet her again.'

This unusually generous tribute struck me not just because it was the strongest testimony yet of the enormous impression Marianne made on those around her. It was clear from Hanna's memory and other details that the main contact between the two *must* have been during Marianne's time underground. Despite living in conditions of permanent threat and uncertainty, Marianne had managed to convey such a sense of liveliness and freedom that Hanna Jordan could not initially believe that her memory dated from Marianne's illegal period. Hanna, as she herself said, had good reason to know what it was like being in hiding, because she too had to go underground in the closing months of the war.

I realized that, for someone like Marianne, 'hiding' was a misnomer. She was living in many ways a very unhidden life, 'passing' as a red-haired Aryan. Her identity was in hiding, but she herself was out in the open.

Food and money

Though she may have given a carefree impression, Marianne was very conscious of what she was asking of her hosts. Not only did she compromise their safety but, since as a non-person she did not qualify for ration cards, the Bund members had to feed her from their own limited resources. Some, like Karin Morgenstern and Hedwig Gehrke, grew food in their gardens. Others were less well placed. Bund members who were not actually putting Marianne up helped by providing some of their own ration cards. But the brunt still fell on her hosts.[55]

Marianne tried to alleviate the burden by eating, whenever possible, at a restaurant or inn that did not ask for food coupons. In Braunschweig there was a smart restaurant where you could get a decent *Stammgericht* without ration cards. But, of course, this meant mixing with strangers in public. On one occasion, the restaurant was very crowded and she had to join a table with a high-ranking Wehrmacht officer. Marianne, being Marianne, played 'Russian roulette' and engaged in a mixture of flirtation and debate. In doing this she was following the Bund policy of imparting political education through one-to-one conversations. She had an idea that the handsome officer guessed there was something odd about her position, but everything remained charming and there were no consequences.[56]

Of course, even if coupons were not an issue, eating a meal in a restaurant required money. I assumed that Marianne bankrolled her time underground from the wad of notes her father had given her. When I asked about this, she insisted that she never touched that money.[57] Mindful of the seriousness with which her father took money and property, and determined to prove herself the dutiful daughter, perhaps also to keep her parents alive in symbolic form, she jealously guarded the billfold and put it in a savings account after the war:[58]

'I didn't really need much money. My friends wouldn't have wanted me to *pay* for what they did for me – it would have been an insult more than anything. So I did whatever I could to make up for it, above all going into the countryside and bartering for food.'

Marianne started going to Essen periodically to visit Maria and Wilhelm Jürgens, the acquaintances of her parents who were storing some of the family's trunks. Here she collected household goods, linen and suchlike which she could use for barter. She would then embark on the 'necessary but dangerous enterprise' of taking the goods to the farmers in the country and bartering them for whatever you could get:[59]

'Persian rug – a hundred grams of bacon. Three eggs for a tailored suit – that sort of rate. The story told after the war that the pigsties were plastered with Persian rugs is quite true. Really, the farmers survived the war with absolutely everything you could think of. You were entirely at the mercy of the farmers and what they would give you.'

The problem with obtaining the family goods for barter was that she had to break open the seals of the trunks at the Jürgens':[60]

'Once I had done that, they started to rob them systematically. Well,

I can't blame them . . . They probably said to themselves that my parents would never come back, and I'd probably be found anyway, so there wasn't much risk.'

On one occasion, arriving at the Jürgens' while Wilhelm was still in bed, Marianne saw her brother's alarm clock, a Barmitzvah present, on the bedside table. But she could say nothing.[61] In fact, the Jürgens provided her with a unique insight into the double standards of at least part of Christian Germany during this period. The Jürgens lived quite near the Blockhaus. The Blockhaus hall was used as a temporary place of worship and, as devout Catholics, Herr and Frau Jürgens would go there for Sunday services. While staying in the Blockhaus, Marianne would, from her hidden vantage point, see the Jürgens come in to prayer:[62]

'They would come to the service . . . and it was really quite ironic that they were praying there in this hall and I could see them coming in and praying. Little did they know that I was just round the corner from them. They went to church and they prayed, then they went home and robbed a little more.'

In addition to bartering the family property, Marianne had learned all kinds of skills as part of her kindergarten training, including making artificial flowers out of felt and leather. (Vivian and I found that a few of the patterns had survived among her things.) She was able to collect the scraps she needed from cases she had deposited with friends. The shops had nothing to sell, and were delighted to buy Marianne's confections. In this way she managed to earn both money and ration cards. In particular, she found a small fashion shop in Braunschweig, whose owner became her main customer because she was prepared to pay for most of the goods in coupons. Marianne had a distinct sense that this woman understood her predicament and wanted to help.[63] Marianne may have had other customers, too. Aenne Schmitz remembered providing Marianne with food but being unable to help her out with cash. She did not enquire about Marianne's own source of money or where she went on her regular journeys during the week. She says she once saw a train ticket to Frankfurt and remembers Marianne making the leather flowers.

Marianne's patterns

Ill health

One of Marianne's biggest fears was that she might fall ill. 'God forbid anything happened and you needed a doctor.' Her first stroke of ill luck came in Göttingen, while tending Hedwig Gehrke's bees. She was stung on the eyelid, potentially a very dangerous place. Luckily, the swelling went down by itself. During air raids, Marianne was almost more afraid of being injured than of dying. As Maria Briel remembered:[64]

'Marianne was frightened, you know, she was frightened, she must have been thinking, for God's sake, just let me not end up in a hospital! And that was a time when there was an air-raid warning every day, when the bombs fell every day.'

In winter 1943 in Wuppertal, a minor disaster struck. Wuppertal is a very hilly town, with many steps carved into the hills to connect the levels. It was a very cold winter and the roads and pavements were frozen. Marianne was coming down some steps when she slipped, grabbed on to the iron rail and wrenched her thumb. She was in agony, unsure whether she had dislocated or broken it. Yet the risk of going to hospital was too great. Marianne was in despair. The injured thumb continued to swell and throb and began to look as if it would be permanently out of joint. After a couple of days, Marianne decided she had to do something.

When she arrived at a nearby Protestant hospital, the staff were surprised when she said she was not covered by insurance and was there as a private patient. Surprise turned to horror when she asked the doctors to set the thumb without anaesthetic. 'Without an anaesthetic they couldn't *possibly* dream of doing that.' Marianne explained that, after her experience with her toe, she was terrified of anaesthetics; what she didn't say, of course, was that she was fearful of betraying herself when anaesthetized. Did they suspect anything? Marianne didn't think so. With her red hair up in a bun, she looked every inch the German girl. Eventually, the staff agreed. There were three doctors and two nurses and 'it was like a medieval procedure', she said. 'I don't think I made a peep, and they were absolutely staggered at this . . . they set my thumb, but it never healed properly.'

In the longer term, stress and poor nutrition did no favours to her health. Because of the rationing, most of her diet consisted of bread and potatoes, with a distinct shortage of fats and proteins.[65] But in this particular deprivation, Marianne was no different from many other Germans at the time.

Games and poison

Trying to imagine the daily struggle to survive in such circumstances, to cope with the kind of fear she must have felt, I asked Marianne where she had found the nerve. 'I'm a fighter, otherwise I wouldn't be here now,' she said. The whole thing had been like a game of chess. 'I wanted to outwit them, it was like a game. I made a very conscious effort never to show fear . . . I couldn't do it now, but then I felt I had nothing to live for.'[66]

In our interview in 1989, she had said, 'For me, the most important thing was to outwit the Nazis whatever happened. I pitched my understanding and my will against their stupidity and their bureaucratic rules.'

Marianne told me that she carried cyanide with her: 'My hope was that I would never be found alive by the Gestapo. I always had enough medication with me, on my person, so that I could take my life at any time. That was the most important thing for me – that I would either get out of this inferno healthy or not at all.'

Marianne mentioned the cyanide several times. It had clearly given her a sense of control, a way to decide the means of her own death, a way to avoid the degradation of incarceration in a concentration camp. The Polish resistance fighter, Jan Karski, in *Story of a Secret State* described his feelings when a nun placed a cyanide capsule under his pillow:[67]

After her departure, I felt a surge of courage and determination. I was now armed against the worst contingencies. The poison gave me a sense of luxury, a feeling that I had a magic talisman against the eventualities which I had dreaded most – torture and the possibility that I might crack and betray the organization.

Marianne said something similar: 'That helped me very much, this possibility. I was not a victim and had it in my power in some way to control my fate – although I was of course completely dependent on others.'

But I thought I detected in Marianne's repeated mention of the poison another resonance, too. When I spoke to her in October 1996, she was tired of life. Every time we met she was drugged up to give her extra energy. She'd said to me about the 'game' she played against the Nazis that she 'couldn't do it now'. Perhaps in 1996 she wished she still had the courage and means to determine her final fate.

The diary

In early December 1997, almost a year after Marianne's death, I was staying with Vivian on what must have been my third visit to go through Marianne's papers. On previous occasions, we had scaled mountains of restitution files and waded through great swaths of post-war reports and correspondence from the Bund. This time, I'd stayed over on Friday night to go through the bulk of the remaining documents. It had also given me the chance to join in Vivian's fiftieth birthday celebrations. Secretive as his mother, Vivian asked me in advance not to discuss our finds with the family and friends at the celebration.

Preparing for my visit, Vivian had sorted through several boxes of papers and unearthed a lot of personal material. There was Marianne's commonplace book from school and her little striped address book with family contacts overseas. I started ploughing through yet more restitution files, but Vivian said he wanted me to look at something. It was another little square, hard-backed notebook, with the same abstract red and blue design as the commonplace book and the same green bound spine. I hadn't finished the file I was working on, but Vivian persisted.

Opening it, I found unruled pages covered with Marianne's handwriting. I had still not fully mastered her Gothic script and the book did not immediately yield its contents. Opening a page at random I made out a heading, 'Mülh., 31.9.44'. 'Mülh.?' Mülheim? Then I went back to the beginning. The first entry was 20 April 1944. I turned to the end, 10 September 1944. No, there was an additional entry folded in from February 1945. Then I realized that there was a typed insert at the beginning as well. The first entry was dated 18 April 1944, Remscheid. And there were typed letters folded in between the pages, some typed during the war, some after. 'Vivian!' I shouted, 'Do you realize what this is?!'

Driving back home that night it was hard to contain my excitement. The idea that we could gain an insight into Marianne's state of mind *while she was on the run* was staggering. Almost as amazing, indeed almost eerie, was the fact that Marianne had never told me about the diary. She could not have failed to appreciate its significance for my book. Perhaps she had withheld it, but if so, why? Because it was too personal? I did not think it could be more personal than her correspondence with Ernst which she had given me. Perhaps she simply could not face looking for it, unearthing it amid all the other papers. Perhaps she had forgotten that she still had it. Either interpretation was possible, not least because the diary pages were so pristine and well-preserved as to make clear that they had been very little read since the war. Either way, the diary surfacing like this opened a window not only on her years on the run, but also on her reluctance to confront the past.

II

Underground Chronicles:
April 1944 – April 1945

The typewritten entry folded into the beginning of the diary was headed 18 April 1944, Remscheid:

Beautiful being on one's own in the open air. Sun, hills, meadows and woods. With all my senses I relish lying on the earth, relaxed, my mind wandering, and yet feeling more connected to myself than I have for a long time! How good, how healing friendship with nature is – no words, no need to say anything; just yielding oneself up to it and listening. There's so much to learn here for our relationships with other people.

Thoughts wander with the brook and buzz with the bees. How good it is to be alone, to find oneself again. The distance from others, from everyday life, the communion with the wind as it slips through the grass and trees, with the hare as it trustingly looks for food just a couple of steps away from me, pointing with its long ears. Listening to the noises of this little world, one is so grateful that it consists of nothing more than a little patch of earth: a sun-drenched meadow, with a stream chattering through it, surrounded by tall pine trees. In this defined space the heart is full of reverence, the gaze is not distracted by the diversions of daily life; the trees bar one's gaze from straying further.

What a powerful experience it is: looking, listening, being with oneself. How much we need this in our everyday life!

. . . I keep thinking of a conversation. It was about how to find one's

self. Does one manage it through turning outwards – devoting oneself to the community – or turning inwards – self-exploration in the peace of solitude? This is not an easy question. A whole lifetime would not suffice to answer it. The important thing is to confront whatever task stands before us, master it and allow ourselves to be sustained by so doing. Facing up to our responsibilities necessarily brings us into the community, makes us links in the chain and no longer just separate individuals. But we will always remain separate beings. How could we find repose, if we were never alone! We need the chance to rest, to draw on our inner reserves. And it is good that this is so, because the strength that we draw on in such moments will benefit the community later. Fields cannot be sown every year. Sometimes they need to lie fallow to gather strength for new seed and future harvests.

My thoughts travel on through time and space. How incomprehensible and awful it is; the enclosed, dreamy peace here, this little world within a larger one in which, every moment, countless fates are sealed. All the people out there, so intensely in our thoughts and yet so far away and so alone; beyond all knowledge, beyond all feeling, how difficult the present is for them, that same present which brings one such happiness and fulfilment. And it makes one think that it is impossible to come through unscathed. How can one get away without sacrifice or pain when, every second, pain and sacrifice is demanded of so many others? What does life hold in readiness? How fortunate that we can only grope our way to the future, blindfolded, step by step.

For that reason we must learn to live so that we can greet tomorrow without regrets, without having to repair what we have done. Every day must be a lifetime; complete, worthwhile; filled with duty, love, and at least one good honest deed and one good thought, one loving word. Each day, something must happen so that one can say in the evening: today I helped to make the wheel turn a little further.

And that reminds me of a thought I had yesterday when I was working in the garden. I thought suddenly how many centuries and how many people were necessary to transform the primordial earth into the soil we plant today. And the thought that what we do now may be of use to those that follow us showed me that life is worth living.

Recognize life's law and act accordingly.

The hand-written diary proper begins on 20 April 1944, two years to the day since Marianne had last seen Ernst:

How my thoughts are with you today! More than for a long time. Two years lie like a chasm between then and now; two years of events, of experiences, of difficulties, pain, horror, and so little that was good. Today you are so much in my feelings, my blood, my heart. It has all come back to me again, so vividly – your being, your love, your understanding. Oh, my love, if only you were always so close to me! Then my flight, my restless searching, would not be necessary. How even and steady everything would be! Often I think with fear and guilt how, how it is possible that I could lose you so. You know, what we experienced, what we shared, all the good things you left in me – I am always aware of them. You could say they are your legacy. They will be there as long as I live and as long as I can pass them on to others; but you, you as a living person, you I can't reach any more.

[...]

Oh, how I yearn to have my friend next to me. If only I could rest my head on his shoulder and close my eyes and feel how good that is.

But then it's the other way round; then I wish with all my heart to draw him in to me completely, to embrace him, to give, to give and to feel.

Oh, my love, how heavy I feel! But perhaps somewhere you sense this too, and know what I'm feeling.

. . . My thoughts travel back, back down the road we took together – the most beautiful time of my life. The first period of being alone was still filled by you; we were so together and yet so far apart. Then came the knowledge of your fate and I had only one thought – to help you and be close to you. And then there was nothing, no word, and slowly you slipped away from me. I didn't want you to go and held on to you desperately. But there are forces stronger than will. And then came a new life; challenges, danger, demands on every part of me. I had to relinquish even the things I wanted to hold on to. I had to have my hands free to master new challenges . . .

And so two years have passed. If you were to find me now? What would that be like? How different we are now. What we share is the past, but the present is something we're experiencing on our own. We have nothing in common there but the past that lives on within us. And the future, could we sustain it together? I don't know! I know only that I would like to preserve you inside me, just as I have over these last two years. And a whole lifetime won't change that, no matter what happens.

Marianne wrote both of these entries in Remscheid, while she was staying with the Briels. The next lengthy account dates from Whitsun. Marianne was taking part in a Bund study trip in the Bergisch area, near Remscheid. The entry begins confusingly enough:

Whitsun, [28/29] May 1944

Marvellous days outside in the Bergisch Land. Whitsun conversation about WA. One hopes that all the Easter wounds have been healed. But have they? The effort is too great! Only we three are aware of it.

It took me a while to figure out that WA was Marianne's abbreviation for *Weltanschauung* or 'view of the world'. But for the moment the 'Easter wounds' remained a mystery. The Whitsun entries continue on 2 June, headed 'at the dam; extract from a letter':

The rain is streaming down, but still how beautiful it is: camping by the lake. How one lives when close to nature, to weather and time, to the animals and the sounds of solitude. I can't tell you how beautiful it is! At first, I was worrying about the weather and thinking I could enjoy it and feel happy only if everything were bathed in sunlight. But now I realize that's not true. Everything, including oneself, is more alive when the clouds and the rain and the wind are all about. I feel like the grass and the leaves, exposed, utterly open to the elements. It's beautiful! Beautiful, beautiful, beautiful.

To be totally oneself, without distortion, without a mask, without qualification. To open oneself fully, to forget oneself and only then to find oneself.

To be all senses; feeling, seeing, hearing. And to want nothing; to just take what comes; to taste and enjoy it.

Waking up in the dawn after an astoundingly warm and good night in the tent; bathing in the reservoir in the morning, surrounded by the mist as it moves across the water. And then hiking through the pouring rain;

woods, fields, meadows. At one point a rain-drenched cart, otherwise no sounds, no evidence of people near by. The path led across a hill through wisps of cloud, then through a wood rich with the fragrance of wet pines. At one point, a horse out to pasture whinnied happily at the unexpected interruption of its isolation. It sniffed me up and down, chewed at my sprig of broom and walked with me to the end of the pasture. Elsewhere, I surprised a couple of cows. Behind a gorse-covered hill two farms squatted together, like children huddled in the rain. A thousand good thoughts wandered with me through mist and rain, above all the strong desire to have a friend by my side, someone to share the experience with me.

Sometimes on the way you explore a stretch through the woods and then have to retrace your steps to the main path. You must erase this detour from your memory so that later you don't lose your way home. And it occurred to me that life's often like that; you can take a wrong path and so easily lose sight of your goal. It's so good to be able to blank out the mistake until you can find the right path. Then you can look at your mistake, evaluate it, and above all, learn to accept it.

Afternoon

[. . .]

I spent a lot of time with farmers today. I wanted to experience people, smell life and hear what they had to say. Oh, what a muddle you get to hear! You need so much time and patience and education! It's easy to get frightened. Learn, understand, and believe with conviction – is that the secret to conquering this fear?

The following day

[. . .]

You know, I'd like to say something about the Whitsun days. Those few days were beautiful. I keep thinking of the discussions about WA, a topic I'm sure you've often pondered and talked about. An endless topic. Much became clear, much more was just touched on and lightly dislodged, to keep rolling forward like a heavy stone. You don't know where it will end up, you just feel it rolling inside you. In those conver-

sations, questions came up that I've been thinking about for a long time. I've made heavy weather of them in the past, but now much was clarified and many uncertainties removed.

WA. What are we to understand by the term? Where can we find a WA? What should it look like?

As I gradually reclaimed these first few entries from Marianne's beautiful but near-impenetrable Gothic script, I felt like an archaeologist stumbling on ancient gold, untarnished and unaltered. The pages were almost pristine. Her writing was so composed that hardly anything was crossed out in the whole diary. There is barely an ink smudge. Possibly, she drafted every entry before inscribing it; often, the entries are extracts from letters she was writing.

In deciphering the diary's contents I felt I was bringing something to the surface that had been doubly hidden, actually three times hidden. The diary had emerged so unexpectedly and unannounced from the clutter in Marianne's house in Liverpool. Its steady, even lines, written behind enemy lines, as it were, had survived a life in hiding in Nazi Germany. Most of all, these first entries were enough to reveal an account strikingly at odds with the world in which it had been composed – or at least with the image we have of that world. I saw already, for example, that my preconceptions about hiding had prevented me almost completely from understanding the freedom Marianne had wrested from the situation. But I also saw that Marianne herself had since lost sight of the life she had once lived and, above all, who she had once been.

Nothing in our interviews had prepared me for the fact that Marianne had been able to do something so light-hearted and independent as camping. Obviously, I could see at once the attraction of doing so. Like many influenced by the youth movement, Marianne was a nature lover. In her situation, with human society so dangerous and unpredictable, solitude in nature offered a vital respite from threat, subterfuge and disguise. But, still, I found such unencumbered freedom of movement almost incredible. We have to pinch ourselves to recall that one unlucky check of her papers would see Marianne unceremoniously switched between two worlds that do not seem to exist in the same universe – the world of camping and the world of the camps.

If Marianne's actions were remarkably carefree, her reflections were anything but. The comments of those who knew her at the time had not prepared me for the diary's maturity, perceptiveness and sophistication. Particularly when writing about Ernst, Marianne evinced a self-awareness that was truly admirable. She recalled her love for him, but at the same time acknowledged the distancing that had necessarily taken place. A year earlier, she had noted in her Essen diary that others might feel she was heartless because of the way she pushed painful issues deep down out of reach. Now, with the metaphor of 'freeing her hands', she was again conscious that the psychological mechanism of displacing painful issues was crucial to her survival. Perhaps most impressive was that she could feel her love and debt to Ernst as strongly as ever, but at the same time wonder if their separate experiences (assuming Ernst had survived) would in fact have made them incompatible.

The diary reveals for the first time that Marianne suffered enormous guilt at surviving, even while she herself was still on the run. There was that striking passage as she wondered 'with fear and guilt' how she could have allowed Ernst to go. Guilt slips easily into fear and back again. When she asks how she could be enjoying such peace and beauty while others are suffering unknown and unspeakable horrors, she wonders fearfully if sacrifice or pain must one day inevitably be her lot, too.

Often, Marianne's preoccupations and judgements do not seem to correspond to her predicament as we understand it. Someone picking up the diary without knowing its background would have no sense that Marianne was on the run. Keeping a diary was in itself, of course, an extremely risky act, as Marianne was well aware. So, she camouflaged some details, never named her hosts and conversation partners, and avoided specifying her address or giving details of her personal identity. To a certain extent, therefore, we have to read between the lines and imagine the thoughts and feelings left out because of her fear of discovery.

But take, for example, the paragraph in which her enjoyment of solitude leads to thoughts about whether one really can find oneself in isolation. The issue of how to reconcile individual freedom with the needs of the community was for the Bund, as for Kant, a central preoccupation. When Marianne exhorted herself to recognize life's 'law' and 'act accordingly', she, in line with her Bund mentors, expressed the Kantian belief in an objective moral imperative which governs action in any situation; men become truly free when they recognize and act on what is objectively right. In various guises, Marianne's diary throughout 1944 was full of reflection on this issue. Cast out of the community by racial laws, on the run, her family imprisoned and facing God knows what fate, her lover blinded, probably dead, Marianne was preoccupied with general reflections about the place of the individual in society; as though such generic philosophical choices were her problem! Yet, as later entries show, her pursuit of these questions was real and earnest. Marianne was redefining, or perhaps burying, her direct experience within the broader framework of the Bund's Kantian questions about self and society.

On 28 April, Marianne noted a recent report that the women in a technical school were doing much better than the men, most of whom were disabled veterans. 'What consequences,' noted Marianne with feeling, 'the depleted physical capacity of a people can have for its spiritual development!' Obviously, she could not have been hoping that Germany would win the war. But she expresses no sense of being an outsider, that it is not her society. One is reminded, too, of what she wrote on 18 April about working in the garden and imagining the thousands of generations who had worked the same soil before her. She unselfconsciously found solace in the idea that her garden work had reconnected her to hundreds of years of settlement and working the soil beneath her. In doing so, she ironically adopted a vision of continuity used by many anti-Semitic conservatives against the 'rootless' Jew. And she ironically adopted this vision of continuity at the very time when the anti-Semites had *turned* her into a rootless Jew.

On the move again

During the Whitsun meeting, the Bund leaders must have decided Marianne should leave the Ruhr again. Marianne's first port of call was not a Bund member at all, but her distant relatives in Beverstedt, the cousin who had 'married out' and her 'rough diamond' of a husband. In a diary entry influenced by the news of D-Day, which came that same day, Marianne described her train journey north:

On 6 June

In B.

Journey through a fateful night. Ignorant of what was happening – and yet so closely linked to the events of the world. On the surface one is still uninvolved, but how long before one is sucked into the whirlpool? Will one survive the struggle?

The train journey took her to Bremen, where she spent the day before travelling on to Beverstedt.[1] Wartime Bremen was a subdued place, but Marianne was still entranced and invigorated by the echoes of its mercantile, cosmopolitan Hanseatic past. She chanced on a restaurant in the Böttcherstrasse, and her description provides some of the earliest evidence of a love of historic objects that was to be Marianne's life-long passion:

I had lunch in the beautiful old restaurant. Wonderful old Worpsweder furniture, hand-crafted lamps, stained glass windows and on the walls old, blue-painted tiles, tin and porcelain plates, wood-cuts and paintings – some of which were so old they were painted on wood and metal.

Here amongst the beautiful old furniture she first heard the news:

Here I first heard of the invasion; I had travelled through the night in blissful ignorance. It's strange and frightening to think that one can experience moments, hours, of such security whilst others are waging such decisive struggles. And yet how much one is involved, inextricably involved! It is so much better to live in danger!

Later in the afternoon, it was on to Beverstedt. The following day Marianne celebrated her twenty-first birthday. In her 1980s article, Marianne wrote that the day brought her some horrific news:[2]

On 7 June 1944 – on my twenty-first birthday, I was back in Beverstedt and heard on the English broadcast that the 18 December 1943 transport from Theresienstadt to Birkenau-Auschwitz had been gassed there in

*the last few days. I knew that my parents and my brother had been on
this transport. And so I had an unforgettable birthday present.*

But there is no diary entry for 7 June and on the 8th, still full of the
Whitsun discussions with the Bund, Marianne wrote calmly and at
length about *Weltanschauungen*. Could she really have heard such
horrific news about the family?

WA

Marianne's lengthy notes on 8 June about 'WA' again reconnected to
the Bund conversations at Whitsun. One of Marianne's Bund friends
wrote to me of the great fascination the Bund's meetings exerted:[3]

*One returned home as if laden with gifts, in the awareness that one had
come a little closer to real independent thought.*

Marianne's intellectual activity throughout the summer of 1944 was
dominated by the questions the Bund meeting had raised for her. She
was, literally, running with an idea.

On 8 June, for example, Marianne embarked on a detailed description
of the meaning of a *Weltanschauung*, outlining the seven components
that any self-respecting WA should contain. A month later, ensconced
in Göttingen, she would still be grappling with the same issues. Waking
up very early one morning and unable to go back to sleep, she wrote a
letter to some friends, which she then noted in her diary:

I. *'Basic principles'; that is the basic question, and one must begin by
asking 'what actually is a basic principle?' A basic principle is a
formula that provides an objective guideline for a particular area
of life (do you agree?)*
And I think we have said something decisive here: an objective guideline.

Was there something 'decisive' in writing 'an objective guideline'? We
may well feel astonished that to someone in Marianne's situation this
dry, ponderous exercise meant anything at all. But it is clear that for her
these concerns were more than an intellectual game. She sought a core

belief or set of principles strong enough to provide assurance in a world full of threats and horrors. One sentence in her ensuing reflections (which go on for pages) is underlined: 'We evolve basic principles to give us confidence and a guiding rule.'

In the 8 June entry, she comments on the absence of objective principles in her time:

We live in a time without Weltanschauung. *Lessons and slogans are taken from all corners, thrown together, all jumbled up, and no one looks to see whether they really fit together. This is no basis on which to build a coherent view. The last two centuries, with all their technological developments, have challenged mankind with radically new challenges – challenges which have yet to be mastered. Technology has changed the whole structure of the world and dislocated basic concepts and values.*

That's why we can't talk of a WA in our time. Above all, a WA has to evolve organically.

In this passage the Nazi era practically disappears from view, absorbed into the generic problems of our 'technological' age. Curiously, many German conservatives in the immediate post-1945 period articulated this very argument as an explanation for what had gone wrong in Germany, not least as a way of suppressing awareness of the Nazis' unique crimes.[4] Marianne's adoption of it is more surprising, particularly as it seems too ready-made, too fully formed, to be just her own view, and presumably stems from the Bund. Neither she nor they had the conservatives' reasons for wanting to deny the Nazis' distinctiveness. But perhaps the Bund as a whole, like Marianne, sought to master the oppressive threats they faced by redefining them in general historical and societal terms. Valid insight thus merged with a form of psychological 'threat-management'.

Dreams, films and broadcasts

If Marianne sought by day to conquer her fears through philosophical reflection, her dreams were not so easily controlled. In Beverstedt, the morning after writing the entry above, Marianne woke early and reached for her pen:

9.6.44

6°

I've woken up from a dream which I feel I must write down: it includes two portraits of H., which represent him clearly, amazingly clearly.

I'm sitting with a few friends when H. enters the room with a young woman, his wife, to tell us about two episodes in his life and 'work'.

In the first he's still a young man, a boy in fact, taking part in a fire drill. He and several comrades are dressed in firemen's uniforms, black, with a steel helmet. In the dream, a new person appears to tell us what we are watching: In his youth, H. belonged to a fire fighters' unit. His own responsibilities were modest; but there was someone else who could climb up the ladder particularly high. Everyone was amazed by this person and everyone admired him. When he reached the ladder's dizzy heights he could even fire a shot, that is, he could stand without holding on. H. couldn't bear this. He had to achieve what the other person could do. One day he managed it. He stood on the top rung with a revolver and fired a shot. But he hit a street lamp which hung above him and put out the light. As we looked round in the dimness, we saw rubble strewn everywhere; walls, remains of houses, torn up streets, all jumbled together. Somewhere there was a blacked-out tram. H. climbs down from the ladder and dares the others to match his feat. Some other young man volunteers, makes it to the top, and as he comes down again, H. shakes his hand with a calm expression and reaches for a box which he opens. The young man thinks that he will receive a medal [with an asterisk here, and at the bottom of the page, Marianne had added the comment 'i.e. I think that'], but H. simply puts something in the box and closes it. I don't remember any more of this bit of the dream.

2.   *We are still sitting together, H. and his young wife among us. He thinks about what else he can do to impress us. Then above us, at a window, we see a man's head, a beautiful, intelligent looking face. H. calls up immediately, 'V.Mst. I would like to talk to you.'*

The man's face darkens, he seems unsettled. Then he comes down accompanied by two other men and greets H . . . One of his companions gives M. something and I see that it's a revolver.[5] Then the four go into a room [with an asterisk here, Marianne inserts the comment 'H. on his own'] and after this we only hear their voices.

H. attacks v.M. over the invasion and holds him responsible, but v.M. proves intelligently and clearly that no other outcome was possible and that it was the logical consequence of all that has already happened. He is completely calm, considered and clear. I imagine I see him smiling, while H.'s voice is loud and agitated. As v.M. finishes his remarks, H. says only, 'I don't understand that, I am not with you.'

Then they come out of the room. H. with his chest puffed out and head held high, looking as if he's just won a battle. Behind him is M. with an indulgent smile which to me signals wisdom. Now I notice that he has no uniform and is wearing knickerbockers. His companions stand behind him and he gives them back the revolver. H. sees it and threatens him but M. stays calm, pauses for a second and says: 'This is only because I want to go with you.' H. says nothing. I understand that if H. had tried to shoot him . . .

Marianne breaks off here at this point, leaving the ending very unclear. The 'H.' is clearly Hitler. 'V.Mst.' or 'v.M.' or 'M.', may be von Manstein, one of Hitler's leading generals. The dream powerfully captures Hitler's character, particularly as a younger man. His shot at the light was a masterful metaphor of Hitler's assault on the German and European order. The armed stand-off between Hitler and Germany's military leaders (though probably indicating that Marianne shared the widely held, though erroneous, view that the army was not deeply implicated in Nazi crimes) anticipated by little more than a month their failed military attempt on Hitler's life. The dream is a masterpiece of precise observation of the Nazi regime, quite different from the normal run of Marianne's daytime reflections, in which she rarely mentioned politics.

Although she never admitted it to me, throughout her life Marianne was to experience in dreams the horror of what she overcame by day.[6]

What Marianne *did* find unbearable by day (and not for the first time) was living with narrow-minded, provincial relatives – in this case the Beverstedt cousins. With typical contempt for the couple's petty-bourgeois outlook, she fumed about their limitations. From her diary entries it is clear that she tried to introduce them to the Bund's ideas while they, unsettled, tried to pick holes in her idealism.[7] After a few days of this, Marianne's restless spirit could stand it no longer and she set off on an expedition that was as risky as it was typical. It was a three-hour journey to the cinema. The film, *The Secret of Tibet*, was, she wrote afterwards to a friend, 'really marvellous, and if I had decided not to take the risks involved in such a journey I would have missed something'.[8]

For Marianne, who felt so limited in where she could go and what she could do, the glimpse of this other universe was overpowering. Afterwards, even wandering round the provincial port of Wesermünde assuaged a little of her thirst for the wider world. The town was grey and ugly, to be sure:[9]

But the sea and the winds of the world. In wartime there's not much going on, but one still senses a little of the wide world coming in with the tide as it laps the shore. I walked a long way along the dyke and took deep breaths of the sea breeze wafting in over the Weser. The current is strong in the river estuary. You could imagine you were already at sea. There's sand on the shore, the air smells of salt and seaweed, gulls are flying over the water and big ships move on the water. Over in the distance, the river winds its way past Oldenburg, past Blexen. There's a small church, a windmill, so far away, like toys. I enjoyed the walk very much and closed my eyes to absorb it all.

Just before she left Beverstedt, Marianne wrote one little diary entry of a completely different kind. A line and a half at the bottom of a page runs: '20 June. Horrific! What will happen now? I'm thinking of my second dream on 9 June . . .' The immediacy and pithiness of that cryptic 'horrific!' breaks through the diary's normal tone. What had happened?

There is good reason to think that this was a reference to some

Marianne's underground diary – at the bottom of the page is the
oblique reference to the murder of her parents

extraordinary and horrific news. It seems it was now that Marianne heard the BBC broadcast containing information about a Theresienstadt – Auschwitz transport which she knew included her parents. The broadcast – the full story of which will be unravelled later – was transmitted on 16 June and contained the prediction that the occupants of the transport would be gassed on 20 June.[10] It was on 20 June that Marianne wrote the horrified entry above. She was in some way reminded of her vivid dream – probably because of its disturbingly accurate representation of Hitler's wild radicalism. Had the dream in some way been a portent? What dark forces she must have felt were governing a world in which a broadcasting service from London could be predicting the precise date of the murder of her family.

Göttingen with Hedwig and Meta

Almost immediately, though, Marianne's normal tone reasserted itself. Here she is, a day or two later, by now ensconced with Hedwig Gehrke in Göttingen:

Gö. 25 VI

Days with He. Marvellous sunshine; garden, bees and child. How attractive the city is! But the people!

In her conversations with me, too, Marianne recalled the pleasures of working in Hedwig Gehrke's garden, tending her bees and helping to look after her child. Göttingen also had other distractions. Marianne went to the cinema, seeing among other things *Nora*, based on the Ibsen play. But the social problems of living with Hedwig's mother-in-law continued, though whether the diary's cryptic 'But the people!' referred to old Frau Gehrke, or to the middle-class Göttingen population, so much less attractive to Marianne than the more anti-Nazi Ruhr working class, is not clear.

The final straw at the Gehrkes, Marianne told me, were the bugs. While on leave from the front, Gustav Gehrke, a skilled joiner, had converted the attic. The conversion was 'beautiful, absolutely beautiful',

Marianne said, although it did get very warm in the hot summer of 1944. But then Marianne started breaking out in awful blisters. Since there was no question of consulting a doctor, it took a while for the cause to emerge. One night, Marianne felt something moving in her bed. Turning the light on, she discovered the woodwork crawling with bugs, which she thought Gustav had probably brought back from the front. Hedwig was so appalled that she practically threw Marianne out. (Marianne never quite clarified this, perhaps not wishing to say that Hedwig assumed Marianne had imported the bugs!)

Thanks to help from other Göttingen Bund members, I tracked down Gustav and Hedwig Gehrke. I knew that the couple, now in their eighties, had broken with the Bund. Another Bund member wrote to me that while on leave from the front, Gustav had said to him that they had fooled themselves with their abstinence from alcohol and tobacco. 'Probably the events of war smashed his youthful ideals,' he wrote.[11] When I rang, Gustav answered and was clearly not sure his wife would want to talk to me at all. Hedwig did come to the phone, but was so poorly and depressed that she was able to tell me little more than that she remembered Marianne staying with her. Evidently the Bund had disappointed her after the war, and Marianne too, she said, had never been in touch again. 'Life is hard,' Hedwig Gehrke told me. She sounded more drained and sad and ill than anyone I have ever spoken to. I wished her well and left it at that.[12]

On or soon after 20 July – the day of the attempted assassination of Hitler – Marianne moved in with Meta Steinmann.[13] Years after the war, Meta, by then remarried as Kamp, published an account of her experiences during the Third Reich for her children and grandchildren. Marianne lent me her copy of the book, and it was thanks to this that I managed to find Frau Kamp. I thought the Göttingen city administration might have had a hand in funding the book's publication, and the friendly staff at the town's cultural affairs department were indeed able to provide me with Frau Kamp's address. It turned out that both Meta Kamp and her younger sister, Elfriede Nenadovic, had been influential in local politics after the war. Frau Nenadovic was still active in cultural affairs and local history at the time I established contact.

Meta was born on 24 July 1907, one of five children, into a working-

Meta Kamp and granddaughter

class family.[14] Her grandfather had been a carpet weaver and a highly respected, well-educated Social Democrat; her parents (her father was a tailor, her mother a housewife) were both Social Democrats and also active in the local workers' chorus. Meta, a bookworm from an early age, became a convinced Social Democrat herself in the 1920s. She and the man who was later to become her husband, Ernst Steinmann, were both enthusiastic members of the youth movement, above all the Natur-freunde.[15] Abstinence from alcohol and tobacco and a commitment to further education are indicative of the group's high-mindedness. Meta remembered reading Dostoevski, August Bebel, Kant ('not all of which we understood') and many other writers.

Meta's contact with the Bund developed during the 1930s through Carlos Morgenstern. Meta felt that, of all her comrades in Göttingen, she had perhaps been the one who most closely identified with the Bund and early on intuited what they were about. Sonja Schreiber was her 'spiritual adviser', and Meta was deeply impressed by Artur Jacobs' personality. She had the feeling of 'coming home', she said, 'as if I had been waiting for such an experience'.[16] Sadly for Meta, she found that her husband did not share her enthusiasm. Their first great source of confrontation was the issue of sexual equality. Meta read the Bund pamphlet: *Man and Woman as Comrades in the Struggle* – and this, for husband Ernst, raised in a traditional farming family, was too much to take. Thus Meta made her spiritual journey very much alone, an independence reinforced by the fact that for much of the 1930s Ernst was working as a mechanic on building sites across Germany.

In 1936, Meta's father was arrested and imprisoned by the Nazis for a few months, his name having been divulged by a former Social Democratic comrade during interrogation. Meta, as her sister told me, learned to be particularly careful, not least because of the hostile neighbourhood. One of the residents in the neighbouring block, a certain Herr Flohr, was or had been a commandant of Moringen concentration camp. The local Block leader lived on the second floor of Meta's own building and was always on the look-out for activities to denounce.[17] Nevertheless, during the war Meta and the other local Bund members tried to put the group's philosophy into practice, providing food to foreign forced labourers – and taking in Marianne.

In order not to endanger her family, and mindful of her husband's lack of commitment, Meta told no one that Marianne was Jewish. Instead, she invented a story that Marianne had been bombed out in Essen and lost her family, becoming psychologically unstable. Her doctor had advised her to move to a new location to recover. The neighbours were fed this tale and it rapidly made the local rounds.

Meta's published account and her conversations with me contained many warm memories of Marianne. Like many other Bund members, she recalled Marianne's beauty and, of course, that hair . . . Its colour, she wrote in her memoir, was a 'warm brown with a reddish sheen'. And Marianne, she wrote, was 'basically a happy, life-affirming young person'.[18] Talking to me, Meta recalled with amazement Marianne's confidence and cheerfulness. But along with the amazement, she seemed to be asking an unspoken question. Frau Kamp could not really understand how Marianne could have been quite so cheerful. Indeed, at the time, she felt some consternation that Marianne was too convivial and gay for someone who had ostensibly lost her family in the bombing:[19]

'When she was so cheerful and confident, sometimes I had to wink at the neighbour with a sad face and point to my head. Which was supposed to imply, "The poor girl is completely confused!"'

At other times, though, Marianne sat quiet and despondent, and although they did not discuss things much, Frau Kamp caught a glimpse of the turmoil beneath.

Meta's book describes a dramatic episode. One day, Marianne was out walking with Meta's son, Ernst junior. The pair were stopped by police and ordered to show their papers. If they had been exposed, it would have meant certain death for Marianne and dire consequences for Meta's family. But Marianne was so jokey and friendly that in the end the patrol decided not to bother and allowed the two to continue unhindered.

Through Meta I obtained young Ernst's phone number, and when I finally caught up with him, now sixty-seven and living near Hamburg, what I really wanted to know was how *he* had coped with that moment. I was astonished to learn that he had no recollection of the incident, though he didn't doubt it had occurred. How could a moment when his life had hung in the balance disappear from his memory? But, as his mother reminded me, none of the family knew Marianne was Jewish. So Ernst had had no idea of the danger he was in, nor of the courage being shown by his companion. The incident was almost a non-event – they were asked for papers, but then didn't have to show them. Thoroughly forgettable.

Another occasion, however, had impressed itself on Ernst's memory. In 1944, he was one of many teenage anti-aircraft auxiliaries. One day he was in the flak emplacement when Marianne suddenly appeared to ask if he had his mother's watch. Evidently, Meta had been upset about losing it, and to relieve her anxiety Marianne had come over to ask if Ernst had got it. As Ernst remarked to me, even ordinary civilians were wary of venturing into designated military areas, so for Marianne – 'that took quite a lot, you know?' 'She had a lot of guts', was his comment on the girl, though just how much he found out only after the war, when

Marianne in underground years

his mother revealed Marianne's true identity.[20] Incidentally, Ernst felt guilty for years at having lost his mother's watch. Twenty years later he finally got round to buying her a new one.

After hearing the BBC broadcast, Marianne must have been consumed with worry about her parents. Meta's much younger sister Elfriede told me a moving story about this. In July 1944 Elfriede was on labour service in Upper Silesia. While she was visiting Göttingen, Meta told her that she had a young guest staying who wished to ask Elfriede something about Upper Silesia. And so the two went for a walk. Elfriede found Marianne very nice and lively, but wondered what she wanted. It soon came out. 'Have you heard of a camp there for political unreliables?' Marianne asked. In this cautious way, Marianne sought to find the truth of the BBC report about Auschwitz. Elfriede, of course, did not know why Marianne was asking, nor had she heard of Auschwitz, so could offer little enlightenment. But they agreed a code by which she would communicate anything she found out. Once back in Upper Silesia, she asked around. A farmer confirmed that special trains came through continually to the camp, but more than that he could not say. In any case, Elfriede told me, her base was relatively far from Auschwitz. Like her brother, it was only after the war that she understood the significance of the encounter: with her seemingly casual question, Marianne had been trying to confirm whether Theresienstadt deportees really were being murdered.[21] Not until 1945 did Elfriede realize how 'spirited' and fearless Marianne had been. Her confident manner had been Marianne's protection, Elfriede said. That and the fact that she 'didn't look Jewish'.[22]

The trials of friendship

Marianne's diary entry from 13 July contained yet another revelation, in the form of excerpts from a letter sent to her by Sonja Schreiber. Sonja gave vent to gentle but firm criticism of Marianne's behaviour in relation to the Briels; in forming a close friendship with Fritz Briel, Marianne, it seems, had been careless of Maria. She also commented on Marianne's relationship with someone called Hermann:

'. . . *And something else, while I'm dispensing maternal advice: I was somewhat perturbed by the fact that you're venturing to advise Hermann on his personal relationships. Really, the only person who can and should give such advice is someone with maturity and experience, someone who has gained first-hand insights into such difficult problems. I hope you have not entangled yourself in difficulties. I also think you should be a little more circumspect towards a man who has a close relationship with another woman. You have known both sides for far too short a time.'* – How right she is! And that's why it's doubly painful!

A letter from a Hermann Schmalstieg is also folded in at this page. Though the tone of the letter is friendly, the writer was clearly concerned at unsolicited advice Marianne had given his girlfriend, Berti. He did not question Marianne's insight, but rather the inappropriateness of her seeking to advise someone whom she hardly knew, on the basis of so little knowledge and experience.[23] Had she thought through the conversation, he wanted to know, since such things required careful thought. Had she discussed it with Hedwig? (Evidently, Hedwig Gehrke was a mutual friend.) He included part of a subsequent letter from Berti to himself, which showed how unhappy she was about the affair.

Of course, I found all this, the diary and letters, only after Marianne's death. Whenever she and I had spoken about Bund members, she had alluded to tensions only with Mrs Gehrke senior, Hedwig's mother-in-law. For the rest, the Briels, the Schmitzes and so on took on an almost saintly quality. Some were closer and more powerful presences, Maria Briel, for example, or Sonja Schreiber; others, such as the Morgensterns, more distant, if only because Marianne had had little contact with them after the war. But there was never a hint of problems between them. Now I looked back into the diary and realized that I had failed to spot the significance of various other passages. When Marianne had talked at Whitsun about 'Easter wounds', of which 'only we three are aware'[24] this was not, as I had thought at first, some kind of quasi-religious reference, but a hint of conflict between herself and the Briels.

If the letter from Sonja was correct, the cause of friction, it seemed, was often, ironically, Marianne's desire to help her hosts. She had been thrust suddenly into intimate familial situations and confronted with other people's marriages in a way that was new to her. (Ernst, too, had written from Izbica about the novelty of living side by side with other families. Nazi policies and the dislocations of war had the effect of roughly pushing aside the screens that normally shielded family life from view.) In addition, as we know, part of the Bund's philosophy was that its moral and political values should be applied just as much to marriage and private life as to the public arena. Its members were engaged in the experiment of creating a moral community, and there was a tradition of open discussion about relationships.[25] For Marianne, who felt her inactivity and her dependence so keenly, here was a forum in which she felt she could actively help. But the impact of the beautiful, headstrong girl had evidently been explosive.

The next couple of weeks were spent in various attempts to make things better. On Sunday 16 July, Marianne noted 'a lovely, clarifying, open exchange with Hermann; Hedwig was there. That was how I wanted it', but 'nevertheless everything in me is dark and heavy'. A letter to Sonja followed, excerpted in the diary. She wrote to the Briels, too.[26] And she wrote to Berti, with more harmless advice on how to decorate her room. Her suggestion was to pick some landscapes by Van Gogh:

Göttingen, 5 August

(Letter to Berti)

The 'Landscape with Vegetable Garden' is one of his peaceful pictures, although he often applies the paint tube directly to the canvas out of impatience and a desire to capture the object completely. How far he penetrates beneath the surface and how much renunciation of self! The painter completely submerging himself in the subject!

This is something one senses in his pictures, and that is why I love them so (not all of them!). Also because they are so life-like (through the thick layers of colour), so luminous, so vivid and so immediate.

For someone like Marianne, so knowledgeable, so conscious of material artefacts and so aware of the environment around her, what torture it must have been to live for two years with virtually no possessions and with no base of her own.

As part of her peace mission, Marianne made a weekend excursion into the Harz mountains to spend time with Hermann Schmalstieg and Berti. In her published account from the 1980s, Marianne made only a brief reference to Hermann Schmalstieg and he did not surface at all in our conversations. Initially, therefore, I made no particular effort to find him. When Meta Kamp mentioned that Hermann was still alive and gave me his address I was, of course, glad to make the connection. But only after discovering the diary did I realize that Marianne had met him more than once in 1943–4 and that they corresponded regularly. As a result, I contacted Herr Schmalstieg on several occasions by telephone or letter, each time with a fresh batch of questions, and finally interviewed him in 1999, at what may prove to be the Bund's last summer meeting.

Like so many in the Bund, Schmalstieg had been born into a modest working-class family.[27] In his teens during the 1920s, he had also been an enthusiastic member of the Naturfreunde. Also like many Bund members, he first came in contact with the group through gymnastics. Responding to a notice advertising classes in Göttingen, run by Georg Reuter, a Bund member, Hermann soon came to realize that there was more than simply physical exercises on offer: here was a movement seeking answers to fundamental questions about life.[28] Though he never lived in the Bund's heartland, the Ruhr area, Hermann retained regular contact through the meetings and Bund holidays, which continued to be held during the Nazi years. These meetings made such an impression on him that after the war he took an entirely new career path, giving up his job as a laboratory technician and becoming a youth worker in order to help shape a different generation of Germans.

During the war, Hermann Schmalstieg worked at the Technische Hochschule in Braunschweig. Because of the air raids, his research section, which tested audio and radio equipment for the military, moved to the Auerhahn mountain, near Goslar in the Harz mountains. Hermann was quartered in a lonely forester's cottage, in an isolated romantic area, ideal for hiding the young Marianne, and it was doubtless there that she went in July 1944. Hermann Schmalstieg had a vivid memory of her visit, and of one incident in particular. In the morning, he left Marianne in the cottage while he went off to work. No one was supposed to know she was there, since a highly sensitive technical project for the military was in the vicinity. Returning home from his day's work, Hermann's blood ran cold. Marianne had opened the windows wide and was sitting with her legs dangling outside, singing happily.[29]

For her part, Marianne's record of the experience was quite different. Lonely, with the recent news of her family behind her, she evidently began to have feelings for Hermann that troubled her:

Monday, 31.7

Weekend in the Harz

Conversation with Hermann in connection with a remark I once made: 'The only things of value in life are things one has called forth from oneself; knowledge that comes from the self.'
[. . .]
Early morning on a superb, beautiful day, and a growing attraction to a somehow familiar and yet so alien person. Around me the open peacefulness; pine-dark hills and valleys.

To feel so divided! Torn back and forth between heart and reason; so close to despair; the abyss so near. At such moments you feel a loneliness without end or, more accurately, you become clearly aware of how lonely you are. Help is to be found only within. From the clear, objective forces which lie within. For human beings, the greatest challenge is to keep these forces alert at all times, at every moment, to never lose the clear judgement of one's critical faculties ('critical', in a good sense). But how close the danger is! If you are not endlessly vigilant. You have to keep renewing that judgement; it's never simply to hand.

But it is so difficult; so difficult, so difficult, so difficult! The heart is so powerful; far too strong a counterweight. Often the weight of reason is not sufficient to balance it. How true the saying: 'Two souls dwell, ach, in my breast.'
The struggle of I against me is so difficult and so lonely.
If one could only learn to say an unequivocal 'Yes' to loneliness!
Perhaps one asks too much, too much from people and from things?
And each step, each new piece of knowledge, each new rung on the ladder, involves so much pain.
To be able to love, to love, to love, to love; uninhibited, unfettered by

one's own conscience, unchallenged by the world outside! But the fact that it's never possible, that I'm never allowed to love, that it always brings so much pain – surely this must mean something?

If only one weren't always desperately waiting for something, always wanting. If only one could let go of the branch, give oneself up, completely and without reservation; give oneself up to something, perhaps that's the secret. Perhaps that's also the way to the other person. If only one could!

[...]

Yesterday during our walk, the conversation about Weltanschauung. *The Jewish question: How is such an attitude possible, given such intellectual capacity and judgement! If only he knew! Oh, my stupid heart.*

A couple of hours later.

Goslar, on the market place.

Ernest, I think I might have lost you now. Or, did you let me go? Forever?

Will you draw me to you again? Who knows?

[...]

This old town is beautiful in its harmonious style. For writing poetry, dreaming and losing oneself.

It is not absolutely certain that the conversation Marianne refers to is the same conversation, the one with Hermann, with which the entry opens, but it seems likely. Clearly, whoever was with her on the walk had stirred feelings of love – and of guilt in relation to Ernst. Taking this entry in conjunction with the letters, I wondered if there had been more than friendship between Hermann Schmalsteig and Marianne. Meta Kamp thought not, but, enclosing transcripts of some of the diary and letters I had found, I wrote to Hermann Schmalstieg and, after apologizing for presenting him with what might be emotionally painful, I asked him whether he could fill in the background.

Hermann Schmalstieg was touched by my letter, but was adamant that there had been no affair. He had been going out with Berti at the time, a vulnerable girl, now long dead, who suffered feelings of inferiority and needed constant reassurance. He remembered Marianne and Berti meeting. Looking back, Hermann was amazed that under the conditions of war and Nazi terror a private life had been possible at all.

To come back to Marianne, she really was a delightful person. I had no idea how close she felt to me until I read the thoughts in her diary. I mean the thoughts and feelings which she wrote in her diary after a conversation with me. Yes, the diary opened up a world of which I was completely unaware at the time. I myself was too preoccupied with Berti, with the events of the war and the work in the institute. Reading Marianne's thoughts and feelings as an older person today, one could gain the impression that her behaviour towards me was more than just friendly. But on my part this really wasn't the case. I've already explained why not. Nevertheless I am moved by Marianne's thoughts. That is because what appears in the diary entries is also my world, one which I've carried around fixed within me, for almost a lifetime.

When we finally met at the Bund conference at the Rüspe in the Sauerland, I found Hermann Schmalstieg a little unsteady on his feet but still with youthful charm and, above all, an enthusiastic innocence, despite being in his nineties. He was accompanied by his attractive wife, she only in her sixties and looking younger still. Hermann told me again how deeply moved he had been to learn of Marianne's feelings for him.

In my letters, I posed some delicate questions, curious whether he realized the full implications of some of Marianne's remarks:

One entry of 31.7.1944, which perhaps *referred to a conversation with you, raised the question for me whether you actually knew at the time that Marianne was Jewish. Or was this information withheld for your safety?*

Of course he had known that she was Jewish, he wrote. And as far as I can tell, the Bund members who protected Marianne *did* generally know this. But Marianne wrote that her 'stupid heart' had left her with strong feelings for someone with intolerable views on the Jewish question, prompting the only entry in the whole diary making even an oblique reference to her Jewish identity. Her remark 'If only he knew!'

either meant 'he' did not know she was Jewish or that 'he', with his views about Jews, did not realize she loved him. But if Hermann Schmalstieg now registered the implication of Marianne's remarks, he did not let on to me.

Where to now?

A diary entry from late August begins with yet another brief encounter:

26. VIII.44

'It's coming to an end, everything's coming apart,' the dentist said. Shame – I'd like to have got to know him better. And I had the feeling he wanted to know more about me. Perhaps at some later time. Who knows!? Sometime, when we can put our cards on the table.

But the tone soon changes, introducing an unexpected twist:

Later, in the train

[. . .]Farewell to Gö. Where to now?
Never have I felt the burdens of my life so acutely as I do now. Homelessness, loneliness. I'm suspended in space! How will the heart-to-heart with Karin go?
[. . .]
Journey into the unknown. After Goslar into the Harz . . . and then? Ach, if only I could rest with someone's loving heart.
But could I? One's own nature is so torn, so ambivalent. One wants to surrender oneself but also to fight; to be carried along but also to set the direction.

Marianne had never even hinted to me that the chain of helpers had been close to breaking. Only the diary revealed that in late summer 1944, after four weeks with Meta Steinmann, Marianne really did not know where she should go next. For a while in Göttingen, she had been anxiously awaiting a letter from Karin Morgenstern. Now, it seemed that Karin was camping in the Harz mountains and some kind of clarification was needed between them before a decision could be made about Marianne's future.

That evening Marianne slept under the open sky:

Evening [in the Harz]

Marvellous to drift along! Just water, sky and God – and the unknown depths below. Evening above the water. Solitude and peace. You feel all your problems flow away. Forests and sky, sun and moon, the untapped harmony of the universe. But life?

Sunday!

[. . .]

Yesterday evening brought a short conversation with Karin, to be continued this morning, and a walk with the other two friends though the moonlit summer evening. We talked about Karin and the difficulty of being with her, above all because of the way she takes every favour for granted. The conversation ended on a positive note.

I'm so preoccupied, thinking about life in this difficult, bloody time. Future; tests and dangers, how are they to be mastered?

To be whole! And to master the horror through reason!

In a letter to Meta Steinmann it emerged that the conversation with Karin Morgenstern had been far from satisfactory.[30] Tensions persisted between Marianne, Karin, and the other two Bund members in the mountains. From shorthand in the diary and some information provided by Hermann Schmalstieg, it seems the others were Hermann and Lene Krahlisch, a couple from Mülheim. The problems were apparently compounded by the fact that not only was Marianne's arrival unexpected but Lene's mother also turned up unannounced. Nevertheless, from the Harz mountains, Marianne now travelled back to Braunschweig with Karin.

Hints at tensions in her relations with Bund friends continue for some weeks. Tucked into the front of the diary I found a letter in someone else's hand addressed to 'Liebe Anya' and clearly directed to Marianne.

23.9.1944

Dear Anya,

I wonder how things are with you? Did you arrive at L's[31] safe and sound? I hope the journey went well. In my thoughts I was with you so much – I'm sure that helped. How are you settling in?

I wanted to send you a parcel but they wouldn't take it. Now I have to pack a smaller one. And send you a little bread and some groceries in it.

Something is weighing on my mind that I wanted to tell you before you started living there. I've had the strong sense that you, in yourself, if you know what I mean, have somehow been thrown off kilter. Recently.

That's the feeling I get from your latest letters. It may partly be the result of ~~the weeks being so insecure~~ of your external situation being so insecure – as you waited for K's[32] letter and didn't know where to go. But M, if we are secure inside, have confidence and know where others stand in relation to us, then we can stay on an even keel.

One has to learn to stop seeing oneself[33] as the centre of every-thing and learn to share more of others' lives.

If you want to take part.

If you want to live with a family.

It's not always easy – but it is something that can be learned.

And so I wanted to say something to you about living together, as a community.

Our whole life consists of experimenting and testing.

But not, as you tend to do when living with others, laying down the law unilaterally. Something which expresses itself in so many small things.

To be sure, M is young and the world is open to her. And she wants to conquer all by 'force'. But that's not the right way.

One must be able to adapt to other people – that has to be learned. One must listen to others and learn how to fit oneself into their lives.

And not always react with a critical attitude to everything that doesn't suit you.

I have some misgivings about you going to L. You will be thinking, is that —-'s [the letter-writer's] business . . .

Yes, I feel that I must say something to you about it.

You see, I'm able to say when something doesn't suit me or, more to the point, when I believe something isn't right. But not everyone can do that. You remember that I too had to learn to tell you when I didn't think something was right. Not everyone learns so quickly. Usually, people think, 'the couple of weeks are soon past and then we'll be on our own again'.

No, it should be a proper life together.

And since you exert a very powerful influence on people, even when you're wrong and aren't seeing things properly, you must always ask yourself, 'Is that right?' and, 'Am I allowed to do that?'

What I find troubling is that in conversation you see that something you've done is wrong and say yes, yes but afterwards you act just as you want, just as you had before.

That's not the point of living and experimenting together. The point is to act on the principles one has already accepted and then experiment further.

I've often found it so draining. Perhaps you do it without realizing. But it's very depressing for the people you're living with.

And when I think of L, she's not a very strong person[. . .]

I think I've expressed myself clearly.

Will you write to me what you think?

For today, loving greetings.

The signature is unclear, and in any case is probably a code. Comparison with other letters does not help identify the handwriting. The letter is not fluent enough to be from Sonja. Most likely, it came from Hedwig Gehrke.

Poor Marianne! What utter loneliness she must have felt in such moments. When those on whom her life depended were exasperated with her, who was there left to turn to? With the exception, perhaps, of the time she actually spent with Meta, this whole period since Beverstedt now seemed so much more conflict-laden and unsettled than I had realized.

It was, above all, the letter to 'Anya' that prompted me to ask Hermann Schmalstieg whether he thought the Bund friends really understood Marianne's situation. When Marianne and Karin Morgenstern had their quarrel in the Harz, Karin had even accused Marianne of not understanding the difficulties of *her* position. Of course, Marianne was not the only one in danger. The heroism of the Bund members is without question. In that sense, they were all in the same boat. But unlike her friends, Marianne had no choice but to continue being heroic. If they stopped defying the regime, they would be safe from persecution. If she stopped defying the regime, she would be murdered. I wondered if Marianne's hosts had made sufficient allowance for her special predicament. Yet, when I considered the situation from their angle, it was clear that they actually found it hard to cope with and contain Marianne. They experienced her not as vulnerable, but as powerful. As Hedwig wrote, they had to learn to say 'no' to her. The indomitable character that was essential for Marianne's physical and psychological survival did not make life easy for her hosts.

The front creeps closer

During an air raid over Braunschweig at the end of August, Marianne and Karin took refuge in a shelter and Marianne penned a letter to Sonja in the anxious hours of the night. She had been on the run for a whole year:

Bra.[34] 29/30.VIII

Night in the shelter

One has the feeling that the war is coming closer with every day. How much it devours and how frighteningly small are the personal sacrifices we've made until now!

Eberhardt [Jungbluth – recently killed in battle] – I still can't believe it! Sometimes you wonder if it always strikes the best of them! (But that's an unworthy thought; it just strikes doubly hard.)

All that's left are the happy thoughts and memories that allow those we have lost to live on. The more they were loved, the more they stay with us. Isn't that so? And I feel we have a duty to do our utmost to live properly, in memory of the dead (because their lives and being are somehow interwoven with ours; on one level they've died and taken part of us with them, but they've also left much behind; though we often don't recognize its value because of the pain).

... and to do our utmost to live, mindful of our own death because we are part of an unending cycle.

That's never been so clear to me as it is now. I've often thought such things but never felt so fulfilled by them.

A remarkable year lies behind me, one in which I've won – and lost – an enormous amount. (But where does the idea of winning begin and the idea of losing leave off?) Is there not a loss entailed in winning and a win in each loss?

[. . .]

The shelter has now emptied. Next to me, two people are talking about the war. Which is never more present than in moments of danger. 'What do you think, will we still win the war?' The other shakes her head: 'What, now? Impossible!' Do many people think like that?

Strange, people at night; quite different from by day!

Signs of the approaching front were ever more apparent; the air-raid warnings unceasing. Marianne's diary entries became more intermittent and her thoughts preoccupied by the mounting chaos around her. Paradoxically, life was now as much under threat from the Allies as from the Nazis. When I interviewed her for the Ruhrland Museum in 1989, Marianne said that the last few months of the war were the most taxing and stressful:

'All these factors built up: the never-ending travelling, the fact that I could never come to rest, the ever-growing danger of being caught or recognized, on top of the problems I shared with the rest of the population – finding food, staying healthy, avoiding the bombs. In the last months of the war and of my illegal existence they all had an effect on me which I was aware of only much later.'

Marianne's first port of call after Braunschweig was Mülheim in the Ruhr, just a few miles from her home in Essen. Here she stayed with

Lene Krahlisch (probably the 'L' of Meta's letter), one of her Bund hosts whom she completely forgot after the war and never mentioned in her article:[35]

Mülheim, 31.9.44

(Letter to Meta)

I've been with Lene for a week now, a very eventful, unsettling week that has given me little chance to rest. The journey here was better than I'd feared. We left early in the morning and arrived late at night. The trains were packed. Every time you meet other people, you are moved and shaken by what they tell you. Dramatic experiences and fates seared by the relentlessness of war. People torn apart, separated from their families, often without a clue to where to find them. Refugees fleeing battles on the borders, or fleeing bombs. The stories they tell are often so horrific that you're left trembling with fear about your own fate.

Travelling has become dangerous. Massive attacks can happen any time. Some people have already been through such horrors. Yes, the war has come very close. The front is not far, and day and night you can hear the thunder of the guns.

Here was further evidence that Marianne made no mental distinction between herself and 'the Germans'. The refugees evoke her sympathy and also elicit anxious identification with their plight. Their dreadful experiences make her fear for her own safety.

As defeat seemed increasingly certain, the regime became even more radical. Half-Jews and Jews in mixed marriages were now targeted for deportation and murder. Typically, Marianne tried to help those around her. Her friend, Grete Menningen, had been relatively protected until the early summer of 1944 because she was married to a non-Jew. She lived in Barmen and had been able to put Marianne up once or twice. But now Grete, too, was assigned to a transport. Marianne told me that, through the help of another Bund friend, Else Bramesfeld, someone was eventually found who lived in an isolated house near Remscheid and was willing to hide Frau Menningen.[36]

Marianne herself struggled to make a virtue of the constant tension and threat. In Duisburg, she was caught up in one of her worst air raids yet:

15.X.44

Attacks day and night. Yesterday and last night Duisburg. The bombs just kept falling. One dies a thousand deaths. And people manage to put up with it!

How salutary the way one's sense of values changes in moments of acute danger. All your own worries seem so tiny. You no longer cling so rigidly to external things. You feel your way, testing, exposed to everything. We should learn from this for our ordinary lives. Really learn: to be detached from everything, to be able to let go. Only then can one live properly and die properly.

Monday, 16.X.44

Still filled with the horror of the previous few hours I went to the cinema yesterday afternoon, because I simply could not relax. My thoughts kept wheeling round and round what had happened.

By the end of October, Marianne was in Remscheid, probably staying with the Briels again:

30.X.44 Rem.

(Letter to Lene)

Yes, these are difficult, bad times. Fear of what is to come creeps up on you. Essen must have been awful. I was so happy when Maria brought news on Thursday that everyone there is well and in good shape. During the raid on Monday evening, I was sitting in a train between D.–S.[37] *It was absolutely dreadful. The planes rumbled overhead, flying very low. Any minute a bomb could have fallen on us. You can imagine the panic. I learned what an effect on others it has if one stays completely calm. I surprised myself with the strength I could convey by staying calm and speaking calmly. Women, trembling, clutched on to my hands, but then they too calmed down. I only hope I'll have the same strength when things really depend on it. But that demands so much!*

31.X

Another day has passed! At midday it seems there was another attack on Essen. I worry so much about our friends! Every day brings new tests. I listen to every rumour and am always on the move.

Half-sedentary, half-nomad.

The image of Marianne sitting in the train providing solace to the women around her is extraordinary, and conveys vividly her divided sense of identity. On the one hand, she feels part of the wider community, and it is natural that she should provide others with assistance. On the other hand, she does not yet consider this the real test. What was probably the high-point of terror in the whole war for those around her is for Marianne just a rehearsal for the challenges she fears are yet to come.

At the beginning of November a letter must have arrived from Meta, bringing not only news that the Göttingen friends were still alive, but also, evidently, some welcome praise for Marianne herself, acknowledging her strength and spirit at such a difficult time. Such words, so important to Marianne after so many difficult encounters, prompted her to put pen to paper straight away.

Friday, 3.XI.44

(From a letter to Meta)

I can't tell you what pleasure your delightful letter gave me! I was a little worried not to have heard from you for so long. The times are so uncertain and one's life so dependent on the bigger picture – at least that's how things are here.[. . .]

Now to your letter: are you sure that you're seeing me properly? I don't feel my thoughts and deeds merit anything like so much praise! I keep learning how much I'm still at the beginning. In that, you're right. Yes, it is time that I do something productive with my life, though not to give (as you think) but to learn – to learn the inner peace and balance required for true freedom and the discovery of the true, clear path to oneself and others. Objective actions are surely the secret. So much confusion in personal things, and in humanity as a whole, would be resolved instantly if everyone heard the call of necessity and simply acted on it! One can and must confront mankind with the basic command: 'Do what you see is necessary; do what it is most important for you to do!'

The diary and identity

With that, and another small entry from 11 November 1944, the diary proper comes to an end. Over the months from April to November 1944 a voice had emerged which I had not heard in any of the interviews. Had I read the diary first, I might have been able to make out faint echoes in some of the things Marianne said to me. But, as it was, my image of the girl on the run had been quite different from the self-portrait she painted. My overriding awareness of that monstrous thing, the Holocaust, and the knowledge that Marianne's flight had been triggered because she was a Jew, had led me to assume that while on the run she would see herself primarily as a Jew in hiding and as a victim caught among her tormentors. My conversations with Marianne had not challenged this image. True, she never paraded her victimhood. She was very conscious of the difference between her experiences and those of people in the camps. But nothing she had said to me revealed, as the diary now suggested, that at the time Marianne had not in any way seen herself or her problems in light of Jewish persecution.

Of course, the diary itself raises problems of interpretation. Fear of discovery may have led to suppression of some issues and thoughts. Marianne may have deliberately omitted, for example, anything that identified her as Jewish. But there are too many sustained observations and judgements (and also too many indiscretions) to see the diary as a document written in terror, in fear of calling a spade a spade. Moreover, as we shall see, Marianne's post-war writing, when the Gestapo had ceased to be a threat, continued in the same vein.

The more important issue surrounding the diary's 'authenticity', though, is what was the relationship between the entries, on the one hand, and Marianne's identity and experience, on the other. The diary is not a stream of consciousness or unmediated outpouring of emotion but a remarkably composed document. It was clearly influenced by a genre of reflective journal-keeping that sought to probe the essence of things, rather than record the day-to-day.[38] Thus Marianne often uses the third-person construction 'one' rather than the more immediate 'I'.[39] The diary was also clearly a way of regaining balance, finding her feet, a deliberate counterweight to the fears of the day. She was able to apply (and be quite conscious of applying) a kind of psychological censorship. The letters to Ernst from 1942 showed her capacity to exclude from her writing the daily threats and humiliations, and to focus on what was enriching or constructive. This did not mean that, off the page, Marianne was not aware of those threats or that they did not influence her sense of her identity.

Should we see Marianne's sustained reflections on *Weltanschauung*, then, as just 'flights' of fancy, an effort to hide from being in hiding? Did her dreams give a better account of what she was going through than her measured daytime reflections? There *was* undoubtedly a degree of escapism here, a refusal to connect the dots in her increasingly well-informed picture of Nazi terror. But the diary also reports authentic experience that did not reinforce a sense of identity as a Jewish victim of Nazi persecution. For one thing, as the war went on, Marianne was increasingly surrounded by German suffering of one sort or another, and she was guiltily, fearfully conscious that she had so far come through the war 'unscathed', while the number of refugees, evacuees, war-wounded, and war-dead grew around her. In her descriptions of encounters with refugees on the train, what comes through is that Marianne saw herself as one of very many people displaced by war. Of course, for us, the moral significance of being an accidental victim of the machinery of war and of being sought out for a programme of genocide is quite different. But Marianne's awareness of others' suffering was probably an important factor in her survival.[40]

Something else that emerges from the diary is how disorientating it must have been constantly to pretend to be someone else. For Marianne, 'passing' as someone else involved maintaining at least *three* identities. She herself and those fully in the know were aware that she was a Jew on the run (although, as noted, this barely seemed to define her identity for herself or them). To Elfriede Wahle, Ernst Steinmann and others, Marianne as Bund member was a politically endangered Aryan, keeping her head down, but not belonging to that most dangerous category – the Jew. And for the wider world, she was quite simply an ordinary German. That last identity kept changing its specific character: sometimes she was a young woman with a child, sometimes a distant relative and sometimes a bombed-out victim. Small wonder that, occasionally, Marianne ached to end the role-playing and simply be herself. The problem was, as she herself acknowledged, that she was no longer sure what that was. In September, for example, she wrote:[41]

I love the 'I' too much; all the different 'I's within me. And the true person one should be and wants to be somehow gets lost. One is always playing a role to oneself and to others. One is never really 'I'.

This comment also reveals perhaps the most subtle and important part of Marianne's experience. With our awareness of the Holocaust, we assume that persecution was the fundamental fact in Marianne's life. Of course, in many ways, it was: it had robbed her of family and friends and sent her into hiding. But for Marianne, a young woman just entering maturity, encountering new ideas and new people, it was not always easy to tell which of her fears and problems were in fact the product of war. Was the loss of the 'I' the result of trying to decide who she was or rather of having to be in hiding? She was not sure. In early August, she wrote, for example:[42]

All one's personal difficulties and problems – don't they stem from the chaos of our time? Events fly by so fast that one follows them in an exaggerated state of wakefulness and tension. Aren't one's own problems inextricably interwoven with all this?

To us, the connection seems so obvious – how could friendships and relationships be other than fraught in such circumstances? But Marianne's insight is phrased as a question; she could not be certain of what is now obvious. And on reflection, we can see that *not* everything she said or experienced, *not* every feature of her life and interactions, could be ascribed to persecution. It was Marianne's tragedy to experience the process of growing up, of finding herself, in those horrific conditions. Marianne had an advantage enjoyed by few other Jews passing as Aryans; a very positive 'Aryan' role model. Looking back on some of the personal difficulties she experienced with her hosts, I realized that the Bund members' refusal to make allowances for Marianne's special predicament had a powerfully uplifting aspect. For Marianne, the letters from Hedwig and Sonja, critical though they were, signalled that they treated her as one of the group. No distinctions were being made. In other words, the Bund provided her not only with safe houses but, even more important, it offered her an identity. More and more, as the diary makes clear, Marianne saw herself as one of them, a fighter for a better Germany. From our interviews, I learned her debt to the Bund; from the diary, I learned that for a while during the war she became, at least subjectively, *part* of the Bund.

The last weeks on the move

As 1944 came to a close, travelling became even more risky as a result of air attacks on the railways and the increasing surveillance by Gestapo and criminal police on trains, stations and public places. According to a Bund member from Düsseldorf, towards the end of 1944 Marianne almost fell into the hands of the criminal police and only escaped by good luck.[43] The number of safe houses dwindled rapidly. In January 1945, Sonja Schreiber was sent into a rural area with her school. Artur and Dore Jacobs went to ground in southern Germany. It was now too risky to travel as far as Braunschweig, Göttingen or Bremen.[44]

On 31 December 1944, Marianne was at Wuppertal-Vohwinkel station, waiting for a train to Solingen-Wald to stay with a woman associated with the Bund called Reni Sadamgrotzky, when suddenly the station came under direct attack in a bombing raid. The following day, by which time she was ensconced at Reni's in Solingen-Wald, waves of bombers suddenly flew over while they were eating lunch; bombs exploded around the house as they fled to the cellar. The house received a direct hit while they were in the cellar and the whole estate was destroyed in minutes. Happily, Reni and Marianne emerged unharmed.[45]

Marianne's restitution testimony reveals that in January 1945 she paid a brief visit to Hammacher, her father's bank manager. She wanted to make it clear that at least one of the family had survived. Whether

her purpose was to establish later claims to the house (which, she knew by then, had been destroyed), or to prevent the bank from doing anything with the records of the family's accounts, I am not sure. In her testimony, she said that she had wanted to ascertain the current state of the family property and finances. She did not tell Hammacher where she had come from or where she was going, and the whole visit lasted no more than ten minutes. There is no evidence that the bank director informed anyone else about it.[46] Marianne also used her visit to Essen to drop in on the Jürgens. This time, she said, there was 'a spanking new table cloth with my mother's monogram' on the dining table, and she had to bite her lip to keep silent.[47]

By February 1945, the Allies had reached the left bank of the Rhine. In view of the war situation, where was best for Marianne to go? Her friends advised her to try Düsseldorf, which they believed would soon fall to the Americans. A Remscheid Bund member, Greta Dreibholz, had an old friend in Düsseldorf, Hanni Ganzer, a teacher at a girls' grammar school. Marianne wrote in *Das Münster am Hellweg*:

On a cold February night I stood at the station in Ratingen because the unceasing shelling meant that the trains couldn't get any closer to Düsseldorf. I waited with many other refugees till dawn, at which point a couple of trucks ventured into the city centre. A driver took me along. I was carrying all the property I had gathered or swapped in the suitcase which had accompanied me on all my travels over the last two and a half years.

At six in the morning, Marianne knocked on the door of a woman she had never met. Marianne knew that she was confronting the stranger with new and serious risks. It turned out she was lucky to have arrived just then, as Hanni Ganzer was generally in the house for only an hour or so in the early mornings and spent the rest of the day in the air-raid shelter. Hanni read Greta's letter and said without hesitation 'Of course you can stay.'[48]

Else Bramesfeld and Hanni Ganzer, after the war

Holed up in Düsseldorf

The Bund had calculated that Marianne would soon be liberated. True enough, the Americans reached the western part of the city, on the left bank of the Rhine, on 3 March, only a few weeks after Marianne's arrival. The left bank was now governed by a mayor appointed by the Americans. But Marianne was in the main part of Düsseldorf, east of the Rhine, and the Wehrmacht destroyed the remaining bridges across the river. The city's Nazi leaders[49] and the Wehrmacht decided to make a last stand; Marianne thus found herself trapped in a bastion of resistance with no escape in view. By April, large parts of the Ruhr were under Allied control, but Düsseldorf was still holding out.

The Bund had made a disastrous mistake. Though 20 February saw the last massive bombing raid on Düsseldorf, the city was now under ceaseless artillery bombardment from the left bank and daily attacks from low-flying American fighters. The city centre dissolved into a crazy world of rubble and craters. During March, gas, electricity and water supplies were cut off.[50]

For more than six weeks, Marianne and Hanni slept on chairs in the air-raid shelter, sometimes spending up to twenty-three hours a day underground. If possible, during the day, Marianne would leave her protector to herself. Whenever there was a lull she would come out of the shelter, sometimes to order a meal from one of the few inns still functioning. In the shelter, Marianne was protected from American shells, but not from the other threat in those last desperate weeks: the incessant patrols searching for deserters and 'enemies' of the state. The offices of the local chief of the NSDAP and other party functionaries were next door to the shelter where Marianne and Hanni spent their time.[51] In addition to Party and Gestapo, army units were also combing the city (though largely looking for male deserters).

At this stage, run-ins with the authorities could go either way. Some officials, mindful that it would not be a bad thing to have post-war witnesses to their humanity, were already tending to play it safe. If Eric Alexander's reminiscence is correct, Marianne *was* stopped on one occasion but not detained. By contrast, the final days of the Reich also saw many party members and others engage in a last outpouring of violence and rage. In Düsseldorf, the killings went on to the very end. On 15 April 1945, just two days before the city fell, an army unit found Moritz Sommer, a Jew, in hiding. The seventy-two-year-old Sommer was hanged in public on the Oberbilker Markt.[52]

We gain a brief glimpse into Marianne's feelings in the inferno from the draft of a letter she wrote to Maria, which is folded into the diary. The draft may have been written just before she moved to Düsseldorf:

Sunday evening, 18.2.45

(To Maria)
I've just got home. Despite two air-raid warnings, the journey was easy and quick, and I want to sit down to write to you.

I must say how lovely the few hours with you were. For me, they set some thoughts rolling and I want to send you my best wishes in acknowledgement. I felt the enormous weight, which presses down on me all the time, day and night, lift from my shoulders for a few hours.

We live with a thousand fears, with danger always just around the corner, with constant premonitions of death by one means or another.

And this evening, while I was sitting in the train and thinking over our conversations, I started wondering why we have such a fear of death. Surely, death is the culmination of life, biologically and spiritually. Fulfilment and release. Shouldn't we in fact fear life rather than death? In life, so many goals and expectations we set ourselves remain unfulfilled.

Perhaps what is so frightening is that death has its own laws. It doesn't ask whether we still have jobs to do, or more accurately, whether we still believe we have a job to do. When the time comes, death cuts the thread, sometimes without notice, sometimes after a warning, sometimes with our full knowledge.

Death's law.

Who knows what law governs our existence? Where we find fulfilment and completion? When we have to cease being here? We often imagine we should be spared because we still have so much to do in the years ahead and we sense enormous energy within ourselves, demanding to be used. But isn't this arrogant and inappropriate? Self-deception! Our true work often lies not in the great challenges but in the smaller ones that we so easily overlook. If only we could always remember this! If only knowledge, and living according to that knowledge, weren't two separate things!

I would like to thank you for all your love and to say (it's easier in writing) how happy I am that you are there!

Never had Marianne written so under the shadow of death.

In a letter written shortly after the war, she looked back on this period.[53] In post-war safety, Marianne's tone was heroic:

Life in the face of death is very different – much more intense, truer, more naked. I wrote like someone possessed in order to keep a record of the crazy, dreamlike, unbelievable life of those days. I hope I'll soon be able to show you my diary entries, Meta.[54] So many thoughts about you are inter-woven with them. . . The greater the danger, the stronger the will to live and the more productive one's thinking and actions.

But then this thought slipped out: 'In this last period I often gave up hope of surviving. And who knows what would have happened had the war lasted longer!'[55]

The impressions I gathered during those eight weeks of almost intimate life with the motley crew in the air-raid shelter . . . it's incredible, when I think back. There was little that was positive in the experience.

Marianne wrote of the egotism and lack of common sense she observed around her, and the tension:[56]

Almost every night there was a raid in search of deserters. I always had to reckon with the possibility of being caught at the last minute, after surviving so many other dangers. It was an incredible feeling.

Finally, though, on 17 April 1945, the Bund's job was done. A US 97th Infantry battalion entered Düsseldorf and the city capitulated quietly, without further resistance. Marianne was saved.

The Bund and Marianne

As we know, Marianne was not the only Jew to survive under the Bund's protection. Lisa Jacob had been in hiding since April 1942. Other Jews had been hidden by the Bund for at least part of the war. A woman called Eva Seligmann hid in the Blockhaus for a while. Hannah Jordan was briefly protected by Bund contacts. Dore Jacobs was under threat after September 1944 when, with some inconsistency, the regime began deporting Jews of mixed marriages. In all, perhaps some eight Jews (and half-Jews) were saved by the group. But, given the length of time and the fact that she was not previously known to any of her hosts, protecting Marianne must rank as their finest achievement.

How did they manage it? The Bund had a number of remarkable advantages. Few other left-wing organizations had been so conscious of the dangers of Nazi racism so early, possibly because Jews had played a prominent role in the group.[57] In any case, Artur was an extraordinary leader – an idealist, but at the same time a master tactician. With scrupulous attention to detail, he laid down rules and procedures for every eventuality.[58] And he practised what he preached. The transcript of his interrogations by the Gestapo – again on file in Düsseldorf – in which he kept returning and adding extra detail in a tone designed to match their assumptions, is a masterpiece.[59] Indeed, several members of the Bund were interrogated by the Gestapo[60] yet no charges were ever brought and monitoring of Jacobs' mail never revealed anything of an incriminating nature.[61]

Studies of people who helped Jews in the Holocaust have often drawn attention to the importance of informal networks.[62] The Bund in this sense was a rather odd hybrid, as much a collection of friends as an organized body. There was no official structure, but there was the rigour of its emphasis on the ethics of the everyday act and a strong internal hierarchy. Unlike other groups, which seemed large but in fact had an active core of only a few members, Bund members were all active, all committed.[63]

The Bund was an odd hybrid, also, in the way it combined dance and politics. Though Dore's school was soon closed, gymnastics lessons provided a basis for activity which could be maintained even into the early years of the war. This gave members a chance to communicate and to conceal their other activities. When Gestapo officers carried out searches and found papers about dance and physical movement, they didn't know what to make of them.[64]

Additionally, the movement's ownership of the so-called Bundeshäuser, where like-minded people could be tenants, ensured a relatively safe framework for meetings and communication in the early years. The Blockhaus, the house in the Dönhoff, where Grete Ströter lived, and the Jacobs' house in Wuppertal remained key addresses for much of the war. The group meetings there and in the wild were crucial in helping members establish the right balance between personal safety and commitment.[65] Above all, the group broke through the sense of isolation that characterized daily life in Nazi Germany.[66] By the time Marianne was on the run, regular group meetings had largely ceased. But even then, as we have seen, the Bund's gatherings once or twice a year could be a crucial source of moral support. Finally, the Bund was lucky. Every member I spoke to had a near-miss story to offer, and Marianne had plenty of her own.

In one of the Bund's post-war bulletins, an article asserted that the Bund members were neither particularly adventurous nor possessed of particular physical courage. And they were well aware of the consequences of what would happen if they were caught.[67] A booklet in memory of August Schmitz, produced by the Bund, offered a comment that could serve for many of its members:[68]

It is astounding how someone possessing no extraordinary gifts could grow, work and influence those around him.
'Man grows in his actions and with his tasks.'
He exemplifies this truth.

In her 1980s article and conversations with me, Marianne suppressed, perhaps even had forgotten, her personal wrangles with various of her hosts. As a result, what she felt about the Bund probably became slightly distorted in her memory. The way she presented her friends then was as miraculous, almost saintly people. Whereas at the time, I think, Marianne knew that the real miracle lay in the fact that they were, in many ways, quite ordinary human beings who, well-led, well-organized, well-hidden and powerfully motivated, found the extraordinary courage and commitment to risk their lives to save hers.

Marianne and the Bund

To dwell on the Bund's qualities is not to question Marianne's own contribution to her survival. Jews in Nazi Germany often said how easy it was to spot one another. Nervous looks, a self-effacing gait, the consciousness of being a pariah all revealed the mark of Cain – or perhaps we should say of Abraham. Marianne under pressure was all coolness and confidence. Hers was an astonishing performance.

What was the relationship between the performance and the person? The diary suggests that Marianne was 'passing' not only on the outside, but also within her most intimate self. She refused to internalize the category 'Jew' which the Nazis imposed on her. In the company of the Bund and inspired by their philosophy, she sloughed off her former identity and slipped into being one of them. To the extent that her

Jewishness was the key reason for her persecution and that she was not really free to redefine her identity, we might say she was in hiding from what she was. But if so, the self-deception undoubtedly helped her to pass as an Aryan.

In addition to her own qualities, Marianne had three other things in her favour. She had capital – her access to the family trunks for bartering was crucial. She had skills and could make things to sell. Above all, she was a woman. As Marianne's youth-group friend Jakov (Klaus) Langer in Israel pointed out:[69]

A man would have been lost. I don't mean that he would not have had the manual skill [to produce felt flowers etc.], but he could not have ventured on to the street.

It was hard enough to explain why a young healthy girl should not have been in employment or in some kind of uniform. But a young man neither in uniform nor working long hours in a factory would have been impossible.

Jakov Langer raised a question I had not considered. Why had the Bund not found Marianne somewhere she could stay for the duration? After all, Lisa Jacob spent the last six months of the war, perhaps longer, at a guest-house in Bodensee run by Bund sympathizers. Marianne's friend, the half-Jewish Grete Menningen, was placed with someone for the last nine months of the war. Of course, they were both older than Marianne, and a neighbour seeing them would perhaps not find it so odd that they were not at work. Even so, was there no remote house where she could have stayed? Perhaps the Bund did not believe her suitable for a lengthy stay in hiding. Artur Jacobs was so conscious of human qualities and human frailties. Had he recognized that Marianne was not reliable enough, perhaps also too disruptive a presence, to stay in hiding? Hermann Schmalstieg's experience of finding her sitting on the window ledge, singing, legs dangling through the open window, might have served as a warning. The very energy that had helped Marianne survive on the edge prevented her from living quietly and unobtrusively. She was outstanding at passing, but she would have been hopeless at staying in hiding.

12

Living Amid the Ruins

As Marianne and I worked through her last months in Düsseldorf, I was looking forward to the day the Allies arrived. I wanted to share in the exhilaration of the moment of liberation. But I didn't get the pay-off I was expecting. Marianne said she had learned for so long to be cautious that when the end of the war came she felt no release. Indeed, for ten days or so, she said, she did not believe she was safe:[1]

'I couldn't believe it. I simply couldn't believe it. I couldn't believe or trust this magic. It took about ten days before my friend could persuade me to register myself officially.'

Of course, I knew that as the battlefront shifted from one locality to another, it was often not clear for a day or two whether the Allies really were in control.[2] And even after the Nazis were finally and definitively gone from the scene, old habits of caution died hard. Ellen Jungbluth recalled with some amusement the very first Bund summer meeting after the war. They were holding a political discussion in the forest on one of their walks and someone said automatically, 'Just check and make sure that no one is coming.' To which the response was: 'Wait, we can shout out as loud as we want to, now!' 'Oh, yes, you're right!'[3]

But still I found Marianne's testimony odd. Even if the first day after the Americans arrived was a day of caution, wouldn't the second have been the day of joy? After Marianne died, I came across a letter she wrote to Bund friends in Göttingen just a few weeks after the end of the war:[4]

*And while a thousand small and big things were happening . . .
salvation came ever closer – but from the East and not, as we had
expected, from the West. I continue to marvel at this strategic and
tactical coup.*

*And one day, there they were. For eight weeks we had expected
them daily. Rumours and pronouncements followed thick and fast,
often contradicting each other. Then, one summer afternoon when
we had given them up for the day, the Americans arrived.*

*The 'historical moment' passed without fanfares. Everyone felt
an enormous sense of release. But that was more of an unconscious
feeling. It's often hard to see the full significance of such an event
as it happens. How should we evaluate it and where does it fit in?
It wasn't obvious at the time that this was a turning point. Instead,
one simply flowed into a new set of circumstances. Something had
ended, but the thing that was beginning wasn't clear at all. Once
you understand this, however, you needn't be disheartened –
indeed you cannot be disheartened – even though the reality is so
different from what many had hoped for.*

*We too have to keep relearning this truth, rather than think that
we have to drive things forward, do more, achieve more.*

Apart from showing what an insightful observer Marianne had
become, this letter does, to some extent, convey more of what we might
have expected. Here she does express a sense of salvation. But the letter
contains a new surprise – the salvation is presented in collective terms.
Under daily bombardment from across the Rhine, in a city where the
most basic services had ceased functioning, the whole population had
of course been in great danger. But still the end of the war meant
something different for Marianne than for her neighbours, yet she makes
no distinction. At the very end of this passage, Marianne does allude to
some differentiation; but it is between the mass of Germans and us, as
Bund members, not herself as a Jew.

I thought of Marianne's perception when I spoke to the two of her
friends who had also experienced the end of the war in the Ruhr. One
was Hanna Aron, who as a half-Jew had initially been protected from
deportation, and later was in hiding in Essen. As the war ended, she was

in Essen. She recalled with delight the moment the Allies arrived in the city. She donned her yellow star and went out to greet them:[5]

'The troops came up Zweigert Strasse and Hufelandstrasse, that's how they came in. I was at the Hufelandstrasse with my star, needless to say, and I said "hello" to these boys, and I was so happy. And they said, "Oh, no, you can't be here, they were all killed! You can't be a Jew, that's impossible!" I saluted them, but the neighbours didn't take that so well, you know?'

'How do you mean?'

'Well, they didn't like us to give them a good hello, you know. They didn't realize that we *had* to give them a good hello.'

For Hanna Aron, her feelings at liberation only deepened the division between herself and the resentful neighbours.

Ludwig, later Lew, Schloss had had the most appalling wartime experiences. Beginning in Riga, he was moved from one labour or concentration camp to another. For a few weeks he was in Stutthof, by common account one of the most bestial sites, even by the Nazis' unique standards. Lew and his father were then sent to Buchenwald and, in 1944, as two of a group of mainly foreign conscripts, to a factory in Bochum. They were within spitting distance of their hometown of Gelsenkirchen. It transpired that Lew's father had known the brother of their Bochum foreman well. And through this personal link they were able to make contact with the outside world. Someone they knew sent them civilian clothing, which the foreman brought in. Lew and his father hid the clothes, along with false papers, in the factory cranes. One day, they changed into the clothes and walked out of the plant in broad daylight. They awaited the end of the war in Essen. Like Hanna, Lew had no doubt about the meaning of the event. On 10 April the Americans moved in, on the 11th he was working for them, on the 12th he had an American uniform. Hanna Aron told me virtually the same story. The Americans set up headquarters in the Nazi Gauleiter's old house in Bredeney, and the very next day Hanna told her mother she was going there to get a job. She 'marched right in' and said she wanted to work as a secretary. Not a woman to be denied, she got the job.

If we contrast these memories with Marianne's letter, we would say that Hanna Aron and Lew Schloss experienced the end of the war as

Jews, while Marianne experienced it as a German. Marianne's letter sustains the tone of the wartime diary, even though the Gestapo and denunciation were no longer any threat. So Marianne's self-presentation during the war was evidently not simply enjoined by self-censorship. She really had understood herself as a member of the Bund, as a young German thinking about how to create the better society of the future.

On the other hand, Marianne's letter was addressed to other Bund members. Mindful of the dangers and privations they too had faced, she may well have been averse to pleading any special privilege as a victim of persecution. In this context, Marianne was all Bund, and probably deliberately underplaying the facets of her identity that did not connect with the Bund members. As the letter goes on there is a distinct sense of clubbiness and a slightly literary bravado.

Putting the letter to one side for a moment, when we contrast what Marianne said to me with the testimonies of Hanna and Lew, what strikes us is how much clearer a story Hanna and Lew have to tell. As comfortably-off, well-integrated Americans in Connecticut and New Jersey, Hanna Aron and Lew Schloss recall the end of the war as a moment of American–Jewish amity. They can, as it were, draw a direct line from the people they were then to their identities today. Whereas Marianne, no less comfortably off but perhaps more uneasy about her past, seemed not to want to acknowledge the end of the war. I wondered if, once again, her memory was shaped by her sense of guilt and loss. Perhaps, in retrospect, she could not allow herself to have experienced the end of the war as a liberation, when it underlined the reality of her family's murder.

What is certain is that the ambivalence in Marianne's testimony is symptomatic of her memories and descriptions of the post-war years in Germany. More than any other phase of Marianne's life, these years refuse to take on a stable shape. One minute they appear as a burst of creative energy and optimism, a time when Marianne was able to commit her energies to building a new Germany. Then, the kaleidoscope of memory twists just a degree or two, and the bright world of cultural life and activism gives way to far more sombre hues of loss and disorientation.

The activist

'From the moment of liberation,' Marianne wrote just after she arrived in Britain, 'I could be active again, and the year and a half in Düsseldorf forms some of my brightest and dearest memories.'[6] Almost fifty years later her judgement was just the same. To me, Marianne described the post-war years – apart from the uncertain days at the beginning – as a time of great joy and enthusiasm. The energy which had been stifled for so long could at last be unleashed.

Liberation brought three important benefits almost immediately. First, *Lebensraum*, living space, was no longer the privilege of the Aryans. For more than three years, Marianne had not had a room to herself and, since August 1943, not even a shared room. Now, Marianne gained a large bed-sitting room in Hanni's apartment at Lindenstrasse 223; Hanni moved her big weaving loom into the front room.[7] 'Now that I finally have my own four walls,' she wrote to friends, 'I'm a completely new person. A room is almost the mirror of one's personality, a piece of oneself.'[8]

Despite its visible scars of war, Marianne loved her new home. To begin with, she furnished it with some old furniture dragged out of a cellar, carefully covering the odd blemish with a table cloth or a vase. But soon after the end of the war, Marianne visited the Jürgens to pick up the furniture and trunks her parents had deposited. Here, she had a most unpleasant surprise. The Jürgens claimed that her parents had given them the possessions! Marianne had to enlist the help of the authorities to reclaim what was hers. 'There was a terrible kerfuffle about that; it was dreadful, really dreadful,' she said.[9] In fact, it was the start of a miserable fifteen-year struggle over family property that was one of the low points of Marianne's post-war life. But by January 1946, Marianne was able to write to Hugo and Grete Strauss in the States:[10]

I have a very pretty room which I have furnished with furniture that was in safe-keeping with acquaintances. This furniture and a few old family pictures (from my mother's side) are about the only things I have left. It is good, to have saved something of the old atmosphere and the old good family tradition.

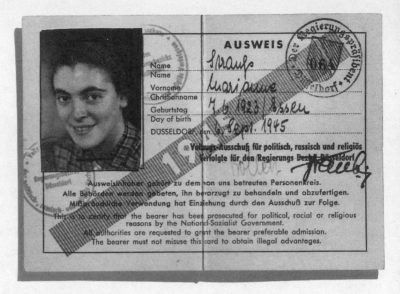

Marianne's post-war pass

A second major post-war bonus was food, not that there was so much of it. For the next three years, German cities were to suffer periodical bouts of real hunger, and nowhere worse than in the Ruhr. Marianne wrote in May 1945 that, 'the food situation is very very bad'. She received no potatoes, only two pounds of bread and less than a quarter-pound of fat per week, and even this meagre allowance required long hours of queuing. 'How good that I no longer have to live illegally! I would simply starve, because even with the best will in the world, you cannot feed two on these rations.'[11]

But Marianne was no longer dependent on others to eat. In that sense, the end of the war brought a decisive improvement. She had her first encounter with society at large when she went to get ration cards. She felt very strange walking into an office and registering as a legitimate person. 'How did you get through the war?' they asked her. The officials were very embarrassed; they'd never encountered anything like her.[12]

Marianne's position in relation to official allocations – foodstuffs, housing, clothes – was transformed overnight. Suddenly, racial discrimination was replaced by privileged treatment for victims of the Nazi regime. In September, Marianne received an official pass from the Regierungspräsident in Düsseldorf, authenticating her as a victim of persecution. She was entitled to the rations normally reserved for someone employed in heavy labour. Marianne could still remember the enormous pleasure of the first loaf she obtained with her own ration card. She was beholden to no one over how much or when she ate. The result, predictably, was that she made a pig of herself on this 'wonderful bread' and became 'quite sick'.[13]

The third great benefit of the post-war period was that Marianne could work and pay her own way. Her wartime experiences had given her an absolute dread of being dependent on others. She wrote to the Strausses in the States about the possibility of emigrating there:[14]

> *What is important for me, however, is that I have the opportunity to work and enjoy full material independence. I say this so bluntly because over the last few years I have gathered enough experience of living with other people and of what can happen to good friendships when one is materially dependent on the other.*

Like her wartime admirer Imo Moskowicz, Marianne had hoped to find a job in the theatre. But whilst Imo was to make his decisive step to stardom in Düsseldorf, Marianne failed in her attempts to find a job in theatre management there. Instead, her route to employment took a rapid and unexpected turn. Within a couple of weeks of the end of the war, Marianne went to the Düsseldorf labour exchange to enquire about possible job openings. The entire labour administration had been deeply implicated in the Nazis' forced-labour programme and was anxious to forestall major purges of its personnel. So the director of the Düsseldorf branch was overjoyed to discover this young woman, who would, as a Jew, enhance the exchange's reputation. Here, again, the tide had turned, and Marianne was now a sought-after item. With no qualifications, she found herself employed as a careers adviser, generally a highly trained profession.[15] Incidentally, I had thought nothing of Marianne's going to the labour exchange for work until Hanna Aron and Lew Schloss told me they had immediately gone to the Allies in search of employment.

Yet again, Marianne's behaviour conveyed a different sense of identity from theirs.

Marianne's memory of her work was very ambivalent. Almost from the beginning she had doubts about the value of what she was doing.[16] Initially, her job was to assist young female school graduates to find employment, but she was soon moved into a special new section. As she wrote to her cousins:[17]

> *My office has to help all those who suffered in the Nazi era get back to work and their careers. That sounds very good, but it's very difficult. On the one hand, the labour force is substantially reduced because of the incredible decline in the German economy (consequence of the war, removal of German competition).[18] On the other hand, the people I'm looking after are physically and psychologically in need of recuperation. They have to find their way back to normal life slowly. Time, patience and sympathy are needed to find the right way forward. The stories I hear at my desk every day are beyond description.*
>
> *The work is not as satisfying as one would wish because we don't have the resources to provide the kind of help that is needed.*

To me, she said the job was 'very bureaucratic and not my cup of tea at all. I'm not cut out to be a civil servant. I'm anti-authoritarian.'[19] Her rapid rise in the profession was 'resented, naturally' by all the 'long-established pen-pushers who'd been there long before'. Moreover, Marianne found it very peculiar working alongside people whose wartime role she knew very well. The director 'saw me as his life saver', she said:[20] 'He had been very much involved with slave labour for Mannesmann and Krupp and all those other great people who were employing all the slave labour they could lay their hands on.'

And here she was working with these 'polite and friendly colleagues' day in, day out. But none of this could gainsay the importance of financial independence.[21]

In addition to work, there was politics. Just three weeks after the end of the war, a fired-up Marianne told Meta Kamp that 'our work has begun' and spoke of her 'impatient, burning desire to act'.[22] From almost the first day of peace, Marianne was travelling around the Ruhr, meeting

Bund activists. In one May weekend alone – at a time when public transport was still largely out of service – Marianne was in Essen, Mülheim and Wuppertal, talking with different local Bund leaders about the possibilities for reshaping society:[23]

> In Mülheim the friends are working very, very actively in the factories and, it seems, with success. They can influence decisions and bring about important changes and improvements. All within narrow limits of course, but it's still a beginning.

One reason Marianne took the labour exchange job was the hope that it would enable her to gain access to youngsters and influence them. Beyond working for the Bund, she also joined the Communist Party.[24] She had seen the courageous way in which the Communists had thrown themselves into resistance against the Nazis. Many of the most active and idealistic Bund members – like the Zenkers and the Morgensterns and, probably most important for her, Ernst Jungbluth – were Communist Party (KPD) members. Within a short period, Marianne was being trained as a youth leader for the Communist-backed youth movement, the Freie Deutsche Jugend (FDJ). With her credentials as a victim of persecution, her Bund contacts and her enthusiasm she soon gained access to the men (and they were very largely men) who played a decisive role in the local political scene.

Hanna Aron heard through the grapevine that Marianne was very left wing. Being rather anti-Communist herself, she went to visit Marianne in Düsseldorf with some trepidation. What she found confirmed her worst fears:[25]

'Her whole apartment was decorated with the red flags. I mean, I walked in there and thought I was in Russia, honestly. Hammers and sickles all over and the red flags. This was just before the break-up of the Allies and so forth, so I wasn't an enemy of the Russians, but I just thought it was going a little bit too far.'

One of Marianne's boyfriends at the time, Johannes Oppenheimer, remembered falling under Marianne's political influence, though he was her senior by several years.[26] Marianne, he recalled, had links with a Düsseldorf Communist group which was just being reestablished, and she dragged him along to meetings.[27] Oppenheimer found some of them interesting, including one with the dramatist Müller-Schlösser, but he soon felt that the KPD was not for him, as a party 'egotistical and fairly unconcerned about the common good', and he stopped attending.[28] Although both Aron and Oppenheimer were struck by Marianne's Communist affiliations, Marianne's writings show that it was the Bund, far more than the KPD, which influenced her outlook and ideas.

Alongside politics, there was education and there was culture. Marianne was enormously conscious of the gaps in her knowledge and read voraciously. She also thought of pursuing a medical career (or so she asserted later in one of her restitution claims), and to that end studied Latin.[29] She remained extremely interested in the theatre – and Düsseldorf was a good place for theatre lovers at the time. As early as July 1945, the Düsseldorf Schauspielhaus was operating again. Its first director was Wolfgang Langhoff, an inspiring though cantankerous Communist who had spent many years in the Burgermoor and Lichtenburg concentration camps. And outside the theatre, too, post-war Düsseldorf offered a very animated cultural life. (The British, who had taken over control of the town from the Americans at the beginning of June 1945, encouraged considerable freedom.)

In January 1946, Marianne ended a letter to relatives saying she would happily write more:[30]

> But time is pressing, there is always so much to do. There's not enough space in my diary for all my appointments. The days pass in a whirl and I come home in the evening and drop into bed exhausted.

New professional opportunities were opening up. In February 1946, Marianne wrote to her cousin Alex Weinberg that she had received a series of good offers from both the military government and the provincial German administration, 'astounding, given the shortage of career opportunities here; and so I have the freedom and the burden of choice'.[31]

Marianne as missionary

Marianne began to write as a freelance theatre critic for the *Düsseldorfer Nachrichten* and as a cultural correspondent for the KPD paper *Freiheit*, and in April 1946 gave up her job with the labour administration to concentrate on writing.[32] She also began to write pieces for the BBC's German language transmission to the British Zone of Occupation, in particular for the *Letter Box* programme. In February, Marianne sent in her first piece, 'Youth problems in Germany'.[33] The basic proposition was that German youngsters had been so misled and disillusioned that they had lost sight of core values. Particularly in the last years of the war, the errors and misjudgements of the adult generation had exposed them to terrible hardship. Now, young people simply wanted to follow their own road. But this, said Marianne in strikingly Bundist tones, was to misunderstand freedom:

The individual who holds to a firm line and does not allow himself to be driven by his desires, drives and instincts is the one who is really free. 'In the ties that bind us, lies our freedom!' – a great truth! But our youth does not yet understand it. Young people are fighting for their own interests. For too long they were forced into a community which was not really a community at all. So now they think only of their own needs at the expense of the good of all.

Youth had to be persuaded, she concluded, that personal happiness does not derive from satisfying one's impulses, but only from 'serious, responsible work'.

Marianne clearly felt a sense of mission towards Germany. She framed her piece as a letter from a German woman, explaining the situation in her country to an English friend. In many ways sympathetic to the situation of young Germans, she implicitly criticized one of the most hypocritical features of post-war German life – the common complaint by adults about young people's loss of values with no reference to their own responsibility for the crimes of the recent past. Interestingly, however, when the BBC broadcast the letter in April, it presented Marianne not as a typical German but as a young Jewish woman and a

Marianne after the war

spokeswoman for the 'Freie deutsche Jugend'.[34] The British, not Marianne, chose to identify her this way.

Praise from the programme's producers prompted a very happy Marianne to submit her two perhaps most impressive pieces.[35] One was entitled 'Taking responsibility for a meaningful life. From a letter to a young student'. In it, she responded to the complaint of a 'young student' (Marianne at this stage herself was not quite twenty-three!) about the difficulties of studying in post-war conditions, and also to reports on the radio about a recent student conference at Göttingen. Marianne argued that young people today were waiting for a leader or for a philosophy to tell them what to do, instead of beginning with themselves. Her young correspondent had forgotten, she argued, the meaning of taking responsibility for oneself:

True, they speak of democracy – just as they used to speak of National Socialism. But they still surround these concepts with lots of words without really giving them living meaning. What is stopping young people from being creative themselves and building something new? This is something I often ask myself.

Of course, the Bund was not the only group to see the emptiness in post-war political rhetoric and attitudes. Others too, particularly on the left, criticized the empty phrase-making and the dutiful and rather nominal acceptance of democracy.[36] A more distinctive Bund line, though, emerged in the second half of Marianne's piece, as she sought to explain why young people were not more active, reflective or creative. Why were so many all appearance and no substance?

What is it that prompts young people to strike such a pose? I have no other explanation than that they simply lack a sense of awe: for the life force that is everywhere present. That is why they cannot be creative. When people cease to listen, they become deaf to the eternal process of renewal and awakening. They live on the surface, they see but they understand nothing. And so they can only reproduce and not actively shape the self.

This insight, she went on, seemed to her to explain the behaviour not only of the young people she was addressing, but of humanity as a whole.

Far more than any Communist line, Marianne's counsel expressed the Bund's efforts to fuse post-religious spirituality with practical, democratic commitment. Her article ended with an appeal to the young '*werde wesentlich*' – lead a responsible life never losing sight of the essential.

Another piece, 'Fate has turned', was broadcast by the BBC on 27 August. It began by describing the queues for food in the cities and the despair and criticism to which food shortages gave rise:[37]

Hunger is terrible and many are only now getting to know its brutal ways. On the streets, German children ask Occupation soldiers, 'You, got bread?' We are reminded of the last years of the war, when grey columns of tired, ragged prisoners from all nations dragged themselves along the same streets where Germans now go hungry. The prisoners' eyes were fixed on the ground in search of every cigarette butt Germans had casually thrown away. Perhaps a couple of puffs would still their fearsome hunger. And we are reminded as well of the wretched foreign conscript worker, nervously approaching the well-dressed Germans on the street, whispering, 'You, got bread?' How readily one turned away, because it was forbidden to give anything to these 'sub-humans' and because a full stomach allowed the 'sleeping beauty' of one's own conscience to slumber on.

And today? Today the same Germans on the street, no longer the secure master race, find themselves mired in the distress and the misery of those to whom they once threw cigarette butts.

Does that make them think? Do they wonder whether some balancing force of justice is at work? One only has to stand in the long queues in front of the shops to hear that they do not!

We Germans have a difficult, difficult time before us. We had better hope that we won't be subjected to equal retribution; we had better hope that the world's conscience will not remain as passive as did the conscience of many Germans when things were the other way round. We had better hope that someone will help us. But we had better hope too that we will not forget the way things were.

Once we grasp the situation and judge it properly, we'll find it easier to understand and to bear and other nations will find it easier to help us out of our distress.

Rarely in Germany in 1946 were the sufferings of the German population so openly and clearly placed in the context of the sufferings
Germany had inflicted yesterday. It is noteworthy that Marianne again
presents herself not as victim, but as one who shares Germany's collective
fate. Clearly, this was partly a literary device. Marianne had calculated
that the message would be much more powerful if delivered not as
accusation from outside – the victim Jew accusing the former oppressors
– but from inside: 'we Germans'. But the very fact that, in the interest of
creating a new Germany, she *wanted* to speak as a German, that her
primary instinct was not to speak out as Jew or as victim is what
impresses itself on our consciousness.

Was this a marvellous testimony to her generosity of spirit and her
ability to distinguish between active perpetrators and bystanders? Was
it an act of self-denial? Or was it, in fact, both, the expression of a young
woman increasingly unsure of who she was and which way her life was
taking her?

The displaced person

Naturally, from the moment the war ended, Marianne had a burning
interest in tracing her immediate family:

'One of my first steps after the war was to open a German bank
account in the hope that maybe they would come back and I could
proudly present my father with the money he'd given me, which seemed
like a lot of money in those days. I don't know, now it probably wouldn't
be much at all.'

It is hard to know how hopeful she really felt. Probably, the survival
of the money had became a symbol of the survival of the family. In
fulfilling her father's admonitions to practise probity and economy,
Marianne had consciously or unconsciously kept something of him alive
within herself.

Almost immediately after the war Marianne wrote to the Strauss
family lawyer in Basel, Marcus Cohn, to tell him she was still alive.
Through Cohn, other surviving relatives learned of Marianne's whereabouts. It was probably in this way that in September 1945, Grete

Sander was able to establish contact from Sweden, offering help and hoping that Marianne had heard some news. It was now that Marianne learned that her parents had managed to get letters out of Theresienstadt to Grete in Sweden; she also obtained her first information about the fate of uncle Alfred and Aunt Lore.[38] In March and April 1946, more information arrived from Erna Ogutsch, the wife of the cantor in Essen, who had been in Theresienstadt and could tell Marianne more about the experiences of her parents and brother and her uncle and aunt. She also had news about some of Marianne's former teachers from Berlin. One had been murdered at Auschwitz, another had survived the camps and gone to Sweden. 'It was good,' Frau Ogutsch reassured her young correspondent, 'that you did not come to Theresienstadt. Your own experiences were hard enough.' Cousins on her father's side, the Ansbachers, wrote from Frankfurt in April 1946. They too had been with Marianne's parents in Theresienstadt.

By the summer of 1946, having heard from Grete Sander, Erna Ogutsch and the Ansbachers, Marianne knew most of what she would ever learn of the fate of her parents, her brother, her aunt and her uncle. (Of Ernst and family she discovered no more than she had in 1943.) In most cases, this was still far from definite knowledge. 'It is agonizing to think about,' she wrote to Hugo Strauss, 'a thousand speculations about a thousand possible different horrible ends. If one knew for sure, everything would be easier.'[39]

At what point, I asked her, did she give up hope?[40]

'I didn't learn ever for definite. There was never, there was always . . . I don't know, for many years, I still thought somebody would turn up. But then I thought rationally that if they were going to turn up they would have turned up in Essen. I knew enough people even if I wasn't living there, and they knew where I was, there wouldn't have been any difficulty with that. And pretty soon it became very clear that it really was an exception for somebody to come back. But I always thought that being a big family somebody might have survived, my brother or Ernst, somebody who was younger, who maybe had more physical or moral resilience or ruthlessness, which they didn't have. Ruthlessness was probably the most important ingredient of survival they didn't have.'

The first of the family with whom she had an actual meeting was her cousin Otto Weinberg, now a proud Lance Corporal Gerald Alexander of the 1ˢᵗ Battalion Glasgow Highlanders. The only one of the three brothers to be stationed in Germany, Gerald managed to locate Marianne in August 1945.[41]

Marianne's attitude to such revived contacts, though, was often mixed. She felt her family had let her down where friends had prevailed. Writing to Alfred in 1947 about her pleasure at seeing Gerald, she said:[42]

> *From the start, we spent many happy hours together and I can tell you that I really enjoyed having some family by me (although in general I don't believe in blood ties but in ties of choice. In difficult times they always proved themselves where the family failed to help.)*

Nevertheless, she did seek to reestablish contact with relatives who had managed to get out of Germany. She regained contact with her maternal uncle Karl, now a decorated war hero, living in Brussels, and with her cousins on her mother's side, the Weinberg boys. Marcus Cohn informed surviving relatives in the USA that she was alive – her father's cousin Hugo Strauss, her maternal uncle Adolf Rosenberg, and Lore's brother Ernst Dahl – and they got in touch with her over the next months. More distant cousins in Britain – the Oppenheimers and the Seligs – also surfaced. Marianne learned (though when, we are not quite sure) that her cousin Richard, now René, Wolf – the son of her father's sister Bertel and her husband Ferdinand Wolf, both interned in France and later murdered in Auschwitz – had also survived. He had made an epic journey across France and Spain as a fifteen-year-old, fought with the French Foreign Legion and entered Germany as part of the French force of occupation. Marianne also made unsuccessful enquiries to trace the child left behind by Lore's sister Ilse when she and her husband were deported from France.

But often, when the family did make contact, one of their first steps was to cement a kind of pact of silence about the past. Karl Rosenberg, for example, helped enforce that silence. Karl had been considered the 'black sheep' of his family, but whatever his misspent youth, he had had an adventurous and heroic war. Trained in Britain, he was parachuted into France to fight alongside the French resistance. Now living with his wife Diane in Brussels, he wrote in the warmest fashion to Marianne. After receiving a letter in reply, he wrote back in November 1945:[43]

We are fine, that's the main thing. What happened, happened. I feel as you do, that it was a hard school and I too am happy that I've come through it – one is stronger for life as a result. But I want to forget it and only think of the here and now. Life is so short, why make it harder than it already is?

A couple of months later Marianne wrote to her cousin Alex:[44]

You'll have heard much about me and about our fate in recent years. It's unnecessary to talk about it. We have no time to think about the past because the present demands all our strength. There is an enormous amount of reconstruction work to do and we're tackling it with courage and hope.

And evidently she must have written something similar to Erna Ogutsch, because the latter responded:[45]

It is good that you have satisfying work that demands all your thoughts and attention so that you don't have to think about the sadness of recent years. I force myself to look to the future.

When I asked Marianne whether her work colleagues tried to talk with her about the past she replied:[46]

'Not then, no, they never talked about it, never. They just knew I was Jewish and that I had come back, one of those that had come back ... but it was never discussed. They were all terrified, naturally. There was no reference ever, no question, nobody wanted to know anything because it was all too uncomfortable. And the people who came back from the concentration camps, all they were interested in was getting a job, earning a living, restoring a normal life. And that's all I was interested in, to restore a normal life. I didn't seek out, wanting to ask questions, I didn't want to go into all my past history. I wanted to forget it as quickly as possible and get on with a normal life and make something ... make up for lost time.'

It is one of the ironies of Marianne's life that although she continually exhorted the Germans to remember, she herself sought to forget. Her 'forgetting' was not 'thoughtless', to use her term, but it was relentless. She avoided almost every connection with her former life. Despite living so close to Essen, for example, she rarely went back there.

She was not sure she had anything in common with her family any more. As she wrote to Hugo and Grete Strauss:[47]

> It's good finally to be able to build a bridge across the time and physical distance which divides us. Above all, it's good to feel meaningful contact reviving again. Between us lies not just the ocean but also the monstrous experiences of the last few years.

Apologizing to her cousin Alex Weinberg in February 1946 for not having written before, she said she had been extremely busy, but also that it was 'not very easy after the long years of such different experiences to find a point of contact'.[48] On several occasions when more distant relatives and family friends located her, she did not follow it up at all.

Reading the correspondence between Marianne and her relatives in Britain, Australia and the USA, we begin to see that she was doubly displaced. On the one hand, she knew she was no longer the person her relatives had known. On the other, in the privacy of the correspondence, she revealed an increasing unhappiness at her situation in Germany. Karl began by reporting Gerald's comments on meeting her:

> Otto told me that you were doing very well, and that you wanted to stay in Germany. In my view, everyone should shape their life as they wish. When I heard that you wanted to stay there I thought, you know best what's right for you. But I see from your letter that you would gladly leave Germany. I hope it is understood that nowhere would you be looked after better than with us.

The offer from Karl and his wife Diane could not have been warmer or more affectionate, but there is no evidence that Marianne responded to it.

In January 1946, Marianne wrote to Hugo and Grete Strauss, thanking them for the parcel they had sent:[49]

> I cannot tell you, my dears, how much pleasure your loving parcel gave me! It contained real treasures – things I haven't seen for such

*a long time – and I had a real day of celebration. I'm surprised I
didn't get indigestion! The stockings and scarf are wonderful. It's
impossible to get them here. All textiles, shoes etc. are unobtainable. Germany is in every respect so poor!*

What echoes must she have heard in her own thanks now that *she*
was the recipient of parcels full of unobtainable treasures! These echoes
led her to give a succinct and poignant account of her wartime experience. At the end she concluded:

*Few have survived these horrors and returned. Only now do we
really learn what went on – but it needs to be broadcast to the
world with far more emphasis and far louder than it has been.
Much too little is being done here to compensate for all the suffering.*

*The few survivors have one thing in common; they have lost
their loved ones. That common fate binds us, but often it's the only
thing we share. The ties are not strong. Everyone thinks and
worries about himself and wants to catch up on all that he's missed
in the last few years. Judaism, religion, does that still exist out
there? There's no trace of it here.*

Marianne said she was thinking of leaving Germany, perhaps only for
a period, but she had trepidations. 'Having finally regained my freedom,'
she explained, 'I value it extremely highly and am very reluctant to enter
into a new dependence.'

To Alex, she wrote in February:[50]

*More and more I feel the desire to leave Germany, at least for a
while. There are no prospects here for young people and there's a
lot I'd like to learn to be able to give real help.*

She had lots of good job offers but, 'Naturally I see all that now as
temporary. I yearn for any possibility of leaving Germany as quickly as
possible.'

It is hard to square all this with her cheerful missive to Alfred Weinberg
in 1947, looking back on the time in Germany as one of the 'brightest
and most beautiful memories' of her life.

Half-way house

The ambivalence of Marianne's position is equally apparent in her friendships. After the Nazi years, one of the luxuries of the post-war period was her freedom to socialize as she chose. It would not be long before such an engaging, lively and attractive young woman made new friends. One day, soon after she began working at the labour exchange, a young man appeared seeking advice. By chance, she had seen him arrive:[51]

'I remember he was pushing a bicycle and left it standing outside in the compound which was very brave, because anything on wheels would move very quickly . . . On my way home in the afternoon I saw him on the Koenigsallee pushing this bike. He came over – he'd seen me, I don't know if he'd been waylaying me, I'm not sure; anyway he came up grinning and was pushing his bicycle and chatting and talking and that's how we got to know each other.'

The man was Johannes Oppenheimer. He was living with a lively group of four *Mischlinge* who had survived the war as labourers in the Organization Todt (OT), the enormous organization entrusted with road and fortification building named after the transport minister Fritz Todt. They were all highly gifted and intent on educating themselves for successful professional careers. 'They had a pretty grotty flat the four of them,' Marianne remembered fondly. 'And trying to make their futures in their very different ways.' Two of them, Johannes Oppenheimer and Wilhelm Jacob, became life-long friends.

Marianne had told me various things about their lives before the war, but when I spoke to Johannes Oppenheimer, retired Vice President of the Federal German Court of Administration, what struck me was how inaccurate most of her information had been. Johannes Oppenheimer was born in Berlin in the closing months of the First World War of a Jewish father and a Protestant mother. His father held a senior position as Oberregierungsrat in the Prussian finance administration until forced into early retirement in 1935. After a failed suicide attempt, he later died in Auschwitz. Johannes Oppenheimer began training as a chemist but was called up in 1939. In 1940, his office duties in the army enabled him to see a communication to the effect that all *Mischlinge 1 Grades* were to be dismissed from the service. In his eighties still every bit the German jurist, Herr Oppenheimer said to me, 'That surprised me, because it differed from the legal position.' But it had been a 'special directive of the Führer'. Oppenheimer dutifully communicated his situation to his superiors, was transferred to the reserve and in November 1940 dismissed. Prevented from continuing his studies, he was drafted into the OT and sent first to Paris, and then elsewhere in France, building fortifications, often in very poor conditions. Shortly after D-Day, he was recalled to Paris and trained to supervise foreign conscripts who were to be taken to Germany for work. Even a half-Jew could thus find his place in the hierarchy of racial subordination. However, the unit was transferred to Wuppertal before Herr Oppenheimer had to perform this duty. Finally, in the middle of February 1945, he ended up in Düsseldorf in an OT camp, where he stayed till April.

Recognizing his administrative abilities, the camp leader asked Oppenheimer to be his deputy and the latter accepted. He 'didn't want to promote the war but wanted to help maintain order'. I didn't keep a precise count, but in our conversation Herr Oppenheimer must have said the word *Ordnung* about thirty times. His success in improving conditions for the many foreign conscripts in the camp was borne out, he said, by the fact that after the war had ended he and the other half-Jewish OT conscripts were able to continue living side by side with the now liberated 'DP's, (displaced persons). Finally, in May 1945, his friend Kurt Zeunert, another OT conscript, prevailed upon the authorities to assign them an apartment that had formerly belonged to some Nazis. Here, sharing two rooms, a kitchen and a toilet, five, then later four of the half-Jewish survivors of the Organization Todt formed the bachelor household Marianne so much enjoyed visiting.

Johannes Oppenheimer remembered meeting Marianne in the labour exchange, although he had forgotten about arriving by bike. He remembered that the bicycle itself had been sold to him by a 'crooked OT comrade'. And that he had no lock[52] – hence the 'reckless' act of leaving the bike unsecured at the labour exchange gates. Marianne, he wrote to me:[53]

was indeed a remarkable person, about nineteen years old [actually twenty-two] when we met. That was in May or June 1945 soon after the end of hostilities in Düsseldorf. If my memory serves, Eduard Marwitz, a so-called quarter-Jew, took me with him to the Düsseldorf labour exchange as so-called 'victims of Nazi persecution' to get advice from 'Sister Marianne Strauss'[. . .]

She was very friendly towards us and showed an ease in dealing with people which suggested a maturity far beyond her years.

'We became friends and were often together outside work,' he added. 'I fell in love with her for a while and she did not reject my advances.' But 'we did not have a really close relationship'.[54] By the end of the year, whatever love affair had existed between them had fizzled out. Marianne, always very reticent about her relationships, admitted there had been more than friendship between them, 'but that didn't really work at all, we were too different in temperament'.[55]

Johannes Oppenheimer recalled what he knew about Marianne at the time:[56]

That she was Jewish was clear from the start. She must have been in a concentration camp and looked after children or the sick as a nurse. How she came to survive the end of the war in Düsseldorf I have no idea; I heard nothing about Düsseldorf relatives.

In other words, despite the fact that they had met within a month or two of the end of the war, he learned next to nothing about her wartime experiences or her life before the war, and what he thought he knew was wrong. Acknowledging the great gaps in their knowledge of each other, Herr Oppenheimer wrote:

From the present vantage-point I find it hard to understand why we did not talk more about our earlier lives and about our fate in the Nazi period. But apparently all that wasn't important once we had got it behind us and felt liberated; we lived and thought only in the present, and looked somewhat hesitantly but full of hope into the future.

In a subsequent interview, I asked again why they had talked so little about the past:

'I don't know why, we had no reason to be silent. We thought of the future. That we had lost relatives was not so dramatic, because ordinary Germans had also lost relatives. We did not see any particular literary material in that. We did not have the feeling we had special reason to complain. I don't even know what happened to Marianne's parents.'

Now I understood why, when referring to his application to the labour exchange, Herr Oppenheimer had placed the phrases 'victim of persecution' and later again 'victim of racial persecution' in quotation marks. To him they were only legal categories and not real ones.

The other member of Oppenheimer's entourage whom Marianne got to know well, and who remained an enduring friend, was Wilhelm Jacob. Once again, Marianne's information about his past life was largely inaccurate, as I learned when I talked to Wilhelm Jacob's widow, Dr Elisabeth Jacob, née Kühne, the daughter of a former Prussian general.[57] Wilhelm Jacob was born in Kösslin, near Danzig, in 1916. His father, Emil, had married a non-Jewish hairdresser from a high-class establishment in the town. Wilhelm wanted to study medicine and spent eight semesters in Zurich. In 1938, while he was studying there, his father was murdered at a police station. The family could no longer support Wilhelm financially and the Swiss predictably chucked him out. He returned to Kösslin and got a job driving a truck collecting rags, working for a man Frau Jacob called a 'decent Nazi', who became a master butcher after the war and maintained friendly contact with the Jacobs. 'You see,' said Frau Jacob to me, 'the mass of the people were not such rabid Nazis!' Like Oppenheimer, Wilhelm Jacob was called up to the OT where, his widow told me drily, he 'protected his life and his glasses'. Engaged in building bridges and laying railway tracks in France, perhaps the saddest thing for Wilhelm, who had dreams of becoming a musician, was that the work ruined his hands. 'But', continued Frau Jacob – a general's daughter to the core – 'from the point of view of survival it was not the worst place to be.' He had ended up in the same OT camp as Oppenheimer, and after the war shared the house with him. He completed his medical studies in Düsseldorf and met Elisabeth Kühne in the process. 'Wilhelm,' Marianne remembered, 'was very Prussian, which was quite amusing, being half Jewish and marrying a general's daughter, it was quite incongruous.'

Whatever Wilhelm may have known about Marianne's history, his widow Elisabeth, with whom Marianne developed a close friendship which lasted from the 1940s until Marianne's death, had no knowledge of it at all. As with the others, Frau Jacobs had constructed her own picture based on signs and assumptions, telling me, for example, that Marianne's relatives had owned a string of department stores – no uncommon thing among wealthier German Jews, but not true of any of the Strauss family.

It is hard not to see this network, the only friendships outside the Bund that survived the immediate post-war years, as symptomatic of Marianne's situation in post-war Germany. It seems entirely appropriate that the people she attached herself to as friends should have been half-Jews. This was a group who did not regard themselves as Jewish, in many ways German to the core, yet they shared a sense of having been defined as outsiders. The group was marked by a common loss of relatives and friends and at the same time by an absolute unwillingness to dwell on their losses or talk about the past.

Marianne, the Bund and post-war society

To add to Marianne's feeling of displacement, she was becoming increasingly frustrated with what she was able to achieve in Germany. Material conditions were dispiriting enough. Only 7 per cent of Düsseldorf's buildings had been undamaged – and Düsseldorf was in a much better state than Essen.[58] In Marianne's age group there were 172 women for every 100 men (not that Marianne was ever going to have to worry about the competition). In the winter of 1945–6, the rationing system virtually collapsed – and worse was to come a year later.[59] Small wonder that so many non-Jewish Germans were also keen to leave the country.

In addition, the Bund as a whole was becoming disenchanted with its role in post-war Germany. Understandably, and with considerable justification, the members felt that history had proved them right. As the Bund proudly announced to its overseas well-wishers and contacts:[60]

What has proved itself above all is the idea. The Bund, its approach to education, its structure, its principles, its view of human beings and its attitude to history all gave each individual the strength to carry on and resist the thousand-fold temptations and influences of the National Socialist un-spirit and the general weakening of character.

Surely, its members reasoned, this wartime achievement proved how vital the Bund was for the challenges that lay ahead.[61] And yet from early on we find the Bund members having to acknowledge that they were not enjoying the resonance they had expected. 'Our flock has dwindled,' commented Artur Jacobs as early as 1947, 'one often feels very lonely. We are having to stand against the current just as we did during the twelve years of Nazism.'[62]

Partly, the Bund felt, the problem was that the Germans were not willing to confront their past:[63]

Everything is judged only from the perspective of today as though there had been no past, no provocation of war, no Lydices, no extermination camps, no arbitrary decrees, no millions murdered.

The Bund also made the painful discovery that they themselves were now seen as implicated in the past. Most young people wanted nothing to do with any kind of organized movement or party, and rituals such as oath-swearing were anathema to a deeply disillusioned generation of youngsters. The Bund itself later acknowledged:[64]

As a result of National Socialism the younger generation were very intolerant of hierarchical structures. For all their undoubted interest in the Bund, they could not commit themselves to new ties.

Artur Jacobs and the other Bund members, insightful as they were, probably could not comprehend, though, how thoroughly out of place the group seemed in the post-war years. I managed to locate and interview a number of young people (of Marianne's age or a little younger) who had come into contact with the Bund in the late 1940s. They had been enormously impressed by what Artur Jacobs and his friends had achieved. Some of them told me that their subsequent choice of career and political orientation were strongly influenced by contact with the

Bund. But they could not cope with the Bund's hierarchical character, its 'inner circle', its veneration for Artur Jacobs and the way youngsters were supposed to sit at his feet. They found the Bund leadership over-sensitive to criticism.[65] And, although unwilling to be directly quoted, some children of the founding Bund generation expressed similar senti-ments. None of them could be persuaded to become full-fledged Bund members.[66]

As a charismatic movement, the Bund's other problem was that some of the fight had gone out of its leaders. Both Artur and Dore had been emotionally and physically drained by their wartime experience. Artur was now nearing seventy, mentally still at the height of his powers, physically no longer really in a position to lead a vibrant movement. Dore, though younger, would never again be completely healthy and had to conserve her strength. They were also, as Maria Briel related in an interview, deeply troubled by the impact the war had had on their son Gottfried (he later committed suicide).[67] A bitter argument between Carlos Morgenstern and Artur Jacobs further weakened the group. The former wanted the Bund to be more politically active and eventually broke away from the group.[68] Artur, by contrast, felt increasingly that the Bund's role should lie predominantly on the spiritual–intellectual plane. He devoted more and more of his time to thinking and writing, culminating in the book *Die Zukunft des Glaubens* (*The Future of Belief*).[69] It is an enormously impressive text, but far too wooden and out of kilter with the times to have much resonance when it finally appeared posthumously in 1971.

So it is not surprising that Marianne had growing doubts about whether she was doing any good. She shared with other Bund members the belief that the great mass of Germans had learned nothing from the past. She bemoaned the political shallowness of the young. She felt that many of the left-wing leaders who might have given guidance were far too fixated on material reconstruction, to the detriment of spiritual renewal.[70] And, like the Bund, steeped in a tradition of searching for organic unity of purpose, she probably also found some of the signs of an emergent pluralist society, with its party politics and interest groups, rather disheartening. A letter to cousin Alex in February 1946 contains her most comprehensive critique yet of German society:[71]

You can imagine how happy I was, after the endless years of being condemned to do nothing, finally to have a clear set of tasks, to know that I was needed and to take part as an equal. I plunged in with real enthusiasm and tried with holy zeal to do my best towards rebuilding. But increasingly one recognizes how illusory were the hopes we placed in Germany's ability to develop and change. Sometimes I feel that the Germans have learned nothing. Party-political interests are more important to them than united reconstruction. Will they ever learn to pull together? Will they ever learn real political convictions rather than just allow themselves to be driven by material interests and gather round the bowl that promises the best meal? Will they ever learn to be tolerant? Unity can emerge only from a foundation of tolerance – the prerequisite for creating new values.

On the one side there are the politically active, with their short-sightedness and dissension. Ranged against them is the unending number of politically indifferent, who represent an even bigger danger than the first group. In part, they are simply ignorant of political matters. But many have resolved on the basis of National Socialism never to tie themselves to a political line so that 'afterwards they're not the ones who did it'. They forget that National Socialism would have failed in 1933 if fewer people had stood on the sidelines.

There is so much talk today about 'democracy' and 'freedom'. The German people are far from being mature enough for democracy and freedom. They must be steered slowly along the right road. It's good that there's a military government in Germany to prevent anarchy (even though it also hinders healthy economic reorganization and regeneration, which is less smart).

But as Marianne's political engagement began to falter, her life was gaining new purpose.

Basil

On 25 November 1945, Marianne received an intriguing letter:

> Captain B. K. Ellenbogen RAMC 13 (BR) FDS BAOR
> 25 Nov. 1945
> Dear Miss Strauss,
> I do not know who you are, but I called here to let you know that
> your cousin Ernst Dahl (now in Canada) has received news of you
> through your relative in England. I was given this information by
> a Canadian officer who knows your cousin. Your cousin's address
> in Canada is:
>> Ernie (Ernst) Dahl
>> c/o Dominion Bridge Coy.
>> Ottawa Canada
> I called here this morning too at 11.15, but there was no one in. I
> should like to meet you, but unfortunately I do not live here but in
> München Gladbach. However, I should try my best to call on you
> again sometime, perhaps during next week.
>> With best wishes
>> B. K. Ellenbogen
>> Captain BAOR

Ernst Dahl, Aunt Lore's younger brother, had gone to Canada before
the war. Having received Marianne's address (probably from Marcus
Cohn), Ernst asked a Canadian officer stationed in Germany to
make contact with her. In the end, the officer had no time to follow up.
Instead, a young Jewish doctor with the British Forces, Captain Basil
Ellenbogen, offered to go. Captain Ellenbogen had made it his mission
to seek out Jews in Germany and offer help where possible. On his
own initiative, he had sought permission to visit Belsen, an experience
recorded in some shocking photographs which survive to this day.
Correspondence in his files attests to the moving and conscientious work
he put in to establishing contact between camp survivors and their
relatives overseas.

Basil Ellenbogen was born in Liverpool in December 1917, the second of three boys. His father, Max, was a credit draper selling clothing and furniture on credit. Basil's grandfather, Gershon, had come from Lithuania and Max, whose first language was not English, still did all his adding up in Yiddish. A pious man, learned in Jewish law, Max had married Gertie Hamburg from Cardiff, the daughter of the cantor at the Cardiff synagogue, and the two had settled in Liverpool. The three boys Gershon, Basil and Raymond were all very bright. Gershon won a scholarship to read classics at Cambridge. Basil and Raymond both went to Liverpool University, where Basil read medicine and Raymond dentistry.

Basil was very different from the people Marianne was mixing with in Germany. Not particularly politically engaged, he was a committed Orthodox Jew. He had been prominent in Jewish student life at university, and for a while chaired the national Jewish student federation. A handsome, witty man, he was popular with women, but apart from a deep attraction to a cousin, he had not experienced a serious relationship before he was called up.

Marianne told me that when Basil came to her apartment she was out at a Communist Party meeting. Knowing their later marriage had been difficult and that a major bone of contention had been the issue of Jewish observance – he was much more Orthodox in practice than she – I found it hard not to see already in this very first non-meeting a symbol of the problems ahead. Basil sought out Marianne because she was Jewish and he wanted to help Jewish people. Marianne was not at home because she was a Communist or, more precisely, because of the political mission she felt the Bund had given her. In a way, the war had brought them together almost on false pretences. He was pursuing an identity which she had sloughed off. But on reflection, this is probably too rigid an interpretation. Marianne's identity, her affiliations and her sense of the future were still much in flux. And love has a way of building bridges between the most unlikely shores.

On Marianne's return, Hanni Ganzer told her that a marvellous-looking man had been to see her. For his part, Basil had apparently been impressed by the various things that Marianne had managed to reclaim – the quality furniture and family portraits. This was not the picture of misery and destitution he was used to finding. On the Saturday, he came back. As she watched a khaki hat ascend the stairs, Marianne thought at first it belonged to one of the other officers she knew. Then suddenly this 'glorious chap' appeared. She was twenty-two, he twenty-eight. It was love at first sight. 'It took over. I knew it would. I wasn't very happy about it, but there was nothing I could do.'[72]

Over the following months, Marianne and Basil came to see more and more of each other. They would take romantic walks along the Rhine, looking out at the devastated bridges. They went to the opera and saw, amongst other things, *Così fan tutte*. Marianne introduced Basil to some of the prominent figures in the post-war Jewish community. By April 1946, when Basil learned that he was to be demobilized, they were deeply in love. Before Basil left, Marianne put together a little book of memories and photos for him to take along. In the accompanying letter, dated 19 April, Marianne wrote (in English):

> *Do not forget*
> *Düsseldorf*
> *And . . .*
> *Marianne*

At the time Basil was demobilized, Marianne was perhaps not yet committed to spending her life with him. Her uncle Adolf Rosenberg had cabled from New York that he had sent two affidavits of support to the American Consulate in Stuttgart and that he was able and happy to pay her passage when required. In April 1946, Marianne was still interested in following this up. A day after writing her farewell letter to Basil she informed the US consulate that Adolf had sent the affidavits and that her family had been about to emigrate to the USA in 1941 when the consulate was closed. Was a new registration necessary, or was the old quota number still appropriate?[73] But when the necessary forms came back in June, Marianne did not fill them out. Her desired destination had by then become clear: she wanted to join Basil in England.

The struggle to get to Britain

The fact that Marianne spent the next six months in Germany was due solely to difficulties the authorities put in the way of her coming to Britain. As she was about to discover, the UK was opposed to special immigration arrangements for German (or other European) Jews. There was a strong anti-Semitic unwillingness to respond to Jewish moaning. There was a principled (but, in view of recent events, scarcely defensible) refusal to make racial distinctions between different groups of Germans. Above all, there was a reluctance to create a precedent of 'special treatment' for European Jews that might in any way bolster their demands to be allowed into Palestine.

In early 1946, Marianne's relatives, the Oppenheimers, made a first attempt to obtain permission for her to come to Britain and failed. Then in March Marianne's cousin Gerald Alexander approached the British Interest Branch of the military government in Lübbecke.[74] The response from the Passport Control Officer was a sure indication of how little the British authorities were listening to the particular sufferings of German Jews. 'A scheme will shortly be put into operation by which distressed persons in Germany may come to England, provided that relatives there can give them a home. The conditions of this scheme will shortly be published.' Reading thus far, Gerald must have felt fairly confident, 'but', the letter went on, 'unless Miss Marianne Strauss has parents in England, I am afraid she will not fall within the limitations of this scheme.'[75]

On 22 March, Basil took up the case, noting that:[76]

> since the parents of Miss Strauss are dead, she will not be eligible for entry into England. This appears to be a particularly harsh decision, since being an orphan would incline one to consider her more a 'distressed' person than one whose parents are, fortunately, still alive.

Basil's letter may have crossed with a further note from the Passport Control Office, offering no more hope than the previous one and helpfully pointing out that 'There are, unfortunately millions of distressed persons in Europe in the same situation as your cousin.'[77] Certainly, Marianne could be assured she was not the only victim of British indifference to the plight of European Jews. When a British rabbi applied early on to go to Berlin to minister to Jewish survivors there, a visa was denied because British citizens were not supposed to provide help to Germans.[78]

A growing collection of letters, applications, health reports and other documentation built up in Marianne's files over the following months. When the couple became engaged in June 1946, the emphasis in the applications shifted from seeking to be united with relatives to wishing to marry Basil. But after being informed by the Public Safety Officer in Düsseldorf that a visa could be expected in six to eight weeks,[79] Marianne heard in July that she did not fall under the category of distressed persons and that 'no travel is at present allowed under these circumstances'.[80]

Marianne grew more and more impatient. Schemes were afoot to marry Basil in Belgium and travel from there to Britain. In October, Basil wrote to his Member of Parliament. Noting that several German brides had already reached the country, he went on:[81]

> It appears to me scandalous that after five months no visa should have been granted, and indicative of the chaotic state of military government in Germany. May I add that as a doctor, I worked amongst the concentration camp victims at Sandbostel (and unofficially at Belsen) and saw the fate that my fiancée had averted but which had befallen her family. She has herself endured much hardship during the war and all the years of Nazi rule – is it not time that British democracy be extended to include her?[82]

Finally, in November 1946, the authorities relented, allowing Marianne to enter as a German national, on the basis that she was going to marry Basil. Among Marianne's papers we find a reference from the *Freiheit* attesting to her journalistic ability and a charming farewell letter from the paper's editorial board hoping 'from our hearts that England may give you all that we are at present still denied in Germany'.[83] Hanni Ganzer too had many moving wishes to send to her young friend.[84]

On or soon after 20 November, Marianne finally arrived in England. Basil's solicitor, a family friend who had been involved in the legal battle for more than six months, felt compelled to write a personal note to his client:[85]

> *The world is in such a terrible state as far as relations between communities and peoples are concerned that one is particularly happy as one goes through it in these days to find that personal relations can be so satisfactory in a tortured universe . . .*
>
> *It was good to see Miss Strauss in the flesh – really here – and it seemed to me at once that you will both be very happy and are in for an interesting time. At any rate, my wishes will follow you. There are so many frustrations nowadays in jobs one does and activities we all want to do, that when one sees one object attained it is all the more satisfying.*
>
> *So – sincerest wishes for all your future happiness, and that Miss Strauss will enjoy being amongst us in England, as I am sure she will after all her experiences.*

13

The Fate of Marianne's Family

Marianne and Basil made rapid plans for their wedding. Given that Marianne's visa would expire within two months unless she married a British national, speed was of the essence. The ceremony took place at London's Hampstead Garden Suburb synagogue on Sunday 29 December and the newlyweds honeymooned in Torquay. Liverpool was where they intended to live. They moved in briefly with Basil's parents, but soon found a flat in the attic of a Victorian house. The flat had previously been occupied by some of Basil's friends. Following her mother's example rather than her advice, Marianne conceived within a few months of the marriage, and Vivian was born on 23 November 1947.

Several months before Vivian's birth, in the summer of 1947, Basil's brother Gershon brought Marianne some remarkable letters from Sweden. With the information they contained, Marianne was as well informed about her family's fate as she would ever be.

Marianne's testimony

Marianne herself shared only some of this knowledge with me. By the 1990s, she had forgotten various details, subtly changed others, and some she probably deliberately withheld. From the papers in her possession and other sources, I had to reconstruct a picture not only of what

The young marrieds – Marianne and Basil

had happened to her family, but also what exactly she had once known.

Marianne knew her parents had been deported from Theresienstadt to Auschwitz in December 1943. As we've seen, in her published account she claimed to have heard this on the run. Her even more startling claim was that, while staying with her relatives in Beverstedt on her birthday, 7 June 1944, she had been listening to the BBC and heard that the occupants of her parents' particular transport had been gassed. This is what she told me in our conversation for the museum in 1989:[1]

'Throughout the war and particularly during my illegal phase we listened to the English broadcasts. That was, of course, extraordinarily dangerous because the opening bars of the Beethoven Symphony [the BBC's call sign] were very distinctive. One had to be careful to turn the volume right down and lie with one's ear next to the speaker. But for my parents and family, and later for me and my friends living illegally, it was a lifeline to hear the real war situation.[. . .] And so on one such lunchtime transmission, we were listening to the broadcast and heard that the transport from 18 December 1943 to Birkenau-Auschwitz had been gassed there in the last few days. I knew that my parents and brother had been on that transport to Auschwitz. So, I had an unforgettable birthday.'

Of all Marianne's revelations about communication, I found this the hardest to believe. Surely she could not have obtained such precise details about which transport her parents were on? And surely, the BBC did not broadcast information about gassings with this kind of precision?

While I was in Düsseldorf just after Marianne died, Dr Angela Genger from the Düsseldorf Museum of Persecution showed me a list they had of deportees to Theresienstadt. From this, I gained the name of a Czech expert on Theresienstadt, Miroslav Karny, who led me to an ongoing project to enter information about all the inmates into an electronic database.[2] I contacted the group by email, and received the following communication from Zdenek Schindler:

A list of our (not yet fully authenticated) data follows. The list needs an explanation:

1. First datum is a code of a transport. VII/4 means Düsseldorf, 9.9.1943[3]

2. *The transport number of a person follows*
3. *[Next in line] is the code of transport from Terezin and the personal number.*
4. *I have added also the destination and the date of deportation from Terezin (please, check it)*

VII/4 3	Ep 128 (Auschwitz 9.10.1944)	Dahl \ Else	born 25.01.1883	Died ?
VII/4 8	Dz 1870 (Auschwitz 15.5.1944)	Jaffe \ Gertrude	born 27.06.1903	Died ?
VII/4 9	Er 881 (Auschwitz 16.10.1944)	Liebrecht \ Reha	born 12.01.1942	Died ?
VII/4 67		Rosenberg \ Anna	born 04.01.1867	Died 09.01.1944 Terezin
VII/4 1	El 497 (Auschwitz 29.9.1944)	Strauss \ Alfred	born 24.04.1891	Died ?
VII/4 2	Ep 127 (Auschwitz 9.10.1944)	Strauss \ Lore Rosa	born 16.08.1907	Died ?
VII/4 5	Ds 2215 (Auschwitz 18.12.1943)	Strauss \ Regina	born 13.01.1896	Died ?
VII/4 6	Ds 2216 (Auschwitz 18.12.1943)	Strauss \ Richard	born 26.10.1926	Died ?
VII/4 4	Ds 2214 (Auschwitz 18.12.1943)	Strauss \ Siegfried	born 24.04.1891	Died ?

total 9 persons

Siegfried, Regina and Richard *had* been deported together on 18 December 1943, leaving Regina's mother, Alfred, Lore and Lore's mother behind. The seventy-seven-year-old Anna Rosenberg had then died in Theresienstadt on 9 January 1944. At the time, I thought this news about Anna was something Marianne had not known. Later I was to discover that this was just one of many facts about the family's life in the ghetto which Marianne *had* in fact known. (Gertrude Jaffe and Reha Liebrecht, incidentally, were the other people transported with the Strauss family from Essen in September 1943.)

So Marianne's information about her parents' transport had been correct. When we spoke about this, she could no longer remember exactly how she had found out. But it is known that, as a 'show camp', Theresienstadt was still allowed postal contact with the outside world. Other inmates remembered, for example, that Theresienstadt inmates could write once every eight weeks, and outside correspondents could write in to the camp once every four weeks.[4] In fact, the regulations varied and there were always many restrictions and limitations, but there is no doubt that post could go in and out.[5] It thus seems likely that either the Strauss family or someone else had sent a letter to an address in Germany that allowed Marianne to learn of their departure.

Subsequent research in Britain and Germany confirmed that, on this rare occasion, the BBC really did broadcast precise information about the fate of a particular transport, a fact of which even much of the specialist literature on the Third Reich seems unaware. The circumstances surrounding the broadcast were quite unusual. The underground resistance movement within Auschwitz had obtained advance knowledge that the people on the December transport from Theresienstadt would be held 'in quarantine' for a period of several months and later murdered. Wanting to convince outsiders of the credibility of their revelations about Auschwitz, the resistance sought to present as much detailed information as possible. The fact that it was able to forecast the impending murder of the occupants of a specific transport was important. In April 1944, Rudolf Vrba and Alfred Wetzler, two Slovakian Jews in the camp underground, hid between the inner and outer perimeter fences and after several days succeeded in escaping. They took with them a wealth of facts and figures from the camp, including the details of the December transport. By the end of April they had written a meticulous report, which delivered in sober language by far the most comprehensive description of Auschwitz-Birkenau yet available to the outside world.[6] One copy reached Dr Jaromir Kopecky, the diplomatic representative in Switzerland of the Czech government, sometime in May. Kopecky showed a copy to the Swiss-based General Secretary of the World Jewish Congress, Gerhard M. Riegner, who had already played a vital role in informing the Allies about the Holocaust.

Because of the urgency and clarity of Vrba and Wetzler's prediction that thousands of Czech citizens would be murdered on 20 June, Kopecky and Riegner decided to inform the Czech government in exile in London. Kopecky made a request to British and US broadcasters: 'Please, broadcast promptly the most urgent warning possible to the German murderers who are managing the slaughter in Upper Silesia.'[7]

This message was sent on 14 June with the help of Elizabeth Wiskemann, the British legate in Bern. On 15 June it was deciphered in London. We know that the first BBC broadcast of the news was made in its Czech and Slovak service on 16 June. On the 17th, a more comprehensive version with a more emphatic warning was transmitted.[8] And on or about this date, a German transmission was made, which is what Marianne must have heard. We don't have the direct transcripts of the German service, but we do find the following item in the BBC's German Service records:[9]

Here is an important announcement. News has reached London that the German authorities in Czechoslovakia have ordered the massacre of 3,000 Czechoslovakian Jews[10] in gas chambers at Birkenau on or about June 20th. These Jews were transported to Birkenau from the concentration camp at Theresienstadt on the Elbe last December.

Four thousand Czech Jews who were taken from Theresienstadt to Birkenau in September 1943 were massacred in the gas chambers on March 7th. The German authorities in Czechoslovakia and their subordinates should know that full information is received in London about the massacres in Birkenau. All those responsible for such massacres from the top downwards will be called to account.

Marianne's diary entry on the 20th – 'Horrific! What will happen now?' – so different in tone from the measured entries preceding it, must have referred to this news.

Why should Marianne in her memory have displaced the date of receiving the news from the 16th or 17th back to 7 June, thereby inventing the notion of her 'unforgettable birthday present'? As in her account of Ernst's death, she had added a slight 'literary' slant to the truth. The shocking nature of the birthday 'present' brought out even more poignantly the horrible contrast of those times: that she could be living in comparative security while her parents had suffered the most hideous fate. A day that should have been shared by her family brought news that the family would never be together again.

We are all familiar with the experience that sometimes the facts don't seem powerful enough in the retelling. We feel the need to add something extra to the story to give it greater punch, though the perceived need might well spring as much from our insecurity as from the insufficient interest of what we have to tell. In Marianne's case, it seems hardly credible that she should have felt the need to embellish her account, but perhaps with the passage of time she had come to feel some lack in the emotional power of the facts and begun, wittingly or not, to add extra details.

On the other hand, Marianne's version omitted perhaps the most gruesome feature of the events – that when she heard the broadcast, the gassings *had not yet taken place*. She had obliterated the traumatic four-day waiting between the broadcast on the 16th or 17th and her diary entry on the 20th; in much the same way, her most painful separations and partings – from Ernst and her parents – had been slightly reworked in her memory.

Incidentally, Marianne was far from the only person in Germany to monitor this broadcast. It was received by the SS in Auschwitz and may have been responsible for delaying the killings for a few weeks. They took place on 11–12 July 1944.[11] Again, although not widely known, this BBC broadcast seems to have been important for other Jews still in Germany (by now almost exclusively Jews of mixed parentage, those in mixed marriages or the very few in hiding). On 20 August, Viktor Klemperer noted in his diary:[12]

I heard: Some time ago many Jews (three hundred? three thousand?) are said to have been brought out of Theresienstadt and afterwards the English radio reported the gassing of this transport. The truth?

Klemperer did not know. The broadcast did not end Marianne's uncertainty, either. Like Klemperer, but far more urgently, she was confronted with the choice of whether or not to believe what she had heard. As the memories of Frau Nenadovic indicated, Marianne probed gently where she could to find out more.

Marianne's documents

I learned about the BBC broadcast from Marianne directly. What I did not learn from her, and discovered only after her death, was that once the war was over she found out quite a lot about how her parents had lived before they were murdered.

As we know, her parents were initially deported to Theresienstadt in September 1943. By that point an extension to the railway line had been built, bringing new inmates directly into the ghetto. For most, the first shock was the *Schleuse* (sluice), the one-, two- or three-day processing period in dark, unhealthy conditions, during which they were robbed of most of what they still had. It is possible that, because they came in a tiny privileged transport, the Strauss family was spared the lengthy processing. But they were not spared the plunder.

We know about the plunder because of letters Vivian and I came across which had been sent to Marianne in March and April 1946 by Frau Erna Ogutsch, the widow of the former Essen cantor. Erna Ogutsch, by then working as a librarian in a DP camp in Bavaria, gave Marianne detailed information about the family's life in Theresienstadt and the circumstances of their departure.[13] The Ansbachers, cousins of Siegfried and Alfred from Frankfurt,[14] also wrote at around the same time; they had maintained regular contact with the Strausses in Theresienstadt.

According to Frau Ogutsch, when the Strausses arrived, the guards found money in Ine's possession. Despite their imprisonment in Essen, the Strausses had still managed to hold on to some of their money. Ine was sentenced to four months' imprisonment. According to Erna, however, Ine in prison had 'more, much more food than we had. She was allowed to work as a cleaning woman and *was completely content.*[15] Ine Strauss, working as a cleaning woman and 'completely content'? Erna Ogutsch was undoubtedly sensitive to the psychological needs of her reader. But, perhaps, in a world turned upside down, it was a credible assertion.

With few exceptions, men and women were not allowed to stay together in Theresienstadt, and so Siegfried, Alfred and Richard were immediately separated from Lore, Else Dahl and Anna Rosenberg. According to Frau Ogutsch, Alfred, Siegfried and Richard lived in the Hanover barracks and Lore and the two grandmothers in the Hamburg barracks. The possibility of meeting was limited to certain times of day, between work and curfew. Conditions were, however, easing a little in this respect, thanks to the Danish government's request to inspect the camp. Another resident of the Hamburg barracks remembered, for example, that as of autumn 1943 one no longer needed a pass to leave the building.[16]

Conditions had been at their worst in 1942, when Theresienstadt had been completely unprepared for the influx. The Strauss family were lucky to the extent that, since September 1942, a number of steps had been taken to improve matters. Nevertheless, housing remained overcrowded and extremely primitive, often double or treble bunks in large dormitories. Compared with even the vastly reduced circumstances of their last years in Essen, the conditions must have been a terrible shock. The Strausses did not experience the worst of the water shortage, which had been resolved by 1943, but they must have been forced to accept the most degrading washing conditions in which tens, sometimes hundreds of people shared the same lavatory and wash basin.[17] In the Hamburg barracks, for example, where Lore, Else and Anna lived, the lavatories were at the distant end of an arcade and far too few.[18] Obviously, misery for an elderly person with any kind of infection.

There were also far too few doctors – one for every 1,600 people, many of whom were the vulnerable young or the vulnerable elderly. Typhus, scarlet fever, jaundice, measles and, particularly, enteritis swept through the ghetto. For the Strauss brothers, the anarchy of corruption, despite the many regulations, and the constant individual battles for survival must have been almost as intolerable. The family was also exposed to the infamous census on 10–11 November, when the ghetto's population was made to stand outside in the rain for some fifteen hours, an ordeal which several of the elderly did not survive.[19]

Apart from Erna Ogutsch's reference to Regina's diet in prison, we do not know how the Strausses fared with nourishment. For newcomers, the food was often awful. Even the official rations fell below absolute minimum levels of necessary protein. To make matters worse, the wide-

spread corruption ensured that a substantial portion of the food allocation never became available for general consumption. Anyone who tried
to protest was removed on the next transport.[20] But what I learned from
Erna's letters was that the Strausses did have the one thing vital to
keeping body and soul together – regular parcels from outside. Provided
they contained no written messages, parcels could be sent to Theresienstadt frequently and were distributed daily.[21] But the Strausses were
possibly the last Jews to be deported from the Ruhr: who was still
outside, supplying them with such precious commodities?

Parcels for the Strauss family

Erna Ogutsch wrote that in 1944 Lore, 'often had news and parcels
from you and once, for her birthday, a small book, perhaps E.T.A.
Hoffmann or someone like that.' Because the polite German word for
'you', *Ihnen*, can also mean 'them', it took me a moment to realize that
Frau Ogutsch meant that the parcels came from Marianne. To confirm
the point, the Ansbachers, too, wrote of Marianne's beneficence, 'All
your parcels arrived and gave your loved ones much pleasure.'[22] So,
suddenly, from these very last letters in her house, I learned that while
Marianne was on the run, she had still been assembling food parcels
and sending them to Theresienstadt. Yet she had never mentioned this
in any of her testimony, even though one would have thought that proof
of Marianne's continued freedom would have given her parents the
greatest consolation, and would comfort her memory of them, too.

When Vivian learned that his mother had been providing for her
parents even while in hiding, he was overcome. It was not just her
heroism, her truly remarkable resourcefulness. It was that he should
discover this only now. His reaction made me aware of the strange
symmetry between his experience and his mother's. Both, it seemed,
were condemned to find out about their parents' lives via a posthumous
paper trail. The same letters which in 1946, two years after the Strausses'
murder, had told Marianne about her parents' experience in Theresienstadt, now in 1997, a year after his mother's death, told Vivian about
who his mother had been.

The Ansbachers' letter contained another surprise. 'Is the name Christian familiar to you? He was a friend of yours and did a great deal of good.'[23] Christian Arras again! When I had spoken to Lilli Arras, she had vaguely remembered sending parcels to the family in Theresienstadt. On one such occasion, she was so brutally shouted at by the clerk in the post office that she simply walked out, too nervous to complete the transaction. She also thought that Christian Arras had visited Theresienstadt once. I was unable to confirm his visit and had rather discounted it. But now the Ansbachers' cryptic comment made it much more likely. Either the Strauss family had simply talked about his help or, more probably, they were still somehow the beneficiaries of his good offices in Theresienstadt. The exact details will never be known.

These striking revelations almost paled into insignificance beside another batch of documents Vivian and I had already turned up; the postcards Basil's brother, Gershon, had brought back from his trip to Sweden in 1947. In Stockholm, Gershon had met Grete Sander who had, it seemed, received some 800 Swedish kronor from the Strauss family. She gave Gershon several cards which on his return he forwarded with a cheery letter: 'We had a most interesting time, particularly in Stockholm, but it came so expensive that I am personally more relieved than disappointed at the ban on foreign travel!'[24]

At this stage, I had not yet discovered who Grete Sander was, and for a while pursued a false trail.[25] But then I learned from Eric Alexander that Grete had lived in München Gladbach, near Krefeld, and was a relative on his side of the family. The family connection to Marianne was so distant that without looking at Eric Alexander's letter I can never quite get it right: Grete Sander was Marianne's mother's sister's husband's sister's husband's sister.[26] Grete would never have featured in this story but for one vital fact: she had emigrated to Sweden, a neutral country with which direct postal contact was possible from Germany.[27]

The first card, complete with Hitler's stern visage on the 15-pfennig stamp, was something I had never expected to see – a postcard from Marianne's father in Theresienstadt. Siegfried's card is dated 1 October, but postmarked 12 January 1944, so apparently lay around for three months before being dispatched. With the rigorous censorship operating in the camp, Siegfried had little choice but to be upbeat. Only the *absence*

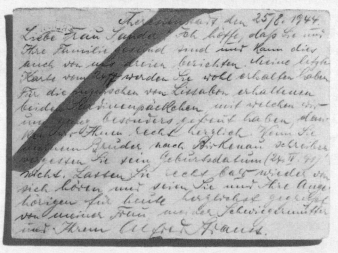

Postcards from Theresienstadt to Sweden

of news tells us that the postcard was not sent from a family holiday in Norderney or Nordwijk:[28]

> *Dear Grete,*
>
> *We arrived here fine and are healthy and hope the same of you and your children. My address is Hauptstrasse 1.*
>
> *We often see Hans Orgeler's parents and Luise Saul. We would be very glad to hear from you soon. All send their best wishes.*

The card did contain one crucial piece of information for the recipient: the address. Later cards indicated that Grete was now able to act both as benefactor and as an important intermediary to Strauss relatives in the States. Parcels were not only being sent from Sweden but also from the USA, commissioned by Hugo Strauss. According to Alfred's cards in 1944, parcels were being sent via Lisbon, received by him (it is not clear whether Siegfried was in Theresienstadt long enough to benefit) and confirmed by mail to Sweden. A post-war letter from Grete Sander to Marianne suggested that Grete Sander had also sent numerous parcels from Sweden direct.[29] Another post-war letter, from the family's Swiss lawyer Marcus Cohn to Hugo Strauss, listed items sent to Theresienstadt between May and December 1944. That made me wonder whether 'Lisbon' was in fact Alfred's neutral code for the USA, and whether Hugo's gifts were in fact coming via Switzerland.[30] In 1947, Cohn evidently also still had in his possession some postcards from Theresienstadt, which Alfred had sent to Switzerland on 10 July and 21 August 1944.[31] The most likely scenario, if 'likely' is a word that can be used in such an astonishing context, is that Alfred wrote to the family in neutral Sweden. They passed on the details to relatives in the USA who, in turn, commissioned the family lawyer in neutral Switzerland to send parcels, receipt of which was confirmed via Sweden.

Deportation to Auschwitz-Birkenau

Most of the postcards I found had been sent by Alfred in 1944, after his brother had gone. Siegfried's upbeat postcard to Frau Sander, written on 1 October 1943, will have been doubly misleading to its recipient since, by the date of the postmark, 12 January 1944, Siegfried had already been deported to Auschwitz. In her letter to Marianne after the war, Frau Ogutsch confirmed that Marianne's parents were indeed deported in December 1943, and ended by suggesting that Marianne should get in touch if she wanted to know more. Marianne rarely responded to such invitations, but in this case was evidently spurred on to respond almost by return.[32] She wanted to know why her parents been singled out for transport in December 1943. In April Erna wrote again:[33]

> You ask why your parents were transported to Birkenau as early as December. There were continual transports. Already in autumn 1942 so many from our transport[34] were sent on, mainly older people. Then there were several large transports in January 1943, including my sister and again many from Essen of every age. There was a constant coming and going. Always the spectre of a transport hanging over us. It is possible that the punishment of your mother led to the earlier transport. In May 1944 there were again many.

And here Erna listed the Essen families who had been transported to Auschwitz – including Rudi's father, Dr Josef Löwenstein, Liesel Sternberg's father Leopold, Marianne's friend Irma Ransenberg, and many others.

In fact, for much of 1943 there were no transports out of Theresienstadt. During the summer, Eichmann even declared that the ghetto would be spared further deportations. But on 6 September 1943, just four days before Siegfried and his family arrived, 5,000 ghetto occupants were deported and the whole place was plunged into uncertainty again, an uncertainty which would last until the end of the war. December 1943 – when Siegfried, Ine and Richard were carted off – was a new peak. In that month over one-eighth of the inhabitants were caught up in deportations.[35]

We do not know in what condition Siegfried, Ine and Richard travelled to Auschwitz. Frau Ogutsch wrote that when Lore was deported the following year, she went off reasonably well equipped (adding, sadly, 'But what good did it do?'). So it is possible that Marianne's parents, too, had possessions as they boarded the train. But since suitcases had to be handed over before departure, that may have been the last they saw of them.

Nor do we know if they had any idea what awaited them. Ever since hearing Christian Arras's information about Izbica they must have dreaded being sent on to Poland. Yet it seems most Theresienstadt inmates did not really know about Auschwitz until December 1944. Between September 1943 and October 1944 there had been occasional 'postcard actions' from Birkenau to Theresienstadt, orchestrated by the Nazis. On at least one occasion, in June 1944, recipients of such cards in Theresienstadt were allowed to reply, though the replies never reached the original writers, most of whom had been killed in the interval.[36] Because of this, the Theresienstadt Jews were far less well informed than the remnants of the Polish Jewish community. Whatever the case, the specific fate of Marianne's parents' transport beggared belief even in a world in which the unbelievable happened every day.

Ruth Elias, a Czech woman who had been in the same barracks as Lore, was on the Strausses' transport.[37] In her published autobiography she provides a vivid account of the departure. Unlike the ordinary train carriages in which the Strauss family had travelled from Essen, they were now sent in cattle cars. SS guards called out the names of the travellers and then chased them on to the trucks, yelling, 'Faster, faster, you Jewish swine!' The cattle cars were filled with fifty, sixty people, sometimes more. There was no straw on the floor, and in any case there was no room to lie down. The deportees were held in semi-darkness. There were two pails on the floor, one filled with water; the other supposed to be a toilet. Since it was virtually impossible to empty the pail out of the small windows, the stink became unbearable.

Elias could not remember whether she spent one night or two on the train – in fact it was two. In the late afternoon of the third day the train stopped, the doors were wrenched open and the inmates confronted with yelling kapos and barking dogs. They had to jump down from the cars and line up in groups of five. Ruth Elias asked one of the men standing near by the name of the place:[38]

Without looking at me, he said, 'Auschwitz.'
That meant nothing to me. It was the name of one of many towns in

Poland. I didn't know how deeply Auschwitz *would be engraved into my very being, so indelibly that it could never be erased.*

More evidence that the Theresienstadt deportees really did not know what awaited them.

In this abnormal world, the 'normal' next step should have been the selection. Siegfried and Ine would probably have been sent one way, to immediate death; Richard, the other, to work. But this was no ordinary transport. For the December transports were the second tranche of two very large waves of deportations from Theresienstadt to the Auschwitz-Birkenau 'family camp', one of the most bizarre elements of the Nazi murder programme.[39] '*Familienlager BIIb*' was established in September 1943 with the arrival of 5,006 Jews from Theresienstadt.[40] In his memoirs Rudolf Vrba recalled:[41]

Nobody who survived Camp A in Birkenau will ever forget September 7, 1943, for it was unlike any day we had ever known. That morning we felt wonder, elation, nostalgia and overwhelming amazement as we gazed on a sight which most had forgotten existed and the rest doubted if they would ever see again.

Into Camp B beside us, separated from us by only a few strands of wire, poured men, women and children, dressed in ordinary civilian clothes, their heads unshaven, their faces bewildered, but plump and unravaged. The grown-ups carried their luggage, the children their dolls and their teddy-bears; and the men of Camp A, the Zebra men who were only numbers, simply stood and stared, wondering who had tilted the world, spilling a segment of it on top of them.

[. . .]

The SS men treated them with consideration, joking with them, playing with the children.[. . .]I noted that each of them, even the youngest children, who were about two years of age, had been tattooed with a special number that bore no relation to Auschwitz; and each had a card on which was written: 'six months' quarantine with special treatment'.

Soon after the arrival of the September transportees, the camp underground learned that the official transport list was headed, 'SB – Transport of Czech Jews with six months' quarantine'.[42] The underground knew that SB was an abbreviation for *Sonderbehandlung*, 'special treatment', itself usually a euphemism for murder. But it was not clear what was intended. In contrast with other transports to Auschwitz, no selection was carried out. All those who arrived were taken to the camp. They retained their personal property, their hair and their clothes. How exceptional these conditions were can be gleaned by comparing them with the fate of 1,260 Jewish children and 53 carers who arrived from Theresienstadt on 7 October. All were gassed on the day of their arrival.[43] On 16 and 20 December, the second wave from Theresienstadt entered Birkenau, amongst them Siegfried, Regina and Richard. They too had the symbol SB6, i.e. special treatment after six months,[44] against their names in the camp files (though, unlike the camp underground, they themselves will not have known this). They, too, arrived in the 'family camp', this strangely privileged area in the heart of the most horrific place of the twentieth century. No one knew why they had this special status.[45]

In Auschwitz terms, the inmates were thus immensely privileged and the sight of them called forth 'nostalgia'. But here is the same experience described from the point of view of the arrivals themselves, not yet having learned the Birkenau scale of horror by which to calibrate their good fortune:[46]

Our pitiful human column in rows of five, flanked by SS men with their rifles at the ready, began to move. Not a word was said. Totally intimidated, we moved forward like automatons. Koni and I had only one thought: Stay together; don't lose sight of each other. The column came to a halt in front of a large building, and we were ordered to undress. Undress? Here we were, women and men and children all together. We couldn't do that! But when the SS men used their whips, we obeyed. It was shortly before Christmas, and the temperature hovered between 10 and 14 °F (−10 to −15 °C). Then the men were separated from the women, and we were led into a large room where showerheads were attached to the ceiling. Ice cold water poured down on us. There was no way to avoid the downpour since we were crowded together like sardines. We cursed. There was no soap; there were no towels. When we

*came out, we were sopping wet. They threw some clothes at us. There
was no sign of my fur-trimmed winter coat that had cost me so much
bartered bread. Instead, I was handed a flimsy dark-blue silk dress and
a lightweight coat; no underwear, no stockings, just wooden clogs.*[47]
*Before we were led into the shower room, we had to bundle our own
clothes and shoes together and turn them in. We never got them back.*

Thinking of Marianne's parents in the cold reminded me of one of
Eric Alexander's letters to me:[48]

*As I am writing this, another conversation comes to mind, so
grotesque and tragic that you could be forgiven for thinking that I
made it up. I do distinctly remember Ine saying to my mother that
if they were ever taken away, she would make sure that she would
take her Persian lamb fur coat with her, because if there was
anything she disliked, it was being cold.*

*Such lovely uplifting conversations. They talked about this kind
of thing without believing what they were saying.*

In three-tiered wooden bunks, with no mattresses and nothing but a
thin blanket, the new arrivals tried to make themselves warm. Their first
food since leaving Theresienstadt was not to come till the following day,
when they were also tattooed. The 1,137 men from the train were given
the numbers 169969 to 171105 and the 1,336 women and girls numbers
72435 to 73700.[49] I hoped I would be able to identify the precise
numbers the Strausses were given and find some record of them in the
Auschwitz archives. But it is not clear how precise a list was kept.
Certainly the Strausses' names are not included among the 50,000 or so
which survive on the Auschwitz lists. Since new lists are being discovered
in Russia, it is just possible that their names may be found in the future.[50]

The daily routine was also unlike that in any other part of Birkenau.
According to some accounts, the new inmates were allowed to write to
family every fortnight and receive parcels. The men did not have to
report to work and a school was opened for the children under the
leadership of the inspirational Fredy Hirsch. The children also had a
small garden area and, initially, somewhat better food than the rest of
the camp.[51] With the exception of the Camp Elder, the Jewish inmates

themselves ran the camp administration. Best of all, because the men's and women's barracks were in the same enclosure, families could meet during the evening visiting hour in the Lagerstrasse.

The inmates, unaware of their relative privilege, felt they were enduring the most horrific experience of their lives. The diet consisted of little more than watery soups, and hunger and disease took an enormous toll. Within the first six months, more than 1,000 of the 5,000 who arrived in September had died of 'natural causes'.[52] There was roll call early in the morning, which involved standing outside in skimpy clothes in freezing weather, sometimes for hours, until all had been accounted for. Senseless, backbreaking work, moving rocks, was their daily lot. One of the most shocking experiences for the second wave of inmates was meeting their former Theresienstadt comrades who had been deported in September. As Ruth Elias recalled:[53]

These people had changed completely their behaviour. We had known each other, we had been friends, after all, and one of them had become Blockälteste, *a person in charge of a block with 400 people or more. Someone approached him as a friend, but he told him: 'We don't play games here,' and started making a speech: 'You've come to a place from which you will not return.' The people we had known became unrecognizable. Those I had known as civilized persons behaved like savages, and it was difficult to explain the change that had come over them.*

And over the next few weeks, rumours about gas chambers and ovens became part of the arrivals' consciousness. The rumours became more urgent and the whole meaning of the camp experience for the December arrivals changed dramatically in March when, almost exactly six months after the arrival of the first transport, instructions came from the RHSA that the September deportees were to be killed. In the camp, the Nazis attempted to maintain the illusion that those affected were being transferred to labour camps in the interior. All were instructed to send postcards to acquaintances; those capable of work were transferred to quarantine camp BIIa, the men in one set of blocks, women in another; and all were allowed to take their things with them. None the less, the suspicions of the underground hardened. On 4 March, the head of the

Auschwitz underground confided his thoughts to Rudolf Vrba, telling him that the group had all been told to write postcards and post-date them by one month. The Sonderkommando had been ordered to stoke the furnaces for 4,000 on the night of 7 March and the SS men had been talking about a special job.[54] The underground leaders hoped that the size of the operation, the certainty of it, and the fact that there were some thirty members of the underground in the group might provide the basis for an uprising. They decided that Fredy Hirsch, the inspirational youth leader who had done so much for the youngsters on the transports, was the man who might enjoy enough confidence throughout the camp to lead the uprising. After Vrba talked to Hirsch, the latter went off, ostensibly to consider, and poisoned himself.

All the September deportees were killed in one night, 7/8 March or, in the Jewish calendar of that year, on Purim, the festival commemorating the defeat of the wicked Haman who had plotted to kill all the Jews. Just as there had been no selection on arrival, there was no selection now (with the exception of a few twins, on whom Mengele practised his experiments, and some medical personnel).[55] From then on, according to the witnesses cited by the historian Otto Dov Kulka, it was clear to those left behind that the life span of transports brought to the special camp was pre-determined at precisely six months. Camp life continued, with concerts and theatrical performances, youth and educational work,[56] but now many inmates were fully aware that they were doomed to extinction. However, A. Schön recollected that even weeks after the March murders, members of the December group remained unaware of the deaths of their compatriots. Their self-delusion was reinforced by the arrival of the victims' post-dated postcards (25–27 March);[57] which also served to convince those still in Theresienstadt that Birkenau was a reasonable camp.[58]

With that, we are almost done, but for one more, tiny glimpse into the lives of the Strauss family. Among the cards received by Grete Sander in Sweden was one in a wild pencil scrawl from Regina Strauss, Labour Camp Birkenau, near Neuberun (Oberschlesien). Dated 15 April, it said:[59]

Dear Grete, I am healthy, things are fine, I hope to hear often from you. With best wishes, your Regina

As we know, cards were sometimes sent to deceive. The designation 'Work Camp Birkenau' was misleading, since this was no work camp. The address 'near Neuberun' was chosen deliberately by the authorities so that no one receiving a card from the family camp would link it with Auschwitz.[60] The dates were also often deceptions and the writers murdered before the cards reached their addressees. In this case, though apparently written in April, the card was postmarked 23 June and may have been sent out deliberately at a time when the Nazis knew that the Vrba/Wetzler report was receiving considerable international attention.[61] My initial feeling of having discovered a miraculous conduit of communication was therefore soon replaced by the insight that virtually nothing interpretable was being communicated. That Ine was healthy is only just possible. That she was still alive in April, the putative date of the card, is quite probable. That she was 'doing fine' is impossible. That a wild scrawl was not her normal way of writing is certain. From Frau Ogutsch and others, Marianne learned after the war that Richard, too, had managed to send one card back to Theresienstadt. And we also know that Grete Sander was able to convey to Lore that she had heard from Ine[62] and also send parcels to Auschwitz.[63]

But Ine will not have received them. In June (though then delayed to July), it was the December transport's turn to be eliminated. The imminent prospect of the murders was what Marianne had heard announced on the radio. What the underground had not predicted, however, and Marianne never knew, was that this time there was a selection. It is possible that this was the result of the publicity about the killings. But in any case, the Nazis were growing more aware of the need to conserve labour.[64] So, unlike the March killings, where all had been sent to the gas chambers without exception, in June those deemed fit to work were taken to labour camps in Germany.[65] According to the historian H. G. Adler, himself a Theresienstadt survivor, of the 2,503 people transported to Auschwitz from Theresienstadt on 18 December 1943, some 443 survived, and of the two December transports overall 705, 13 percent, survived.[66] I do not know what Marianne would have made of this, if she had lived long enough for me to tell her that this was the case. Possibly some of the Strausses, perhaps Richard, made it through at this stage. If they did, there is no trace of them in the records.

These two six-month quarantine periods surely form one of the most bizarre and macabre twists in the Auschwitz chronicle. What can have been the purpose of this murder by clockwork? One thing is clear: the killings were planned from the very beginning. It now seems certain that the family camp was one of the actions the RSHA undertook to conceal the murder programme. There was some fear that Red Cross representatives visiting Theresienstadt might also wish to see Auschwitz. The family camp, the mail facilities, the receipt of parcels sent under the auspices of the International Red Cross and so on were all part of an elaborate smoke screen. In May 1944, for example, Himmler agreed to conduct a tour of inspection of 'one Jewish labour camp [in Birkenau]' with representatives of the German and International Red Cross.[67] Not until the Red Cross decided that a visit to Theresienstadt on 23 June 1944 had 'satisfied all expectations' and that a further visit to Auschwitz was unnecessary did the regime decide to wind up the special family camp and dispose of its last inmates.[68]

Among all the Holocaust's grotesqueries, this must rank as one of the strangest. There is something about the 'special treatment' within the 'special treatment' that seems to capture the Holocaust's essence. What makes the Holocaust so singular and so impenetrable is the macabre interplay between procedure, irrational hatred and murderous brutality. In this case, a special procedure was imposed on the general pattern; the virtues of murder were carefully weighed up against the importance of public relations; a precise timetable of premeditatedly delayed murder was substituted for the usual clockwork. The story of the Theresienstadt transports stands as a symbol for the impenetrability of the whole.

From another perspective, the family camp was for the Strausses the final phase of their privileged status, though they will not have experienced it as such. As well-connected, affluent Jews, the men boasting a distinguished war record, they had long escaped the treatment received by other Jews. Through their connections they had escaped early deportation. When they were deported, they went to Theresienstadt, the ghetto for *Prominente*, prominent Jews. And now, along with other inmates of that ghetto, they still had a limited, special worth, essentially as propaganda. But at each stage, the value of their prominence had diminished. Initially, it had ensured them relative freedom and prosperity. Then, in 1941–3, in increasingly straitened circumstances, they had continued to enjoy the privilege of the use of part of their home and part of their savings. Then, in Theresienstadt, privilege had spared them the extermination camps. Now it meant just a few extra months of life in excruciating conditions.

What sense can they have made of it all? Would Siegfried have seen in the 'Germanness' of the enterprise around him the ultimate repudiation of his cherished beliefs? Or would he simply have shaken his head at the circumstances which had allowed a band of criminals to subvert the strengths of his German homeland? Throughout her life, Marianne tortured herself wondering how they had reacted to the concentration camps. Yet at no time did she mention what must have been the single, dazzling ray of light for her parents: that they went to the gas chambers knowing their daughter had escaped and was probably still alive.[69] One of them had managed to outwit the Nazis. From our perspective, Marianne's survival must have been their sole consolation. Yet Marianne seemed to take no comfort from this at all.

Alfred and Lore in Theresienstadt

Meanwhile, the rest of the family was still in Theresienstadt. Anna Rosenberg died of 'old age', as Erna Ogutsch put it, three weeks after her daughter's deportation.[70] Both Alfred and Oe found useful jobs to do. Alfred supervised the queues at the post counter, where parcels were collected. This explains the frequency with which he managed to send post out to Grete Sander. With assistance from Herr Ogutsch, Oe was able to gain a position in a children's home. She moved in and took charge of about fifteen boys. According to Erna Ogutsch, who worked as a nurse across the way and spent much time with Oe in the summer of 1944, Oe found genuine fulfilment in her work. How much contact Alfred and Oe had with each other, we do not know.

In March 1944, Alfred Strauss wrote a card acknowledging receipt of a parcel.[71] A month later, he sent a lengthier postcard, which yet again sat for three months before it was sent off:[72]

Alfred and Lore in happier times

Dear Frau Sander,

I acknowledge with thanks the packet sent from Lisbon to our brother. He and his family are not here. We three are healthy and hope the same is true of you and your family. Aunt Anna died 8.1.1944 after a short illness. My wife and her mother were with her to the last. Have you heard from Siegfried and his wife? We would be very happy to hear from you very soon. Many thanks, dear Frau Sander, and best wishes also from my wife and my mother-in-law.

Your Alfred Strauss

In May or June 1944, Alfred received a postcard that Siegfried had sent from Birkenau in January. These delays! This was a time when it was possible for letters sent from German troops on the Eastern front to reach their destination within a few days. We also know that, in May, Alfred and Lore received a card from Richard, which seemed to suggest that he was on his own but gave no address.[73] On 3 June, Alfred wrote to Frau Sander:[74]

I hope that my card of April has reached you. For the parcels sent from Lisbon I thank you most warmly. They are very valuable to us. My brother wrote in January that he and his family are well and that they receive post punctually. We three are also well and hope that this is true of you and your family.

For now, accept my best wishes also from my wife and my mother-in-law!

Your Alfred Strauss

In July, he wrote again:[75]

Dear Frau Sander! I hope my cards of 7/6 and 24/6 have reached you. Have you heard anything from my brother? What else do you hear from our relatives? Please tell my cousin Hugo that we are delighted with his Lisbon parcels, which are very valuable to us. Please send best wishes to all our loved ones, accept our thanks and good wishes for you and your family from my wife, my mother-in-law and myself.

Alfred's postcard of August 1944 was anxious that letters sent to his brother should have his birth date on the parcel. In all probability, though, Siegfried was already dead:[76]

Dear Frau Sander, I hope that you and the family are well and I can report the same of us. You will have received my last card of 24/7. For the parcels of sardines from Lisbon which we were particularly delighted to receive, many thanks. If you write to my brother in Birkenau do not forget his date of birth (24.IV.91).[. . .]

A short card, dated 18 September 1944, confirmed that they still had no news of Siegfried and family.[77] It was Alfred's last communication.

I tried to contact Grete Sander and her family to find out what it had meant to them. I learned that Grete's nephew, Paul Alsberg, had been Chief Archivist for the Israeli government, had done some work on the family tree, and might have information. He told me that Grete herself, 'an extraordinarily active and intelligent woman,' had died, but her daughter, Erna Morting, was still living in Sweden.[78] I wrote to Mrs Morting in Sundbyberg to ask her what she remembered. But other than a fascinating snippet of information about the Strausses' Swiss bank accounts and a rather sad hint that there had been recriminations from Marianne about money after the war, she could add little. Her closing comment was that she, her husband and her mother had been in such financial difficulties during the war that there was little they could do other than send some parcels to deported relatives. Clearly, it was impossible to have survived the Holocaust and not feel guilty.

I also telephoned Gershon Ellenbogen, but, as the gay tone of his original letter implied, he had passed on the postcards without realizing what they were and was rather taken aback to discover fifty years later that he had been so casual with the last signs of life from Theresienstadt and Auschwitz. Typically, Marianne had never explained what he had given her.

The deportation of Alfred and Lore

It is not clear why the closing stage of the war should have seen another major wave of deportations from Theresienstadt. The Nazis probably felt some fear of the former Jewish military officers in the camp. Most of the officers were now deported.[79] Whatever the reason, the new wave of deportations began on 28 September. Because those dispatched in the first of the transports were selected for work fitness, it was widely believed within Theresienstadt that they really were going to some new camp or labour centre.[80] During the journey, the men were enjoined to send their wives postcards confirming that they had reached their ostensible destination and that food and accommodation were good and the work not too harsh. In reality, the transports, as before, were going to Auschwitz-Birkenau. Over the next few weeks, a whole series of transports followed, the last on 23 and 28 October. The scale of the operation is clear from the figures: on 28 September there were still 29,481 people in Theresienstadt, a month later only 11,077.[81]

On 29 September, eleven days after writing his last postcard, Alfred was deported. By the time the authorities deigned to frank and send his missive, not only Alfred but Lore and her mother too had gone to Auschwitz. Frau Ogutsch wrote to Marianne that when Lore was included on one of the very last transports out of Theresienstadt (on 9 October[82]), Lore's mother Else volunteered to go with her.

The end of two journeys

When the final Theresienstadt transports arrived in Birkenau, they were subject to a selection. We do not know if Alfred survived it, but Else Dahl cannot have done. In Marianne's letter to Hugo and Grete Strauss dated January 1946, she assumed that Alfred, Oe and Else had all died in Birkenau. But later that year, Marianne told me, Erna Ogutsch wrote to her from a hospital in Sweden, where she had ended up after liberation, completely emaciated and almost dead. According to Marianne, Frau

Ogutsch had been in Birkenau and knew that Oe had been selected to work and dispatched to some distant concentration camp:[83]

'She witnessed how my aunt was shot by the SS on the retreat. As the Russians were marching forward, they [the SS] emptied the concentration camps of the ones who were still there and drove them away, and whoever sat down by the wayside was shot. And apparently she just couldn't make it and she just sat down and they shot her. And I think a few miles later the people who were still alive – within a matter of probably hours – were rescued, they were liberated. So she really could, just for a matter of a few hours, have survived the war. That is the only story I have of all these near relations where I know what happened up to the end.'

Oe 'was not a well woman ever', Marianne pointed out, 'but she was pretty tough and resilient, so I think that if it hadn't been for that, she might well have been here even now. She was born I think in 1906 or 1909[84] and so there would certainly have been the possibility that she would still be around.' Marianne told me that Frau Ogutsch said Oe's last words to her had been, 'tell Alfred what happened to me'.[85] Marianne said she would find Erna Ogutsch's letter for me, but never did. I rather think she could not bear to look for it.

Though Vivian and I had gone through most of the papers in her house, we failed to find the Ogutsch letter. But we did find a number of contradictory references to Oe's death. In the 1950s, another survivor, Frau Julia Böcker, made a rather different statement:[86]

Declaration under oath

I saw Frau Lore Strauss from Essen, earlier resident Hufelandstrasse 23, arrive in the concentration camp in Auschwitz. All occupants of this transport were gassed immediately after their arrival.

I can say with certainty that Frau Lore Strauss, whom I knew from Essen, was among the people who were gassed on 22 November 1944.

This report simply cannot be true. We know that Oe left Theresienstadt on 9 October and that the gassings stopped in Auschwitz on 2 November 1944. We have already seen that the same witness made an inaccurate statement regarding family possessions.[87] It is of course possible that Oe had been killed after disembarking from the October transport. According to H. G. Adler, there were only twenty-two survivors of the 1,600 people on the transport that left for Auschwitz on 9 October 1944.[88] But even this figure is a little suspect. We know that other healthy younger people were selected for work from this transport.

In 1978, Marianne filled out 'pages of testimony' for Yad Vashem. These recorded the deaths of her parents and brother at Auschwitz, date probably June 1944, and of her grandmother at Theresienstadt, date unknown. Evidently, she had forgotten by this point that Anna died in January 1944. For Alfred, she had put a question mark next to the date of death, followed by 1944, but for Oe's place of death she had entered Treblinka or Maidanek 1945. Treblinka, however, had been shut down as a killing centre after the 1943 uprising and Maidanek was not a destination for Jews sent from Auschwitz in the last months of its existence. So neither of these could be correct. It suggested that during the 1970s Marianne had lost track of the letter describing the death of her aunt.[89]

In the 1980s, Marianne received another set of Yad Vashem memorial pages, this time in German and sent by the Alte Synagoge in Essen. Marianne dutifully filled out this set as well. For her parents and brother, this time she did not guess at a date but wrote simply that they had been transferred from Theresienstadt to Auschwitz and had been recorded as dead in May 1945. She recalled the precise date of her grandmother's death, and for Oe she wrote that she had been shot by the SS at Treblinka in the final days of the war.[90] As noted already, this is not possible since Treblinka no longer existed.

In the very last plastic bag of papers, the one in which we also found Ernst's ring, Vivian and I finally found Frau Ogutsch's letter, which indeed contained many details of the Strausses' experience in Theresienstadt. What Erna Ogutsch's letter did not contain was the one item Marianne had described to me, namely the account of Oe's death. Indeed, it could hardly have done so – Frau Ogutsch had never left Theresienstadt, and when she wrote to Marianne it was not from Sweden but from a DP camp in Bavaria.

But the plastic bag contained another letter, dated May 1 1946 from Ludwig Ansbacher and his wife Selma.

Ludwig explained the coincidence which had brought them news of Marianne:[91]

> *Your best friend Trude Schloss, who was with you in Berlin, went from here to Bremerhaven and from there to America. Her uncle, a good friend of mine, was with her. We talked; he said here is my only surviving relative. I asked the girl where she was from, she said I come from Essen. Can you imagine what I was feeling? I asked her then, and as luck would have it she was able to tell me about you. I went home straight away and told Aunt Selma; naturally she was very excited.*

Selma Ansbacher added that their daughter Sigrid had been deported from Theresienstadt a few days after Oe and her mother. On 22 December 1944, Selma and Ludwig, still in Theresienstadt, had received a letter from Sigrid sent on 19 October. Through an agreed secret code, they were able to figure out that Sigrid was in Auschwitz. Sigrid had written that she had met Oe there. Selma continued:

> *When we were liberated by the Russians and the war came to an end, we knew that something awful had taken place in Auschwitz. We arrived in Frankfurt on 22 June and found none of our dear children here. But let me tell you straight away that Sigrid is alive and has been in Sweden since July last year. But our dear Heinz never came back. I know that you are on your own. How often we talked about you in Theresienstadt. Your parcels all arrived and gave your loved ones much pleasure. We were together every day.*

The next section of the letter made clear that it was the Ansbachers' daughter who had been working with Lore:

> *Now I have to tell you something very, very sad. We have been in contact with our Sigrid since last October. We discovered through Julius, my husband's brother in America, that Sigrid was alive and Sigrid discovered through America that we had been saved. Sigrid wrote and told us her awful story, all the places she was taken. She was with aunt Lore until 24 January 1945 in Kursbad b/ Trachenburg über Breslau.*

Frankfurt den 1. Mai 1946
  Liebe Marianne!
Wir erfuhren von einem Fräulein Trude
Schlass durch einen Zufall. Deine Adresse.
Wir freuen uns dass Du Gott sei Dank am
Leben bist. Erinnerst Du Dich unser? Mein
l. Mann ist der Vetter Deines l. Vaters
u. Onkel Alfred und waren wir in
Theresienstadt mit Deinen l. Eltern u.
Richard u. Tante Lore u. Onkel Alfred
zusammen. Wir kamen schon 1 Jahr
vorher mit unserer Sigrid dorthin.
Leider kamen alle Deine Lieben schon
sehr bald nach transdwärts und zwar am
18. Dez. 1943. Deine l. Grossmutter ist
bald darauf in Theres. gestorben. Im Mai
1944 kam einmal eine Karte an Onkel
Alfred von l. Richard. Wir entnahmen
daraus, dass er allein ist. aber wir wuss-
ten damals nicht genau, wo er ist, den
es war keine Adresse angegeben Anfangs
Oktober 1944 kam Onkel Alfred weg u.
Tante Lore mit ihrer Mutter kam 14 Tage

Extract from the Ansbachers' letter

The letter went on to explain that Sigrid had gone from Auschwitz to the Gross-Rosen concentration camp. Even before this letter emerged, I had begun to think that Gross-Rosen might have been Lore's destination. Much less well-known than some of the other camps, it has begun to receive more attention from Western historians only in the last few years. In the latter stages of the war its network of satellite work camps made it one of the largest labour constellations in Germany. The use of female labour (almost exclusively Jewish women) in the Gross-Rosen satellites began in 1944. Thirty-nine female labour camps were created in the course of that year and another three in 1945, absorbing some 26,000 women prisoners.[92] I already knew of one inmate, Felice Schragenheim, who had been on the same transport as Oe and was sent to a Gross-Rosen sub-camp, as had been two survivors of Birkenau family camp, Ruth Klüger and her mother.[93]

My problem was that Kursbad does not appear as a location in any accounts of the camp. But a number of indications began to suggest that the Ansbachers had got the name slightly wrong. Under the rubric of 'Operation Bartold', four new sub-camps of Gross-Rosen were created in late autumn 1944 to build fortifications against the advancing Red Army. These four camps were Birmbäumel, Hochweiler, Kurzbach and Schlesiersee. In addition to the similarity of the name, other facts suggested that it was Kurzbach and not Kursbad that marked the end of Lore's journey. Kurzbach, which was indeed north of Breslau, was opened in November 1944, around the time that Lore would have been transferred from Auschwitz, and it closed 20–21 January, just when Sigrid remembered her having been killed.[94] Other sources confirm that the inmates of Birnbäumel, Christianstadt, Hochweiler and Kurzbach were marched to Bergen Belsen, where Sigrid ended up.[95]

The 1,000 women in Kurzbach came mainly from Hungary and Poland. German Jews such as Lore Strauss and Sigrid Ansbacher were in the minority.[96] The women were quartered in the stables of a large estate, surrounded by barbed wire and watched over by Wehrmacht soldiers. Because they worked in the open, visible to the general population, they wore civilian clothes rather than striped convict uniforms. Like Sigrid Ansbacher, most of the women were in their early twenties or even younger. But even for them the extremely taxing work must have been barely manageable in their undernourished state. For Oe, it must have been torture, as testimony preserved in Yad Vashem confirms.[97] The women knew, though, that prisoners deemed no longer capable of working were either shipped back to Auschwitz or sent to the Gross-Rosen main camp, where they were murdered by injection. The only redeeming feature compared with other camps was that, by and large, the female overseers in the women's camps seem not to have murdered inmates for sport or for minor misdemeanours.[98]

Towards the end of January, the Red Army moved closer and all four Operation Barthold camps were shut down. Selma wrote:

> Then the Russians came and the inmates had to flee with the SS. Aunt Lore had typhus and lay in the sick bay and here comes the terrible thing, Marianne; Aunt Lore was shot. Sigrid wrote that it was terrible. Aunt Lore said she should tell everything to Uncle Alfred. Our Sigrid suffered terrible things, she was in the KZ Gross-Rosen, Mauthausen and finally in Bergen-Belsen. There she got typhus and arrived in Sweden in July with a weight of five stones, a girl of seventeen.

The effect of reading this letter was heightened by the fact that it was virtually the last document left to find. It seemed the end of two journeys. That the letter was so well hidden away conveyed anew how dreadfully painful the memory had been. For several weeks I was involved in a fruitless search for Kursbad, unaware that the letter itself contained a misremembering. But I knew immediately that Oe's fate was not quite what Marianne had told me. As in her memory of Ernst's fate, so here she had gently embellished the original with a literary touch. Unlike her treatment of Ernst's death, though, she had not rendered Oe's more brutal. Rather, by moving Oe's death from the camp's sick bay, still some months away from the end of the war, to a forced march just a few hours before liberation, she had intensified the picture of senseless waste.

Living with a Past in Hiding

From an early stage in my conversations with Marianne I knew that I wanted to ask her about her post-war life in Britain. Having read many survivor autobiographies or biographies which took their subjects' lives no further than the liberation or the end of the war, I had often felt I was being offered a false sense of closure. It was obvious that survivors' problems long outlived the war.[1] Indeed, the condition of *being* a survivor was one that existed only after 1945.[2] For me, Marianne's post-war life raised many questions. I wanted to understand how a woman with the courage to take on the Nazis had felt confining her strength and talent to her home and family. I wanted to understand the irony behind her comment that 'the Jewish festivals are celebrated in this house'. Had she been a martyr to her Jewishness all her life? And I wanted to understand the tragedy, the unspeakable (the word comes up unbidden) tragedy, that having lost her parents and her brother Marianne should lose her daughter. In short, I wanted to understand how Marianne's past reached into her post-war life.

The problem was that these issues, or most of them, were precisely the reason why Marianne did *not* want to talk about her life in Liverpool. She had brought me in to commemorate the heroism of her friends and helpers, to remember her lost family and to create a memorial for Ernst. She saw no logic in advancing beyond 1945 and, indeed, believed it would cause pain to others if she did so. I tried to persuade her that to understand her persecution one had to make sense of the way the past had hounded her to the present. Reluctantly, Marianne accepted that we might look at some specific aspects of what the Germans call *Vergangenheitsbewältigung*, dealing with the past. Restitution, for example, was an area on which she provided information. But we were not to pry into her private life in Britain. Nearly all my arguments with her, and subsequently with Vivian, were about determining the precise boundary between *Vergangenheitsbewältigung* and privacy.

Evidence of a settled life

Marianne's first months in England were far from easy. Encountering Basil's parents, with whom she and Basil lived in 1947, was a culture shock. She found their form of Orthodox piety very different from her own liberal background and their attitudes very old-fashioned. 'To my in-laws a dowry was very important. Quite incredible! They had attitudes which go back to ghetto years, ghetto life. A dowry was something that was quite essential.'[3] If I had known more about her own family background at that stage, I would have pointed out that Siegfried had not objected to his 60,000 marks, either.

Basil and Marianne soon moved into an attic flat, but it was the 'most primitive flat you can imagine', Marianne said. There were 'tiny little English fireplaces for the servants' quarters. There was no fridge, no proper heating and these two small open fireplaces. There was a very primitive bathroom with a gas heater which exploded now and then with great aplomb and terrified the wits out of me. The water tank in one of the rooms (for the whole house) made a great deal of noise.' Every morning, the heavily pregnant Marianne had to go down to the cellar and carry two buckets of coal up several flights of stairs. Never having learned to light a coal fire, her first efforts were a disaster. Someone told her to fan it, but nothing happened. In the end, she used more fire lighter than coal. It was an icy cold winter and droplets froze on her nose.[4]

Over 1946–7, Marianne taught German literature at what would now be A-level standard in a Liverpool girls' school. Despite her fractured English and their fractured German, all passed. She stopped working, however, after Vivian was born in November 1947. It was a lonely period. Basil was studying hard to become a consultant physician and had little free time. Marianne did not get on with her parents-in-law. Being on the top floor, it was hard to get the baby any fresh air. She remembered one day leaving the pram in the garden while she sat upstairs. Looking down, she saw that Vivian had managed to crawl out of the pram and was hanging by his harness. How she managed to get down the stairs so fast, she did not know!

All this was delivered as a fond recollection of early adversity, not imbued with any existential misery. What came through, in fact, was how quickly Marianne adapted to her new life. Married to someone settled in England, she avoided many of the problems of survivors finding their feet in a new country. The English language came easily to her – she learned 'with great aplomb', she might have said. Just nine months after leaving Germany she dreamed in English for the first time. When she woke up, she knew she had arrived.

I had been prepared to see her domestic role as the trap from which she had *not* managed to escape. But I soon realized that Marianne did not see her life this way at all. On the contrary, creating her own family was a mission she took up gladly. In 1949, she and Basil bought a pleasant four-bedroomed semi in the Allerton district of Liverpool, where she was to spend the rest of her life. In January 1951 their second child, Elaine, was born. Marianne's cousin René, writing to her in 1950, was clearly surprised by the speed with which she had settled down:[5]

> *I am personally astonished that you are buying a new house. From my perspective, I have put my savings in liquid form, i.e. money. My idea is never again to allow oneself to be settled anywhere. But in England perhaps one thinks differently about this problem.*

One might observe that attitudes towards house-buying were different in England and France and Marianne's gesture was therefore less signifi- cant than it appeared to René. But Marianne really did settle into her new life in Britain with remarkable speed and enthusiasm. She and Basil soon acquired a circle of close friends in Liverpool that lasted forty years or more. By marrying a 'local', Marianne had gained access to a settled circle, many of them from Liverpool's sizeable Jewish medical scene. The Millers and the Benders, whom I interviewed, were soon enormously impressed with Marianne's learning and culture, her knowledge of English literature (which put most English speakers to shame) and her expertise on antiques.[6] The Millers told me that Marianne knew England much better than they did. No matter how obscure the village, Marianne would know where there was a nice coffee shop and the address of a good antique dealer.[7]

For his part, Vivian recalled a rich and stable family life. Like any good 1950s middle-class family, they always ate a proper dinner together. Friends of the children remembered the family dinners as good-humoured, civilized affairs where one had to be on one's best behaviour. Not only Vivian but also other family and friends confirmed Marianne's prowess and creativity as a cook.

Many authors have commented on the fact that in the USA it is easy to be an immigrant and still feel American, but in England (or indeed in Britain) to have a foreign accent or manner was, until recently at least, to be clearly not English.[8] Marianne certainly retained a foreign air. Vivian remembered feeling quite protective of her (particularly in relation to schoolmates) because of this. Yet Marianne did not appear displaced or stateless. There is no evidence that she felt cut adrift as she had in post-war Germany. Rather, she conveyed an air of gracious cosmopolitanism.[9]

A remarkable coincidence brought me some extra insights into Marianne's family life in the 1950s and 60s. In autumn 1998, I asked my final-year students at Keele University to look at some of the contradictory testimony from Marianne's fellow school pupils. Before the seminar, one of the students, Rob Gray, knocked on my office door and said that the name Marianne Ellenbogen had rung a bell. He had checked with his parents and it was as he had thought: for almost the entire 1950s and 1960s his father and aunts had grown up literally next door to the Ellenbogens. I travelled to London to interview Rob's father, David Gray, and to Romsey to talk to his aunt, Jane Dalton, about their memories of the Ellenbogen family.[10] Jane, for a while a close friend of Elaine, remembered Marianne in the early 1960s as a glamorous and slightly racy mum. There were exciting trips for Jane and Elaine in

Modelling photo from the 1950s

The proud parent – Marianne and family in Stratford

Marianne's convertible, for example, or they were left to enjoy themselves at a funfair and once, famously, Marianne used contacts to get them tickets to a Beatles concert.[11]

Like many German-Jewish émigrés, Marianne missed aspects of German life and retained a soft spot for German landscape. She quoted Heine's dictum to me:

> *Think I of Germany in the night*
> *I sleep no more until daylight*

Marianne felt a painful mixture of nostalgia and aversion for locations that had been frequented by her family. In 1970 she and Basil visited Ahlen for the first time since the war. They went to the Dutch resort of Nordwijk, too, and stayed at the family's regular old hotel, the Haus der Dönen. The hotel was being converted to flats and not much frequented but was still beautiful, 'still very grand' and absolutely 'bang on the sea'. Marianne rarely went back to Essen. Returning there in response to an invitation to Essen's former Jewish citizens, she could not face the official reception.[12] Unlike other émigrés, however, she did have a way of maintaining links with Germany that were both strong and not too painful, namely through her relationships with the Bund. Warm correspondence with various Bund members continued up to her death. Some of her Bund friends visited her in Liverpool, others she met on occasional trips to Germany. Vivian remembered meeting Hanni Ganzer and others in the Black Forest.

Between secrecy and restitution

Towards the end of what proved to be our last lengthy conversation, I asked Marianne about her battle for compensation from the German government. Like most people, I had only a vague sense of what was involved. I assumed that 'it' was a single something which you managed to 'get' or not, though obviously the exact amount would depend on what you had lost and what you had suffered. But Marianne said that restitution became 'more and more involved and difficult, the more they unravelled the whole thing. The law was still very raw, very much at the beginning. It was all very difficult, very involved; nothing was very clear. Oh God, it went on for years.'

The process took a heavy toll:[13]

'I remember sitting up night after night, writing reams and reams of letters. I've still got all that correspondence lying around, about restitution. Absolutely dusty old things lying around ... It went on for years and years and years and years and years. I went to Germany every eight months or so to keep an eye on things and speed things up ... There were many court cases.'

It was only after Marianne's death, when Vivian began to unearth those 'absolutely dusty old things' lying around, that I realized that I had had absolutely no conception of what was involved. Scattered around the house were enough files, folders, boxes, stuffed envelopes and loose piles of papers to form a private archive. And as I waded through the letters, affidavits and court proceedings, something of the

Marianne and family visit the Bund in 1963.

simply enormous demands of the process began to emerge. There were demands on her purse (because, as in any legal process, there was outlay before compensation), demands on her time, demands on her energy and health and, above all, emotional demands. The first letters date from September 1945, when Marianne applied in Düsseldorf for an advance to help re-equip her room.[14] The last legal letters date from the 1970s. For almost thirty years restitution was on her mind, with a particularly intense phase which extended from 1950 to the mid-1960s.

The problems were legion. The law itself began to take shape only in the late 1940s. Adequate legislation on many issues emerged only in the mid-1950s. Initially, Marianne used British lawyers who, in turn, dealt through German colleagues, and the dual chain in an uncertain law field proved disastrous. It was not until 1956, after a most acrimonious correspondence and a trip to Germany, that she finally ditched her 'worse than useless' lawyers (a judgement which the documentation suggests not to have been unfair) and engaged Carl Hermann, a distinguished advocate in Cologne who was handling restitution cases for the big Jewish concerns of Ullstein and Wertheim.[15]

By the mid-1950s, the Strausses' major property sales had been dealt with, but for the rest work had only just begun. An idea of the scale involved can be gained from a far from exhaustive list her lawyer presented her in 1958 of still unresolved claims:[16]

Claims in the name of Siegfried Strauss
Loss of liberty; Household goods; Gold and silver; Insurance policies;
Special payments (Reich Flight Tax; Judenvermögensabgabe;
Other payments, including payments to the Jewish community, social payments, payments arising from racially based tax rates);
Transfer damages (damages arising from the emigration to Sweden; damages arising from transfers to Cuba); Professional losses, including damages arising from enforced closure of the business.

Claims in the name of Regina Strauss
Loss of liberty; Gold and silver goods; Judenvermögensabgabe; Securities.

Claims in Marianne's own right
Loss of liberty; Damages in her education and training; Damages to health; Gold and silver; Judenvermögensabgabe; Damages to her career.

Claims in the name of Richard Strauss
Gold and silver; Damages to his education and training;[17] Judenvermögensabgabe.

Sundry other issues were also listed at the end. Not included in the list are the property matters already dealt with as well as all the claims being handled by René Wolf's lawyers in which he and Marianne were co-beneficiaries – particularly with regard to the estates of Alfred and Lore Strauss and Leopold Strauss. On these, too, Marianne was regularly consulted and had to provide declarations, estimates and lists.

But what constituted the biggest challenge was the mix of moral, emotional and psychological problems interlaced with the purely legal complexities. Marianne was torn between needing to delve into the documents and wishing to forget what had happened, and torn too between her desire to preserve the family wealth and her distaste at haggling over the remains.[18] Particularly painful for her were cases where her memory or her experiences were challenged. For example, Marianne wished to claim compensation for her loss of liberty, both as a wearer of the yellow star from 1941 to 1943 and for her years underground. Marianne noted 'with amazement' in January 1957 that, despite the well-known Nazi directive of September 1941, the Restitution authorities in Essen wanted *proof* she had worn the yellow star between 19 September 1941 and 31 August 1943.[19] However, the job of finding witnesses to prove something that Nazi law had required was small beer compared with what followed. Hermann wrote apologetically to Marianne in June that, based on recent court decisions, the official at the Düsseldorf Restitution Office believed that Marianne's underground years did not constitute loss of liberty or living under inhuman conditions. The official would, however, accept her claim if she could prove that she had worn the yellow star while on the run.[20] Not surprisingly, Marianne could scarcely believe what she was reading. To have worn the yellow star while passing as an Aryan would have been madness. She responded by return with a moving and powerful account of the stresses of life underground.[21]

Nevertheless, on 5 December the state rejected Marianne's claim for compensation, arguing that the presence of her circle of friends and her ability to earn ration points by selling felt flowers meant that her life was not, as the law required, of or below the level of a prisoner.[22] In other words, Marianne's extraordinary courage in breaking through the constraints of wartime life was now being used to prove that the conditions had been bearable.[23] It was only by dint of further representations, which Marianne found enormously taxing and stressful, and a court hearing in May 1958, that a compromise was reached. And this was just one claim under one of the many headings of restitution.[24]

In some cases, the emotions of yesterday were aroused particularly acutely, and nowhere more so than with the family banker, Hammacher, and with the Jürgens. In the case of Hammacher, Marianne had already suffered the shock in the early post-war months of finding him ensconced in a flat with many of the family possessions. Now there was the question whether they had been purchased at a fair price or under duress. Hammacher, however, did have something to offer Marianne's lawyers – considerable help in tracing Deutsche Bank documentation about the transfer of family funds to Sweden. So Marianne was faced with the problem of whether to accept a compromise figure from Hammacher for the family goods he had received, in recognition of his efforts in tracking down the funds.[25] After some months, Marianne agreed to the compromise, though the tone of her English solicitor's letter to their German lawyer indicates the depth of her bitterness.[26]

The single most painful and upsetting case for Marianne had to do with the Jürgens. In the immediate post-war period, Marianne had gone to reclaim the furniture and trunks left in trust with them, but the Jürgens claimed that these were a gift from her parents. 'I had to get the authorities to come to the house and say you have to give it back. It was all really dreadful.'[27]

What was?

'Well, the way they behaved, it was so undignified, so absolutely awful, I felt, I really felt as if I was in the wrong, stealing what was really legally theirs, terrible, really terrible. Amazing how people can behave.'

In conversation, she returned to the Jürgens several times. She particularly resented that she should have been depicted as the importunate claimant, 'because it throws such a bad light on what's your right. So, that was all pretty awful. Really awful. And what hurt me most was that they didn't give me all the family portraits back.'

As I discovered from the documents, her claim against the Jürgens went on for years. From October 1950 we find a deposition by Frau Jürgens to the Office for Restitution, Essen, the only document I found among all the restitution papers that has Marianne's annotations all over it. Clearly, what was extraordinarily painful was that Maria Jürgens made public Marianne's poor relationship with her parents (something Marianne could scarcely deny) and used it to claim that Marianne had no knowledge of the arrangements between Regina Strauss and the Jürgens:[28]

The applicant, Frau Marianne Ellenbogen née Strauss, was not informed about the personal relationships I had with her parents, particularly as she was on very poor terms with them. At that time, I did the Strauss parents great favours without compensation. During the war, as the food supply, particularly for Jews, was very difficult, I kept them well supplied with food.

Here were all the burdensome strands of the past coming together. The mixture of truth and lies must have cut her to the quick. She had covered Maria Jürgens' statement with underlining and exclamation marks, often doubled, which grew ever larger through the document, until the final paragraph, which is adorned by two huge exclamation marks as large as the paragraph itself.

Restitution also imposed a strain on relations between the various branches of the family. She fell out with Adolf Rosenberg over the Ahlen inheritance (as indeed did Karl, who ended up taking legal action against his brother); with Hugo Strauss over money deposited in a US account; there were irritable exchanges with Lore's brother Ernst Dahl and an angry letter to Erna Morting about money Anna Rosenberg had deposited in Switzerland. Marianne's underlying feeling that the extended family had not done enough for her parents and brother no doubt influenced her attitude. Probably, too, she was deflecting the anger she felt towards her parents on to relatives who were a more acceptable target. Certainly, the documents suggest that on occasion she was less than indulgent towards her relatives. On the other hand, her many years of close co-operation with René Wolf proved an essential ingredient of her success. René's indefatigable efforts on both their behalfs in relation to Alfred and Lore often helped her with regard to her own claims. Given the similar situations of Alfred and Siegfried, often all her own lawyer had to do was simply duplicate René's successful applications.

Overall, Marianne pursued restitution with determination, perseverance and great success. Apart from René's assistance, she was also aided by the huge range of documentation the family had managed to deposit with the bank, the Jürgens and others. By 1967, when the last significant payments were handed over, Marianne had received many hundreds of thousands of Deutschmarks:

'I've not inherited this to squander it or use or do whatever with it but to hand it on, to make something with it. And that's really why I started buying antiques, selling antiques as well, not an awful lot but also selling. And investing the money so that I could feel that I had done right by my parents – that I had not done, what so often happens, that one generation builds up something and the next generation tears it down. That's what they usually say. . . . And I really do think that I haven't done too badly in that respect.'

She had been her father's daughter.

Silence and suffering

Looking at Marianne's ability to adapt to her new surroundings, the energy with which she threw herself into motherhood, her ease with the English language and culture, her circle of friends, the success with which she tackled the complexities of restitution, would anybody knowing her in the 1950s and 1960s have said that she was struggling to cope with the past? I think probably not. Vivian was hesitant about delving into the minutiae of his childhood, but it did not seem that Marianne had flinched every time she saw a policeman, or told her children always to have their passports with them, or kept a suitcase ready-packed in the bedroom – characteristics which many other second-generation survivors noted of their parents.

As in the war years, she gave no impression of being vulnerable or a victim. She was formidable. I certainly found her so. Even in our last interview, weeks before her death, Marianne never gave me cause to feel that I was powerful or that she was fragile. She was very self-controlled and, as I and others experienced, quite ready to control others.

Was this self-control, though, merely the iron lid on boiling turmoil beneath? Marianne certainly did show signs of stress. Up to the 1980s, she was an extremely heavy smoker. Despite her asthma, she would smoke upwards of forty cigarettes a day. Most of her acquaintances also commented on her rows with Basil. But neither smoking heavily nor shouting at one's spouse are the preserves of a Holocaust survivor. More significant as an indicator of Marianne's pain (and of the control she had to exert) was her silence. Just as in the immediate post-war period so now, Marianne hid her past behind an almost complete blackout. Even those closest to her found their questions deflected and discouraged. I was never able to ask Basil what he had or had not learned. But from the urgent instructions on the packets full of letters that Marianne had sent on ahead of her in 1946 – 'Marianne, private, not to open' – through to her unwillingness to include Basil in our conversation in 1989, I deduced that she was little more forthcoming with him than with others. To close family friends, the Millers, the Benders and other relatives she imparted, at best, snippets of information. And of course, the wartime letters and diaries lay untouched and unread for forty years. Indeed, Marianne's habit of secrecy, of divulging past information a nugget a time, became such a habit that it extended to every area of her life. Her grandchildren would find her as loath to disclose her chopped-liver recipe as to provide information about Nazi Germany for a school project. (She *did* provide a recipe for chopped liver. But they discovered that it lacked her secret ingredients.)

Yet the past would not disappear. Marianne's accounts and memories have already made clear her complicated feelings towards her family. They were compounded by her sense that she had let the Bund down after the war. Bruno Bettelheim reminds us that rescued Jews often felt they had to prove they were worthy of having been saved.[29] Marianne said:

'After the war, after it was finished I always felt that I let the Bund down, because I took on an entirely humdrum, bourgeois existence bringing up a family and not really doing anything else – not being, you know, a politically active person, which I had intended to be after the war. You know, when I was in Düsseldorf first after the war I joined the party and did whatever I thought was expected of me. I didn't enjoy it, but I felt I had that obligation. *I* had taken on that commitment[. . .]But I couldn't say I was committed – that I was convinced that that was the way for me. When I got married, and I really had no choice in taking that step, I felt I also have a life to live at last and I have to live the sort of life that means something to me, bringing up my children. I always felt guilty about it because it didn't leave me any sort of leeway, any time for doing something else, which I knew would have been important to them [the Bund]. They never *said* anything. But I felt I let them down.'

For Vivian and Elaine, the past made itself felt above all as unearthly, heavy silence. They learned early not to ask questions for fear of upsetting their mother. They dimly sensed but could not see the forces pressing down on Marianne's shoulders. Vivian said that as a youngster he was aware of his mother's guilt-feelings towards her parents, and above all her brother. But when I asked him why he thought this, he volunteered only that that was what *he* would feel were he in her situation. The one thing he did strongly remember was his mother sitting up during the night, typing away at her restitution correspondence, and himself having a keen sense that she was engaged in something burdensome and painful.

Jane Dalton, Elaine's friend and neighbour, gave me an extraordinary, brief glimpse into Marianne's inner world. During the summer months when the windows were open, she said, you would hear Marianne crying out loudly in German in her sleep. This was to repeat itself several times over the years. On the other side of their road lived the German consul in Liverpool and his wife (with whom Marianne was on very friendly terms). Sometimes, the consul's wife would have nightmares too, and fearful German would echo from both sides of this suburban Liverpool street.

Yet almost as arresting as this image was the fact that Vivian had no memory of his mother's nightmares at all. Indeed, he challenged the assertion and I had to go back to Jane to confirm it. If Jane was right, this seemed to me a telling example of the way the children learned to hide from signs of their mother's pain.

Mastering the past

Thinking about Marianne's life after the war made me look again at the wartime experiences that had now become memories. Clearly, her situation could not be compared with that of a survivor of the camps. She had not suffered the arbitrary brutality, the powerlessness or the shame and degradation which were the camp inmate's daily fare.[30] She had not had to endure seeing the extremes to which people were driven in order to survive. Nor did she have to reconstruct her essential humanity after the war.[31] No one was more conscious of this difference than Marianne herself:[32]

'That was something I always feared when thinking of ending up in a concentration camp – how I would behave, whether I'd behave like a civilized human being, how long it would take before I wouldn't care any more how civilized I was, and survival become the main thought, as it did for so many. That you just did anything in order to survive . . .'

The difference between camp survivors' memories and Marianne's was reflected in the quality of her testimony. Her flow of speech was not impaired by memory, as was that of some survivors.[33] What she had to tell did not defy her capacity of expression.[34] She spoke, and wrote, when she had to, smoothly and articulately. She did not weep in the telling or pause mid-sentence, nor did she have to adopt the mechanical voice of the automaton.

Yet her own past had been traumatic enough. Bruno Bettelheim could have been describing her when he wrote that to be considered a survivor it was not necessary to have been in the camps:[35]

Having to live for years under the immediate and continuous threat of being killed for no other reason than that one is a member of a group destined to be exterminated, and knowing that one's closest friends and relatives are indeed being killed – this is sufficient to leave one for the rest of one's life struggling with the unsolvable riddle of 'Why was I spared?'

A central feature of Marianne's psychological predicament was that her traumatic memories revolved remarkably little around what had happened to herself. Her wartime friends had been astonished by the insouciance with which she brushed off the threats to her life and liberty. I myself sometimes found it hard to remember how much danger she had faced. In her testimony, Marianne devoted precious little emotional energy to describing the close shaves with police and Gestapo. The most detailed account of a near arrest came not from Marianne but from Meta Kamp. Instead, Marianne's most vivid and painful stories had to do with leaving or losing her family and fiancé. Almost equally powerful were the moments when Marianne learned of their fates. Even in her diary, it is only the news of her parents on the BBC that broke through the normal tone. And also in her diary, guilt already vied with fear as her predominant emotion.

Marianne's long years of silence over these incidents suggest that she fought to prevent the past from taking control of the present. But the way her memory altered events also suggests that the present reached back to try to take control of the past. All memory is subject to change. In inconsequential matters of information Marianne's memory was prone to the usual inaccuracies. But when she related incidents as if they had happened yesterday, incidents which seemed to be permanently etched into her consciousness, the differences between what she said and what I later learned to be true took on a different significance. Lawrence Langer has argued that it is inappropriate to talk about inaccuracy in Holocaust testimony and has talked of the survivor's 'insomniac memory' – the memory that never goes away.[36] But Marianne's memory suggests that even those traumatic memories which were always with her were subject to change. Moreover, the alterations followed certain common patterns, adding to my sense that what was happening in her mind was no accident.

One thing I'd noticed was that in a number of cases a kind of polarization had taken place in her testimony. On the one hand, there were small exaggerations or magnifications of experience. Particularly where there had been some traumatic event, the circumstances surrounding that event had often taken on slightly larger dimensions in Marianne's memory. Periods of time were doubled or trebled: the duration of her father's internment in Dachau after Kristallnacht in 1938 became in her memory six weeks; in reality it was three. Similarly, after her flight in 1943, her family was imprisoned in Essen just over a week; Marianne remembered the period as three weeks. Something true not only of her own testimony but that of other Jewish witnesses was that uniform wearers of very different provenance metamorphosed in memory into 'SS men'. Wehrmacht soldiers, railway officials, ordinary police on the trains and other figures became fused with the archetypal threat figure: the SS man. This was evident in both Marianne's and Imo Moszkowicz's memories of Christian Arras. On the other hand, in contrast to these forms of magnification, there were occasions where time had served to diminish or underplay past events. This was most marked in relation to the Bund, where Marianne's desire not to tarnish their memory had led her to forget or suppress the arguments and tensions that I discovered in the diary.

More interesting than this tendency of memory to expand or diminish the good and the bad, however, were the various points in her personal narrative where the chain of events, as described by her, did not match with the events as described by other sources. The most striking and consistent pattern was the reworking or obscuring of episodes of separation and loss. Marianne's memory was that she had accompanied Ernst to the barracks; in reality she had left him in his apartment. In her memory of her own escape, she believed she had slipped out of the house while the Gestapo men assessed the loot in the basement. In reality, she had asked them if she could get bread for the journey and had left the house while ostensibly in the kitchen. In her memory, she had heard on the BBC that her parents had already been murdered. She had forgotten the waiting period between the announcement and the date on which the gassings were due to take place. All these partings or farewells – *the* central traumas of Marianne's life – had subtly changed.

Marianne, it seemed, 'defused' traumatic and guilt-ridden partings by amending them. In Ernst's case, she adopted Hanna Aron's story and, in so doing, sought to delay the moment at which she had let Ernst go. In the story of her own escape, she again adopted a story – this time taking Pastor Keinath's attempted route out of the house for her own. For a while I wondered why escaping down the stairs and locating the Gestapo in the cellar had seemed preferable as a memory to asking for bread and slipping out of the kitchen. Did Marianne wish to deny the fact that her escape depended on a gesture of humanity from the Gestapo? It is possible, but unlikely, since she was very alive to the nuances of goodness and evil in those around her. I came to the conclusion that Marianne had invented an escape route that her brother could have taken with her. Both could have sneaked down the stairs whilst the Gestapo were in the cellar. Fetching bread from the kitchen was a ruse which allowed the escape of only one.

What was the point of these changes? Even if they had been true, would they have made her any less 'guilty'? From our perspective, she was not guilty anyway. From Marianne's perspective, even if she *had* slipped out of the house by a route which Richard could have taken, even if she *had* spent the night with Ernst, she would probably not have felt any less guilty after the war. She might well have felt the need to make other changes to cope with the past. The important thing was to impose some mastery on the moments that caused such pain.

In other words, it seemed to me that the inaccuracies in Marianne's memory were evidence of her pain and loss and a sign that she had sought to control the past within her, just as she sought to limit communication about it to the outside world. The stories had gently been changed into metaphors. As 'parables' of her and her family's fate they were very slightly more bearable.

As the past moved further and further away, the painful reliving of these separations began to be joined by a new emotion that she commented on several times, namely, a sense of disconnection from the past. The murders of her family and loved ones were not just senseless – they also began to become more remote. Probably this new 'parting', a separation enforced by time and distance, occasioned new feelings of guilt. Indeed, there are hints in the wartime diary entries that in relation to Ernst Marianne felt this guilt at 'letting go' of memory as early as 1944. So she began to embellish the stories of her loved ones' fates. Ernst's horrible accident became a medical experiment – just as Enrique, several thousand miles away in Buenos Aires, invented the image of the SS stabbing. Marianne 'rescheduled' the announcement of her parents' death to her birthday, whereas there were in fact some ten days between birthday and broadcast. She moved Lore's shooting forward from January 1945 to a few hours before liberation. We might well feel that the changes themselves were trivial – the original facts were awful and poignant enough. Here again, the 'gesture' of reworking the past, in this case to try and keep it alive, was the important thing.

I did not know whether such changes were deliberate or unconscious. But after Marianne died, I listened again to my conversation in September 1996 and was struck by a passage I had forgotten. Marianne was talking about returning with Basil to Noordwijk:[37]

'So, that was going back to traces of my childhood. I didn't like doing that ever. And, er, I never, I'm not a person who likes looking back anyway. I don't like to look back on what went on before, all these experiences, which are bound up with one's existence, because I always find I get very unsettled. I always think that one's memory's always different from the reality of it. And, not only is that *mostly* the case, it's not always, but you certainly are frightened of it that it's always the case, that you always are disappointed.'

Vivian, too, told me he recalled his mother making similar comments. It seemed to me, therefore, that Marianne saw herself as more the victim than the master of her memory.

Losing touch with the past

Once, when Marianne and I were looking at old photographs of the Strauss family in the Gruga Park or at Norderney, I asked her what she felt. She felt nothing, she said. It was like looking at somebody else's life. 'My life seems to be fragmented in so many different parts, it's as if it's not me.'[38] It made me realize anew how many abrupt changes in her environment and identity Marianne had endured between 1933 and 1946. As a child, she had been an acculturated Jew, not particularly aware of her Jewishness. The Nazis forced her Jewish identity to the fore, initially at school as a stigma, but more positively in the late 1930s and early 1940s as a source of identity (though still very much within a German intellectual and cultural framework). During 1941–2, she referred often to God, cited portions of the Bible, and observed the Jewish calendar. With the Bund, she had acted out three identities – the ordinary 'Aryan' for outside consumption, the fellow-comrade with her hosts, and the Jewish girl the regime sought to murder her for being. But while 'passing', she increasingly saw herself as the Bund fighter. After the war, she was torn between the activist and the exile. Finally, she came to Britain as Jewish wife and mother. Given so many transitions, it was not surprising that Marianne should feel disembodied.

It is perhaps also not surprising that Marianne should have lost sight of some of her earlier incarnations. Yet it did not seem accidental that the two 'selves' which had slipped from view were the religious self and the wartime Bund fighter. As far as the latter was concerned, I felt that what blocked Marianne's vision of the person she had been in the diary was the same thing that had made the diary so unexpected for *me*: namely, the public perception of the Holocaust that emerged after the war. As a 'claimant' to special treatment – post-war rations, access to Britain, restitution – Marianne had been encouraged to present herself as Jewish victim. When she broadcast, the BBC chose to label her as a young Jewess talking to the Germans. The family members with whom Marianne re-established contact after the war of course viewed her in this light. And in the Anglo-Jewish circles in which she moved in Liverpool, particularly once public discussion of the Holocaust became more open, this was how she must have been seen. In this post-war context, it was perhaps inevitable that her wartime self-image as Bund comrade should disappear from view.

Marianne's experience here may be a sign that people who survived by 'passing' as an Aryan were prone to wartime shifts in their self-image. We are familiar with the idea that Jewish children taken in by non-Jewish parents or institutions sometimes underwent a permanent change of identity and emerged from the war as Christians. Adults rarely underwent such permanent conversions. But it may be that, like Marianne, for a while they too did not just *pretend* to be someone else, but really took on a new identity, an identity which they then discarded some time after the war. (We can rarely observe such changes because we usually only have oral testimony at our disposal – and interviews are ill-placed to reveal to us what the memory has hidden. Marianne's diary provided a very unusual window into her wartime state of mind.) On the other hand, few Jews passing as Aryans had such positive role models to emulate as Marianne found in the Bund. Few had such a strong motive to take on a new identity within as well as without. Moreover, afterwards it was not only the pressures of victimhood that compelled Marianne to abandon her wartime role. Had Marianne been a man actively embraced during the war by a non-Jewish political grouping, it is hard to imagine an equivalent post-war reabsorption into an observant Jewish household. Such feats of domestic adaptation are seldom expected of men. So the discontinuities Marianne underwent seemed to me possibly unique, but certainly the experience of a woman.

Having abandoned the political activist, Marianne was also unable to reconnect to the earlier self who had talked and thought seriously about God. It was clear from things she said that the Bund's influence blocked her way back. In addition, the Ellenbogens' Jewishness was so alien to her own and Basil's expectations (though Basil was in no sense an intolerant man), so at odds with hers, that Jewish religious life became conflict-laden and difficult. And when Elaine died, Marianne gave up on religion completely.

Elaine's death

In June 1968, Marianne started a letter to her Bund friends. It was summer but she did not feel at all summery:[39]

> Even the sunshine cannot make the world look any more bearable today. Elaine has been in hospital for almost five months and there has been no improvement in her condition or her weight. As long as she is so negative in her attitude to life, all we can do is hope and pray.

Marianne talked about what a strange disease anorexia was and went on:

> My thoughts and well-being are so completely entwined with hers. Often I ask myself how we have managed to survive this long year, from one day to the next existing and hoping. And who knows for how much longer and what is still to come!
> And the world around us looks so sad, after . . .

And here the letter ended, unsent, joining the growing pile of papers in Marianne's house. On 29 September 1969, the eighteen-year-old Elaine died.

'For my own part', Vivian said of his mother, 'I felt it was an extreme injustice, I still do, for somebody who'd been through what she'd been through and lost what she'd lost, to have to suffer losing a child as well, although nobody should have to lose a child.'[40]

I was never able to probe the question of a connection between Elaine's death and Marianne's experiences.[41] The matter was too painful for

Marianne to discuss. Vivian's feelings were also still extremely raw. After Marianne's death, Vivian's distress was compounded by the discovery of letters Elaine had written but not sent to his parents during her stay in hospital. He had never read them, and his parents had denied any such letters existed. Twice Vivian told me a story in the first person, but when I quizzed him about it, he looked at me confused and said 'No, not me, her.' Vivian had theories about Elaine's death, but refused to discuss them with me. I raised the matter with some of the Ellenbogens' family friends and with Jane Dalton, Elaine's girlhood neighbour and friend. I even managed to gain contact with Elaine's psychiatrist. A family friend, he had been asked by Basil to destroy his case notes and could not bring himself to talk about it.

I do know that Elaine's death almost destroyed Marianne. She lost all remnants of her religious faith. The marriage survived, despite hints from Basil to Vivian that it went through a very rocky patch in the wake of the tragedy. But Marianne's life was never the same again.

How far Vivian was aware of it I do not know, but the loss of his sister represented an eerie reprise of his mother's loss of her brother Richard. Both mother and son had lost an eighteen-year-old younger sibling. Both felt that the child who had died had been brighter and more promising than them. Both felt enormous guilt towards their sibling – Marianne felt she had abandoned Richard; Vivian felt that his studies had prevented him giving Elaine enough attention when she was ill. For both Vivian and Marianne, the deaths also intensified a sense of guilt towards their parents. Vivian had long felt that he fell short of Basil and Marianne's academic expectations. After Elaine's death, it was incumbent upon him to do twice as well. Incumbent on him also to survive – in 1971 Vivian was involved in a near-fatal car crash and felt intense guilt at the burden of worry he was placing on his parents. And because he so often felt guilty, he, like his mother, was unable openly to acknowledge how important his survival had been for his parents' happiness. Just as the knowledge that Marianne was free must have been the one comfort for Siegfried and Ine as they faced their deaths, so I knew that in her later years Marianne's principal source of happiness was Vivian's family and children. And, of course, Vivian felt angry with his parents, as Marianne had with hers – she because they had held

Coffee and cakes with the Bund. Clockwise from left: Tove
Gerson, Else Bramesfeld, Doris Braune and Marianne

Richard back in the country for too long, he because they had withheld
much that Elaine had communicated to them. That anger could never
be properly dealt with for either of them.

Seeking recognition for the Bund

Another source of sadness in the latter part of Marianne's life was her
failure to have the Bund included among the ranks of 'righteous gentiles'.
In 1984, Lisa Jacob sought to have her Bund saviours recognized in Yad
Vashem, the museum and memorial to the victims of the Holocaust in
Jerusalem. Marianne supported the application and added those from
the ranks of her own helpers who were not on Lisa's list. But when the
Commission for the Designation of the Righteous considered the Bund
at its session on 28 January 1986, the outcome was inconclusive and the
matter fizzled away. In 1994, Basil and Marianne were in Jerusalem.
Lisa Jacobs having died, Marianne felt it was up to her to pursue the
case. In March, she and Basil met Mordechai Paldiel, the director of that

part of Yad Vashem which deals with recognition, to make another attempt. Again, she failed to achieve her goal.

Marianne was very bitter and disappointed to have again failed her friends, as she saw it, and I too felt frustrated on her behalf. When visiting Israel in 1998, I arranged to meet Paldiel to ask him about the case. Even before I met him, however, I already had a fair idea of what had gone wrong. The very peculiarities of the Bund that had helped it elude the Gestapo now perplexed those who were in a position to award it honours. I had already discovered that the major history of resistance and persecution in Essen did not mention the Bund – except to belittle reference to its achievements made in an earlier study.[42] It really was remarkable that in a thick, well-researched book focusing purely on Essen, the Bund should warrant nothing more than one condescending footnote. As a circle of friends that did not resemble a formal political grouping and as a dance movement in which seemingly unpolitical women played a major role, the Bund failed to fit the image of what resistance was supposed to look like.

What I now discovered was that Yad Vashem had made various enquiries in Germany to try to substantiate Lisa's claims – Dr Paldiel handed over the file of letters to prove the point – and all their enquiries had drawn a blank. No one knew of the Bund, the group no longer had links to senior people in the SPD who might have been able to speak for them, and the claims sounded so implausible. In addition, Dr Paldiel had not been clear who was gentile and who was Jewish in the Bund – an essential piece of information in a programme designed to reward gentiles. And, no doubt, as Dr Paldiel regretfully acknowledged, there had been probably been a degree of scepticism on their part, and they had let the matter drop.

Then something unexpected happened. Since I had indicated my willingness to help put the case together, Dr Paldiel handed me their file. 'Look through that,' he said, 'take copies of what you need, and do what you can.' Suddenly, the responsibility for pursuing the case rested on *me*. My first duty, I told him, was to this book, but afterwards I would indeed make the case to Yad Vashem. Perhaps I shall be able to fulfil Marianne's wish, albeit posthumously.

Marianne's story

While she was alive, Marianne herself never volunteered – and I never managed to elicit – any kind of judgement or view of her life overall. The forays we made into the post-war years were confined to particular details. She told no over-arching story. I suspected that, if Elaine had survived and prospered, Marianne might just have managed a happy ending. Her post-war family would have given some meaning to her wartime survival. But Elaine's death precluded this. Although Vivian and his children were very precious to Marianne, indeed in the final years her principal source of pleasure, she could not call her post-war life a success.

Marianne was an intensely private person. Even if she had been able to put a more positive gloss on her biography, she might well still have chosen to say little about her post-war life. Divulging *any* personal information came hard to her. During my final research trip in Germany, long after Marianne had died, I rang Liverpool and spoke to Vivian's wife. I was wondering what Marianne would have made of all the connections I had uncovered. 'She would have hated it,' was the friendly but regretful reply. Probably she would.

Shortly before completing the book, I learned from Vivian just how hard he had worked to keep his mother reasonably composed while talking to me. Looking back to the day of our first meeting, I was suddenly confronted by the blindingly obvious fact that it had been *Vivian* who had persuaded us to record her story. When Marianne and I had set off to have lunch with him, we had been considering what to do with Ernst's letters. By the time lunch was over, we were talking about a book. Recognising Vivian's role reassured me that the impulse for the book had come not just from me – but it did not stop me worrying whether I was doing what Marianne herself had wanted.

Yet ever since the war, Marianne knew there was a story she wanted to tell. In January 1946, sensing the communication gap between herself and her overseas relatives, Marianne wrote to Hugo and Grete Strauss:[43]

Last photo of Marianne, Liverpool, October 1996

What I went through, experienced and learned in those two years – one day I will write a whole book about it; a single fate that gives an insight into the general political, spiritual and cultural constellation of Germany in the Nazi period.

She never wrote her book, but it is surely significant that she threw none of her papers away. I learned from her friends that before I made contact Marianne had already been looking for someone to translate the documents. After we began working together, there had been the incident when Marianne dropped in on the Benders and launched into an account of her years underground. Clara Bender said to me, 'you could almost feel her heaving a sigh and saying I must get this down on paper.'[44] In January 1997, when visiting Mathilde Jamin at the Ruhrland Museum, I read a letter Marianne had written in December, just a week away from death. Marianne wrote of her desire 'to do justice to everything and not to leave too much unfinished business behind'. She went on:

Mark Roseman and I have been working through my memories.
Currently this is still in a very rough form and sketchy. We'll see
what form it takes. It is a binding duty and burdens me greatly.

What was it that Marianne wanted told? Above all, she was concerned to show the value of friendship and the heroism and selflessness of the Bund. When Marianne wrote to Mathilde Jamin about her 'binding duty' (doubtless the last time in her life she used the Bund's word *Verpflichtung*) it was to commemorate what her helpers had done. At the same time, she was not ashamed of admitting that she herself had been a fighter and that she herself had contributed to her survival. One of the titles she suggested for the book was the Dylan Thomas quotation, 'Do not go gentle into this good night'.[45] She never sang her own praises, but there was no denying that her courage and stubborn refusal to be subdued had been an essential precondition of staying alive.

Her other concern was more universal. The Holocaust, she said, could have happened anywhere. She had bitter arguments with her father-in-law about whether it could have taken place in Britain:

'I said to him, "Oh, well, you're lucky, it could have happened here." The reaction was absolutely explosive. "Of *course* it could not happen here. This is a democratic country." The usual sort of piffle. I mean . . . it's indescribable that people think . . . it can happen anywhere. It's happening anywhere, it's happening everywhere.'

On one occasion, I asked her if Christian Arras had made any comment to her about what he had seen in Izbica. She didn't remember any specific observations. And then she said:[46]

'The Germans, or anybody in that situation if it comes to that, you look at television every night and you see the atrocities that are going on now everywhere, in every part of the world. Well, after a while, you become immune. It's the most dreadful thing and I could never understand – and I still don't – how people come to think that six million makes an enormous difference from sixty or six thousand. It's what you do, not how many you do it to – *that* is at the root of the thing. The enormity for me lies in the fact that it happened at all – and that it is still happening. And that's what matters. That – is – what – matters. Yes. And nothing else. Not the six million. And those people in Izbica, they're

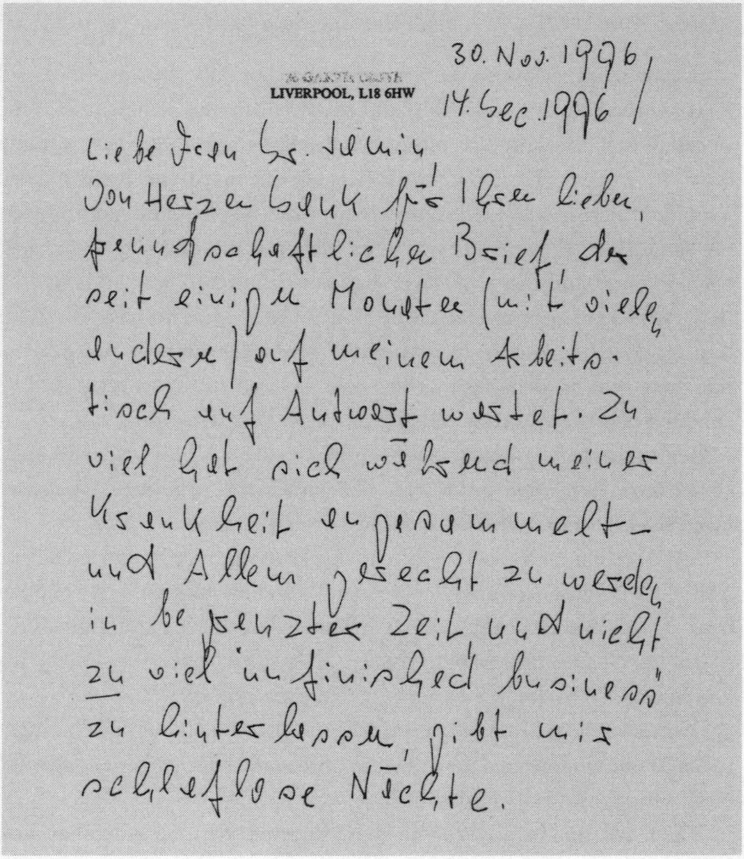

LIVERPOOL, L18 6HW

30. Nov. 1996 /
14. Sep. 1996 /

Liebe Frau Dr. Jamin
Von Herzen Dank für Ihren lieben,
freundschaftlichen Brief, der
seit einigen Monaten (mit vielen
anderen) auf meinem Arbeits-
tisch auf Antwort wartet. Zu
viel hat sich während meiner
Krankheit angesammelt –
und Allem gerecht zu werden
in begrenzter Zeit, und nicht
zu viel 'unfinished business'
zu hinterlassen, gibt mir
schlaflose Nächte.

Last letter to Mathilde Jamin

Augenblicklich bin ich wieder
in Marie Curie Centse [auf
etwa 14 Tage] um mich etwas
auszuruhen; so finde ich
endlich Zeit Ihnen zu denken —
nicht nur für Brief — auch
für den so reichhaltigen Katalog.
Vieles darin erweckt alte Er=
innerungen.
Mit Mac Roseman arbeite wir
meine Erinnerungen, augenblick=
lich noch sehr roh und
"sketchy". Wir werden sehen

not six million they're, what, a few, a handful of people, they're the epitome of what happened then to six million and more and is still happening. And that's it.'

I think she would have liked to use this statement to end the book.

For Marianne, man's inhumanity to man was the important issue, far more significant than the difference between killing sixty people or six million. I was not sure I could agree. I could see that to lose one's mother, one's father, one's brother and one's first love, was to sustain a loss, and to learn something about others' capacity for evil, that made the overall numbers almost irrelevant. To that extent, the murders of the Krombachs in Izbica and the Strausses in Auschwitz encapsulated the killings of all. But to kill six million required such a commitment, such a 'utopian' project of murder, such an infrastructure and such broad involvement and co-operation. It was not just the sheer numbers involved, but even more the aspiration to genocide that was so distinctive. Man's basic potential for inhumanity seemed a necessary part of the explanation, but very far short of a sufficient one.

The idea that every modern society is equally poised to commit genocide also did not ring true to me, even if all contain some of the elements that made the Holocaust possible.[47] At the time of our discussions, I wondered if Marianne had ever really come to terms with the Holocaust's scale or the extent of German society's involvement. In retrospect, I think she may have been provoked into such a blanket assertion of the Holocaust's universality. She could not stand the complacency she found in Britain. It reminded her too strongly of the naïve trust in one's homeland that had proved so misplaced in Germany. Above all, the simplistic anti-German attitudes she encountered in Britain were too much at odds with her own experience.

Marianne knew that there was an 'other' Germany, a Germany of culture and ideas, of idealism and public service, whose values had influenced both Jews and non-Jews. Marianne saw the Bund's intellectual world as in many ways typically Weimar. She knew that the tradition of integrity and public service which guided David Krombach was as German as it was Jewish. She did not deny that other facets of German society and culture had the potential to call forth great evil, particularly in the wake of the political, economic and cultural crisis of the early

1930s. She could not doubt the depth and breadth of German anti-Semitism. But from her I gained the insight that, in their different ways and different generational styles, Artur and Dore Jacobs, David Krombach, the young Ernst and (though she would never have claimed this) the young Marianne herself were the very best of Germans.

Marianne experienced enormous variation in human responses to herself and her family. Despite the threats and dangers, some had found the freedom to offer selfless assistance; others had provided help, but only in return for material rewards; many others had cold-shouldered the family and some had had a hand in their murder. Marianne knew that a remarkable range of relationships had been struck up or maintained with her family at a time when Jews were publicly vilified. The bank director, the priest, the Wehrmacht soldier, the Catholic family and of course the Bund, to name but some. Not all of these relationships were 'bought' by the Strausses' wealth and not all were unique. It was understandable that, for Marianne, the crucial distinction should not be between the 'Germans' and others, but between one individual and another.

The Bund members themselves would have rejected the idea that it was a question of individuals. What proved itself, they wrote after the war, was 'the idea', the principles they shared. Certainly, the fact that they were a group, working together, was crucial, both in giving each individual confidence and strength and in making joint action possible. For all their German roots, they do seem to offer a more universal message of hope. An informal network of upright and courageous individuals, inspired by a common idea, may be able (given some luck) to uphold standards of decency, provide support for the persecuted and elude capture, even in a dictatorship.

Some time after Marianne's death, Vivian and I made our final foray to her house in search of documents. The house was cold and dilapidated. After Elaine's death, Marianne had not been able to tolerate work being done in the home. When I met her, despite her love of cooking she was still making do with a primitive 1950s kitchen. With so many of Marianne's possessions already removed, it was apparent that in fact the whole house needed renovating. There were serious settlement cracks in the back bedrooms. It was as if the whole structure were gradually sinking under the weight of her unmasterable past. Standing in the empty house, I was reminded of Marianne saying that she felt she had lived a series of lives, and that she was increasingly disconnected from all of them. She had suggested a second title for this book, a quotation from Rückert's poem, set by Mahler: 'Ich bin der Welt abhanden gekommen', 'I am lost to the world'.[48]

And yet it was impossible to think of Marianne as lost, or as a victim, for long. The house, forlorn as it appeared, held out another message. Marianne had insisted on her privacy. The subsidence had not been dealt with because she did not want workmen in; she had calculated, rightly, that the walls would hold up for as long as she needed them. Looking at the now defunct stair-lift reminded me that she had managed to look after herself pretty well to the last. Only two days before her death she had still been out and about. She had been resolute in relation to me, insisting on setting the boundaries. I could not help a wry smile when I thought how successfully Marianne had thwarted my efforts to bridge her pre- and post-war lives. She had kept the latter largely off limits.[49] The past *had* been unmasterable for her, yet she had managed it in the best way she could and had remained a fighter – resolute, dignified and in control. Marianne had succeeded, in the end, in telling her story. It seemed entirely fitting, almost a tribute to her, that some parts of her past should for ever remain in hiding.

Abbreviations

ADStE	Gestapo Aussendienststelle (Gestapo Branch Office) Essen
AfWGE	Amt für Wiedergutmachung (Office of Restitution), Essen
AS	Alfred Strauss
ASE	Alte Synagoge, Essen
BAB	Bundesarchiv, Berlin
BDC	Berlin Document Centre
CH	Carl Hermann
CV	Central-Verein deutscher Staatsbürger jüdischen Glaubens (Central Association of German Citizens of the Jewish Persuasion)
DB	Deutsche Bank
DBE	Essen branch of the Deutsche Bank
DBF	Deutsche Bank Historisches Zentrum, Frankfurt
DRK	Deutsches Rotes Kreuz (German Red Cross)
EK	Ernst Krombach
EP	Ellenbogen Papers
HStAD	Hauptstaatsarchiv, Düsseldorf
JFB	Jüdischer Frauenbund (Jewish Women's League)
JPF–MH	Jüdischer Pfadfinder–Makkabi Hazair (combined Jewish Scouts and Maccabi Hazair Youth Group)
JSK	Jüdisches Seminar für Kindergärtnerinnen und

	Hortnerinnen, Berlin (College for Kindergarten Teachers, Berlin)
KPD	German Communist Party
KriPo	Kriminalpolizei (Criminal Police)
LBINY	Leo Baeck Institute, New York
LG	Landgericht (State Court)
LGD	Landgericht Düsseldorf
LGE	Landgericht Essen
ME	Marianne Ellenbogen
MS	Marianne Strauss
NRW	North-Rhine Westphalia
NSDAP	Nationalsozialistische Deutsche Arbeiterpartei (National Socialist German Workers' Party – Nazi Party)
ODD	Oberfinanzpräsident, Düsseldorf, Devisenstelle (Currency Section of the Finance Office, Düsseldorf)
OFD	Oberfinanzpräsident, Düsseldorf (Finance Office, Düsseldorf)
OKW	Oberkommando der Wehrmacht (Armed Forces High Command)
OT	Organisation Todt
RjF	Reichsbund jüdischer Frontsoldaten (Reich Association of Jewish Combat Veterans)
RSHA	Reichsicherheitshauptamt (Reich Security Main Office)
RV	Reichsvertretung der deutschen Juden, later Reichsvereinigung der Juden in Deutschland (Reich Association of German Jews, later Reich Association of Jews in Germany)
RW	René Wolf
SD	Sicherheitsdienst (Security Service of the SS)
SStr	Siegfried Strauss
StAE	Stadtarchiv, Essen
StAE NJ AJD	Stadtarchiv, Essen Nachlaß Jacobs, Artur Jacobs diary
StaPo	Staatspolizeileitstelle (Gestapo Main Office)
StaPoD	Staatspolizeileitstelle Düsseldorf

StAW	Stadtarchiv, Wuppertal
VE	Vivian Ellenbogen
WGK	Wiedergutmachungskammer (Court for restitution matters)
YVJ	Yad Vashem, Jerusalem

Dramatis Personae

Eric Alexander (formerly *Alex Weinberg*), oldest of the three Weinberg brothers, Marianne's cousins on her mother's side.

Gerald Alexander (formerly *Otto Weinberg*), youngest of the Weinberg brothers, Marianne's cousins on her mother's side.

Nancy Alexander, Stamford, second wife of *Eric*.

Uri Aloni, (formerly *Hans Eulau*) contemporary of Marianne's from Essen in the 1920s and 1930s.

Paul Alsberg, distant relative of Marianne's. His aunt, *Grete Sander*, played an important role as addressee for family letters from Theresienstadt and Auschwitz-Birkenau.

Hanna Aron (née *Drucker*), near contemporary of Marianne's from Essen. Hanna's mother, *Irene Drucker*, worked with Marianne at the Jewish Community Office 1942–3. Hanna, Irene and Hanna's brother *Wolfgang* lived with Marianne for six months March–September 1943.

Christian Arras, soldier who acted as courier for Marianne to Izbica; also the name of his father. His son, also *Christian*, continues the family truck business.

Lilli Arras, wife of *Christian Arras*, Marianne's courier to Izbica.

Waltraud Barkhoff-Kreter (née *Kreter*), contemporary of Marianne's at the Luisenschule.

Saul and *Clara Bender*, friends of the Ellenbogens in Liverpool.

Thomas Toivi Blatt, Sobibor survivor who grew up in Izbica.

Else Bramesfeld, Bund member.

Fritz and *Maria Briel*, Bund members living in Remscheid. Their son, *Wolfgang*, was a small child when Marianne stayed with the family.

Chaja Chovers (formerly *Klara Kleimann*), contemporary of Marianne's from the Essen Jewish community.

Jane Dalton (née *Gray*), lived next door to the Ellenbogens in the 1950s.

Ruth Davidsohn (née *Mendel*), Jewish fellow-pupil of Marianne's at the Luisenschule.

Inge Deutschkron, journalist and author of *Ich trug den gelben Stern*; a contemporary of Marianne's at the College for Kindergarten Teachers in Berlin.

Edith Dietz, near contemporary of Marianne's at the College for Kindergarten Teachers in Berlin.

Greta Dreibholz, Bund member in Remscheid.

Ruth Elias, author of *Triumph of Hope*; at Theresienstadt at the same time as the Strauss family and took the same transport to the Family Camp in Auschwitz.

Basil Ellenbogen, Marianne's husband.

Elaine Ellenbogen, Marianne's daughter.

Gershon Ellenbogen, older brother of *Basil*.

Raymond Ellenbogen, younger brother of *Basil*.

Vivian Ellenbogen, Marianne's son.

Hanni Ganzer, friend of the Bund, living in Düsseldorf; Marianne's last protector before the end of the war.

Ruth Gawse (née *Ferse*), near contemporary of Marianne's in the Essen Jewish community; at the Luisenschule until 1938.

Karin Gerhard, Essen; successor to Lisa Jacobs as Director of the Dore Jacobs school.

Tove Gerson, Essen; Bund member who was in the USA during the war years.

David, Sandra and *Rob Gray*, London; Rob was my student who alerted me to the fact that his father David had grown up living next door to the Ellenbogens in Liverpool. Rob's mother Sandra had also met the Ellenbogens on many occasions.

Werner and *Hanna* (née *Heumann*) *Hoffmann*; Werner was an employee of the Strauss brothers from 1924 until he left Germany for Argentina in 1936 with his fiancée Hanna. They have a son, *Tomas*.

Waltraud Horn, non-Jewish contemporary of Marianne's at the Luisenschule.

Lisa Jacob, Jewish member of the Bund, also in hiding.

Artur and *Dore* (née *Marcus*) *Jacobs*, founding members and leaders of the Bund.

Elisabeth Jacobs, wife of *Wilhelm Jacobs*, one of the group whom Marianne met in Düsseldorf after the war.

Mathilde Jamin, historian at the Ruhrland Museum who made the original contact to Marianne.

Hanna Jordan, near contemporary of Marianne's. Her quaker parents had close links to Bund circles. Hannah met Marianne during the war and she (herself half-Jewish) was protected by the Bund for a brief period. After the war worked in theatre with *Imo Moszkowicz*.

Ellen Jungbluth (formerly *Ellen Hube*, née *Brandt*) Wuppertal Bund member since the 1930s, had only limited contact with Marianne, but after the war married *Ernst Jungbluth*, one of the Bund's central figures. In the last decade or more Ellen has been the central figure ensuring the Bund's survival.

Meta Kamp, (formerly *Meta Steinmann*, née *Wahle*) Bund member and Marianne's main host in Göttingen. Her sister *Elfrieda Nenadovic* and son *Ernst Steinmann* also had contact with Marianne.

Hermann and *Lene Krahlisch*, Bund members from Mülheim; Lene protected Marianne in October 1944.

David Krombach, father of Marianne's fiancé, *Ernst*. Died in Izbica 1942.

Enrique (formerly *Heinz*) *Krombach*, Buenos Aires; brother of *Ernst* who left Germany before the war.

Ernst Krombach, Marianne's fiancé.

Minna (*Minne*) *Krombach*, *Ernst's* mother; disappeared from Izbica November 1942.

Rosemarie Lange (née *Hahn*), Bobingen; non-Jewish contemporary of Marianne's from the Luisenschule.

Jakov (formerly *Klaus*) and *Tsofia Langer*, Kiryat Tivon; Jakov was in Marianne's youth group and managed to leave Germany just after the outbreak of war.

Rudi and *Grete Löwenstein*, friends of Ernst in Izbica; they had come to Essen in 1938. Rudi's father, *Josef*, had operated on Marianne's toe in 1941.

Hilde Machinek, Wuppertal, Bund member.

Grete Menningen (née *Ransenberg*), sister of *Irma Ransenberg*. Because she was in a mixed marriage she was protected from deportation until 1944 and sheltered Marianne a couple of times. In 1944 Marianne helped her find safety.

Monte and *Phyllis Miller*, Liverpool; friends of the Ellenbogens.

Eva Morting, Sundbyberg, Sweden; daughter of Marianne's very distant relative *Grete Sander*. Eva was married to *Ivor Morting*, notary.

Imo Moszkowicz, Ottobrunn; celebrated TV and theatre director after the war; met Marianne in 1942 before being deported to Auschwitz in 1943.

Elfrieda Nenadovic (née *Wahle*), Göttingen; younger sister of *Meta Kamp*; met Marianne in July 1944.

Johannes Oppenheimer, Berlin; one of Marianne's half-Jewish friends in Düsseldorf after the war, who later became a distinguished judge.

Irma Ransenberg, nurse with Jewish community; worked with Marianne in the home for the elderly until Irma's deportation July 1942.

Adolf Rosenberg, Marianne's maternal uncle who emigrated to the USA in 1941.

Anna Rosenberg, Marianne's maternal grandmother.

Isaak Rosenberg, Marianne's maternal grandfather.

Karl (later *Carlos*) *Rosenberg*, Marianne's maternal uncle who fought with the resistance in France.

Hannah Rosenberg, see *Hannah Weinberg*.

Reni Sadamgrotzky, friend of the Bund, living in Solingen.

Grete Sander (née *Alsberg*), Marianne's distant relative who was the Strauss family correspondent in Sweden.

Lew (formerly *Ludwig*) and *Trudy* (née *Ullmann*) *Schloss*, Teaneck, New Jersey; both had met Marianne independently before they knew each other. Lew came from Gelsenkirchen and his former girlfriend worked for the Strausses. Trudy met Marianne in the Children's Hospital in Berlin in 1941.

Hermann Schmalstieg, Göttingen; Bund member based near Goslar during the war, for whom Marianne may have had a secret passion.

Aenne Schmitz, Wuppertal; Bund member (along with husband *August*) with whom Marianne stayed for a while in the small village of Berringhausen.

Eva Selig, London; distant cousin of Marianne's on her mother's side.

Robert Selig, Denmark; son of *Eva*; provided me with a family tree of the Rosenbergs and some anecdotal evidence about Marianne.

Tillie Stein, Atlanta, Georgia; second cousin of Marianne's on her father's side who provided me with information about the Strausses.

Ernst Steinmann, Achim; son of *Meta Kamp*; encountered Marianne in 1944.

Fritz Stern, Siegfried's cousin (Fritz's mother, Bertha Strauss, was a sister of Leopold Strauss). Resident in the USA since 1907 and a US citizen since 1915. Successful businessman; the Strausses' guarantor in their efforts to emigrate to the USA.

Liesel Sternberg, Birmingham; former employee and friend of *David Krombach*.

Alfred Strauss, Marianne's paternal uncle.

Leopold Strauss, Marianne's paternal grandfather.

Lore (Oe) Strauss (née *Dahl*), wife of Alfred and Marianne's aunt by marriage.

Regina (Ine) Strauss (née *Rosenberg*), Marianne's mother.

Richard Strauss, Marianne's paternal uncle who died in the First World War.

Richard Strauss, Marianne's younger brother.

Rosalie (Saly) Strauss (née *Stern*), Marianne's paternal grandmother.

Siegfried Strauss, Marianne's father.

Grete Ströter, Essen; Bund member; visited the Strausses in prison in September 1943.

Reinhold Ströter, Mettmann; Bund member; formerly married to *Grete*.

Alex Weinberg, see *Eric Alexander*.

Alfred Weinberg, see *Uri Weinberg*.

Ernst Weinberg, husband of *Hannah*, Marianne's uncle by marriage, father of *Alex*, *Alfred* and *Otto*, deported to Łodz 1941.

Hannah Weinberg (née *Johannah Rosenberg*), Marianne's maternal aunt, mother of *Alex*, *Alfred* and *Otto*, deported to Łodz 1941.

Otto Weinberg, see *Gerald Alexander*.

Uri Weinberg (formerly *Alfred Weinberg*), second of the three Weinberg brothers, Marianne's cousins on her mother's side.

Abraham and *Anna Weyl*, Marianne's great-uncle and great-aunt (Abraham was Anna Rosenberg's brother); moved to Essen 1938, deported to Theresienstadt 1942.

Bertel Wolf (née *Strauss*), Marianne's paternal aunt, married to *Ferdinand Wolf*.

René (formerly *Richard*) *Wolf*, Marianne's cousin (son of her father's sister *Bertel*); survived the expulsions to French concentration camps and service in the French Foreign Legion and played a major role assisting in Marianne's restitution claims.

Hélène Yaiche-Wolf, Paris; daughter of *René Wolf*.

Kurt Zeunert, Berlin; member of the group of part-Jewish survivors whom Marianne befriended in Düsseldorf.

Notes

Introduction

1. Marianne Ellenbogen, 'Flucht und illegales Leben während der Nazi-Verfolgungsjahre 1943–1945', *Das Münster am Hellweg*, vol. 37 (1984), pp. 135–142. Reprinted in Alte Synagoge (ed.), *Stationen jüdischen Lebens. Von der Emanzipation bis zur Gegenwart* (Verlag J. W. Dietz Nachf., Bonn, 1990), pp. 248–252.
2. Only years later did I learn that Basil was in fact a fluent German speaker – a fact which merely underscored Marianne's wish to keep her memories shielded from him.
3. Sadly, Mrs Liesel Sternberg died before publication of the book.
4. Viktor Klemperer, *Ich will Zeugnis ablegen bis zum letzten*, vol. 1: *Tagebücher 1933–1941*; vol. 2: *Tagebücher 1942–1945* (Aufbau-Verlag, Berlin, 1995).

1 Childhood in a German-Jewish Family

1. Several authors choose not to use this label to describe the events of 9 November 1938 because it belittles the real violence and terror on that day. Indeed, the term *has* contributed to obscuring the reality of what went on, but since the discovery that this is so is the theme of a later chapter, it is appropriate to retain the customary label, at least for now.
2. With many thanks to Dr Vera Bendt for her assistance. See Hermann Simon, *Das Berliner Jüdische Museum in der Oranienburgerstraβe. Ges-*

chichte einer zerstörten Kulturstätte (Stadtgeschichtliche Publikationen II ed. Berlin Museum, Berlin, 1983).

3. In the Orthodox Jewish service, it is the cantor or chazan, and not the rabbi, who leads the congregation in prayer.

4. The following sources for Leopold's career were consulted: Tillie Stein to author, 16.1.1998 and 8.9.1999; LBINY, *Jüdische Bibliothek* (Hamburg), no. 324, 31.12.1931; *Jüdisches Nachrichtenblatt*, 30.6.1939; Kurt Tohermes and Jürgen Grafen, *Leben und Untergang der Synagogengemeinde Dinslaken* (Verein für Heimatpflege 'Land Dinslaken' e.V., Dinslaken, 1988), p. 60; Bürgermeister, Dinslaken, to Leopold Strauss, 1.8.1903; *Dinslakener Generalanzeiger*, 1.4.1927.

5. Information about Isaak Rosenberg was provided by Marianne, her cousins Eric Alexander and Uri Weinberg and Hans W. Gummersbach, 'Sozialhistorische und soziologische Forschungen zur jüdischen Minderheit in der westfälischen Stadt Ahlen vor und während der Zeit des Nationalsozialismus unter besonderer Berücksichtigung lebensgeschichtlicher Selbstzeugnisse' (PhD, University of Paderborn, 1996). Gummersbach's principal source was Marianne's uncle, Karl Rosenberg.

6. The white garment worn on some religious occasions and in which one is buried.

7. The prayer shawl worn by the officiant and by married men for morning prayers.

8. The clumsy term acculturation is preferred to assimilation because the latter implies a loss of identity, which was not the case here. See Marion Kaplan, 'Tradition and transition: the acculturation, assimilation and integration of Jews in Imperial Germany, a gender analysis', in *Leo Baeck Year Book*, vol. 28 (1982), pp. 3–36.

9. Amongst the wealth of studies on the evolution of Jewish identities in Germany, see Reinhard Rürup, *Emanzipation und Antisemitismus. Studien zur 'Judenfrage' der bürgerlichen Gesellschaft* (Vandenhoeck & Ruprecht, Göttingen, 1992); Trude Maurer, *Die Entwicklung der jüdischen Minderheit in Deutschland. Neuere Forschungen und offene Fragen* (Niemeyer, Tübingen, 1992); Helmut Berding, 'Antisemitismus in der modernen Gesellschaft: Kontinuität und Diskontinuität', in Jörg K. Hoensch, Stanislav Biman and L'ubomir Liptak (eds.), *Judenemanzipation – Antisemitismus – Verfolgung in Deutschland, Österreich-Ungarn, den böhmischen Ländern und in der Slowakei* (Klartext, Essen, 1999), pp. 85–100; Falk Wiesemann, 'Jewish burials in Germany – between the Enlightenment and the authorities', *Leo Baeck Institute Year Book*, vol. 37 (1992), pp. 17–31, at p. 31. For the region, see Michael Zimmermann, 'Die Assimi-

lation und ihre Relativierung. Zur Geschichte der Essener jüdischen Geme-
inde vor 1933', in Dirk Blasius and Dan Diner (eds.), *Zerbrochene
Geschichte. Leben und Selbstverständnis der Juden in Deutschland* (Fischer
Taschenbuch Verlag, Frankfurt am Main, 1991), pp. 172–186.

10. Avraham Barkai, 'Die sozio-ökonomische Situation der Juden in Rheinland und Westfalen zur Zeit der Industrialisierung (1850–1914)', in Kurt
Düwell and Wolfgang Köllmann (eds.), *Rheinland-Westfalen im Industriezeitalter*, vol. 2: *Von der Reichsgründung bis zur Weimarer Republik*
(Peter Hammer, Wuppertal, 1984), pp. 86–106.

11. Interview, Uri Weinberg, Jerusalem, 30.7.1998.

12. Werner Hoffmann to author, 29.4.1997; Industrie und Handelskammer
für die Stadtkreise Essen, Mülheim & Oberhausen, 26.4.1939, 'Bescheini-
gung', signed Dr Herbig; copy, CH to Oberstadtdirektor Essen, 9.5.1959,
Entschädigungsantrag der Frau Marianne Ellenbogen geb. Strauss ...
nach Siegfried Strauss 50, 8/St 24 a (statement of Paul Petry); Siegfried
Heineberg, Düsseldorf, 'Zeugnis', 7.1.1919.

13. Befähigungs-Diplom, 9.3.1916.

14. Quabecks Handelsschule, 1.4.1918, reference for Regina Rosenberg,
signed F. Pratje.

15. John Dippel, *Bound Upon a Wheel of Fire. Why Leading Jews Stayed in
Nazi Germany* (Basic Books, New York, 1996), p. 17.

16. Ibid.

17. When Ine interceded with the Gestapo on Siegfried's behalf in 1938 and
listed the reasons for which he deserved release from his post-Kristallnacht
imprisonment, she named various decorations but not the Iron Cross,
which she undoubtedly would have, had he received it.

18. On Alfred, see his pay book and several letters from Lieutenant Kiss to
Sergeant Strauss, July and August 1918.

19. HStAD RW58 74234, file Alfred Strauss; Staatliche Kriminalpolizei,
Kriminalpolizeistelle Essen, Strafanzeige 12.5.1941, Aussage von Alfred
Strauss.

20. And indeed of a populist, right-wing politics in general. See Peter Fritzsche,
Germans into Nazis (Harvard University Press, Cambridge, Mass.,
1998).

21. Dippel, *Bound Upon a Wheel of Fire*, p. 20.

22. Saul Friedländer, 'Political transformations during the war and their effect
on the Jewish question', in Herbert A. Strauss (ed.), *Hostages of Modernisation: studies on Modern Anti-Semitism 1870–1933/39. Germany–Great
Britain–France* (Walter de Gruyter, New York and London, 1993),
pp. 150–164.

23. This is not to claim that Nazism was inevitable in 1918. For recent work on the Jews and anti-Semitism in Weimar, see below, notes 66–68.

24. Copy, CH to Oberstadtdirektor Essen, 9.5.1959, Entschädigungsantrag der Frau Marianne Ellenbogen geb Strauss . . . nach Siegfried Strauss 50, 8/St 24 a (statement of Paul Petry).

25. The date of founding the business is taken from René to ME, 12.3.1955; a copy of the registration in the family possession, however, places the official registration date at 30.9.1919.

26. Werner Hoffmann to author, 29.4.1997.

27. File, Salta GmbH I Liqu. documents in folder 'Zuwachssteuererklärung Mackensenstr. [Brunnenstrasse] 69; Debitoren und Creditoren. Waren und Inventarbestand'.

28. Undated (clearly 1939) CV, 'Lebenslauf Siegfried Strauss Essen, Ladenspelderstr. 47'.

29. 'Debitoren und Creditoren. Waren und Inventarbestand'.

30. Interview, Werner Hoffmann, Buenos Aires, 19.6.1998; Werner Hoffman to author 29.4.1997.

31. SStr to Ine, 7.6.1923.

32. The French occupied the Ruhr at the beginning of 1923 to enforce reparations transfers.

33. SStr to Mieteinigungsamt der Stadt Essen, 23.6.1928.

34. Typewritten 'Aufstellung über Mobilar und Hausrat u.s.w. *Siegfried Strauss*'.

35. Unsigned copy, *Eidesstattliche Versicherung*, produced by Frau Selig, May 1955.

36. Trude Maurer, 'Reife Bürger der Republik und bewußte Juden: die jüdische Minderheit in Deutschland 1918–1933', in Hoensch, Biman et al. (eds.), *Judenemanzipation*, pp. 101–116, at p. 112.

37. ASE, INo.75, Bernd Simon, 29.08.94, a236.

38. Interview, ME, 10.9.1996.

39. Interview, ME, 31.10.1996.

40. MS to her father, 3.5.1932.

41. MS to her mother, 7.5.1932.

42. Undated New Year's card with Magen David on front, MS to parents.

43. MS to parents, 1 Tischri 5695.

44. MS to her parents, 5695.

45. Interview, ME, 31.10.1996.

46. Ibid.

47. Marianne's father's money was by then frozen in blocked accounts. He was allowed to draw a certain amount each month, including monthly

transfers to Berlin to pay for Marianne's tuition there. This is the 'stipend' referred to.

48. Interview, ME, 31.10.1996.
49. Interview, ME, 10.9.1996.
50. Werner Hoffmann to author, 5.3.1997.
51. Interview, ME, 31.10.1996.
52. Ibid.
53. Ibid.
54. Ibid.
55. House of the Dunes.
56. The small town south of Mönchen-Gladbach where the Weinberg boys grew up.
57. NS-Documentationszentrum der Stadt Köln (eds.), *Die jüdischen Opfer des Nationalsozialismus aus Köln. Gedenkbuch* (Böhlau Verlag, Cologne, 1995), pp. 490–49, 536–537.
58. Phillippe Burrin, *Hitler and the Jews: the Genesis of the Holocaust* (Edward Arnold, London, 1994), p. 126.
59. The hats worn by some very traditional Jews.
60. Benzion Patkin, *The Dunera Internees* (Cassell Australia, Stanmore, N.S.W., 1979) confirms all the details Uri gave me.
61. I should point out that in 1922 the daily falls in currency value were still pretty modest; nevertheless, it's a nice end to a good story.
62. Michael Zimmermann, 'Zur Geschichte der Essener Juden im 19. und im ersten Drittel des 20. Jahrhunderts. Ein Überblick', in Alte Synagoge (ed.), *Jüdisches Leben in Essen 1800–1933* (Klartext, Essen, 1993), pp. 8–72.
63. Ibid., pp. 32–33.
64. Photo and description in Hermann Schröter, *Geschichte und Schicksal der Essener Juden. Gedenkbuch für die jüdischen Mitbürger der Stadt Essen* (printed by the city of Essen, Essen, 1980), pp. 109–110. At some point, it moved to the Herkulesstrasse and then to Frohnhausen. In 1978 *Das Münster am Hellweg* published an account of the school.
65. On this, see Kaplan, 'Tradition and transition'.
66. Berding, 'Antisemitismus', pp. 85–91; Reinhard Rürup, 'Jüdische Geschichte in Deutschland. Von der Emanzipation bis zur nationalsozialistischen Gewaltherrschaft', in Blasius and Diner, *Zerbrochene Geschichte*, pp. 79–101, at pp. 94ff.; Zimmermann, 'Zur Geschichte der Essener Juden'.
67. Angela Genger, 'Hakoah – Die Kraft. Ein jüdischer Turn- und Sportverein in Essen', in Alte Synagoge (ed.), *Zwischen Alternative und Protest. Zu Sport- und Jugendbewegungen in Essen 1900–1933* (Exhibition cata-

logue, Essen, 1983), pp. 8–25, at p. 13; Zimmermann, 'Zur Geschichte der Essener Juden', p. 36.

68. Recent work on Jews in the Weimar Republic includes Michael Brenner, *The Renaissance of Jewish Culture in Weimar Germany* (Yale University Press, New Haven, 1996); Friedländer, 'Political transformations'; Anthony Kauders, *German Politics and the Jews: Düsseldorf and Nuremberg, 1910–1933* (Clarendon Press, Oxford, 1996); Donald L. Niewyk, *The Jews in Weimar Germany* (Manchester University Press, Manchester, 1980).

2 *Schoolgirl in the Third Reich*

1. Marion Kaplan, *Between Dignity and Despair: Jewish Life in Nazi Germany* (Oxford University Press, Oxford and New York, 1998), p. 18.

2. Testimony of Marta Appel, née Insel, in Monika Richarz, *Jewish Life in Germany: Memoirs from Three Centuries* (Indiana University Press, Bloomington and Indianapolis, 1991), p. 351.

3. Alfred Strauss, income tax return for 1932; Copy, ME to René, 19.11.1961; J Clemens, estimates; folder, 'Mischanlage'.

4. Copy, CH to Drs Kessler and May, 8.6.1962.

5. International comparisons are notoriously difficult, since they involve not only converting currencies fixed in the 1930s at rather artificial exchange rates but also taking into account different standards of living. In 1937, when Alfred earned around RM20,000 before tax, this was equivalent to dollar income of around $8,000. Their cousin, Fritz Stern, a successful businessman in the USA, was at that stage earning three times this amount. So by US middle-class standards, 'the Strausses' was not a great income. The sterling value of Alfred's earnings in 1937 would have been about £1,600. This was a fair middle-class income in the UK at the time. By way of comparison, a skilled engineering worker in Britain would be earning less than £200 a year. See Statistisches Reichsamt (ed.), *Statistisches Jahrbuch für das Deutsche Reich 1932* (Berlin, 1932); and *1939/1940* (Berlin, 1940), sections on German prices, earnings, currency rates, foreign prices, foreign earnings.

6. Copy, Gebr. Strauss to Deutsche Gesandtschaft, Sofia, 27.6.1934; Deutsche Gesandtschaft to Gebr. Strauss, 2.8.1934; draft, Declaration re Winterhilfswerk. October 1934–March 1935; 'Mitgliederverzeichnis, Großmarkt für Getreide und Futtermittel e.V., Essen 1.4.1936.

7. Werner Hoffmann to author, 5.3.1997.

8. Dirk von Laak, ' "Wenn einer ein Herz im Leibe hat, der läßt sich von einem deutschen Arzt behandeln". Die "Entjudung" der Essener Wirtschaft von 1933 bis 1941', in Alte Synagoge (ed.), *Entrechtung und Selbsthilfe. Zur Geschichte der Juden in Essen unter dem Nationalsozialismus* (Essen, Klartext, 1994), pp. 12–30, at p. 22; Kaplan, *Between Dignity and Despair*, pp. 24–31.

9. Kurt Düwell, *Die Rheingebiete in der Judenpolitik des National-sozialismus vor 1942* (Ludwig Röhrscheid Verlag, Bonn, 1968), p. 191.

10. I am indebted to Jacob Borut for this insight.

11. On the economic measures, see Raul Hilberg, *Die Vernichtung der euro-päischen Juden* (Fischer, Frankfurt am Main 1993) vol 1, pp. 140–141, 149; Avraham Barkai, *From Boycott to Annihilation: the Economic Struggle of German Jews, 1933–1943* (University Press of New England, Hanover, 1989), pp. 99–100, 144; Kaplan, *Between Dignity and Despair*, p. 71.

12. Werner Hoffmann to author, 5.3.1997.

13. Ibid.

14. Marta Appel, in Richarz, *Jewish Life in Germany*, p. 356.

15. Marion Kaplan, 'Jewish women in Nazi Germany: daily life, daily struggles, 1933–39', in Peter Freimark, Alice Jankowski and Ina S. Lorenz (eds.), *Juden in Deutschland: Emanzipation, Integration, Verfolgung und Vernichtung* (H. Christians Verlag, Hamburg, 1991), pp. 406–434, at p. 420.

16. Barkai, *Boycott*, p. 100.

17. Interview, Werner Hoffmann, 19.6.1998

18. Including land costs. The figures of Hufelandstrasse 25 are taken from typewritten sheet 'Gestehungskosten Hufelandstr. 25'.

19. See, for example, Theodor Kruse, to Strauss brothers, 17.10.1936; Alfred and Siegfried Strauss to Th. Kruse, 17.10.1936; letters from Kruse to brothers, Dec. 1936 and Feb. 1937.

20. The family papers did at least include a clipping from the *Essener Allge-meine Zeitung* of 20.8.1936 with the headline, 'Neubauten in der Hufel-andstraße'.

21. File, Einkommenssteuer, Einkommensteuerbescheid für Alfred Strauss 1937.

22. Interview, ME, 31.10.1996.

23. Ibid.

24. Interview, ME, 1989.

25. Interview, ME, 31.10.1996.
26. Undated, untitled typewritten manuscript, evidently for broadcast on the BBC, produced some time in 1946.
27. Not her real name. References that follow are from an interview on 28.7.1997.
28. A guest of the family whom she had previously mentioned.
29. Dr Lange here refers to people associated with the oppositional 'Confessing Church'. Heinemann later became Federal President in post-war Germany.
30. Interview, Waltraud Barkhoff-Kreter, Essen, 23.6.1999.
31. On the characteristic philo-Semitic patterns in post-war discourse, see Frank Stern, *Am Anfang war Auschwitz. Antisemitismus und Philosemitismus im deutschen Nachkrieg* (Bleicher Verlag, Gerlingen, 1991), pp. 227ff.
32. Letter from Ruth Gawse, August 1991, printed in *125 Jahre Luisenschule 1866–1991*.
33. Interview, Ruth Davidsohn, née Mendel, and Chaja Chovers (Klara Kleimann), Haifa, 27.7.1998.
34. Telephone conversation with Ruth Davidsohn, Israel, 18.10.1997.
35. Interview, Ruth Gawse, née Ferse, Jerusalem, 30.7.1998.
36. Ruth Gawse to author, July 1997.
37. Interviews with Uri Aloni (Hans Eulau), in the Museum of Kibbutz Lochamei Hagetaot, 28.7.98, and Lew Schloss and Trudy Schloss, nee Ullmann, Teaneck, New Jersey, 11.8.98.
38. Interview, Jakov (Klaus) Langer, 27.7.98, Kiryat Tivon.
39. Clara Asscher-Pinkhof, *Star Children* (Wayne State University Press, Detroit, 1986).
40. Charles Hannam, *A Boy in Your Situation* (Adlib Paperbacks/André Deutsch, London, 1988).
41. Arbeitsbericht des Zentralauschusses der deutschen Juden für Hilfe und Aufbau, Reichsvertretung der Juden in Deutschland, July to December 1934, p. 24, cited in Werner T. Angress, 'Jüdische Jugend zwischen nationalsozialistischer Verfolgung und jüdischer Wiedergeburt', in Arnold Paucker (ed.), *Die Juden im nationalsozialistischen Deutschland* (J. C. B. Mohr/Paul Siebeck, Tübingen, 1986), pp. 211–232, at p. 213.
42. Cited in Ruth Röcher, *Die jüdische Schule im nationalsozialistischen Deutschland 1933–1942* (Dipa, Frankfurt am Main 1992), p. 69.
43. Unsigned copy, *Eidesstattliche Versicherung*, May 1955, produced by Frau Selig.
44. A medical questionnaire carried out in April 1940 by the Reichsvereini-

gung der Juden in Deutschland in 1940 – presumably to support applications for emigration – has been preserved and records Marianne's medical history.

45. Interview, ME, 31.10.1996.

46. Arnold Paucker, 'Zum Selbstverständnis jüdischer Jugend in der Weimarer Republik und unter der nationalsozialistischen Diktatur', in Hans Otto Horch and Charlotte Wardi (eds.), *Jüdische Selbstwahrnehmung. La Prise de conscience de l'identité juive* (Max Niemeyer Verlag, Tübingen, 1977), pp 111–128, at p. 115.

47. Jutta Hetkamp, *Die jüdische Jugendbewegung in Deutschland von 1913–1933* (Lit, Münster and Hamburg, 1994), p. 32; Zimmermann, 'Zur Geschichte der Essener Juden', pp. 54–55.

48. Kaplan, *Between Dignity and Despair*, p. 111.

49. LBINY, Bundesleitung des JPF–MH (ed.), *Unser Weg zum Volk. Ein Beitrag zur Ideologie des Makkabi Hazair*, (Berlin, 1936), p. 25.

50. LBINY, Bundesleitung des JPF–MH (ed.), *Unser Weg im Zionismus. Eine Sammelschrift des jüdischen Pfadfinderbundes Makkabi Hazair* (Berlin, no date).

51. Jakov Langer to author, 16.3.1997.

52. Jakov Langer to author, 25.2.1997.

53. Interview, Uri Aloni (Hans Eulau), in the Museum of Kibbutz Lochamei Hagetaot, 28.7.98.

54. For instance, Dr Lange, Frau Horn, and Frau Hochwald.

55. For example Dr Martha Jenke in her farewell speech to the school in 1956, in *Mitteilungen der Altschülerinnenbund der Luisenschule Essen*, vol. 30 (1998), pp. 50–51 and vol. 31 (1999) pp. 51–52.

56. See also Moshe Zimmermann, 'Vom Jischuw zum Staat – die Bedeutung des Holocaust für das kollektive Bewußtsein und die Politik in Israel', in Bernd Faulenbach and Helmut Schütte (eds.), *Deutschland, Israel und der Holocaust. Zur Gegenwartsbedeutung der Vergangenheit* (Klartext, Essen, 1998), pp. 45–54.

57. As I was to realize later, the British context served rather to enhance her feeling of disembodiment. See pp. 479ff.

58. Interview, ME, July 1996.

59. *Blätter des Jüdischen Frauenbundes (BJFB)*, vol. 9 (1933), no. 5, p. 11.

60. *BJFB*, vol. 13 (1937), no. 7, p. 1.

61. Ibid.

62. Interview, ME, 31.10.1996.

63. Edith Caspari to MS, 8.1.1943.

64. This is probably an error. If Marianne had been fifteen, she would have

been in Wyk in 1938. There is no certain proof that Marianne was in fact in Wyk in 1936, the date Marianne remembered; but there is a fitness questionnaire Marianne completed in 1940 which said that her bronchitis had become particularly bad at age thirteen, which suggests that she had remembered correctly. See note 44 above.

65. Max Eschelbacher, *Der zehnte November 1938* (Klartext, Essen, 1998), p. 32.

66. On the worsening conditions, see Saul Friedländer, *Nazi Germany and the Jews: the Years of Persecution, 1933–1939* (Pheonix Giant, 1997); Barkai, *Boycott*, pp. 121–130; Dippel, *Bound Upon a Wheel of Fire*, pp. 209–222, 234.

67. René Wolf to May, 14.2.1958.

68. Schröter, *Geschichte und Schicksal*, p. 52.

3   Shattered Glass, Shattered Lives

1. Events in Essen arc chronicled in Michael Zimmermann, 'Die "Reichskristallnacht" 1938 in Essen', in Alte Synagoge, *Entrechtung*, pp. 66–97.

2. Information from Mrs Liesel Sternberg, Birmingham.

3. Gummersbach, 'Ahlen', pp. 176ff.

4. Not her real name.

5. Not her real name.

6. Not her real name.

7. Stern, *Am Anfang war Auschwitz*, p. 204.

8. Zimmermann, ' "Reichskristallnacht" ', p. 78.

9. Interview, ME, 31.10.1996.

10. HStAD RW58,45264, 'Einlieferungsanzeige', 12.11.1938.

11. Undated, untitled typewritten manuscript, evidently for a BBC broadcast, produced some time in 1946.

12. See note 3 above.

13. Information from Uri Weinberg.

14. René to ME, 18.5.1961, copy attached: 'Eidesstattliche Erklärung, 11.5.1961', from Johann Mund.

15. Yitzhak Sophoni Herz, *Meine Erinnerung an Bad Homburg und seine 600jährige jüdische Gemeinde (1935–1942)* (privately published, Rechovoth, Israel, 1981), pp. 284–294, cited in Anselm Faust, *Die 'Kristallnacht' im Rheinland. Dokumente zum Judenpogrom im November 1938* (Schwann, Düsseldorf, 1987), pp. 81ff.

16. Ibid.

17. Krankenunterstützungskasse des NS Lehrerbundes KUK Hauptverwaltung, Bayreuth, to Leopold Strauss, 22.11.1938.

18. Brandkasse der Lehrer Rheinlands u. Wesfalens, Bochum, to Leopold Strauss, 19.12.1913.

19. Brandkasse westdeutscher Lehrer a.G., Bochum, to Leopold Strauss, 1.8.1933.

20. Brandkasse westdeutscher Lehrer a. G, Bochum, to Leopold Strauss, 'date as postmarked', [1938].

21. English original in Archive Ernst Schmidt, Ruhrland Museum, file 19–490. See also Walter Rohr, 'Die Geschichte meines Lebens', in Ernst Schmidt, 'Walter Rohr – 1938 aus Essen vertrieben, 1945 als US-Soldat zurückgekehrt', Alte Synagoge, *Entrechtung*, pp. 98–117, at pp. 106ff.

22. HStAD RW58, 45264, letter from Ehefrau Siegfried Strauss to Gestapo Essen, 23.11.1938.

23. HStAD RW58, 45264, letter from Ehefrau Siegfried Strauss to Gestapo Essen, 27.11.1938.

24. Schröter, *Geschichte und Schicksal*, p. 53.

25. Ibid., p. 368.

26. HStAD RW58, 45264, draft of letter from the Stapo IIB4 5629/38 dated 2.12.1938 to the KL Dachau.

27. She said six weeks to me. See also file Restitution 'A', CH to ME, 4.12.1956, annex: CH, Cologne, to Stadtverwaltung Essen, Amt für Wiedergutmachung, 12.10.1936.

28. Marta Appel, in Richarz, *Jewish Life in Germany*, p. 355.

29. Interview, ME, 10.9.1996.

30. Typed sheet: 'Abschrift, Judenvermögensabgabe Familie Siegfried Strauss'; figure includes bank charges and stock exchange taxes.

31. The total tax paid by Essen's 2,000 Jews was RM6,903,000: Schröter, *Geschichte und Schicksal*, p. 5.

32. For Essen more generally, see Schröter, *Geschichte und Schicksal*, p. 53; Zimmermann, 'Reichskristallnacht', p. 78.

33. Sterbeurkunde, Standesamt Essen-Rüttenscheid, 15.6.1939.

34. Draft, Ine Strauss to Fritz Stern, 19.6.1939.

35. United States Lines Affidavit of Support, signed 2.12.1938.

36. A slight mystery is offered by Ine's comment in her letter to the Gestapo on 23 November, in which she stated that she already had the affidavit in her possession. Probably she had received a cabled confirmation by then from Fritz Stern that he had provided an affidavit, but the actual document took a little longer to arrive.

37. Geburtsurkunde, Essen, 24.11.1938.

38. 'Empfangsbescheinigung', Essen 2.1.1939.
39. On what they submitted, see CH to ME, 21.2.1958, annex: Übersicht über die Entschädigungs- und Rückerstattungssachen der Frau Marianne Ellenbogen; copy, WGK beim LGE, Beschluß RüSp 58/54, 23.1.1956.
40. Herbert Schein, MD, 'Medical certificate', Essen, 9.5.1939.
41. Copy, 'Recommendation', Vorstand der Synagogen-Gemeinde Essen, 27.7.1939.
42. German Jewish Aid Committee, Immigration Section, Ref BA 4382 to SStr, 19.7.1939 and 15.8.1939.
43. British Consulate-General, Cologne to Siegfried and Alfred Strauss, 21.8.1939.

4   Blossoming in a Harsh Climate

1. Interview, ME, 10.9.1996.
2. Sozialpädagogisches Seminar zur Ausbildung von jüdischen Kindergärtnerinnen und Hortnerinnen in Berlin.
3. For use of the term, see Kaplan, *Between Dignity and Despair*.
4. Luisenschule zu Essen, Schuljahr 1938/9 Abganszeugnis für MS, 10.11.1938.
5. Schröter, *Geschichte und Schicksal*, p. 110.
6. Information from Dieter Corbach, *Die Jawne zu Köln. Zur Geschichte des ersten jüdischen Gymnasiums im Rheinland und zum Gedächtnis an Erich Klibansky 1900–1942* (Scriba Verlag, Cologne, 1990); Joseph Walk, 'Das jüdische Schulwesen in Köln bis 1942', in Jutta Bohnke-Kollwitz, Willehad Paul Eckert, Frank Golsczewski and Hermann Greive (eds.), *Köln und das rheinische Judentum. Festschrift Germania Judaica 1959–1984*, (Cologne, 1984), pp. 415–426.
7. By the Law Against Overcrowding of Schools and Universities of 25 April 1933.
8. Walk, 'Jüdisches Schulwesen', p. 420.
9. Ibid.
10. See the reminiscences of Anni Adler in Barbara Becker-Jakli (ed.), *Ich habe Köln doch so geliebt. Lebensgeschichten jüdischer Kölnerinnen und Kölner* (Volksblatt Verlag, Cologne, 1993), pp. 182, 205.
11. Interview, Eric Alexander, Stamford, 16.7.1998
12. Eric Alexander to author, 17.1.1997; interview, Eric Alexander, Stamford, 16.7.1998.

13. Walk, 'Jüdisches Schulwesen', speaks of seventy (p. 422), but Corbach, *Jawne*, p. 29, refers to the higher figure.

14. Marta Appel in Richarz, *Jewish Life in Germany*, p. 359.

15. Hilberg, *Vernichtung*, vol. 1, p. 153.

16. Authenticated copy of the Abgangszeugnis from the Jawne Schule, 30.3.1939.

17. Joseph Walk, *Jüdische Schule und Erziehung im Dritten Reich* (Verlag Anton Hain, Frankfurt am Main, 1991), p. 225.

18. Röcher, *jüdische Schule*, p. 219.

19. Deutsche Bank Historisches Zentrum, Frankfurt (DBF) F67/56, Der Oberfinanzpräsident Düsseldorf, Devisenstelle, to Siegfried Israel Strauss, 23.11.1939.

20. Interview, ME, 31.10.1996.

21. Ibid.

22. Bundesarchiv, Berlin (BAB), R4901, 10575/42, document 6, memo, 25.5.1934; document 7, circular, Prussian Ministry for Science, Art and Education to Herren Oberpräsidenten, 27.7.1934.

23. Marianne and other contemporaries referred to Frau Fraenkel as 'Dr', but it seems that this title was purely honorary. Information from her son via Gudrun Maierhof.

24. 'Die Kindergärtnerin und Hortnerin', in LBINY, *BJFB*, vol. II (1935), no. 3, p 6.

25. The Bishop's Avenue is a road of very expensive houses in Hampstead, north London. Marianne's comparison here reminded me that her knowledge of British social geography was now at least as good as her sense of place in Germany.

26. LBINY, *BJFB*, vol. 13 (1937), no. 2, p. 13.

27. 'Die Kindergärtnerin und Hortnerin', in LBINY, *BJFB*, vol. II (1935), no. 3, p. 6.

28. On Hannah Karminski (1897–1942), see Richarz, *Jewish Life in Germany*, p. 342, note 8; correspondence is LBINY AR330 (ex. A.154) LOC. K1/6/E Hannah Karminski, circular letter, 2.7.1939; interview, ME, 31.10.1996.

29. Interview, ME, 31.10.1996.

30. Her testimony was recorded in Switzerland in 1946, see Zentrum für Anti-Semitismusforschung A.15, Edith Dietz, 'Freiheit am Ende des Weges' (recorded 1946 in Zurich). An abbreviated version was later published – Edith Dietz, *Den Nazis entronnen. Die Flucht eines jüdischen Mädchens in die Schweiz. Autobiographischer Bericht 1933–1942* (Dipa Verlag, Frankfurt, 1990).

31. Dietz, 'Freiheit', p. 18.

32. Copy, RV, Abteilung Zentralwohlfahrtsstelle, 23.7.39; Jüdisches Seminar für Kindergärtnerinnen und Hortnerinnen, Berlin (JSK), 'Zeugnis', 20.10.1941, signed Margarethe Fraenkel.

33. 'Zeugnis' from Rosie Zenik [?] Berlin Charlottenburg Uhlandstrasse 179, 28.7.1939. See also reference from Henriette Klein, Berlin, 10.12.1939.

34. Interview, ME, 31.10.1996.

35. Ibid.

36. Ibid.

37. Interview, ME, 10.9.1996.

38. Inge Deutschkron, *Outcast: a Jewish Girl in Wartime Berlin* (Fromm International, New York, 1989). German edition, *Ich trug den gelben Stern* (Deutsche Taschenbuch-Verlag, Munich, 1995).

39. *Ab Heute Heißt Du Sara.*

40. Interview, Inge Deutschkron, Berlin, 28.5.1999. In addition to the interview, some information stems from Inge Deutschkron, *Mein Leben nach dem Überleben* (DTV, Munich, revised edn, 1995).

41. Deutschkron, *Ich trug den gelben Stern*, p. 64.

42. I have slightly stretched the truth here. In fact, number 36 did not match Marianne's description, whereas number 45 did. I stood in front of 45 and thought that changes in the street numbers meant that 'this' was the house. But with the help of Frau Leonore Maier of the Jewish Museum and Herr Andreas Matschenz of the Landesarchiv Berlin I was able to find out that there had been no number change and 36 was still where it always had been. It is possible that the house has been rebuilt, of course.

43. Interview, ME, 31.10.1996. The comment about Goering was off the tape.

44. Ibid.

45. Erica Fischer, *Aimée & Jaguar: a Love Story, Berlin 1943* (paperback edition, Bloomsbury, London, 1996), p. 70.

46. Interview, ME, 31.10.1996.

47. Jüdische Wohlfahrts- und Jugendpflegestelle, Taubstummenheim und Gehörlosenschule, Berlin-Weissensee, Parkstrasse 22, report, 20.9.1940 and additional note Jüdische Gemeinde zu Berlin eV, Jüdische Wohlfahrts- und Jugendpflegestelle to Jüdisches Seminar für Kindergärtnerinnen und Hortnerinnen, Berlin, Wangenheimstrasse 36, 24.9.1940.

48. Interview, ME, 31.10.1996.

49. Ibid.

50. This may indeed have been its original home, since the College's founding address was in Meineckerstrasse.

51. Interview, ME, 31.10.1996.

52. Carola Sachse (ed.), *Als Zwangsarbeiterin 1941 in Berlin: die Aufzeich-nungen der Volkswirtin Elisabeth Freund* (Akademie Verlag, Berlin, 1996), p. 112; Wolf Gruner, *Judenverfolgung in Berlin 1933–1945. Eine Chronologie der Behördenmaβnahmen in der Reichshauptstadt* (Edition Hentrich, Berlin, 1996), pp. 9–11.

53. Interview, ME, 31.10.1996.

54. Dietz, 'Freiheit', p. 21.

55. Sachse, *Als Zwangsarbeiterin 1941 in Berlin*, p. 96.

56. Ibid, p. 116.

57. Gruner, *Judenverfolgung*, p. 78.

58. Interview, ME, 31.10.1996.

59. Gruner, *Judenverfolgung*, p. 79.

60. Sachse, *Als Zwangsarbeiterin 1941 in Berlin*, p. 82.

61. Ibid., p. 92.

62. Dietz, 'Freiheit', p. 82.

63. Sachse, *Als Zwangsarbeiterin 1941 in Berlin*, pp. 51–52, 58, 79–80. In the course of 1941, however, the women became too tired and their courses came to an end (p. 89).

64. Jüdische Kultusvereinigung zu Berlin e.V., Säuglings und Kinderheim, to JSK, Marburgerstr. 5, 6.10.1941.

65. Ludwig and Selma Ansbacher, Frankfurt, to MS, 1.5.1946. Marianne knew Trudy (then 'Trude') in Berlin by her maiden name Ullmann, but she married very soon after the war, so Marianne had the opportunity to see her in Germany as Mrs Schloss.

66. On the demanding nature of the course, see also Ruth Arndt, cited in Ingrid Littmann-Hotopp, *Bei Dir findet das verlassene Kind Erbarmen. Zur Geschichte des ersten jüdischen Säuglings- und Kleinkinderheims in Deutschland (1907 bis 1942)* (Edition Hentrich, Berlin, 1996), pp. 90–91.

67. Jüdische Kultusvereinigung zu Berlin e.V., Säuglings und Kinderheim, to Jüdisches Seminar für Kindergärtnerinnen und Hortnerinnen, Berlin, Marburgerstr. 5, 6.10.1941.

68. Littmann-Hotopp, *Bei Dir findet das verlassene Kind Erbarmen*, p. 114.

69. Dietz, 'Freiheit', p. 21.

70. Richarz, *Jewish Life in Germany*, p. 447, note 1.

71. Sachse, *Als Zwangsarbeiterin 1941 in Berlin*, p. 149.

72. Richarz, *Jewish Life in Germany*, p. 448, note 4.

73. Camilla Neumann, née Salinger, in Richarz, *Jewish Life in Germany*, p. 435.

74. Dietz, 'Freiheit', p. 24.

75. RV Abteilung Fürsorge, 19.1.1942.

76. Trudy was still in close contact with her former fellow-nurse, Ruth Arndt, who now lives in California.

77. EK to MS, 'Mittwoch Abend' [4.2.1942].

78. As noted above, Ernst had studied in Berlin in the 1930s and Marianne had come to know some of his former friends.

79. Sometimes he signed himself Ernst and sometimes Ernest.

80. According to the *Wegweiser durch das jüdische Berlin* (Berlin, 1937), p. 13 Iranischestrasse 3 is listed as the Kindergarten and Hort of the Jewish Community. This was presumably the last home of the Seminar. Iranischestrasse 4 must have been the place of the halls of residence. I am grateful to Dr Jörg H. Fehrs for this information.

81. An asterisk links this quotation to Ilmenau.

82. EK to MS, 'Monday' [9.2.1942].

83. Ibid.

84. MS to EK, 11.2.1942.

85. In German, as in English, the normal phrase would be 'life and death'.

86. MS to EK, 17.2.1942.

87. MS to EK, 11.2.1942.

88. MS to EK, 13.2.1942.

89. MS to EK, 14.2.1942.

90. Ibid.

91. Walk, *Jüdische Schule*, p. 323

92. See, for example copy, Hermann to Regierungspräsidenten, Dezernat für Wiedergutmachung, 28.2.1958.

93. This was to be the last exam. On 1.4.1942, the College was disbanded. BAB R4901, 10575/41, Stadtpräsident der Reichshauptstadt Berlin to Reichsminister für Wissenschaft, Erziehung und Volksbildung, 23.4.1942.

5   *The Family, the Gestapo, the Abwehr and the Banker*

1. Dippel, *Bound Upon a Wheel of Fire*, pp. xix, 222.

2. Copy, SStr to Fritz Stern, 16.1.1941.

3. Certificate, dated 30.7.1941.

4. Copy, SStr to Grete and family, 5.3.1941.

5. Hugo Strauss to Siegried and Ine, 31.1.1939.

6. Copy, RW to Ernst Dahl, 22.7.1960.

7. Copy, SStr to Hugo, Essen, 9.12.1940.

8. Hugo Strauss to SStr and family, 7.1.1941.

9. Copy, AS (Lore) to Uncle Markus and family, 6.9.1941; see also copy in Siegfried's hand, Fritz Stern to Strauss family, 9.5.1941.

10. Copy AS to Marcus Strauss and family, 6.9.1941.

11. DBF F67/56, various memos from the Zollfahndungszweigsstelle, Essen, later from the Oberfinanzpräsident, Düsseldorf, Devisenstelle (ODD).

12. Sachs, *Als Zwangsarbeiterin 1941 in Berlin*, p. 123.

13. Joseph Walk, *Das Sonderrecht für die Juden im NS-Staat* (C. F. Müller, Heidelberg, 1981), pp. 312, 314, 328.

14. I am indebted to Michael Zimmermann, as for so much, for alerting me to the documents in the Essen Stadtarchiv. Those documents cited without a class-mark are in the Ellenbogens' possession.

15. StAE Rep. 102/1/33, Stadtrat Schlicht to Herrn Oberbürgermeister Dillgardt, 5.12.1940.

16. StAE 45 – 2515, Schwarzlose to Grundstücksamt, 23.12.1940.

17. StAE 45 – 2515, memo: E d29/1/1941.

18. This was the only way to circumvent the punitive currency conversion rates.

19. StAE 45 – 2515, Vermerk 25–2–1047/40 E d4/2/1941. And again in February, EP, Schwarzlose to Siegfried Israel Strauss, 8.2.1941.

20. StAE 45 – 2515, letter from Dipl. Kaufm. Ricco Arendt to Oberbürgermeister, 3.6.1941.

21. Wolfgang Dressen, *Betrifft: 'Aktion 3'. Deutsche verwerten jüdische Nachbarn* (Aufbau Verlag, Berlin, 1998).

22. HStAD RW58 74234, Alfred Strauss, Kripo Essen, Strafanzeige, 12.5.1941.

23. Ibid.

24. HStAD RW58 74234, ADStE to StaPoD, 26.5.1941.

25. HStAD RW58 74234, Alfred Strauss, Kripo Essen, Strafanzeige, 12.5.1941.

26. HStAD RW58 74234, copy of judgment to ADStE, signed Oberstaatsanwalt i.A. Dr Cohausz, 22.5.1941.

27. HStAD RW58 74234, ADStE to StaPoD, 26.5 1941.

28. Note from Polizei Präsident, Essen, 5.6.1941.

29. Reichsgesetzblatt I S. 1709.

30. StAE 45 – 2515, SStr to Hernn Oberbürgermeister, 4.7.1941; memo, 25–2–1047/40; StAE document 17817 Beurkundungsregister A Nr 49/41; Beurkundungsregister A Nr 50/41 verhandelt Essen.

31. Copy, SStr to Gilka, 17.9.1941.

32. Copy, SStr (Ine) to Grete and family, 4.9.1941.

33. Copy [draft] ME to LG Essen, Wiedergutmachungskammer (WGK), 2.10.1952. There is more than one copy of this document; only in one is the head of the Wohnungsamt identified by name.
34. Copy, JSK, 'Zeugnis' Fräulein Marianne Sara Strauss.
35. The date is clear from copy of a letter to EK, dated 25.10.1942.
36. Schröter, *Geschichte und Schicksal*, p. 346.
37. HStAD RW36, 19, StaPoD to Aussendienstellen, 11.10.1941; Schröter, *Geschichte und Schicksal*, p. 56.
38. StAE, Rep 102/I/33, copy Der Oberbürgermeister als Preisbehörde St.A. 34–5 Gr.1643, Genehmigung, 24.10.1941, signed Dr Zwick, Direktor.
39. Interview, ME, 1989.
40. HStAD RW58, 45264, memo headed 'Dauerdeint: Essen 25.10.1941', clearly lists those due for transportation as Siegfried Strauss, Regina and Richard. The deportation list in Schröter, *Geschichte und Schicksal*, p. 368 also does not list Marianne.
41. Interview, ME, 1989.
42. HStAD RW36, 19, StaPoD to Aussendienstellen, 11.10.1941.
43. Interview, ME, 1989.
44. Interview, ME, 10.9.1996.
45. Ibid.
46. Telephone conversation with Hanna Aron, 20.10.97.
47. Author to Imo Moszkowicz, 24.10.1997.
48. Interview, Imo Moszkowicz, Munich, 14.6.1999.
49. Winfried Meyer, *Unternehmen Sieben. Eine Rettungsaktion für vom Holocaust Bedrohte aus dem Amt Ausland/Abwehr im Oberkommando der Wehrmacht* (Verlag Anton Hain, Frankfurt am Main, 1993), pp. 100–102; Heinz Höhne, 'Canaris und die Abwehr zwischen Anpassung und Opposition', in Jürgen Schmädeke and Peter Steinbach (eds.), *Der Widerstand gegen den Nationalsozialismus* (Munich and Zurich, 1985), pp 405–416, at p. 407; Eberhard Bethge, *Dietrich Bonhoeffer. Theologe. Christ. Zeitgenosse* (Chr. Kaiser Verlag, Munich, 2nd edn, 1967), pp. 702–708.
50. HStAD RW58, 45264, telegram Bremen to ADStE, 22.10.41.
51. HStAD RW58, 45264, telegram ADStE to StaPoD, 25.10.1941.
52. HStAD RW58, 45264, StaPoD to RSHA, 25.10.1941.
53. Ibid.
54. Ibid.
55. See HStAD RW58, 74234, memo II B 4/71.02/Strauss Düsseldorf, [25]. 10.1941, added in typescript to StaPoD telegram to RSHA, which is a copy of the telegram in the Siegfried Strauss file.

56. HStAD RW58, 45264, memo headed 'Dauerdeint: Essen 25.10.1941'.

57. HStAD RW58, 74234, draft of StaPoD IIB4 to StaPo Bremen, 28.10.1941.

58. HStAD RW58, 74234, telegram, Bremen to StaPoD, 4.11.41.

59. HStAD RW58, 74234, ADStE to StaPoD, 6.11.1941.

60. Meyer, *Unternhmen Sieben*.

61. For this and the following sections, the sources used, other than Meyer, *Unternehmen Sieben* and Bethge, *Dietrich Bonhoeffer*, are Elisabeth Chowaniec, *Der 'Fall Dohnanyi' 1943–1945* (R. Oldenbourg Verlag, Munich, 1991), pp 10–17; Christoph Strohm, *Theologische Ethik im Kampf gegen den Nationalsozialismus. Der Weg Dietrich Bonhoeffers mit den Juristen Hans von Dohnanyi und Gerhard Leibholz in den Widerstand* (Christian Kaiser, Munich, 1989), pp. 231–289.

62. Meyer, *Unternhmen Sieben*, p. 336; Bethge, *Bonhoeffer*, pp. 898ff.

63. Meyer, *Unternhmen Sieben*, pp. 100–102; the proportion of active opponents is based on Höhne, 'Canaris und die Abwehr', p. 407.

64. Meyer, *Unternhmen Sieben*, pp. 206ff.

65. Ibid., pp. 213, 223.

66. Ibid., pp. 209–212, 235.

67. HStAD RW58, 74234, letter from Wilhelm Hammacher DBE to ADStE, 2.7.1943.

68. Copy, W. Hammacher to CH, 27.6.1957.

69. See note 33 above.

70. Interview, Hanna Aron, West Hartford, Connecticut, 7.8.1998.

71. Copy, Öffentliche Sitzung des II.WGK beim LG Dortmund, Dortmund, 4.11.1960.

72. 'Eidesstattliche Erklärung', signed ME, Liverpool, 14.11.1961.

73. Interview, Hanna Aron, West Hartford, Connecticut, 7.8.1998.

74. LBINY, SAFE ME805, Arthur Prinz, *Plunging Into Chaos*.

75. NS-Documentationszentrum der Stadt Köln (eds.), *Die jüdischen Opfer des Nationalsozialismus aus Köln. Gedenkbuch* (Böhlau Verlag, Cologne, 1995), pp. 490–491, 536–537.

76. YVJ file 0.48/1630.2 Archiv 13390, very tattered mail, no envelope, from Rosenberg/Strauss to Alfred Weinberg, Essen, 5.11.1941.

77. YVJ file 0.48/1630.2 Archiv 13390, George Morel Delegate in Australia and New Zealand of the IRC to Alfred Weinberg, Internment Camp, 20.8.1942.

78. Schröter, *Geschichte und Schicksal*, p. 379.

79. HStAD RW58, 45264, AStDE to StaPoD, 7.11.1941, and enclosure, Bremen Nr 7137, 6.11.41, 1800 hrs.

80. ASE, AR.8043, Leopold to Walter Sternberg, 20.3.1942.

81. ASE, AR.8043, Leopold to Walter Sternberg, 8.6.1942.

82. Copy, SStr to Fritz Stern, 17.11.1941.

83. The somewhat later Wannsee conference in January 1942, once viewed as the moment at which murder policy was decided on, is now seen more as establishing responsibility and procedure.

84. HStAD RW58, 45264, return from Finanzamt Essen Süd to ADStE, 5.6.1941.

85. Copy, Finanzamt Essen-Süd to Schroetter, 7.2.195[2?].

86. Rheinisch-Westfälische Bank, Filiale Essen, Tagesauszüge, SStr 60 723.

87. Copy, 'Teil-Beschluss in der Wiedergutmachungssache der Erben nach SStr und AS . . .', Gericht der Wiedergutmachung des LGE, Essen, 1.9.1953.

88. The fact that Alfred was able to make the transfer on that date raises questions. Had the contact with the Abwehr begun earlier in October? In which case, it is not obvious why the Abwehr representative visited on the 24th. Possibly, the brothers were able to use their assets *before* Abwehr intervention, but this seems unlikely. Possibly the date in the restitution papers is wrong.

89. RW to ME, 12.3.1955, attached schedule in respect of AS; copy, RW to May, 19.5.1961, annex, copy, Hammacher to Schroetter, 14.8.1951.

90. Copy, RW to Oberstadtdirektor Essen, Gutachterausschuß für Grundstückswerte, 3.3.1954; copy DBE to RW, 12.6.1963.

91. WGK des LGE, Beschluß Rü Sp 18–54 Rü 1171–50 in der Rückerstattungssache der Erben nach dem Kaufmann AS, Essen, 15.5.1956.

92. DBE to LGD, 7. Entschädigungskammer, 5.3.1965; Meyer to Schroetter, 21.5.1952, enclosures: copy of letter from lawyer Beyhoff to SStr, 29.1.1942; excerpt from Abtretungserklärung from SStr, 19.11.1941.

93. Copy, Finanzamt Essen Süd to Schroetter, 7.2.1955.

94. RW to ME, 12.3.1955, attached listing of claims in respect of AS.

95. HStAD RW58, 74234, ADStE Abt II B 4 IA, telegram to StaPoD, 20.11.1941.

96. HStAD RW58, 74234, copy with Geheim stamp ADStE II B 4 to Polizeipräs Abt II, 24.11.1941. We also do not know what the situation was in relation to Lore's mother, Else Dahl.

97. HStAD RW58, 74234, StaPoD draft telegram to RSHA IV B 4, 20.11.1941 (Eichmann) (sent 21.11.1941).

98. HStAD RW58, 74234, RSHA IV B 4 b 3182/41g (1445), telegram to StaPoD, SS Obersturmbannführer Oberreigerungsrat Dr Albath persönlich, 2.12.1941, signed Eichmann.

99. HStAD RW 58, 74234, draft, StaPoD to StaPo Bremen, 6.12.1941; draft StaPoD to ADStE, 8.12.1941; additional memo 10.1.1942, noting that no response has yet been received from Bremen.

100. HStAD RW 58, 45264, StaPoD to ADStE, 24.3.1942, betrifft den Juden Siegfried Israel Strauss.

101. HStAD RW 58, 74234, ODD Gen. Abt III/Ausw./Tal to StaPoD, 2.6.1942.

102. HStAD RW 58, 74234, StaPoD II B 4 to ODD, 19.6.1942.

103. HStAD RW 58, 74234, ODD Gen. Abt III/Ausw./Tal to StaPoD, 20.7.1942.

104. HStAD RW 58, 74234, RSHA IV B 4 a 3182/41g (1445) to StaPoD, 16.7.1942; ADStE to StaPoD telegram 10.8.1942; draft, StaPoD to RSHA, 12.8.1942.

105. EK, Izbica report.

106. Hugo Strauss to ME, 27.3.1948, annex: invoice from Marcus Cohn, Austrasse, Basel dated 19.5.1947.

107. HStAD RW 58, 74234, ADStE II B 3 – 285/42g to StaPoD, 6.11.1942.

108. HStAD RW 58, 74234, RSHA IV B 4 a 3028/42, letter to StaPoD 5.10.1942, signed Moes.

109. HStAD RW 58, 74234, draft telegram StaPoD to ADStE, 14.10.1942.

110. HStAD RW 58, 74234, ADStE II B 3 – 285/42g to StaPoD, 6.11.1942.

111. HStAD RW 58, 74234, draft StaPoD II B 3/Tgb Nr 421/42g/Strauss to RSHA IV B 4 a, 18.11.1942.

112. A copy of his letter to Abwehr is in HStAD RW 58, 74234, RSHA telegram to StaPoD, 19.12.1943.

113. This date does not correspond to any particular document in the Gestapo files. It may correspond to a decision within the RSHA that the Strausses should be at least temporarily reprieved. The formal approval of the Strausses' exemption, as noted above, was sent to Düsseldorf only in March 1942.

114. HStAD RW 58, 74234, RSHA Roem 4 B 4 – 3182/42g (1445) to StaPoD 19.12.1943, signed Eichmann; Meyer, *Unternehmen Sieben*, p. 421.

6 Love Letters in the Holocaust

1. Interview, ME, 31.10.1996.

2. Oberbürgermeister der Stadt Essen to Alfred Israel Strauss, 23.4.1940.

3. Interview, ME, July 1996.

4. Interview, ME, 31.10.1996.

5. MS, private diary, 10/11.10.1942.

6. Interview, ME, 31.10.1996.

7. Postcard, EK to MS, 30.3.1942.

8. Enrique Krombach to author, 31.12.1996.

9. This section draws also on interviews Enrique recorded with Angela Genger and Benno Reicher, ASE, reference IN 002, 10.6.1983 and IN 260, 26.10.1987.

10. On Herzfeld and the RV's creation, see Otto Dov Kulka (ed.), *Deutsches Judentum unter dem Nationalsozialismus*, vol 1: *Dokumente zur Geschichte der Reichsvertretung der deutschen Juden 1933–1939* (Mohr Siebeck, Tübingen, 1997), pp. 56–63; LBINY file ME 287 Herzfeld.

11. Schröter, *Geschichte und Schicksal*, pp. 48, 193, 623.

12. Enrique's account of his father's life in 'Dr David Krombach, ein Leben aus dem Glauben', in Schröter, *Geschichte und Schicksal*, pp.193–194; Bernd Schmalhausen, *Schicksale jüdischer Juristen aus Essen 1933– 1945*, (Klartext, Essen, 1994), pp. 81f.; E. G. Lowenthal, *Bewährung im Untergang. Ein Gedenkbuch* (Deutsche Verlags-Anstalt, Stuttgart, 1965), p. 110.

13. Lowenthal, *Bewährung*, p. 110.

14. ASE interview, IN 260, 26.10.1987; ASE interview, IN 002, 10.6.1983.

15. The CV Youth was later renamed and absorbed into the 'Ring – League of German Youth' (Ring – Bund jüdischer Jugend). On the German-Jewish wing of the youth movement, see Kulka, *Deutsches Judentum*, p. 466.

16. Enrique Krombach to ME, 20.6.1988.

17. See *50 Jahre Jubiläum der Schüler der Israelitischen Gartenbauschule Ahlem* (no date, no place), in the Wiener library, London.

18. See Schmalhausen, *Schicksale*.

19. ASE AR 4434, Liesel Sternberg to Dr Alexander, 20.8.1945.

20. Interview, Liesel Sternberg, Birmingham, 11.9.1997.

21. Sadly, Mrs Sternberg has since died. Britain was distinctive in admitting many Jewish refugees as domestic servants; see Tony Kushner, *The Holocaust and the Liberal Imagination: a Social and Cultural History* (Blackwell, Oxford and Cambridge, Mass., 1994), pp. 90–118.

22. Letter-diary, final entry, New Year's Day 1943.

23. Undated pencilled note in Marianne's handwriting on the back of the timetable.

24. EK to MS, 'Sonntag Abend' [8.2.1942].

25. Ibid.

26. The couple were Harry and Grete Höllander, neé Levy. Both were soon

deported and murdered; see Schröter, *Geschichte und Schicksal*, pp. 590, 387.

27. MS to EK, 6.2.1942.

28. MS to EK, 8.2.1942.

29. EK to MS, 'Sonntag Abend' [8.2.1942].

30. EK to MS, 'Montag Abend noch 7 Tage!' [16.2.1942].

31. EK to MS, 'Sonntag Abend' [8.2.1942].

32. EK to MS, 'Dienstag' [10.2.1942].

33. EK to MS, 'Montag' [16.2.1942].

34. EK to MS, 'Dienstag, noch 6 Tage' [17.2.1942].

35. MS to EK, 18.2.1942.

36. Ibid.

37. MS to EK, 19.2.1942.

38. Interview, ME, 31.10.1996.

39. MS, private diary, 5.2.1943.

40. Hand-posted letter from EK to MS, 26.3.1942.

41. EK to MS [pencilled date is 30.3.1942. This is a Monday, and from the card which followed, I think the date has been added by MS, and is the day she received it. I think the letter was written late the day before].

42. Letter-diary, final entry, New Year's Day 1943.

43. Interview, ME, July 1996.

44. Essen Alte Synagoge (ed.), *Essen unter Bomben: Märztage 1943* (Klartext Verlag, Essen, 1984), pp. 46–47.

45. Artur and Dore Jacobs' role is explored more fully below. See pp. 269 ff.

46. StAE, Nachlaß Jacobs, Artur Jacobs diary (henceforth StAE NJ AJD), 13.3.1942. A number of later references place it beyond doubt that 'Dr K' is David Krombach.

47. Schröter, *Geschichte und Schicksal*, pp. 380–402.

48. Michael Zimmermann, 'Die Deportation der Juden aus Essen und dem Regierungsbezirk Düsseldorf', in Ulrich Borsdorf and Mathilde Jamin (eds.), *Überleben im Krieg. Kriegserfahrungen in einer Industrieregion 1939–1945*, (Rowohlt, Hamburg, 1989), pp. 126–143.

49. Schröter, *Geschichte und Schicksal*, p. 380.

50. All this from Zimmermann, 'Deportation der Juden', pp. 127–131.

51. StAE NJ AJD, 14.4.1942.

52. Franciszek Zabecki, *Wspomnienia dawne i nowe* (Warsaw, 1977), p. 45.

53. In full: Lublin, Belzyce, Izbica Lubielska, Kamionka, Luszawa, Ostrow, Piaski, Rejowiece and Zamosc. The standard work remains Hans-Günther Adler, *Der Verwaltete Mensch. Studien zur Deportation der Juden aus Deutschland* (JCB Mohr/Paul Siebeck, Tübingen, 1974).

Adler's extraordinary painstaking research has never been given the acknowledgement it deserves.

54. Postcard from Ernst Israel Krombach, III/418, Transport Essen Izbica a.d. Wilpez, krs Krasnyetaw b. Lublin, Gen. Gouvern., Post Ältestenrat., 25.4.1942.

55. Martin Gilbert, *The Macmillan Atlas of the Holocaust* (Macmillan, New York, 1982), p. 91.

56. *Gedenkbuch Opfer der Verfolgung der Juden* (Bundesarchiv, Koblenz, 1986), pp. 1759ff.

57. The main part of the journey began only on 22 April. But the Essen Jews were taken on 21 April to spend a night in Düsseldorf before deportation.

58. Schmalhausen, *Schicksale*, p. 82.

59. Interview, ME, July 1996.

60. It is possible that she had known Jacobs for longer, since she said in a letter to Yad Vashem in 1984 that she met Jacobs in 1941.

61. See note 57 above.

62. 'Erinnerungen an das Lager am Holbeckshof', in *Stationen jüdischen Lebens*, pp. 232–235.

63. Interview, Hanna Aron, West Hartford, Connecticut, 7.8.1998. See also Mark Roseman 'Surviving memory: truth and inaccuracy in Holocaust testimony', *British Journal of Holocaust Education* (1999); 'Erinnerung und Überleben: Wahrheit und Widerspruch in dem Zeugnis einer Holocaust-Überlebenden', *BIOS*, vol. 11 (1998), no. 2, pp. 263–279.

64. MS, letter-diary, 26.4.42.

65. Interview, ME, July 1996.

66. Enrique Krombach to ME, Buenos Aires 28.5.1989.

67. Interview, ME, 10.9.1996.

68. MS, letter-diary, 30.4.1942.

69. This is clearly an oblique reference to Cuba.

70. Postcard, 21.4.1942, 'nach Mülheim', postmarked Duisburg.

71. Postcard, 'Wednesday early' [22.4.1942].

72. Zimmermann, 'Deportation der Juden', p. 132.

73. Ibid., p. 135.

74. Postcard, 'Wednesday early' [22.4.1942], postmarked Düsseldorf.

75. EK to MS, 22.8.1942. This is the first of two letters sent on that day. This one, an eighteen-page account which must be one of the most remarkable contemporary documents of the Holocaust, will be referred to henceforth as 'Izbica report', the other as 'Arbeitsbericht'. See the following chapter.

76. I.e., as one of the Jewish orderlies.

77. Zimmermann thought the transportees were then taken on to the extermination camps Belzec, Kulmhof, Sobibor, Maidanek or Treblinka within a few days. However, it is clear from EK's letters that this was not the case.

78. Letter, Thursday, 23.4.1942

79. We do not know to what he refers.

80. Dr Rudolf Löwenstein, b. 6.3.1900 in Essen Steele. He had practised as a doctor in Soest until 1938; after his licence was withdrawn, he had moved to Essen. Rudi was deported with his wife Grete (Margarete, née Katzenstein), b. 18.9.1901, and his son Klaus, b. 16.3.1930. His daughter Klara, b. 9.6.1932, seems to have survived, though she too was deported – see the deportation list in Schröter, *Geschichte und Schicksal*, p. 392; see also Ingrid Niemann and Ludger Hülskemper Niemann, *Vom Geleitbrief zum gelben Stern. 450 Jahre jüdisches Leben in Steele* (Klartext, Essen, 1994), p. 172, note 94.

81. Postcard, Ostrowo, 23.4.1942.

82. EK talks of a *coupé*, which suggests they were in passenger carriages, although Michael Zimmermann states that they were in goods trucks.

83. The first reports from Düsseldorf, as Jacobs noted, were very negative.

84. See Schröter, *Geschichte und Schicksal*, pp. 40, 472, 500. I discovered that Herta's sister had emigrated to Birmingham and was living just a mile and a half away from my home, in a nursing home. Sadly, though, in the opinion of the nursing staff, her physical and mental state precluded an interview. She has since died.

85. Postcard from Ernst Israel Krombach, III/418, Transport Essen Izbica a.d. Wilpez, krs Krasnyetaw b. Lublin, Gen. Gouvern., Post Ältestenrat., 25.4.1942.

86. MS, letter-diary, 24.4.1942.

87. MS, letter-diary, 30.4.1942.

88. MS, letter-diary, 26.4.1942.

89. StAE NJ AJD, 5.5.1942.

90. MS, letter-diary, 26.4.42.

91. MS, letter-diary, 3.5.1942.

92. Pencil-written letter EK to MS, 5.7.1942.

93. Pencil-written letter EK to MS, 9.8.1942.

94. Postcard, 31.5.1942.

95. MS, letter-diary, 6.8.1942.

96. Letter, 11.8.1942.

97. Ibid.

98. Letter in pencil from 11.8.1942.

99. In copy of letter to 'Hetty', 29/30.6.1942. Ernest is here referred to as Arthur – a name in which he also signed some of his cards. I was not able to ascertain Hetty's identity.

100. Unsigned note from 3.5.1942, probably from Rudi Löwenstein.

101. Entry: 'Pfingstmontag, den 25.5'.

102. MS, entry 'Mittwochabend' [27.5.1942].

103. Yitzhak Arad, *Belzec, Sobibor, Treblinka – the Operation Reinhard Death Camps* (Indiana University Press, Bloomington, 1987), pp. 383, 390. On what EK knew, see the next chapter.

104. Copy, MS, letter to Hetty, 29/30.6.1942.

105. MS, letter-diary, 4.6.1942.

106. MS, letter-diary, 7.6.1942.

107. EK, 'Izbica report', p. 6.

108. MS, letter-diary, 29/30.6.1942.

109. Letter from EK, 5.7.1942.

110. EK, 'Izbica report'.

111. Copy, MS, letter to Hetty, 6.8.1942.

112. From other references, it seems likely that this refers to Melitta Levy, a young woman of about Marianne's age, who with her rather older husband Kurt had been one of the couples Marianne enjoyed visiting in the Holbeckshof and who now, after the July deportations, had been moved into the Jewish Community building at Hindenburgstrasse 22. See Schröter, *Geschichte und Schicksal*, pp. 428, 447. Both were eventually deported to Auschwitz on the last major Essen transport of 1 March 1943. It is not clear why Ernst was sending letters via Melitta (or why Marianne was sending messages via Hetty). Possibly they wished to avoid attracting attention by sending too many letters to the same addressee.

7 Report from Izbica

1. Interview, ME, 31.10.1996.

2. MS, letter-diary, 2.8.1942.

3. The surviving copy of the letter has no heading or date. Typed on it is simply 'Mit Christian'.

4. No heading, attached to the above.

5. MS, letter-diary, 17.8.1942.

6. MS, letter-diary, 27.8.1942.

7. MS, letter-diary, 3.9.1942.

8. Letter in pencil from EK [from Izbica], 23.8.1942, henceforth 'cover note'.

9. Hand-written note from Rudi and Grete Löwenstein, 21.8.1942.

10. Letter in pencil, dated 22/23.8.1942, henceforth 'Task list'.

11. Ibid.

12. In German, the convention is to write the date in the form 'Izbica, the 9th August 1942'.

13. E. Thomas Wood and Stanislaw M. Jankowski, *Karski: How One Man Tried to Stop the Holocaust* (John Wiley & Sons, 1994) suggest that in 1942 Polish underground fighter Jan Karski visited Izbica and not Belzec, as Karski claimed.

14. Thomas Toivi Blatt, *From the Ashes of Sobibor. A Story of Survival* (Northwestern University Press, Evanston. Ill., 1997). Mr Blatt kindly also sent me a copy of *Sobibor, the Forgotten Revolt: a Survivor's Report* (HEP, Issaquah Wash., 1996).

15. I.e. should the Strauss family be deported, Marianne might well choose to accompany Christian to Izbica.

16. See previous chapter, note 80 and text.

17. With whom the Krombachs had been living before deportation.

18. This is something of an exaggeration. Perhaps two-thirds of the town's Jews had been deported.

19. Ernst's comment in German is 'Sie sind nicht so wie wir auf das Judentum gestossen worden und zu ihm zurückgeführt worden.'

20. This section is not clear in the German. It seems that the members of the transport had to come up with a certain amount of gold to avoid its leaders being shot.

21. In the German, the list of presents include 'Nuss-Maske', the meaning of which eluded me.

22. This is hard to square with his earlier letter in which he said he did not work, it was not customary. Perhaps he had now forgotten his first weeks of idleness.

23. Evidently a brand of medicine.

24. Postcard, Ostrowo, 23.4.1942

25. Blatt, *Ashes*, pp. 16ff.

26. Thomas Blatt to author, 19.2.1997.

27. YVJ, Hejnoch Nobel, b. 1.2.1896 in Izbica, testimony 19.5.1946.

28. As an example of the quality of Ernst's information, with the aid of the historian Peter Witte, I was able to establish that his listings of the transports to Izbica was highly, possibly completely accurate.

29. Arad, *Belzec, Sobibor, Treblinka*, p. 243.

30. Blatt, *Ashes*, p. 33.

31. Arad, *Belzec, Sobibor, Treblinka*, p. 244.

32. Interview, ME, 10.9.1996; supplementary information interview, ME, 31.10.1996.

33. Christian and Lilli Arras to MS, 7.9.1946.

34. Interview, ME, 31.10.1996.

35. The first massive raid on Essen took place on 5 March 1943, when 442 planes bombarded the city for about an hour. Some 50,000 residents lost their homes and another 20,000 had to move out temporarily. *Essen unter Bomben*, p. 26.

36. Interview, Lilli Arras, 10.1.1997.

37. Lilli Arras to author, 30.1.1997.

38. Ibid.

39. Interview, Lilli Arras, 10.1.1997; Lilli Arras to author, 1.3.1997.

40. Herr Bartnick, Bundesarchiv, section III Z 4 to author, 26.2.1997.

41. Lilli Arras to author, 1.3.1997.

42. Interview, Lilli Arras, 10.1.1997.

43. StAE NJ AJD, 4.9.1942.

44. Conversation between Gummersbach and Moszkowicz recorded June 1988, reproduced in Gummersbach, 'Ahlen', p. 250.

45. Ibid.

46. Imo Moszkowicz to author, 2.9.1997.

47. Interview, Hanna Aron, West Hartford, Connecticut, 7.8.1998.

48. Email, Hanna Aron to author, 27.9.1999.

49. After completing the manuscript, I discovered Christian's De-Nazification Panel report from the post-war period. This too confirmed that he had been a member of neither the SS nor the Nazi Party. See HStAD NW 1005–6. 11 119.

50. Email, Hanna Aron to author, 27.9.1999.

51. ASE Izbica 4431, Archiv der Zentralen Stelle der Landesjustizverwaltungen in Ludwigsburg, Akten, Vermerke des Unterabteilungsleiters Türk, Chef der Unterabteilung Bevölkerungswesen und Fürsorge in der Inneren Verwaltung beim Distriktchef von Lublin, 20.3.1942; Dieter Pohl, *Von der 'Judenpolitik' zum Judenmord: der Distrikt Lublin des Generalgouvernements 1939–1944* (Lang, Frankfurt am Main, 1993), p. 119.

52. This was the deportation of most of the ghetto's inmates, not the assault against the Warsaw Underground, which took place in May 1943. See Israel Gutman, *Resistance: the Warsaw Ghetto Uprising* (Mariner, Boston and New York, 1994).

53. Christopher Browning, 'Foreword', in Blatt, *Ashes*, pp. xiii–xix, at pp. xvi–xvii; Pohl, *Judenpolitik*, pp. 128–139.

54. MS, private diary, 'Sonntag' [4.10.1942]; entry 'den 12.[10.42]'.

55. MS, letter-diary, 22.10.1942.

56. Pohl, *Judenpolitik*, p. 138.

57. Ibid., p. 137.

58. Blatt, *Ashes*, p. 42

59. Pohl, *Judenpolitik*, p. 165.

60. MS, private diary, 25.11.1942. By this time most of the deportees to Izbica had been murdered.

61. Interview, ME, 31.10.1996.

62. Interviews, ME, 10.9.1996, 31.10.1996.

63. Presumably Carl Austerlitz, in Glogau, brother of a close friend of the Krombachs.

64. Emil C. Fuchs to MS, 8.1.1943.

65. Deutsches Rotes Kreuz (DRK), Der Beauftragte beim Generalgouverneur, Krakau, to Marianne Sara Strauss, 26.1.1943.

66. DRK, Der Beauftragte beim Generalgouverneur, Krakau, to Marianne Sara Strauss, 10.2.1943.

67. Copy, Marianne Sara Strauss, Hindenburgstr. 75, to DRK Krakau, 17.2.1943.

68. DRK, Der Beauftragte beim Generalgouverneur, Krakau, to Marianne Sara Strauss, 13.3.1943.

69. Copy, Marianne Sara Strauss, Hindenburgstr. 75, to DRK Präsidium, Berlin, 1.4.1943.

70. Copy, Marianne Sara Strauss, Hindenburgstr. 75, to DRK Krakau, 13.4.1943.

71. DRK, Presidium Berlin VII/4 Br.-Pu. to Marianne Sara Strauss, 15.4.1943.

72. Copy, MS to Julie Koppel, 16.5.1943.

73. Schmalhausen, *Schicksale*, pp. 81–82.

74. Julie Koppel to MS, 25.6.1943.

75. Thomas Blatt to author, 11.3.1997.

76. StAE NJ AJD, 31.12.1942.

77. ASE AR 4434, Liesel Sternberg to Dr Alexander, 20.8.1945.

78. Julie Koppel to MS, 25.6.1943.

79. Blatt, *Ashes*; YVJ Nobel, Hejnoch, testimony, 19.5.1946.

8 *Deportations, Death and the Bund*

1. Walk, *Sonderrecht*, pp.364–387; Fischer, *Aimée & Jaguar*, p. 89; interview, Hanna Aron, West Hartford, Connecticut, 7.8.1998; hand-written note, 'An jüdische Kultusvereinigung, Synagogengemeinde Essen e.V.,

Essen', 19.11.1941, signed Siegfr. Isr. Strauss, with added note of when the objects were handed in.

2. Copy, Else Sara Dahl to Postamt Wuppertal-Barmen, 8.2.1942.

3. Postamt 1, Essen, to Frau Else Sara Dahl, 16.2.1942.

4. HStAD RW58, 74234, OFD to StaPoD, 7.6.1943.

5. EK to MS, 'Sonntag Abend', 8.2.1942.

6. Corbach, *Jawne*, p. 29.

7. Interview, ME. 10.9.1996.

8. Interview, Frau Sparrer, 28.7.1997; Waltraud Horn to author, 26.2.1998.

9. Transport to Izbica, 15.6.1942. See Schröter, *Geschichte und Schicksal*, pp. 403f.

10. Schröter, *Geschichte und Schicksal*, p. 686.

11. On the deportation, see Michael Zimmermann, 'Eine Deportation nach Theresienstadt. Zur Rolle des Banalen bei der Durchsetzung des Monströsen', in Miroslav Karny, Raimund Kemper et al. (eds.) *Theresienstädter Studien und Dokumente* (Edition Theresienstädter Initiative Academia, 1994), pp. 54–73, at. p. 56; *Stationen jüdischen Lebens*, p. 246; copy of MS to Julie Koppel 16.5.1943; StAE NJ AJD, 25.7.1942.

12. MS, letter-diary, 21.7.1942.

13. Interview, ME, 31.10.1996.

14. Dried peas.

15. MS, letter-diary, 31.7.1942.

16. War Organization of the British Red Cross and Order of St John, postal message scheme, enquirer Klaus Langer to Erich Israel Langer, 17.9.1942. Copy in possession of the author.

17. Interview, ME, 1989; interview, ME, July 1996.

18. MS, letter-diary, 31.7.1942.

19. Imo Moszkowicz to author, 29.8.1997.

20. Imo Moszkowicz to author, 2.9.1997.

21. MS, letter-diary, 24.4.1942.

22. MS, letter-diary, 7.6.1942.

23. Whether in her community Shavuot was presented in this light we do not know. More usually, Shavuot – which among other things commemorates the giving of the ten commandments – is associated with study rather than contemplation.

24. In the Jewish morning service on the Sabbath and festivals, and also in the afternoon service on the Day of Atonement, a section of the Five Books of Moses, the Torah, is read from the scrolls. For each Torah portion there is an appropriate Haftorah, a selection from the remaining post-Mosaic books of the bible, which is also read.

25. Isaiah, chapter 57, verse 14 to chapter 58, verse 14. In her transcription, Marianne wrongly cites the second part of the passage as chapter 58, verses 1–4.

26. Paucker, 'Zum Selbstverständnis jüdischer Jugend,' p. 114.

27. MS, letter-diary, 28.9.1942.

28. MS, letter-diary, 7.10.1942.

29. MS, private diary, 3.10.1942.

30. Edith Caspari to MS, 31.12.1942. The letter was folded in Marianne's private diary.

31. Richarz, *Jewish Life in Germany*, p. 342, note 8. Caspari talks of eighteen escapees, Richarz of twenty.

32. There is an additional blank sheet with the letter-diary which looks as if it has faint lines of typing on it. Whether this is a faded carbon of further entries or whether it had simply rubbed off from existing entries is impossible to say.

33. Else Bramesfeld, Doris Braune et al. (eds), *Gelebte Utopie: Aus dem Leben einer Gemeinschaft, Nach einer Dokumentation von Dore Jacobs* (Klartext, Essen, 1990). Henceforth *Gelebte Utopie*.

34. The best known being the Internationaler Sozialistischer Kampfbund (ISK), also known as the Nelsen-Bund. There were, in fact, a number of similarities between the ISK and the Bund, see Werner Link, *Die Geschichte des Internationalen Jugend-Bundes und des Internationalen Sozialistischen Kampf-Bundes. Ein Beitrag zur Geschichte der Arbeiterbewegung in der Weimarer Republik und im 3. Reich* (Meisenheim am Glan, 1964).

35. Artur Jacobs, *Der Bund* (Bund Verlag, Essen 1929), p. 41.

36. *Gelebte Utopie*, p. 63.

37. *Gelebte Utopie*; Zum Gedenken an Artur Jacobs, 'Worte zur Gedenkstunde für Artur Jacobs im Bundeshaus am 17. März 1968', in unpublished Bund Manuscript pp. 7–8 (Sonja Schreiber); interviews with Meta Kamp, Ursula Jungbluth.

38. *Gelebte Utopie*; unpublished, printed and bound volume, produced by the Bund in 1989 'Für Lisa Jacob'. The volume contains the article 'Leben und Lernen mit Lisa Jacob', by Ellen Jungbluth.

39. A point also made by Monika Grüter's excellent dissertation 'Der "Bund für ein sozialistisches Leben": Seine Entwicklung in den 20er Jahren und seine Widerständigkeit unter dem Nationalsozialismus' (Examensarbeit, University of Essen, 1988), pp. 59ff.

40. Interview Tove Gerson, Essen, 8.1.1997.

41. Der Bund, *Mann und Frau als Kampfgenossen* (Bund series 'Die Bresche', Essen, 1932).

42. Der Bund. Gemeinschaft für sozialistisches Leben (ed.), *Aus der illegalen Arbeit des Bunds. Zweiter Auslandsbrief* (printed pamphlet, 1948), p. 3.

43. A point made by Grüter: 'Bund', p. 46.

44. *Zweiter Auslandsbrief*, p. 5.

45. Interview, Aenne Schmitz, Wuppertal, January 1997.

46. 'Zum Gedenken an Artur Jacobs', p. 13 (Lisa Jacob).

47. 'Worte zur Gedenkstunde für Artur Jacobs', p. 13; conversation with Ellen Jungbluth, 13.7.1999.

48. Interview, Tove Gerson, Essen, 8.1.1997.

49. *Zweiter Auslandsbrief*, pp. 8f.

50. Der Bund. Gemeinschaft für sozialistisches Leben (ed.), *Leben in der Illegalität. Dritter Auslandsbrief* (printed pamphlet 1948), p. 3.

51. Interview, Tove Gerson, 8.1.1997; video by Jochen Bilstein with Frau Briel, Herr Jost, 9.11.1990.

52. *Sie wußten was sie taten*, WDR broadcast.

53. StAE NJ AJD, 8.11.1941.

54. Interview, ME, 10.9.1996.

55. StAE NJ AJD, 10.8.1942.

56. StAE NJ AJD, 22.9.1942.

57. Ibid.

58. StAE NJ AJD, 20.11.1942.

59. StAE NJ AJD, 31.12.1942.

60. MS, private diary, 26.1.1943.

61. Interview, ME, 10.9.1996.

62. Schwester Tamara to MS, 23.6.1943.

63. MS, private diary, 26.1.1943.

64. MS, private diary, 17.11.1942.

65. MS, private diary, 23.11.1942.

66. Ibid.

67. Dore Jacobs, 'Ein Auslandsbrief', in *Gelebte Utopie*, pp. 109–121, at p. 112.

68. Folded, typed sheet in MS private diary.

69. 'Liste der am 25 Juni 1943 von Düsseldorf nach Theresienstadt evakuierten Juden', Gestapo document kindly provided by Michael Zimmermann.

70. *Essen unter Bomben*, pp. 26–47.

71. Interview, ME, 31.10.1996.

72. Some information here was gleaned in a telephone conversation with Hanna Aron, 20.10.97; the remainder in the interview in West Hartford, Connecticut 7.8.1998.

9 The Escape

1. See the note attached to HStAD RW58, 74234, draft StaPoD IIB 4/Tgb Nr 248/43/Strauss, telegram to StaPo Prag, Polizeigefängnis Theresienstadt, letter sent 31.8.1943.

2. Copy, RW to May, 19.5.1961, annex; copy, Hammacher to Schroetter, 14.8.1951.

3. DBF F67/56, copy, DBE to SStr, 10.5.1943; SStr to DB, 10.5.1943; copy, DBE to SStr, 18.5.1943. In Marianne's papers, see DBE to LGD, 7 Entschädigungskammer, 5.3.1965 and attached letter describing the contents of DB's communication to the lawyer Schroeter of 6.7.1955.

4. Copy, CH to AfWGE, 19.7.1963.

5. Copy, Schroetter to Koplowitz, 18.4.1955, containing copy of Alfred Strauss to DBE, 2.6.1943; copy, RW to May, 19.5.1961, annex, copy, Hammacher to Schroetter, 14.8.1951.

6. Schwester Tamara to MS, 23.6.1943.

7. HStAD RW58, 74234, letter from Wilhelm Hammacher in Firma DBE to ADStE, 2.7.1943.

8. HStAD RW58, 74234, draft letter, StaPoD to ADStE, 19.7.1943.

9. Interview, ME, 31.10.1996.

10. Interview Tove Gerson, Essen 8.1.1997.

11. HStAD RW58, 74234, draft telegram, StaPoD to RSHA IV B 4, 27.5.1943.

12. See HStAD microfilm A28, StaPoD II B 4 to RSHA IV B 4, 9.6.1943.

13. HStAD RW58, 74234, telegram, Berlin Chef d. SIPO und d. SD Roem 4 B 4 Kl., signed Eichmann to StaPoD, 9.6.43.

14. HStAD RW58, 74234, OFD to StaPoD, 7.6.1943.

15. Ibid., memo *verso*, 10.6.1943.

16. Meyer, *Unternehmen Sieben*, pp. 241, 411–412.

17. Ibid., pp. 412, 417.

18. HStAD RW58, 74234, telegram, RHSA IV B 4a to StaPoD, 6.8.1943 (it may have been sent 5.8.1943).

19. HStAD RW58, 74234, draft telegram, StaPoD to ADStE, 9.8.1943.

20. HStAD RW58, 74234, draft of letter to Herr OFD, 9.8.1943.

21. Memo attached to HStAD RW58, 74234, draft StaPoD to StaPo Prag, 31.8.1943.

22. Copy, Schroetter to Koplowitz, 18.4.1955, containing copy of AS to DBE, 2.6.1943; copy, RW to May, 19.5.1961, annex, copy, Hammacher to Schroetter, 14.8.1951.

23. Copy, Hammacher to CH, 27.6.1957.

24. Copy, Ernst Dahl to RW, 3.3.1961.

25. Marianne slightly misremembered his name.

26. Marianne's description of the garment was a 'ski suit', but it was clearly closer to a modern tracksuit than a padded ski suit.

27. Interview, ME, July 1996.

28. Sadly, I was not able to add any details about Pastor Wilhelm Keinath. He and his wife Margarethe died before I began my researches and left no children. Marianne remained in contact with his niece, Frau Hedda Keinath. I contacted Frau Keinath, but she owed to Marianne what she knew about her uncle's past connections with the Strauss family and could add nothing.

29. Interview, ME, 1989.

30. Interview, ME, 31.10.1996.

31. Interview, ME, 1989.

32. Interview, ME, 31.10.1996.

33. Ibid.

34. Information from Angela Genger, Düsseldorf.

35. Robert Gellately, *The Gestapo and German Society*, (Oxford University Press, Oxford, 1990).

36. HStAD RW58, 74234, ADStE to StaPoD, 1.9.1943.

37. Typed manuscript provided by Michael Zimmermann, 'Gespräch mit Herrn Borghoff über die Ermittlungsverfahren 1964 bis 1986 zu den Deportationen der Juden aus dem Gebiet der Gestapoleitstelle Düsseldorf'.

38. HStAD RW58, 74234, draft telegram, StaPoD IIB, Ratingen to Police Prison in Theresienstadt FAO SS-Hauptsturmführer Dr. Seidl., 1.9.1943 (sent 2.9.1943).

39. Copy, AfWGE, in der Wiedergutmachungssache Marianne Ellenbogen nach Siegfried Strauss, witness statement from Erna Rosenberg, 9.11.1959.

40. HStaD RW58 74234 Betriff: Flucht der Jüdin Marianne Sara Strauss geboren am 7.6.1923 in Essen Wohnhaft hier Ladenspelderstr. 47, Essen 3.9.1943.

41. Email, Robert S. Selig to author, 24.8.1998.

42. ME, Eidesstattliche Erklärung (Declaration under Oath), 14.11.1961.

43. ME, Eidesstattliche Erklärung (Declaration under Oath), 22.5.1957.

44. Declaration under Oath, 14.11.1961.

45. Interview, Hanna Aron, West Hartford, Connecticut 7.8.1998.

46. Hanna was working as a seamstress at the time.

10 *Memories Underground: August 1943 – Spring 1944*

1. Interview, ME, 10.9.1996.
2. StAE NJ AJD, entries for 25, 26 and 29/30.8.1943.
3. Extract reproduced in a letter from Dore Jacobs to ME 24.9.73. The September extracts are missing from the copy of the diary in the Essen City Archive. They are, however, present in another copy of the diary in the Blockhaus.
4. Interview, ME, July 1996.
5. ME, 'Flucht', p. 140.
6. Biographical information from an unpublished Bund Manuscript, 'Zum Gedenken an Sonja Schreiber' (Doris Braune and others) (no date [1987]).
7. HStAD RW 58, 1808.
8. See copy, ME to CH, 3.2.1958, annex: Eidesstattliche Versicherung.
9. Interview, ME, 31.10.1996; undated carbon copy (1983), 'Flucht und illegales Leben während der Nazi-Verfolgungsjahre 1943–45 der Marianne ELLENBOGEN STRAUSS.'
10. Interview, ME, 1989.
11. Interview, ME, 31.10.1996.
12. Copy, Julia Böcker, 'Eidesstattliche Erklärung', Essen, 26.2.1955.
13. Ibid. See below, chapter 13, note 87.
14. Copy, witness statement of Julia Böcker, 28.3.1955.
15. Copy, ME to LGE, in Sachen Ellenbogen/Hammacher, 2.10.1952.
16. ME, 'Flucht', p. 140.
17. Interview, ME, 31.10.1996.
18. HStAD RW 58, 74234, draft letter StaPoD II B 4/Tgb Nr 248/43g/Strauss to Bahnhof M-Gladbach 6.9.1943.
19. According to Frau Jürgens in 1960; see copy, Öffentliche Sitzung des II. WGK beim LG Dortmund, 4.11.1960.
20. HStAD RW 58, 74234, StaPoD II B 4/Tgb Nr 248/43g/Strauss, draft memo, Düsseldorf, 21.9.1943.
21. HStAD RW 58, 74234, Quittung, Theresienstadt 10.9.1943.
22. Zimmermann, 'Eine Deportation nach Theresienstadt'; HStAD RW 58, 74234, draft, StaPoD to RSHA IV B 4, Düsseldorf, 21.9.1943 (posted 24.9.1943).
23. HStAD RW 58, 74234, StaPoD, memo, 21.9.1943.
24. Kaplan, *Between Dignity and Despair*, pp. 207ff.
25. Konrad Kwiet and Helmut Eschwege, *Selbstbehauptung und Widerstand.*

Deutsche Juden im Kampf um Existenz und Menschenwürde 1933–1945 (Hans Christians Verlag, Hamburg, 1984), p. 154.

26. Emphasized particularly in a typewritten early draft of ME's article in *Das Münster am Hellweg*; presumably for reasons of space, the paragraph was omitted from the final draft.

27. Reprinted in 'Zum Gedenken an Sonja Schreiber'.

28. Jacob, ' "Der Bund" ', p. 112.

29. ME, 'Eidesstattliche Erklärung', 22.5.1957; copy CH to Oberstadtdirektor, Essen, 4.6.1957.

30. Interview, ME, July 1996.

31. 'Eidesstattliche Erklärung', 25.9.1957, signed Johanna Ganzer.

32. Telephone conversation with Fritz Briel, Remscheid, 10.1.1997.

33. In Jewish ritual, the stone-setting, which takes place up to a year after the burial, is accompanied by a short ceremony and a eulogy and concludes the formal period of mourning.

34. Interview, Sol and Clara Bender, Chester, 17.10.1997.

35. Interview, Lew and Trudy Schloss, Teaneck, New Jersey, 11.8.98.

36. Telephone conversation with Eric Alexander, 21.8.98.

37. Born Margarete Ransenberg, 27.9.1881, Schröter, *Geschichte und Schicksal*, p. 686.

38. Interview, ME, 31.10.1996.

39. See chapter 11, pp. 359ff.

40. ASE, A6418, copy of Ruth Kotik, 'Ein Vorläufer alternativer Lebensformen: Der Bund – Gemeinschaft für sozialistisches Leben.' 16.11.1984, 20.15–21.00 WDR3.

41. 'Hilfe für Juden war für die Briels selbstverständlich', *Bergische Morgenpost*, 21.4.1994.

42. Video, Frau Briel, Herr Jost, 9.11.1990, made by a historian of Remscheid, Jochen Bilstein, Wermelskirchen, in whose possession the video resides.

43. Interview, Aenne Schmitz, January 1997.

44. Video, Frau Briel, Herr Jost, 9.11.1990.

45. Ibid.

46. Interview, Aenne Schmitz, January 1997.

47. Interview, ME, July 1996.

48. Video, Frau Briel, Herr Jost, 9.11.1990.

49. Telephone conversation, Fritz Briel, January 1997.

50. Video, Frau Briel, Herr Jost, 9.11.1990.

51. Ibid.

52. Interview with Maria Briel, in Jochen Bilstein and Frieder Backhaus, *Geschichte der Remscheider Juden* (Remscheid, 1992), p. 135.

53. Janina Fischler-Martinho, *Have You Seen My Little Sister?* (Valentine, Mitchell, London and Portland, Oreg., 1998), p. 236.
54. This and following information from my conversation with Hannah Jordan, Wuppertal, 29.7.1997.
55. Interview, ME, July 1996.
56. Ibid.
57. Ibid.
58. Interview, ME, 31.10.1996.
59. Ibid.
60. Ibid.
61. Interview, ME, July 1996.
62. Interview, ME, 31.10.1996.
63. ME, 'Flucht', p. 138.
64. Video, Frau Briel, Herr Jost, 9.11.1990.
65. See copy, ME to CH, 3.2.1958, annex: Eidesstattliche Versicherung.
66. Interview, ME, July 1996.
67. Jan Karski, *Story of a Secret State* (Houghton Mifflin, Boston, 1944), p. 185.

11   *Underground Chronicles: April 1944 – April 1945*

1. Typed letter folded into the diary headed 'Beverstedt, den 12. Juni 44'.
2. ME, 'Flucht', p. 139.
3. Hermann Schmalstieg to author, 4.5.1997.
4. Mark Roseman, 'The organic society and the Massenmenschen. Integrating young labour in the Ruhr mines 1945–1958', in Robert Moeller (ed.), *West Germany Under Construction: Politics, Society, and Culture in the Adenauer era* (Ann Arbor, University of Michigan Press, 1997), pp. 287–320.
5. The alternation between 'v.Mst', 'M' and v.M' are in the original.
6. See chapter 'Living with a Past in Hiding', p. 474.
7. Typed letter, headed 'Beverstedt, den 12. Juni 44.'
8. Ibid. *Geheimnis Tibet* deals with Schäfer's expedition to Tibet in 1940, and not with the escape to Tibet of Heinrich Harrer in 1944, as portrayed in the film *Seven Years in Tibet*.
9. Incidentally, Marianne said that she was writing the above while sitting in a little wood on an old tree trunk. But the letter which contains all this is typed (and contains several mistakes and crossings out, suggesting that she typed as she thought and was not writing it up later), so I wondered if

she was travelling around with a portable typewriter. On the other hand, the typeface here is not the same as that in her first letter in April, nor the later ones from Düsseldorf, so she may well have borrowed a portable from her hosts and taken it into the woods with her.

10. See chapter 13.

11. Hermann Schmalstieg to author, 10.10.1998.

12. Telephone conversation, Hedwig Gehrke, 21.1.1997.

13. The date from telephone conversation with Elfriede Nenadovic, neé Wahle, 24.1.97.

14. The following information is taken from Meta Kamp, *Auf der anderen Seite stehen* (privately published, Göttingen, 1987) and from telephone conversation with Meta Kamp, 24.1.1997.

15. Kamp, *Auf der anderen Seite stehen*, p. 11.

16. Telephone conversation with Meta Kamp, 24.1.1997.

17. Telephone conversation with Elfriede Nenadovic, 9.12.1997.

18. Kamp, *Auf der anderen Steite stehen*, p. 45.

19. Telephone conversation with Meta Kamp, 24.1.1997.

20. Telephone conversation with Ernst Steinmann, 24.1.1997.

21. Telephone conversation with Elfriede Nenadovic, 24.01.1997.

22. Ibid.

23. Letter from Hermann Schmalstieg, 12.7.1944.

24. See p. 347.

25. Hermann Schmalstieg to author, 2.4.1998.

26. MS, diary entry, 31.7.1944.

27. The following information derives from a telephone conversation with Hermann Schmalstieg, 24.1.1997, subsequent letters from him to me, 4.5.1997, 2.4.1998 and 10.10.1998, and an interview 25.8.1999.

28. Hermann Schmalstieg to author, 4.5.1997.

29. Telephone conversation with Hermann Schmalstieg, 24.1.1997.

30. MS, diary entry, Friday, 3.11.1944 (from a letter to Meta).

31. Lene Krahlisch in Mülheim.

32. Presumably Karin Morgenstern.

33. 'Oneself' is underlined in pencil (the rest of the letter is in ink) suggesting that, while she was reading, Marianne wanted to emphasise this section for herself.

34. Braunschweig.

35. Another one of her wartime helpers who later slipped from view was Albert Schürmann, whom Marianne thanked in a submission made on behalf of Ernst Jungbluth after the war, but who did not surface in her later article. See Stadtarchiv Wuppertal (StAW) Wiedergutmachungsakte,

Jungbluth, Ernst, 115, 24, statement from Marianne Strauss, Düsseldorf 24.8.1945. It is unknown what Schürmann's role was.

36. See ME, 'Flucht', p. 139; diary, Mülheim, 31.9.1944 [Brief an Meta].

37. Possibly Düsseldorf and Solingen.

38. I am grateful to Michael Zimmermann for this insight.

39. This is not always apparent in my translation. The repetition of 'one' (in German 'man') was so clumsy in English, that I have rendered it sometimes as 'you', sometimes as 'we', occasionally as 'I', depending on the context.

40. Interview, ME, 31.10.1996.

41. MS, diary entry, Braunschweig, 2.9.1944

42. MS, diary entry, 9.8.1944.

43. Copy, Johanna Ganzer, 'Eidesstattliche Erklärung', Düsseldorf, 25.9.1955.

44. ME, 'Flucht', p. 140.

45. Ibid., p. 139.

46. Copy, draft, ME to Landgericht Essen, 2.10.1952.

47. Copy, ME to RW, 14.10.1960.

48. ME, 'Flucht', p. 141.

49. Gauleiter Florian, Kreisleiter Walter and police president Korreng.

50. Peter Hüttenberger, *Düsseldorf. Geschichte von den Anfängen bis ins 20. Jahrhundert*, vol. 3, *Die Industrie- und Verwaltungsstadt* (Schwann, Düsseldorf, 1989), pp. 635–646.

51. Copy, Johanna Ganzer, 'Eidesstattliche Erklärung', Düsseldorf, 25.9.1955.

52. Hüttenberger, *Düsseldorf*, pp. 631, 648.

53. In diary, copy MS to Meta, Hedwig, Elli and Hermann [Meta Kamp, Hedwig Gehrke, Elli Schlieper and Hermann Schmalstieg] 30.5.1945.

54. Unfortunately, this later diary does not seem to have survived.

55. Copy, MS to Meta, Hedwig, Elli and Hermann, 30.5.1945.

56. Ibid.

57. A comprehensive study shows that those who helped Jews were more likely to have had Jewish friends before the war than the bystanders. Samuel P. Oliner, *The Altruistic Personality. Rescuers of Jews in Nazi Europe* (The Free Press, New York, 1998), p. 115.

58. Unpublished Bund manuscript, 'Zum Gedenken an Artur Jacobs'. Here, 'Worte zur Gedenkstunde für Artur Jacobs im Bundeshaus am 17. März 1968', p. 13 (Lisa Jacob).

59. HStAD RW58, 1593 (Jungbluth); RW 58, 19223 (Jacobs); RW 58, 71703 (Jacobs).

60. Jacob, '"Der Bund"', p. 109; HStAD RW 58, 19223, various papers.

61. HStAD RW 58, 71703 Jacobs, Dr Artur, copy of statement dated 6.8.1944, and attached note Gestapo AStE IV 3 a 6812/44 to StaPoD.
62. Oliner, *Altruistic Personality*, p. 130.
63. *Dritter Auslandsbrief*, pp. 9–10.
64. Comment by Herr Jost in video, Frau Briel, Herr Jost, 9.11.1990.
65. Interview, Frau Gerson, Essen, 8.1.1997.
66. *Zweiter Auslandsbrief*, pp. 8f.
67. *Dritter Auslandsbrief*, p. 5.
68. 'Unsere toten Freunde – Lebenszeugnisse des Bundes' (anonymous unpublished printed booklet from the Bund, no date).
69. Interview, Jakov Langer, 27.7.1998.

12 Living Amid the Ruins

1. Interviews, ME 1989; July 1996.
2. See, for example, Klemperer, *Tagebücher 1942–1945*, pp. 750–760.
3. Interview, Frau Jungbluth, 29.7.1997.
4. Copy MS to Meta, Hedwig, Elli and Hermann, 30.5.1945, folded into diary.
5. Interview, Hanna Aron, West Hartford, Connecticut, 7.8.1998.
6. YVJ, file 0.48/1630.2, archiv 13390, MS to Alfred Weinberg, 26.6.1947.
7. Interview, ME, 31.10.1996.
8. Copy, MS to Meta, Hedwig, Elli and Hermann, 30.5.1945.
9. Interview, ME, 31.10.1996.
10. Copy, MS to 'Meine sehr Lieben [Hugo and Grete Strauss], 24.1.1946, folded into diary.
11. Copy, MS to Meta, Hedwig, Elli and Hermann, 30.5.1945.
12. Lisa Jacob had a similar story to tell; see ' "Der Bund", Gemeinschaft für sozialistisches Leben und meine Rettung vor der Deportation', in *Das Münster am Hellweg*, vol. 37 (1984), pp. 105–134.
13. Interview, ME, July 1996.
14. Copy, MS to 'Meine sehr Lieben' [Hugo and Grete Strauss], 24.1.1946.
15. Interview, ME, July 1996.
16. Copy, MS to Meta, Hedwig, Elli and Hermann, 30.5.1945 [postscript from 8 June].
17. Copy, MS to 'Meine sehr Lieben' [Hugo and Grete Strauss], 24.1.1946
18. It is interesting that Marianne subscribed to the widely held myth that German industries were being shut down because of Allied fear of competition.

19. Interview, ME, 31.10.1996.

20. Ibid.

21. Arbeitsamt Düsseldorf, 'Zeugnis', Düsseldorf, 30.4.1946.

22. Copy, MS to Meta, Hedwig, Elli and Hermann, 30.5.1945.

23. Ibid.

24. Interview, ME, July 1996.

25. Interview, Hanna Aron, West Hartford, Connecticut, 7.8.1998.

26. Telephone conversation with Johannes Oppenheimer, 27.3.1997.

27. Johannes Oppenheimer to author, 3.3.1997.

28. Telephone conversation with Johannes Oppenheimer, 27.3.1997.

29. Copy, ME to Koplowitz, 4.2.1956.

30. Copy, MS to 'Meine sehr Lieben' [Hugo and Grete Strauss], 24.1.1946.

31. Copy, MS to Alex [Eric Alexander, formerly Alex Weinberg], 4.2.1946, folded into diary.

32. According to copy, ME to CH, 9.1.1956 [sic = 1957], she left the job in January, but a surviving reference from the Arbeitsamt Düsseldorf suggests that she was there until 30 April 1946. Though I contacted various people who had worked for the *Freiheit* at that time, only the wife of the paper's former editor, Gerd Leo, vaguely remembered her. A few of Marianne's manuscripts are preserved, though it is not always possible to identify the newspaper in which they were published.

33. Copy, MS to Braun, BBC, 2.2.1946.

34. BBC, German Service, Funkbriefkasten Programme no. 48, 12.4.1946, transcript.

35. Copy, MS to Christina Ogilvy, 12.7.1946.

36. Roseman, 'The organic society'.

37. The text here is taken from Marianne's own copy. The transmission date confirmed by undated postcard from G. H. Gretton, BBC, evidently enclosed with some other letter or parcel.

38. Grete Sander to MS, 22.8.1945.

39. Copy, MS to 'Meine sehr Lieben' [Hugo and Grete Strauss], 24.1.1946.

40. Interview, ME, 31.10.1996.

41. YVJ file 0.48/1630.2, archiv 13390, letter from ME to Alfred, 26.6.1947.

42. Ibid.

43. Karl Rosenberg to MS, 18.11.1945.

44. MS to Alex [Eric Alexander, formerly Alex Weinberg], 4.2.1946, folded into diary.

45. Erna Ogutsch to MS, 20.4.1946. We don't have Marianne's letter, but Erna Ogutsch thanks her for her letter of 31.3.1946.

46. Interview, ME, 31.10.1996.

47. Copy, MS to 'Meine sehr Lieben' [Hugo and Grete Strauss], 24.1.1946.

48. Copy, MS to Alex [Eric Alexander, formerly Alex Weinberg], 4.2.1946.

49. Copy, MS to 'Meine sehr Lieben' [Hugo and Grete Strauss], 24.1.1946.

50. Copy, MS to Alex [Eric Alexander, formerly Alex Weinberg], 4.2.1946.

51. Interview, ME, 31.10.1996.

52. Telephone conversation with Johannes Oppenheimer, 27.3.1997.

53. Johannes Oppenheimer to author, 3.3.1997.

54. Ibid.

55. Interview, ME, 31.10.1996.

56. Johannes Oppenheimer to author, 3.3.1997.

57. Including Jacob's place of origin, the fate of his father and so forth. The following is based on a lengthy telephone conversation with Frau Elisabeth Jacob, 24.1.1997.

58. Hüttenberger, *Düsseldorf*, p. 660.

59. Ibid pp. 667–668

60. *Zweiter Auslandsbrief*, p. 2.

61. Ibid.

62. 'Erster Auslandsbrief', p. 7.

63. Ibid.

64. *Gelebte Utopie*, p. 15.

65. Interviews with Helmut and Helga Lenders, Düsseldorf; Kurt and Jenni Schmit, Wuppertal; Alisa Weyl, Meckenheim.

66. Much more will be explored here in my and Norbert Reichling's forthcoming publication on the Bund.

67. Video, Frau Briel, Herr Jost, 9.11.1990.

68. Information from Reinhold Ströter, Mettmann.

69. Artur Jacobs, *Die Zukunft des Glaubens. Die Entscheidungsfrage unserer Zeit* (Europäische Verlagsanstalt, Frankfurt am Main, 1971).

70. Copy, MS to Meta, Hedwig, Elli and Hermann, 30.5.1945.

71. Copy, MS to Alex [Eric Alexander, formerly Alex Weinberg], 4.2.1946.

72. Interview, ME, July 1996.

73. Copy, MS to Herrn Generalkonsul des Amerikanischen Konsulats, Düsseldorf, 20.4.1946.

74. Copy, Gerald Alexander to Officer i/c British Interests Branch CCG (BE), Lübbecke.

75. Passport Control Office c/o Political Division CCG Lübbecke BAOR, to L/Cpl G. Alexander, 14.3.1946.

76. Copy, Cap. B. K. Ellenbogen to Passport Office, 22.3.1946.

77. Passport Control Officer, Lübbecke to L/Cpl G. Alexander, 25.3.1946.

78. Ursula Büttner, *Not nach der Befreiung. Die Situation der deutschen Juden*

in der britischen Besatzungszone 1945–1948 (Hamburg, 1986), p. 17.
79. Copy, Basil Ellenbogen to Scholefield-Adams, 20.10.1946.
80. HQ Military Government, North Rhine Region, Deputy Inspector General Senior Public Safety Officer (J. T. Baldock), 5.7.1946 to 320 Detachment Mil. Govt, attention of Public Safety.
81. Copy, Basil Ellenbogen to Scholefield- Adams, 20.10.1946.
82. Many German Jews at the time were deeply upset that it was no easier for them to come to Britain than for non-Jewish Germans. See Gerda Rother to MS, 2.11.1946.
83. *Freiheit* Hauptschriftleitung, Düsseldorf Pressehaus, to MS, 1.11.1946; *Freiheit* Hauptschriftleitung, Düsseldorf, to MS, 4.11.1946, signed G. Eisenhütte, Gerhard Leo, Nora Leibnitz and another.
84. Hanni Ganzer to MS, undated.
85. Herbert Perrett to Ellenbogen, 21.11.1946.

13   *The Fate of Marianne's Family*

1. Interview, ME 1989.
2. 'Project of Automated Data Processing of Terezin Prisoners', conducted by the Institute of Information Theory and Automation at the Academy of Sciences of the Czech Republic, in co-operation with the Terezin Initiative Foundation and the Terezin Memorial.
3. This is a correction. In the original communication, Dr Schindler put a date in December. Two transports had the same code.
4. Fischer, *Aimée & Jaguar*, p. 196.
5. Hans-Günther Adler, *Theresienstadt 1941–1945. Das Antlitz einer Zwangsgemeinschaft. Geschichte. Soziologie Psychologie* (J. C. B. Mohr/ Paul Siebeck, Tübingen, 1955), p. 124.
6. The Vrba report: 'The extermination camps of Auschwitz (Oswiecim) and Birkenau in Upper Silesia' [1944, author Rudolf Vrba] microfiched in the Leo Baeck Institute, New York.
7. On the Czech connection and Kopecky's role, see Miroslav Karny, 'The Vrba and Wetzler report', in Yisrael Gutman and Michael Berenbaum (eds.), *Anatomy of the Auschwitz Death Camp* (Indiana University Press, Bloomington and Indianapolis, 1994), pp. 553–568, at p. 557.
8. These details from Karny, 'Vrba and Wetzler report', pp. 557–558.
9. BBC Written Archive Centre, German Service, Sonderbericht scripts Jan. 1943 – Apr. 1945. I am very grateful to Gabriel Milland for this reference.
10. In describing all the occupants as Czech, the report echoed the Auschwitz

camp's own description of the transport, but it was misleading, since the Jews were not just of Czech origin. See Adler, *Theresienstadt*, p. 53.

11. Danuta Czech, *Kalendarium der Ereignisse im Konzentrationslager Auschwitz Birkenau 1939–1945* (Rowohlt, Hamburg, 1989), pp. 800–801.

12. Klemperer, *Zeugnis. Tagebücher 1942–1945*, p. 565.

13. Erna Ogutsch to MS, 22.3.1946.

14. Ludwig's mother was a sister of Siegfried's mother, Rosalie, née Stern.

15. Erna Ogutsch to MS, 22.3.1946.

16. Ruth Elias, *Triumph of Hope. From Theresienstadt and Auschwitz to Israel* (John Wiley & Sons, New York, 1998), p. 97.

17. Adler, *Theresienstadt*, pp. 129 and 316ff.

18. Elias, *Triumph of Hope*, p. 95.

19. Adler, *Theresienstadt*, p. 157; Elias, *Triumph of Hope*, p. 197.

20. Adler, *Theresienstadt*, pp. 339ff.

21. Fischer, *Aimée & Jaguar*, p. 196.

22. Ludwig and Selma Ansbacher to MS, 1.5.1946.

23. Ibid.

24. Gershon Ellenbogen to Marianne and Basil Ellenbogen, 12.9.1947.

25. Schröter, *Geschichte und Schicksal*, p. 710 refers to a Grete Sander from Essen who went to Sweden and for a while I believed her to be the woman in question.

26. Marianne's mother Ine's sister, Hannah, was married to Ernst Weinberg. Ernst Weinberg's sister, Helene Weinberg, married Alfred Alsberg. Alfred Alsberg's sister became Grete Sander by marriage. After completing the book I learned there was a closer connection – Grete's mother was a cousin of Marianne's maternal grandmother, Anna Weyl (information from Uri Weinberg).

27. Eric Alexander to author, 9.7.1997.

28. Postcard, SStr to Grete Sander.

29. Grete Sander to MS, 22.8.1945.

30. Hugo Strauss to ME, 27.30.1948, annex: invoice from Marcus Cohn, Austrasse, Basel, dated 19.5.1947.

31. Marcus Cohn to ME, 19.5.1947.

32. We do not have the letter, but Erna Ogutsch thanks her for her letter of 31.3.1946. See Erna Ogutsch to MS, 20.4.1946.

33. Erna Ogutsch to MS, 20.4.1946.

34. The transport from Essen to Theresienstadt in July 1942.

35. Adler, *Theresienstadt*, p. 158.

36. Ibid., p. 46.

37. Elias, *Triumph of Hope*, p. 105. Elias does not give the exact date of the

transport. But from her own dating, and from the circumstances of the transport, we know that she went on one of the big December transports. She and her partner missed the first of these and went a few days later. According to Danuta Czech's *Kalendarium*, there were only two big transports in that month, one arriving in Auschwitz on 16 December and one arriving on the 20th. The latter, we know, was the one which took the Strausses to the camp. Elias also notes that they arrived 'shortly before Christmas', and her tattooed number is one of those assigned to this transport, all facts confirming she was on the same train.

38. Elias, *Triumph of Hope*, P. 106.

39. The following information stems largely from the Vrba report, 'The extermination camps of Auschwitz (Oswiecim) and Birkenau in Upper Silesia'; Adler, *Theresienstadt*, pp. 53–56, 692; Rudolf Vrba and Alan Bestic, *I Cannot Forgive* (Sidwick & Jackson/Anthony Gibbs and Phillips, London, 1963); Otto Dov Kulka, 'Ghetto in an annihilation camp: Jewish social history in the Holocaust period and its ultimate limits', in *The Nazi Concentration Camps. Proceedings of the Fourth Yad Vashem International Historical Conference Jerusalem, January 1980* (Yad Vashem, Jerusalem, 1984), pp. 315–330; Czech, *Kalendarium*; Martin Gilbert, 'What was known and when', in Gutman and Berenbaum, *Anatomy*, pp. 539–552; Miroslav Karny, 'The Vrba and Wetzler report', in ibid., pp. 553–568; Nils Keren, 'The family camp', in ibid., pp. 428–441.

40. Czech, *Kalendarium*, p. 600

41. Vrba and Bestic, *I Cannot Forgive*, pp. 180ff.

42. Adler, *Theresienstadt*, p. 53.

43. Czech, *Kalendarium*, p. 670.

44. Michael Zimmermann has pointed out to me that sometimes 'special treatment' meant that people were *not* murdered. I.e. the special treatment in this case may have meant the six months *before* murder.

45. Kulka, 'Ghetto', p. 318.

46. Elias, *Triumph of Hope*, p. 107.

47. According to information provided by Ruth Elias in a letter, those on the September transport were allowed to keep their own clothes. Those on the December transport were not.

48. Eric Alexander to author, 18.7.1998.

49. Czech, *Kalendarium*, p. 684.

50. Staatliches Museum Auschwitz-Birkenau (ed.), *Sterbebücher von Auschwitz. Fragmente*, vols. 1 and 2 (Verlag K. G. G. Sauer, Munich, London, Paris etc., 1995); Dr Franciszek Piper, Panstwowe Muzeum, Oswiecim to author, 26.5.1997.

51. Czech, *Kalendarium*, pp. 600ff.

52. Kulka, 'Ghetto', p. 318.

53. Cited in Keren, 'Family camp', p. 430.

54. Vrba and Bestic, *I Cannot Forgive*, p. 185.

55. Czech, *Kalendarium*, pp. 700ff; Kulka, 'Ghetto', p. 318.

56. Kulka, 'Ghetto', p. 324.

57. A. Schön, 'Co byl Birkenau' (Ms. 1945), cited in Adler, *Theresienstadt*, p. 730.

58. Adler, *Theresienstadt*, p. 128.

59. Postcard, Regina Strauss, Arbeitslager Birkenau, bei Neuberun (Oberschlesien) 15.4.1944, franked Berlin 23.6.1944, to Grete Sander, Stockholm.

60. Gilbert, 'What was known and when', pp. 548.

61. Karny, 'The Vrba and Wetzler Report', pp. 558ff.

62. Erna Ogutsch to MS, 20.4.1946.

63. Grete Sander to MS, 22.8.1945.

64. Though this did not prevent them from subjecting the Hungarian Jews to the most intensive murder programme yet. In two months in the summer of 1944 300–400,000 Hungarian Jews were murdered, one-third of the total number of people murdered during Auschwitz's existence. See Deborah Dwork and Robert Jan van Pelt, *Auschwitz: 1270 to the Present* (W. W. Norton, New York and London, 1996), p. 343.

65. Kulka, 'Ghetto', p. 318.

66. Adler, *Theresienstadt*, pp. 53–56, 692.

67. Kulka, 'Ghetto', p. 329.

68. Ibid, p. 319.

69. It is not known exactly when they received the last sign of life from Marianne. The letter from the Ansbachers might suggest that Marianne's parcels to Theresienstadt began before her parents were deported. If so, they left for Auschwitz knowing she was still well. Thereafter, they are very unlikely to have heard any news of her.

70. Erna Ogutsch to MS, 22.3.1946.

71. Postcard, AS Hauptstr. 195/1, Theresienstadt Protektorat, to Grete Sander, 22.3.1944, franked 4.4.1944.

72. Postcard, AS geb. 24.IV.1891 Hauptstr. 195/1, Theresienstadt Protektorat, to Grete Sander, 3.4.1944, franked 20.7.1944.

73. Ludwig and Selma Ansbacher to MS, 1.5.1946.

74. Postcard, AS geb 24.IV.1891 Hauptstr. 195/1, Theresienstadt Protektorat, to Grete Sander, 3.6.1944, franked 8.7.1944.

75. Postcard, AS Hauptstr. 195/1, Theresienstadt Protektorat, to Grete Sander, 24.7.1944, franked 31.8.1944.

76. Postcard, AS Hauptstr. 195/1, Theresienstadt Protektorat, to Grete Sander, 25.8.1944, franked 12.9.1944.

77. Postcard, AS geb 24.4.1891, Theresienstadt Hauptstr. 195/1, to Grete Sander, 18.9.1944, franked 12.10.1944.

78. Professor Paul Alsberg to author, 29.7.1997.

79. Cited in Adler, *Theresienstadt*, p. 185.

80. Ibid., p. 187.

81. Ibid., p. 191.

82. Felice Schragenheim, whose fate has become famous through the book *Aimée & Jaguar*, was deported on the same transport as Oe and her mother, namely transport EP, 9 October 1944. Listed in Fischer, *Aimée & Jaguar*, p. 197, as passenger number EP 342 on 9.10.1944.

83. Interview, ME, 31.10.1996.

84. Actually, 16.08.1907.

85. Written notes, off the tape, interview, ME, 31.10.1996.

86. Copy, declaration, Julia Böcker, Essen Stadtwald, Drosselstrasse 51, 26.2.1955.

87. Frau Böcker was not to blame here, I suspect. Marianne and her cousin René wanted to establish for the courts that Oe had predeceased Alfred so as to avoid problems with the inheritance and Frau Böcker was an obliging witness. Marianne knew, though, that Alfred had probably died first.

88. Adler, *Theresienstadt*, p. 694.

89. Several sheets bearing the heading 'Yad Vashem Daf-ed. A page of testimony'.

90. Several sheets bearing the heading 'Yad Vashem Daf-ed. Gedenkblatt' and dated July 1983.

91. Ludwig and Selma Ansbacher to MS, 1.5.1946.

92. Isabel Sprenger, *Groß-Rosen. Ein Konzentrationslager in Schlesien* (Böhlau Verlag, Cologne, Weimar and Vienna, 1996), pp. 261–262.

93. Ruth Klüger, *Weiter leben. Eine Jugend* (Wallstein, Göttingen, 1992).

94. Gudrun Schwarz, *Die nationalsozialistischen Lager* (revised edn, Fischer, Frankfurt am Main, 1996), p. 198; Internationaler Suchdienst, Arolsen, *Vorläufiges Verzeichnis der Haftstätten unter dem Reichsführer-SS 1933–1945* (1969), p. 110.

95. Israel Gutman (ed.), *Encyclopaedia of the Holocaust* (Macmillan, London, 1990), p. 625.

96. Details on Kurzbach in Sprenger, *Groß-Rosen*, pp. 263ff.

97. Cited in Sprenger, *Groß-Rosen*, p. 282.

98. Ibid. p. 284.

Living With a Past in Hiding

1. The value of incorporating the post-1945 period has been marvellously demonstrated recently by an autobiographical account, sadly not yet available in English: Ruth Klüger, *Weiterleben*.

2. The literature about Holocaust survivors is vast. Texts cited in this chapter are Martin S. Bergmann, Milton E Jucovy and Judith S. Kestenberg (eds.), *Kinder der Opfer. Kinder der Täter* (Fischer, Frankfurt am Main, 1995); Bruno Bettelheim, *Surviving the Holocaust* (Flamingo, London, 1986); Cathy Caruth (ed.), *Trauma: Explorations in Memory* (Johns Hopkins University Press, Baltimore, 1995); Israel Charny (ed.), *Holding on to Humanity: the Message of Holocaust Survivors: the Shamai Davidson Papers* (New York University Press, New York, 1992); Shoshana Feldman and Dori Laub, *Testimony: Crises of Witnessing in Literature, Psychoanalysis and History* (Routledge, London, 1992); Roger S. Gottlieb, *Thinking the Unthinkable: Meanings of the Holocaust* (Paulist Press, New York, 1990); Henry Greenspan, *On Listening to Holocaust Survivors: Recounting and Life History* (Praeger, Westport, Conn., 1998); Geoffrey Hartmann (ed.), *Holocaust and Remembrance – the Shapes of Memory* (Blackwell, Oxford, 1995); Lawrence L. Langer, *Holocaust Testimonies: the Ruins of Memory* (Yale University Press, New Haven, 1991); Dalia Ofer and Lenore J. Weitzman (eds.), *Women in the Holocaust* (Yale University Press, New Haven and London, 1998); Gabriele Rosenthal (ed.), *The Holocaust in Three Generations: Families of Victims and Perpetrators of the Nazi Regime* (Cassell, London and Washington, DC, 1998).

3. Interview, ME, 31.10.1996.

4. Ibid.

5. RW to ME, 13.1.1950.

6. Interview, Sol and Clara Bender, Chester, 17.10.1997; interview, Monte and Phyllis Miller, Liverpool 17.10.1997.

7. Interview, Monte and Phyllis Miller, Liverpool 17.10.1997.

8. See Marion Berghahn's sensitive exploration, *German-Jewish Refugees in England: the Ambiguities of Assimilation* (Macmillan, London and New York, 1984), esp. pp. 173ff; Rebekka Göpfert, *Der jüdische Kindertransport von Deutschland nach England 1938/9* (Campus, Frankfurt am Main and New York, 1999), pp. 186ff; on the pressures on wartime German-Jewish refugees to be English, Kushner, *Holocaust and the Liberal Imagination*, pp. 57ff.

9. Berghahn too talks about the way the diffuseness of British identities allowed German-Jewish refugees to feel both at home and 'cosmopolitan'. Berghahn, *German-Jewish Refugees*, p. 176.

10. Interviews David and Sandra Gray, London, 30.1.1999; Jane Dalton, née Gray, 6.2.1999.

11. Interviews, VE, 5.12.1997; David and Sandra Gray, 30.1.1999; Jane Dalton, 6.2.1999.

12. Marianne told the Millers that she went back to Germany and went into the fish shop where her parents used to shop. The owner nearly collapsed at seeing her. Interview, Monte and Phyllis Miller, Liverpool 17.10.1997. But I do not know if this was in the immediate post-war years or later.

13. Interview, ME, 31.10.1996.

14. MS to Düsseldorf Vollzugsausschuβ der rassisch, politisch und religiös Verfolgten in Düsseldorf, 12.9.1945.

15. Interview, ME, 31.10.1996.

16. CH to ME, 21.2.1958, annex: 'Übersicht über die Entschädigungs- und Rückerstattungssachen der Frau Marianne Ellenbogen'.

17. This was inapplicable, as it turned out, since this particular claim could not be inherited.

18. This was a common dilemma. See Berghahn, *German-Jewish Refugees*, p. 208.

19. Copy, ME to CH, 9.1.1956 [sic = 1957].

20. CH to ME, 4.6.1957.

21. Copy, ME to CH, 8.6.1957.

22. Copy, Regierungspräsident 14 I, vol ZK 620 480, Teilbescheid in der Entschädigungssache der Frau Marianne Ellenbogen, 5.12.1957.

23. Copy, CH to LGD Entschädigungskammer, 13.12.1957.

24. Copy, '*Persönlich!*', ME to Hermann, 28.12.1957; ME to CH, 3.2.1958, annex: Eidesstattliche Versicherung.

25. G. Meyer to ME, 21.1.1952.

26. Copy of letter, ME to G. Meyer, 18.9.1952; copy of letter G. Meyer to Schroetter, 18.9.1952.

27. Interview, ME, 31.10.1996.

28. AfWGE, Eing. 12.10.1950, In der Wiedergutmachungssache Strauss ./. Jürgens, Geschäftsnummer Rü 1190/50, signed Maria Jürgens.

29. Bettelheim, *Surviving*, p. 37.

30. This is not to argue that the camps brought out only selfishness – as Bettelheim movingly shows.

31. See Charny, *Shamai Davidson Papers*, p. 35.

32. Interview, ME, 10.9.1996.

33. Friedhelm Böll, 'Halblar o callar sobre la persecucion nazi en Alemania', *Historia Antropologia y Fuentes Orales*, vol. 20 (1998), no. 2, pp. 45–52.

34. See Dori Laub, 'Truth and testimony: the process and the struggle', in Caruth, *Trauma*, pp. 61–75, at p. 68.

35. See 'Trauma and reintegration', in Bettelheim, *Surviving*, pp. 31–48.

36. Langer, *Holocaust Testimonies*, p. xv.

37. Interview, ME, 10.9.1996.

38. Written notes off the tape, interview, ME 31.10.1996.

39. Unfinished letter, ME to Sonja [Schreiber], Hanni [Ganzer] and Else [Bramesfeld], 11.6.1968

40. Interview, VE, 5.12.1997.

41. Eating disorders are far from unknown among second-generation survivors, but there is no easy connection between the two syndromes. The literature on anorexia reveals how diverse its causes can be. On second-generation survivors, see Bergmann et al., *Kinder*; Shamai Davidson, 'The clinical effects of massive psychic trauma in families of Holocaust survivors', in *Journal of Marital and Family Therapy*, vol. 6 (1980), no. 1, pp. 11–21; Rosenthal, *Holocaust in Three Generations*. On anorexia, see R. L. Palmer, *Anorexia Nervosa: a Guide for Sufferers and their Families* (Penguin, Harmondsworth, 1989), p. 6; Hilde Bruch, *The Golden Cage: the Enigma of Anorexia Nervosa* (Open Books, London, 1978). I am also grateful to Helena Fox, a psychiatrist specializing in eating disorders, for information.

42. Hans-Josef Steinberg, *Widerstand und Verfolgung in Essen* (Hanover, 1969) referring to Günther Weisenborn, (ed.), *Der lautlose Aufstand. Bericht über die Widerstandsbewegung des deutschen Volkes 1933–1945*, (Rowohlt, Hamburg, 1953), pp. 102–103.

43. Copy, letter to US relatives (not named but clearly Hugo Strauss), 24.1.1946.

44. Interview, Sol and Clara Bender, Chester, 17.10.1997.

45. Written notes off the tape, interview, ME, 31.10.1996.

46. Interview, ME, 31.10.1996.

47. See Zygmunt Bauman, *Modernity and the Holocaust* (Polity Press, Cambridge, 1991); Mark Roseman, 'National Socialism and Modernisation', in Richard Bessel (ed.), *Fascist Italy and Nazi Germany: Comparisons and Contrasts* (Cambridge University Press, Cambridge, 1996), pp. 197–229.

48. Written notes, off the tape, interview, ME, 31.10.1996.

49. Marianne's relationship with Basil, for example, remained largely a mys-

tery to me, as did Basil himself. I could, of course, have asked his surviving relatives more questions but, given Marianne's strictures, it seemed wrong to do so. I am grateful, though, for the information provided by Gershon, Raymond and Michael Ellenbogen.

Bibliography

The bibliography is restricted to works cited in the text. Interview partners and archives consulted are listed in the acknowledgements. Unpublished sources listed in the endnotes with no archival attribution are Marianne's own papers.

50 Jahre Jubiläum der Schüler der Israelitischen Gartenbauschule Ahlem (no date, no place) (held in Wiener library, London)

Adler, Hans-Günther, *Theresienstadt 1941–1945. Das Antlitz einer Zwangsgemeinschaft. Geschichte. Soziologie. Psychologie* (J. C. B. Mohr/Paul Siebeck, Tübingen, 1955)

— *Der Verwaltete Mensch. Studien zur Deportation der Juden aus Deutschland* (J. C. B. Mohr/Paul Siebeck, Tübingen, 1974)

Alte Synagoge, Essen (ed.), *Essen unter Bomben: Märztage 1943* (Klartext, Essen, 1984)

— *Stationen jüdischen Lebens. Von der Emanzipation bis zur Gegenwart* (Verlag J. W. Dietz Nachf, Bonn, 1990)

— *Jüdisches Leben in Essen 1800–1933* (Klartext, Essen, 1993)

— *Entrechtung und Selbsthilfe. Zur Geschichte der Juden in Essen unter dem Nationalsozialismus* (Klartext, Essen, 1994)

Andreas, Nachama and Julius H. Schoeps (eds.), *Aufbau nach dem Untergang. Deutsch-Jüdische Geschichte nach 1945* (Argon Verlag, Berlin, 1992)

Angress, Werner T., 'Jüdische Jugend zwischen nationalsozialistischer Verfolgung und jüdischer Wiedergeburt', in Arnold Paucker (ed.), *Die Juden im nationalsozialistischen Deutschland* (J. C. B. Mohr/Paul Siebeck, Tübingen, 1986), pp. 211–232

Arad, Yitzhak, *Belzec, Sobibor, Treblinka – the Operation Reinhard Death Camps* (Indiana University Press, Bloomington, 1987)

Barkai, Avraham, 'Die sozio-ökonomische Situation der Juden in Rheinland und Westfalen zur Zeit der Industrialisierung (1850–1914)', in Kurt Düwell and Wolfgang Köllmann (eds.), *Rheinland-Westfalen im Industriezeitalter*, vol. 2, *Von der Reichsgründung bis zur Weimarer Republik* (Peter Hammer, Wuppertal, 1984), pp. 86–106

— *From Boycott to Annihilation. The Economic Struggle of German Jews, 1933–1943* (University Press of New England, Hanover, 1989), pp. 99–100

Bar-On, Daniel, *Legacy of Silence: Encounters with Children of the Third Reich* (Harvard University Press, Cambridge, Mass, 1989)

Bauman, Zygmunt, *Modernity and the Holocaust* (Polity Press, Cambridge, 1991)

Becker-Jakli, Barbara (ed.), *Ich habe Köln doch so geliebt. Lebensgeschichten jüdischer Kölnerinnen und Kölner* (Volksblatt Verlag, Cologne, 1993)

Benz, Wolfgang, 'Zielsetzung und Maßnahmen der deutschen Judenverfolgung', in Jörg K. Hoensch, Stanislav Biman and L'ubomir Lipták (eds.), *Judenemanzipation, Antisemitismus, Verfolgung* (Klartext, Essen, 1999), pp. 131–141

Berding, Helmut, 'Antisemitismus in der modernen Gesellschaft: Kontinuität und Diskontinuität', in Hoensch et al., *Judenemanzipation*, pp. 85–100

Berghahn, Marion, *German-Jewish Refugees in England: the Ambiguities of Assimilation* (Macmillan, London and New York, 1984)

Bergmann, Martin S., Milton E. Jucovy and Judith S. Kestenberg (eds.), *Kinder der Opfer. Kinder der Täter* (Fischer, Frankfurt am Main, 1995)

Bethge, Eberhard, *Dietrich Bonhoeffer. Theologe. Christ. Zeitgenosse* (Chr. Kaiser Verlag, Munich, 1967)

Bettelheim, Bruno, *Surviving the Holocaust* (Flamingo, London, 1986)

Bilstein, Jochen and Frieder Backhaus, *Geschichte der Remscheider Juden* (Wermelskirchen, 1992)

Blasius, Dirk and Dan Diner (eds.), *Zerbrochene Geschichte. Leben und Selbstverständnis der Juden in Deutschland* (Fischer Taschenbuch Verlag, Frankfurt am Main, 1991)

Blatt, Thomas Toivi, *From the Ashes of Sobibor: a story of survival* (Northwestern University Press, Evanston, Ill., 1997)

Böll, Friedhelm, 'Halblar o callar sobre la persecucion nazi en Alemania', *Historia Antropologia y Fuentes Orales*, vol. 20 (1998), no. 2, pp. 45–52

Borsdorf, Ulrich and Mathilde Jamin (eds), *Überleben im Krieg. Kriegserfahrungen in einer Industrieregion 1939–1945* (Rowohlt, Hamburg, 1989)

Bramesfeld, Else, Doris Braune et al. (eds), *Gelebte Utopie: Aus dem Leben einer Gemeinschaft, Nach einer Dokumentation von Dore Jacobs* (Klartext, Essen, 1990)

Brenner, Michael, *The Renaissance of Jewish Culture in Weimar Germany* (Yale University Press, New Haven, 1996)

— *Nach dem Holocaust. Juden in Deutschland 1945–1950*, (Beck, Munich, 1995)

Burgauer, Erica, *Zwischen Erinnerung und Verdrängung – Juden in Deutschland nach 1945* (Rohwohlts Enzyklopädie, Rheinbek, 1993)

Brewer, W. F., 'What is biographical memory?', in D. C. Rubin (ed.), *Autobiographical Memory* (Cambridge University Press, Cambridge, 1988), pp. 25–49

Bruch, Hilde, *The Golden Cage: the Enigma of Anorexia Nervosa* (Open Books, London, 1978)

Bundesleitung des Jüdischen Pfadfinderbundes Makkabi Hazair (ed.), *Unser Weg zum Volk. Ein Beitrag zur Ideologie des Makkabi Hazair* (Berlin, 1936)

— *Unser Weg im Zionismus. Eine Sammelschrift des jüdischen Pfadfinderbundes Makkabi Hazair* (Berlin, no date)

Burrin, Phillippe, *Hitler and the Jews: the Genesis of the Holocaust* (Edward Arnold, London, 1994)

Büttner, Ursula (ed.), *Not nach der Befreiung. Die Situation der deutschen Juden in der britischen Besatzungszone 1945–1948* (Hamburg, 1986)

— *Die Deutschen und die Judenverfolgung im Dritten Reich* (Hamburg, 1992)

Caruth, Cathy (ed.), *Trauma: Explorations in Memory* (Johns Hopkins University Press, Baltimore, 1995)

— *Unclaimed Experience: Trauma, Narrative and History* (Johns Hopkins University Press, Baltimore and London, 1996)

Charny, Israel (ed.), *Holding on to Humanity: the Message of Holocaust Survivors: the Shamai Davidson Papers* (New York University Press, New York, 1992)

Chowaniec, Elisabeth, Der *'Fall Dohnanyi' 1943–1945* (R. Oldenbourg Verlag, Munich, 1991)

Conway, M. A. et al. (eds.), *Theoretical Perspectives on Autobiographical Memory* (Kluwer Academic Press, Dordrecht, 1992)

Corbach, Dieter, *Die Jawne zu Köln. Zur Geschichte des ersten jüdischen Gymnasiums im Rheinland und zum Gedächtnis an Erich Klibansky 1900–1942* (Scriba Verlag, Cologne, 1990)

Czech, Danuta, *Kalendarium der Ereignisse im Konzentrationslager Auschwitz Birkenau 1939–1945* (Rowohlt, Hamburg, 1989)

Davidson, Shamai, 'The clinical effects of massive psychic trauma in families of Holocaust survivors', *Journal of Marital and Family Therapy*, vol. 6 (1980), no. 1, pp. 11–21

Davidson, Shamai (ed.), *Holding on to Humanity – the Message of Holocaust Survivors* (New York University Press, New York, 1992)

Der Bund. Gemeinschaft für sozialistisches Leben (eds.), *Aus der illegalen Arbeit des Bunds. Zweiter Auslandsbrief* (printed pamphlet, 1948)

— *Leben in der Illegalität. Dritter Auslandsbrief* (printed pamphlet, 1948)

Deutschkron, Inge, *Ich trug den gelben Stern* (Deutsche Taschenbuch-Verlag, Munich, 1995), translated as *Outcast: a Jewish Girl in Wartime Berlin* (Fromm International, New York, 1989)

Dietz, Edith, *Den Nazis entronnen. Die Flucht eines jüdischen Mädchens in die Schweiz. Autobiographischer Bericht 1933–1942* (Dipa Verlag, Frankfurt am Main, 1990)

Dippel, John, *Bound Upon a Wheel of Fire: Why Leading Jews Stayed in Nazi Germany* (Basic Books, New York, 1996)

Dressen, Wolfgang, *Betrifft: 'Aktion 3'. Deutsche verwerten jüdische Nachbarn* (Aufbau Verlag, Berlin, 1998)

Düwell, Kurt, *Die Rheingebiete in der Judenpolitik des Nationalsozialismus vor 1942* (Ludwig Röhrscheid Verlag, Bonn, 1968)

Dwork, Deborah and Robert Jan van Pelt, *Auschwitz: 1270 to the Present* (W. W. Norton, New York and London, 1996)

Elias, Ruth, *Triumph of Hope. From Theresienstadt and Auschwitz to Israel* (John Wiley & Sons, New York, 1998)

Ellenbogen, Marianne, 'Flucht und illegales Leben während der Nazi-Verfolgungsjahre 1943–1954', *Das Münster am Hellweg*, vol. 37 (1984), pp. 135–142

Eschelbacher, Max, *Der zehnte November 1938* (Klartext, Essen, 1998)

Faust, Anselm, *Die 'Kristallnacht' im Rheinland. Dokumente zum Judenpogrom im November 1938* (Schwann, Düsseldorf, 1987)

Feldman, Shoshana and Dori Laub, *Testimony: Crises of Witnessing in Literature, Psychoanalysis and History* (Routledge, London, 1992)

Gottlieb, Roger S., *Thinking the Unthinkable: Meanings of the Holocaust* (Paulist Press, New York, 1990)

Fischer, Erica, *Aimée & Jaguar: a Love Story, Berlin 1943* (paperback edn, Bloomsbury, London, 1996)

Fischler-Martinho, Janina, *Have You Seen My Little Sister?* (Valentine, Mitchell, London and Portland, Oreg., 1998)

Friedländer, Saul, 'Political transformations during the war and their effect on the Jewish question', in Herbert A. Strauss (ed.), *Hostages of Modernisation. Studies on Modern Anti-Semitism 1870–1933/39, Germany–Great*

Britain–France (Walter de Gruyter, New York and London, 1993), pp. 150–164

— *Nazi Germany and the Jews: the Years of Persecution 1933–1939* (Pheonix Giant, London, 1997)

Fritzsche, Peter, *Germans into Nazis* (Harvard University Press, Cambridge, Mass., 1998)

Gedenkbuch Opfer der Verfolgung der Juden (Bundesarchiv Koblenz, 1986).

Gellately, Robert, *The Gestapo and German Society* (Oxford University Press, Oxford 1990)

Genger, Angela, 'Hakoah – Die Kraft. Ein jüdischer Turn- und Sportverein in Essen', in Alte Synagoge (ed.), *Zwischen Alternative und Protest. Zu Sport- und Jugendbewegungen in Essen 1900–1933* (Exhibition catalogue, Essen, 1983), pp. 8–25

Gershon, Karen, *Postscript: a Collective Account of the Lives of Jews in West Germany Since the Second World War* (Victor Gollancz, London, 1969)

Gilbert, Martin, *The Macmillan Atlas of the Holocaust* (Macmillan, New York, 1982)

— 'What was known and when', in Gutman and Berenbaum, *Anatomy*, pp. 539–552

Gill, Anton, *The Journey Back from Hell. Conversations with Concentration Camp Survivors* (HarperCollins, London, 1989)

Göpfert, Rebekka, *Der jüdische Kindertransport von Deutschland nach England 1938/39. Geschichte und Erinnerung* (Campus Verlag, Frankfurt and New York, 1999)

Goldhagen, Daniel J., *Hitler's Willing Executioners. Ordinary Germans and the Holocaust* (Abacus, London, 1997)

Greenspan, Henry, *On Listening to Holocaust Survivors: Recounting and Life History* (Praeger, Westport, Conn., 1998)

Gruner, Wolf, *Judenverfolgung in Berlin 1933–1945. Eine Chronologie der Behördenmaßnahmen in der Reichshauptstadt* (Edition Hentrich, Berlin, 1996)

Grüter, Monika, 'Der "Bund für ein sozialistisches Leben": Seine Entwicklung in den 20er Jahren und seine Widerständigkeit unter dem Nationalsozialismus' (Examensarbeit, University of Essen, 1988)

Gummersbach, Hans W., 'Sozialhistorische und soziologische Forschungen zur jüdischen Minderheit in der westfälischen Stadt Ahlen vor und während der Zeit des Nationalsozialismus unter besonderer Berücksichtigung lebensgeschichtlicher Selbstzeugnisse' (PhD, University of Paderborn, 1996)

Gurewitsch, Bonnie, *Mothers, Sisters, Resisters: Oral Histories of Women*

Who Survived the Holocaust (University of Alabama Press, Tuscaloosa and London, 1998)

Gutman, Israel (ed.), *Encyclopaedia of the Holocaust* (Macmillan, London 1990)

— *Resistance. The Warsaw Ghetto Uprising* (Mariner Books, Boston and New York, 1994)

Gutman, Israel and Michael Berenbaum (eds.), *Anatomy of the Auschwitz Death Camp* (Indiana University Press, Bloomington and Indianapolis, 1994)

Hannam, Charles, *A Boy in Your Situation* (Adlib Paperbacks/André Deutsch, London, 1988)

Hartmann, Geoffrey (ed.), *Holocaust and Remembrance – the Shapes of Memory* (Blackwell, Oxford, 1995)

Henschel, Hildegard, 'Gemeindearbeit und Evakuierung von Berlin', in *Zeitschrift für die Geschichte der Juden* (Tel Aviv), vol.9 (1972), nos. 1/2, pp. 33–53

Hetkamp, Jutta, *Die jüdische Jugendbewegung in Deutschland von 1913–1933* (Münster and Hamburg, Lit, 1994)

Hilberg, Raul, *Die Vernichtung der europäischen Juden* (Fischer, Frankfurt am Main, 1993)

Höhne, Heinz, 'Canaris und die Abwehr zwischen Anpassung und Opposition', in Jürgen Schmädeke and Peter Steinbach (eds.), *Der Widerstand gegen den Nationalsozialismus* (Munich and Zurich, 1985), pp. 405–416

Hoensch, Jörg K., Stanislav Biman and L'ubomír Lipták (eds.), *Judenemanzipation, Antisemitismus, Verfolgung* (Klartext, Essen, 1999)

Hüttenberger, Peter, *Düsseldorf. Geschichte von den Anfängen bis ins 20. Jahrhundert*, vol 3, *Die Industrie- und Verwaltungsstadt* (Schwann, Düsseldorf, 1989)

Internationaler Suchdienst, Arolsen, *Vorläufiges Verzeichnis der Haftstätten unter dem Reichsführer-SS 1933–1945* (1969)

Jacob, Lisa, '"Der Bund", Gemeinschaft für sozialistisches Leben und meine Rettung vor der Deportation', *Das Münster am Hellweg*, vol. 37 (1984), pp. 105–134

Jacobs, Artur, *Die Zukunft des Glaubens. Die Entscheidungsfrage unserer Zeit* (Europäische Verlagsanstalt, Frankfurt am Main, 1971)

Jacobson, Kenneth, *Embattled Selves: an Investigation into the Nature of Identity, Through Oral Histories of Holocaust Survivors* (Atlantic Monthly Press, New York, 1994)

Kamp, Meta, *Auf der anderen Seite stehen*, (privately published, Göttingen, 1987)

Kaplan, Marion, *The Jewish Feminist Movement in Germany* (Greenwood Press, New York, 1979)

— 'Tradition and transition: the acculturation, assimilation and integration of Jews in Imperial Germany: a Gender Analysis', *Leo Baeck Institute Year Book*, vol. 27 (1982), pp. 3–36

— 'Jewish women in Nazi Germany: daily life, daily struggles, 1933–39', in Peter Freimark, Alice Jankowski and Ina S. Lorenz (eds.), *Juden in Deutschland: Emanzipation, Integration, Verfolgung und Vernichtung* (H. Christians Verlag, Hamburg, 1991), pp. 406–434

— *Between Dignity and Despair: Jewish Life in Nazi Germany* (Oxford University Press, New York and Oxford, 1998)

Karny, Miroslav, 'The Vrba and Wetzler Report', in Gutman and Berenbaum, *Anatomy*, pp. 553–568

Karski, Jan, *Story of a Secret State* (Boston, Houghton Mifflin, 1944)

Kauders, Anthony, *German Politics and the Jews: Düsseldorf and Nuremberg, 1910–1933* (Clarendon Press, Oxford, 1996)

Keren, Nils, 'The family camp', in Gutman and Berenbaum, *Anatomy*, pp. 428–441

Klemperer, Viktor, *Ich will Zeugnis ablegen bis zum letzten*, vol. 1, *Tagebücher 1933 – 1941*; vol. 2, *Tagebücher 1942–1945* (Aufbau-Verlag, Berlin, 1995)

Klüger, Ruth, *Weiter leben. Eine Jugend* (Wallstein, Göttingen, 1992)

Kogon, Eugen, *Der SS-Staat. Das System der deutschen Konzentrationslager* (21st edn, Wilhelm Heyne Verlag, Munich, 1989)

Konieczny, Alfred (ed.), *Die Völker Europas im KL Groß-Rosen* (Staatliches Museum Groß-Rosen, Walbrzych, 1995)

Kulka, Otto Dov, 'Ghetto in an annihilation camp. Jewish social history in the Holocaust period and its ultimate limits', in *The Nazi Concentration Camps: Proceedings of the Fourth Yad Vashem International Historical Conference Jerusalem, January 1980* (Yad Vashem; Jerusalem 1984), pp. 315–330

— *Deutsches Judentum unter dem Nationalsozialismus, vol. 1, Dokumente zur Geschichte der Reichsvertretung der deutschen Juden 1933–1939* (Mohr Siebeck, Tübingen, 1997)

Kushner, Tony, *The Holocaust and the Liberal Imagination: a Social and Cultural History* (Blackwell, Oxford and Cambridge, Mass., 1994)

Kwiet, Konrad and Helmut Eschwege, *Selbstbehauptung und Widerstand: Deutsche Juden im Kampf um Existenz und Menschenwürde 1933–1945* (Hans Christians Verlag, Hamburg, 1984)

Laak, Dirk von, ' "Wenn einer ein Herz im Leibe hat, der läßt sich von einem deutschen Arzt behandeln". Die "Entjudung" der Essener Wirtschaft von 1933 bis 1941', in Alte Synagoge, *Entrechtung*, pp. 12–30

Langer, Lawrence L., *Holocaust Testimonies: the Ruins of Memory* (Yale University Press, New Haven 1991)

Laub, Dori, 'Truth and testimony: the process and the struggle,' in Caruth, *Trauma* pp. 61–75

Link, Werner, *Die Geschichte des Internationalen Jugend-Bundes und des Internationalen Sozialistischen Kampf-Bundes. Ein Beitrag zur Geschichte der Arbeiterbewegung in der Weimarer Republik und im 3. Reich* (Meisenheim am Glan, 1964)

Littmann-Hotopp, Ingrid, *Bei Dir findet das verlassene Kind Erbarmen. Zur Geschichte des ersten jüdischen Säuglings– und Kleinkinderheims in Deutschland (1907 bis 1942)* (Edition Hentrich, Berlin, 1996)

Lowenthal, E. G., *Bewährung im Untergang Ein Gedenkbuch* (Deutsche Verlags-Anstalt, Stuttgart, 1965)

Lütkemeier, Hildegard, 'Einrichtungen der Jugendwohlfahrt für Kinder im Vorschulalter in jüdischer Trägerschaft in Deutschland 1919–1933' (Hausarbeit, Erziehungswisenschaft, Universität Dortmund, 1991)

Maurer, Trude, *Die Entwicklung der jüdischen Minderheit in Deutschland. Neuere Forschungen und offene Fragen* (Niemeyer, Tübingen, 1992)

— 'Reife Bürger der Republik und bewußte Juden: die jüdische Minderheit in Deutschland 1918–1933', in Hoensch et al., *Judenemanzipation*, pp. 101–116

Meyer, Winfried, *Unternehmen Sieben. Eine Rettungsaktion für vom Holocaust Bedrohte aus dem Amt Ausland/Abwehr im Oberkommando der Wehrmacht* (Verlag Anton Hain, Frankfurt am Main, 1993)

Niemann, Ingrid and Ludger Hülskemper Niemann, *Vom Geleitbrief zum gelben Stern. 450 Jahre jüdisches Leben in Steele* (Klartext, Essen, 1994)

Niewyk, Donald L., *The Jews in Weimar Germany* (Manchester University Press, Manchester, 1980)

NS-Documentationszentrum der Stadt Köln (eds.), *Die jüdischen Opfer des Nationalsozialismus aus Köln. Gedenkbuch* (Böhlau Verlag, Cologne, 1995)

Ofer, Dalia, and Lenore J. Weitzman (eds.), *Women in the Holocaust* (Yale University Press, New Haven and London, 1998)

Oliner, Samuel P., *The Altruistic Personality: Rescuers of Jews in Nazi Europe* (The Free Press, New York, 1998)

Palmer, Robert L., *Anorexia Nervosa: a Guide for Sufferers and their Families* (Penguin, Harmondsworth, 1989)

Patkin, Benzion, *The Dunera Internees* (Cassell, Stanmore, N. S. W, 1979)

Paucker, Arnold, 'Zum Selbstverständnis jüdischer Jugend in der Weimarer Republik und unter der nationalsozialistischen Diktatur', in Hans Otto Horch and Charlotte Wardi (eds.), *Jüdische Selbstwahrnehmung. La Prise de conscience de l'identité juive* (Max Niemeyer Verlag, Tübingen, 1977), pp. 111–128

Pohl, Dieter, *Von der 'Judenpolitik' zum Judenmord: der Distrikt Lublin des Generalgouvernements 1939–1944* (Lang, Frankfurt am Main, 1993)

Richarz, Monika, *Jewish Life in Germany: Memoirs from Three Centuries* (Indiana University Press; Bloomington and Indianapolis, 1991)

Röcher, Ruth, *Die jüdische Schule im nationalsozialistischen Deutschland 1933–1942* (Dipa, Frankfurt am Main, 1992)

Rohr, Walter, 'Die Geschichte meines Lebens', in Ernst Schmidt, 'Walter Rohr – 1938 aus Essen vertrieben, 1945 als US-Soldat zurückgekehrt', in Alte Synagoge, *Entrechtung*, pp. 98–117

Rohrlich, Ruby (ed.), *Resisting the Holocaust* (Berg, Oxford, 1998)

Roseman, Mark, 'National socialism and modernisation', in Richard Bessel (ed.), *Fascist Italy and Nazi Germany: Comparisons and Contrasts* (Cambridge University Press, Cambridge, 1996), pp. 197–229

— 'The organic society and the Massenmenschen: integrating young labour in the Ruhr mines 1945–1958', in Robert Moeller (ed.), *West Germany under Construction: Politics, Society, and Culture in the Adenauer Era* (University of Michigan Press, Ann Arbor, 1997), pp. 287–320

— 'Erinnerung und Überleben: Wahrheit und Widerspruch in dem Zeugnis einer Holocaust-Überlebenden', *BIOS*, vol. 11 (1998), no. 2, pp. 263–279

Rosenthal, Gabriele (ed.), *The Holocaust in Three Generations: Families of Victims and Perpetrators of the Nazi Regime* (Cassell, London and Washington, DC, 1998)

Rürup, Reinhard, 'Jüdische Geschichte in Deutschland. Von der Emanzipation bis zur nationalsozialistischen Gewaltherrschaft', in Blasius and Diner, *Zerbrochene Geschichte*, pp. 79–101

— *Emanzipation und Antisemitismus. Studien zur 'Judenfrage' der bürgerlichen Gesellschaft* (Vandenhoeck & Ruprecht, Göttingen, 1992)

Sachse, Carola (ed.), *Als Zwangsarbeiterin 1941 in Berlin: die Aufzeichnungen der Volkswirtin Elisabeth Freund* (Akademie Verlag, Berlin, 1996)

Schmalhausen, Bernd, *Schicksale jüdischer Juristen aus Essen 1933–1945* (Klartext, Essen, 1994)

Schröter, Hermann, *Geschichte und Schicksal der Essener Juden. Gedenkbuch für die jüdischen Mitbürger der Stadt Essen* (City of Essen, Essen, 1980)

Schwarz, Gudrun, *Die nationalsozialistischen Lager* (revised edn, Fischer, Frankfurt am Main, 1996)

Simon, Hermann, *Das Berliner Jüdische Museum in der Oranienburgerstraße. Geschichte einer zerstörten Kulturstätte* (Stadtgeschichtliche Publikationen II ed., Berlin Museum, Berlin 1983)

Sophoni Herz, Yitzhak, *Meine Erinnerung an Bad Homburg und seine 600jährige jüdische Gemeinde (1335–1942)* (privately printed, Rechovoth (Israel), 1981)

Sprenger, Isabel, *Groß-Rosen. Ein Konzentrationslager in Schlesien* (Böhlau Verlag, Cologne, Weimar and Vienna, 1996)

Staatliches Museum Auschwitz-Birkenau (ed.), *Sterbebücher von Auschwitz. Fragmente*, vols. 1 and 2 (Verlag K. G. Sauer, Munich, London, Paris etc., 1995)

Steinberg, Hans-Josef, *Widerstand und Verfolgung in Essen* (Hanover, 1969)

Stern, Frank, *Am Anfang war Auschwitz. Antisemitismus und Philosemitismus im deutschen Nachkrieg* (Bleicher Verlag, Gerlingen, 1991)

Strohm, Christoph, *Theologische Ethik im Kampf gegen den Nationalsozialismus. Der Weg Dietrich Bonhoeffers mit den Juristen Hans von Dohnanyi und Gerhard Leibholz in den Widerstand* (Christian Kaiser, Munich, 1989)

Tec, Nechama, *When Light Pierced the Darkness: Christian Rescue of Jews in Nazi-Occupied Poland* (Oxford University Press, New York and Oxford, 1986)

Tohermes, Kurt and Jürgen Grafen, *Leben und Untergang der Synagogengemeinde Dinslaken* (Verein für Heimatpflege 'Land Dinslaken' e.V., Dinslaken, 1988)

Vrba, Rudolf and Alan Bestic, *I Cannot Forgive* (Sidwick & Jackson/Anthony Gibbs and Phillips, London, 1963)

Walk, Joseph, *Das Sonderrecht für die Juden im NS-Staat* (C. F. Müller, Heidelberg, 1981)

— 'Das jüdische Schulwesen in Köln bis 1942', in Jutta Bohnke-Kollwitz, Willehad Paul Eckert, Frank Golsczewski and Hermann Greive (eds.), *Köln und das rheinische Judentum. Festschrift Germania Judaica 1959–1984* (Cologne, 1984), pp. 415–426

— *Jüdische Schule und Erziehung im Dritten Reich* (Verlag Anton Hain, Frankfurt am Main, 1991)

Weisenborn, Günther (ed.), *Der lautlose Aufstand. Bericht über die Widerstandsbewegung des deutschen Volkes 1933–1945* (Rowohlt, Hamburg, 1953)

Wiesemann, Falk, 'Jewish burials in Germany – between the Enlightenment and the authorities', *Leo Baeck Institute Year Book*, vol. 37 (1992), pp. 17–31

Wood, E. Thomas, and Stanislaw M. Jankowski, *Karski: How One Man Tried to Stop the Holocaust* (John Wiley & Sons, New York, 1994)

Zabecki, Franciszek, *Wspomnienia dawne i nowe* (Warsaw, 1977)

Zimmermann, Michael, 'Die Deportation der Juden aus Essen und dem Regierungsbezirk Düsseldorf', in Borsdorf and Jamin, *Überleben im Krieg*, pp. 126–143

— 'Die Assimilation und ihre Relativierung. Zur Geschichte der Essener jüdischen Gemeinde vor 1933', in Blasius and Diner, *Zerbrochene Geschichte*, pp. 172–186

— 'Zur Geschichte der Essener Juden im 19. und im ersten Drittel des 20. Jahrhunderts. Ein Überblick', in Alte Synagoge, *Jüdisches Leben in Essen 1800–1933*, pp. 8–72

— 'Eine Deportation nach Theresienstadt. Zur Rolle des Banalen bei der Durchsetzung des Monströsen', in Miroslav Karney, Raimund Kemper et al. (eds.), *Theresienstädter Studien und Dokumente* (Edition Theresienstädter Initiative Academia, 1994), pp. 54–73

— 'Die "Reichskristallnacht" 1938 in Essen', in Alte Synagoge, *Entrechtung*, pp. 66–97

Zimmermann, Moshe, 'Vom Jischuw zum Staat – die Bedeutung des Holocaust für das kollektive Bewußtsein und die Politik in Israel', in Bernd Faulenbach and Helmut Schütte (eds.), *Deutschland, Israel und der Holocaust. Zur Gegenwartsbedeutung der Vergangenheit* (Klartext, Essen 1998), pp. 45–54

Index